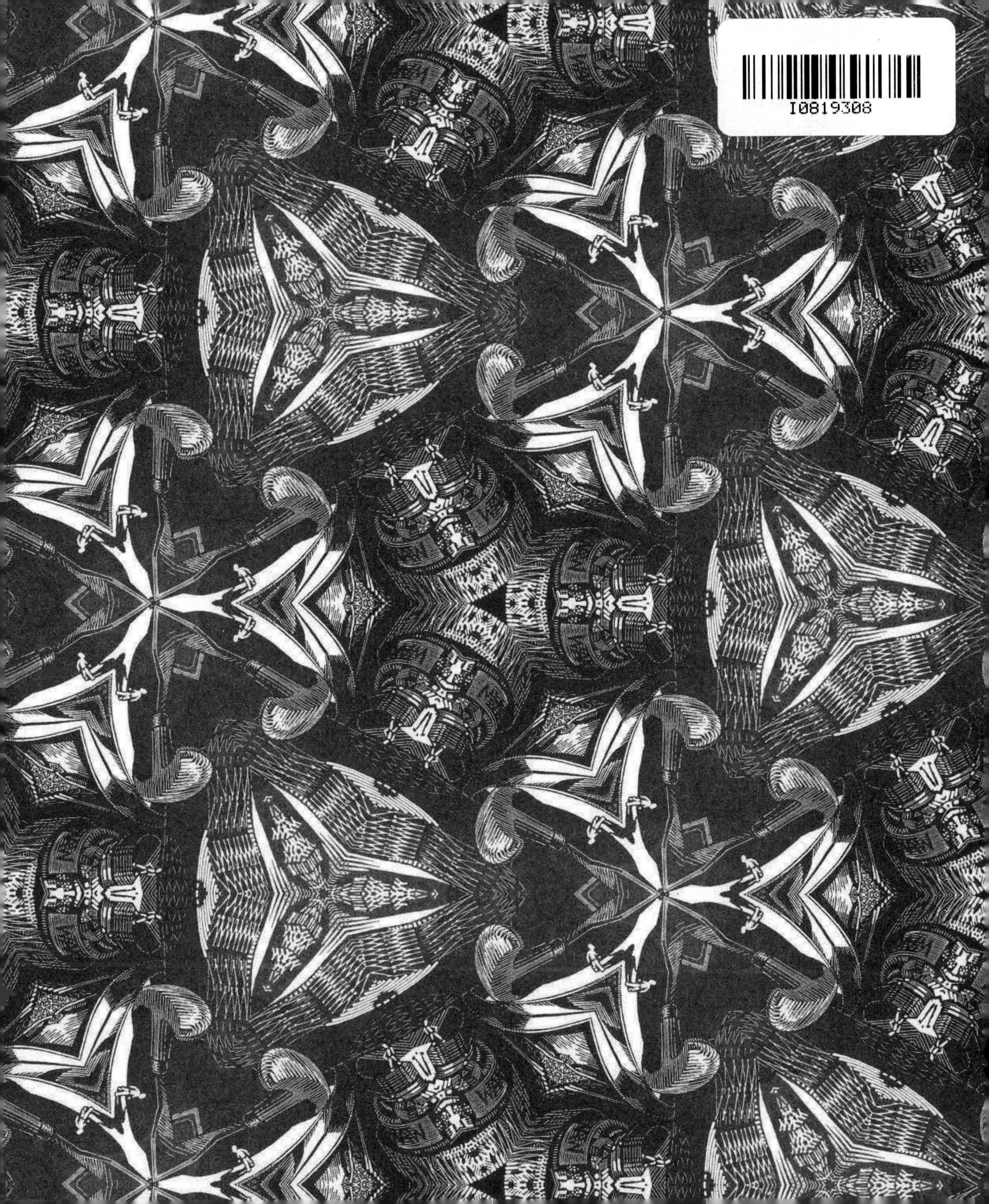

I0819308

WOOD ENGRAVING

A Personal Approach

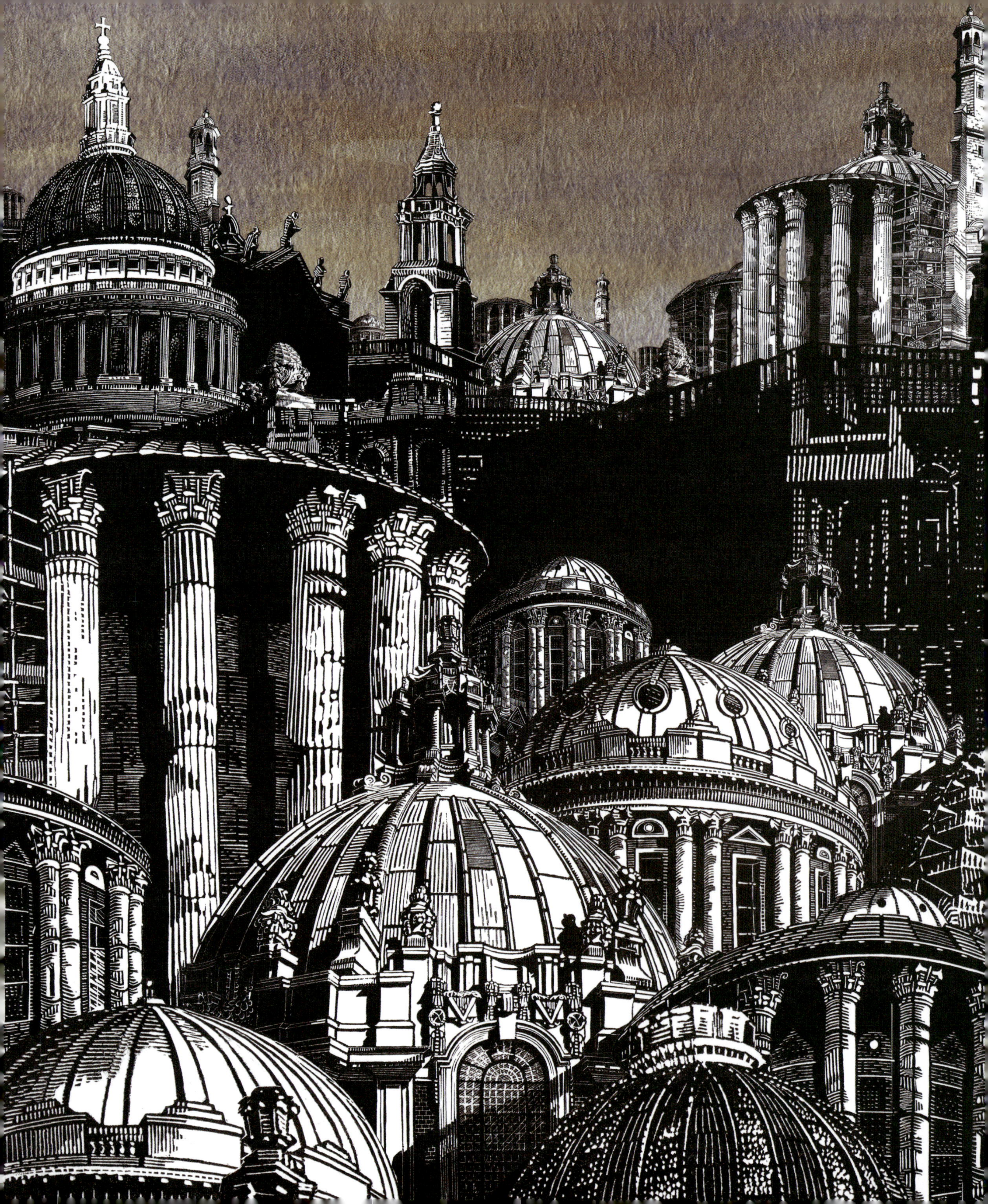

Anne Desmet RA

WOOD ENGRAVING

A Personal Approach

THE CROWOOD PRESS

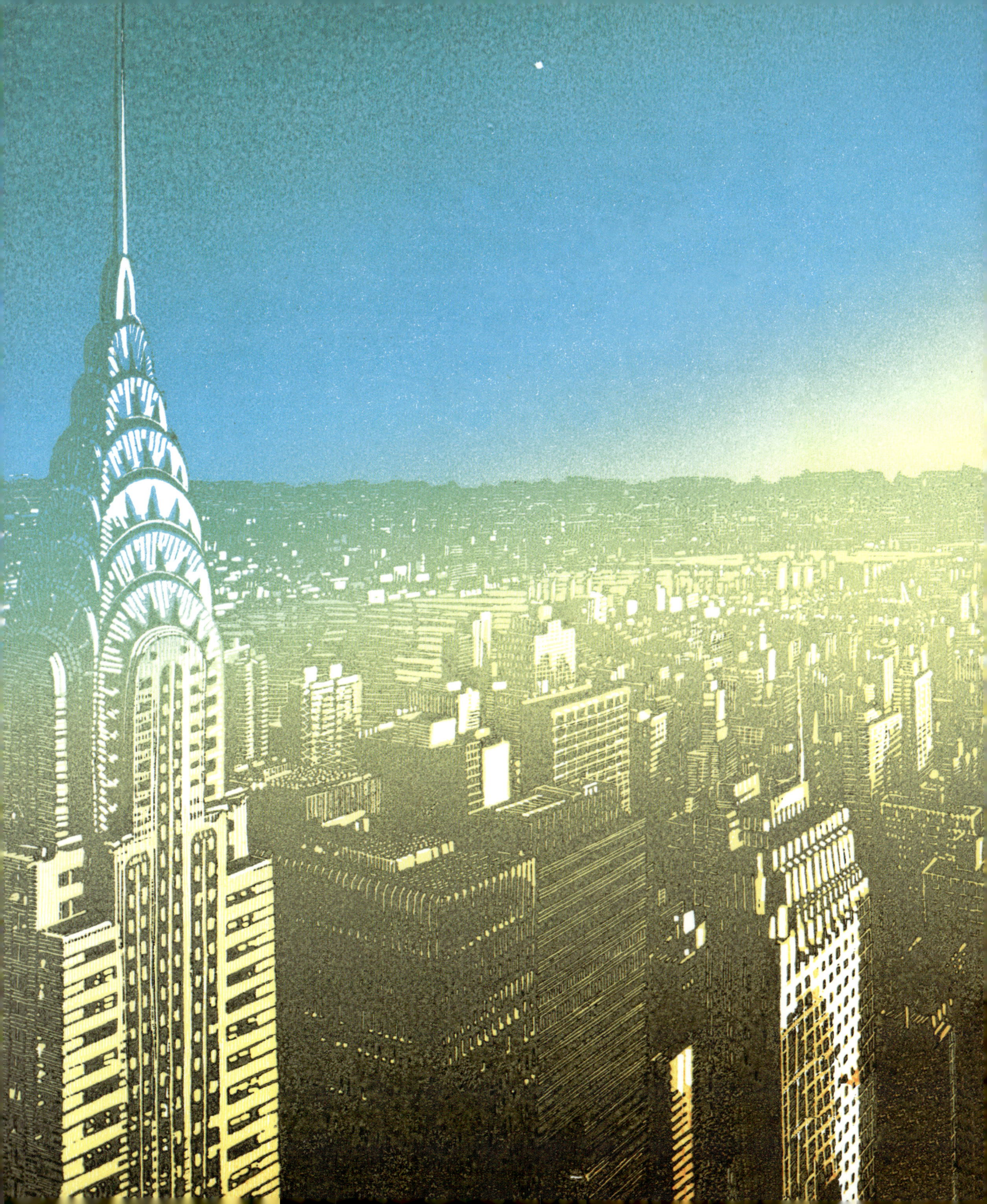

CONTENTS

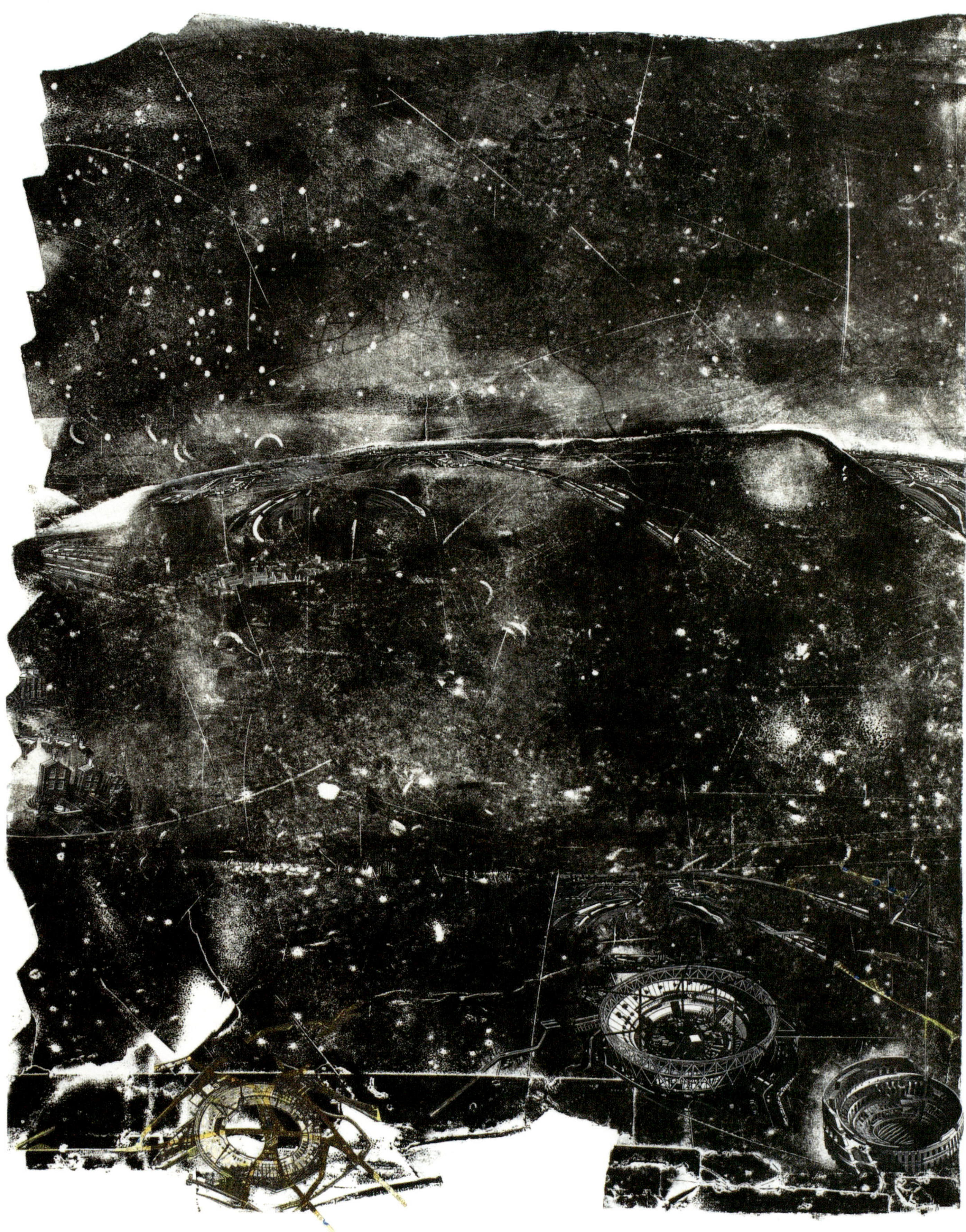

INTRODUCTION

People come to art in all sorts of ways, for lots of reasons and from diverse experiences. My evolution as a printmaking artist and wood engraver happened slowly and grew from a most unpromising start.

As a baby, born in Liverpool, I developed severe hip problems and thus began a childhood of repeated long stays in hospital undergoing many operations to try to 'normalise' my legs. At that time (mid 1960s to early 1980s), each episode of orthopaedic surgery was invariably followed by months in bed before you'd be taught how to walk again and, once competent with a pair of crutches, you'd go home. So, for much of my time in hospital (about five years spread out over my first twenty years), I wasn't exactly ill, but was stuck in bed trying to stave off boredom, while my legs took time to heal. So, what did I do with my time? I read numerous books and drew loads of pictures. What did I draw? Anything in my sightline.

I can't claim to have been a child genius! I definitely wasn't. My early drawings were entirely average. My first hospital drawings, when I was about four, were cartoons of children in adjacent beds with all the medical paraphernalia: drip stands, monitors, wheelchairs and walking frames. I carried on making increasingly detailed cartoons during every hospital stay for the next five years.

Later, I took to drawing representational images in a less linear, more tonal style with a stronger focus on chiaroscuro to suggest three-dimensionality. Most were only about A5 size. I drew what surrounded me at even closer proximity than children in nearby beds: bowls of fruit on my bedside

London Dreams (2010), wood engraving details collaged on a lino print (made from old, scuffed floor lino salvaged from a London Primary School on the brink of demolition) on Kozu paper, 81.2 × 63.8cm (32 × 25in), in the Museum of London collection.

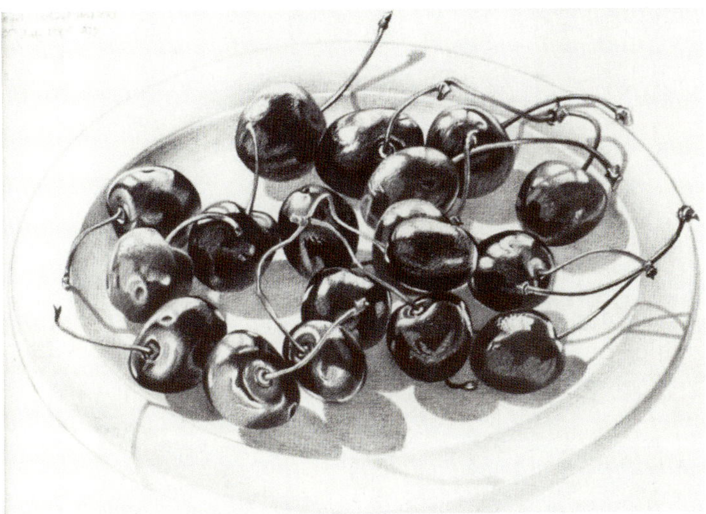

Pencil drawing, 14.5 × 19cm (5¾× 7½in), on a sketchbook page, which I made in hospital in Liverpool in 1985.

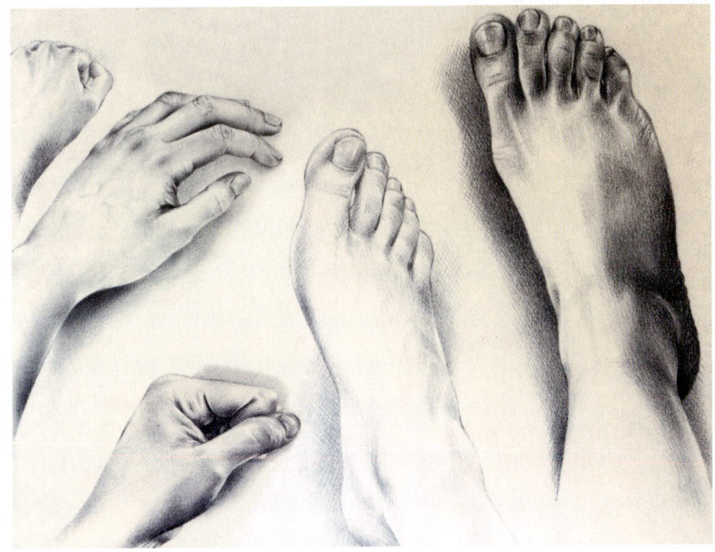

Small studies, in HB pencil, conté pencil and Bic biro on paper, of my left hand and right foot, made from my hospital bed in Liverpool in 1982.

locker, my face reflected in a reading lamp's bulb, my reflection in a tea mug, or detailed studies of my hands and feet.

For a long time, these drawings weren't very good but, as I spent so much time working at them, they improved. My path to any ability was definitely via the 90 per cent perspiration and 10 per cent inspiration route. By the time I was eleven or twelve, I was beginning to be told that I was 'good at art', which was encouraging, though I don't think I had any idea of what that might lead to, coming from a family with no artists in it. My English Mum was a children's surgeon (specialising in general surgery on newborn babies) and my Belgian Dad was an oyster farmer turned hotelier.

By seventeen, I couldn't imagine a life without art-making playing a key part, and I applied to art school. Because, after A-levels, I was scheduled to spend another six months in hospital having yet another major operation, Oxford University's Ruskin School of Drawing and Fine Art offered me a deferred-entry place and assured me I wouldn't need a Foundation course before enrolling, because Oxford's Bachelor of Fine Arts degree would teach me all I'd need to know… So, at eighteen, still unsteady on my legs, I embarked on my degree with a portfolio from school and hospital, full of small, intensely-wrought drawings – almost all in black and white and made with basic materials: HB and B pencils, fine-line drawing pens, biros, watercolour pencils and some in white and black crayons on grey sugar paper.

I'd come from a comprehensive school in Crosby, Liverpool, where the art teaching was good but equipment was limited, into an environment where most of my peers had come from private schools with generously funded art

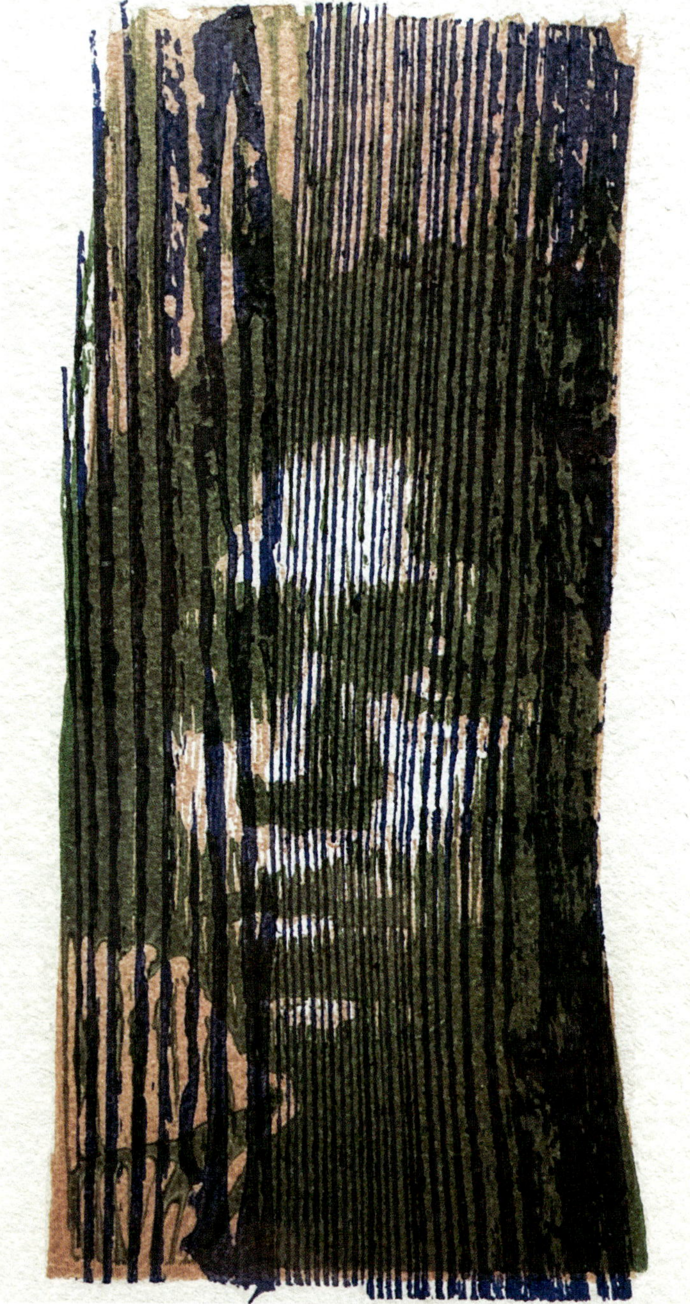

Ephigenie (1994), three-block woodcut, 25 × 12cm (9¾ × 4¾in), by Jean Lodge (b.1941). Printed on rag paper that Jean made herself in the Ruskin School of Art printmaking studio, it is typical of her work in which each block's wood grain is usually an enhanced, vital feature.

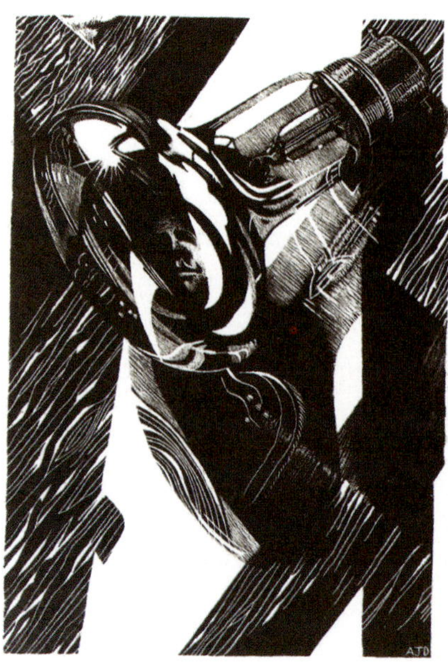

An Idea (1986), stone lithograph, 19 × 12.5cm (7½ × 5in), on BFK Rives paper. Based on studies of my face in various reflective surfaces, having painted the image on the litho stone in black tusche (a special greasy ink used in lithography), I scratched into the design with a scalpel blade to simulate wood grain effects in the print.

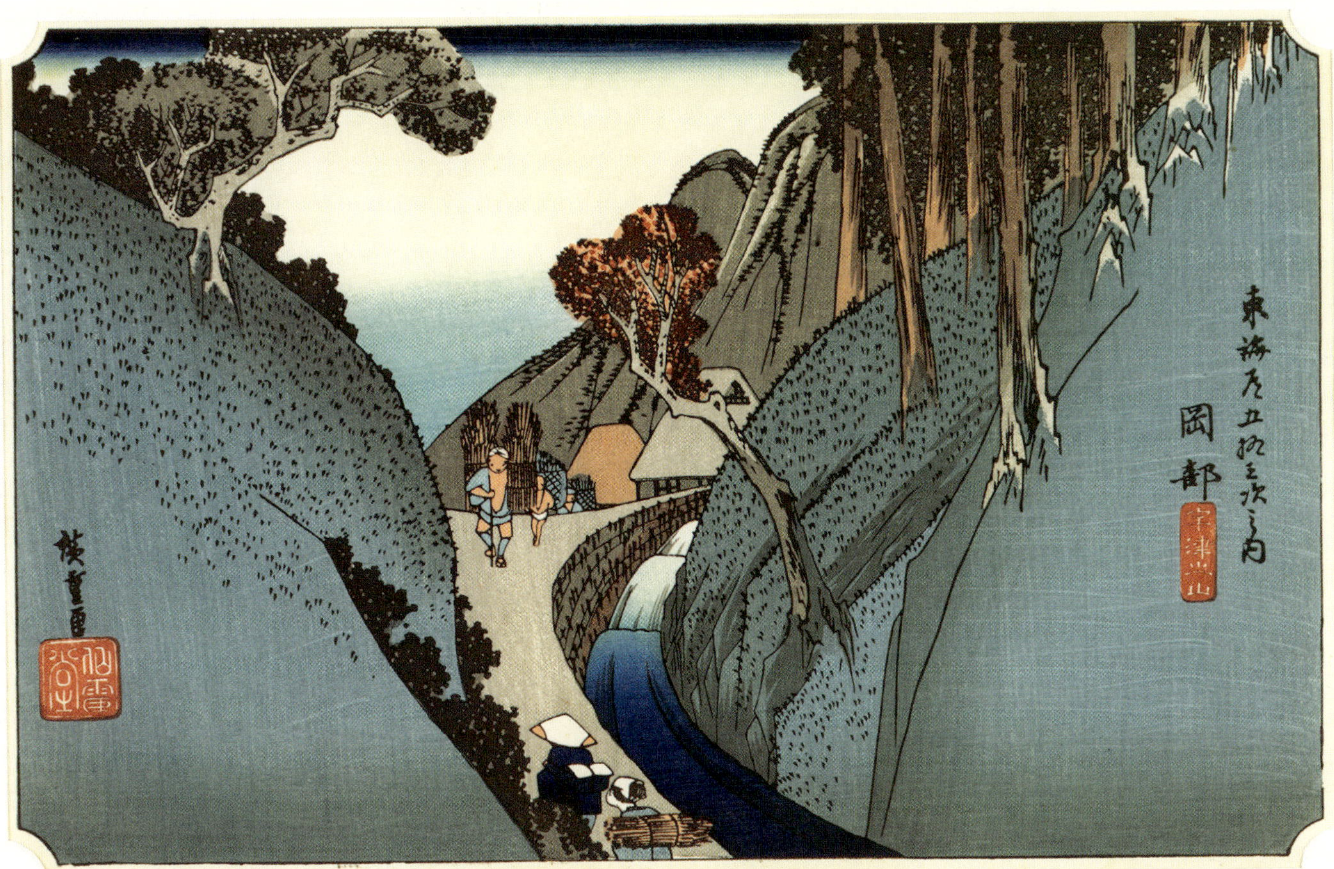

Mount Utsu, Okabe (Station #22)* (1833–4), woodcut, 24.7 × 36.2cm (9¾ × 14¼in), by Utagawa Hiroshige on thin Japanese paper. An outstanding example of the detailed cutting and extraordinary watercolour blend effects achieved by Japanese artists cutting and printing the long grain of wild mountain cherry wood, known for its extremely fine grain and resistance to splintering.

departments offering every possible technique from oil painting to pastels, woodwork to welding. So, as it turned out, the Ruskin's assurance that a pre-degree Foundation wasn't necessary was misleading. Most students arrived there with a great grounding in a whole range of art materials and methods. Many of the art school's tutors, rather than trying to fill in anyone's technical gaps, tended to assume a level playing field, as if we had all come to university with the same range of artistic experience. A significant exception was the Ruskin's printmaking department headed by an extraordinary artist, Jean Lodge, a specialist in woodcutting and etching techniques.

Jean's department offered introductory sessions in all kinds of printing processes: woodcut, etching, metal and wood engraving, screenprint and even stone lithography plus assorted photographic techniques. After a shaky start at the Ruskin, trying my hand at oil painting, I found my 'home' in its printmaking department and never looked back.

At that time (early 1980s), few British secondary schools seemed to teach printmaking – apart from very basic linocut, often done on rock-hard lino with poor-quality, blunt gouges – an off-putting introduction. So the Ruskin's printmaking modules sensibly assumed no prior knowledge and set out to teach techniques few students would have encountered. Until then, I had no clear idea of what artists' printmaking was. I was aware of some of the intense monochrome woodcuts by the great German artist Albrecht Dürer (1471–1528) and, as a teenager, my Mum had taken me to London to see the Royal Academy of Arts' *Great Japan Exhibition* (1981–2), so I had been exposed to some of the great woodblock prints by Katsushika Hokusai (1760–1849),

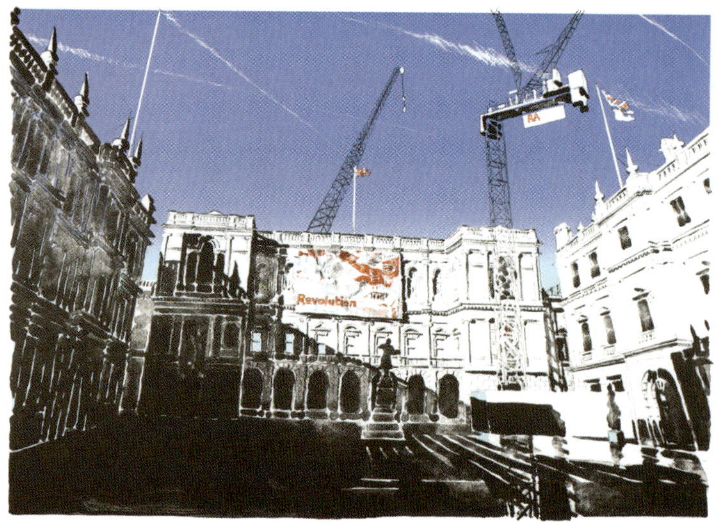

RA Revolution (2017), stone lithograph, 30.5 × 42cm (12 × 16½in), on Somerset Satin paper. I made this at Hole Editions, Newcastle, UK. It looks very like my watercolour and pencil-and-wash sketchbook drawings and has a very different character to my wood engravings.

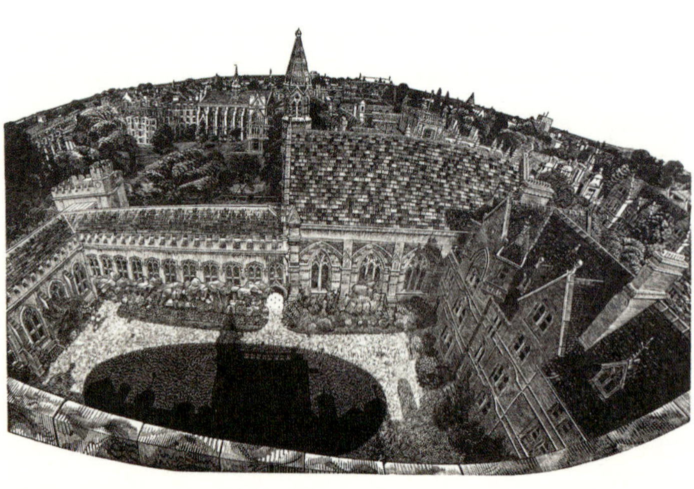

Balliol College Oxford (1995), wood engraving on boxwood, 16.5 × 24.6cm (6½ × 9¾in), on Gampi Vellum paper. I was commissioned by the college to make this, and it demonstrates the detail and tonal range possible in this medium. While similar, compositionally, to *RA Revolution*, its character and mark-making differ significantly from stone lithography.

Utagawa Hiroshige (1797–1858) and others. I of course realised that illustrated books and all kinds of card and paper packaging materials must involve reproductive print processes of various sorts, but I wasn't yet tuned in to printmaking as a means of creative expression and one that can result in the most extraordinarily compelling works of art.

Although I tried etching, photo-etching, copper engraving, screenprint and woodcut, I quickly became enthralled by wood engraving and stone lithography. Drawing on the specially prepared limestones to create lithographs resulted in images with the closest connections to my sketchbook drawings, whereas wood engraving allowed for an extraordinary level of highly detailed work and greater potential for a wider and infinitely variable array of marks from assorted steel burins, each with its own unique cutting tip. Wood engraving also involved 'drawing in light' and produced images with amazing depth and chiaroscuro, effects I loved – and still love all these years later.

After graduating from the Ruskin, then studying postgraduate printmaking at London's Central School of Art, my career unfolded primarily in London, but with a truly inspiring scholarship year at the British School at Rome in 1989–90 and, later, many sketching expeditions in Italy. During my year in Rome, in my mid-twenties, I extended my wood engraving into collage-making.

Back in London and some years later, having children, I had less time for sketching but found myself, instead, beachcombing on English and Welsh seaside holidays. It was then I realised the potential of found materials such as seashells, pebbles, pottery shards and broken glass as supports for collages involving wood engravings on paper.

I've tried to keep an open-minded, experimental, playful approach to printmaking throughout my career. While my work involves a wide range of print-based techniques, wood engraving has been my focus for over forty years. It's a technique steeped in history and tradition, yet I always try to bring to it something new. My most recent experiments have involved reconfiguring my wood engravings via a kaleidoscope app and image creation software to make entirely new digital compositions retaining the look and feel of wood engravings.

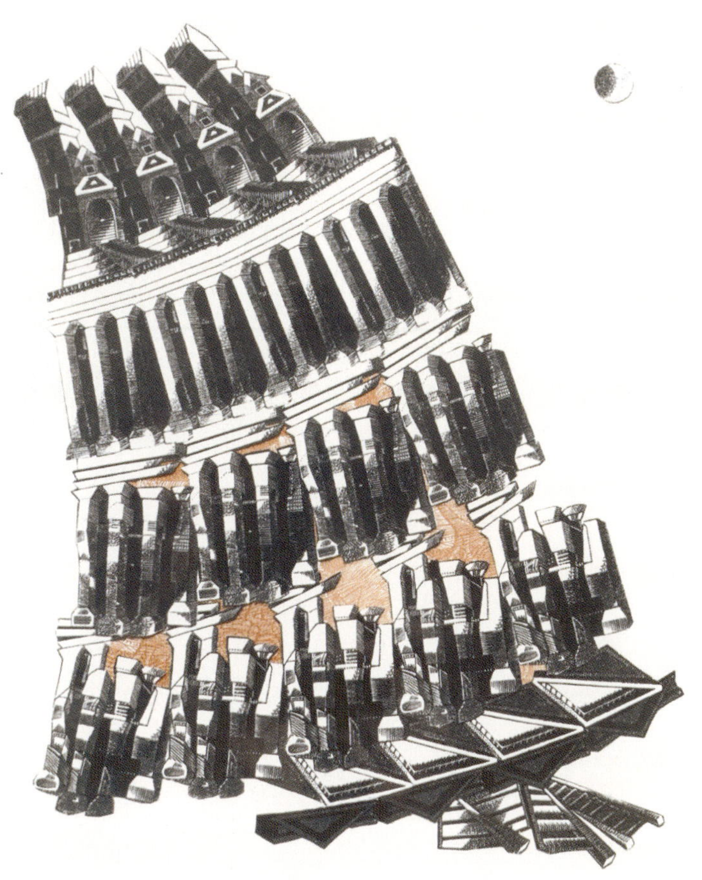

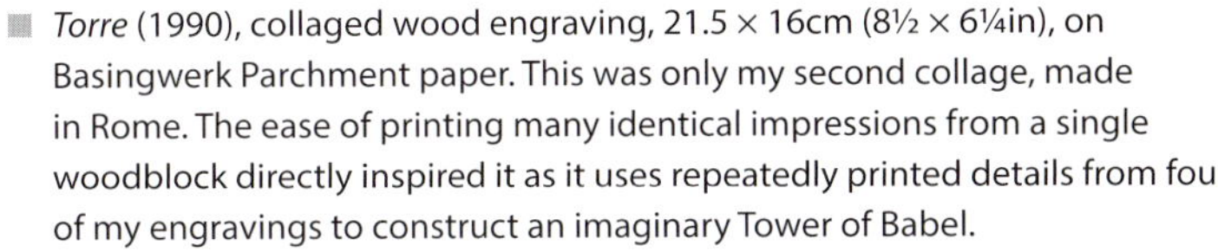

Torre (1990), collaged wood engraving, 21.5 × 16cm (8½ × 6¼in), on Basingwerk Parchment paper. This was only my second collage, made in Rome. The ease of printing many identical impressions from a single woodblock directly inspired it as it uses repeatedly printed details from four of my engravings to construct an imaginary Tower of Babel.

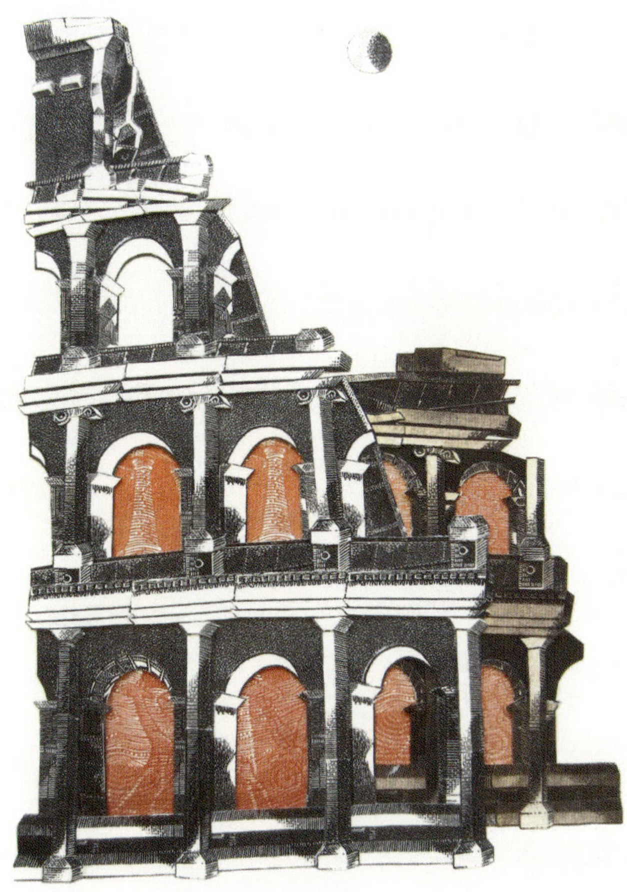

Il Colosseo (1990), collaged wood engraving with grey ink wash, 18.5 × 12.5cm (7¼ × 5in), on Basingwerk Parchment paper (in the Ashmolean Museum collection). Inspired by Rome's colosseum, I made this by using details from several impressions of the same four prints I had used to make *Torre*.

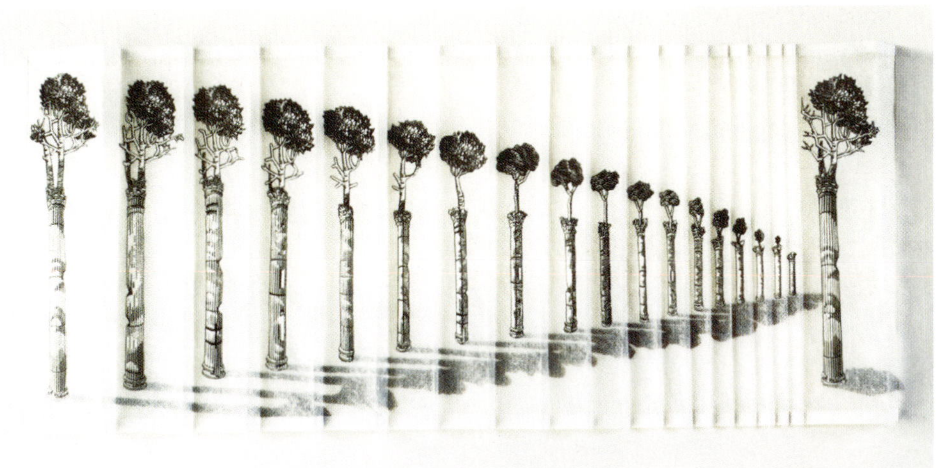

Via Appia (1994), wood engravings and coloured papers collaged on the front and back of concertina-folded, semi-transparent, Japanese tissue, 17 × 40.6 × 1.4cm (6¾ × 16 × ½in). The colonnade is created entirely from columns culled from printings of *Rotunda × 4* (illustrated in Chapter 9).

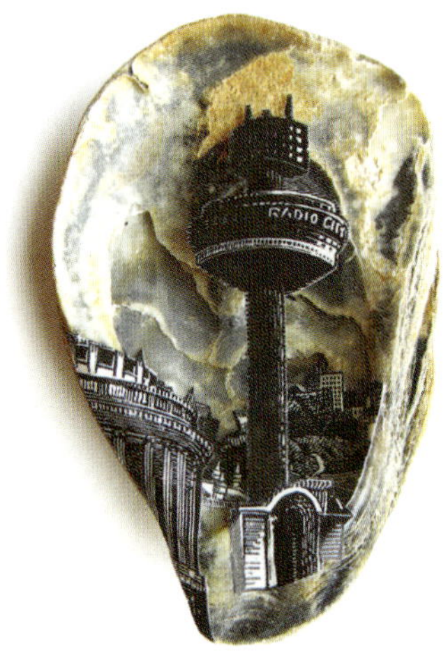

Radio Waves (2014), wood engravings on paper collaged on the concave surface of an oyster shell (scavenged from a beach in Mumbles, Wales), 8 × 5 × 1.3cm (3¼ × 2 × ½in). Its central component depicting Liverpool's Radio City tower is attached at the base only, so that it projects in front of the shell.

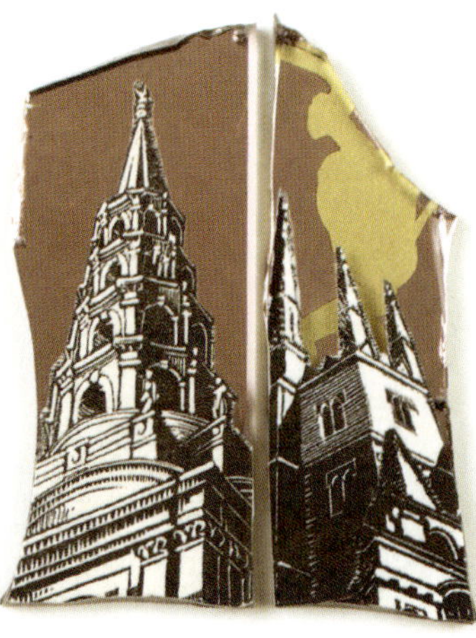

Two London Churches (2018), wood engravings on paper collaged on two mirrored-glass shards, 5 × 4 × 0.3cm (2 × 1½ × ⅛in). Its silvering has a pinkish hue and gold-coloured patterning.

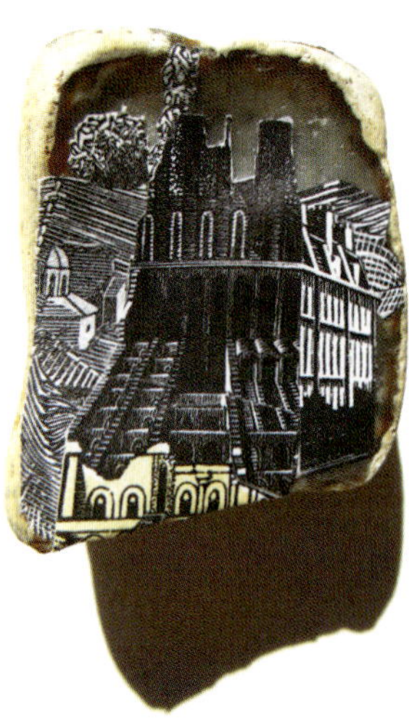

Grand Tour (2012), wood engravings on paper collaged on a pebble, 5 × 3.9 × 2.5cm (2 × 1½ × 1in). The stone's smooth, slightly translucent, reasonably flat, surface with paler rim seemed to suggest a frame for a miniature composition.

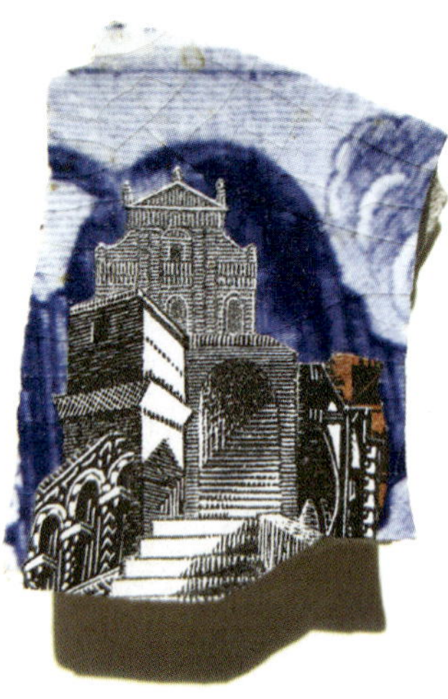

Blue Archway (2012), wood engravings on paper collaged on a glazed pottery shard, 4.8 × 3.4 × 1cm (2 × 1¼ × ⅜in). Dug up in my London garden, this tiny ceramic fragment's blue pattern suggested a dark archway, which inspired this composition.

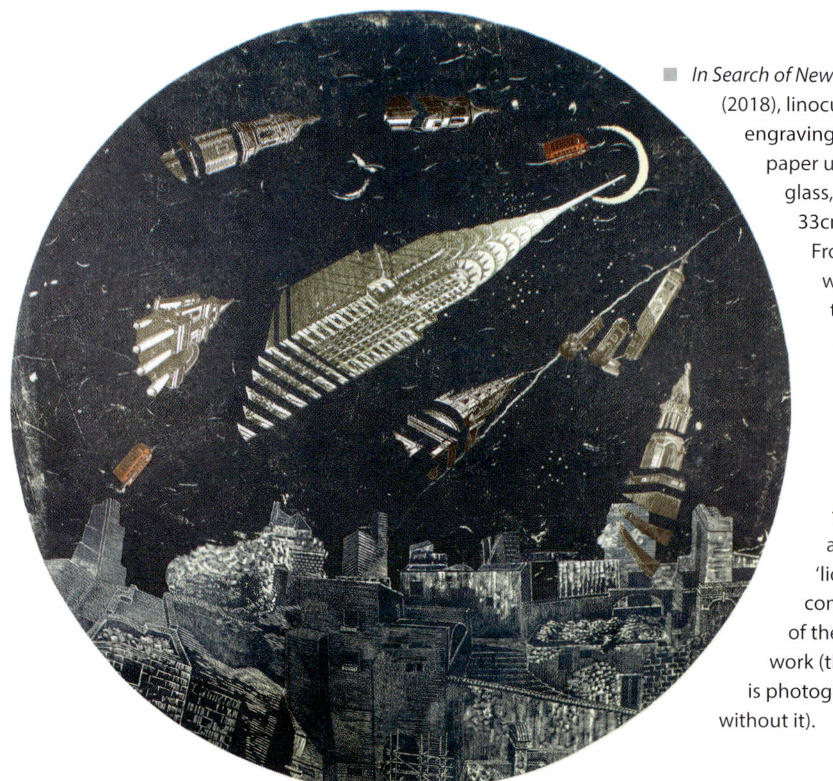

In Search of New Worlds (2018), linocut and wood engravings collaged on paper under convex glass, diameter: 33cm (13in). From a series of works aiming to suggest convex glass mirrors, it was made on papier mâché formed to the shape of a convex glass 'lid'. That lid comprises part of the finished work (though it is photographed without it).

Over the years I have taught numerous short wood engraving courses at museums, colleges, print workshops and public galleries. Aspects of any technique can be conveyed step by step but, beyond the essentials, that is not how I teach engraving. Anyone interested in this amazing medium has the potential to bring something new, individual and entirely unique to even the tiniest woodblock. In this book, I aim to explain some of the more productive creative directions and processes I've taught as well as those I've used in my own work, including mixed-media methods. I hope they may inspire you to take wood engraving in even more experimental, surprising directions. I'd love to see what you do with it. Good luck!

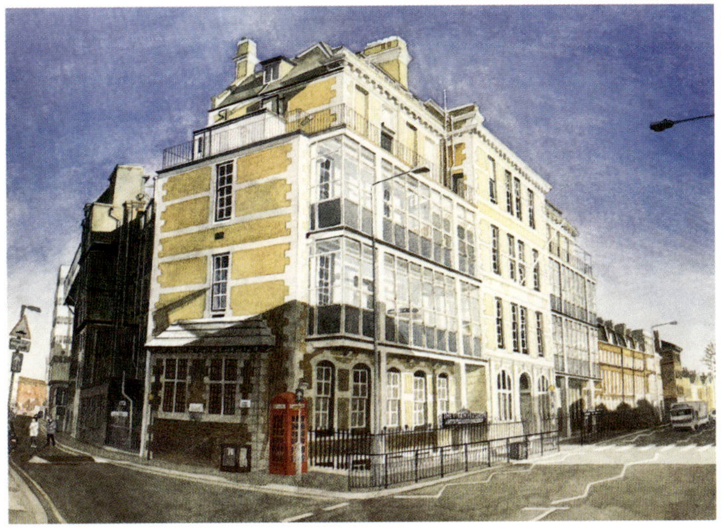

Queen Elizabeth Hospital for Sick Children (1994), watercolour on paper, 21 × 30cm (8¼ × 11¾in). Commissioned by the hospital, this provided source material for my wood engraving, four years later, of the same subject.

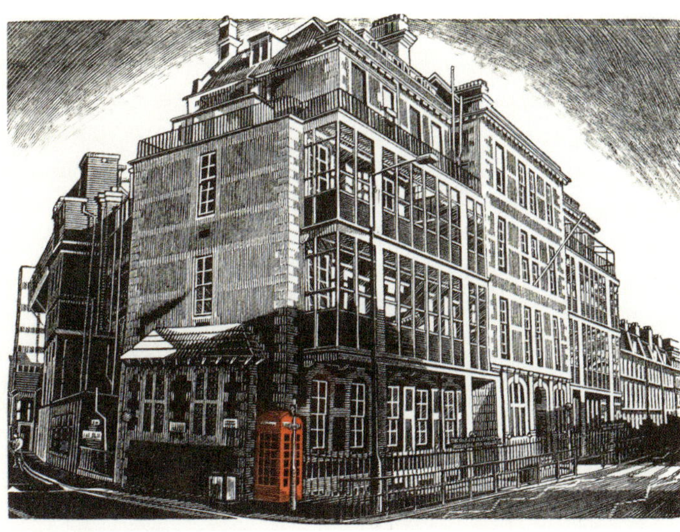

QEH (1998), wood engraving on boxwood, 10 × 13.3cm (4 × 5¼in), printed on Gampi Vellum paper, with linocut for the phone box's red colouring. Commissioned by the former Queen Elizabeth Hospital for Children in East London, this later provided the source material for a completely new digital print.

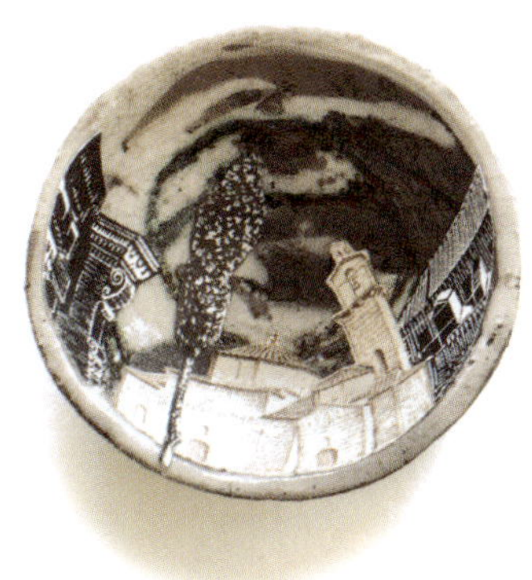

Greece – Storm Light (2019), wood engravings on paper and fragment of Greek (pre Euro) banknote collaged on glazed ceramic bowl, diameter: 4.2cm (1¾in).

Last Dance (2023), digital print, (developed from wood engraving and stone lithograph via kaleidoscope app and Photoshop), 27.6 × 20.7cm (10¾ × 8¼in), on Somerset Satin paper.

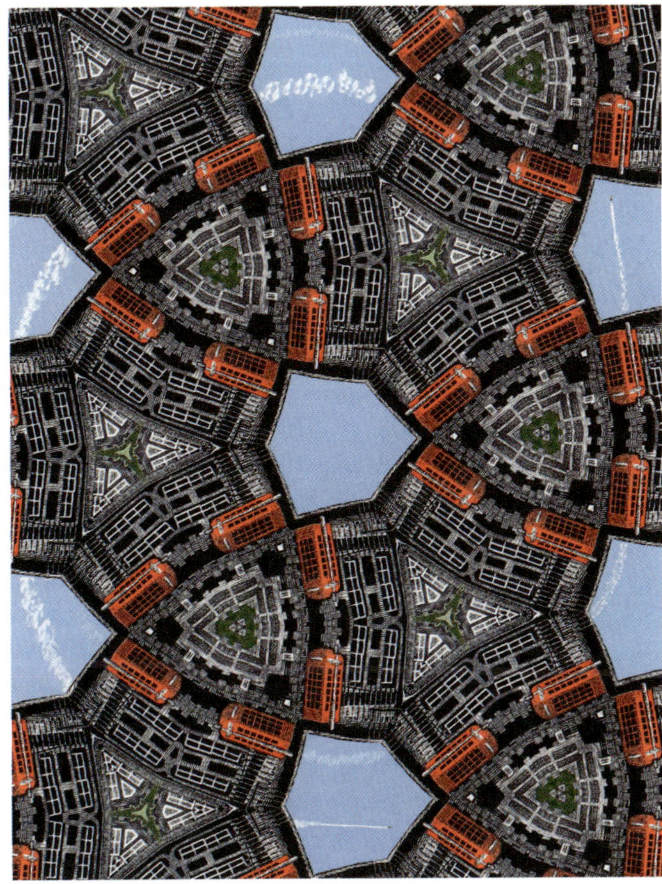

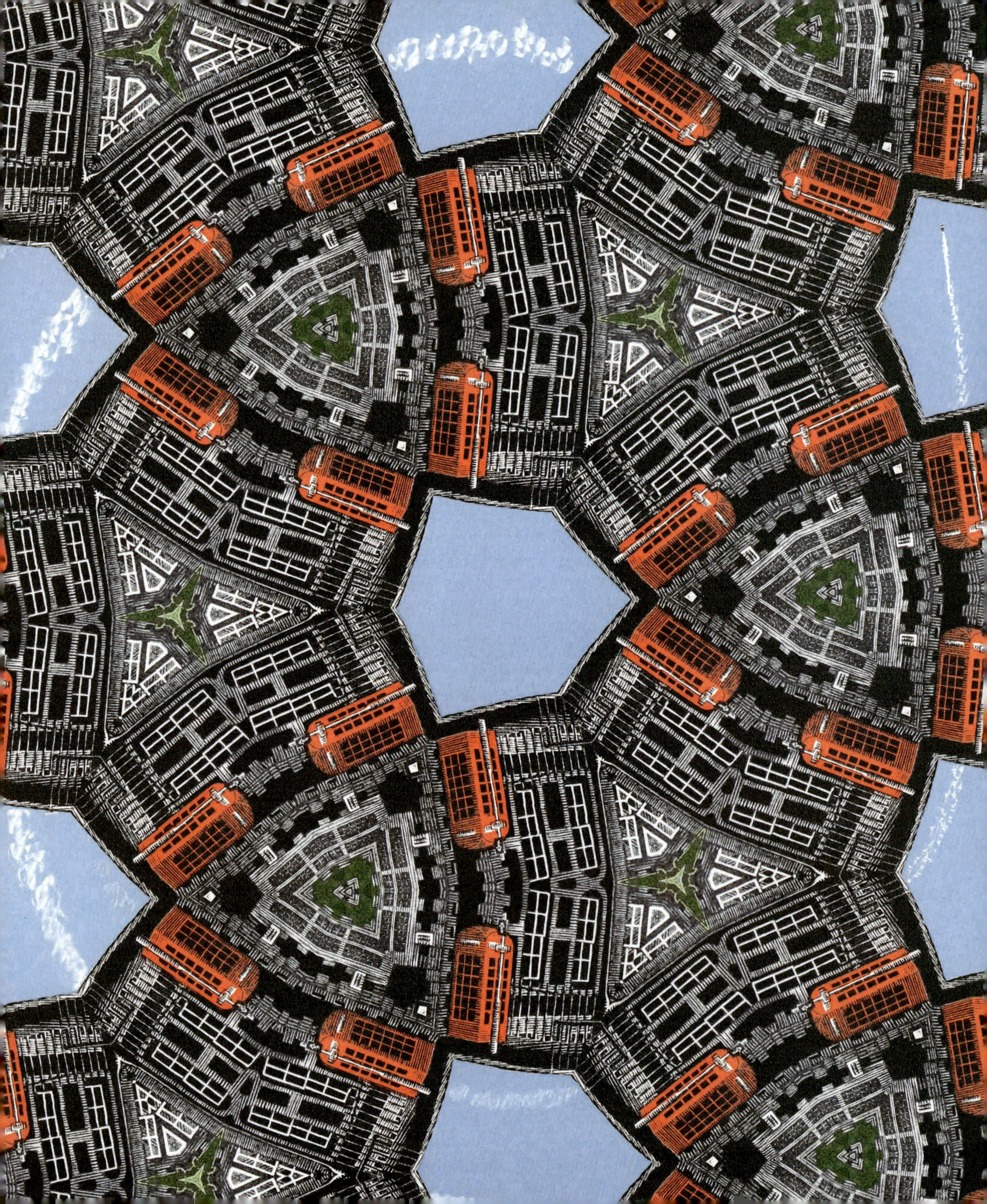

CHAPTER 1

WHAT IS A WOOD ENGRAVING?

Printing on textiles (later on paper) from carved woodblocks was a Chinese invention from at least two thousand years ago. The Tang and Song dynasties (spanning the seventh to the thirteenth centuries) developed the technique, even inventing the first moveable type for printing text alongside images. The process reached its apex in Japan in the eighteenth and nineteenth centuries with the vibrant *Ukiyo-e* (pictures of the floating world) woodblock prints of people and landscapes by Hokusai, Hiroshige and others: their complex, multi-layered images cut on woodblocks by professional block-cutters and printed using liquid water-based inks, specially made papers, and a method of hand-printing using a disc-shaped implement called a 'baren'. The woodblock remained East Asia's most widely used printing method for artistic and commercial applications until the early twentieth century. Its influence on Western artists was profound and still resonates today.

In Europe, the invention of the printing press in about 1440 by German goldsmith Johannes Gutenberg (1393/1406–68) led to an explosion of printing in the West, including the production of chapbooks: a form of medieval, mass-produced, woodblock-printed booklet used for disseminating illustrated ephemera of all kinds including almanacs, folktales, children's stories, poems and ballads, as well as religious and political tracts.

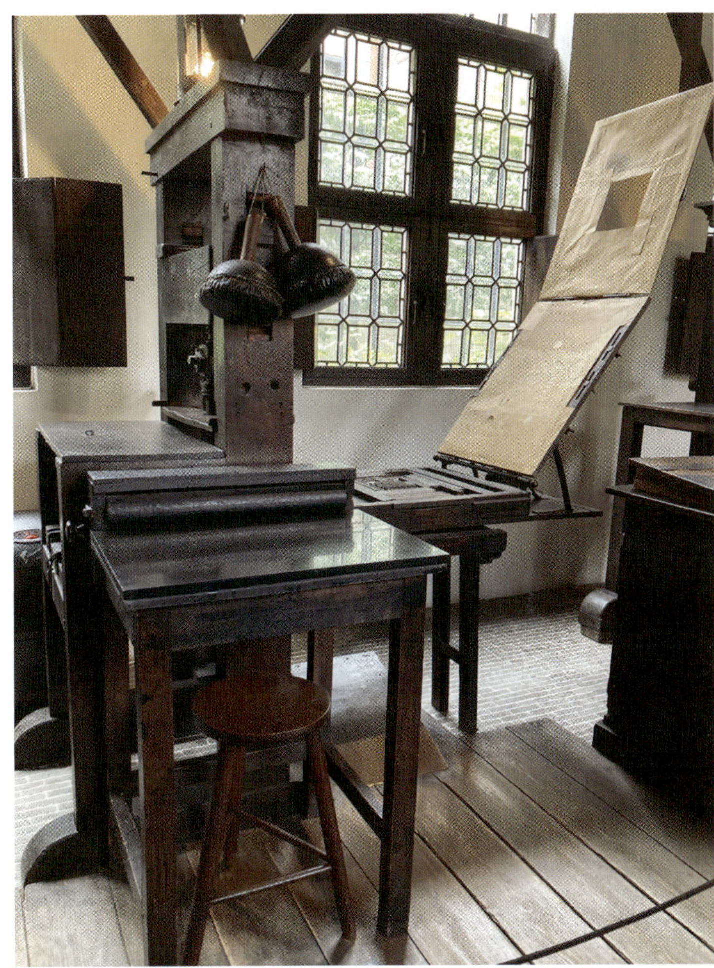

One of many wooden presses in the Plantin-Moretus Museum, Antwerp, Belgium, Western Europe's oldest surviving print workshop established over 400 years ago. A UNESCO World Heritage Site, it houses leather ink dabbers (which pre-date the nineteenth century innovation of printing rollers) and many presses including the world's two oldest surviving wooden ones. This particular press, along with many others in the museum, has intact tympans and frisket – rarities today.

Last Dance (2023), digital print, 27.6 × 20.7cm (10¾ × 8¼in), on Somerset Satin paper. I made this by photographing my engraving *QEH* through a kaleidoscope app. Then, in Photoshop, I copied and pasted blue sky details (from my lithograph *RA Revolution*) into which I drew aeroplanes and vapour trails digitally, and added hints of green to suggest garden squares.

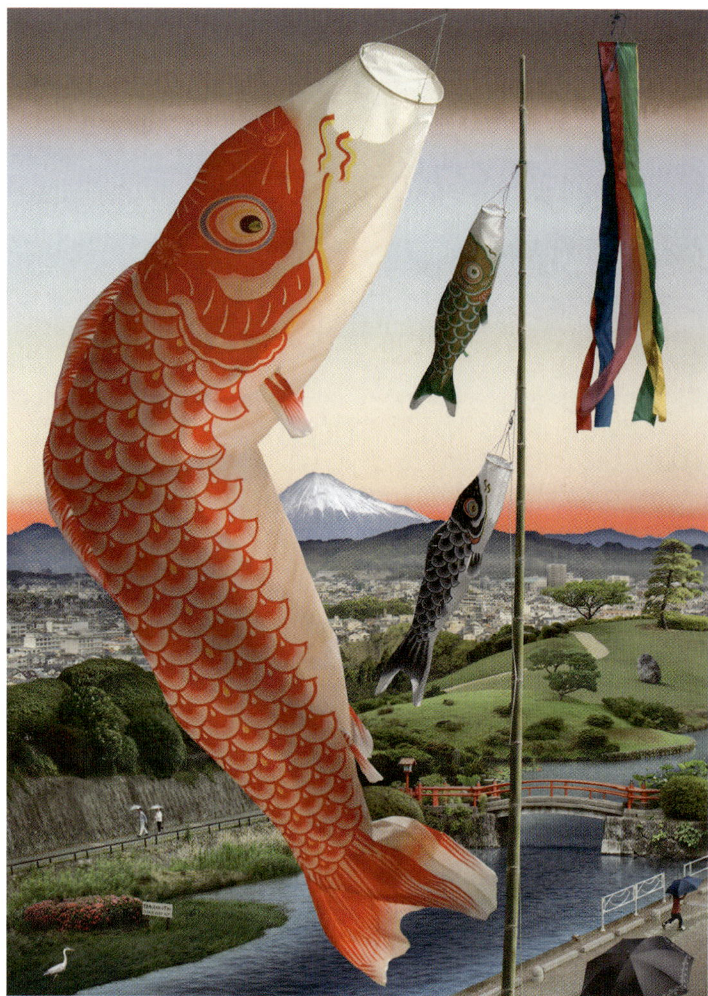

Spring Festival (after Hiroshige) (2020), archival pigment print, 27 × 19cm (10½ × 7½in), on A4 Hahnemühle photo rag paper, by Emily Allchurch (b.1974) who here recreates, using her own location photographs, one of Hiroshige's *One Hundred Famous Views of Edo* (1856–58). This is one of a substantial series, all inspired by Hiroshige's woodblock prints.

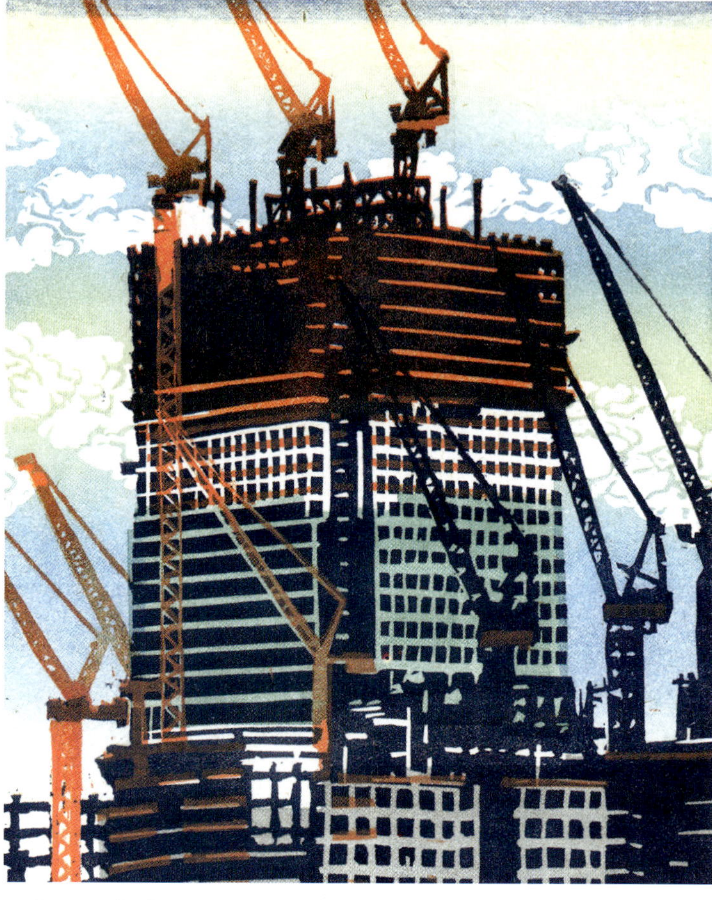

Canary Wharf in Construction (1998), multi-block linocut on Kozo-Shi No. 15 paper, 23 × 18.5cm (9 × 7¼in) by Janet Brooke (b.1947). Part of an ambitious series of London-themed works collectively titled *36 Views of Canary Wharf*, this was inspired by Hokusai's famous woodblock print series *36 Views of Mount Fuji*.

DÜRER'S LEGACY

An early outstanding European exponent of woodblock prints was the German artist Albrecht Dürer. By the time he reached his teens, Dürer's hometown of Nuremberg was awash with woodcutting craftsmen. His godfather, goldsmith-turned-printer Anton Koberger (c.1440/45–1513), became Germany's most successful printer-publisher with twenty-four printing presses and multiple offices at home and abroad. Koberger's best-known publication – one of the best-documented early printed books – is the *Nuremberg Chronicle* (1493), a sophisticated colour-woodblock-illustrated encyclopaedia comprising accounts of human and world history, including biblical, secular and mythological narratives from antiquity. It contained an unprecedented 1,809 woodcut illustrations, including some probably worked on by Dürer during his apprenticeship. Later, as a mature painter-printmaker, Dürer could fairly be described as the Western world's first internationally celebrated artist – his reputation resting on widespread dissemination of his prints on paper. Like the Japanese artists mentioned earlier, Dürer would have used professional block-cutters to carve woodblocks with his detailed pen drawings.

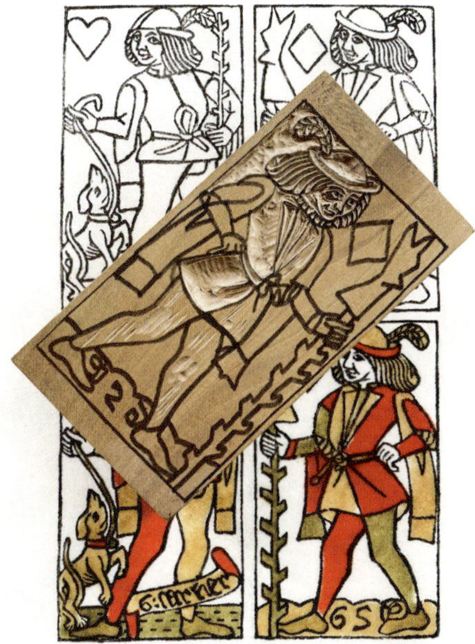

These facsimiles of medieval playing cards (with stencilled colours) were commissioned by the V&A (2008) for a video of historic woodcut processes, for one of its Medieval and Renaissance galleries. The long grain pearwood block is one of two: this one was intentionally unfinished, being used to film me cutting with gouges. A finished block was used to print both figures.

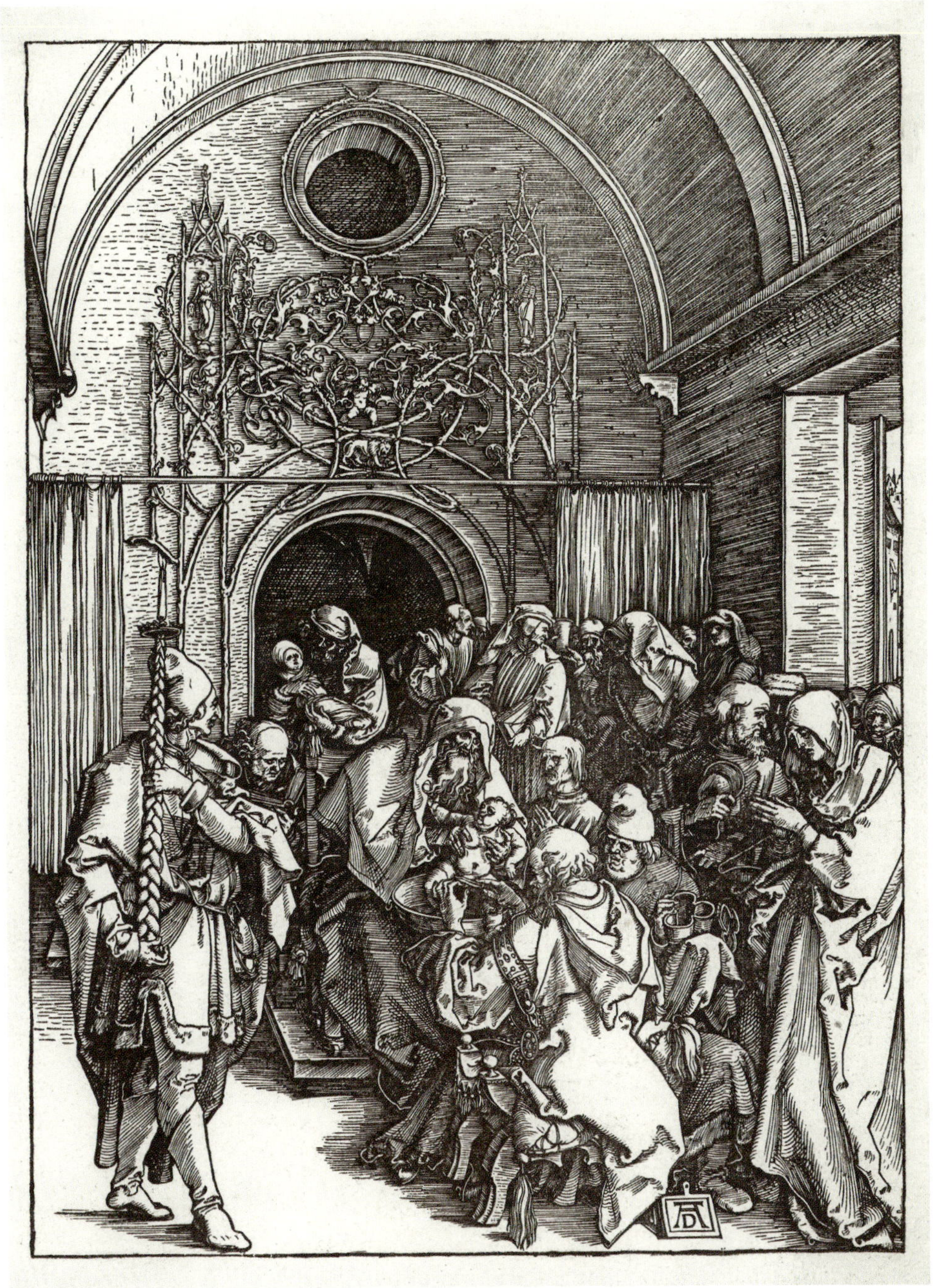

The craftsmanship in retaining, in each block's cutting, Dürer's intricate penmanship of crosshatched effects, was phenomenal – especially when you consider that, in all relief printing techniques (such as woodcut, wood engraving and linocut and, at its most basic, the humble potato-cut), what you leave uncut on the block's smooth surface is the part that is inked and printed, while all the cut parts will be the paper-white areas of the finished print. So, to achieve in a relief print the effects of pen-drawing and so simulate the look of his drawings, artisans cutting Dürer's blocks would have had to cut out all the little diamond-shapes between the crosshatched black lines drawn on the wood's surface.

The Circumcision (1505), woodcut on paper, 29.8 × 21.2cm (11¾ × 8¼in), by Albrecht Dürer. Many artists engraving end grain boxwood couldn't achieve this degree of detail. The fact that this is cut on long grain rather than on end grain wood makes its finesse even more remarkable. Image supplied by fine print dealer Elizabeth Harvey-Lee.

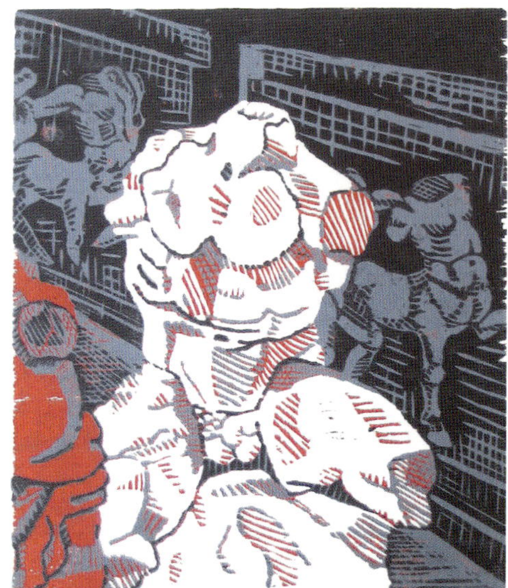

Belvedere Torso (1984), reduction woodcut on paper, 30.2 × 25.4cm (12 × 10in). This was only my second woodcut, made on thin plywood that printed well but splintered readily. Cut with U- and V-gouges, it is closer in character to the woodcuts of twentieth century German Expressionists than to Dürer's.

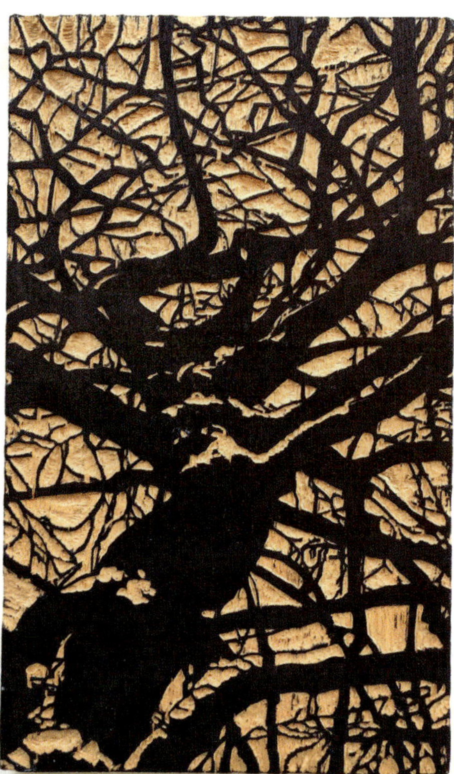

This tree with snow was cut with U- and V-gouges on a long grain plywood block. It gives a strong print but has a very different character to prints engraved on end grain wood.

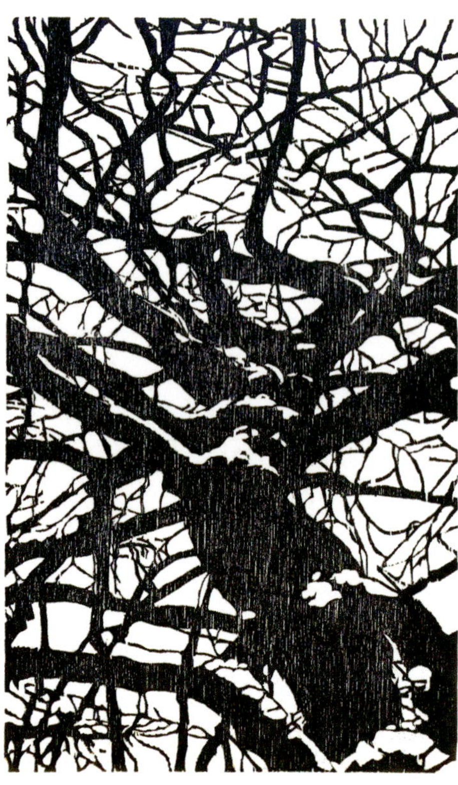

Tree with Snow (1985), woodcut print on paper, 30.5 × 17.9cm (12 × 7in). This image, of a tree in the gardens of Worcester College, Oxford, which I made as a student, clearly shows the wood grain texture running vertically up block and print.

Prints by Dürer and contemporaries in Renaissance Europe and by the historic Japanese and Chinese artists are known as woodcut or woodblock prints. In them, the images are cut using steel gouges and special knives on the plank or long grain of the wood. The wood grain direction may affect the image's character and cutting. You can see wood grain texture very clearly in woodcut prints closer to our own times – by the early twentieth century German Expressionists such as Käthe Kollwitz (1867–1945).

Wood engraving, by contrast, is closer to the technique of engraving on metal, using steel tools with sharp points as opposed to the U- or V-shaped gouges used for woodcutting. Another crucial difference is that engravings are cut on the cross grain (also known as end grain) rather than the plank, so grain direction plays no part whatsoever in how an image is cut on an engraving block. What is more important in end grain engraving wood is that the tree's rings are tightly and evenly spaced (from a slow-growing tree) and that the wood is receptive to detailed cutting. On the ideal piece of wood, the artist can cut easily and crisply in any direction on its planed, smooth-as-glass surface, like a skater gliding in perfectly choreographed loops across a frozen lake.

The origins of engraving on end grain wood – particularly boxwood – are unknown. Fabric printing, using carved end grain woodblocks, has been practised in India for centuries and other examples of end grain woodblock printing exist prior to the life of British craftsman, Thomas Bewick (1754–1828), a Newcastle-born engraver of, primarily, rural subjects. However, it was Bewick's developments in the medium – notably his use of tools designed for copper engraving to engrave his woodblocks – that raised the method to hitherto unknown finesse, such that he is often erroneously credited with having invented it. Bewick's

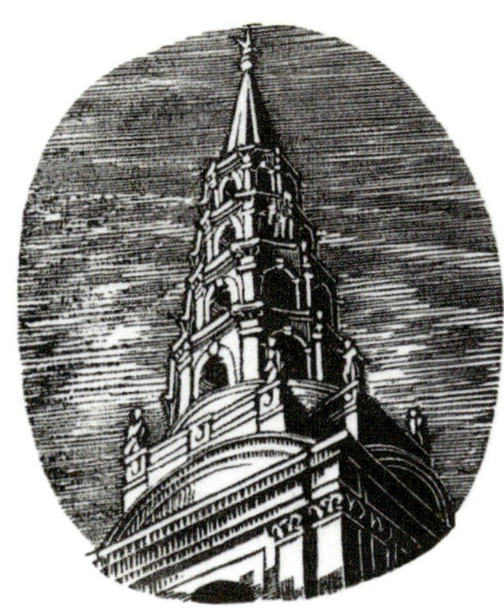

St Bride's (2014), wood engraving on a tiny boxwood roundel, 4.5 × 3.7cm (1¾ × 1½in), on Gampi Vellum paper.

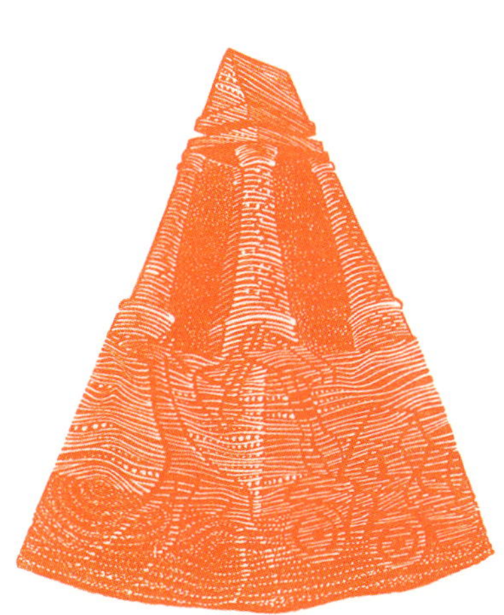

Development (1990), wood engraving on boxwood, 6 × 5cm (2¼ × 2in), on Basingwerk Parchment paper. I engraved this with a simulated wood grain pattern. To make a print of genuine wood grain, you would need to use long grain wood.

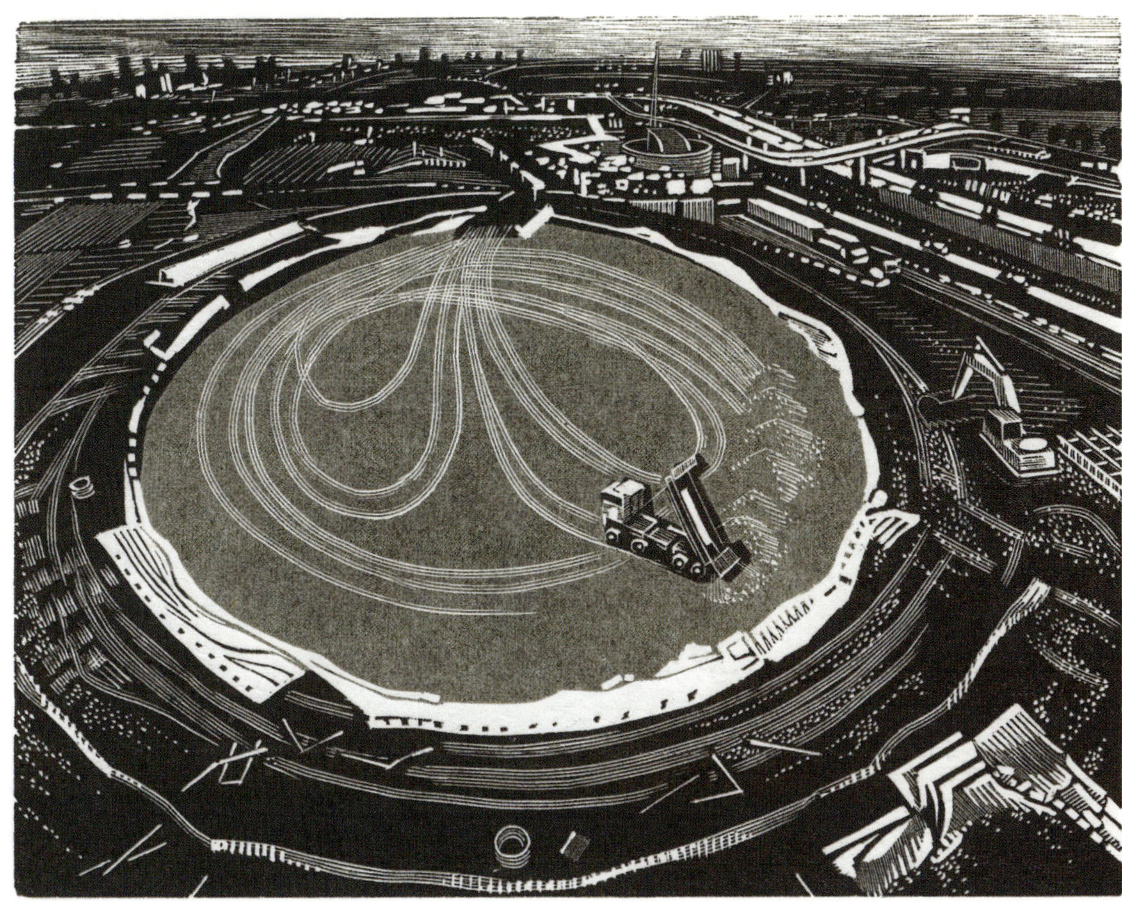

London Olympic Velodrome Site (2010) wood engraving on boxwood (with stencil), 10 × 12.5cm (4 × 5in), on Gampi Vellum paper. I was able to engrave spontaneous, fluent swirls (using a multiple tool) for the lorry's tyre tracks because the end grain block offers no resistance to cutting in any direction across its smooth surface.

sophisticated technique with its particular suitability for graphic images of extraordinary detail was swiftly adopted by the burgeoning newspaper industry since, at this time, although photography existed, the means to mass-reproduce photographs did not.

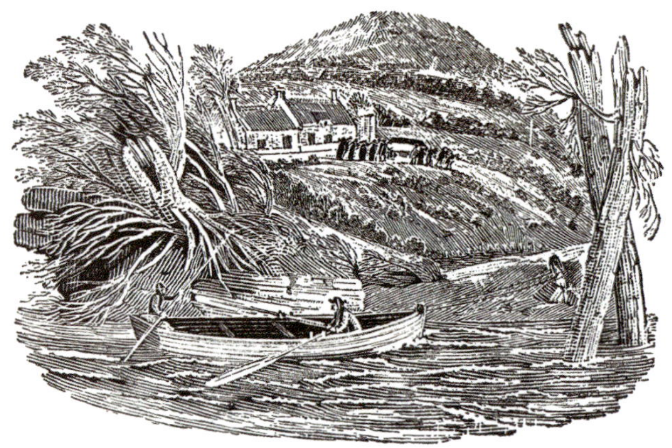

Thomas Bewick's final tailpiece, wood engraving on boxwood, 5.5 × 8.5cm (2¼ × 3¼in). This characteristically detailed image mixing rural life with human incident concludes Bewick's *Memoir*, completed in 1828. It shows a coffin being borne from Cherryburn, where he was born, to a boat to take it to Ovingham churchyard, where he was buried that same year.

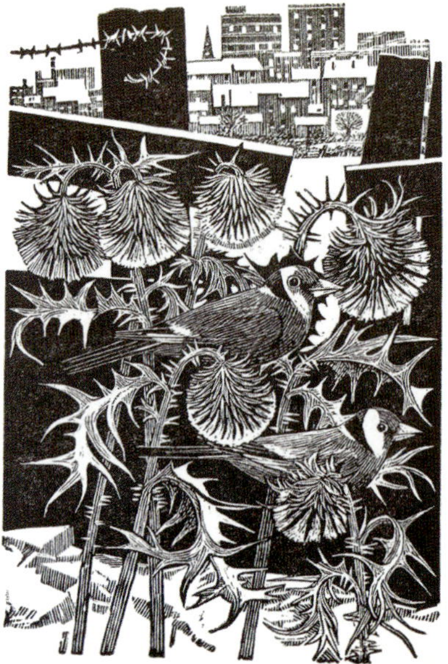

Boundary Lane (2007), wood engraving on boxwood, 8.7 × 5.7cm (3½ × 2¼in), on white paper, by Ian Corfe-Stephens (b.1940), whose engravings demonstrate Bewick's influence in their tiny scale, the character of their tool cuts and their subjects – of rural life and unexpected vignettes – such as these two birds camouflaged among weeds.

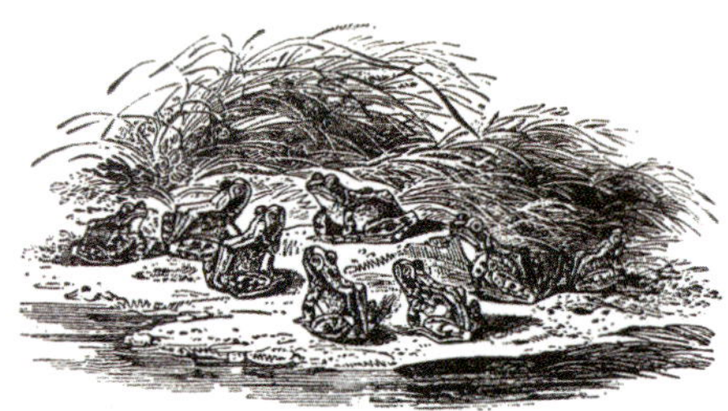

Frogs by Thomas Bewick (1753–1828), wood engraving on paper, 3.5 × 6.4cm (1½ × 2½in). Apparently this so impressed art critic John Ruskin (1819–1900) that he examined a frog's skeleton to confirm how accurate was the depiction of the twin peaks on the backs of Bewick's frogs.

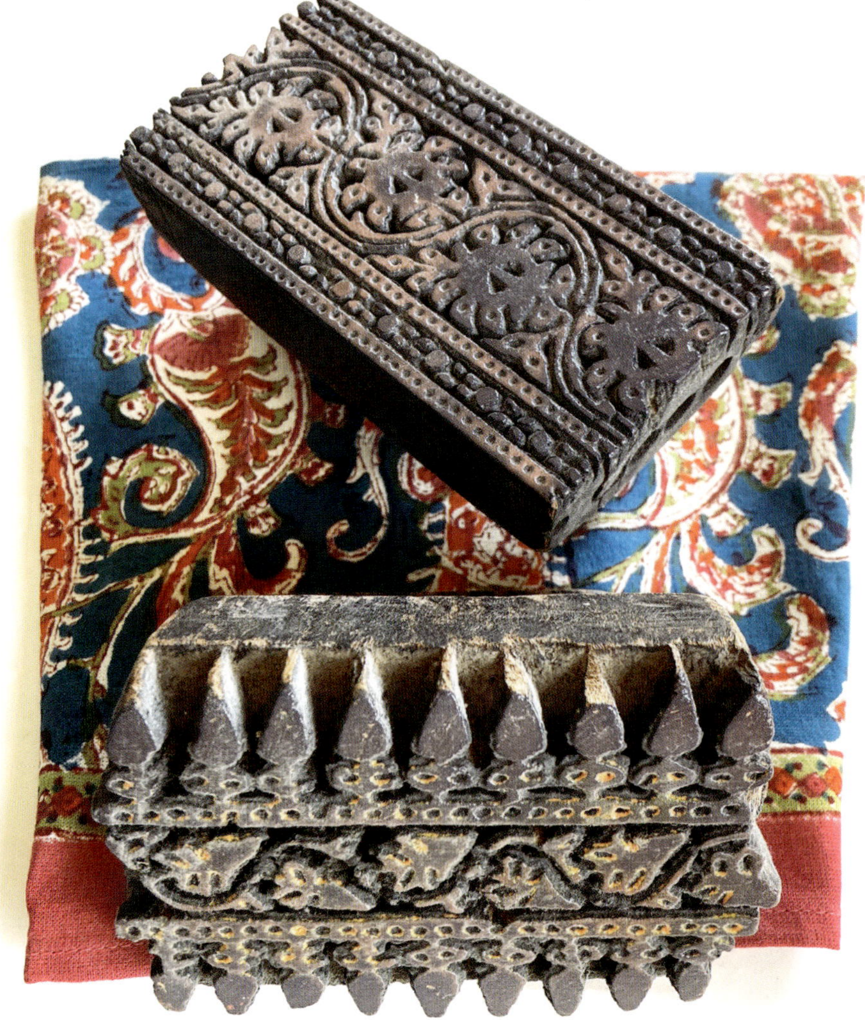

End grain woodblocks such as these are still carved and used in India today to hand-print beautiful, multicoloured, woodblock-printed fabrics.

COMMERCIAL WOOD ENGRAVING

Hundreds of firms of wood engravers arose to produce imagery for commercial purposes – many employing numerous engravers. With tight deadlines (especially for newspapers), this multitude of skilled engravers would have worked long, unsocial hours, probably for quite low pay – perhaps the sweatshop workers of their day.

Each firm would have had one or more master craftsmen who would transfer their drawings or photographic images onto large blocks, each of which comprised perhaps a dozen or more small blocks, all of identical height and clamped together with entirely flush edges. With the image delineated across its entire surface, all the small blocks would then be taken out of the clamp and divvied out among the workforce. Experienced engravers would, no doubt, be charged with trickier areas: figures or architectural details for instance, while novices would be tasked with easier parts such as foliage or skies (for which there existed a mechanical device for engraving tonal parallel lines). All the team would work with tools of the same gauge so that all marks were at a similar scale across blocks comprising a single image before the blocks were bolted back together to create one large image for printing. Firms developed house styles so their engravers would cut particular areas of an image in specific directions with a character of almost invisible tool marks.

Skies were often rendered in horizontal lines with varying amounts of uncut wood between each cut line so as to create different tones of grey in the engraving – much as halftone dots in newspaper photographs create those effects today. The cutting direction was also significant because, when small blocks were engraved and reassembled to form a single image for printing, each one needed to link seamlessly with adjacent blocks by other hands. If one engraver, for instance, had engraved a sky with diagonal lines or swirls when all other engravers' tones comprised horizontal lines, the differently cut one would have stuck out like a sore thumb! These trade engravings featured extraordinarily consistent cutting across all blocks, as well as incredibly tiny tool marks so that any minor stylistic errors would be virtually indiscernible in the prints.

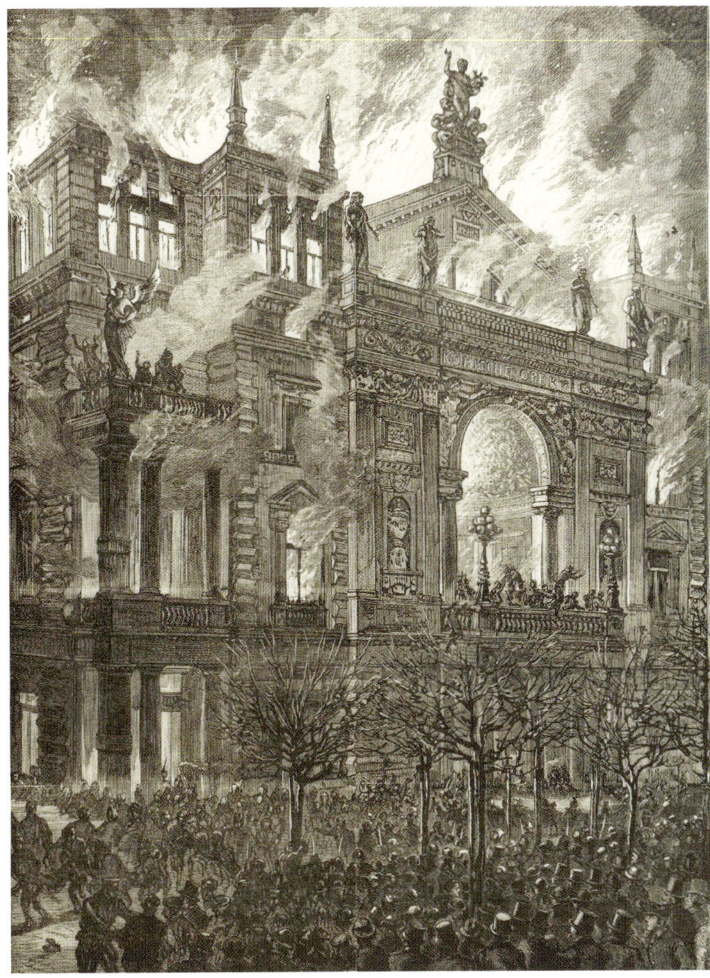

Burning of the Ring Theatre, Vienna (1881). Wood engraving (engravers unknown) simulating fine pen drawing, printed from ten blocks locked together after engraving to print the complete image, 31.7 × 23cm (12½ × 9in), on newsprint. Drawn from a sketch by a 'Herr Mangold of Vienna' and published in the *Illustrated London News*, 17 December 1881.

Boxwood (*Buxus sempervirens*) – from that very slow-growing hedge often used for creating living mazes or intriguing topiary in stately homes – could be engraved with extraordinary precision and was strong enough to take thousands of printings with no visible deterioration in quality. This made it ideal for the newspaper and book printing trades until photomechanical techniques replaced it in mass-produced commercial publications from the early twentieth century.

Bewick's advances in wood engraving were, however, slower to catch on in the field of fine art. His contemporary – English visionary poet-painter-printmaker William Blake (1757–1827) – created only seventeen small wood

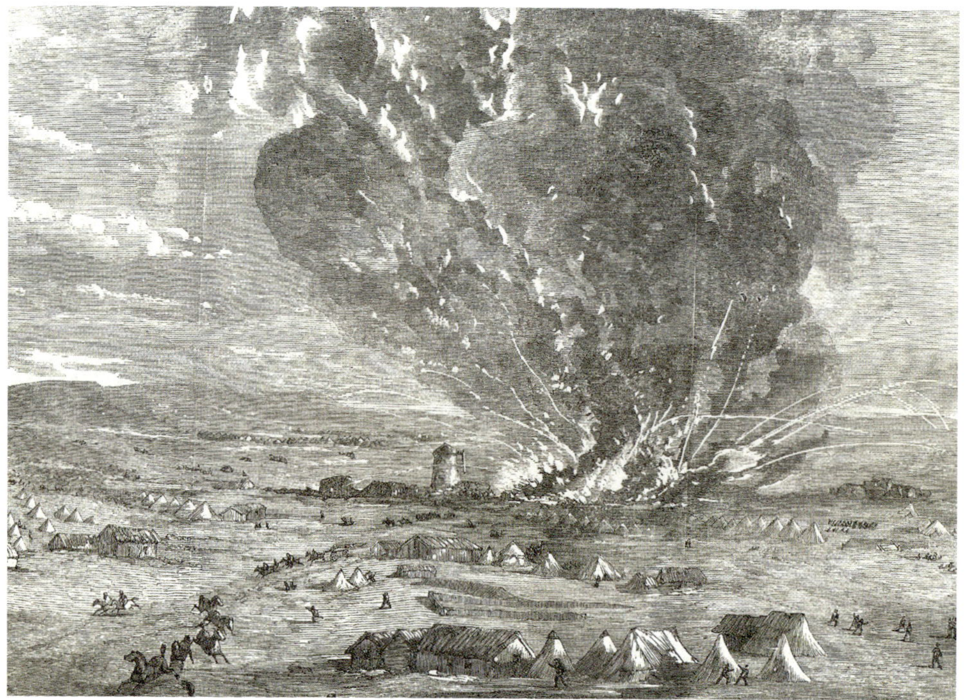

The Explosion of the Right Siege-Train, Near Inkerman Hill, Crimea (detail, 1881). Wood engraving with tint tool cutting to create subtly variant sky tones, printed from many blocks locked together to print the complete image, 23 × 33cm (9 × 13in), on newsprint. From a sketch by an 'E A Goodall', it was published in the *Illustrated London News*, 17 December 1881.

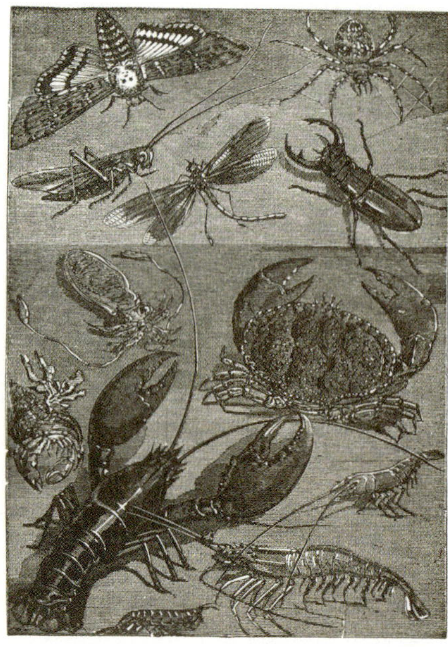

Zoological illustration (untitled), nineteenth century wood engraving on white paper, engraver unknown, 10 × 7cm (4 × 2¾in). The finesse of its tonal cutting is phenomenal, yet its unsung maker is entirely unknown. This was a gift on the birth of my son, from the wonderfully adept tonal wood engraver Monica Poole (1921–2003).

engravings (for a publication of Virgil's *Eclogues* in 1821). Blake's acolytes, Samuel Palmer (1805–81) and Edward Calvert (1799–1883), produced just one and seven engravings respectively. Yet their influence on early twentieth century British artists was profound because of their showing in a V&A exhibition (1926): *Drawings, Etchings and Woodcuts by Samuel Palmer and Other Disciples of William Blake*. This was seen by Paul Nash (1889–1946), the young Eric Ravilious (1903–42) and others who adopted wood engraving for fine art purposes (much as Andy Warhol took on screenprinting in the mid twentieth century) and used it to great effect.

Meanwhile, the parallel influence of Dürer can be seen in engravings by William Morris (1834–96), Edward Burne-Jones (1833–98), Lucien Pissarro (1863–1944) and other pioneers of Britain's Arts and Crafts Movement. Their blocks are phenomenally intricate and, like Dürer's, simulated black-line drawings, hence their technical term: black-line engravings. By contrast, Bewick's engravings began to explore the medium's white-line possibilities:

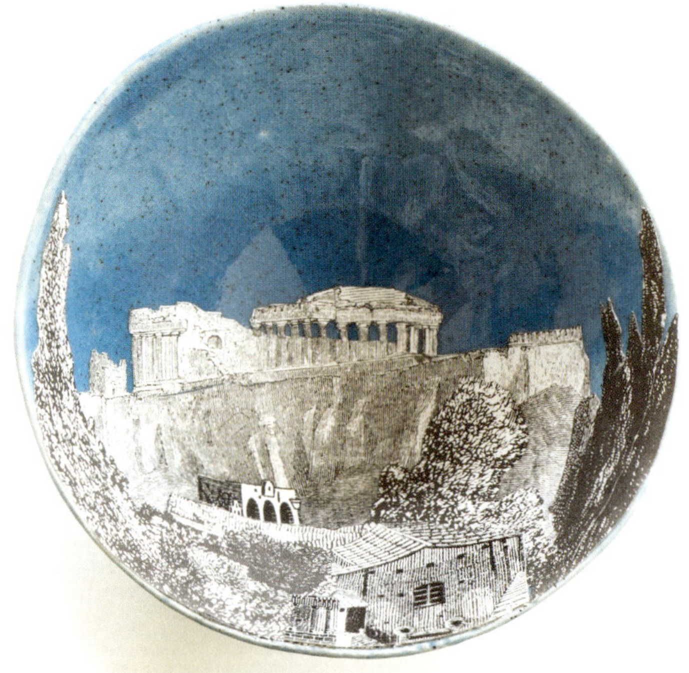

Grecian Sky (2019), my wood engravings and details of nineteenth century engravings on paper collaged on glazed ceramic bowl, diameter: 8.7cm (3½in) × depth: 5cm (2in).

images that at first sight resemble pen drawings but which, on closer inspection, reveal a range of tonal marks that come directly from an engagement with inventive white-on-black tool cuts, rather than merely trying to reproduce pre-existing pen lines. To make such revolutionary images, artists needed to create images *in light*, which required a thinking process akin to that of making drawings in white chalk on black paper. It's that white-line effect – known as white-line engraving – that inspired the twentieth century's great British artist-engravers including Gwen Raverat (1885–1957), Gertrude Hermes (1901–83), Clare Leighton (1898–1989), Monica Poole (1921–2003), Simon Brett (1943–2024) and many others. It's those same effects and their seemingly infinite possibilities that continue to inspire artists today.

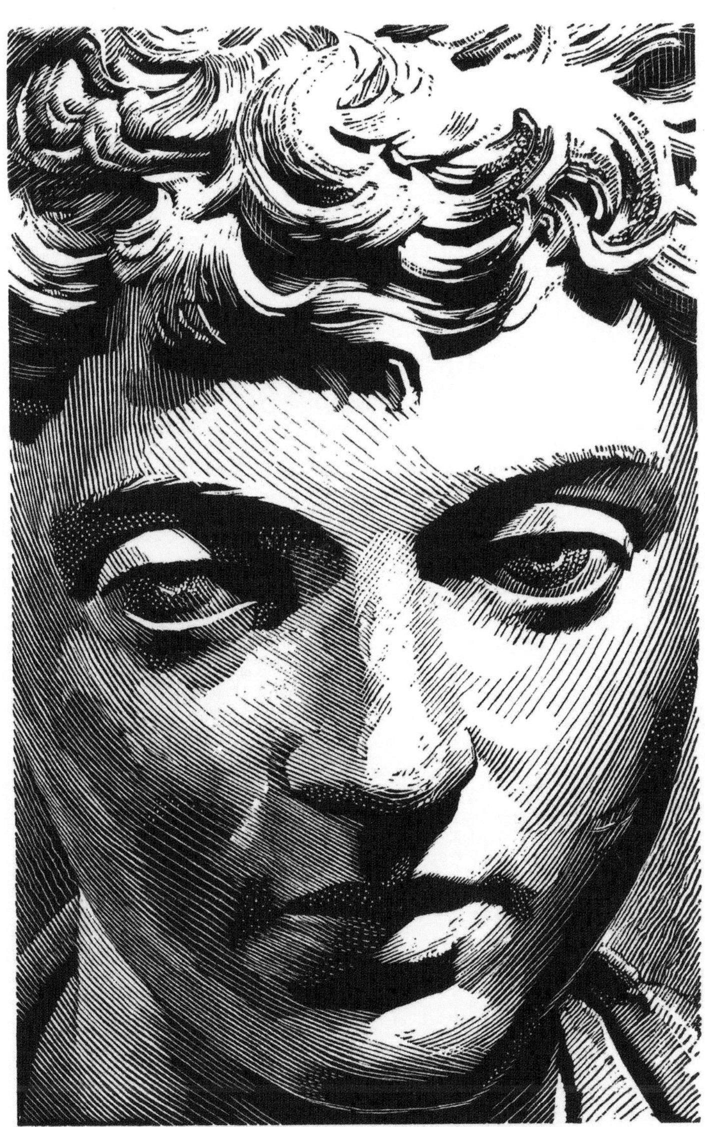

Marcus Aurelius I for *The Meditations of Marcus Aurelius*. Folio Society (2002). Wood engraving on lemonwood, 15 × 9.2cm (6 × 3½in), on Zerkall paper, by Simon Brett. © Estate of Simon Brett. This has some features of black-line engraving but also wonderful white-line cutting with wider and narrower parallel lines spaced far apart or closer together to create its tones.

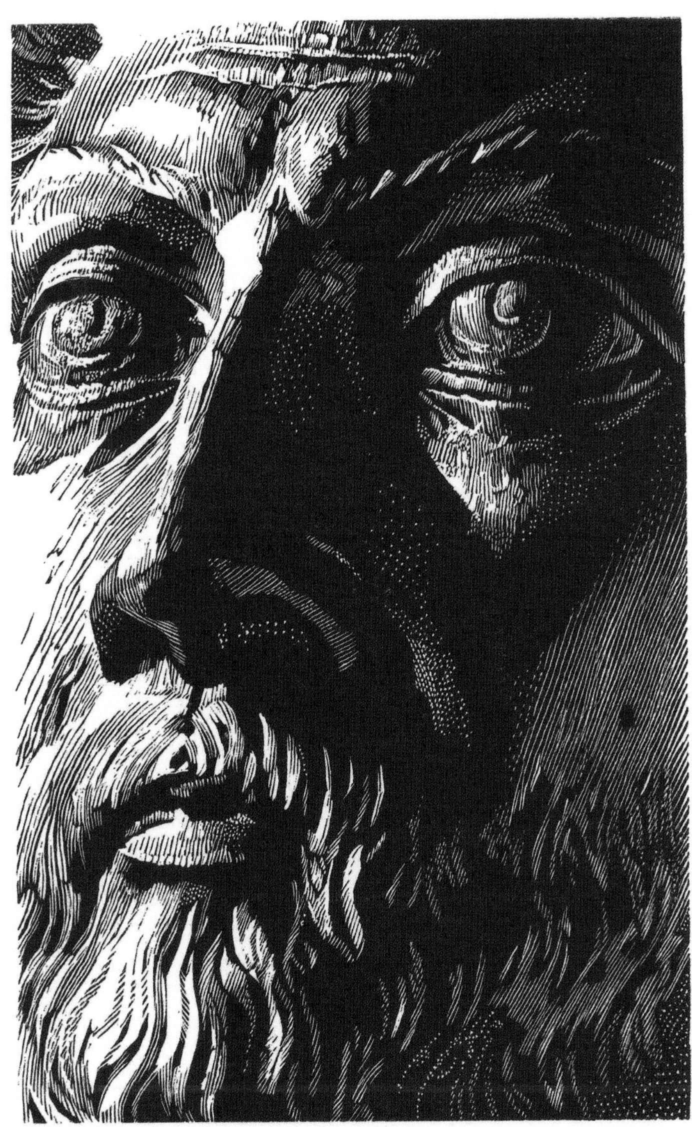

Marcus Aurelius III for *The Meditations of Marcus Aurelius*. Folio Society, 2002. Wood engraving on lemonwood, 15 × 9.2cm (6 × 3½in), on Zerkall paper, by Simon Brett. © Estate of Simon Brett. This expertly combines both black-line and white-line tonal effects and adds scatterings of crisply stippled dots to provide even subtler tones and beautifully contrasted tool marks.

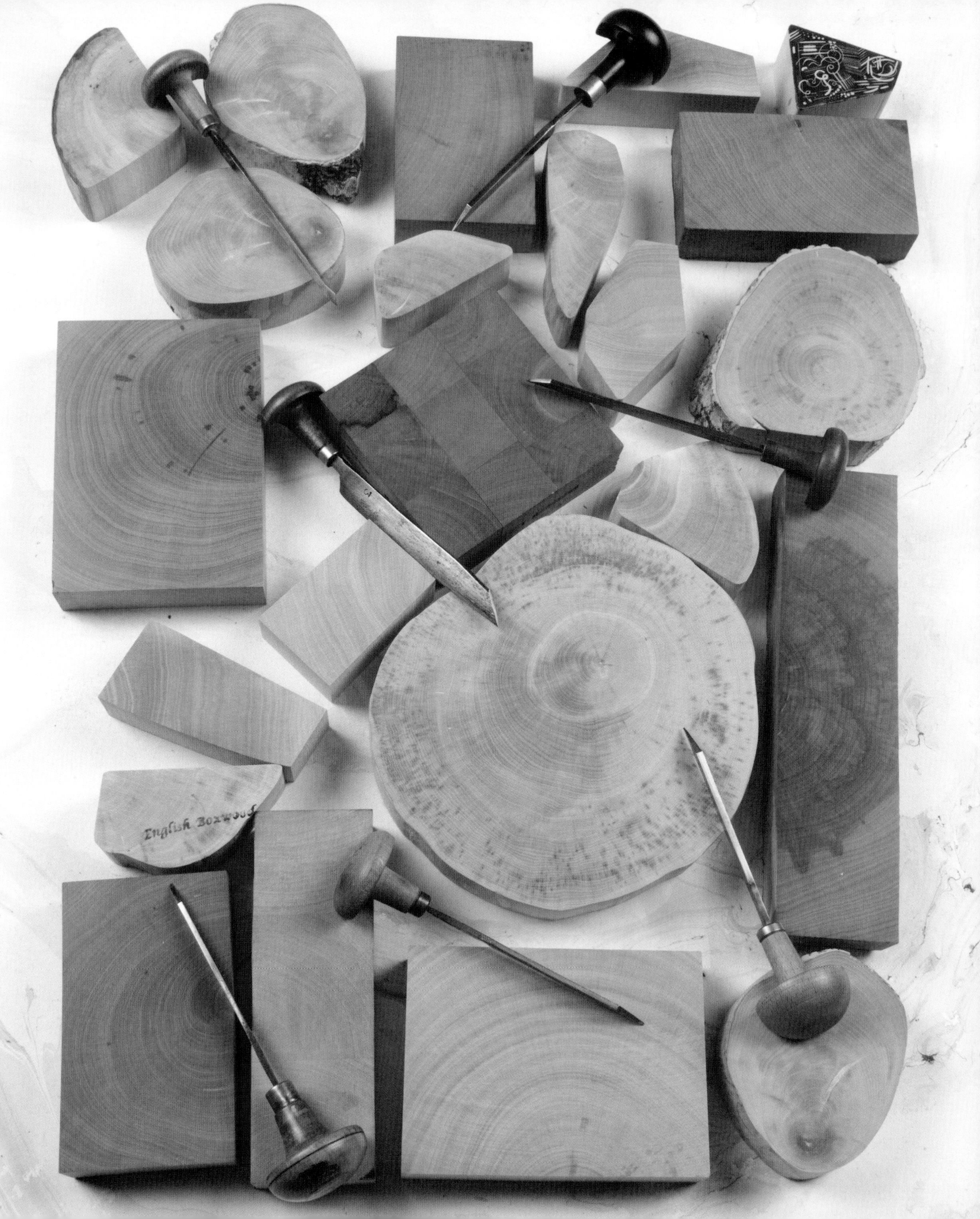
English Boxwood

CHAPTER 2

WOOD, GRAVERS AND OTHER MATERIALS

Suppliers of specialist materials are listed towards the end of this book and detailed information about wood, tools, printing rollers and inks are included here and in other chapters describing their use.

DIFFERENT WOODS FOR ENGRAVING

Not all woods are suitable for engraving. Like Goldilocks trying out the beds in the house of the three bears: some are too hard, some too soft and others just right. Woods I have used include box, lemon, holly, pear and American maple. I'm told that certain varieties of cherry, apple and magnolia can be engraved too. I've also heard of engravers working on large end grain kitchen chopping boards, which comprise lots of small hardwood pieces carefully joined with glue and carpentry joints. In fact, because engraving wood is so slow-growing, larger blocks do have to be specially made by expertly joining smaller pieces together, so that the joins are perfectly aligned and invisible in the printing.

While there are lots of useful sundries for wood engraving, essentially all you need is a woodblock, two tools with different cutting tips, a small inking slab, a roller, printing ink, a teaspoon and some paper.

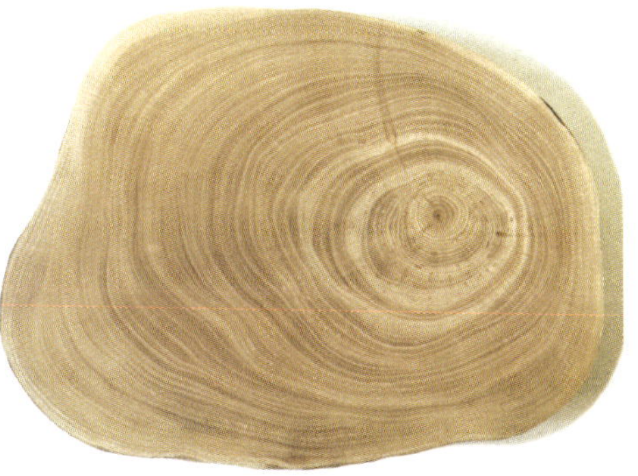

A block prepared for engraving from my mother's holly bush. You can see clearly the closely spaced tree-ring patterns in this large roundel.

A selection of my wood engraving blocks from various different tree species, plus a selection of engraving tools.

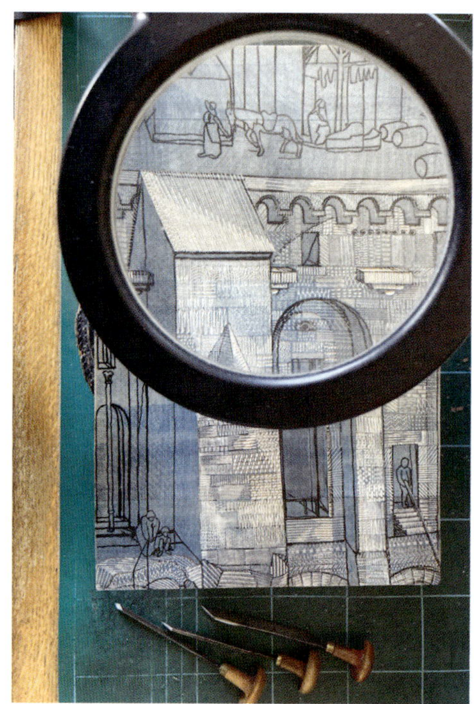

My magnifying lens attaches to my desk with a small G-clamp and provides extremely helpful magnification of my engraved marks.

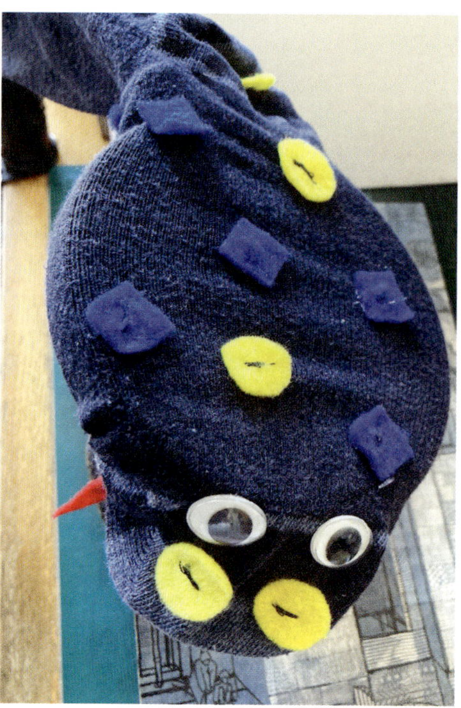

If using a lens, never leave it unattended within range of direct sunlight. Lenses can cause housefires! This sock-puppet (made years ago by one of my children) is a perfect lens cover. If you don't have a handy puppet – an old sock will do the job!

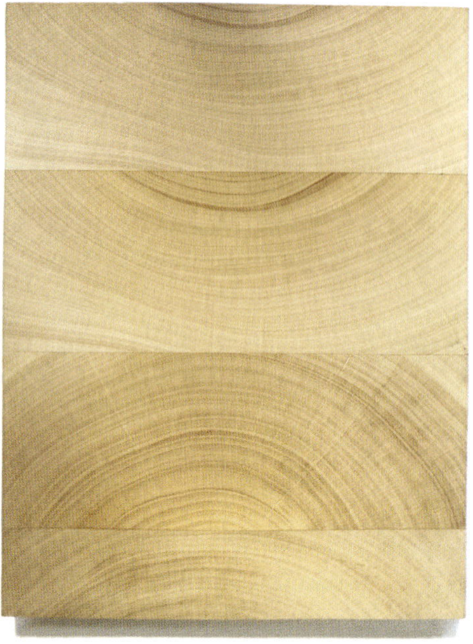

This lemonwood end grain block comprises four pieces joined perfectly with glue, plus carpentry joints at the sides (not visible in this image) to provide extra strength. The joins on a composite block should be seamless so that they don't affect either engraving or printing.

Box

Boxwood is what you might call the Rolls Royce of engraving woods. It's very slow-growing. Its rings are closely spaced and of more or less equal width. Trees that grow fast in summer and slow in winter make terrible engraving woods. The winter rings can be too tough to engrave while the wider summer rings are too soft. Box grows at a consistent rate all year round and cuts cleanly without splintering. When seasoned and planed to glass-like smoothness, its amber-coloured surface is perfect for engraving and can withstand thousands of printings without wearing out. Traditionally, English boxwood has been considered the best. That's because we have such miserable weather that British box is especially slow-growing and so is prized over faster-growing trees from warmer climes! Unfortunately, because a box tree needs about 200 years to grow to sufficient girth to make decent-sized blocks, supplies of it are limited because of the quantities used for engravings (and other purposes) in earlier centuries.

Lemonwood

Lemonwood – nothing to do with lemons and sometimes called Castello Boxwood – is a deciduous, fast-growing tree native to Paraguay, Nicaragua and other parts of Central and South America, the leaves of which, when rubbed, give off a citrus scent. An excellent, less pricey alternative to boxwood, it's faster-growing and thus available in larger sizes. Many engravers can't discern a difference between engraving the pinkish-grey surface of end grain lemon rather than box. I find lemon marginally softer but the difference is negligible and both give great results. For larger-scale engravings, lemonwood is a great choice. Since a block-maker can create blocks larger than any tree's girth by joining pieces together, the number of smaller blocks required to make a larger composite is generally far fewer, if using lemonwood, than for box where available pieces tend to be much smaller and thus the labour involved for the block-maker makes larger boxwood blocks notably more expensive than lemonwood ones of the same size.

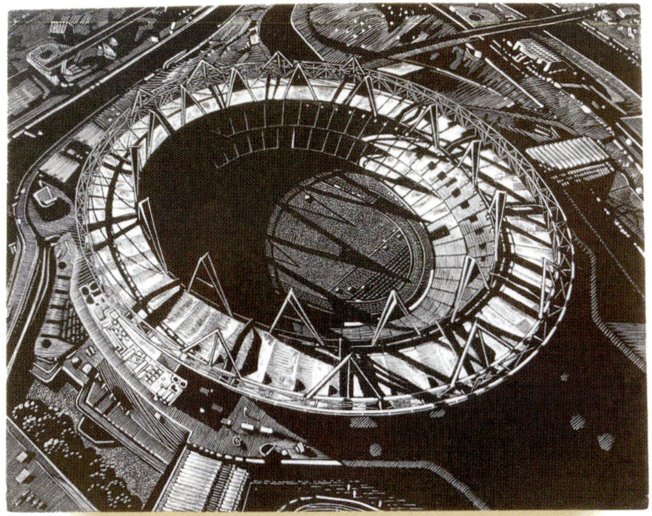

I engraved this image of London's Olympic stadium in 2011 on a boxwood block. It cut cleanly and crisply. There is some talcum powder rubbed into the engraved marks of this and most of the other blocks illustrated so as to enhance the visibility of the tool-marks.

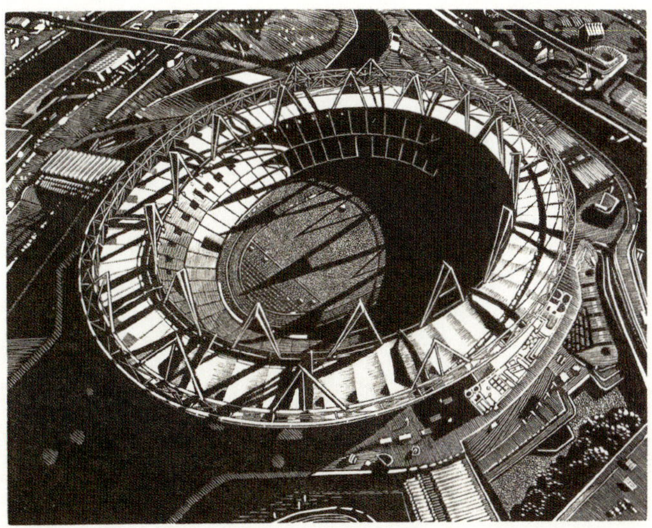

Olympic Shadows (2011), wood engraving on boxwood, 10.3 × 12.8cm (4 × 5in), on Gampi Vellum paper. Boxwood facilitates particularly fine, complex, engraving. Also, note that the finished print is a perfect mirror image of what was engraved on the block.

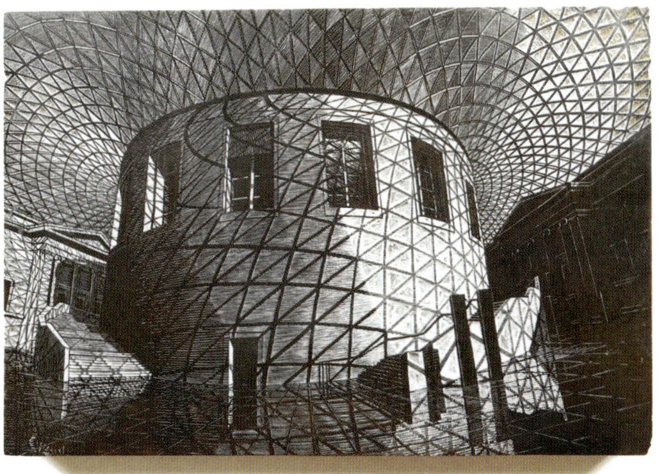

I began engraving this large lemonwood block in 2004 and printed three variants of it before it reached this stage of cutting in 2005. It cut as finely as any boxwood block I've ever engraved.

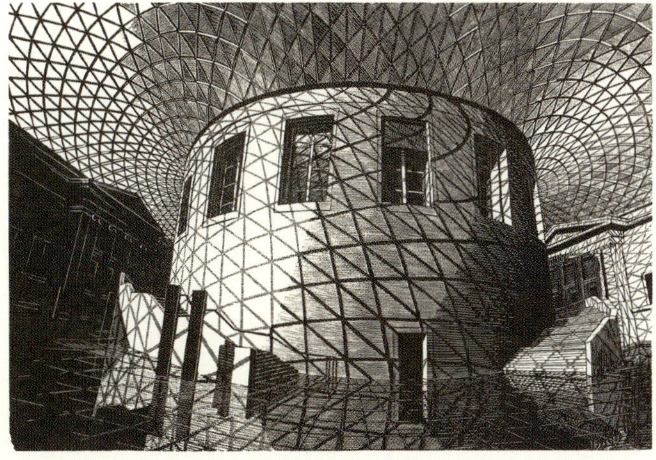

British Museum Series No. 4 (2005), wood engraving, 17.4 × 24.8cm (6¾ × 9¾in), on Gampi Vellum paper. Lemonwood, like box, can be cut with precision and great finesse, and can provide a larger surface area at a lower price than box on which to work.

Detail of an engraving on holly in progress, seen through a magnifying lens. (PHOTO: LUKE HALSTEAD)

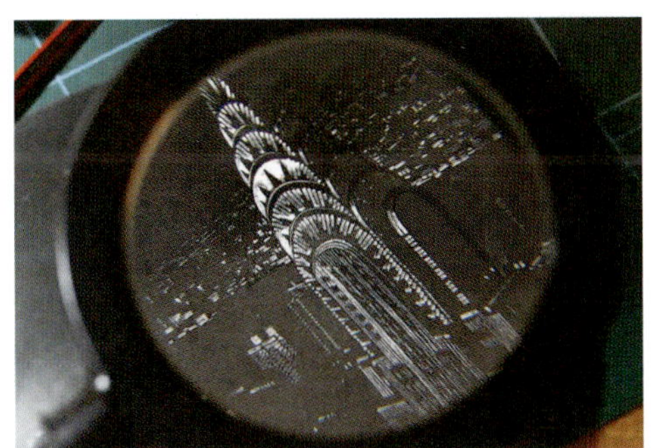

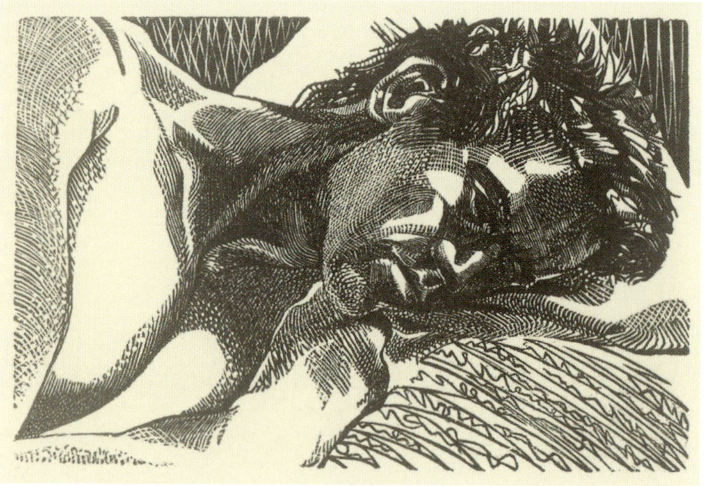

Sam Sleeping (1988), wood engraving on maple, 10 × 15cm (4 × 6in), on buff Japanese paper. This portrait of a friend from my student days is on a composite block of several maple sections. The joins were flush and engraved and printed seamlessly but the wood, overall, was a bit soft and didn't engrave as crisply as box, lemon or holly.

Holly

Holly engraves very well. It is a pale pinkish-white wood, which makes it especially easy to see the image appearing as you engrave (having stained its surface a darker tone). I've engraved several large roundels of holly from a bush at my family's home in Liverpool. My Mum had the bush cut down in the early 1980s and asked the tree surgeon to cut me some roundels, which she stored in the bottom of a wardrobe. We then both forgot about them for about thirty years! I rediscovered them in 2014 and sent them to a block-maker to prepare them for engraving. I ended up with three large blocks, each side of which was planed to a level, smooth-as-glass surface giving me wood for six new engravings.

Maple

The pinkish end grain of maple has a distinctive stripy appearance. It's a popular, readily available wood widely used by engravers, especially in the USA. It engraves reasonably but sometimes is a little soft and doesn't always cut as cleanly as box, lemon or holly.

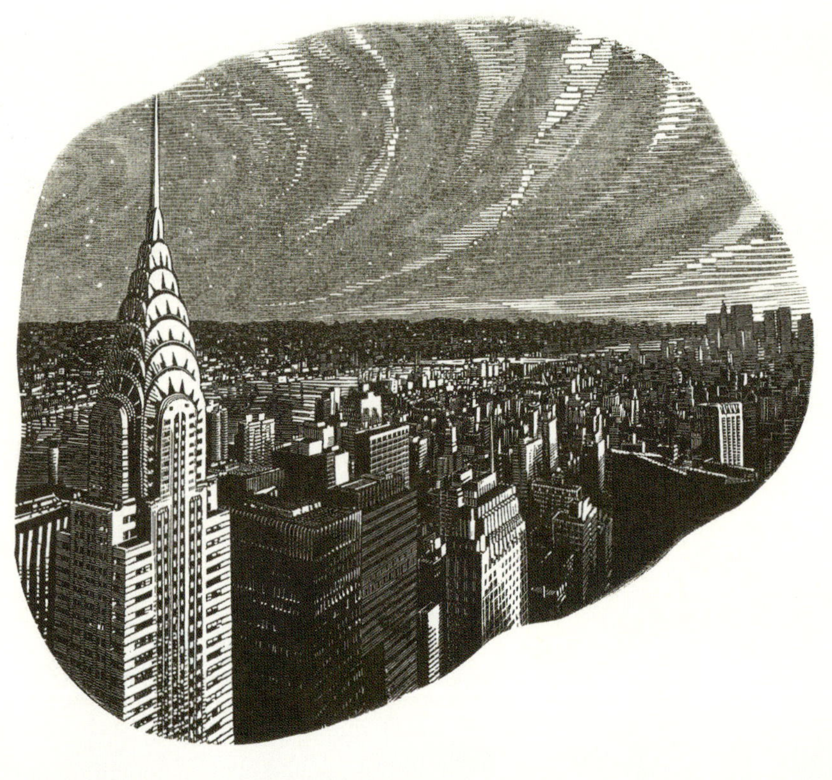

Manhattan Sky (2017), wood engraving (and stencilling to lift off some of the ink's intensity in the sky area) on holly, 19 × 20.3cm (7½ × 8in), on Japanese paper. This image was engraved on a roundel from the same holly bush from my childhood home in Liverpool.

Pear

Used for sculptural carvings and (when cut along the plank) for woodcut prints, pear can also be engraved on the end grain. Its darkish pink/beige hue can make it difficult to see how the engraved marks will translate into the paper-white of the final image and, like maple, it can cut reasonably well, but is sometimes a bit too soft for really crisp cutting.

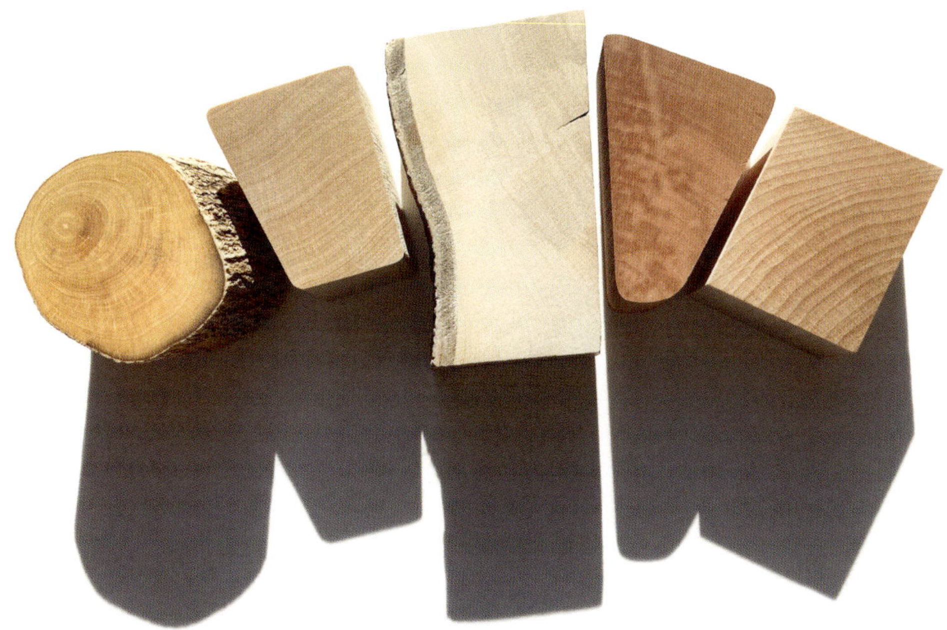

From left to right, small end grain blocks of: box, lemonwood, holly, pear and maple woods.

ORDERING SUPPLIES

Wood can be purchased from printmaking suppliers or ordered to bespoke sizes from a specialist blockmaker. Practice packs are ideal for beginners and useful for experienced practitioners, each pack containing a collection of planed blocks of assorted wood varieties, all more-or-less 'type-high' (2.33cm or 0.918in). Carved wood or cast metal letters for printing text were made to this standard height and printing presses were set to print type-high blocks. Woodblocks intended for engraved images were also made type-high, since many were designed to print alongside text. Although most engravings today are created as independent images, the convention of the type-high block continues, not least because the cast-iron, relief-printing presses created to print them in the nineteenth and early twentieth centuries were designed for type-high blocks. Plenty of these presses are still in use in print workshops, colleges and in the homes and studios of private practitioners worldwide. My own Albion press was made in London in 1859 and is still in excellent working order.

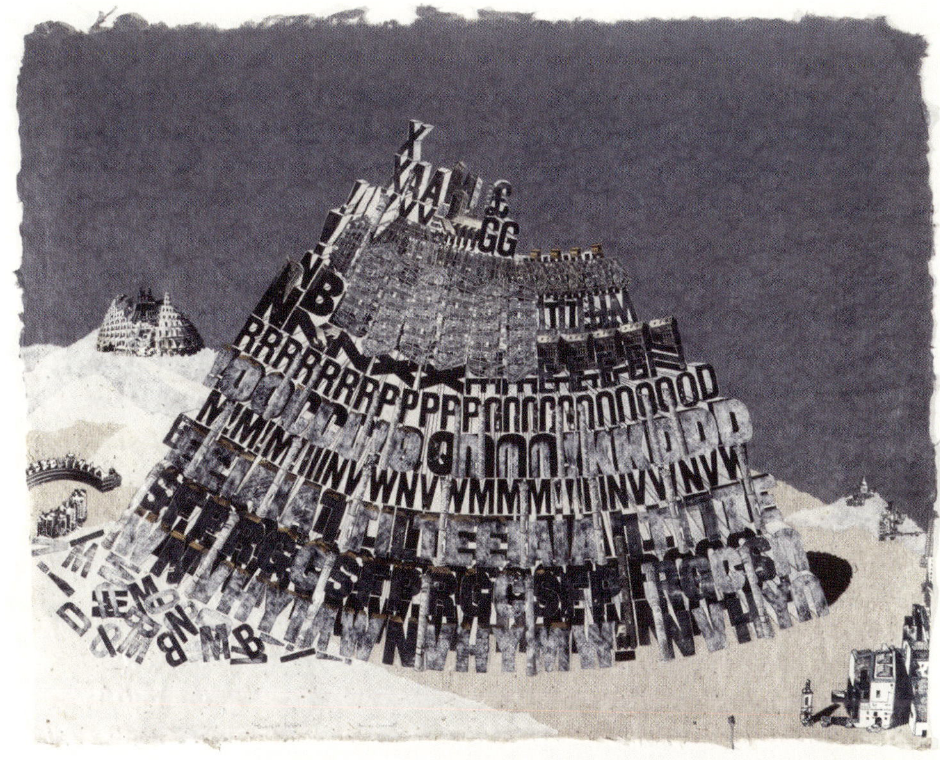

Towers of Babble (2002), wooden type, wood engraving, linocut, solarplate print and collage on various papers, 66 × 81.3cm (26 × 32in). This involved collaging printed wooden-type letters to create an invented architectural tower-like structure. The letter forms were printed separately from the engraved image blocks, but all the woodblocks used were type-high.

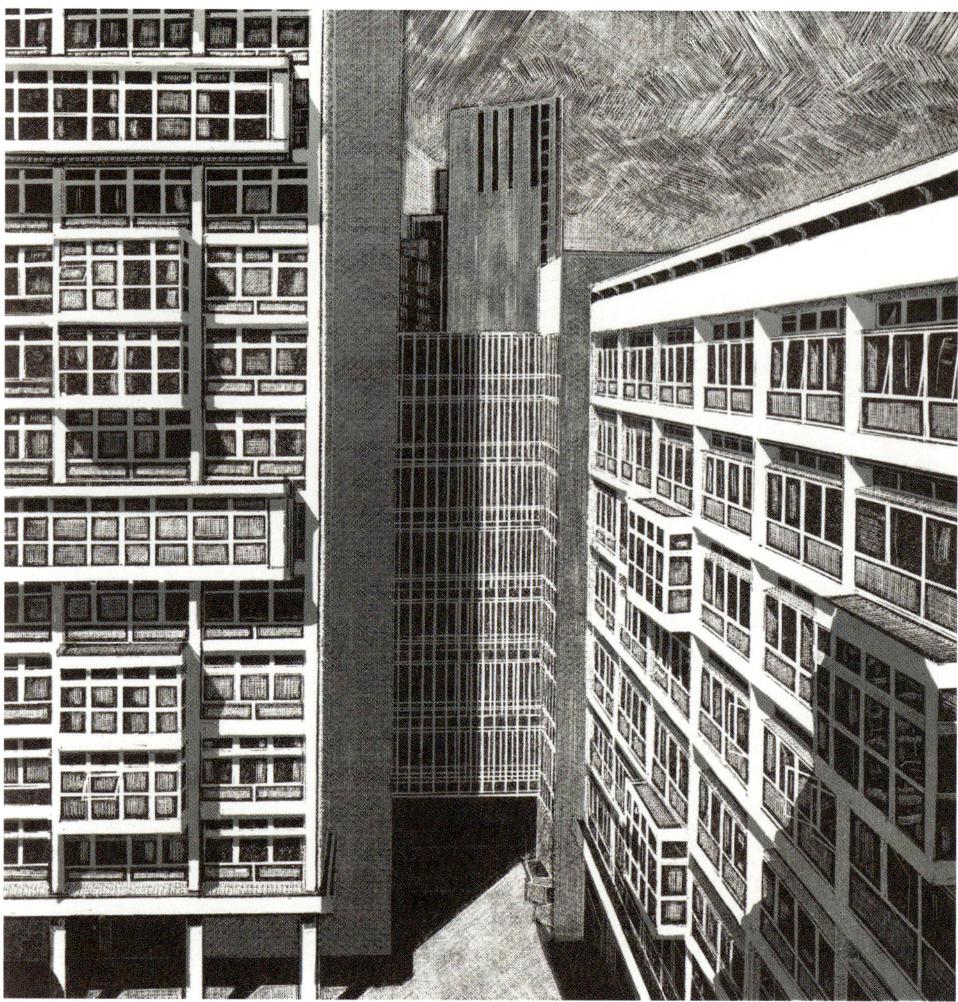

Metro Central Heights (2022), engraving on two blocks of engraving plastic, 21 × 20.5cm (8¼ × 8in), on Zerkall paper, by Louise Hayward (b.1963). This artist almost always engraves on wood substitutes such as the engraving plastic used here, and also *TroLase*®. Her work clearly demonstrates the fine results such plastics can yield.

The nineteenth-century firms of engravers were well served by numerous suppliers of wood and tools. With the decline in the medium's mass-use for commercial purposes and its re-emergence as a specialist technique employed by relatively few artists and illustrators, the quantity of suppliers has declined such that, at the time of writing, there is only one professional block-maker in the UK and not many more elsewhere. There are, however, various inexpensive plastic/polymer plates available for engraving. When printed, the results look indistinguishable from woodblock prints but they feel rather different to engrave. Some varieties used by today's engravers include TroLase® – a 2-ply high-quality acrylic-based engraving plastic (manufactured by Trotec) – and Corian® – a material combining acrylic polymer and natural minerals, which is frequently used to make durable kitchen worktops, among other things.

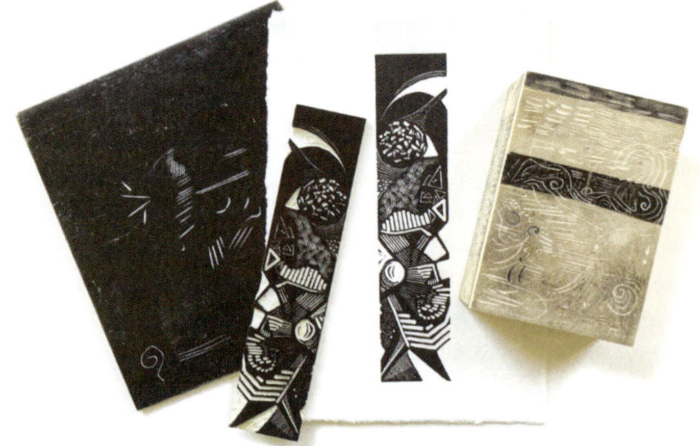

Two pieces of engraving plastic and print, plus *Resingrave*® – a (discontinued) white-coloured polymer surface laminated on MDF. I darkened it with marker pen and dilute ink-wash stripes before testing tool cuts on it. Thin engraving plastic with bevelled edges can be printed on etching presses but laminating such thin blocks on MDF is a good way to make type-high polymer blocks.

MATERIALS CHECKLIST

To get started in wood engraving, you may find this a useful equipment list.

- **End grain practice blocks**. In the UK, these usually come in packs of ten small pieces in a mixture of wood varieties. (Progress to ordering practice packs of larger pieces and/or rectangular or square blocks, at bespoke sizes for your needs, or irregular-shaped roundels.)
- At least **two engraving tools**: ideally a medium spitsticker and medium round scorper. You can do a great deal just with these but, with a larger budget and to develop your skills, add a large lozenge or square graver, medium tint tool, small-medium square scorper, flat chisel and a multiple tool with three or four teeth. Later you may want to expand your tool set with duplicates of any of these tools, but in a range of different gauges to produce different widths of cut from each one.
- A pot of **water-washable fountain-pen ink** in a dark colour – blue or brown are ideal.
- A **square-ended soft-hair watercolour brush** of about one-centimetre brush-head width, and a small flat-tipped bristle brush.
- A **square-tipped indelible marker pen** in blue or green rather than black.
- An **HB or B pencil** and **pencil sharpener**.
- A **fine line black pen**.
- **Chinagraph pencils** (designed for writing on china or glass) in white, red and black.
- **Tracing or carbon transfer paper** (coloured varieties and/or black).
- **Scrap paper** (newsprint, photocopier/printer or cartridge paper).
- **Scissors**.
- A small pot of **French chalk** (aka talcum powder).
- A **small mirror** (helpful if you want to see how your engraving-in-progress will look when printed).
- **Visual aids**: a good magnifying lens (if your eyesight isn't great) or, failing that, off-the-shelf or prescription reading glasses. An Anglepoise lamp for strong directional light on the block is also very helpful.
- A **sandbag**: this specialist piece of equipment comprises two circles of polished leather – each about 12–15cm (4¾–6in) in diameter – stitched together around their edges and packed tight with sand. It can definitely help the engraving process but isn't essential, or not initially, as it's quite possible to make good engravings without one.
- A tube of **stiff, oil-based, black ink** for relief/letterpress printing. Black is a good place to start, but you can add tubes of coloured inks and extender, aka reducing medium (a medium to make coloured inks more translucent) later.
- **Printing paper**: plenty of European and Asian (especially Japanese) printing papers are available from specialist printmaking suppliers. For wood engraving, look for papers with a very smooth surface (like newsprint) but not a shiny/glossy surface like photographic papers.
- A **toughened glass or Perspex inking slab** (or smooth glazed tile, or piece of old Formica from a kitchen worktop, or any other rigid, smooth, easily-cleaned surface). Excellent toughened-glass (with bevelled edges) or Perspex inking slabs of 14.8 × 21cm (5¾ × 8¼in) or 40 × 30cm (15¾ × 11¾in) can be purchased inexpensively from printmaking suppliers.
- A small, hand-held, **printing roller**.
- A **palette knife** (or use an old plastic store card).
- A **metal teaspoon** (or small, smooth, wooden spoon) for hand-printing in the absence of a relief printing press.
- **Clean rags** and/or **paper towel** – though Dorothea Braby's wood engraving manual of 1953 recommends 'discarded silk underwear' as excellent for cleaning up!
- A packet of *Blu-Tack*.
- **Vegetable (cooking) oil**, **washing-up liquid** and/or an alternative non-toxic cleaning fluid.
- An **apron or old T-shirt** to protect clothes, as the printing ink is permanent and doesn't wash off fabrics.
- **Barrier cream** or **disposable gloves** (optional) to keep printing ink off your hands.
- **Sticking plasters** and **antiseptic ointment** in case of a tool cut to the hand (an avoidable but common hazard).
- **Silicon carbide abrasive paper** of extra fine grit: P400, for tool sharpening and fine jewellers' emery polishing paper, grade 4/0, for tool honing.
- An **extra-long steel ruler** for tearing/cutting printing paper.
- A **sharp scalpel** or other hand-held cutting knife for cutting paper.
- A large **self-healing cutting mat** to protect your table if cutting paper. These are usually marked with grids in centimetres as a cutting guide.
- A **comfortable chair and table/desk**. A padded, adjustable, office chair is ideal because you can adjust it to the perfect height so as not to get a stiff neck or back by sitting in an uncomfortable position while engraving.
- **Source material** to inspire engravings. This might be your own drawings or photos or imagery from illustrated books/ magazines or pictures sourced online (but be careful not to infringe anyone's copyright if using source material that you didn't create yourself).

PREPARING WOODBLOCKS AND CARING FOR THEM

If you have a box hedge, holly bush, maple, cherry or pear tree and wish to use it for engraving, this, briefly, is what to do (but keep in mind that not all varieties of these trees will engrave equally well).

1. Have your tree surgeon cut the larger branches and/or trunk into roundels, across the grain. Each roundel must be a bit deeper than type-high to allow for levelling and planing after seasoning. The roundels should be a consistent depth as it is difficult to plane a roundel that is thicker at one side than the other.

2. Store the roundels in a cool, dry environment where the temperature is reasonably consistent. The bottom of a wardrobe or airy cupboard away from radiators or heaters but within a central-heated house is ideal. Garden sheds, greenhouses, garages or conservatories aren't suitable because they get cold and perhaps damp in winter and too hot and dry in summer. Store each piece on a short edge rather than laid flat. Blocks are less likely to warp if they season upright. (Seasoning is the process of drying timber so as to remove moisture from its cells: essential prior to engraving so it doesn't warp, expand or shrink while you're engraving.) Leave a gap between each roundel so that moisture can escape easily from each piece. Leave the wood for three or four years to season fully: its moisture needs time to evaporate slowly to leave the wood hard and firm for engraving. Any warping, cracking or splitting will probably happen if it's going to, during this time. Warps and cracks are more likely if the wood is stored somewhere where the temperature is too variable or if the environment is very hot, which can make the moisture evaporate too quickly.

3. When seasoned, level the wood's end grain surface(s) with a wood plane and use successively fine grades of abrasive paper to give it as smooth a surface as possible. You will, however, probably get a better result if you let a professional block-maker prepare the seasoned roundels for you. Remember that, in an end grain block, there is no right or wrong side, so you can plane both sides, giving you two engraving surfaces from each one.

4. If both faces of the block have been planed, protect one side from scratches (while you're engraving the other) with a sturdy sheet of smooth paper cut a bit larger than the total surface area and taped in place around the block's sides.

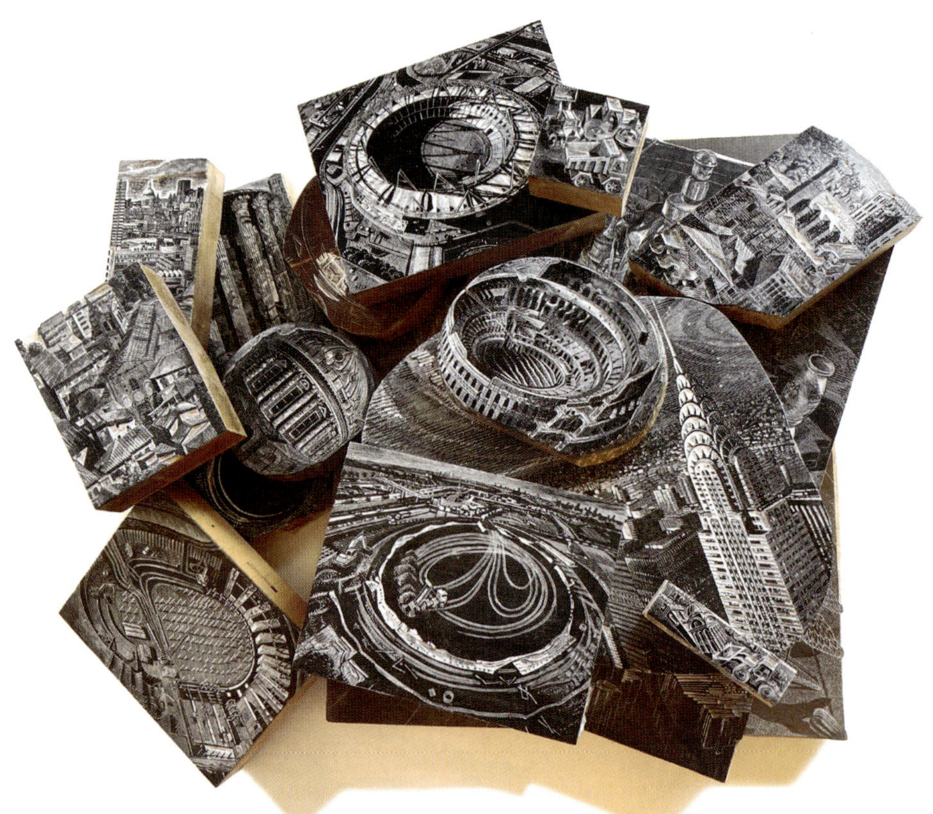

A collection of my engraved blocks in box, lemonwood and holly. Along the visible side of the block in the bottom left, you can see two narrow carpentry joints. These serve to strengthen the composite block which comprises three separate boxwood pieces joined/glued seamlessly together by a professional block-maker.

5. The speediest route to getting started is simply to buy already prepared end grain wood from a block-maker or printmaking supplier.

6. The safest way to store blocks before use is to leave them in their paper and/or card packaging. Otherwise, and after engraving, wrap them in paper so that they don't scuff one another. Store them upright on their short edges rather than flat. They are less prone to warping if upright. Never leave them on a windowsill where they may be in direct sunlight, which will cause them to crack. Even when blocks have been well seasoned and prepared, they can still warp or split if you don't look after them. I store unengraved blocks in a lidded wooden storage box in my studio. For years I kept my engraved blocks in a plan-chest drawer but, as I eventually needed that space for prints, I now store them in large, lidded plastic tubs away from windows and radiators. Also, take care if using a desk lamp: a hot bulb near the block can warp or crack it.

TOOLS AND THEIR USES

If you own lino- or wood-cutting V-gouges, U-gouges or Japanese knives, put them away as they are not suitable for engraving end grain blocks! They will skid across the surface and won't cut it cleanly, if at all. An exception is a flat chisel, which can be used both for woodcutting and engraving. Wood engraving tools closely resemble those used for engraving metal, as used by artists including Dürer and Gustave Doré (1832–83). Today, there are diverse tools (known as burins or gravers), with variously shaped cutting tips for making different marks. Each tool type comes in different gauges designed for larger or smaller marks: size 1 is the narrowest and 12 the widest, but the gauge size varies from brand to brand.

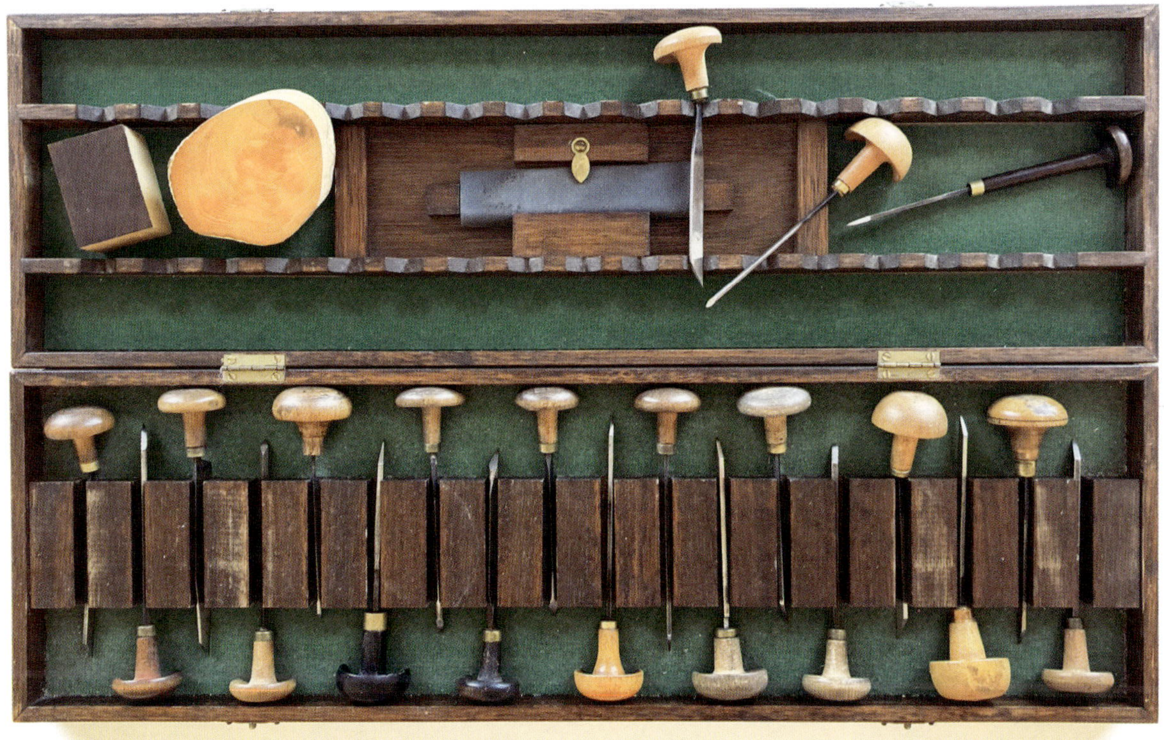

My wooden toolbox (open) made by my artist/engraver husband. It is lined with green baize (to avoid damage to tool blades) and holds my preferred eighteen tools. This is not my complete tool set but, of these, I only use half a dozen regularly. The box also contains a slot for a small tool-sharpening stone.

Lozenge graver

This tool (also known as a *diamond graver* or *lozenge burin*) is the traditional tool still used by metal engravers and jewellers today. With a distinctive diamond- or lozenge-shaped face, sharp cutting tip, sharp straight back, even sharper belly and flat sides, it's designed so that its belly sits in the engraved groove you've begun, enabling you to keep it running easily in a straight line. It's ideal for making straight lines or crosshatched tones but not for curves or circles because its sharp belly will dent the wood behind the curve.

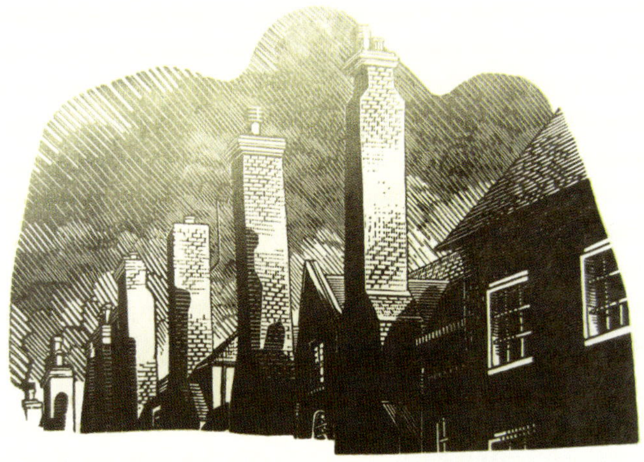

Approaching Storm (2016), wood engraving on boxwood, 8.3 × 11.6cm (3¼ × 4½in), on Gampi Vellum paper. It features lozenge graver cutting in the thinner lines in the sky area and in the thicker and thinner lines and dashes in the rooftop on the extreme right. (It was printed with a colour blend to enhance its drama.)

Varying the pressure of tool on wood can result in fatter or thinner lines. A square graver is essentially the same tool but with a square cutting face, facilitating wider marks. Old lozenge and square gravers sometimes have the top edge of their cutting face ground down a bit.

Spitsticker

The spitsticker (also known as a *spitzsticker*, *spitstick*, *spitz*, *onglette graver*, *point graver* or *elliptical tool*) has a face the shape of a simple boat or upside-down teardrop. Its cutting tip comes to a sharp point. Its belly is notably less sharp than the lozenge graver and has gently curved sides. It also often, but not invariably, has a deeper belly than other tools. (This is especially true of older tools, which can sometimes still be found, second-hand.) Any engraving tool designed with curved sides or curved cutting tip is designed to make curving or wavy lines. Conversely, tools with straight edges and angular cutting tips are designed for straight lines. It's not easy to make successful curves with a straight-line tool, but straight lines can be made easily with tools designed for curves, so the spitsticker, in particular, is highly versatile. Its belly is still sharp enough to guide a straight line just like a lozenge graver. But, if used for its intended purpose of curving lines and wide or tight circles, its belly, being much less sharp, is unlikely to bruise the wood.

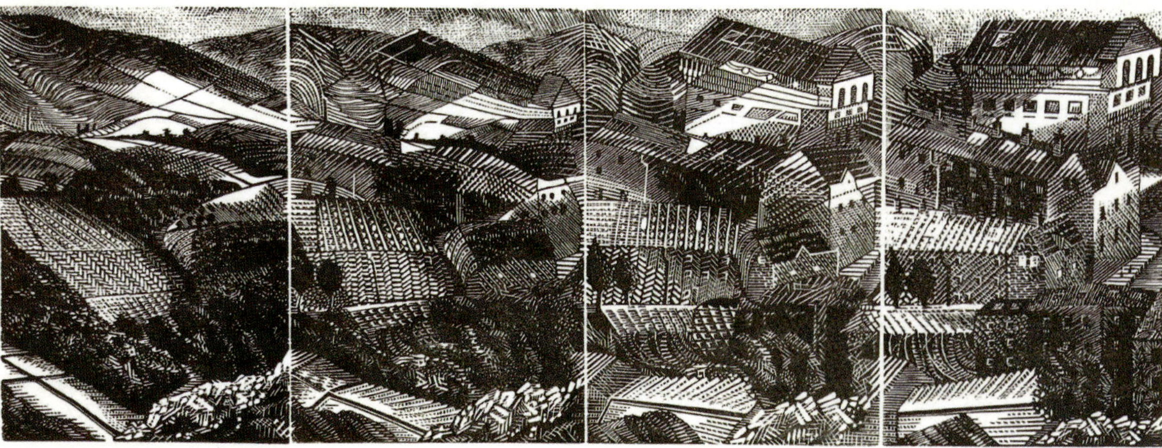

A Second Development (1991), four engravings on boxwood, total size: 7.6 × 20cm (3 × 8in), on China White paper. This sequence was made with several tools but all its curving lines: notably in the top third of each image (where distant hills gradually morph into the Yorkshire town of Hebden Bridge) were made with a spitsticker, making fatter and thinner curves.

Bullsticker

The bullsticker (also known as an *oval graver*) is also designed for curving or wavy lines, circles or swirls. It has a leaf-shaped face, a less sharp belly than a lozenge graver, and sides which are more strongly curved than the spitsticker. Some engravers find it can make tighter curves than the spitsticker but I find little to choose between them. They're both highly versatile and capable of making much the same marks – both curving and straight. As with the lozenge graver, you can increase or reduce the pressure with a bullsticker or spitsticker, as you're engraving, to make lines thicker or thinner, with calligraphic qualities.

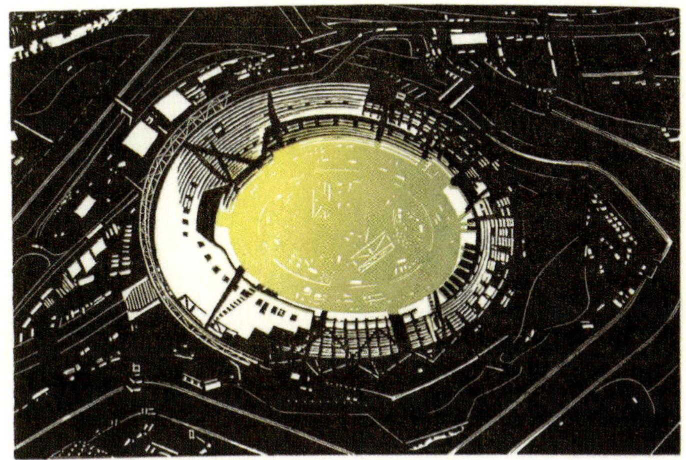

Olympic Site in Construction 2 (2009), engraving on boxwood with stencilling, 10 × 15cm (4 × 6in), on Gampi Vellum paper. All the curving white lines here were made with a bullsticker, using more and less pressure to generate thicker and thinner linework accordingly.

Tint tool

The tint tool (aka *knife graver* or *angle tint tool*) was designed to create tints or tones. At first glance, it looks much like the spitsticker with an upended teardrop-shaped face and sharp, pointed tip. There the similarities end because the tint tool more closely resembles the lozenge graver with its sharp belly and flat sides. It's designed for making very fine, straight lines, which, when positioned close together, parallel to one another, read as assorted grey tones. It can also be used for delicate crosshatching. It differs from tools already described in that it's designed to be used with light pressure to create lines of consistent thinness. (If you increase the pressure to create a fatter line, the likely result will be that the tool's fine, narrow tip will chip off.) In a newspaper photograph, tone is achieved by halftone dots, which you perceive as shades of grey, though the only ink involved is black. In just the same way, an artist can engrave lines and dots and endlessly inventive patterns which, though printed in black, register on the eye as shades of grey, much like halftone dots. The tint tool facilitates particularly fine gradations of tonal engraving.

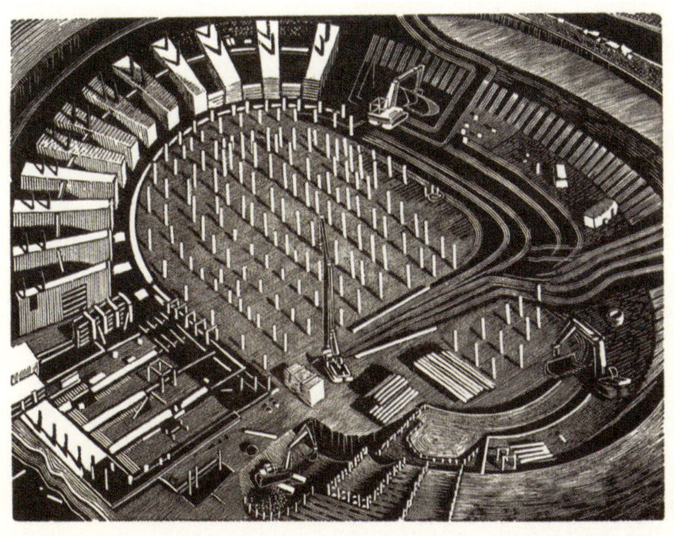

Olympic Velodrome in Construction (2010), engraving on boxwood, 9.7 × 12.5cm (3¾ × 5in), on Gampi Vellum paper. Most of its thin straight parallel lines in the central area, between the velodrome's foundation posts, are closely spaced tint tool marks engraved under a magnifying lens. The effect is a grey tone with individual tool cuts barely evident.

Multiple tool

Viewed from the front, this tool looks like a square scorper (described next) because it appears to have a wide, squared-off cutting tip with flat sides, flat back and flat belly. However, when you turn the tool over, you find its belly is not flat at all, but comprises a parallel row of fine steel teeth which can be used to create series of identical, parallel lines or dots. Multiple tools come in various sizes with teeth very closely spaced or sometimes a little wider apart. The number of teeth per tool varies too – anything from two to about a dozen. Holding it at the precise angle required to enable all its teeth to cut simultaneously is not easy, making it often most effective for short tonal marks, including very delicate hatching, rather than for longer lines, which are easier to accomplish with tools previously described (though multiple tools used to be fixed into ruling machines to engrave large areas of parallel lines in trade engravings).

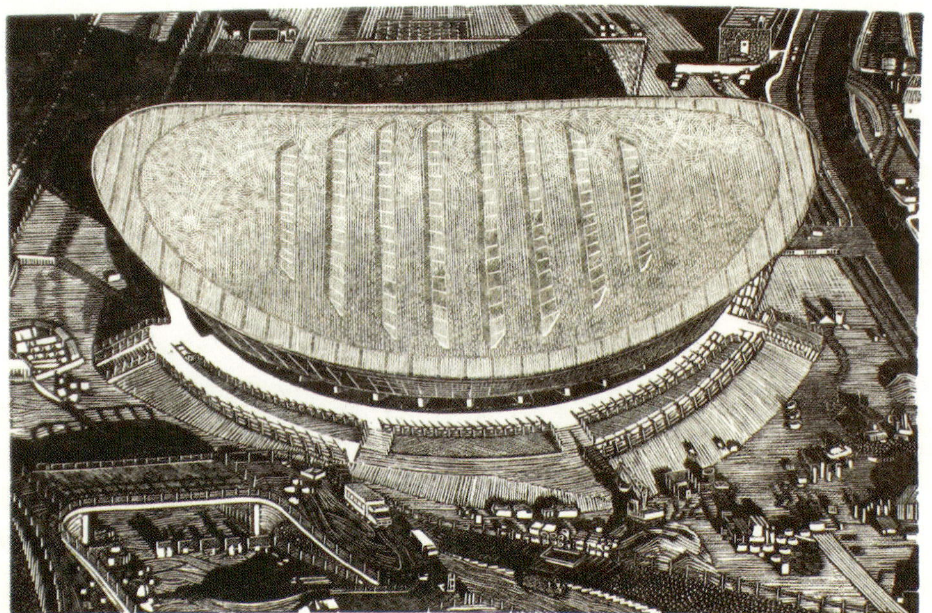

Olympic Velodrome Unveiled (2012), engraving on boxwood, 10 × 15cm (4 × 6in) with stencil (to lighten the tone of the velodrome's roof), on Gampi Vellum paper. The pattern of crosshatching on the left-hand side and top edge of the velodrome's roof was made using a multiple tool with three teeth.

Multiple tools are generally a lot pricier than other tools. I have several but use them rarely, so I wouldn't say they're essential but they can create very distinctive, subtle marks. The engravings of Iain Macnab of Barachastlain (1890–1967) are worth studying for his particularly lively and varied use of the multiple tool.

Square scorper

The square scorper (aka *scauper*, *flat edge graver* or *flat graver*) has a wide, squared-off cutting tip with flat sides, a flat, smooth, straight back and an equivalent flat, smooth belly. It comes in various gauges from very narrow to about 0.5cm (¼in) wide and is designed to make wide lines that

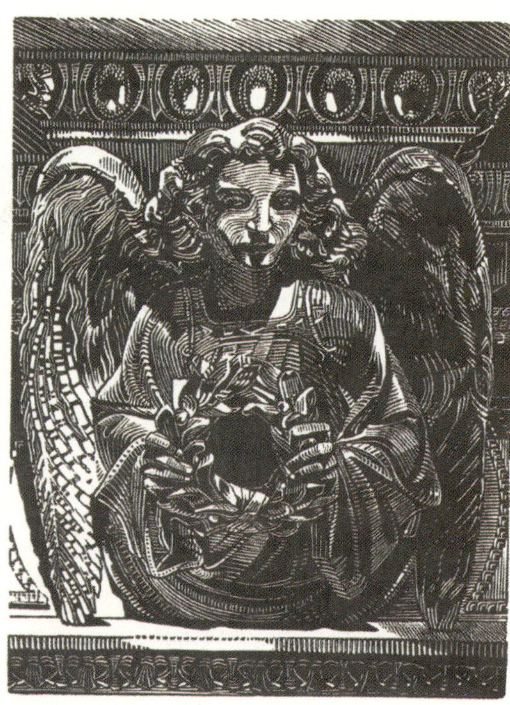

Angel with Laurel Wreath (2020), engraving on boxwood, 9.6 × 7.1cm (3¾ × 2¾in), on Gampi Vellum paper. The pattern of white squares and rectangles on the angel's paler-toned wing on this image was made with one square scorper. The clearing out of areas intended to read as pure white was done with the same tool.

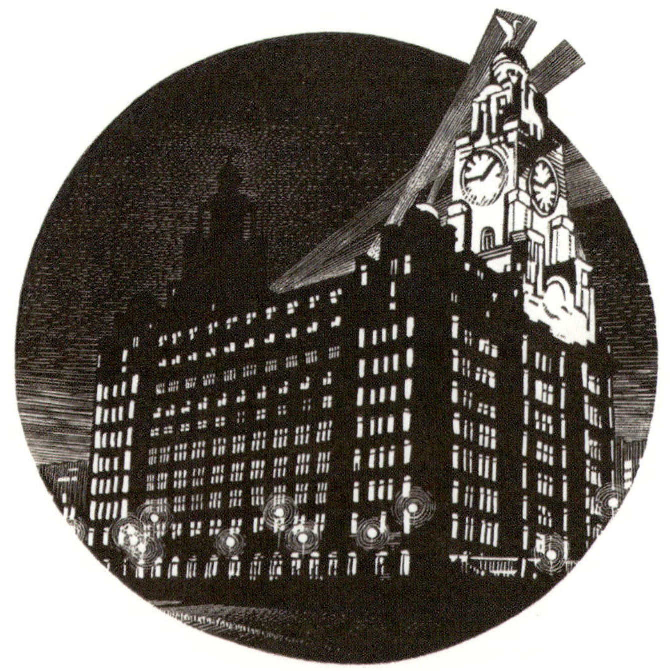

Liverpool Night (2014), engraving on boxwood, 9.9 × 10cm (4 × 4in), on Gampi Vellum paper. In this view of Liverpool's famous Liver Building, nearly all the windows were cut with square scorpers of various gauges to create bigger or smaller white squares or short rectangles, each cut having distinctive squared-off top and bottom edges.

engrave at exactly the width of the cutting tip and can't be varied by pressure changes in the cutting. Its lines have a distinctive squared-off appearance at both ends. It can also make square-shaped dots. If trying to engrave the illusion of a crosshatched drawing, use this tool to cut out all the tiny squares in between the drawing's hatched pen lines on the block. The uncut parts between neat rows of tiny, engraved squares will print to give an illusion of crosshatching. This tool's other use is for clearing away larger areas of the block's surface to achieve the whites in the print. I have various square scorpers in assorted sizes but, invariably, it's the narrower ones I use most often and the wider ones rarely. The wider the cutting tip, the harder the tool is to control and the more pressure it requires to keep it running across the block rather than skidding off course. That said, the great Gertrude Hermes (sculptor and engraver) made extensive use of the widest square scorpers in combination with fine-line tools to create an extraordinary range of lively, diverse engraved marks. The wider square scorpers (and flat chisels) can, however, be used effectively to make zigzag patterns.

Round scorper

The round scorper (aka *scauper*, *round edge graver* or *round graver*) also has a wide cutting tip but, unlike the square scorper's, its cutting tip is semicircular in profile with a related rounded belly. It has flat sides and comes in various gauges from very narrow to about 0.5cm (¼in) wide. Like the square scorper, it can make relatively broad lines, though cutting deeper or more shallowly with it will use more or less of the full extent of its cutting tip to make very marginally wider or narrower lines accordingly. Round scorper lines have a distinctive rounded look at both ends. Its curved belly facilitates engraving curved or wavy lines, which the flat belly of the square scorper does not. This tool too is also designed for clearing away larger areas of the image intended to be paper-white in the print. Its rounded tip is often easier to use with greater precision than the square scorper. Its other wonderful use is for large, medium and small stippled dots, either round or ovoid in profile depending on how far you push the tool along the wood and on the gauge of the scorper. Very light pressure can create the tiniest round dot, while different amounts of pressure with the same tool produces dots of a wide array of shapes and sizes.

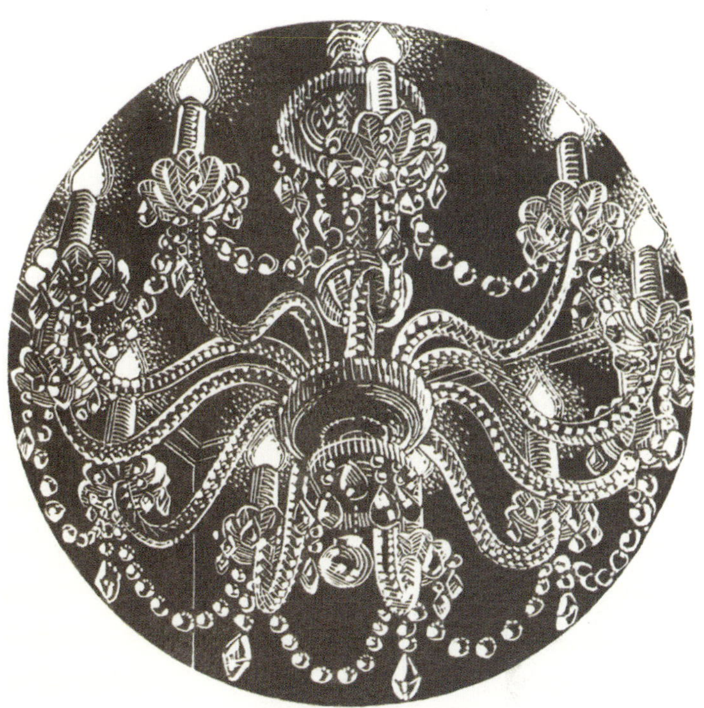

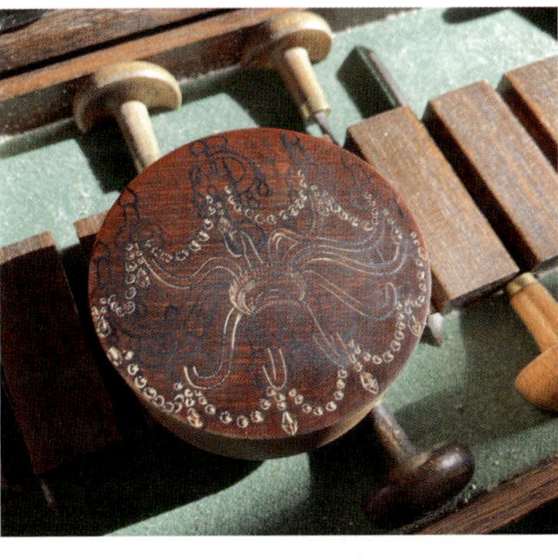

A Little Sparkle (2022), engraving on boxwood, diameter: 6.5cm (2½in), on Gampi Vellum paper and the engraving block at an early cutting stage. In this tiny roundel I used a large round scorper to create large circular-shaped white highlights on each of the chandelier's glass droplets, in contrast to square scorper marks which I used to suggest the texture of its glass octopus-tentacle-like arms.

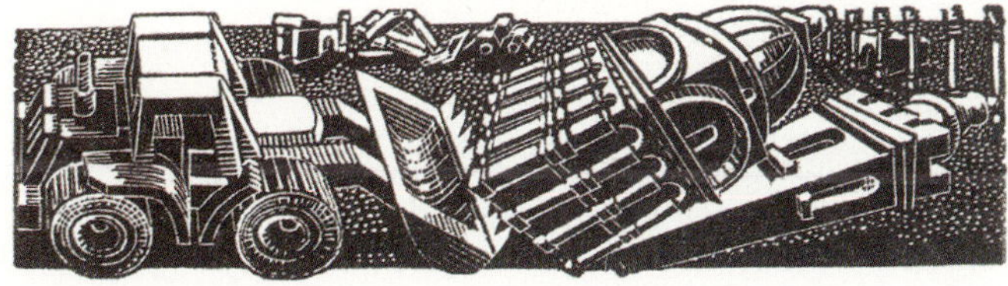

Redevelopment (1994), engraving on boxwood, 0.8 × 6.2cm (¼ × 2½in), on China White Laid paper. In this tiny engraving I used a small round scorper for all the stippled background dots and a slightly larger (medium) round scorper to clear away the larger white areas of the image.

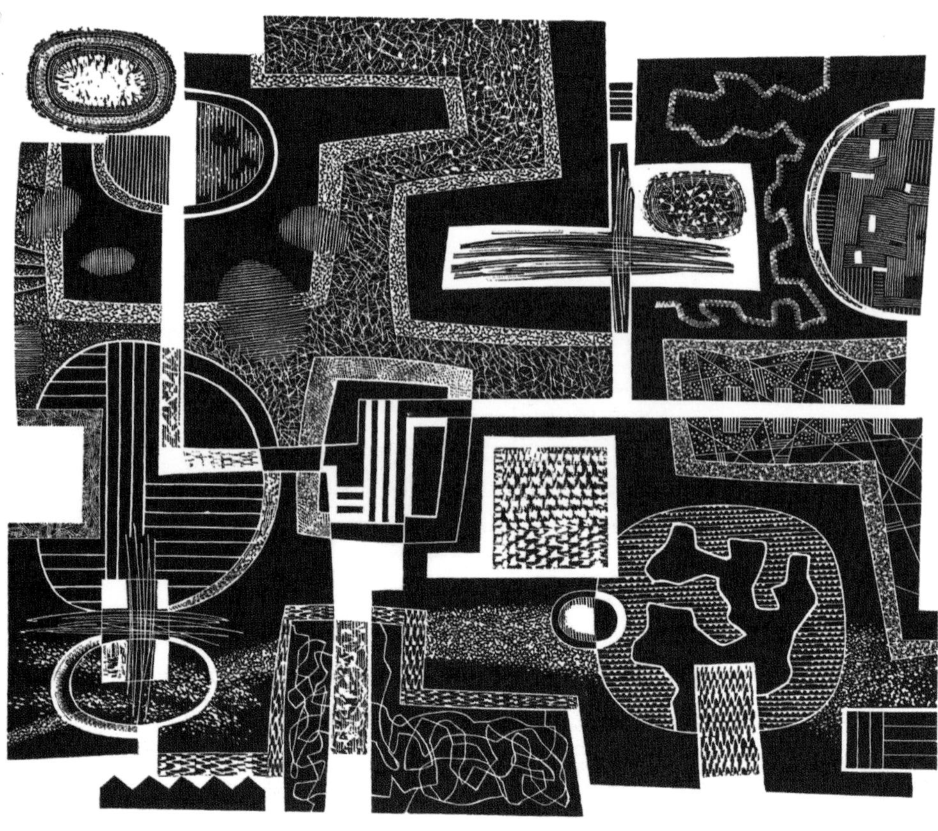

Dark Corners (2002), engraving on Resingrave, 15 × 17cm (6 × 6¾in), on Zerkall paper by Peter Lawrence (b.1951). He also engraves on Corian® blocks (which he says cut more cleanly than Resingrave). He gets Corian® from kitchen suppliers who will cut blocks to order in bespoke sizes. Some of the engraving's scratchier marks were made with a sharpened metal screw.

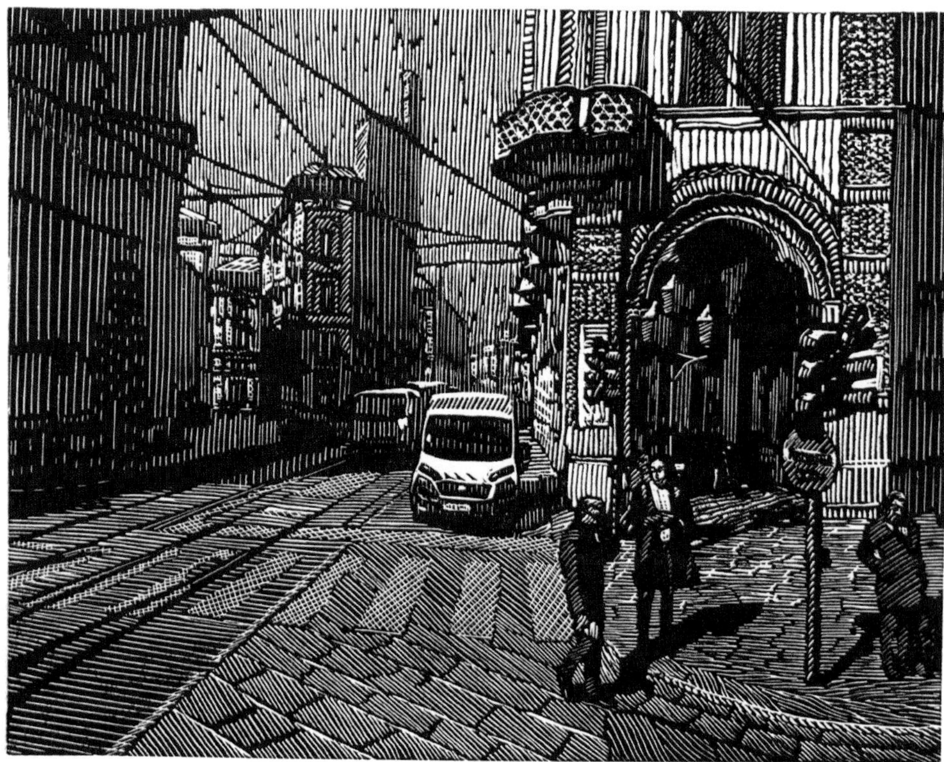

Travel the World Freely No. 95 (2020), engraving on acrylonitrile-butdiene-styrene, 12 × 15cm (4¾ × 6in), on watercolour paper, by Song Hongyu (b.1976). This artist, from Heilongjiang Province, China, is relatively new to engraving (taught by Peter Lawrence) yet this work is from an impressive portfolio of 100 engravings about European travel destinations which Song engraved during the Covid 19 pandemic.

Flat chisel

A flat chisel tool is a useful extra. It is too wide to make a clean cut across a block without skidding. However, like a wide square scorper, it can create effective zigzag zipper-like patterns. It's also useful for planing off any bits of wood that haven't been cleared off the block properly during the engraving process.

Unorthodox tools

As well as the traditional tools described, you can make effective marks using a roulette wheel: a tool for etchers. It comprises a handle to which is attached a small metal wheel, the circumference of which is serrated with tiny, regularly spaced teeth. Applied to an engraving block, these make effective tiny indentations that print as lines of tiny dots. Etching needles and sharpened metal nails can be used to create interesting textures on a woodblock, as can a Dremel drill.

For best results, I'd recommend getting at least a medium-large spitsticker and a medium round scorper. All the other tools are useful, but not essential, for getting started.

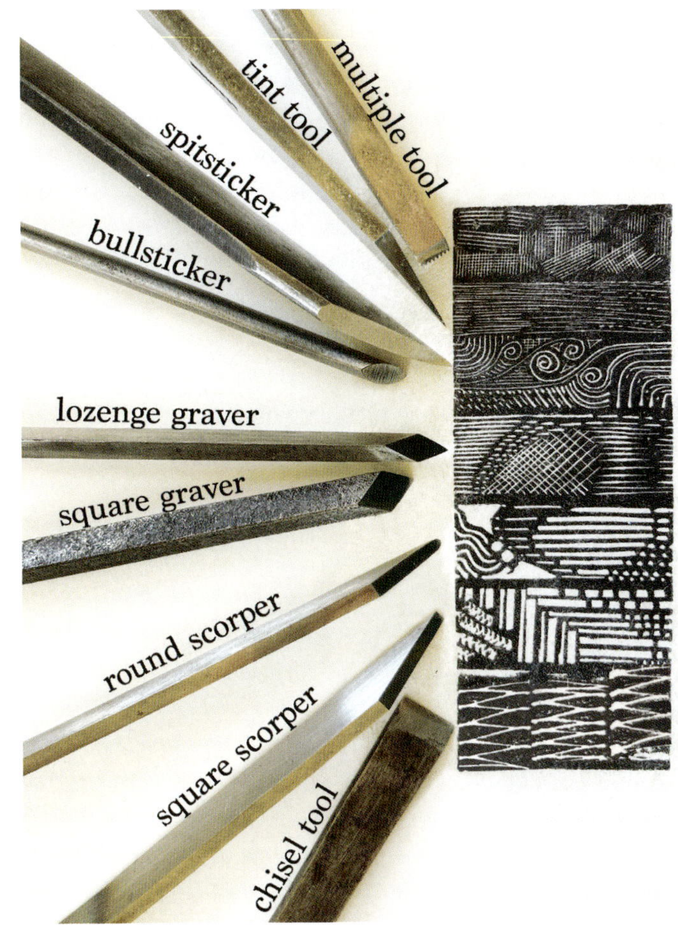

A range of wood engraving tool blades with examples of marks made by each tool shown adjacent to its cutting tip.

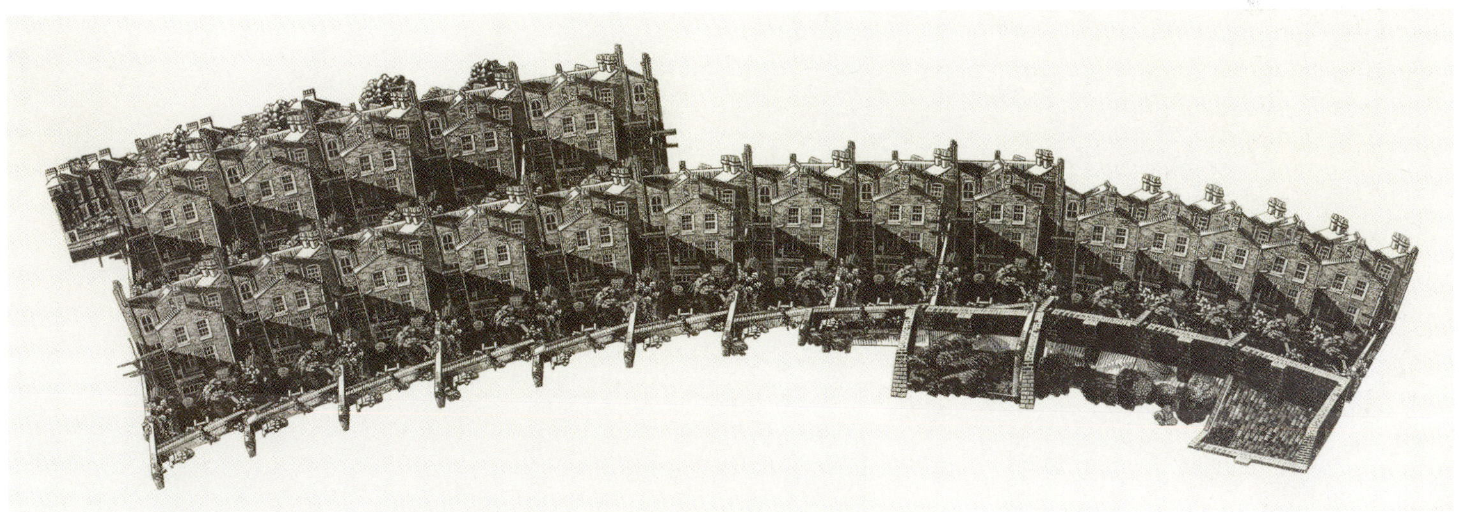

London Terraces (1996), 14 × 45.1cm (5½ × 17¾in), collage on Gampi Vellum paper, comprising nineteen repeated details from the engraving *London Gardens (Diptych)* – *see* Chapter 11.

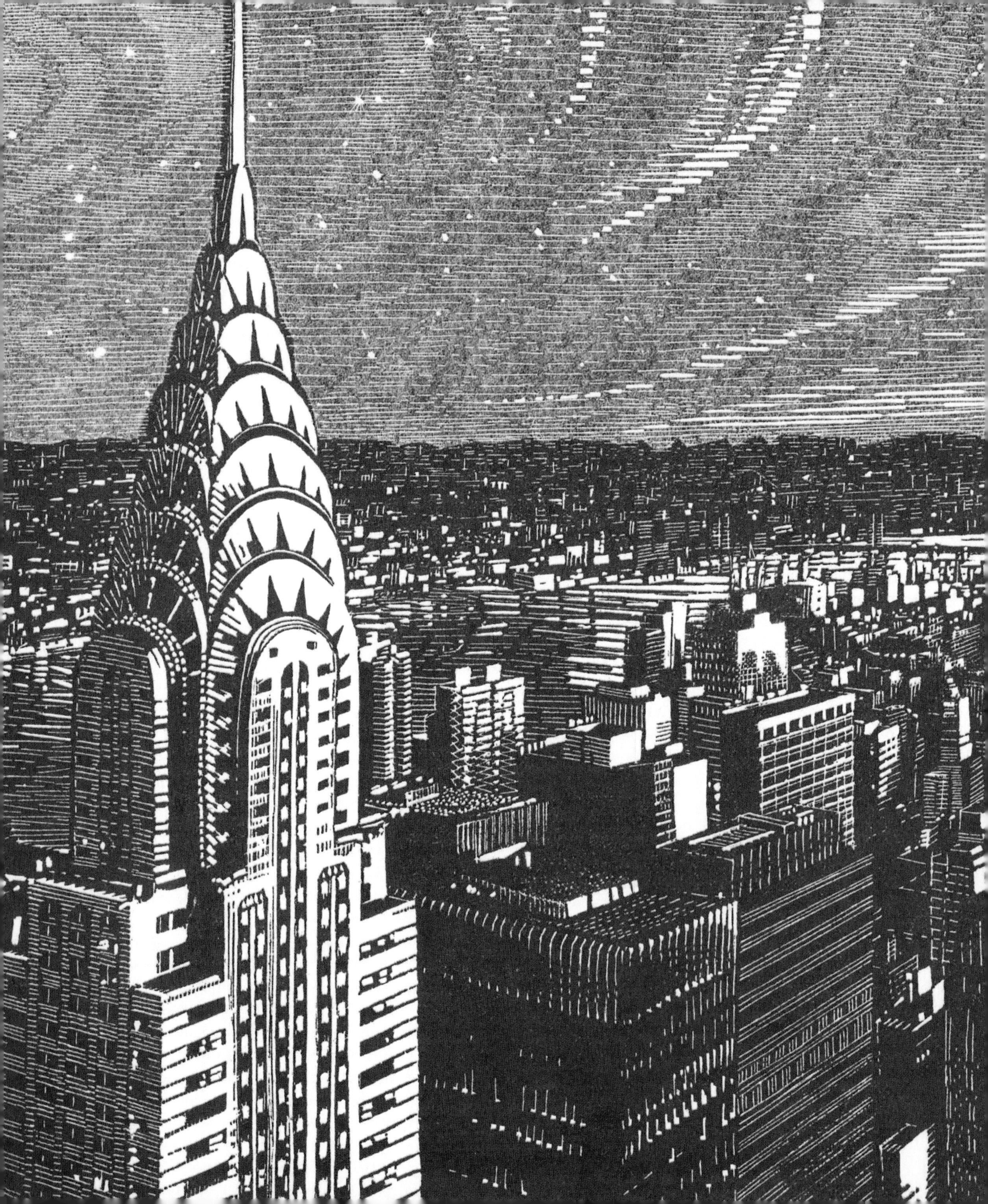

CHAPTER 3

GETTING STARTED

If you were to draw in pencil or pen, straight onto the pale-coloured woodblock, your drawing would be highly visible, but your engraved marks would be largely indistinguishable from the wood's uncut surface. It's helpful to paint or stain its surface a dark colour so that everything you engrave will show up as pale tones against a darker surface. Different artists have different ways of doing this. Some draw on the pale wood first, in pencil, then reinforce their drawing with black pen, gouache or Indian ink before staining the block's surface over the top of the drawing. I have always stained my blocks before drawing on them, but do try out both methods and see what best suits you. There is no right or wrong approach.

STAINING THE BLOCK

For boxwood, my preferred method is to paint the wood's smooth surface with a very thin layer of undiluted, water-soluble, fountain-pen ink straight from the pot. I favour blue Parker Quink ink rather than black, because a black ink drawing can be made on top and remain visible despite the surface being darkened. However, paint the block with caution because, if you were to look at it under intense magnification, you would see that its smooth surface is actually pitted with innumerable microscopic holes comprising the wood's structure. When the tree is cut into end grain roundels, the 'grain' (orientation of wood-cell fibres) runs at right angles to the engraving surface, and the wood-cell fibres – effectively incredibly tiny 'tubes' running up a tree's length – are exposed, creating a surface susceptible to absorbing liquids. Applying too much liquid ink could cause the block to swell, distort in shape or become too spongey. However, if done carefully, it causes no damage and gives a darkened but still entirely smooth surface.

The secret is to apply only the tiniest quantity of ink at a time. Dip your clean, soft-haired, square-tipped, watercolour brush in the ink pot, then wipe off most of the ink on the pot's rim before applying brush to wood. Paint the block in stripes, leaving no unpainted sections and no pools of wet ink. If you apply too much, rub it off straight away with a clean rag. It's only seconds' work to paint a tiny block. Don't worry if you can see the tree-ring pattern through the ink layer, or if your brushstrokes have overlapped, causing some areas to look darker than others. You just need to create sufficient tonal contrast between the wood's surface and its natural colour for engraved marks to show up clearly. Don't make the surface darker by adding extra ink layers because, the less ink you apply, the faster the block will dry and the better a pencil or pen drawing will show up on it. If you apply too much liquid ink, it may bleed a little down the block's sides. This doesn't usually cause problems but, if the wood soaks up too much ink deep into its fibres, your engraved marks will appear the same dark hue as the wood's painted surface, rather than a pale contrasting tone. (But this can be remedied by rubbing talcum powder into the cuts, as you make them, which will help you to see them very clearly indeed.) Leave the block to dry thoroughly for 15 or 20 minutes before you draw or engrave on it. Don't use Indian ink or other inks involving shellac because, while they may initially appear to adhere well to the polished surface, inks with shellac can gradually chip off as you're engraving.

Manhattan Sky (2017), detail of a wood engraving (and stencil – used to lift off ink in the sky area to produce a grey tone) on holly wood, on Japanese paper.

Alternative staining methods

My other method, which I use for all woods except box, is simply to colour in the surface with a square-tipped permanent marker. Use a dark blue or green colour, ideally, as these dry to a dark tone, but not so dark that you can't see a black line drawing on top (or underneath). Avoid red or paler colours as they don't provide enough contrast. Any waterproof permanent marker should work well, but avoid highlighter pens (too pale) or whiteboard markers as they don't adhere well to the wood. I don't recommend this method for box, because it's usually denser than other engraving woods. This means that, when planed for engraving, it tends to acquire a shinier finish. If you colour in that ultra-smooth shiny surface with marker pen, it seems initially to bond to the wood's surface but, after a few hours' engraving, the colour rubs off onto your hand. Conversely, I rarely use the liquid ink method for blocks other than box because, generally, they are from faster-growing trees and therefore less dense, which increases the risk of liquid ink soaking in and causing the wood to become too spongey. I favour the brush and ink method for box and a marker pen for all other woods.

Alternatively, paint (or rub with a clean rag) the surface of any engraving wood with a very thin layer of dark-coloured gouache. Personally, I don't like this technique because, even with the thinnest layer, I find a gouache-painted surface has a very slight gritty texture and this can stop the tool's blade from cutting cleanly. That slightly roughened surface is, however, easier to draw on, without the drawing smudging, and takes a traced pencil drawing or carbon transfer very readily. It is a popular method for many engravers.

Another method is to put a smaller-than-pea-sized blob of dark-hued oil-based printing ink onto a clean rag and rub it all over the block's surface, wiping off any excess straight away. Alternatively, roll the ink out as if for printing (but using even less ink) and lightly ink the block's surface. This is effective but leave it to dry for a day or two before drawing on it (press-printing the freshly inked block on paper to take off excess ink will hasten the block's drying time). Rest a piece of smooth paper on top while it dries, to prevent dust particles from sticking there while the ink is drying. Be aware, however, that printing ink doesn't always adhere sufficiently to a highly polished block and may rub off while you're engraving. To avoid this, lightly rub the shine off the block's surface with fine emery polishing paper before applying the printing ink.

For high visibility of image on block, you can paint the surface with a thin layer of white gouache – or rub on the dilute pigment with a clean rag. Then, when the paint has dried, draw your design on it in pencil or black ink. I don't, however, recommend this method because it can lead to rather dull prints in which the mark-making has been finalised in the drawing and the engraving becomes a somewhat mechanical clearing of the wood's surface around and between the pen lines. It's hard to see tool cuts against a white surface, making it difficult to create inventive tonal ranges in the cutting. It can also be confusing having a white surface on which engraved marks will look darker, whereas, in the final print, the uncut surface will be dark and the cut areas paper-white. Finished prints that began in this way tend to look like exquisite pen drawings, but rarely demonstrate the special capacities of engraving tools for making original marks, patterns and complex tones quite unlike a pen.

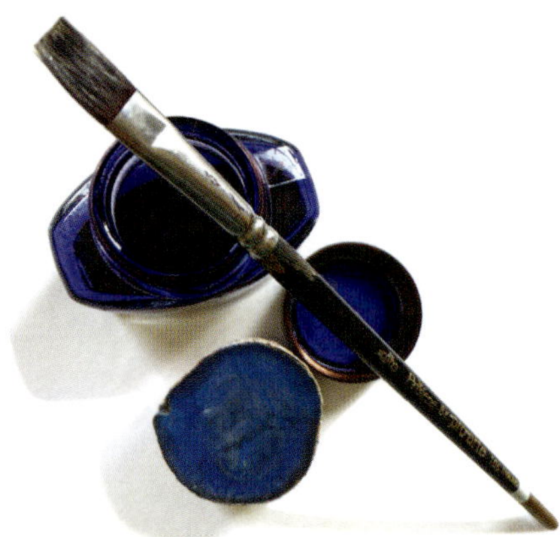

Square-tipped watercolour brush with blue fountain-pen ink used in a very thin layer to stain the surface of boxwood blocks before engraving.

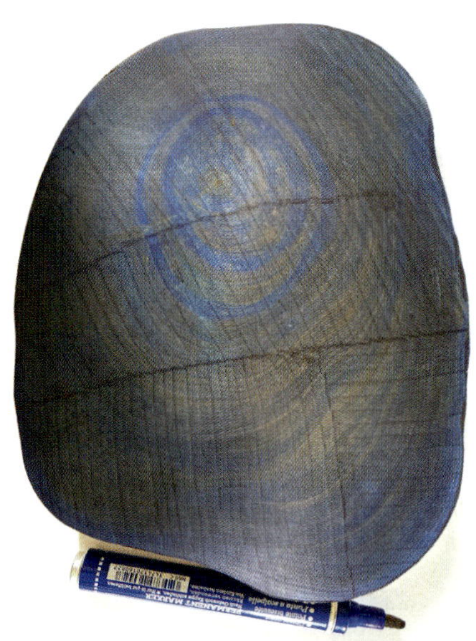

Holly block stained using a square-tipped marker pen. You can see darker tones where pen marks have overlapped plus the wood's ring pattern. You can add more pen layers, if desired, but I find one layer ample to provide sufficient visual contrast between engraved marks and uncut surface.

TOOL HANDLING

The tool has several parts and is designed for both right- and left-handed people:

- **mushroom handle**: made of turned wood, this should sit comfortably in the palm of your hand.
- **ferrule**: a small (often brass) ring keeping the handle firmly attached to the blade.
- **tang**: the non-cutting end of the blade, its tapered end is heated up by the tool maker in order to fix it firmly in place in the handle.
- **blade**: made of tempered steel. Its face is ground to a cutting angle of between about 30 and 45 degrees.

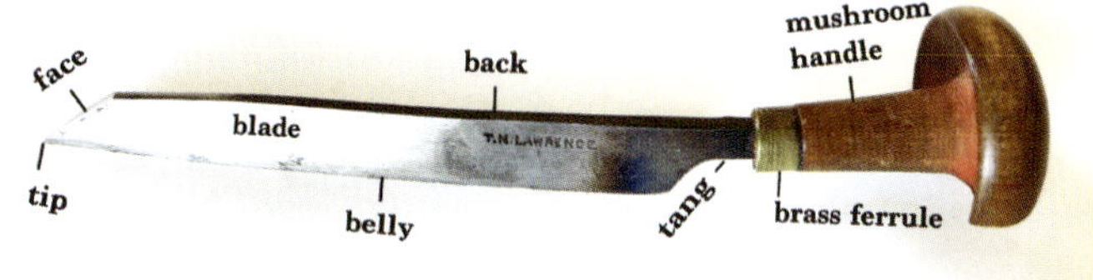

The flat front including the tip is called the 'face'; the top edge is the 'back', the underside is the 'belly'. This example shows a tool with handle more or less in line with the blade, but the handle is sometimes angled slightly upwards to prevent any danger of its underside bruising the woodblock.

Never hold the tool like a pen or pencil: its cutting tip will be at too steep an angle and engraving will be extremely difficult. Place the rounded part of the handle towards the back of your palm so that it nestles comfortably there. The wooden handle's flat part should always face outwards so that the cutting tip is downwards to make correct contact with the woodblock. Traditionally, your little finger should be tucked into the lip of the handle and the other three fingers ranged along the blade's outer edge, with your thumb acting as support and piston on the other side of the blade. When holding the tool this way, the tool's cutting tip shouldn't project more than a few centimetres beyond the end of your thumbnail. If it does, the tool may be too long for your hand, making it harder to control. You can compensate for this either by tucking the tool handle further towards the back of your palm or having the blade professionally shortened.

A more archaic tool-hold is little used today but was practised to excellent effect by the great engraver Clare Leighton, among others. It involves placing the tool handle in the crook of your little finger with the blade running horizontally across the underside of your other fingers, which grip the tool on one side while your thumb acts as a piston along the other side.

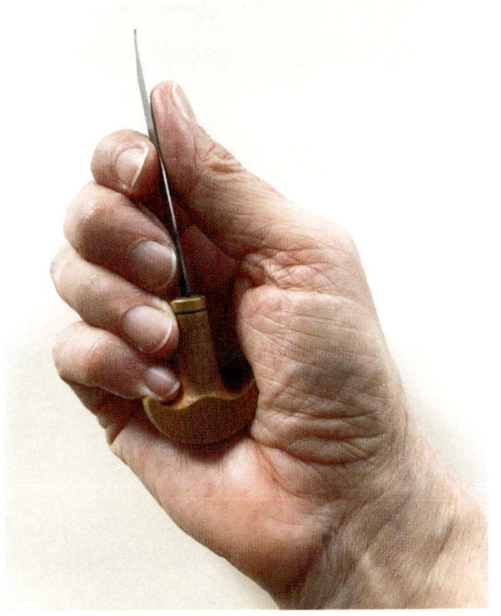

Traditional way of holding a tool and probably the most widely used among engravers today.

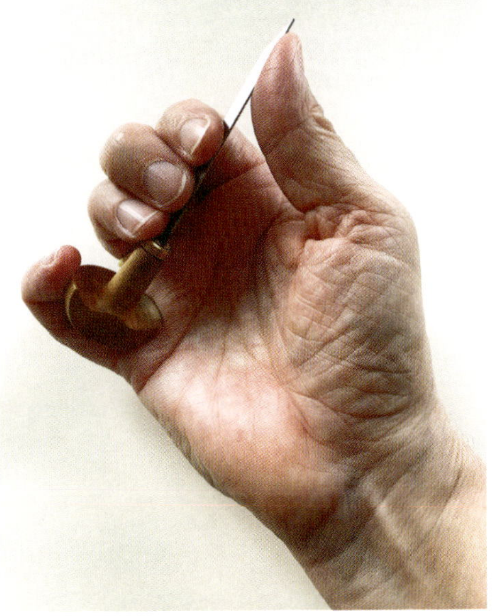

Archaic tool-hold, little used today but can be effective and may allow greater wrist flexibility while engraving.

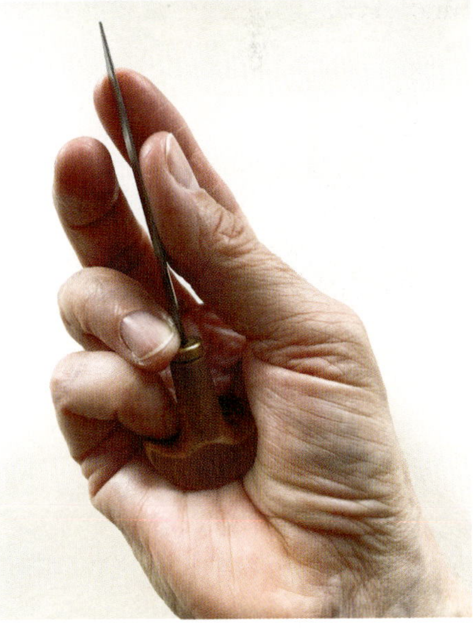

My unorthodox tool-hold. It works effectively and feels somehow right for my hand!

Although I was introduced to wood engraving at art school, there wasn't a practitioner there and, at the time, I didn't have a useful instruction manual, so I taught myself and have consequently had a 40-year-long unorthodox approach. I have gone on to teach my method to students alongside the traditional method. But my approach appears to work as effectively as any other!

My ring finger and little finger hold the tool in the conventional way while my middle finger sits on the block and acts as a brake to stop the tool slipping during engraving. My index finger rests lightly on top of the blade (but it's important to resist the urge to press down with that finger because it will impair the tool's smooth running). My thumb rests on the inner side of the blade in the conventional way and guides the cutting. If this is how you hold the tool, your index finger needs to be close to the cutting tip for optimum engraving control. If there's a gap of more than about 1cm (3/8in) between the tool's tip and where the tip of your index finger meets the blade, then the tool is probably a bit long for your hand. Adjust for this by moving the handle further towards the back of your hand or get the blade shortened.

MAKING A MARK

Make sure you're sitting comfortably and that your chair's height is such that you don't need to bend your neck too acutely over your work. If wood engraving engrosses you, you may be sitting at that desk for extended periods and you'll get aches in neck, shoulders and back if you're uncomfortable in any way. Notice what feels most comfortable or otherwise, as you proceed, and make whatever adjustments are necessary. For your general health, you should get up and walk around for a few minutes at least every half hour.

If you have a sandbag, rest the prepared block in the middle of it. It will help you manoeuvre the block, especially for curved lines. It will also enable you to keep the fingers of your other hand out of the blade's path. Remember the tools are very sharp, so use them with caution. *Always ensure that the fingers of your non-engraving hand are safely out of the blade's path.* As you're working on end grain wood and so can turn the block in any direction to engrave it, it isn't hard to keep your free hand out of harm's way, but it's something to keep in mind at all times. If using a sandbag, the free hand should be used to hold the block at its sides but with none of that hand in range of the blade's trajectory across the block's surface. If you don't have a sandbag, rest your block on a smooth surface so it can be turned and moved easily. A small, toughened-glass inking slab is ideal or, to simulate the extra height a sandbag provides, put your block on a small hardback book with a smooth cover. Otherwise, if your desk has a Formica or equally smooth surface, this will be fine for turning and moving the block while engraving. But if your desk is wood, be aware that the block's movements may scuff the desk's surface.

It's useful to have some small practice blocks in progress at all times. If you're a beginner, this is a great way to learn how the tools work without trying to create specific images. If you're experienced, it's still useful to use practice blocks to check your tools' sharpness and to assess how well they're running before and after sharpening.

Engraving straight lines

Take the lozenge graver (or spitsticker, bullsticker or tint tool). Holding it in one of the ways described earlier, touch the tool's tip into the wood. Before you start to push, lower your hand such that the tool's blade is almost flat against the wood. Then push it along the surface – while holding the block in a fixed position – to create a straight line. Straight lines can be made either in one continuous

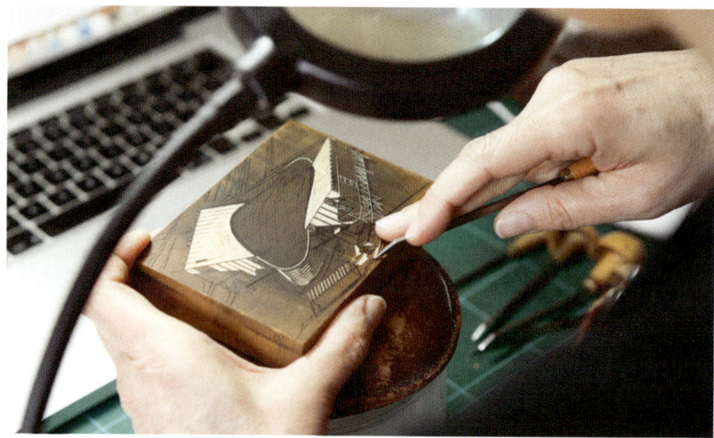

Engraving a block using a magnifying lens and working from a pencil drawing scanned on my laptop. I guide the block with one hand and engrave with the other. To raise this block higher on my desk, I placed it on the sandbag which itself was resting on a plastic canister.
(PHOTO: DAVID ROBERTSON)

movement or, just as effectively: make repeated, short, connecting cuts, using the tool's tip to find the end of each previous cut so as to create seamless longer lines. Make sure you see a tiny curl of wood appearing in front of the blade as you cut, otherwise you are probably only denting (bruising) the wood rather than actually engraving it. A bruised line will print initially but not cleanly or consistently. Although you don't need to dig deep into the wood, you do need to see that curl appearing as you cut. It should readily fall away from the block with each cut you make, though this may not happen if you are engraving on man-made polymer/plastic blocks. Here the curls tend to remain attached and need to be carefully shaved off with a chisel tool used as a plane.

There's a 'sweet spot' to discover, which is the ideal angle of blade to wood. If too steep, the tool will dig in and not run cleanly, your hands will quickly feel strained and the tool will resist your efforts to move it through the wood. If too shallow, the tool may skid and scratch the surface uncontrollably. The sweet spot is the angle at which the tool runs as freely and fluently as your favourite pen and doesn't strain your hands.

Use that sweet spot to aid your engraving and the type of marks you make. For a line that tapers like a blade of grass, slowly flatten tool against block so its cutting tip is forced, gradually, out of the wood. A series of such cuts will create a collection of gradually tapering delicate lines, each of which will end at a somewhat unpredictable place to create a ragged line. Conversely, for a line ending at a very specific place, run tool along block using the sweet spot but, to end each line, tilt the blade to a slightly steeper angle; this will force it to a standstill and provide a controlled stopping point.

If an engraved line does not start or finish exactly where you intended, you can extend it in either direction very easily. The tool's tip easily slots back into the groove of any previously engraved line, which can then be extended or otherwise modified in any direction. To achieve a line of varying thickness for a more calligraphic look (with lozenge graver, spitsticker or bullsticker, but not recommended with tint tool), increasing or decreasing the pressure as you engrave will cause it to become accordingly fatter or thinner. Consistent light pressure along a cut's length will create a line of uniform thickness, but you can always work back into that line by re-engraving certain parts to make it look wider in selected areas.

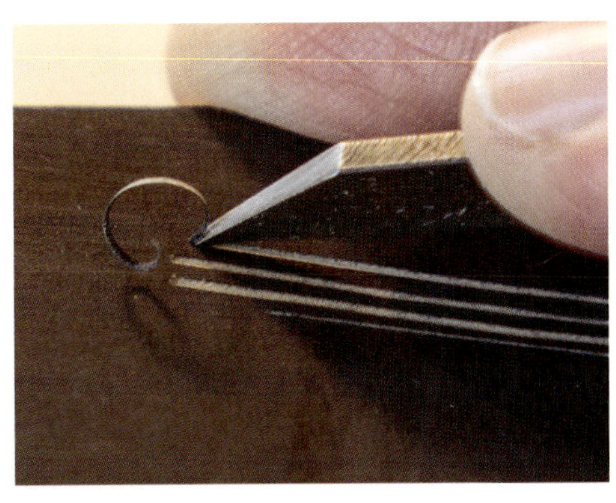

A relatively large curl of wood produced by a scorper. Curls from tools with finer tips will be thinner but still evident as you engrave.

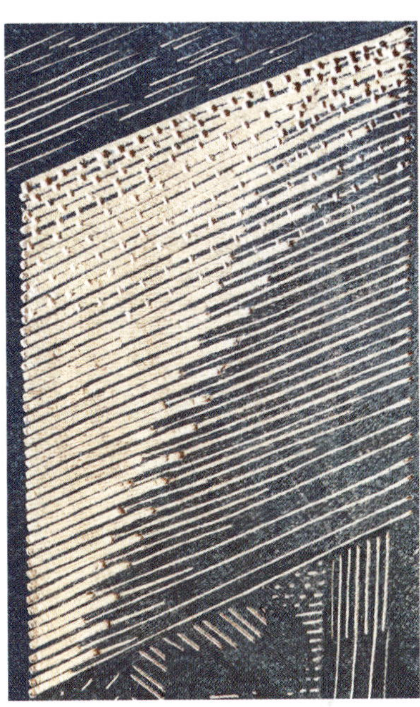

The thin straight lines of the parallelogram shape on this block were made with a lozenge graver while fatter lines were made with a square scorper. All these lines end at very specific, intended places (and some are interrupted by stippled dots). Meanwhile, the lines in the triangular shape (top left) taper off, ending in more random places.

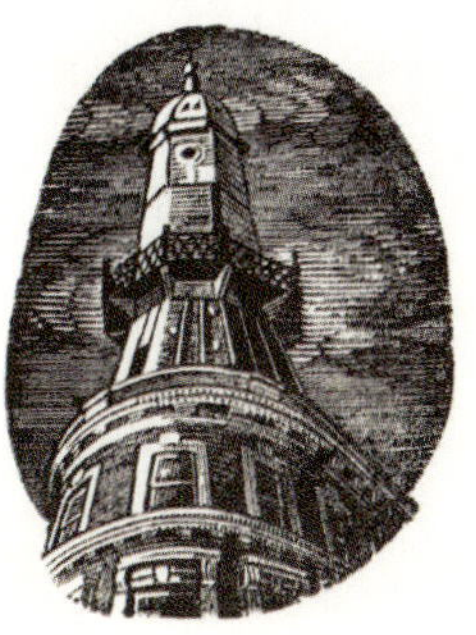

Kings X Lighthouse (2014), engraving on boxwood roundel on Gampi Vellum paper, 4.8 × 3.6cm (2 × 1½in). The sky in this example comprises parallel lines of varying lengths and widths made with assorted tools.

Engraved marks can be very shallow cuts that shouldn't strain your hands in the cutting. Multiple tools and scorpers, having wider cutting tips, need a bit more pressure or they will skid rather than cutting cleanly.

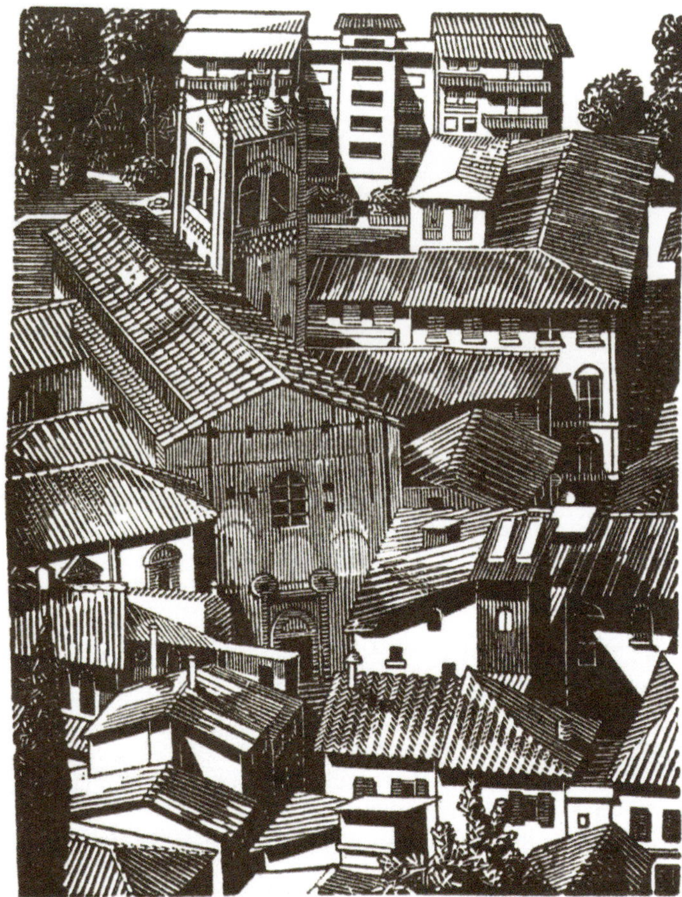

San Severino Marche (2016), engraving on boxwood, 10 × 7.5cm (4 × 3in), on Zerkall paper. This involved tint tool lines of different widths and spaced wider apart or closer together to create different tones and effects of sunlight; and round scorper dashes to suggest terracotta roof tiles, plus stippled areas to enhance certain tones and textures.

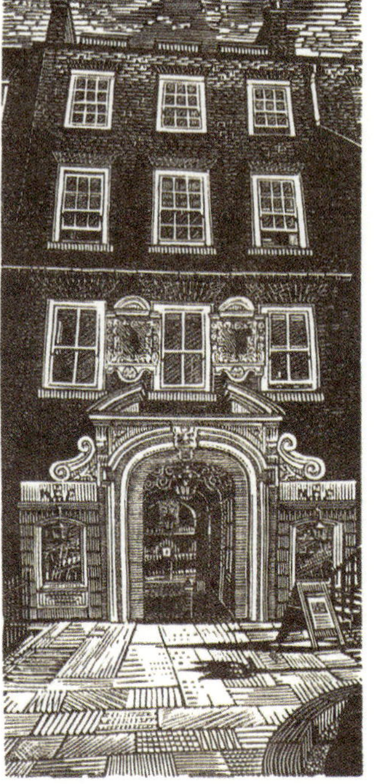

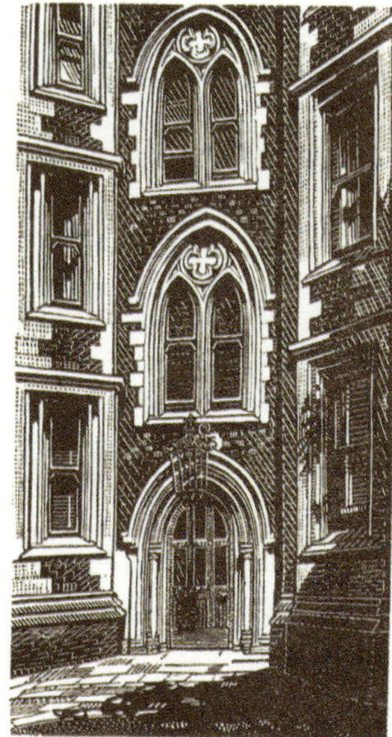

Wildy's Gate, 11.2 × 5cm (4½ × 2in), and *Old Square*, 9.8 × 5cm (3¾ × 2in), engravings on boxwood on Gampi Vellum paper. Both commissioned by Lincoln's Inn Law Chambers, in 2022, to celebrate its 600th anniversary. Both involved the full range of tools to create different tonal effects with lines and dots of diverse shapes and sizes.

Stippling

To make straight lines or stippled dots with any of the tools, dig the tool into the wood (very lightly for the tiniest dots) and then flip the tool tip upwards to clear the engraved wood from the block. (If you dig the tool in and then reverse it out rather than flipping its tip upwards, you will get a series of engraved dots, but each may have a tiny, raised lump of uncleared wood next to it, which impedes printing.) A small- or medium-round scorper is ideal for making pleasingly round-shaped dots in a wide range of sizes from a single tool. A square scorper makes a square-shaped dot. Lozenge gravers, spitstickers and bullstickers also stipple effectively with dots shaped like miniature spearheads. Tint tools stipple too, the narrower gauges often producing a miniature dash rather than a round dot, but avoid undue force as vigorous stippling or deep gouging with a delicate tint tool can break its tip. Remember that tonal effects are often most effectively achieved with several different tools, one applied on top of cuts made by another.

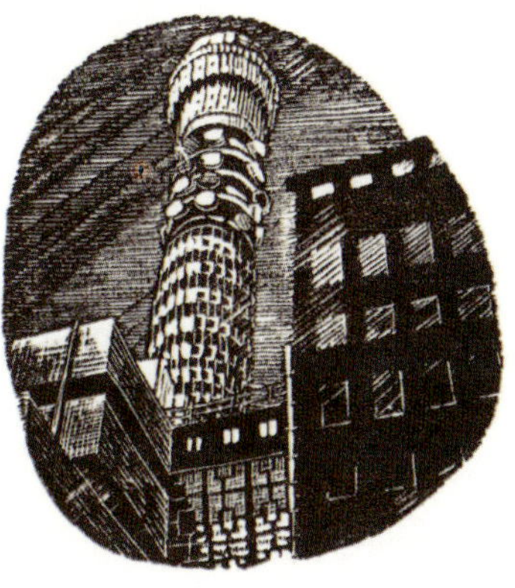

BT Tower (2014), engraving on tiny boxwood roundel, 4.2 × 3.7cm (1¾ × 1½in), on Gampi Vellum paper. Most details on the tower were made with round and square scorpers while the linear, tonal sky was created with one very fine tint tool.

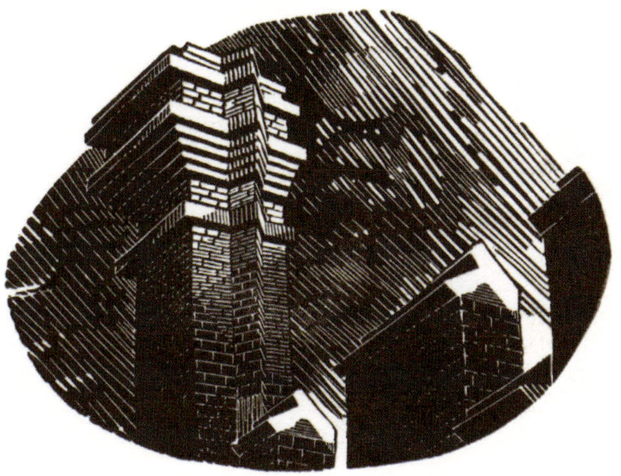

Tudor Chimney (2016), engraving on boxwood, 5.3 × 7cm (2 × 2¾in), on Gampi Vellum paper was cut with square scorpers and a tint tool.

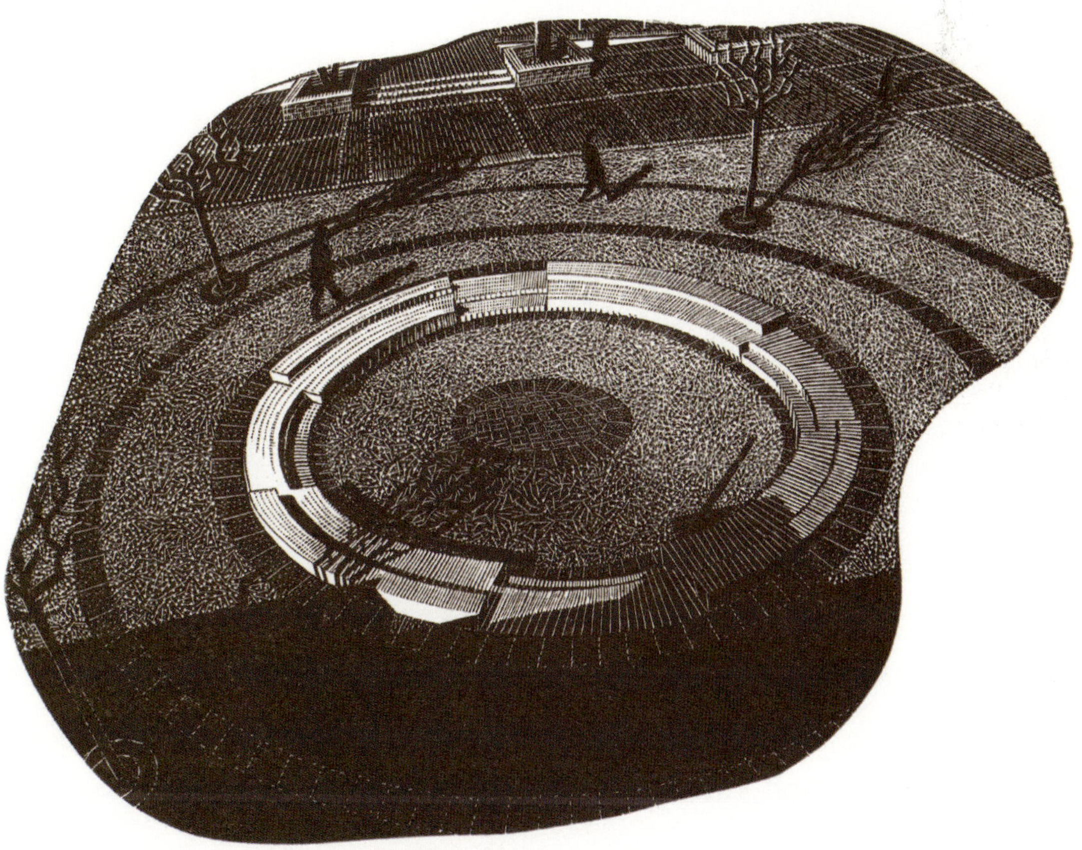

Crossing the Courtyard (2016), engraving on boxwood, 12 × 16cm (4¾ × 6¼in), on Zerkall paper. The paler areas within and surrounding this rendition of the amphitheatre (on Eton College's arts campus) involve stippled dots of various sizes made with one round scorper and overlaid with a network of short lines, each made with a tint tool, intentionally cutting the wood in many different directions.

Curves, circles and swirls

Take the spitsticker or bullsticker. Holding it as earlier described, touch the tool's tip into the wood which, ideally, should be resting on a sandbag. Lower your hand so that the tool's blade is almost flat against the wood. While, with one hand, you push the tool's tip lightly into the wood's surface, use the other hand to turn the block in whichever direction you want the curve or circle to go. You can make a curve in one continuing motion of moving block under tool or, just as effective, make repeated connecting cuts, using the tool's tip to find the end of the curve, each time, before you seamlessly extend it. As previously described, ensure that a tiny wood curl comes up in front of the blade as you cut. Applying more or less pressure will generate curving lines of increasing and decreasing width accordingly. Alternatively (as for the lozenge graver, when making straight lines) you can engrave lines of consistent width, but then go back into them and re-engrave any parts you want wider. Curving lines of a consistent wider width can also be achieved in the same way with a round scorper.

Don't tilt any tool to left or right in the process of engraving. For best results while cutting, you should only be able to see the tool's top edge, never either of its sides. If you have the tool tilted slightly to one side (as is tempting, especially when engraving curves), it will impede the blade from cutting cleanly.

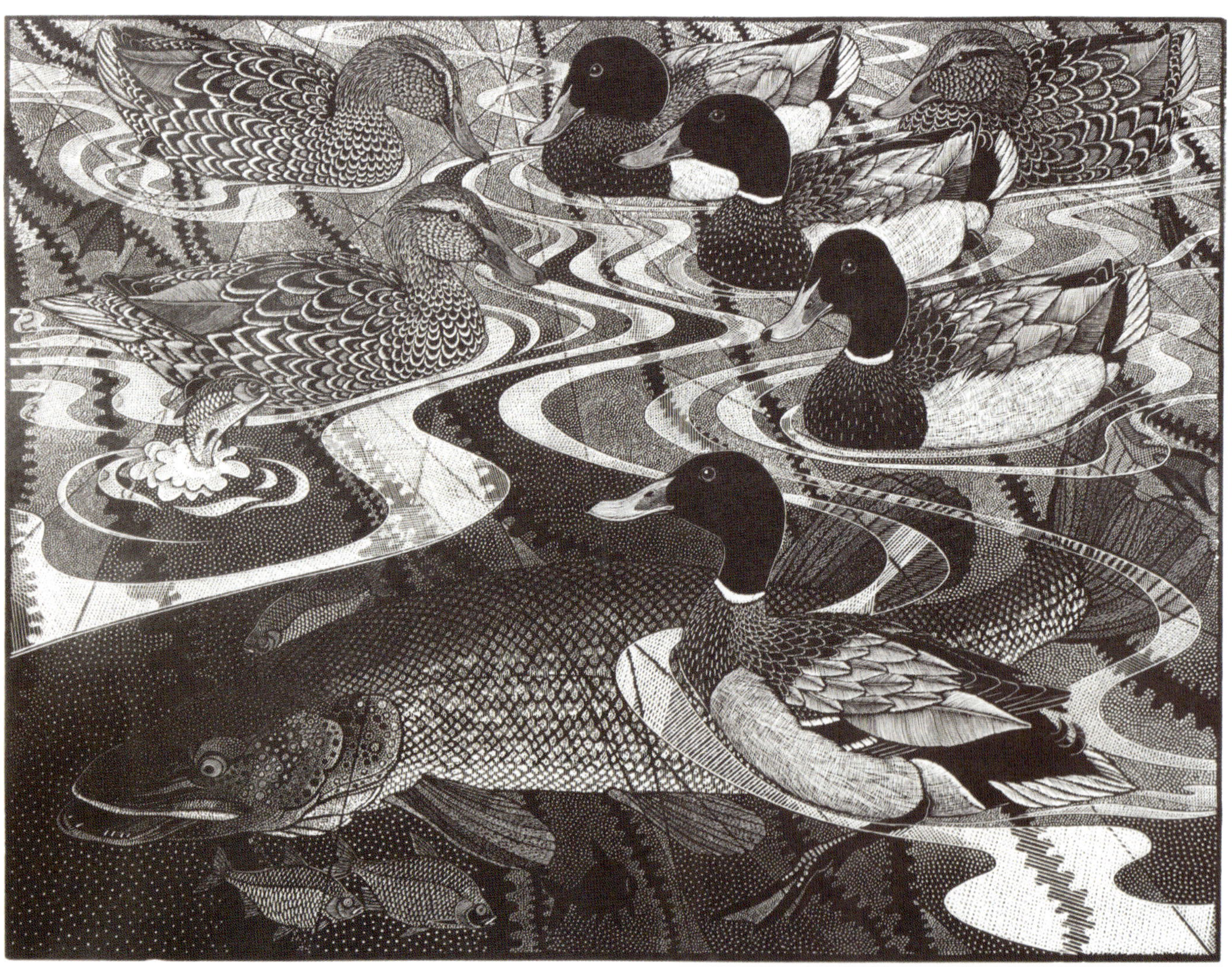

Mallard and Pike (1986), engraving on boxwood, 19.5 × 25.1cm (7¾ × 10in), on Zerkall paper, by Colin See-Paynton (b.1946). This is a typical example of the artist's extraordinary facility with diverse pattern-making to create a wide range of tonal effects. Divisions between each pattern are clearly defined by sinuous spitsticker/bullsticker curves.

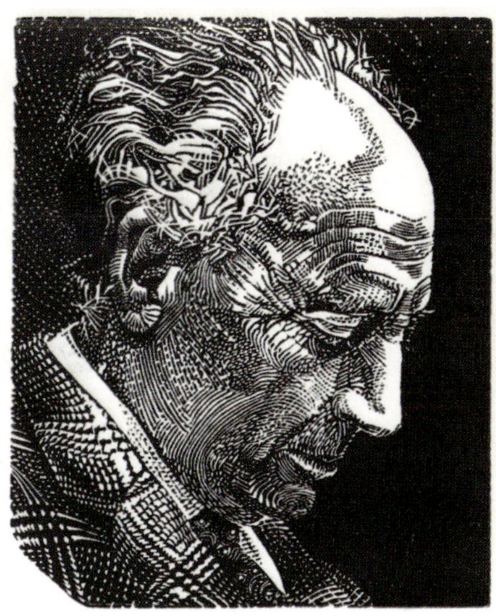

Louis Desmet (1987), engraving on boxwood, 7 × 5.6cm (2¾ × 2¼in), on Basingwerk Parchment paper. In this portrait of my father, much of the skin tone, textures of tweed jacket and patterned areas of background are composed of stippled scorper dots and dashes of various sizes cut in different directions and patterns.

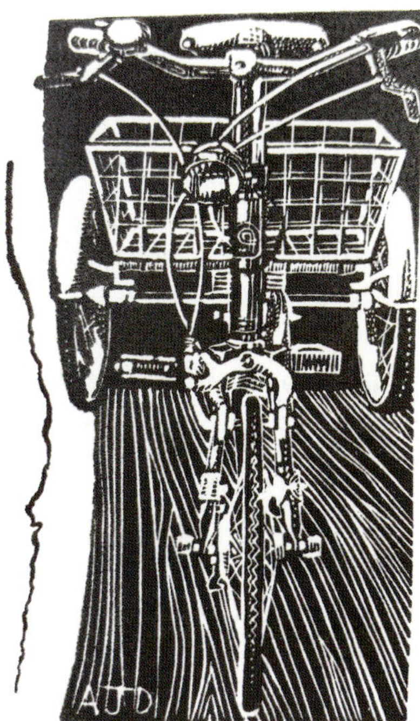

Tricycle (1986), engraving on holly, 8 × 4.8cm (3¼ × 2in). Think of each tool as if you are riding a tricycle: you mustn't lean left or right to navigate turns because that will unbalance it, so it won't run smoothly. Definitely don't think like a cyclist on a two-wheeler who would certainly lean into every curve!

Clearing out

If cutting away areas that you want to read as page-white in the print, these must be cut deeper than any lines or dots because, when you ink the block, the uncut area around each tiny cut keeps the roller from depositing ink there. However, when cutting away a larger area (for which you need either round- or square-scorpers), if the cutting is too shallow, the roller can't help but dump ink there. Inadequate clearing out can result in unexpected textural/tonal effects, occasionally more effective than a clean white. So, it is worthwhile to avoid cutting those intended white parts too deeply initially, and then take a trial print to determine whether you want a clean white after all. Before starting to clear out a section, you may want to outline it with a light line first. That line serves either as a useful start or stop for scorpers pushing away from it and/or towards it as you clear the section. The chisel tool can help to smooth an already scorper-cleared part of a block.

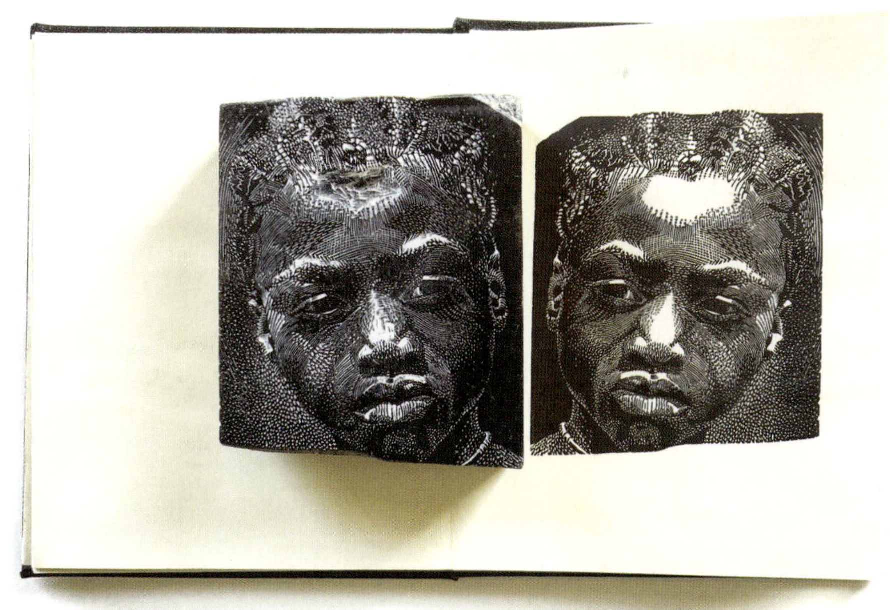

Tompieme's Daughter (1987), engraving on holly, 8.2 × 6.6cm (3¼ × 2½in), printed (in handmade artist's book) on Basingwerk Parchment paper. For white highlights, such as the child's forehead and nose, I cut away the wood to a deeper level than surrounding areas, cutting dish-like, concave indentations to keep those areas clear of the roller during inking.

Making zigzags

Chisel tools, larger square scorpers and wider multiple tools can make surprising zigzag patterns. Hold the tool at right angles to the block's surface with the full length of the squared-off cutting tip in contact with the wood. Imagine the tool is a penguin (its handle the bird's head, its blade the body and the two corners of the cutting tip its feet). Now take the 'penguin' for a walk, rocking the tool from side to side, in a penguin-like waddle, while also moving the tool fractionally forward each time. This produces a distinctive zigzag pattern across the block. Different gauges of tool will produce different-sized patterns. Don't be tempted to use any other tools at this radical angle – you will damage their cutting tips.

DEVELOPING YOUR SKILLS

To improve your skills, engrave one or more small blocks with different marks using the full range of tools at your disposal. With lozenge gravers, spitstickers and bullstickers, see how many different widths of line you can create with a single tool and also lines that swell and narrow as they progress. Practise cutting parallel straight lines with lozenge gravers and tint tools; and curving, looping ones with spitstickers and bullstickers. With round scorpers, as well as making broader lines, see how many sizes of dot you can achieve with just one tool. With tint tools, cut parallel lines of uniform width very closely together and further apart to create illusions of different greys. These exercises will improve your tool-handling skills and you will learn some of the scope of each tool.

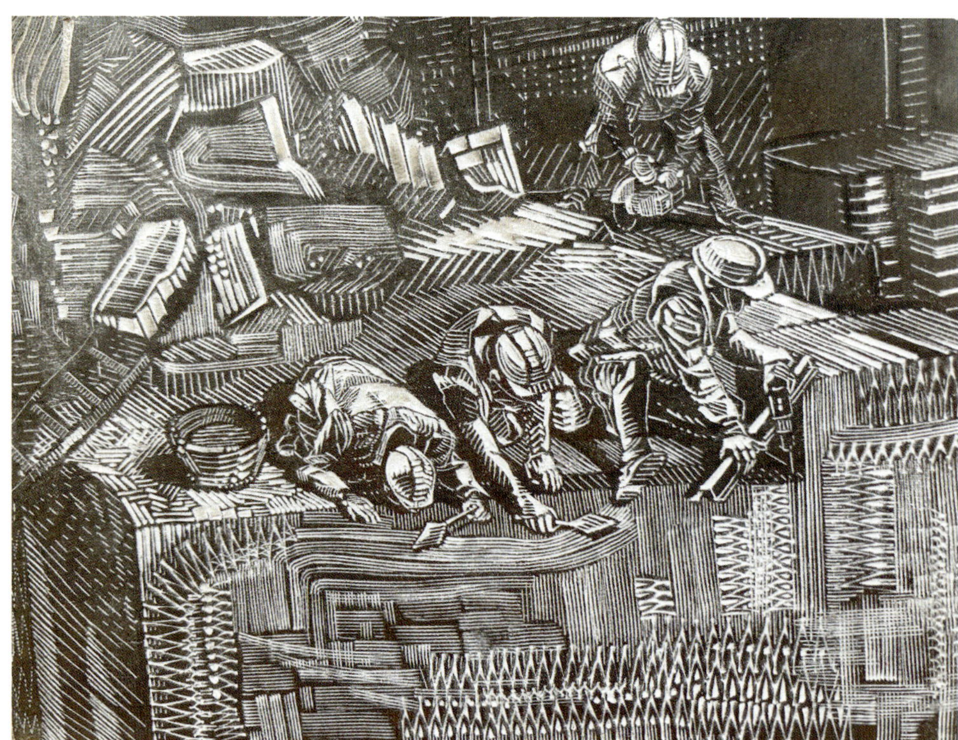

This detail of one of my woodblocks shows repeated zigzag patterns (underneath and to the right of the three foreground builders) made with a chisel tool (with a 6mm/¼in wide cutting tip) for the larger zigzags and square scorpers for the smaller ones.

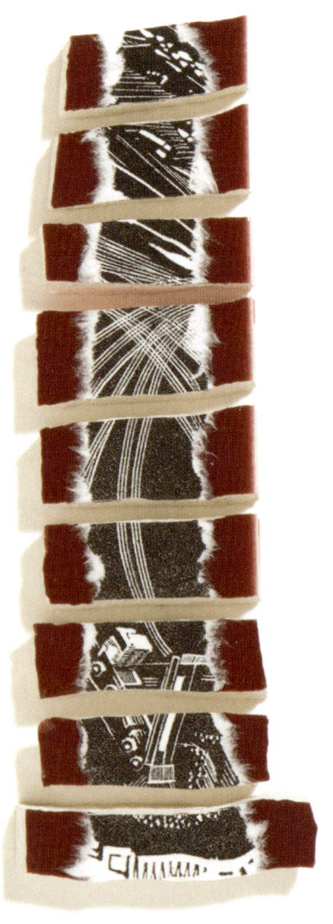

Construction Tower (2010), wood engraving (involving curves made with a multiple tool) on paper collaged on nine ceramic tile fragments, 10.2 × 3.3 × 0.4cm (4 × 1¼ × ¼in).

VISUAL AIDS

For twenty years, I engraved without visual aids. I took care of my eyesight by engraving, almost always, in a daylit room with an Anglepoise lamp by my side to create a raking light across the block. I feared that, with the natural process of ageing, my eyes might become less able to cope with such fine work. However, for nearly two decades, as my eyesight has naturally deteriorated, I have engraved with assorted highly effective visual aids. Initially I used a jeweller's monocular loupe. Subsequently, I have engraved with prescription glasses – both varifocals and reading glasses and with non-prescription cheap reading glasses.

Magnifying lenses of various sorts are invaluable. Some are highly portable and can be worn like glasses or goggles. Others (designed for embroiderers) hang on a cord around your neck, propped on your chest so you can view your work underneath. Others have stands so as to sit, free-standing, on a desk. I use one which attaches with a G-clamp to the lip of my desk; it has a bendable stalk so it's very manoeuvrable and has a good strong lens which, crucially, doesn't distort towards its edges, which some lenses do. It has LED lights around its circumference (battery- or mains-operated) but I've not found those helpful as they create too much direct illumination whereas light from one side, via an Anglepoise lamp or window, creates the raking light better suited for engraving. Through this strong, wide (9cm [3½in] diameter) lens, reasonably finely engraved marks can look quite roughly cut – so it's

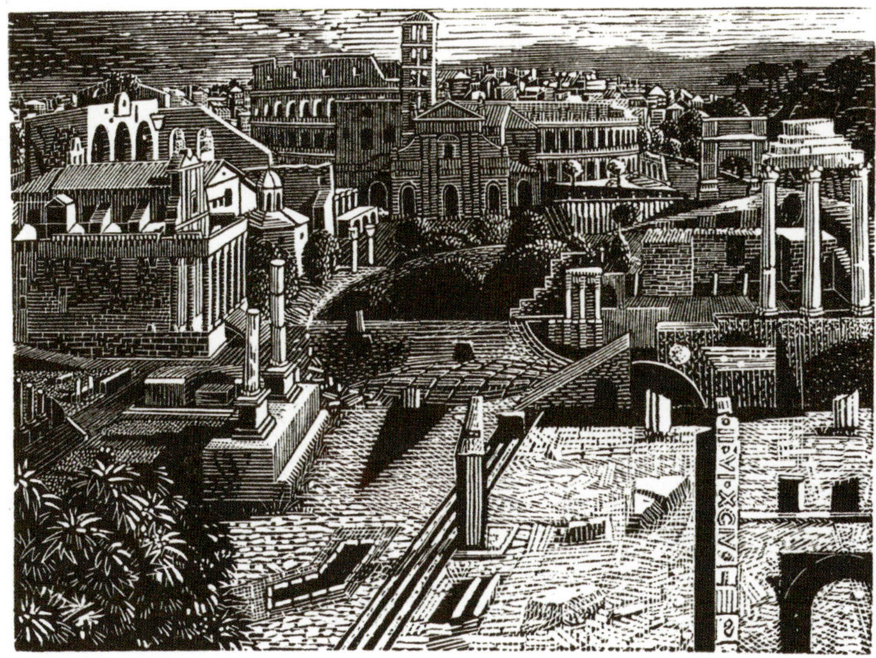

Forum (1994), engraving on boxwood, 7.6 × 10cm (3 × 4in), on Zerkall paper, by me and Roy Willingham (b.1957). This joint effort (the top half is by me, the lower half by my husband) was engraved when we both had great eyesight, so it was made without any visual aids beyond daylight and good desk-lamps.

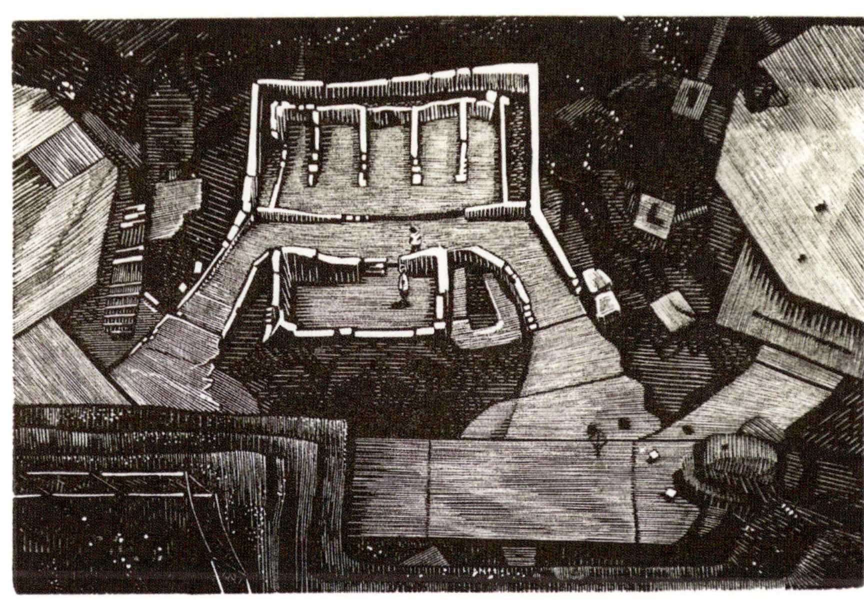

London Olympic Site – WWII Archaeology (2010), engraving on boxwood, 7.7 × 11.5cm (3 × 4½in), on Gampi Vellum paper. Engraved under my magnifying lens using tint tools (with square scorper highlights), its tonal range is subtle and hard to see without magnification. Its character differs from my earlier engravings made without visual aids, but it retains precision.

TROUBLESHOOTING

In wood engraving, bruising is described as a type of damage where the wood fibres are crushed or compressed. Such 'bruises' are usually caused by pressing too hard with an engraving tool.

Avoiding indentations

If you press too hard with the tools – especially lozenge gravers and tint tools, each of which has a particularly sharp belly – you will leave linear indented bruises on the wood behind each engraved line, which will show up in the print. This is a problem especially if you try to use these tools for curves. These tools weren't designed for loops or circles: if put to that use, their very sharp bellies almost inevitably bruise the wood in a series of radiating dents around the outside of each curve. Similarly, although designed for curves, if you press too hard with either spitsticker or bullsticker, your curve will also acquire bruises in the same way. Avoid these dangers by using each tool for its intended function and by not applying too much pressure, especially while engraving curves. Alternatively, place a piece of thin card (a sliver of a postcard perhaps) under the tool's belly and running along the tool's length as you cut. The tool's sharp belly will indent the card rather than the wood.

Filling in mistakes

If you slip and make a longer cut than intended, or cut small dots in an area you intended to leave uncut, assuming you plan to print the block in black ink, you can fill in minor unwanted tool cuts with a black chinagraph pencil, the tip of which is made of hardened, coloured wax. Simply colour in these small errors on the block, pressing quite hard. Waxy deposits will fill the indentations. (Take care not to fill in more than you intend.) Plane off any excess waxy pigment on the surface with your fingernail. This wax repair can sometimes fill small marks permanently and will certainly remain in place for a reasonable number of prints to be taken. Should you clean the block after printing, you will need to redo the repair before printing it again. This is not a suitable repair for large errors as the waxy pencil won't stay within larger cuts. Avoid re-engraving areas filled with these waxy deposits as any recutting will lift out the wax and the block won't re-engrave cleanly. For these reasons, this repair method should only ever be applied sparingly.

Correcting bruises

If the wood is simply bruised rather than engraved, place a small drop of water on the bruise (using a pipette, syringe or small watercolour brush). Strike a match and hold the flame as close to the water droplet as you can. The excess water should evaporate speedily but some liquid will soak into the end grain wood making it swell slightly and the bruise disappear. This repair, however, must be carried out before the block is inked with oil-based printing ink because, even if the ink is cleaned off, the slightest residual oil trace will repel the water droplet and make its absorption, and thus this repair method, virtually impossible.

Inserting a plug

Historically, a chunk of wood on which an engraving error had occurred would be cut out of the block and replaced with a large patch or small wooden plug (depending on the error's size), which was then planed to sit flush with the rest of the block and engraving could recommence. I have never tried either method, but I suspect it would need to be done by a professional block-maker for a seamless repair.

Modifying an error

A better solution may be to modify the design of the engraving to make a virtue from an initial error, though there are ways of making invisible corrections to finished prints, which I'll describe later.

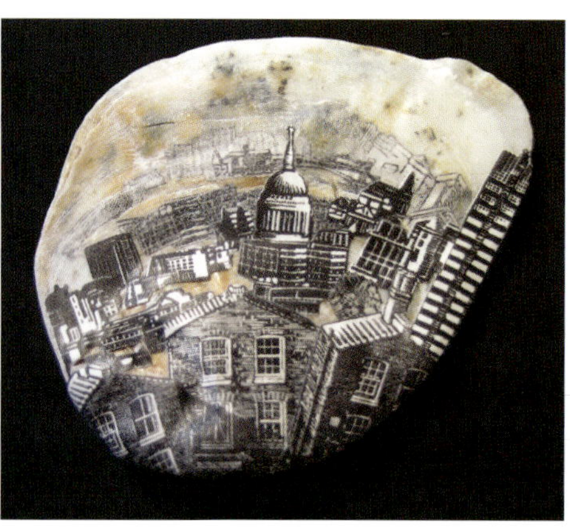

From Hackney to St Paul's (2008), wood engraving on paper collaged on oyster shell, 6.2 × 7.5cm (2½ × 3in).

tempting to re-engrave the block, under the lens, making increasingly fine marks, which are virtually impossible to see with the naked eye. As a result, engravings made after my eyesight became less than perfect actually have finer mark-making than those I made before. So, imperfect eyesight may not be an obstacle to engraving if you invest in visual aids.

Bear in mind, however, that most engravings are studied with the naked eye, so avoid cutting marks so fine that the viewer would need a magnifying glass to discern them. It can help to rub talcum powder into the engraved marks as you make them. This is an excellent visual aid and gives a clear idea of the balance of light and dark tones on your block (assuming you had darkened the block first). If you take a trial proof and then decide the block needs more engraving, all the newly cut marks will look much brighter than earlier ones which, however careful you are in cleaning the block post-printing, will look duller and dirtier than fresh marks, making it difficult to see the tonal range on the block. Again, rub talcum powder into the marks as it evens out any tonal mismatch between old and new cutting. The talc flattens out the block's three-dimensional appearance too, enabling you to see clearly how it will look when printed, substantially reducing the need to print trial proofs along the way. Ensure your block is completely dry after inking, printing and cleaning before you apply talc: any residual moisture will turn it into an unhelpful paste.

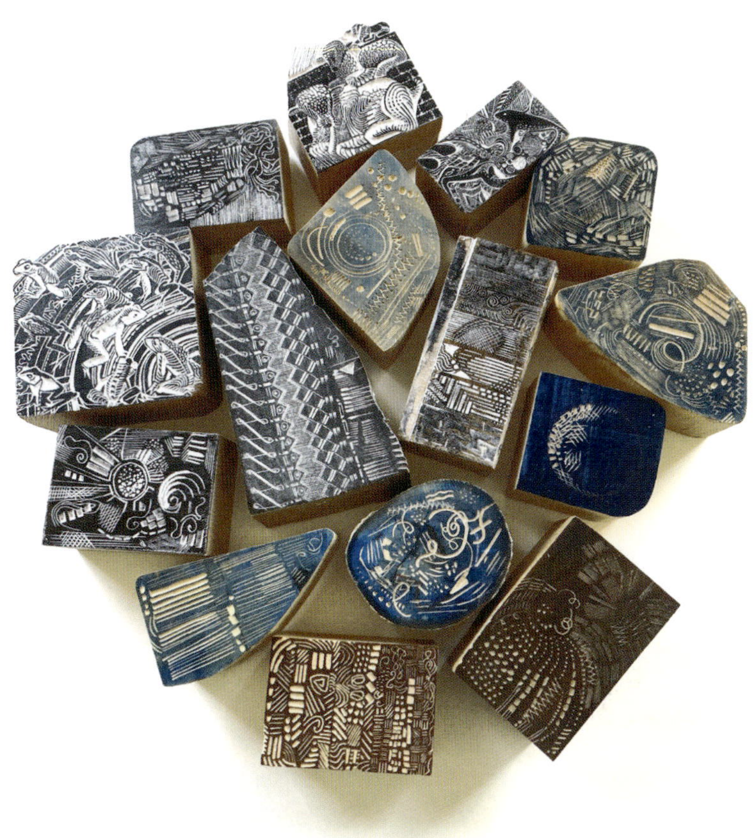

Practice blocks showing engraved marks made with the full range of tools. Some have previously been printed and so have talcum powder rubbed into the cuts to aid visibility, while others, never printed, simply show the engraving against the blocks' blue- or black-stained surfaces.

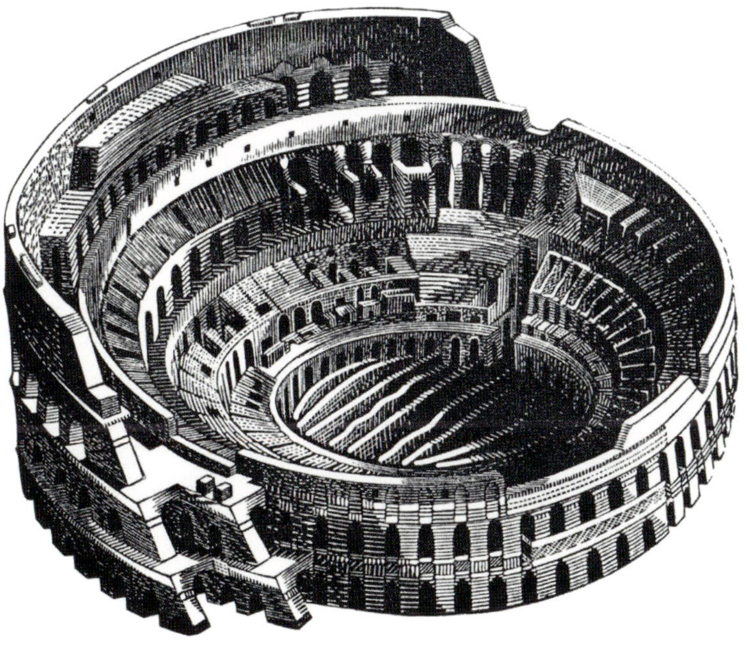

Colosseum (1991), engraving on boxwood roundel, 8 × 9.5cm (3¼ × 3¾in) on China White paper. This was made without the aid of any magnifying lenses and its composition was inspired by the block's beautiful ovoid shape.

TOOL SHARPENING, SHORTENING AND STORAGE

Wood engraving tools are made of strong tempered steel and, if looked after, will last a lifetime. They need sharpening and honing from time to time. The frequency with which they become blunt depends on how much you use a particular tool and how much pressure you apply in the cutting. Tint tools' fine cutting tips are particularly susceptible to snapping if you engrave too forcefully and also, obviously, if you drop them, tip down, on the floor. You may find some tools need sharpening every few days, while others remain sharp for weeks. Follow the advice below to check for bluntness and to sharpen them.

Thumbnail test

Touch the tool's cutting tip very lightly against your thumbnail. If it's sharp enough, it will usually stick slightly into your nail whereas, if blunt, it will slide across without sticking. It's a useful, literal, thumbnail test!

Tool test

Before sharpening a tool, first make a few marks with it on a practice block, sharpen it, then make more marks to see whether its cutting has improved. If it still doesn't cut well, continue sharpening until it does.

Area to sharpen

Unlike woodcutting and lino-cutting tools, wood engraving tools should only be sharpened on the front cutting face. Don't sharpen the sides or belly of any wood engraving tool as this will change its shape and damage it. Sharpening the front face is all that's needed. The only exception is if there is a burr of metal on the cutting edge. Test for that by running a fingernail along the belly of the blade. If your nail catches at the blade's tip, it indicates a burr which needs removing.

Sharpening methods

Traditionally, wood engraving tools are sharpened using a carborundum stone for serious sharpening and a diamond stone for honing. The recommended method is to put a few drops of mineral oil on the stone's surface, then to place the tool's face flat on the oiled stone and grind it by making figure-of-eight motions across the stone's flat surface, keeping the tool's face perfectly flat on the stone as you do so. You then hone the tool by repeating that procedure on a smooth diamond stone. This sounds easy in principle, but I have never managed it successfully! Using that method, I did manage to make my tools a little sharper each time, but their flat faces gradually became somewhat convex, taking on the appearance of the backs of miniature teaspoons – not ideal! However, I have devised a simpler method which works much better for me. I consider myself a fairly poor tool sharpener with the standard method, but have achieved far more successful and easier results like this:

1. First, colour in your blunt tool's cutting face with a permanent marker pen. Having done this, when you are sharpening it, you will know whether you are sharpening its entire face effectively because the marker pen will rub off completely, but it will remain in place in some parts if you aren't managing to sharpen the entire face.

2. Put a folded newspaper on your desk. On top, place a sheet of abrasive paper of a mild grit. My preferred type is silicon carbide (aka wet-and-dry) P400 (used dry). Hold the blunt tool so that its coloured-in cutting face is face down on the abrasive paper and press down hard. Pull the tool towards you with a short, sharp, movement, while keeping its face pressed firmly down. Repeat this half a dozen times. You should see a clear impression or indentation of the tool's cutting face on the abrasive paper with each pull you make. If you can't see that or if you can see only a mark made by part of the tool's face, adjust the way that you are holding the tool to ensure that its entire face gets sharpened.

3. Remove the P400 paper and replace it with a sheet of fine jewellers' emery polishing paper: grade 2/0, 3/0 or 4/0 are all ideal. To hone the tool, repeat exactly the same procedure on the emery paper that you just did with the P400.

4. Repeat the thumbnail test and make a few more marks on the practice block. If there's no improvement, repeat the entire procedure with both the sharpening and polishing papers and continue thumbnail testing and cutting the practice block until the tool cuts well. Usually, sharpening and honing is a very speedy process

and only requires about half a dozen short sharp pulls with the tool, across each of the papers described, before the tool is working perfectly once more. However, if you aren't detecting improvement and are sure you pressed hard with each pull, carry out these checks:

5. Run a fingernail along the belly of the blade. If your nail meets a snag at the cutting tip, however minimal, this is probably a burr which needs removing. You may be able to see it if you inspect the tool's tip under a magnifying lens. Sometimes new tools that haven't been honed perfectly or tools that have been shortened for you may have a burr before you've even used them. If this is the case, they won't engrave effectively, but the cure is quick and simple.

6. To remove a burr, lay the belly of the tool flat on either the abrasive or the polishing paper so that the back of the tip is in contact with the abrasive surface. Holding the tool with its handle in the palm of your hand, as if you were going to engrave a woodblock, drag the tool towards you with a short pull. Don't rub any more than absolutely necessary as there is a danger of damaging the tool's cutting edge if you overdo it. A few light strokes should do the job of removing the burr.

7. If you dropped the tool on the floor and it then doesn't cut well, it's likely that its cutting tip has been chipped or bent by the impact. You can see this under a magnifier. In this case, I recommend you return the tool to its maker or supplier who can usually repair and regrind it mechanically, for a small fee, whereas trying to regrind it by hand to repair such damage is feasible but would likely take days and be tedious work.

Historically, wood engraving tools were made to measure for your hand. Therefore, if you buy second-hand ones, you may find some that are long and others too short – though this shouldn't deter you because the quality of the steel of 100-year-old tools can sometimes be especially strong, and they seem to need sharpening with less frequency than newer ones. Tools bought new usually err on the shorter side, which is fine because, in general, it's easier to work with a tool that is the right size or a bit short for you, but harder working with one that's too long as you will have less control with it. A specialist toolmaker will shorten over-long tools for a small fee to better fit your hand.

When not in use, store your tools carefully. Don't leave them anywhere very cold or damp or they may rust. Smear the blades with a thin layer of rust-preventing oil before storing them for any length of time. I have a baize-lined wooden toolbox (homemade) with a slot for each tool, but an alternative, convenient, lightweight storage solution is a fabric roll. You can buy these from printmaking suppliers or make your own. Alternatively, if storing tools in a box or pot, save some old wine-bottle corks and push the blade of each tool into its own cork to prevent the blades' tips damaging one another.

A round scorper, its face coloured with red marker pen ready for sharpening, resting on an abrasive paper on which tool-tip-shaped indentations from the sharpening of other tools are clearly visible.

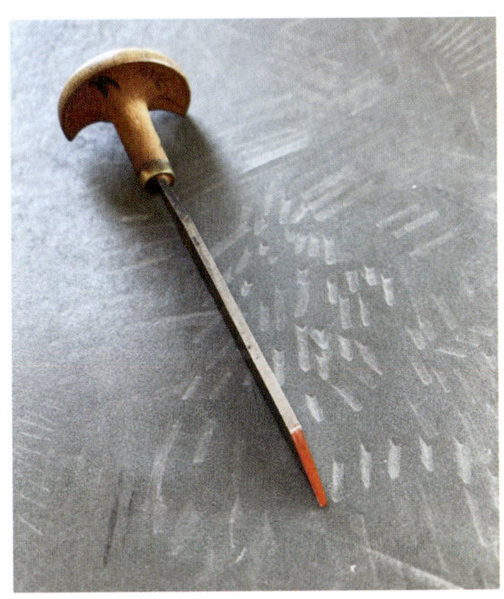

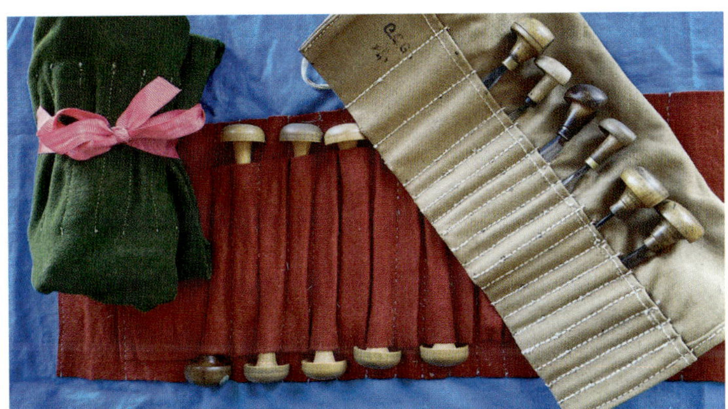

Fabric rolls – one rolled and tied with ribbon. I acquired the beige roll with a second-hand toolset. Underneath it is a roll I made using a blue cotton napkin on which I sewed two brick-red felt layers – one to give more padding than the thin base layer and the other to make pockets for each blade.

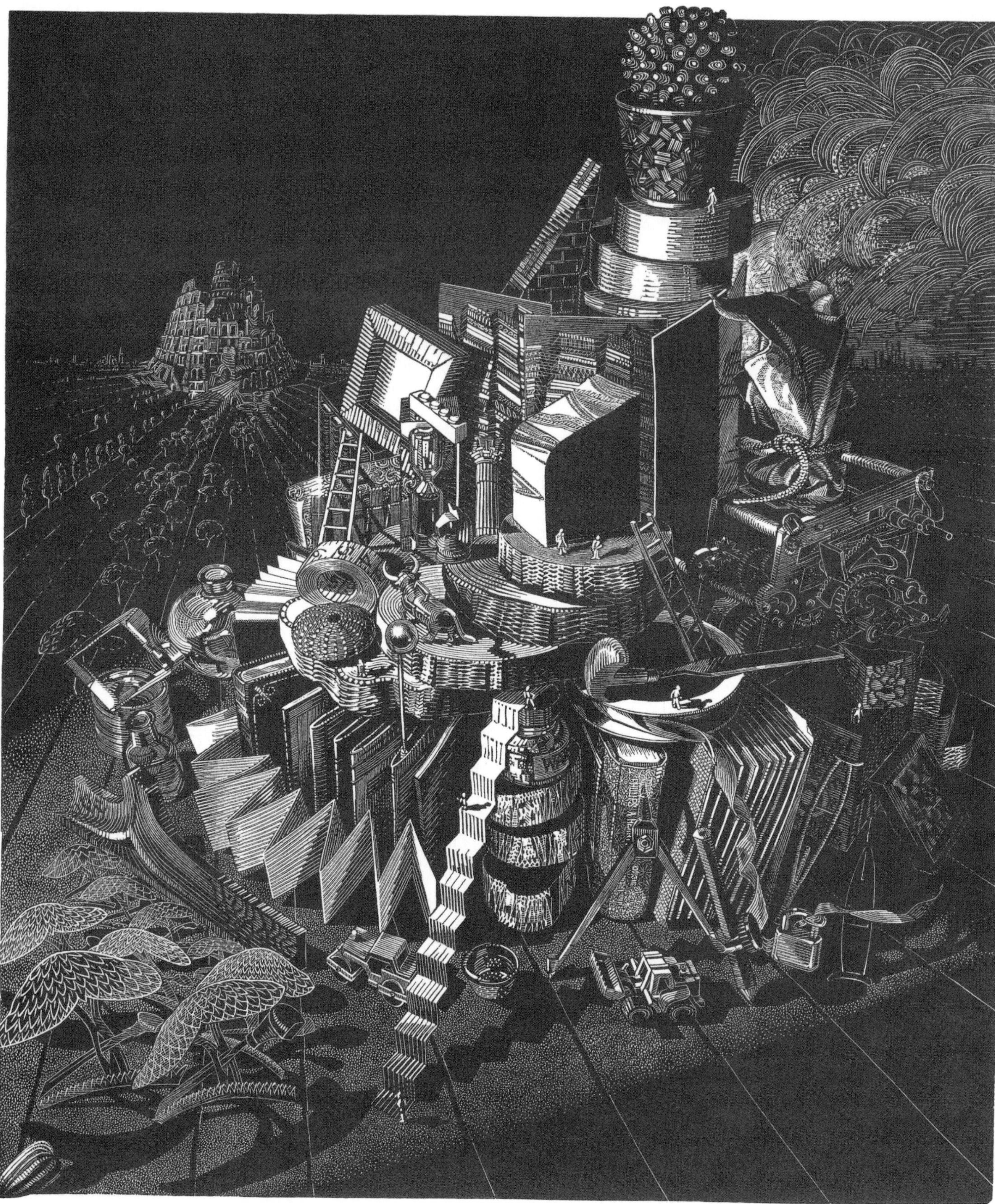

CHAPTER 4

WORKING IN LIGHT

It can be really helpful to study other engravers' work and to learn about their mark-making techniques by trying to replicate a small block-sized detail from a selected engraving. To do this:

Stain the surface of a practice block in a dark tone.

Trace the block's outline shape onto the middle of a piece of scrap paper of about A5-size.

Cut out, using scissors or scalpel, the drawn shape to create a paper viewing window with a block-shaped hole in the middle.

Research in books and/or photocopy engravings by artists whose work you like – or search them out online and bring them up on your monitor. The latter approach means you can scale images to whatever size you like, provided the image file is large enough not to lose focus if enlarged. There are innumerable images you might choose but, as a place to start, the larger engravings of Eric Ravilious and Gertrude Hermes are especially good for this exercise because they generally include a wide range of vibrant, clearly defined tool marks. Alternatively, if you're struggling to make delicate marks, look at the engravings of Paul Nash or Henry Moore (1898–1986), which employ bold yet often quite coarse cutting to excellent effect.

Wood Engraver's Tower (2020), engraving on boxwood, 30 × 25cm (11¾ × 9¾in), on Gampi Vellum paper, commissioned by Manchester Metropolitan University Special Collections Library to celebrate 2020's centenary of the founding of the UK's Society of Wood Engravers. All the tower's components relate to wood engravers past and present and include autobiographical and library-related references.

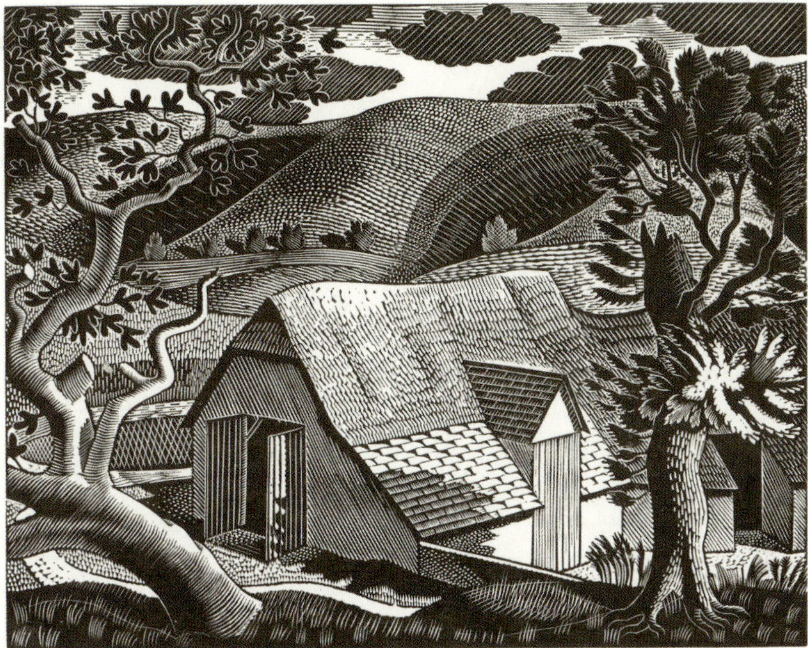

Sussex Landscape (1931), engraving on boxwood, 13 × 16cm (5 × 6¼in) on off-white paper, by Eric Ravilious. Multi-directional tool-marks are especially interesting here in that they follow the form of the hills and thus describe their contours. Also, the various sizes of dots, dashes and lines create vibrant patterns as well as a wide range of tones.

If rescaling, ensure the individual marks on your selected engraving look the same size as cuts you made on earlier practice block(s). This will show you whether you are setting yourself a feasible engraving challenge. If the marks on the selected engraving look much smaller than your marks, either scale up the selected image or choose a different engraving with larger marks in it.

Move the viewing window around the image until you find a section with a wide range of different tool marks and which makes a pleasing composition in your paper window.

Remember that, as you're copying another artist's work, the final result isn't something you should later present as your own original work (unless the source material is out of copyright). But it is, nonetheless, a worthwhile exercise.

Use a small piece of sticky tape (that can later be easily peeled off) to attach your viewing window to the desired place on your photocopy or computer monitor/ipad/mobile phone screen so that the composition is on view exactly as you want it through the paper window.

Draw the composition's simple outlines onto the block in pencil. Don't draw small details, which will unnecessarily complicate the exercise.

If drawing with pencil and wanting to rub something out, don't use an eraser as it won't work well and will leave a smut on the wood. Instead, run your index finger across your forehead or down the side of your nose, then use that finger as an eraser. The small amount of facial grease works as a highly effective eraser and even shines up the block's surface!

The pencil drawing may get rubbed off by your hand as you engrave, so reinforce it with, ideally, a black drawing pen or a red or white chinagraph* pencil. (*This waxy pencil doesn't smudge easily but, to remove it, just scratch it off with a fingernail.) Alternatively, you could fix the pencil drawing on the block using a spray fixative.

Engrave slowly, analysing the artist's marks carefully. Replicate them by using whichever tools you think the artist probably used for each dot and line. Remember that your analysis is of white marks not black ones. The tool marks of the selected engraving are the white areas of the image. The black parts represent the block's uncut parts, so keep your focus solely on the whites.

Notice that some effects are made by combinations of tool marks: for example, a passage of multiple-tool cuts might be overlaid with scorper marks, or lozenge graver cross-hatching might be overlaid with stippled dots.

Remember: you can engrave the block from any direction and can recut and refine any previously engraved marks, modifying them to make your work look more like what you're copying.

When you have completed the exercise to the best of your ability, print the block. The result will be a mirror image of its source material because everything engraved on a woodblock prints in reverse. But, other than that, your print should be a recognisable copy and, in engraving it, you should have learned a lot about controlling and placing each tool mark as well as ways of engraving different marks, singly or in combination, to create tones or patterns in a finished image.

Don't be discouraged if your work looks more roughly cut than its source material. The artist whose work you copied was an experienced engraver, so it would be surprising if you could copy it exactly within hours of first handling an engraving tool! But lessons learnt from this exercise will usefully inform subsequent engravings.

With this engraving and with your randomly cut practice block(s), print them on white paper so you can see what you've engraved clearly. You could also try printing on unusual papers such as coloured street maps or patterned giftwrap (paper that isn't too glossy or shiny).

If you repeat this copying exercise using work by different engravers, you will find that every good engraver of the last 100-odd years has cut their blocks in different ways and with different combinations of tool marks to create varying effects of light and dark, texture and structure, stillness and movement. This is the crux of what makes engraving so fascinating and each engraver's work unique. Having learned some of the diverse marks that can be used to describe similar forms – representational and abstract – try to bring to your engravings a spirit of your own creative invention and make the medium your own.

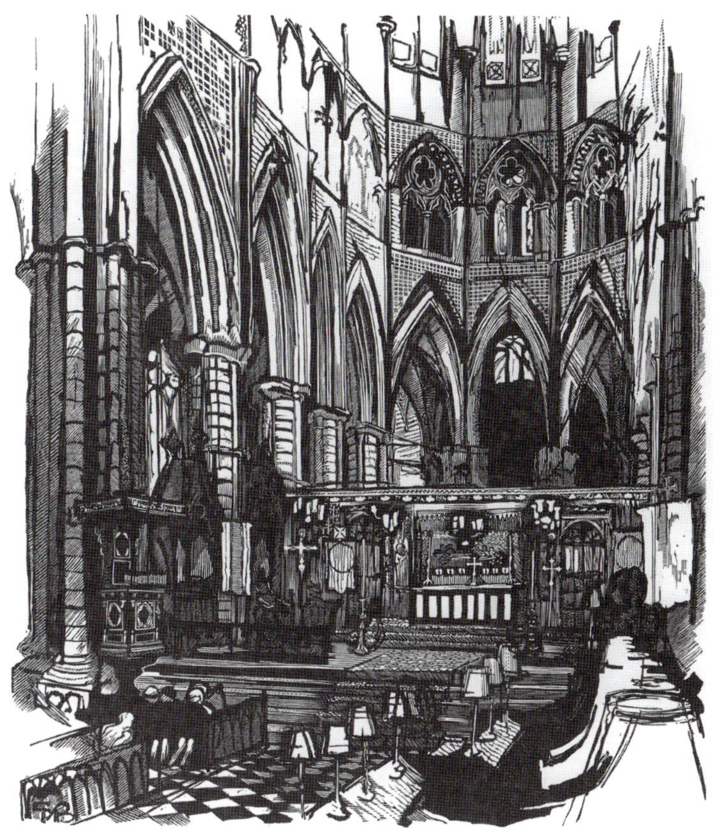

Westminster Abbey 1 – The High Altar (1965), wood engraving, 25.5 × 21.5cm (10 × 8½in), on white paper, by Simon Brett. © Estate of Simon Brett. A small detail of an arched window in this lively engraving inspired the work of a student, Lydia Uglow, on one of the many wood engraving courses I have taught.

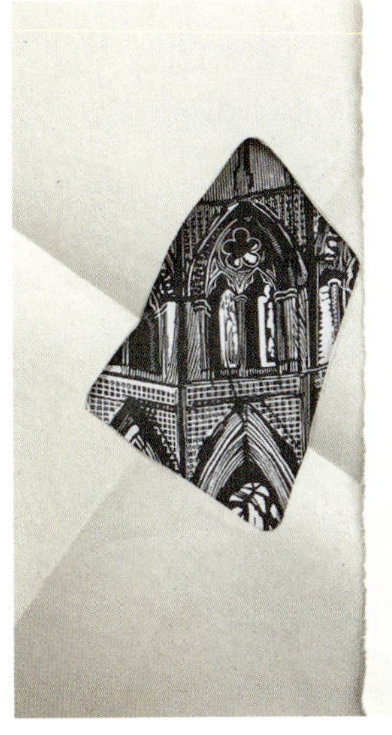

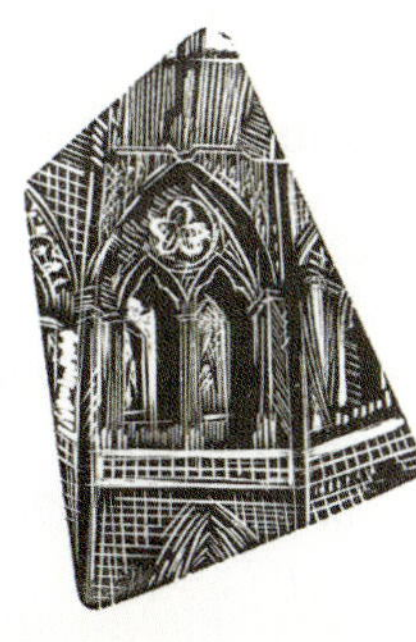

Untitled (2024), wood engraving, c.7 × 5cm (2¾ × 2in), on Zerkall paper by Lydia Uglow (right), next to a detail of Simon Brett's engraving (left) seen through a newsprint viewing window the same size as Uglow's irregularly-shaped block. As Uglow's first wood engraving, it's a creditable copy and was a useful learning exercise.

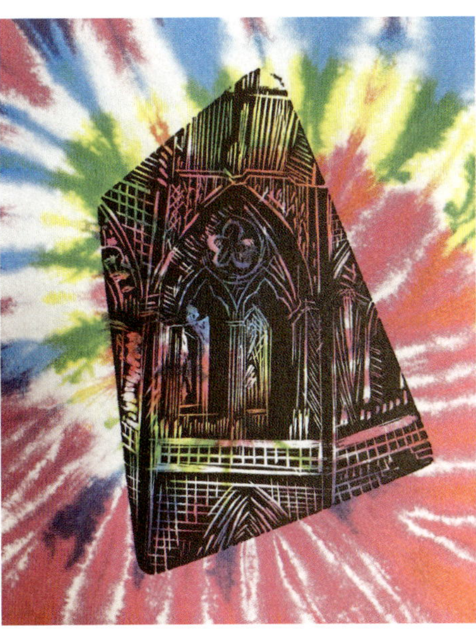

This was printed (by hand-burnishing) from the same block, by Lydia Uglow, onto a sheet of patterned paper designed for origami. The multicoloured paper creates an effect not unlike sunlight on stained glass, which felt appropriate for this image.

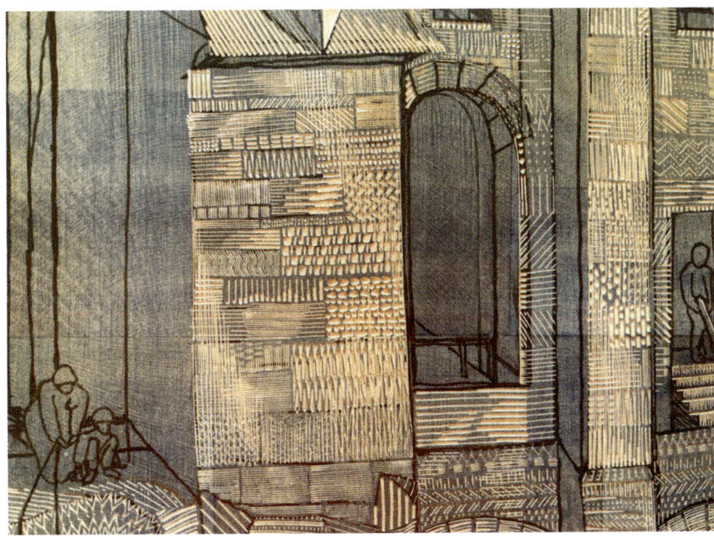

In this small section of an engraving in progress, I have been treating the brickwork as a series of different patterns, almost like a fabric, rather than treating the entire surface in a single way. It's always worthwhile to try out unexpected approaches.

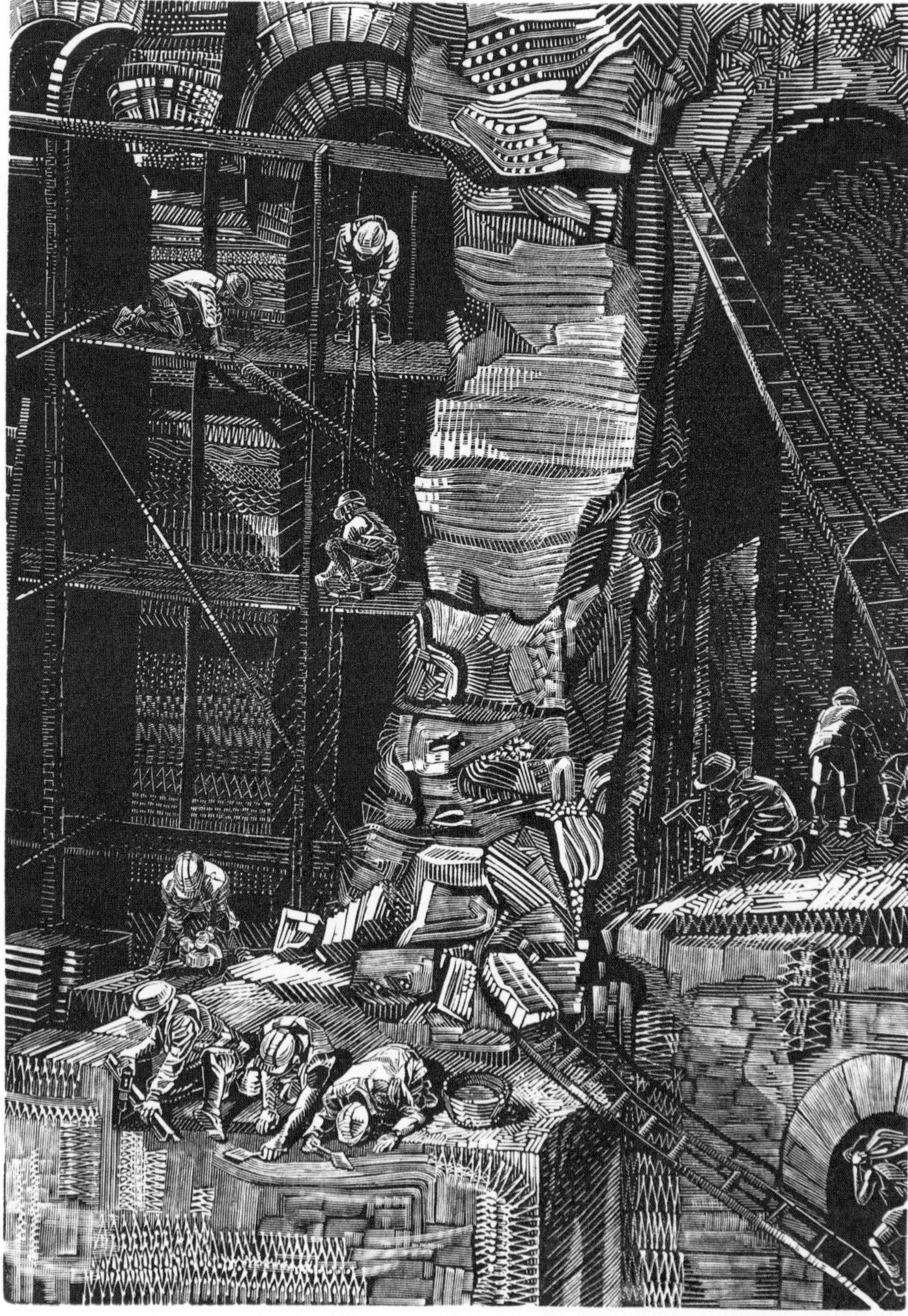

Homage to Bruegel (2023), engraving on boxwood, 24.2 × 16.8cm (9½ × 6½in), on Gampi Vellum paper. Based on a detail of Pieter Bruegel the Elder's *Tower of Babel* (1563) painting in Vienna's Kunsthistorisches Museum, I have depicted its areas of stonework and brickwork via different patterns contrasted with minimal stippled tones in darker areas.

Tonal ranges in a wood engraving can be created via infinitely varied patterns of narrower or wider engraved lines: straight or curving, close together or far apart; and in all sorts of combinations of differently sized and spaced dots and dashes. I can't helpfully teach you how to engrave sunlight or moonlight, plant life, seas, skies, human or animal forms, architectural or abstract compositions. To make original, inspiring work you need to study your specific source material to decide exactly what it is about it that you'd like to depict. Look especially carefully at its balance of light and dark tones and consider how you might best convey them. Then aim to find your own personal engraving language to do so (though this may include ideas absorbed from other artists). This language will develop and expand over time. Some tool marks may seem more useful than others and you may feel instinctively drawn to some tool types more than others, but those choices are different for every engraver. The language you're working on is an ongoing process of discovery and reinvention with every block you engrave.

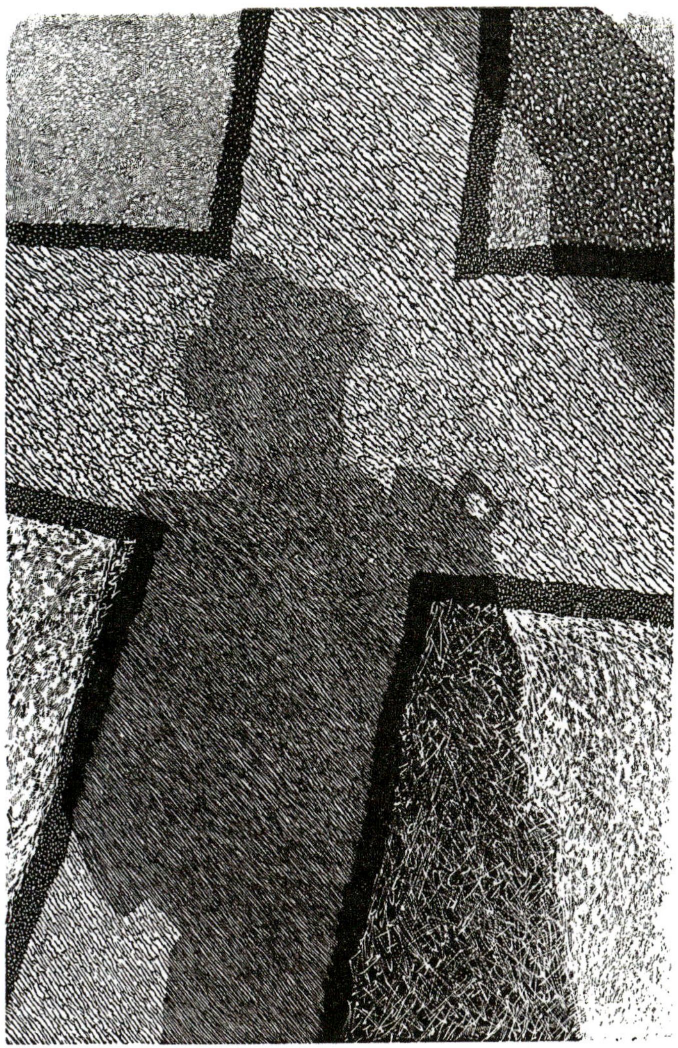

Across The Station (2016), engraving on boxwood, 14 × 9cm (5½ × 3½in), on Zerkall paper, by Peter S Smith (b.1946) involves tonal layers cut to make it intentionally difficult to identify the tools used. This, like many of his engravings, is inspired by innumerable sketchbook studies of his own shadow across roads, pavements and train platforms.

DARK SIDE OF THE MOON

A useful exercise for improving tonal skills is as follows:

1. Take a practice block and a 10p or 2p (British) coin or a Euro coin or any equivalent with a diameter of roughly 2.4cm (1in).

2. Stain the block a dark tone.

3. Place the coin wherever you like on the block, but ensure it fits within the block's surface area. Draw around it with pencil or black pen.

4. Imagine this circle as the moon with light and dark sides. Engrave tones on it, starting within the moon's circumference and going from very light/white on one side, to graduated mid-tone, to either full black or nearly black on the other. You can achieve this using fine lines (maybe tint tools) to create varying tones; or round scorpers to make stippled dots; or some lozenge graver crosshatching; or random tonal patterns of all sorts using the full range of tools. It can be as simple or as complex as you like, so long as it demonstrates a clear transition of tone across the moon's surface. Try to avoid outlining the moon, but use only subtle tonal marks to convey its three-dimensionality.

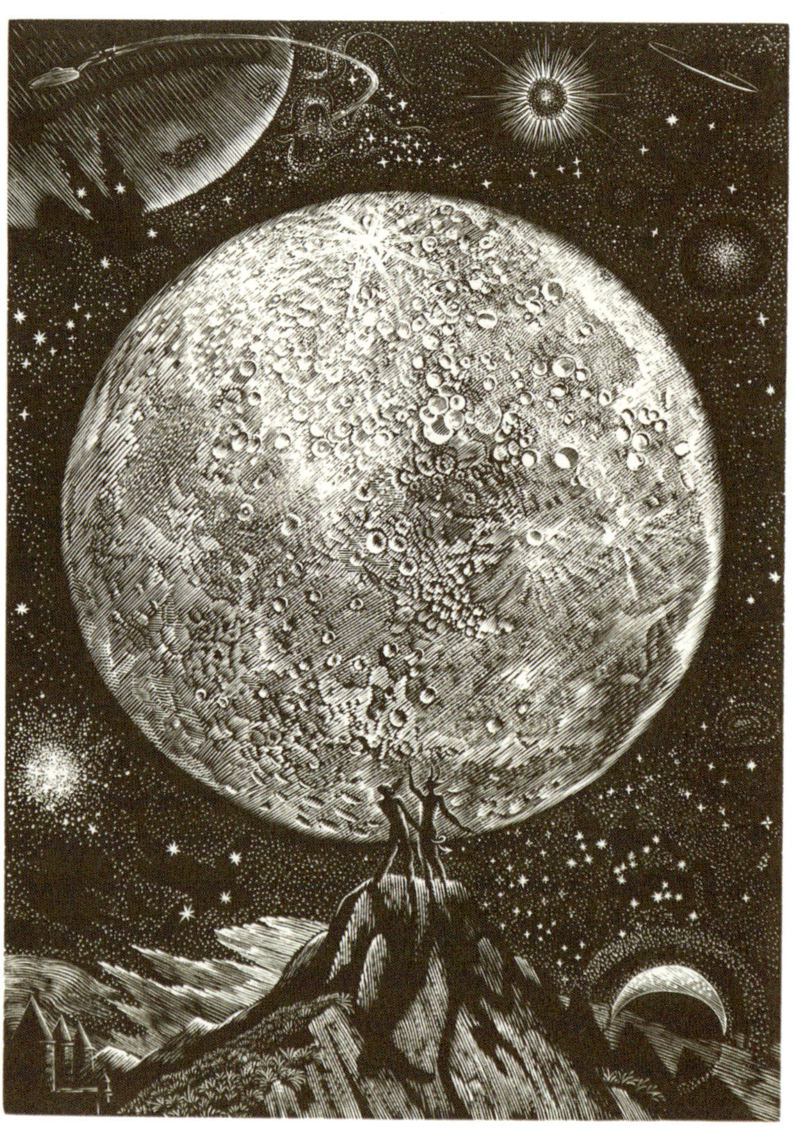

Mephistopheles Showing Faust The Heavens (1995), wood engraving, 17.5 × 12.4cm (7 × 5in), on white paper, by George Tute (b.1933). The drama and exquisite tonal cutting in this image are extraordinary. Many of my students have made excellent tiny tonal engravings inspired by it.

5. Consider working on the background night sky with another graduated tone, from light to dark, so that the lightest side of background meets the darkest side of moon and vice versa, or try combining areas of stars and background tone – have fun with it!

6. Repeat this exercise on one or more practice blocks using different combinations of marks to achieve a graduated range of similar or different tones each time.

Moon studies made by my students in 2024 and 2025. From left to right by Paul Cave, Chiara Occhipinti, Nigel Harriss, Jane Giscombe, Amy Trindall, two by John Cloake above one by Anna Walsh, and a demonstration block in progress by me.

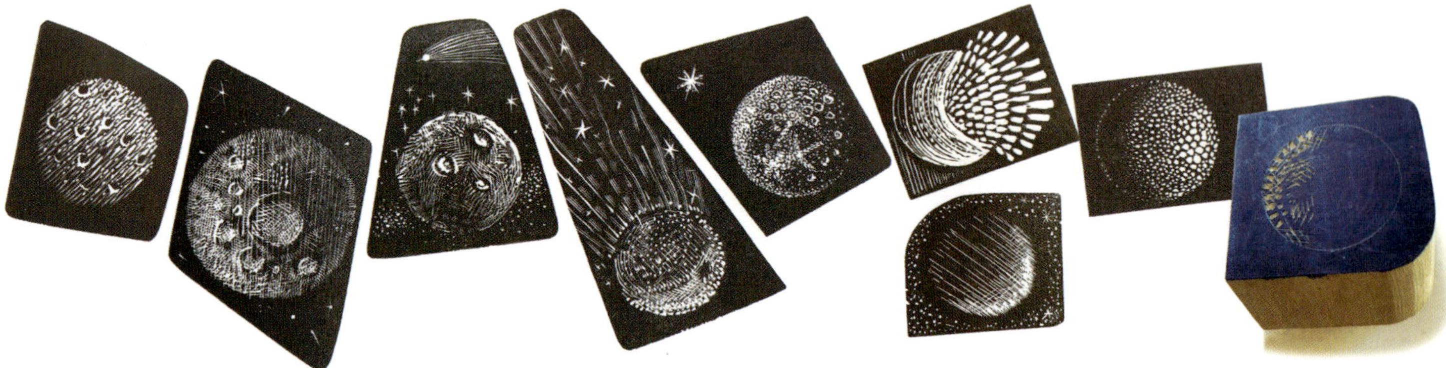

PREPARATORY WORK

Having done these exercises, try making an image from your own preparatory work. For me, sketchbook drawing is vital preparation for engravings, though I also work from my own photos and, occasionally, other material such as old topographical postcards or online images. If you didn't generate the source material yourself, ensure your engraving is sufficiently original and different from it so as not to infringe anyone's copyright.

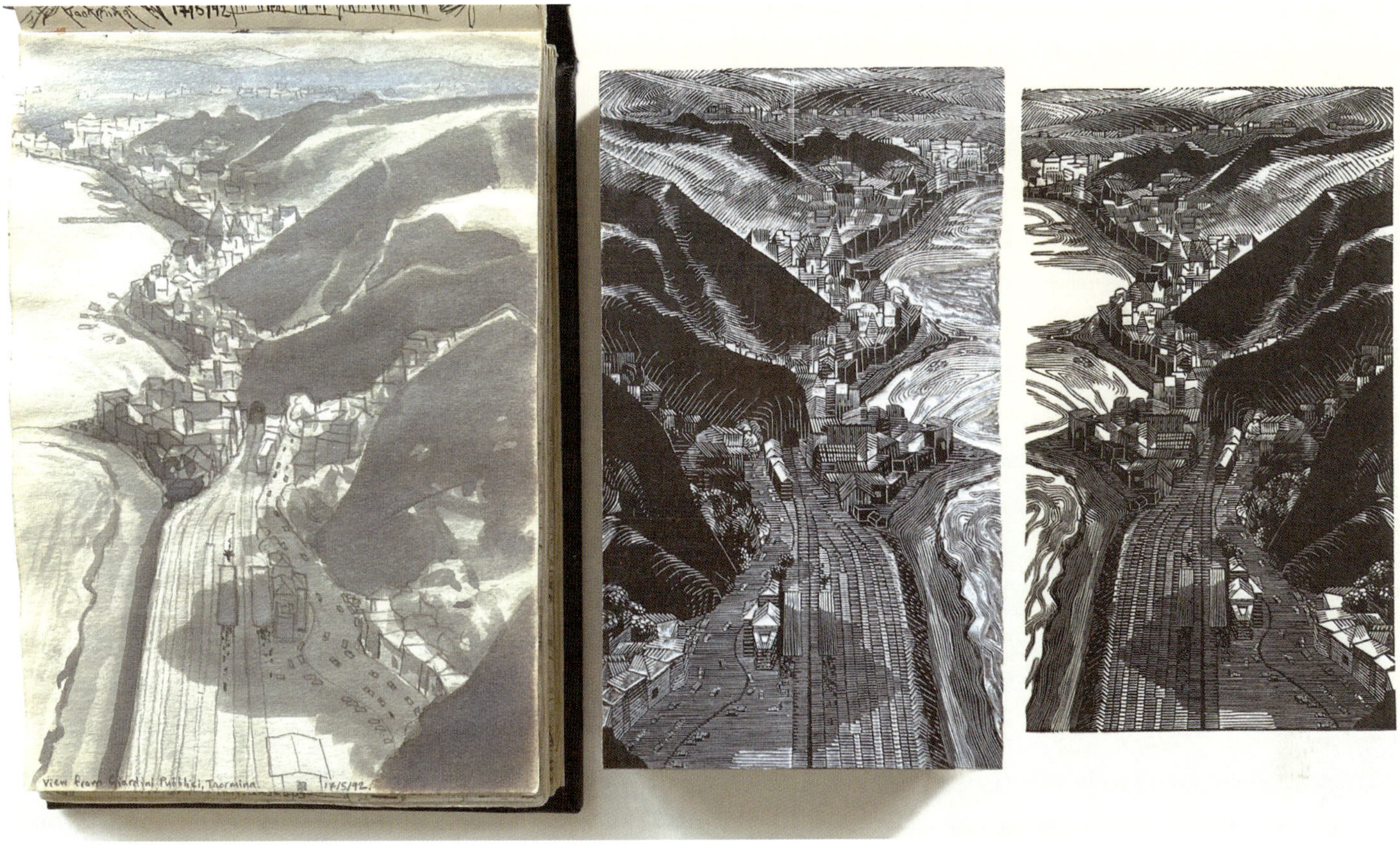

■ Sketchbook study, 14.5 × 10cm (5¾ × 4in), of Taormina railway station, Sicily (1992), seen from above (from a public park), made in pencil and diluted ink wash, plus my engraved boxwood block and finished print: *Sicilia* (1993), wood engraving, 12.7 × 7.3cm (5 × 3in), on China White paper.

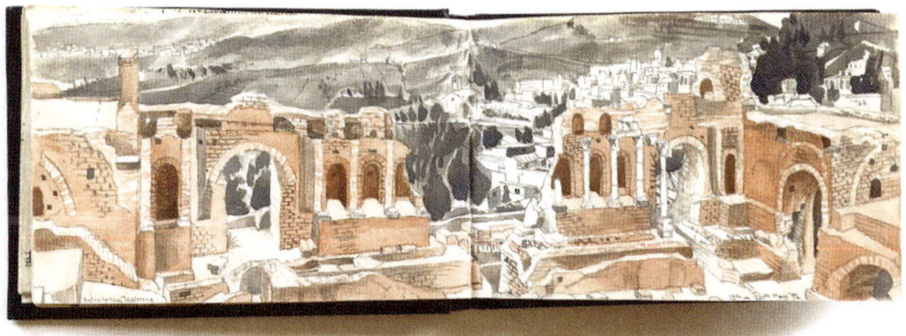

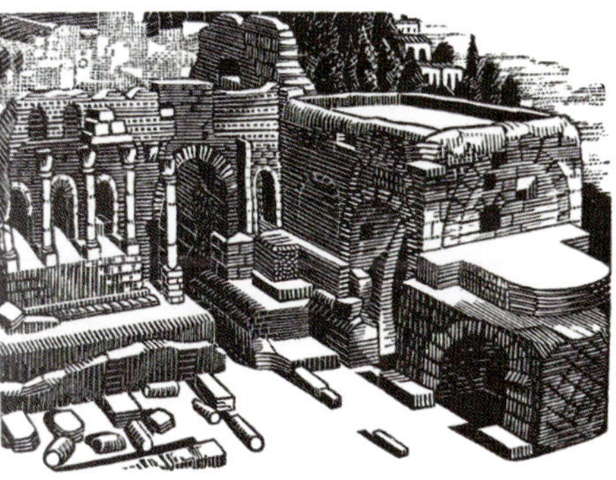

■ Sketchbook study (1992), 10 × 30cm (4 × 11¾ in), of Sicily's Teatro Greco at Taormina, made in watercolour, diluted ink wash and pencil, plus *Teatro Greco* (1994), a boxwood engraving, 5 × 6.7cm (2 × 2½in), on Zerkall paper, based on a detail of this sketch.

SKETCHING FOR ENGRAVING

Sketches and detailed drawings are invaluable source material. Because my work focuses on a highly tonal approach to my subject matter, it's important that my drawings capture a range of light and dark tonality – which is, often, what draws me to a subject in the first place and is essential in my engravings. I draw in various media including pencil, black pen and watercolour, but my favourite – which most often inspires my engravings – is using pencil or pen for defining outlines and details, with diluted ink wash for darker tones and shadows, leaving areas of sunlight page-white.

I use very diluted black Parker Quink ink for tonal washes – about one part ink to seven or eight parts water – applied with soft-haired, square-tipped brushes of various sizes. It's a speedy way to capture shadows. As I've generally

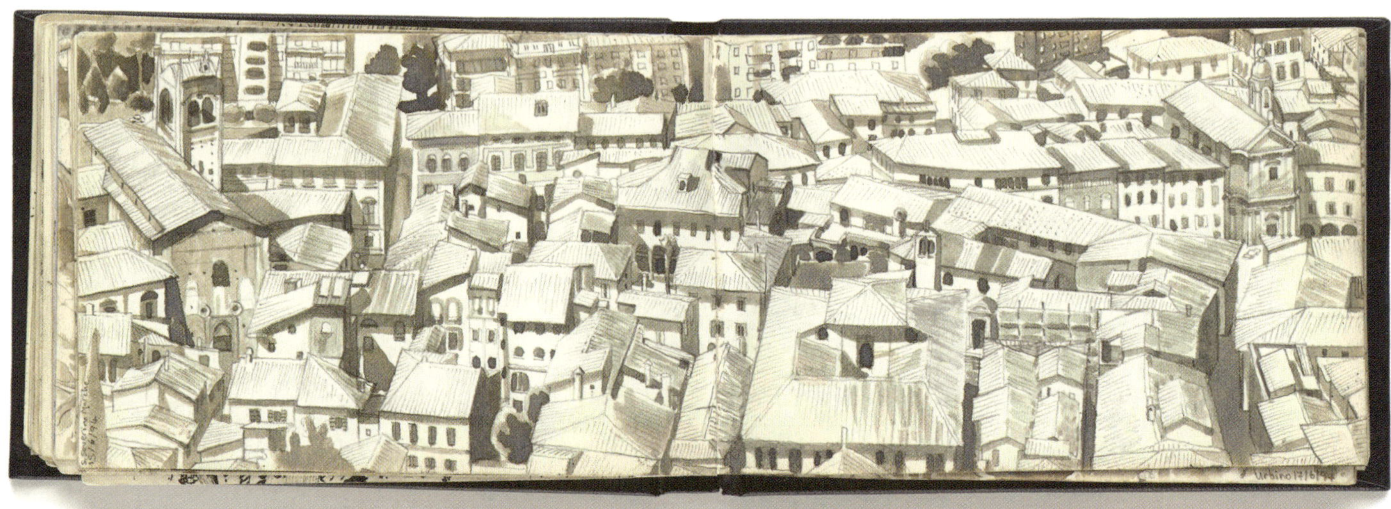

Sketchbook study, 10 × 30cm (4 × 11¾in), of the Italian town of San Severino in the Marche region (1994), seen from a grassy hill looking down on the town. Made in pencil and diluted ink wash, this provided the source material for my engraving of the same subject.

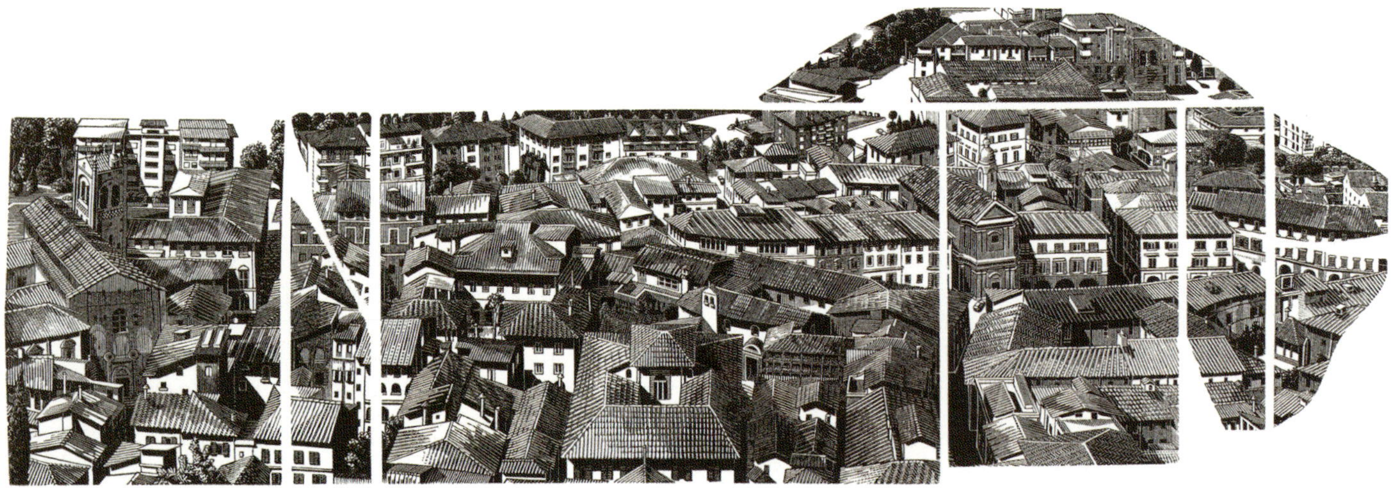

Panorama (1995), engraving on nine boxwood blocks, total printed area on Zerkall paper: 12.8 × 37.2cm (5 × 14¾in). This composite engraving was directly based on my sketchbook drawing of San Severino Marche with some additional photographic references. Its light and shadows are sourced directly from the drawing.

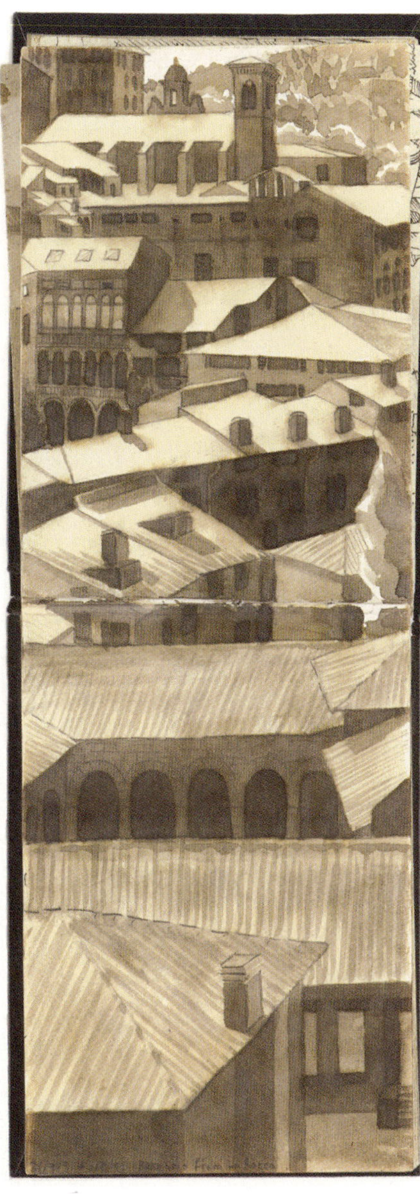

Sketchbook study, 30 × 10cm (11¾ × 4in), of Bergamo (1991). In this case, having these pages of my sketchbook open on my desk for a month or more while making my engraving of this Italian town was enough to cause the ink wash to fade a little and change from grey to sepia.

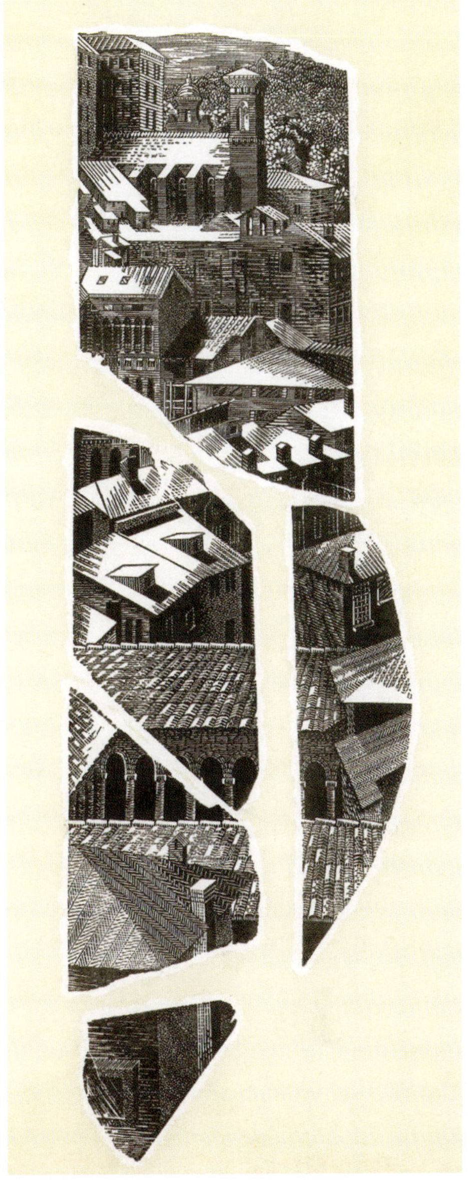

Bergamo fragments (1992), wood engraving on five blocks, printed area: 28.5 × 8.2cm (11¼ × 3¼in), on China White paper collaged on Kozu-shi. Directly inspired by my sketchbook drawing, this image is intended to recall fresco fragments. To enhance this impression, I printed it on white paper, then tore around the margins of each print and collaged them on off-white paper.

chosen to draw a view because its strong light and shade attracted me, I don't want to spend so long drawing that, by the time I get to rendering shadows, the light has totally changed and is perhaps less interesting. If that's likely to happen, sometimes I paint the shadows before drawing anything in pen or pencil. The shadows themselves create the structural masses of buildings or landscape features and it can be a speedier way to capture a scene's essence. This particular ink, however, will fade over time, if exposed to light, and may also change from grey-blue to sepia tones.

The most useful drawings for your engravings will vary depending on the effects you're looking for. If you adopt a strongly linear approach to engraving – such as in the nineteenth and twentieth century black-line prints by Lucien Pissarro, then pen drawings with a particularly linear quality will be most useful. If you're interested in working more tonally and are concerned with effects of light and dark and strong shadows, preparatory studies with clearly defined light and shade will be more useful. But, if you enjoy sketching, you probably choose your medium based on how, in the moment, it seems most appropriate to tackle the subject before you.

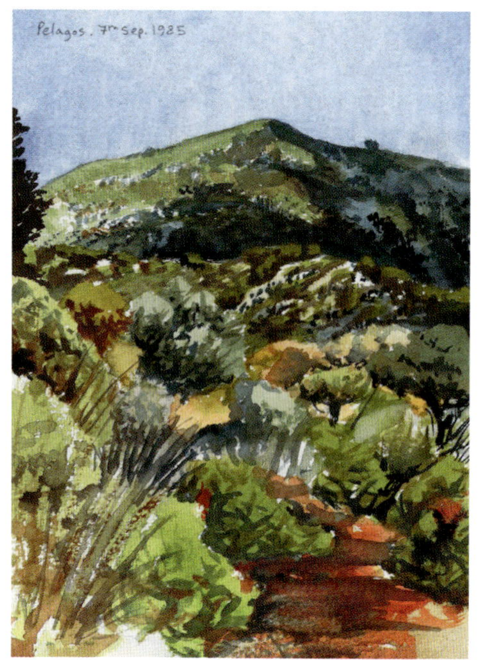

■ *Pelagos* (1985), watercolour on paper, c.16 × 12cm (6¼ × 4¾in). This study of a Greek island was made in response to the landscape, in all its vivid colours, in front of me. It was later that I decided to use it as source material for a monochrome engraving, for which it still supplied sufficient tonal information.

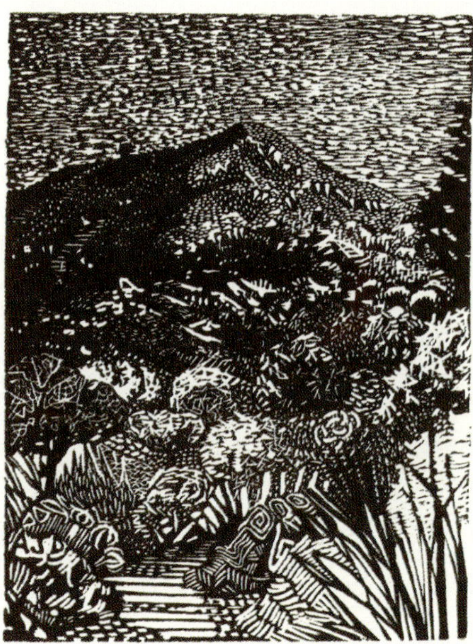

■ *Pelagos* (1986), engraving on maple, 10.1 × 7.5cm (4 × 3in), on Basingwerk Parchment paper. Although based directly on my watercolour, I didn't reverse the image before engraving because I decided that this composition would be stronger if the foreground path went from left to right and the hillside from dark to light.

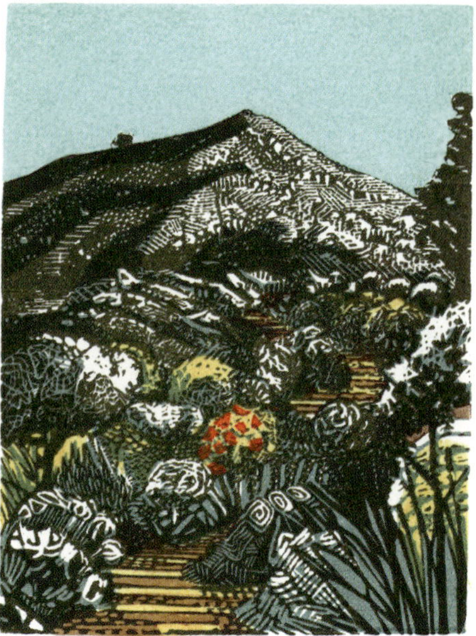

■ *Pelagos Revisited* (2019), engraving on maple with linocut and pochoir, 10.1 × 7.5cm (4 × 3in), on Zerkall paper. Over thirty years later, the same watercolour inspired this colour variant using the same woodblock but with additional newly cut lino blocks and stencils printed on top.

Your drawings must provide enough information for you to understand the structure of whatever your subject happens to be, which will enable you to engrave it with confidence, but be careful that they aren't so finished that engraving becomes merely a way of reproducing them. This can make the engraving boring to make, which may show in its cutting. The most effective, lively engravings are invariably those that bring something new to a subject and which bring greater richness and depth to it, rather than ones that try slavishly to reproduce something that already exists, fully formed, in another medium.

In my teens, I used A4-size sketchbooks but quickly found them too large. I'm a slow sketcher so am more comfortable with an A6 page (or double-page spread). That allows me to make drawings outdoors, in detail but in a reasonable time-frame. Each sketch, even at that size, takes me anything from half an hour to over five hours. Another advantage to this small scale is that I rarely have to rescale my imagery much for transferring it to woodblocks (though it's detailed enough to scale up successfully for making larger linocuts).

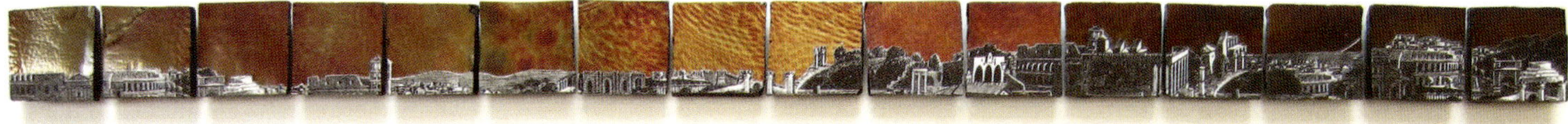

■ *Sense of Rome* (2012), wood engravings on paper collaged on sixteen ceramic mosaic tiles, 2.6 × 43 × 0.5cm (1 × 17 × ¼in).

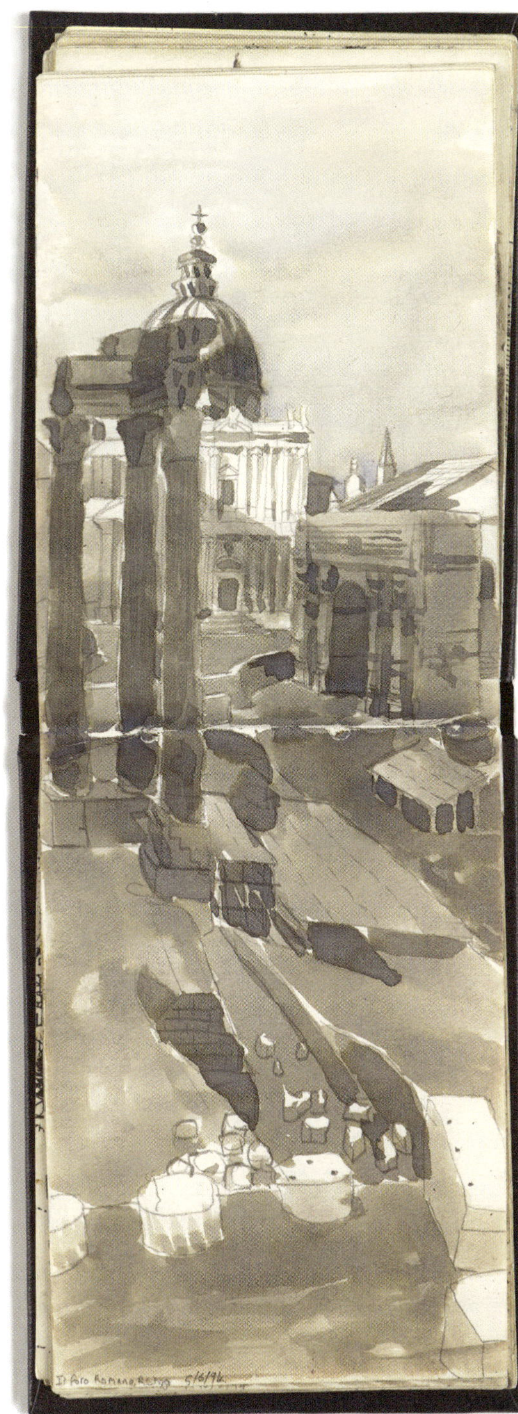

Sketchbook study, 30 × 10cm (11¾ × 4in), of Rome's ancient forum viewed from the Campidoglio (1994), in pencil and diluted ink wash. My aim was to capture the triangle of sunlight on the church's façade contrasted strongly with the shadowed foreground ruins.

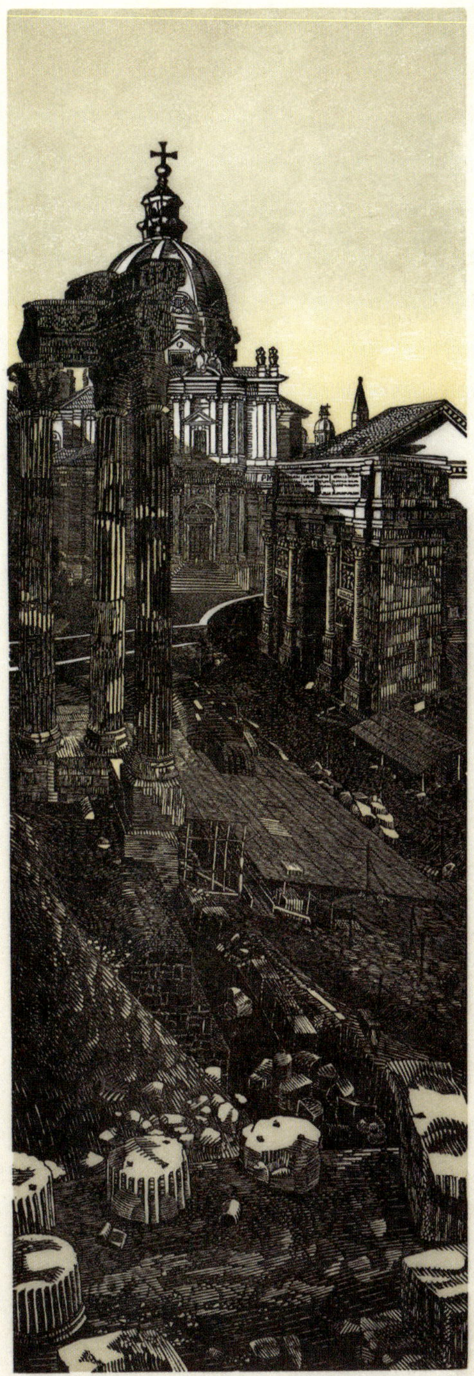

Excavations, Early Evening (2000), two-block linocut, 61 × 20.3cm (24 × 8in), on Kozu paper. The drawing had to be doubled in size for transfer to the much larger lino block. The print's surface textures reinterpret the drawing's tonal washes using tool marks comparable to my wood engravings.

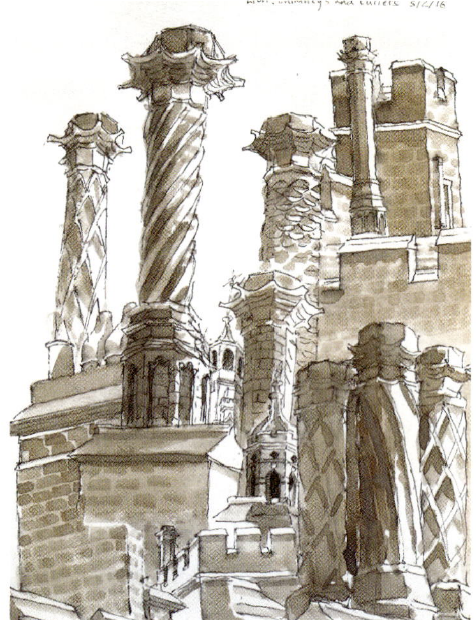

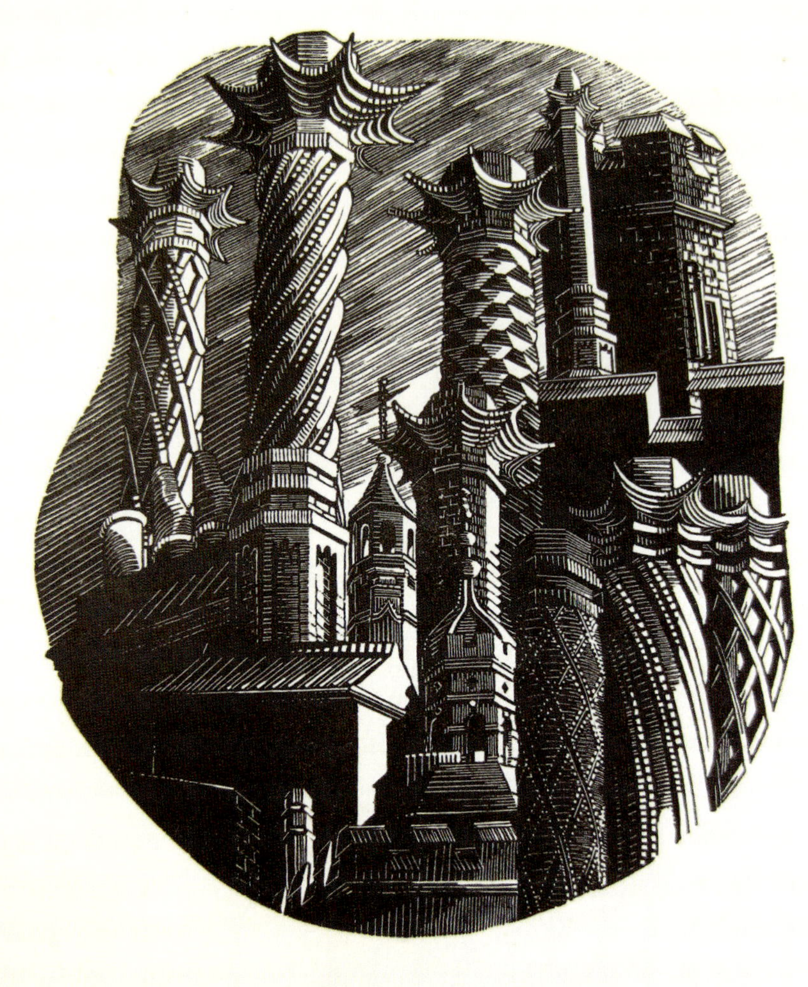

Sketchbook studies (2016), in pen and ink wash, 14.5 × 10cm (5¾ × 4in), of various Tudor chimneys and turrets, made on a winter afternoon on Eton College's campus. The chimneys from assorted buildings were rather randomly placed on the page, yet provided a composition for *Towers and Tudor Chimneys* (2016), engraving on boxwood, 13 × 10.8cm (5 × 4¼in), on Japanese paper.

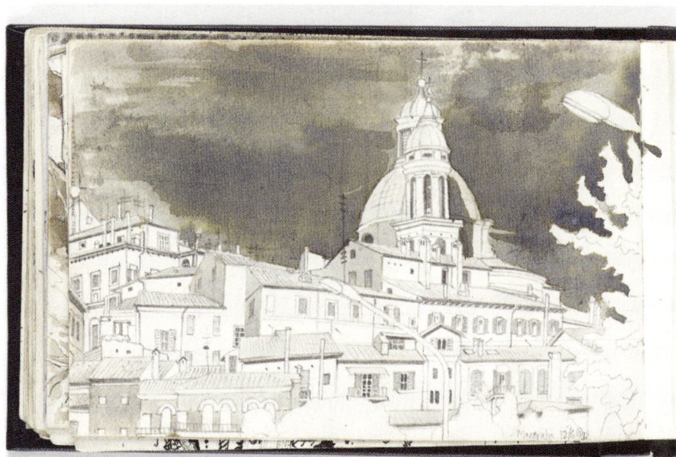

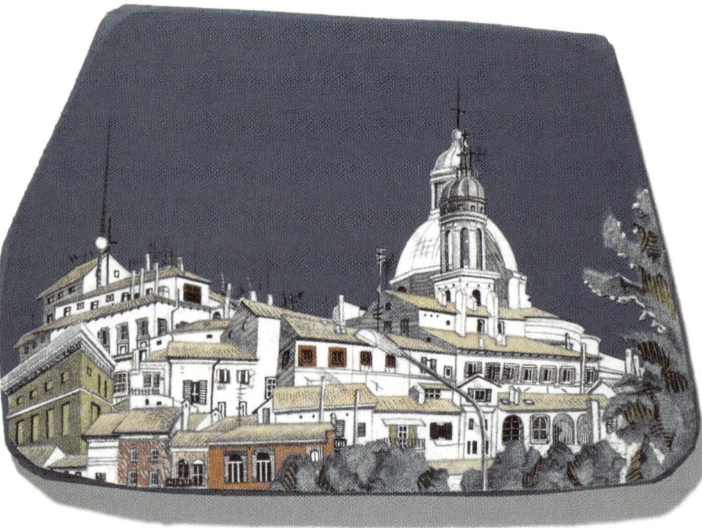

Sketchbook study (1994), 10 × 14cm (5½ × 4in), in pencil and ink wash, of Macerata, Italy, and a collage it inspired: *Italy, Storm Light* (2003), pencil drawing on paper on painted wood panel, collaged with wood engraving and linocut prints on paper, 11.8 × 16.8 × 0.6cm (4½ × 6½ × ¼in).

WORKING FROM PHOTOGRAPHS

Photos are useful, though I find I have greater structural understanding of a subject if I've drawn it. If using photos, ideally take several from different angles to inform your three-dimensional understanding of the view. Although my photos are in colour, I sometimes convert them to black and white and exaggerate their contrast in Photoshop to make them more translatable into wood engraving. Working from my laptop, I can also flip an image horizontally to work from it in the same orientation as it is on the block. But it's not necessarily helpful to be slavishly faithful to a photo. Your source material is only ever a starting point. How you work from it to make the most creative, original, powerful engraving, is what counts.

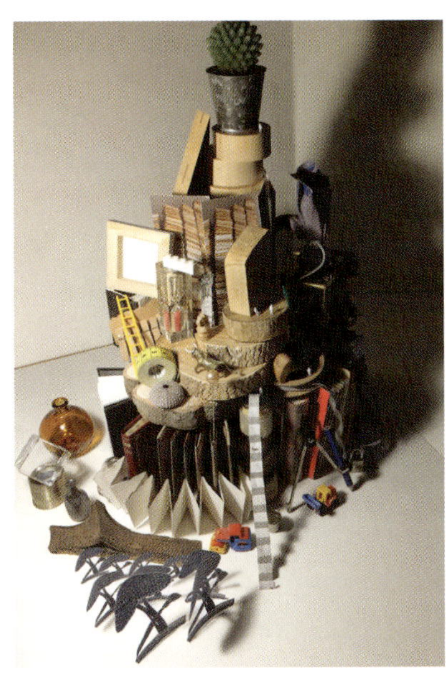

One of many colour photos I took (from different angles) of a tower-like construction I created in my studio: preliminary studies for a complex wood engraving of still-life objects.

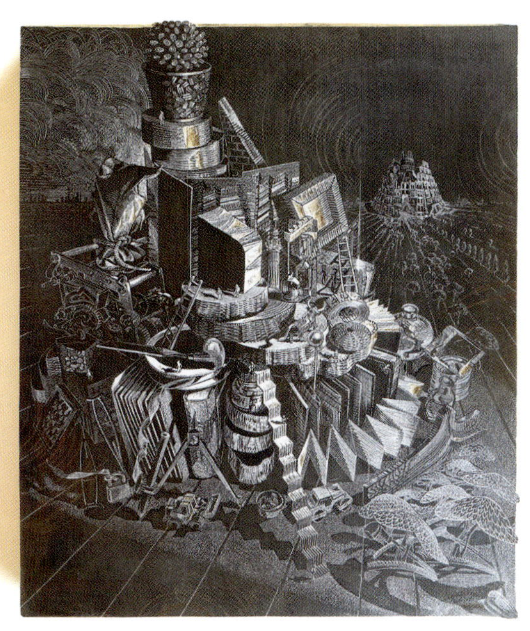

I made the tower shorter and wider to better fit the block's proportions and cut back the block's top, bottom and right-hand edges to allow compositional elements to break out of the rectangle.

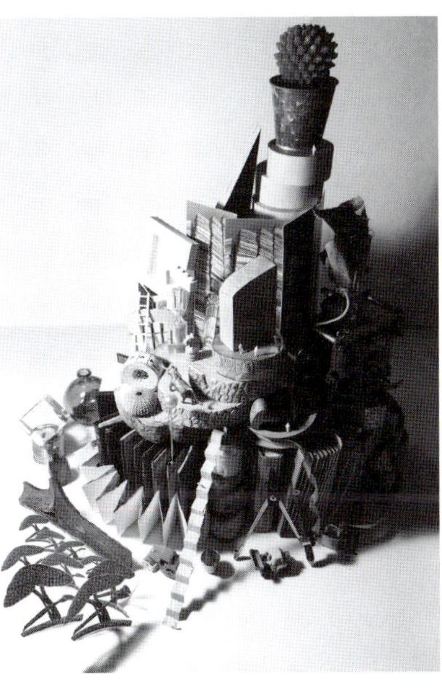

This photo (with colour removed and contrast enhanced) was, ultimately, the direct source material for the wood engraving.

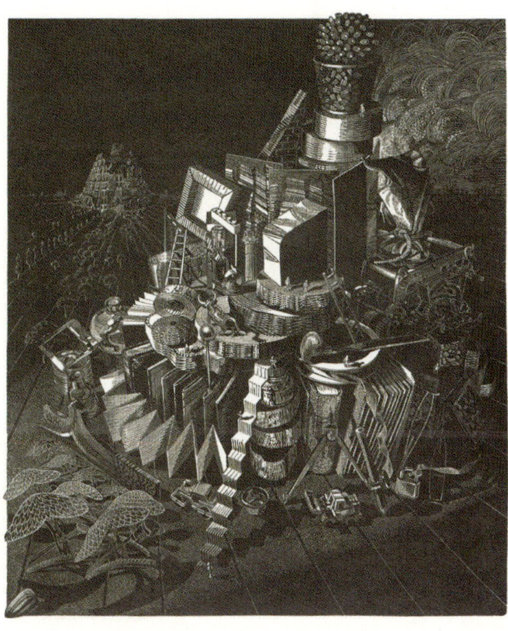

Wood Engraver's Tower (2020), engraving on boxwood, 30 × 25cm (11¾ × 9¾in), printed on Gampi Vellum paper. The horizon line with trees and *Tower of Babel* (after Bruegel) were added to the composition after the foreground tower had been engraved.

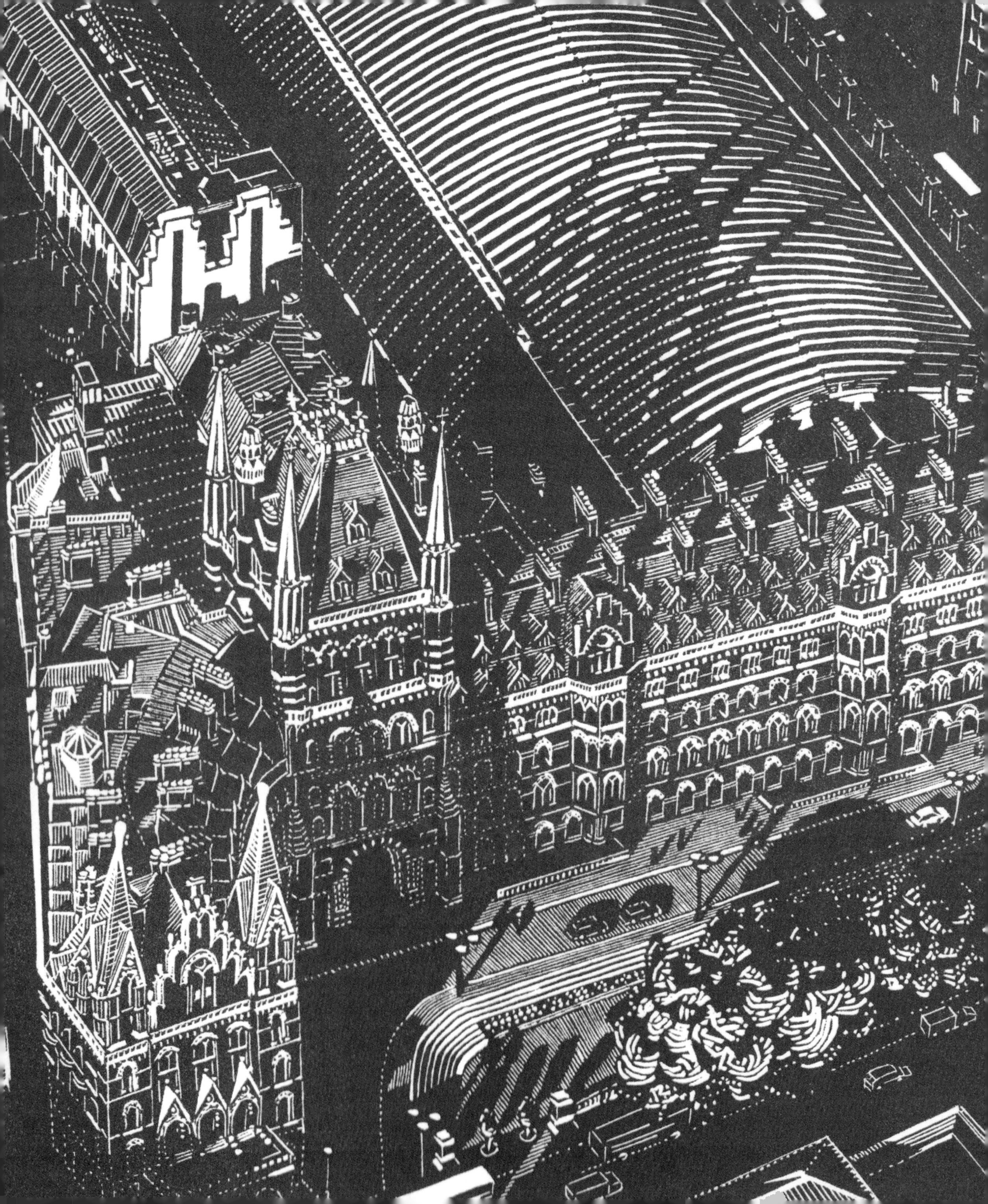

CHAPTER 5

COMPOSITIONAL PLANNING

The block comprises the entire image. That sounds obvious but it can be tempting to regard it like a sketchbook page and position the key compositional feature in the middle, at often unnecessarily small scale, leaving a lot of background to deal with, which maybe wasn't your original plan. Also, if scaled too small, that main compositional element might become too tiny for effective engraving. Also note that different areas of contrasting tool marks can make an engraving visually lively while improving its clarity.

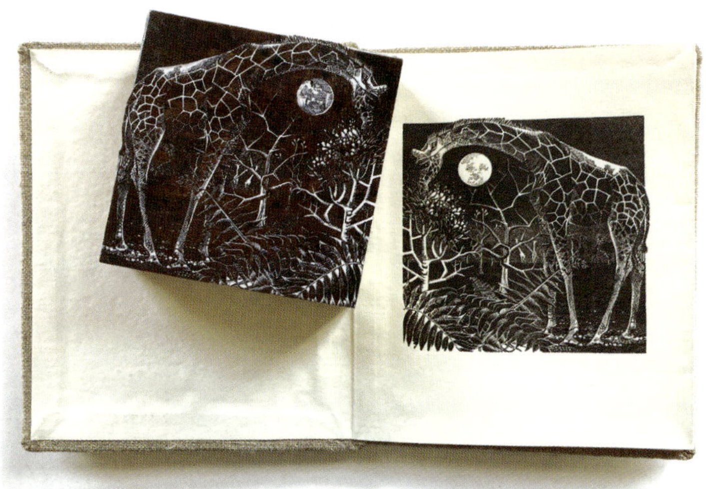

Giraffes (1988), lemonwood engraving block, 7.5 × 7.5cm (3 × 3in), printed on Basingwerk Parchment paper (in handmade artist's book). The giraffe is the compositional focus and fills the available space. I cut away parts of the block's edges to make the animal appear larger and more three-dimensional.

St Pancras - Renaissance (2024), detail of an engraving on holly (on a large wood roundel sourced from my mother's garden in Liverpool), on Gampi Vellum paper.

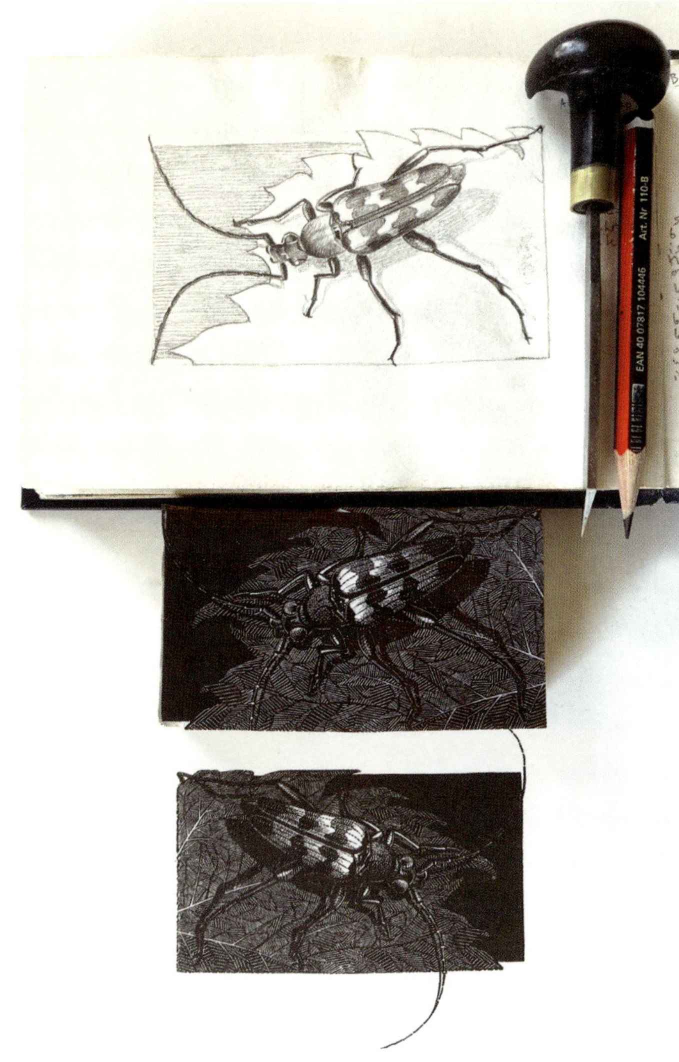

The pencil study for *Beetle* (2020), 8 × 8.8cm (3¼ × 3½in), aimed to fit both antennae on its boxwood block (shown beneath the drawing), but its commissioner wanted them wider. I scaled the beetle to fill the block. Its larger-than-life size allowed me to render its carapace in detail. Ultimately, each antenna tip was hand-drawn on each print.

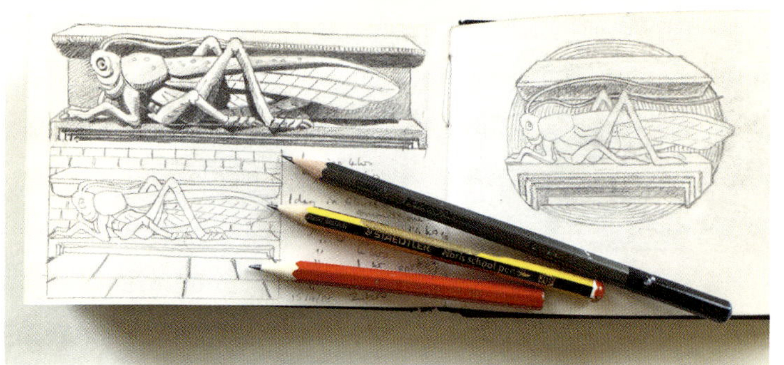

Grasshopper compositional studies in pencil (2014), each sketchbook page: 10 × 14.5cm (4 × 5¾in). These compositional designs for a commissioned engraving tested out ideas for three blocks (a roundel and two rectangles of different proportions) at the actual size of each block. The long narrow boxwood block proved the strongest contender, its sides providing straight edges for the stone bench depicted.

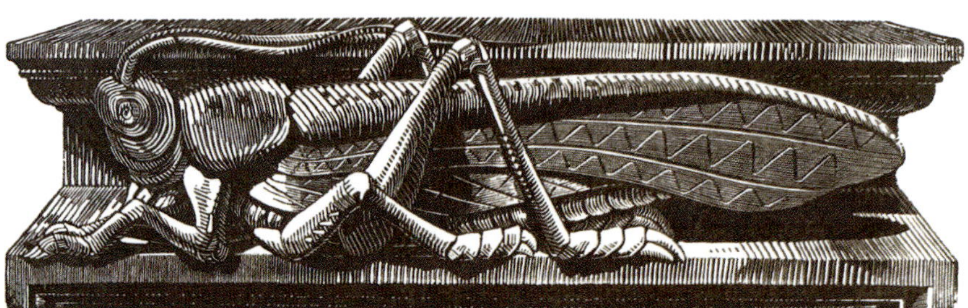

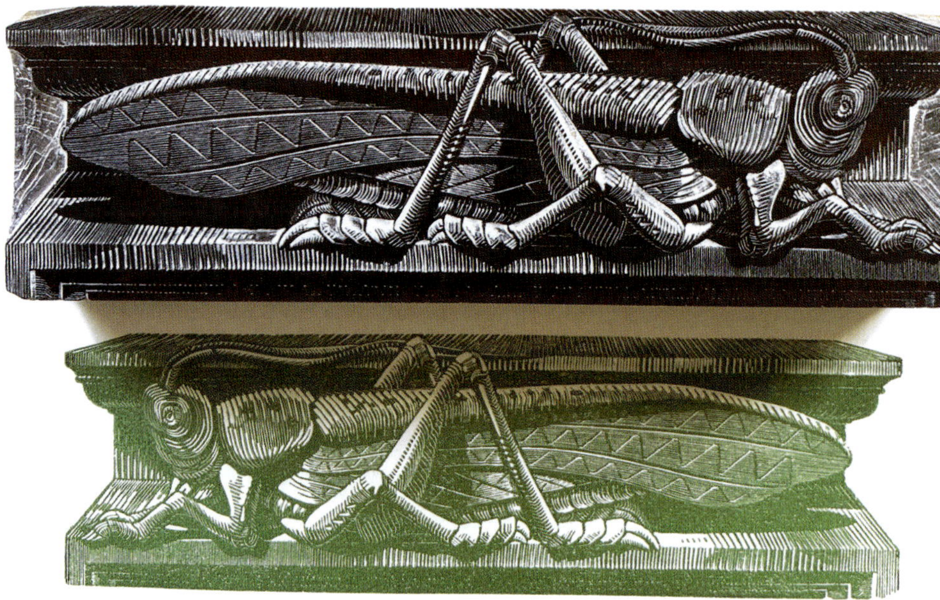

Grasshopper (2014), wood engraving, 4 × 12.9cm (1½ × 5in), on Japanese papers (two variants in black and green ink), and its block. Scaling the bench to the full size of this relatively small block allowed me to engrave plenty of tone, pattern and strong light and shade which, if scaled smaller, would have been much harder to accomplish effectively and the impact of the image overall would have been weaker.

If engraving portraits, to examine textures and tones of skin and hair, you may want to scale them so the head fills the block, giving you room for subtle details. If scaled too small, the key features may be reduced to mere outlines. This is fine if your aim is for a simple, linear, study but less good for depicting light, shade, tone and texture in depth. Wood engravings by Tirzah Garwood (1908–51) are great examples of highly characterful, boldly cut, portrait studies at quite small scale while Simon Brett's larger, tonal portraits balance strong chiaroscuro and three-dimensionality with minute subtleties of skin tone.

If your block is very small, consider engraving just a small portion of a larger image on it or treat the compositional elements in a simplified way, rather than trying to squeeze large complex images onto very tiny blocks. It will be easier to do justice to a striking detail rather than cramming in too much, which will leave you little room for more than engraving structural outlines.

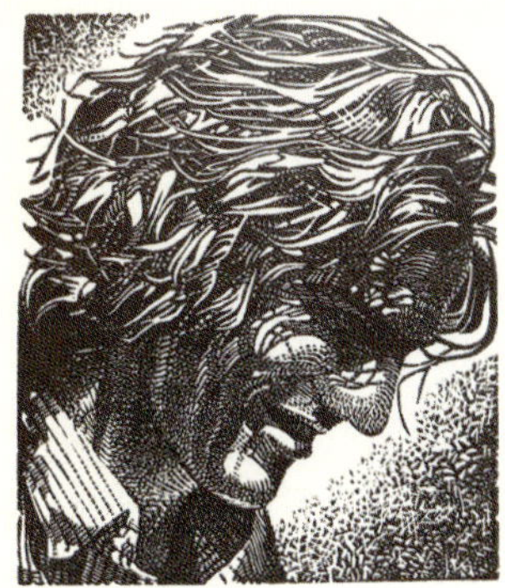

Charlie (1988), engraving on boxwood, 6 × 5cm (2¼ × 2in), on cream Zerkall paper. This portrait gets its strong light and shade by using stippled dots between both totally uncut parts and completely cleared out areas.

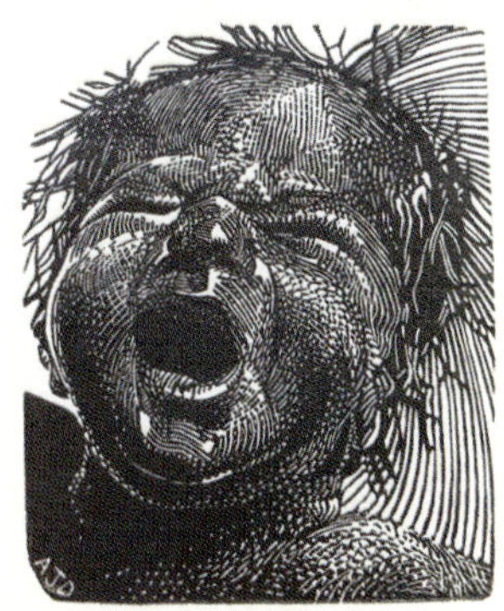

Hush Little Baby (1987), engraving on boxwood, 6 × 4.8cm (2¼ × 2in), on Basingwerk Parchment paper. This involves fine lines interspersed with large and small stippled dots (made with round and square scorpers).

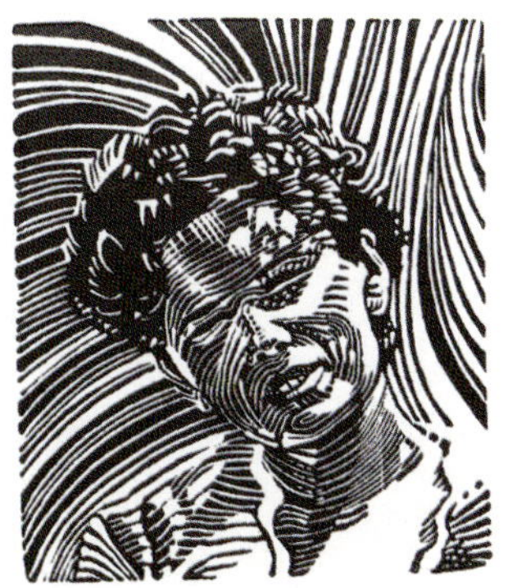

Andrea (1986), engraving on lemonwood, 6 × 5cm (2¼ × 2in), on Zerkall paper. This is treated in a much more linear fashion, its lines (variously spaced to create different tones) following contours of head and neck.

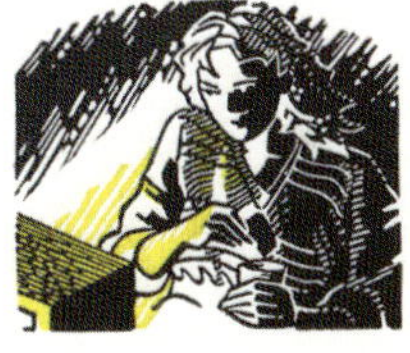

TV (1991), engraving on boxwood with linocut, 3 × 3.5cm (1¼ × 1½in), on China White paper. This self-portrait is much simpler and more stylised to create drama, movement and clean, clear definitions at a tiny scale.

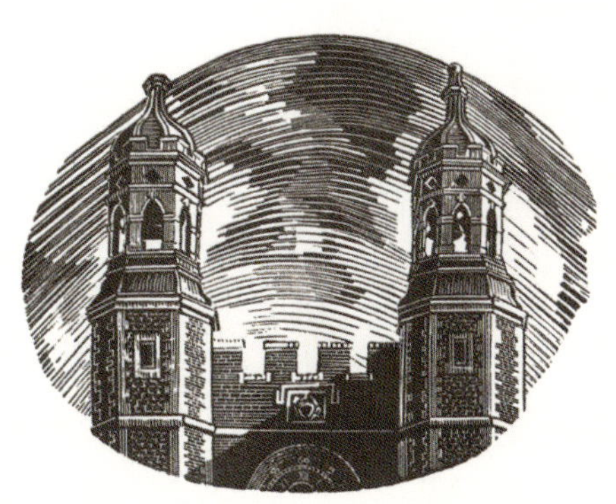

Two Towers (2016), engraving on boxwood, 6.3 × 7.8cm (2½ × 3in), on Gampi Vellum paper. This fits a recognisable detail of Eton College on a small roundel. The sky was invented, its lines following the block's shape to create a sense of movement.

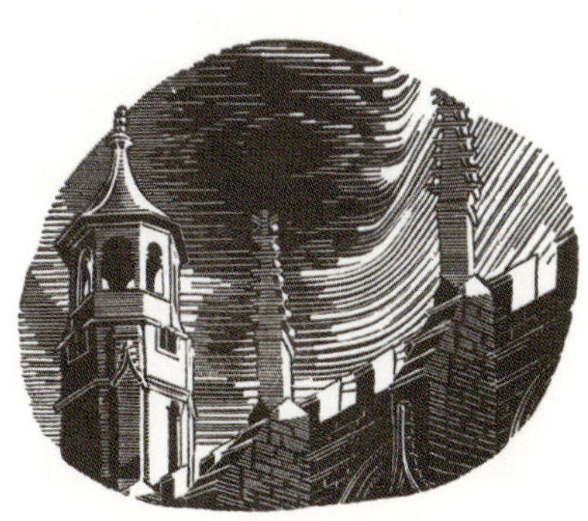

Church and Thunder Cloud (2016), engraving on boxwood, 5.3 × 6.2cm (2 × 2½in), on Gampi Vellum paper. Here I focused on a small yet distinctive detail of Eton's chapel roof, rather than trying to cram more of the building into such a tiny roundel.

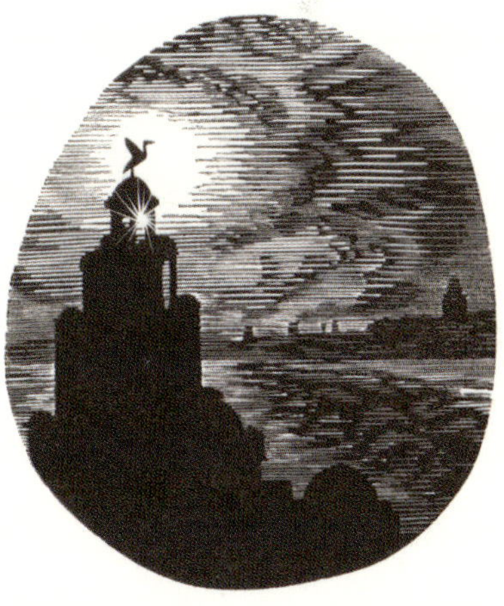

Mersey Light (2014), engraving on boxwood, 7.2 × 6.2cm (2¾ × 2½in), on Gampi Vellum paper. Liverpool's famous Liver Building has impact at this tiny scale by contrasting its clearly defined silhouette against a busy tonal background of lines of different widths.

Before you set to work on a block, try to decide what strikes you most forcibly about the subject you want to engrave. If you're drawn to its strong contours (in a landscape or architecture perhaps), you could engrave it as an elegant, linear design, without any tonal detail. If it's very strong contrasts of light and shade that appeal to you, you could consider treating it as a series of semi-abstract black and white shapes – like the *Dazzle Ships* woodcuts of English war artist Edward Wadsworth (1889–1949). You may need a larger or a smaller block to do justice to your chosen subject depending on how much or how little detail you may choose to include.

If you want a full range of tones, textures and surface qualities, consider engraving a larger image across a series of tiny blocks to assemble later, like jigsaw pieces or Scrabble tiles, to make one larger image. Alternatively, buy a block large enough to do justice to a complex subject.

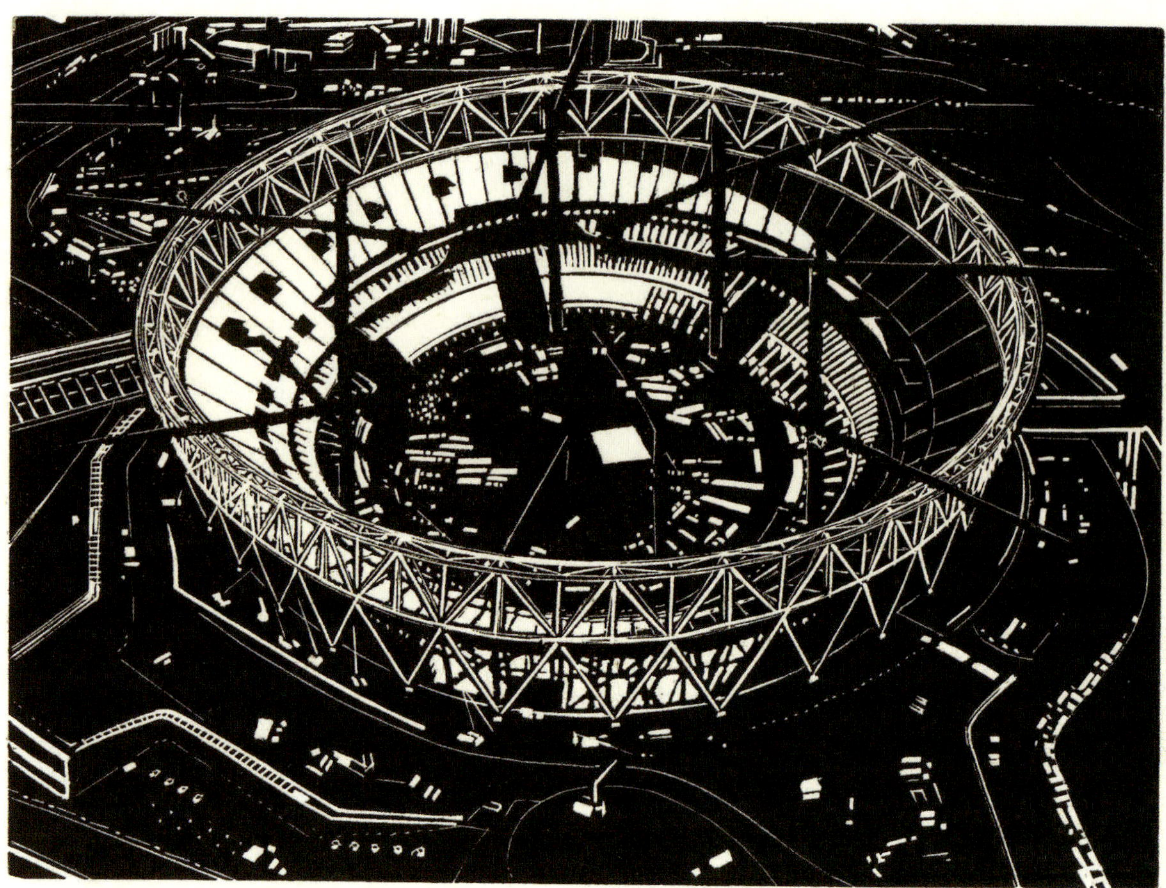

Olympic Stadium with Cranes (2009), engraving on boxwood, 11 × 15cm (4¼ × 6in), on Gampi Vellum paper. I began by engraving all parts intended to be white. As that approach seemed to define the stadium's shape and structure so clearly, I felt it would diminish its impact to add any tonal cutting; the image felt complete at this point.

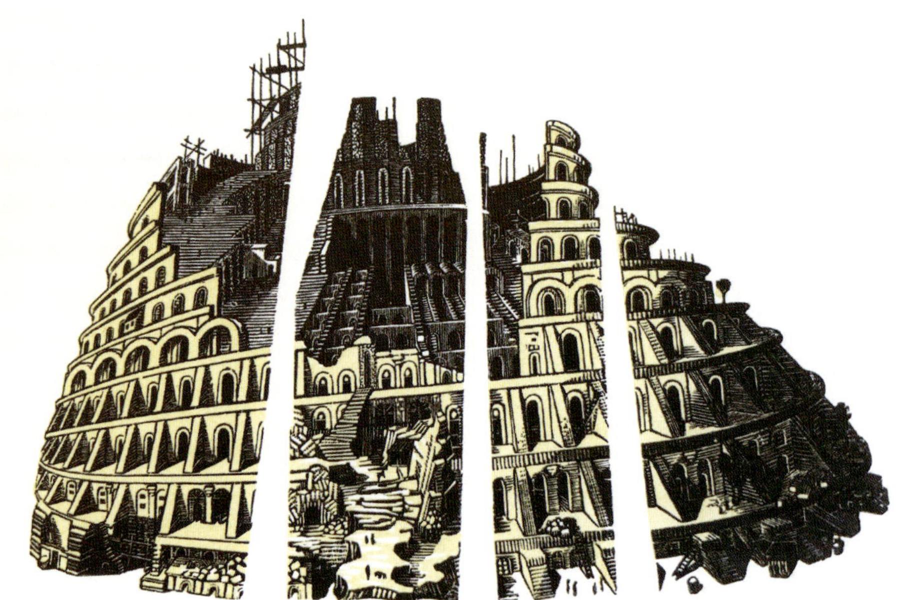

Babel Tower in Pieces (Homage to Bruegel) (1999), engraving on four boxwood blocks with linocut on Zerkall paper, total printing area: 7.5 × 10.8cm (3 × 4¼in). The outline shape of these tiny blocks, arranged as a group, called to mind Bruegel's great *Tower of Babel* and directly inspired the engraving.

VIEWING AND SCANNING

A paper viewfinder, as described earlier, is invaluable for deciding the strongest composition for the block. Draw around the block onto tracing paper but, this time, don't cut out the window. I scan source material onto my computer, bring it up on the monitor and lightly stick the tracing paper over it, on screen, with the paper window in front of the image area that I want to engrave. As the window is on tracing paper, the image shows through and I either move it about on screen until a strong composition presents itself or I keep the image fixed and move the paper window around. An advantage of scanning the source image is that it can be scaled up or down easily to experiment with different compositional ideas. Keep the image on screen in the same orientation as your intended print. The process of transferring image to block will create the mirror image needed for engraving.

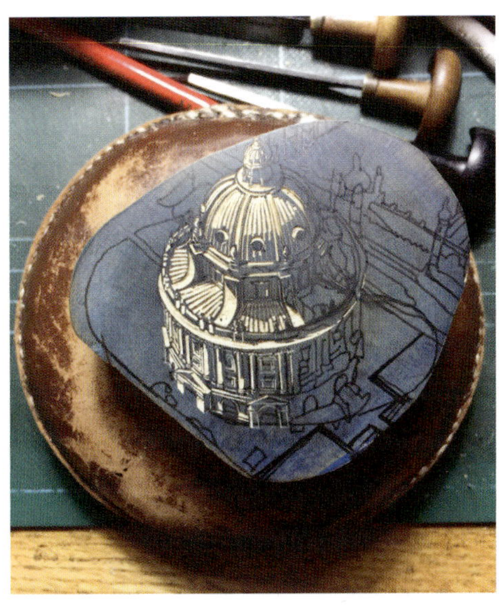

The engraving taking shape on the boxwood roundel.

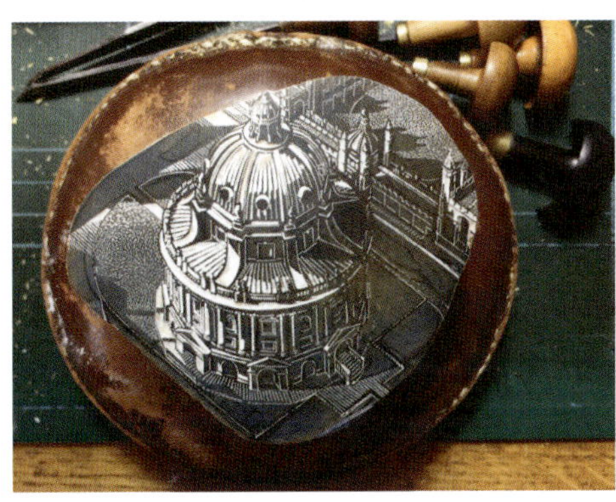

The engraving block finished and ready for printing.

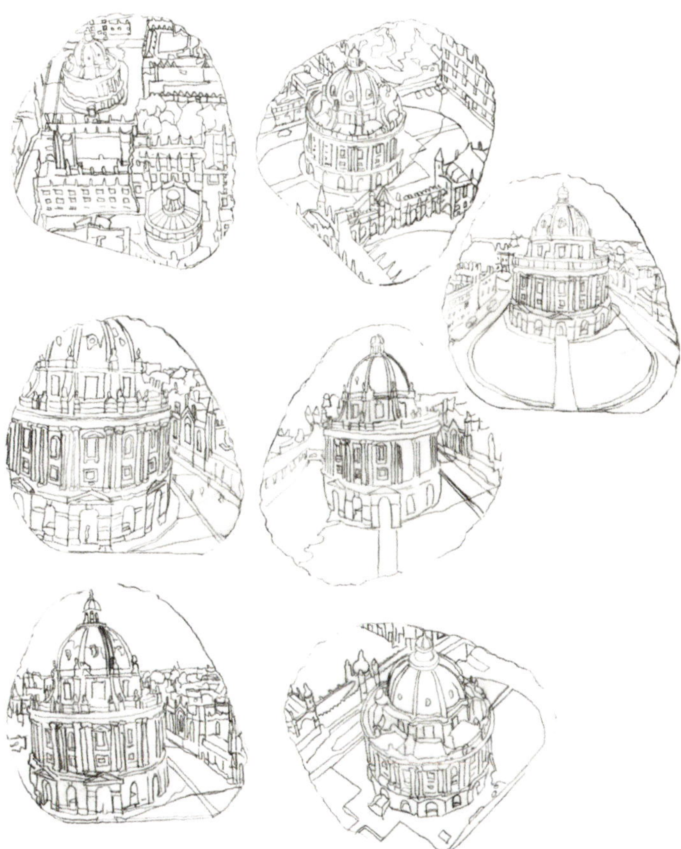

These compositional experiments for a commissioned engraving were made by tracing different options (from photos on my computer scaled up or down as necessary) within separate tracings of the block's outline shape.

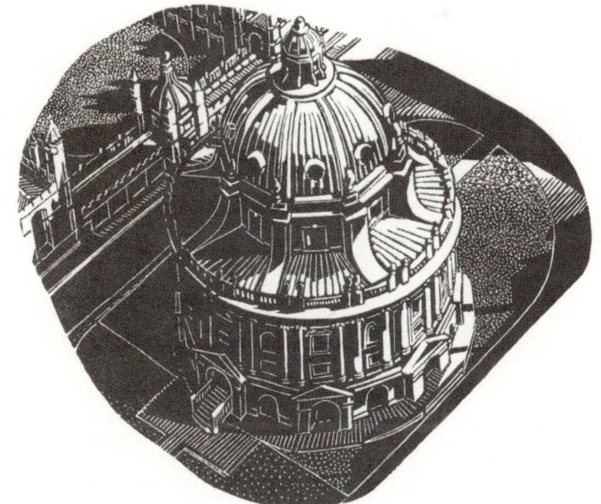

Oxford Light (2021), engraving on boxwood, 7.5 × 8.4cm (3 × 3¼in), on Gampi Vellum paper.

TRANSFERRING IMAGE TO BLOCK

The downside to tracings of any sort is that they might lose some of your drawing's vigour – if your source material was indeed a drawing. If you prefer, you can copy your image, freehand, directly onto the block or you can transfer it using coloured transfer paper (white or red transfers are often more visible on the block than black) rather than directly tracing it. Alternatively, draw a grid of carefully measured squares over your original drawing (or on tracing paper laid on top). Draw an equivalent grid on your block with squares of the same size or rescaled smaller or larger on the block as desired. Copy, by hand, into each square on the block, as accurately as possible, the key lines within the equivalent square of the drawing. As you complete each square, the full composition will take shape on the block.

There are ways to offset drawings in water-soluble ink onto blocks, using a press for the transfer. It's also possible to offset photocopies using acetone but, because I prefer to avoid solvents, I don't use these methods. There is also a danger that, because they involve liquids close to the block's surface, they might adversely alter the wood's engraving quality.

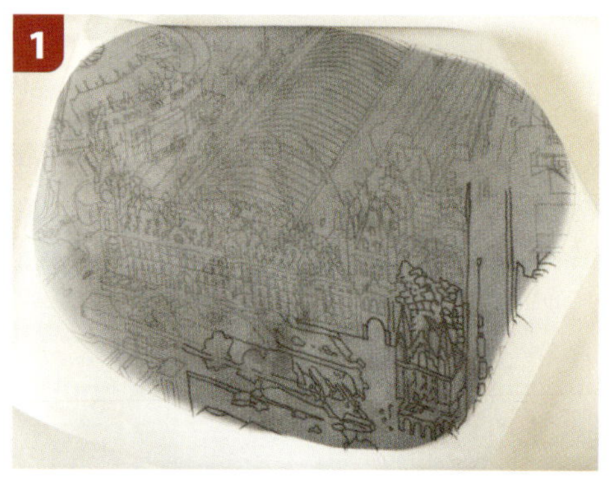

1 Place the tracing of your composition pencil-side-down on the block. Tape down two edges. Transfer it by tracing its outlines through the paper using HB or B pencil (harder pencils may bruise the wood).

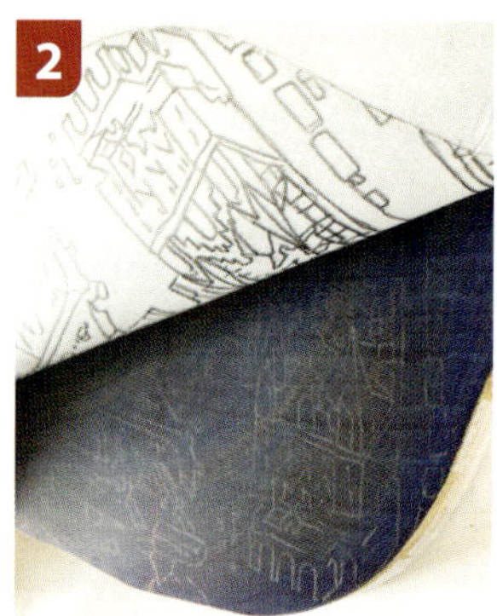

2 Peel paper from block. The tracing should appear as a shiny outline in a mirror image of the print's intended orientation.

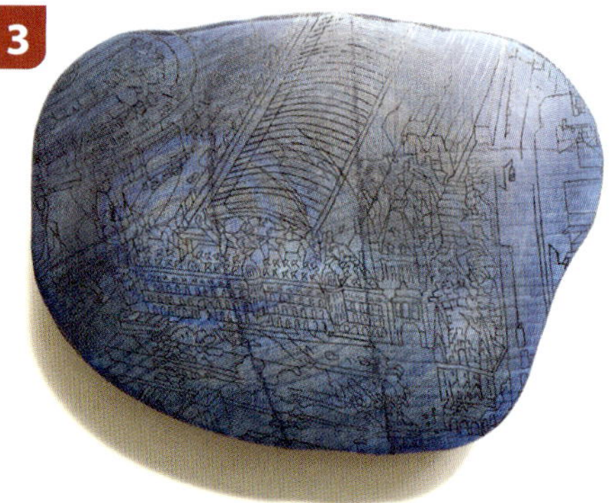

3 Reinforce the drawing using a fine-line drawing pen or a brush with Indian ink as the pencil will smudge as you're engraving. Alternatively, use a spray fixative on the pencil outlines.

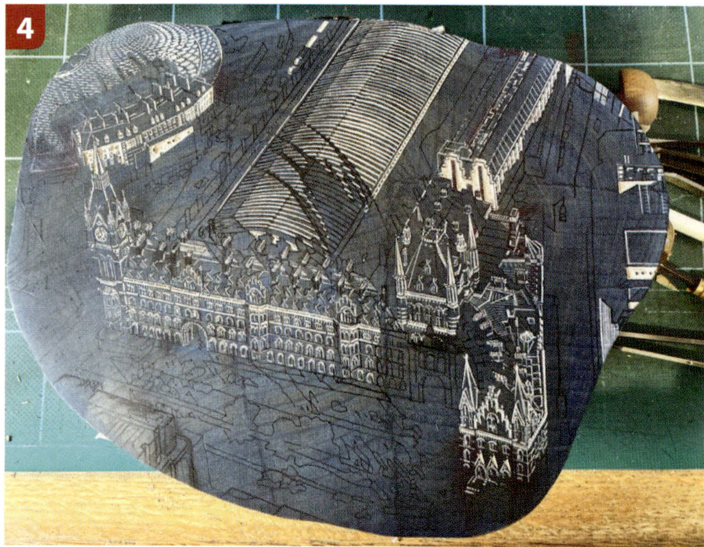

4 The engraving in progress.

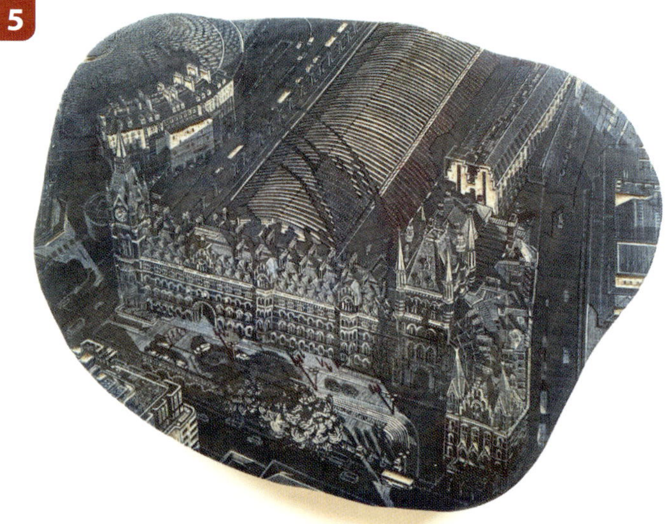

5 The finished block ready for printing.

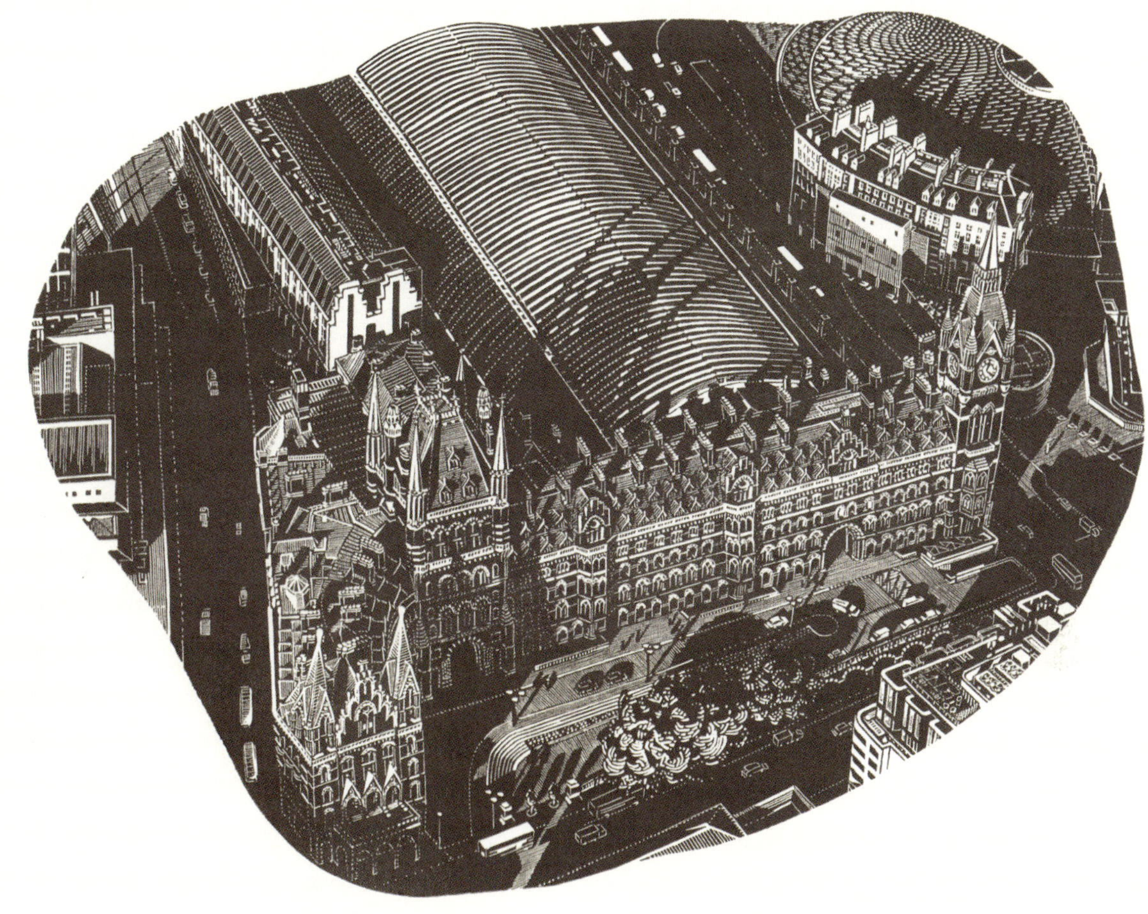

St Pancras - Renaissance (2024), engraving on holly, 17.2 × 22cm (6¾ × 8¾in), on Gampi Vellum paper. The block's irregular shape wouldn't quite accommodate the full roof-curve at the back of St Pancras station, so I hand-drew those few final curving lines on each print.

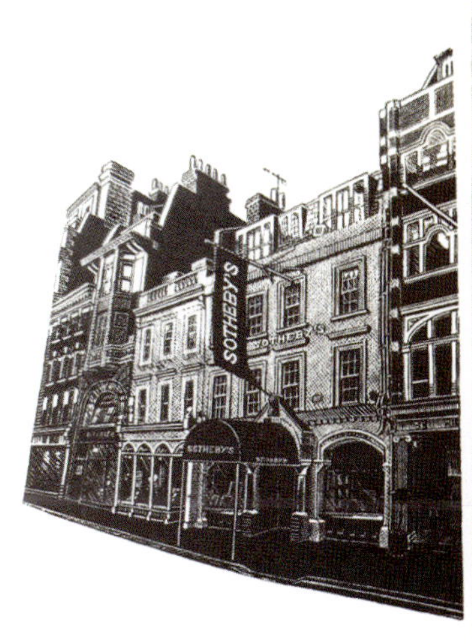

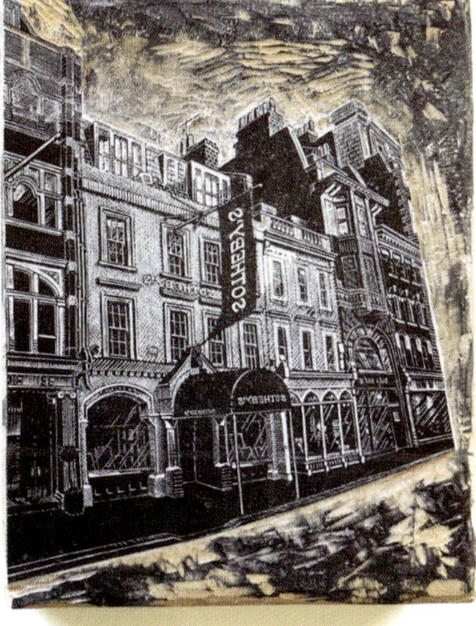

Sotheby's, New Bond Street (1996), engraving on boxwood, 9.3 × 7cm (3¾ × 2¾in), on Zerkall paper. The print will be a mirror image of what's on the block. Before engraving it, check the block's drawn image in a mirror to ensure that the final print – especially if it involves letters or numbers – will print as intended.

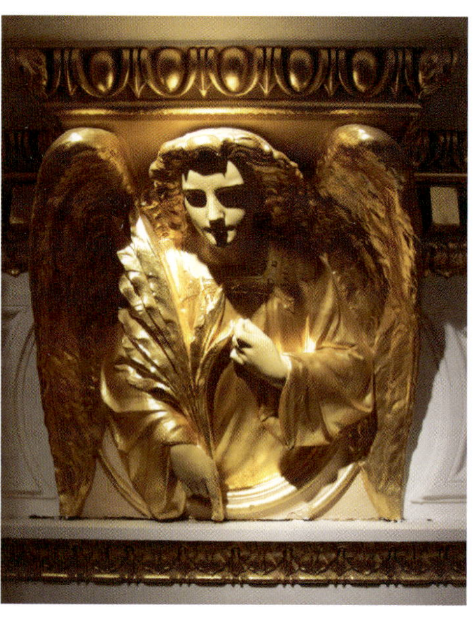

I took this photo of a ceiling decoration in London's Royal Academy of Arts in 2014, from a raised platform forming part of an exhibition at the time.

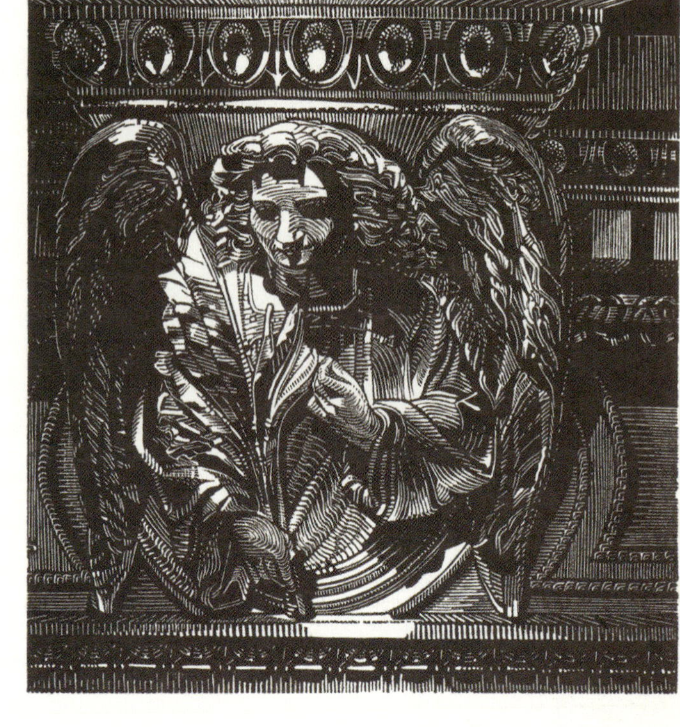

Angel with Palm Leaves (2020), engraving on boxwood, 9.7 × 8.8cm (3¾ × 3½in), on Gampi paper. I tried, in the engraving, to retain the dramatic light and shade of the photo.

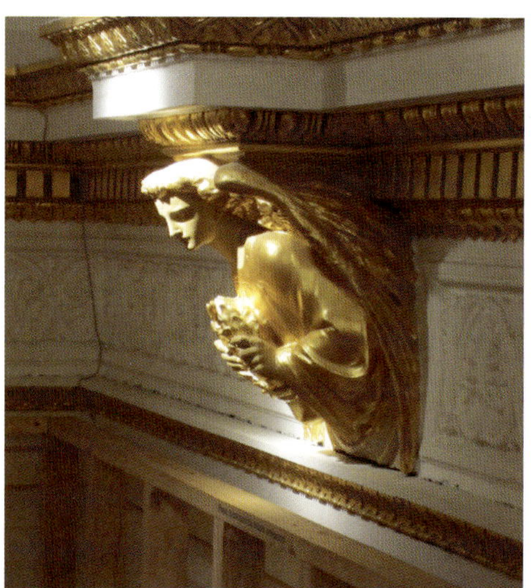

Another photo from the RA's ceiling decorations. A close-up formed the composition for my *Guardian Angel* engraving.

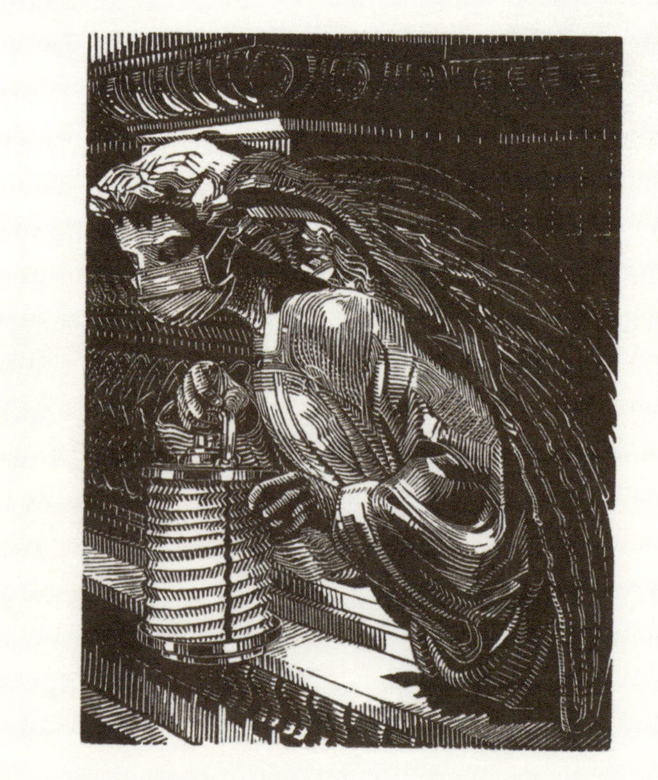

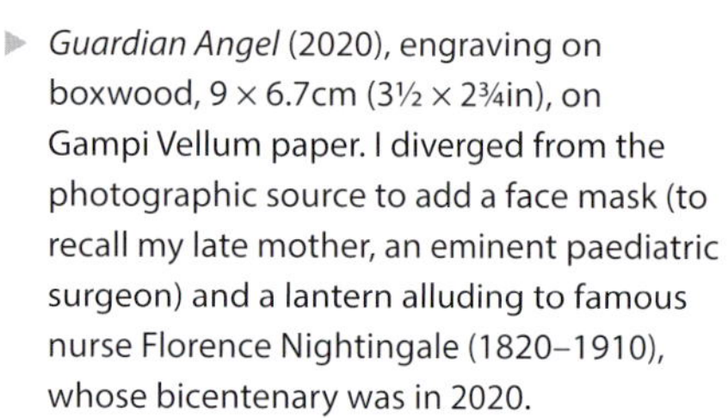

Guardian Angel (2020), engraving on boxwood, 9 × 6.7cm (3½ × 2¾in), on Gampi Vellum paper. I diverged from the photographic source to add a face mask (to recall my late mother, an eminent paediatric surgeon) and a lantern alluding to famous nurse Florence Nightingale (1820–1910), whose bicentenary was in 2020.

THINKING AHEAD

It can be tempting to start by cutting white lines around the main contours of a composition to fix it in place. Don't! Somehow, white marks on black read much more emphatically than black on white. If drawing in black on white paper, you might well start by sketching outlines: a perfectly reasonable approach. But such drawings – especially in pencil – can be erased, revised and reworked whereas everything engraved on a block is fixed and permanent. Engraving a firm outline can be an over-emphatic start and may limit your options for developing any three-dimensional illusion later, because engraved white outlines tend to make an image look two-dimensional. So, unless you're aiming for a flat, linear design, avoid engraving outlines. Instead, maybe start with really tiny, stippled dots to fix a few outlines if that feels like it might be a useful opening move. Ultimately, you might join up some of those dots to create some lines but, in the short term, simply fixing their boundaries, without over-emphasising them, can be a more flexible starting point leaving the engraving with more potential directions to take. The engraver Peter Lawrence has likened wood engraving to playing chess: you need to think several moves ahead to avoid getting into checkmate from the off!

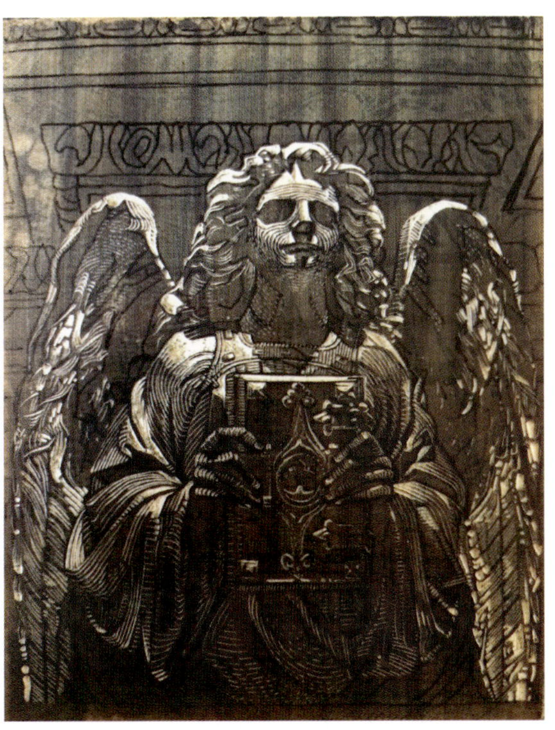

I began by engraving the angel's face, then body and wings, leaving background until last. At this point the background wasn't engraved and stippled areas on face and neck needed more work.

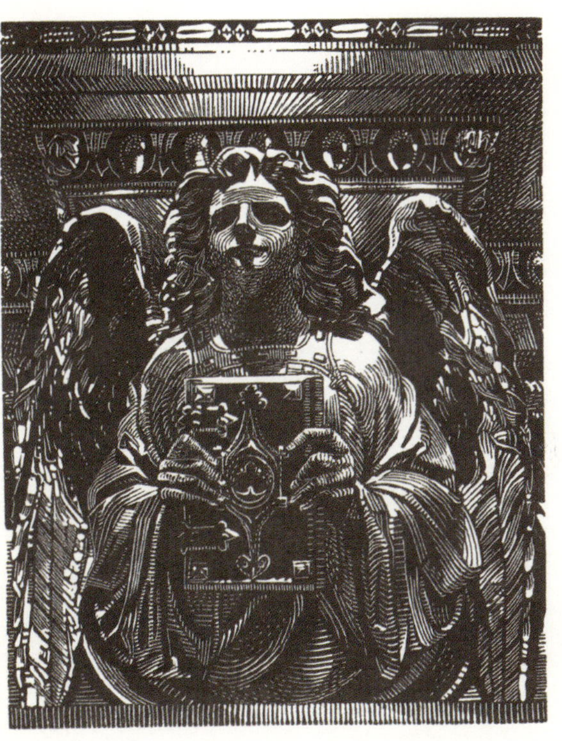

Angel and Book (2020), engraving on boxwood, 9.7 × 7.4cm (3¾ × 3in), on Gampi paper. The engraving aimed for a sense of dramatic chiaroscuro.

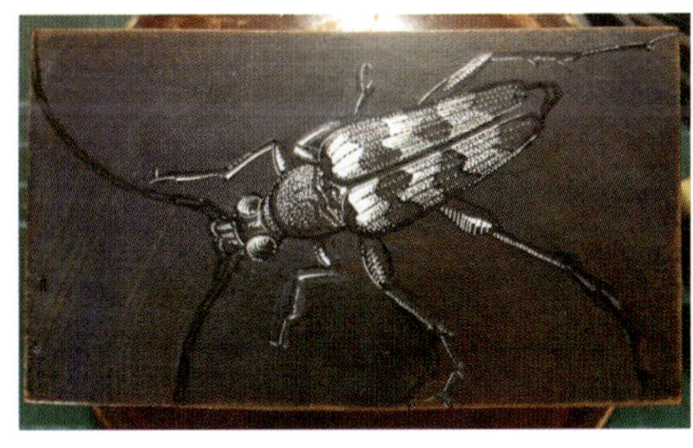

Partially cut block for the *Beetle* engraving illustrated earlier. I began by engraving the insect's carapace, then its head and legs. The last area engraved was the leaf, which I kept quite minimally cut and tonally dark so as not to detract from the compositional focus: the beetle's shiny wing cases.

FROM FIRST CUTS TO FINISHED BLOCK

Once the drawing is on the block, different engravers have different views on where best to start engraving. Some start in the middle and work outwards, or in a corner, or along the bottom edge and work up, or vice versa, or jump about engraving different parts of the image as the mood takes them – in all cases engraving whatever light or dark tones they require as they go along.

Others start with a compositional focal point – the eyes in a portrait for instance (though this is risky as it may produce a better outcome if you practise on 'easier' compositional areas before tackling more challenging or more important parts).

Another view is that you should start with marks that will make the darkest tones and work on the block from dark to light, leaving areas you want paper-white until last. Technically, this would probably involve having a clear plan for the image's full tonal range from the outset and wouldn't allow much room for changing course.

Personally, although I do sometimes use the working-from-the-middle-outwards or the composition focal-point-outwards approaches, I usually find it more satisfying and more flexible to start by engraving all the areas I'd like strong white in the final print. Having done that, I pause frequently to consider the block: to decide how many more tones it needs; and whether I'm in danger of over-cutting it and losing parts that will provide the print's pure blacks. In this way, I can change my mind as I go along, depending on how the block is looking, and can decide to keep the cutting minimal (less can be more!) or introduce a wide tonal range along the way. For me, this is the best way of keeping the image's options open for the longest possible time which can yield unexpected and worthwhile results. It gives me the option of printing at various cutting stages and each printing can yield successful results in its own right. There may not be just one printed outcome for any block. It may well have potential for various outcomes – all equally effective and worth printing. But there is no right or wrong method. Different approaches will suit different personalities and intentions.

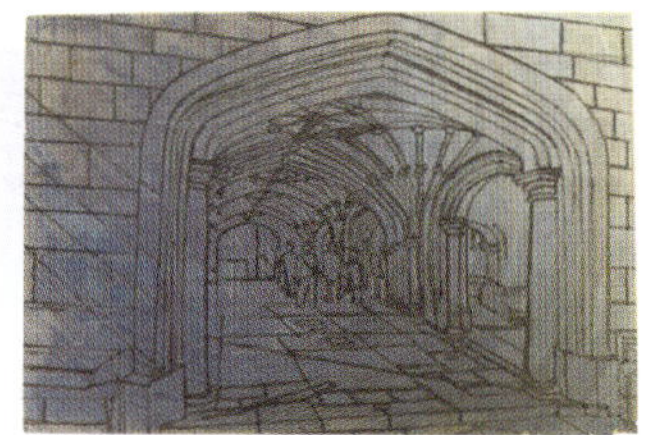

The design drawn in black pen on the stained block.

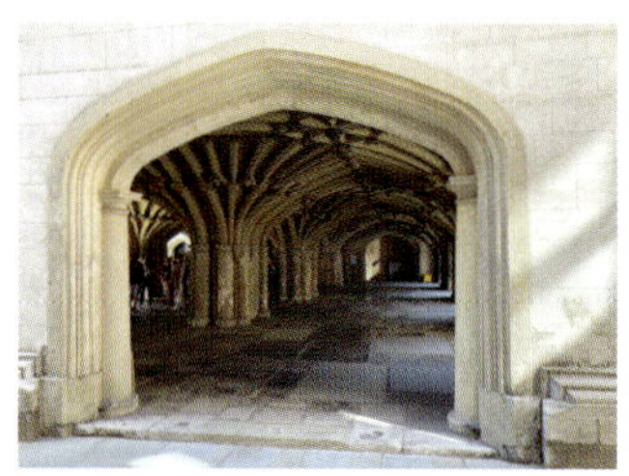

One of my photos for a commissioned engraving for Lincoln's Inn Law Chambers.

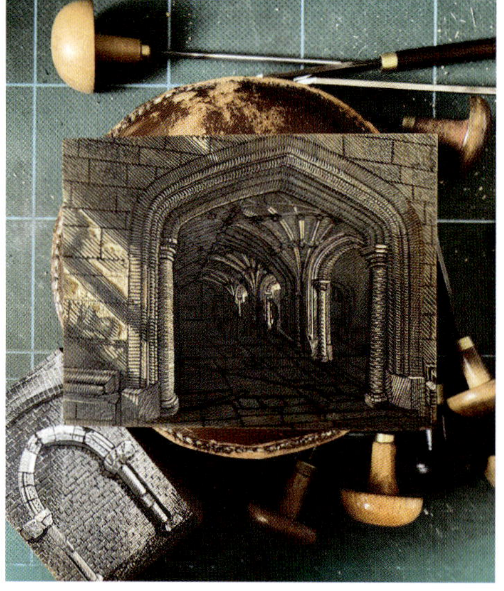

I began by engraving the foreground wall, then the structural curves of the fan vault behind it.

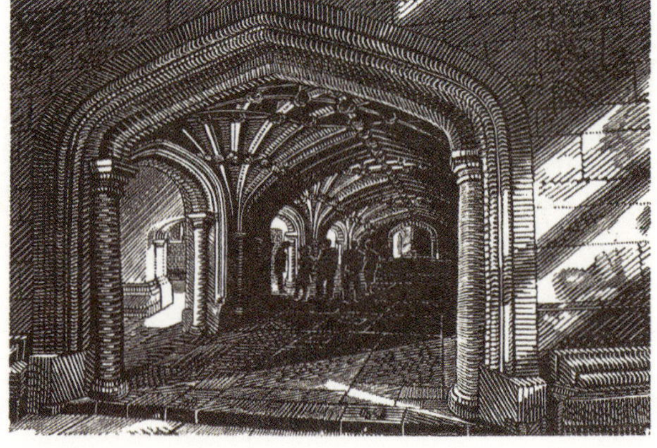

Chapel Undercroft (2016), engraving on boxwood, 15.7 × 3.1cm (6¼ × 1¼in), on Gampi Vellum paper. The first part engraved was the foreground wall with diagonal sunlit streaks.

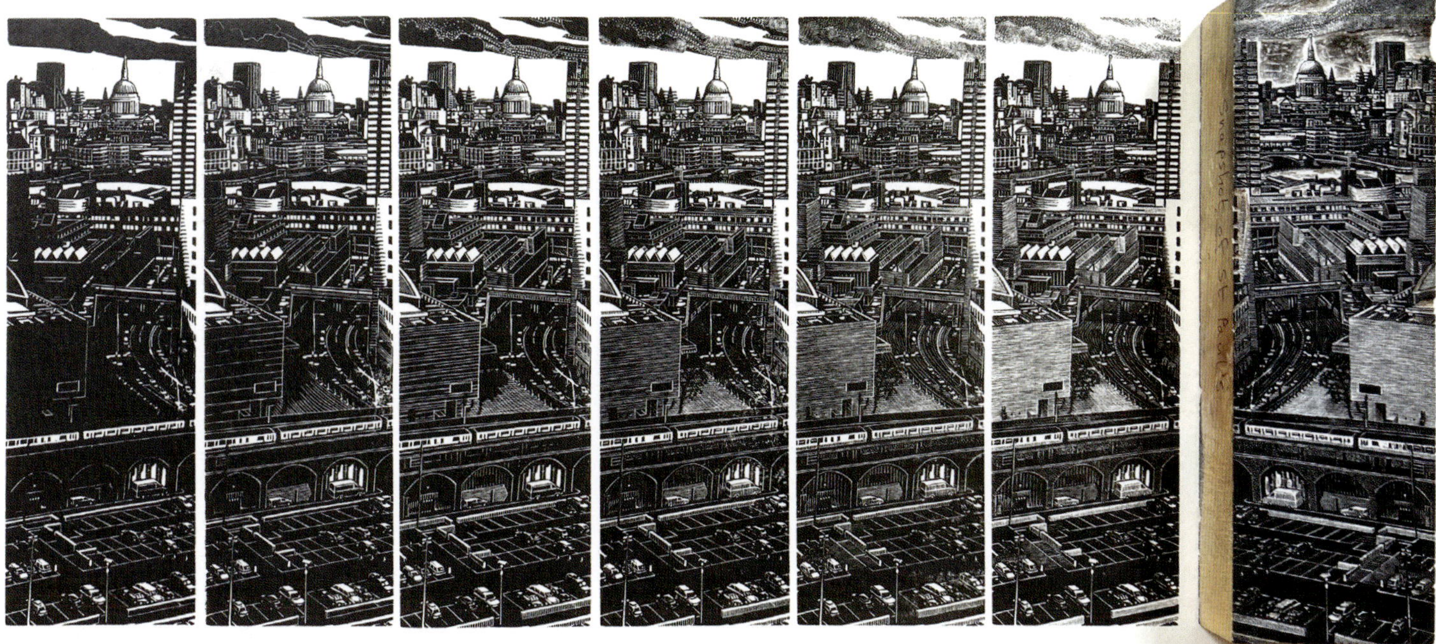

Six Snapshots of St Paul's (2002), reduction engraving on boxwood block, 16 × 5cm (6¼ × 2in), on Zerkall paper, total printed area: 16 × 31cm (6¼ × 12¼in). This London view is printed from one block at different stages of cutting, beginning with white highlights and gradually adding tones. The result is a sequential, filmic image suggesting time passing and subtly changing light.

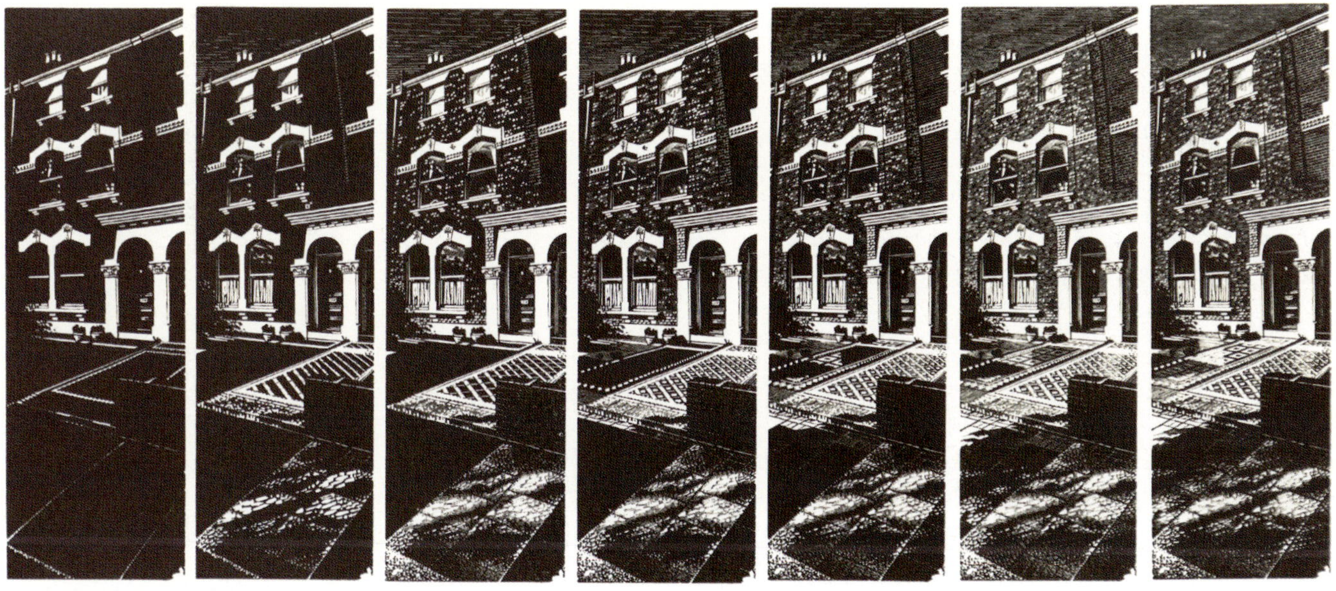

Urban Development (1998), reduction engraving on boxwood block, 16 × 5cm (6¼ × 2in), on Zerkall paper, total printed area: 16 × 37.2cm (6¼ × 14¾in). Printed from a single block at different stages of cutting, each of its stages increases the amount of light and detail in the image.

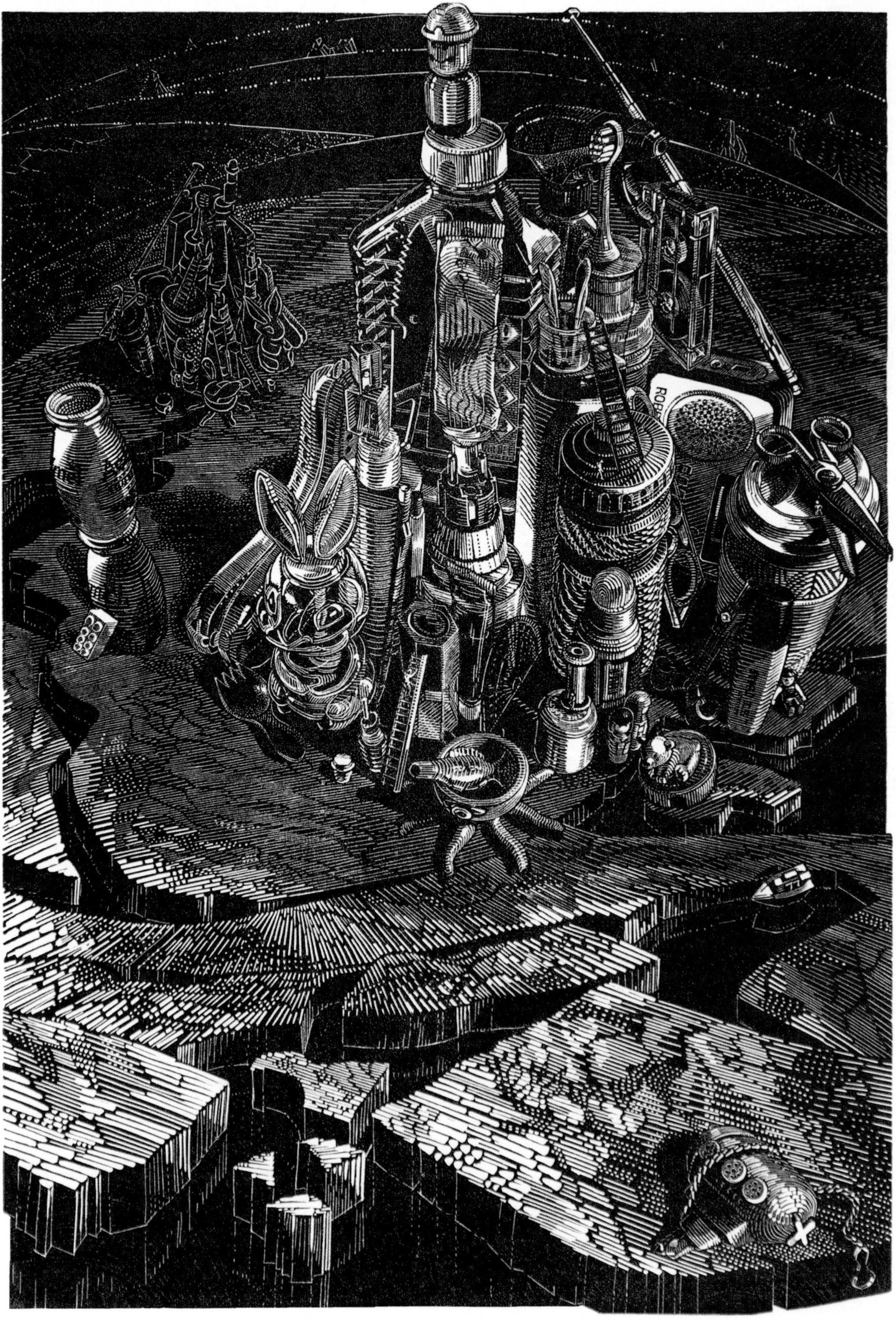

CHAPTER 6

PRINTING BY HAND AND PRESS

A useful practicality of working in wood engraving is that your work space can occupy a surprisingly small area. You only need a well-lit desk for engraving and, if printing by hand, you need no more extra space at all.

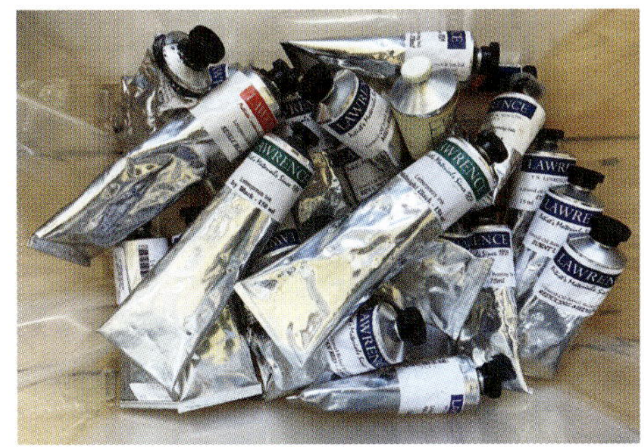

Tubes of TN Lawrence's printing inks in assorted shades of black plus other colours and extending/reducing medium.

PRINTING INK

Unless you regularly print other, larger, relief prints such as woodcuts or linocuts, I wouldn't recommend buying tinned ink. You will use so little for each engraving that a single tube of oil-based, relief printing black ink can last for years. The larger ink quantities in tins tend to dry up before you've used more than a fraction of the tin.

Different engravers favour different inks and there are many brands to choose from. Years ago, I was given a tin of Hostmann-Steinberg black ink – a stiff, intense black producing great results. But, for decades, I have used British retailer T N Lawrence's linseed oil-based letterpress and relief printing inks: five subtly different blacks (the letterpress range) and many colours (the relief printing range) as well as tubes of own-brand 'extender' for extending the inks' pigments to give colours more translucent/transparent qualities. Cranfield make these inks for T N Lawrence (contact details at the back of this book).

Water-based inks, such as the extremely liquid varieties for Japanese woodblock printing, are also made of natural, non-plastic ingredients and, being water-washable, pose no threat to the environment but are not suitable for end grain blocks because the water will cause the wood to swell, filling in engraved marks and making the block unprintable. Water-washable inks as used by printmakers in the Western world are generally made with acrylic resins or hybrid blends of acrylic resin and polyurethanes bound in vegetable oil. There are varieties that print linocuts and other relief prints well, but they are too oily or runny to print wood engravings and, while they can be readily cleaned with washing-up liquid and water, they do contain microplastics.

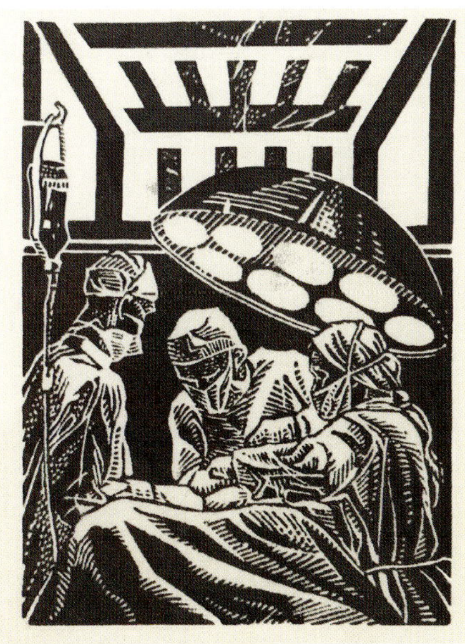

Irene Irving (1988, revised 2020), wood engraving and stencil, 7.6 × 5.4cm (3 × 2¼ in), press printed on Japanese paper. (The surgeon on the right is my late mother, after whom this print is named.)

Land of Beacons (2022), engraving on boxwood, 29 × 19cm (11½ × 7½in), press-printed on my Albion platen press, on Gampi Vellum paper.

Oil-based printing inks have unjustly gained a reputation of being bad for the environment. This is unfair as the inks often comprise powdered plant- or mineral-based pigments bound in a natural oil so they are not environmentally damaging at all. Any environmental issue is from the white spirit or turpentine traditionally used to clean them up. You can, however, easily clean up oil-based inks without using solvents, like this:

- Scrape as much ink residue off the slab with a palette knife (or old plastic store card).
- Pour about a teaspoonful of any cooking oil from your kitchen cupboard (sunflower oil, for instance) onto the ink slab and another teaspoonful onto the inky roller.
- Roll the roller over the ink on the slab to spread the cooking oil thoroughly all over both the roller's surface and the ink on the slab to dilute the pigment.
- Wipe off excess oily ink from both slab and roller with a clean rag or paper towel.
- Clean up the last inky remnants with a clean rag dipped in water and a small squirt of washing up liquid, taking especially good care to clean the roller's edges and the area around its spindle (the thin metal rod on which the roller is threaded) and any ink splashes on its frame or handle.
- Alternatively, there are many non-toxic cleaning fluids on the market, for printmakers' use, which work fine for this final cleaning stage.
- Alternatively – enabling you to dispense with the vegetable oil cleaning stage – try Lincoln Wash from Hawthorn Printmakers. It is a hydrocarbon solvent nearly as effective as white spirit, but with no smell or toxicity.
- Dry the ink slab and roller thoroughly with another clean rag. Never leave the roller to air-dry as its metal parts may rust.

CHOOSING A ROLLER

For small blocks, you will ideally need a small, hand-held, artist's quality Durathene roller – with a minimum diameter and roller length of about 5cm (2in) in both dimensions – or an equivalent rubber roller of similar specifications. Durathene is a pliant plastic and is the contemporary, more resilient, equivalent of traditional gelatine rollers, which had a semi-transparent appearance and were reasonably firm, though not hard, to the touch. Avoid hard, small-diameter, cheap rubber rollers (often used for printing in schools). They are too hard and narrow to ink even the smallest engraving blocks effectively.

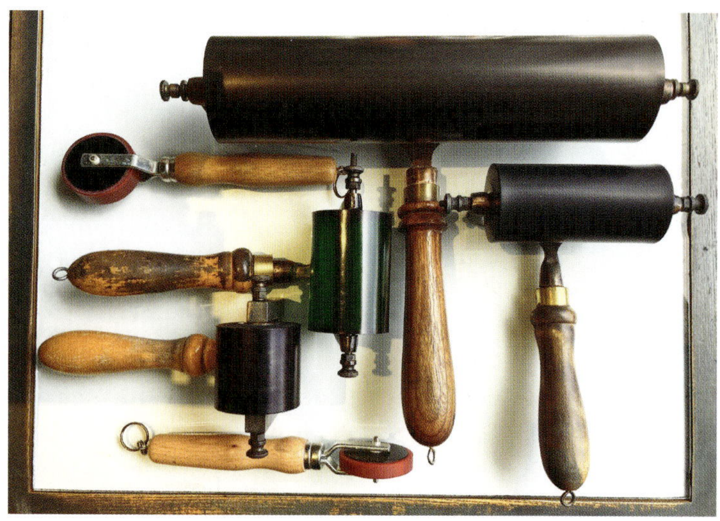

Rollers of different types and sizes, some are Durathene, some are rubber.

For bigger blocks, you need a larger roller with a length just slightly longer than your block's shortest edge and a relatively wider diameter. If inking a larger block with a too-small roller, it's hard to avoid getting ink lines, from the roller's edges, on the block and these will impair the print. Rollers in different sizes are available from diverse suppliers. They're not cheap but, if looked after, you will get a lifetime's use from the metal (often brass) and wood handle and frame of each one. The roller part is usually replaceable, but will last a good decade if cleaned thoroughly after each use. I prefer rollers with a frame that allows you to sit the inked roller on its back, without the inked part being in contact with your work surface. Rollers which don't have this type of frame are still useful, but more likely to generate unwanted inky mess in your printing area, as they will leave an ink residue wherever you set them down. Also, attach a teacup hook into the handle of any such rollers so you can hang them up after use. If you leave them on a worktop, the roller in contact with the flat surface will tend to flatten along one edge over time.

PRINTING PAPERS

Japanese papers are made with much longer plant fibres than European equivalents, which makes them stronger, despite their deceptive thinness. You can print very effectively on Japanese tissue, whereas European tissue will tear. For printing by hand, it's easier to work with thin, semi-transparent, Japanese papers in which the engraved image, when burnished, can be seen through the back. Opaque papers – Western/European or Japanese – can also be hand-printed effectively provided they aren't too heavy: a heavy (thicker) paper may shift on the block – especially a very small block – when you are burnishing, causing a blurred result.

The art of paper-making in Japan dates back to about 610CE and, by 800CE, the country's papermaking skills were unrivalled. Specialist printmaking papers flourished in tandem with the development of Japan's *Ukiyo-e* woodblock prints from the seventeenth to the nineteenth centuries and continue to this day. Traditionally, papers were made by Japanese farming communities in winter, when crops weren't ready for harvesting and little work could be done on the land. The papers are made from different plants, which may include fibres from the inner bark of the gampi tree, or the paper mulberry (kozo) bush, or the mitsumata shrub.

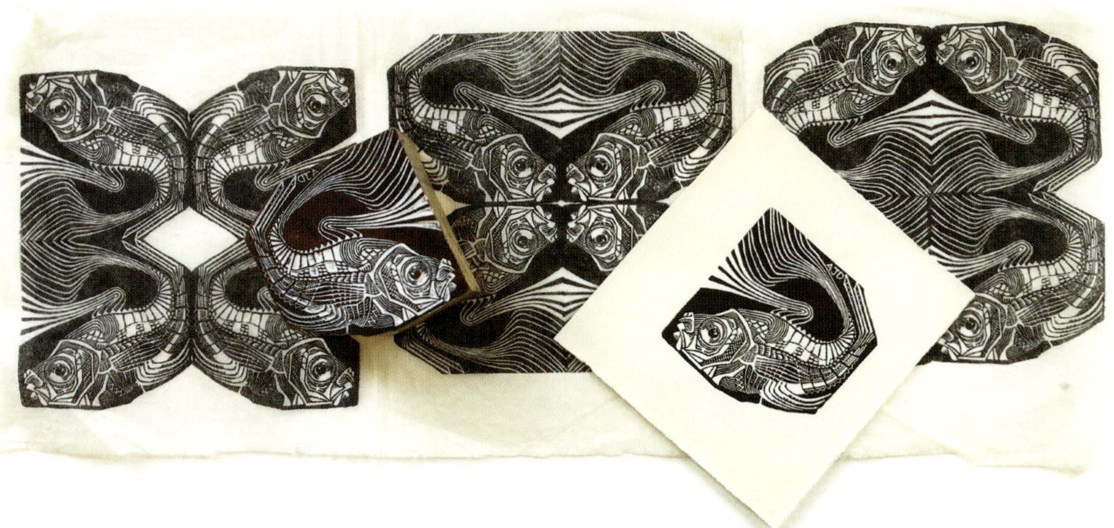

This block (1986), 6 × 5.7cm (2¼ × 2¼in), was press-printed on opaque Basingwerk Parchment paper. The repeat-pattern variant was hand-printed on semi-transparent Japanese tissue, printing on the front and back of the paper, which is so transparent that the image appears equally strong on both sides, making it possible to create assorted repeat patterns from a single block.

Ideal City (1991), wood engraving and collage on semi-transparent Japanese tissue, with glass-headed pins, 9 × 32 × 0.3cm (3½ × 12½ × 1/8in). This involved printing a single square block four times, printing it, alternately, on the front and back of the paper to create a mirror image effect. Coloured papers are collaged behind the printing paper and show through to the front.

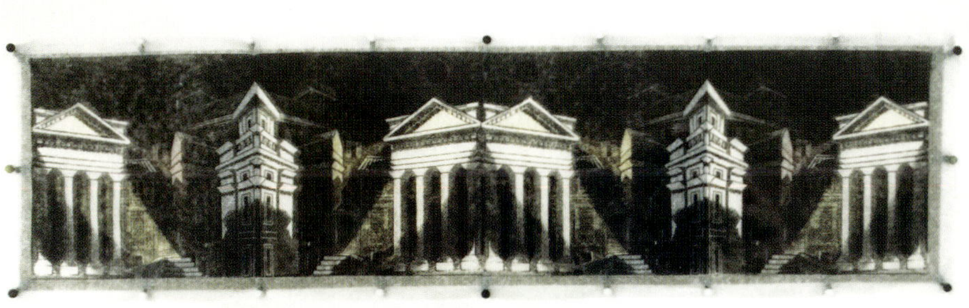

Choosing paper

Washi is a term that describes handmade Japanese paper. *Yōshi* denotes paper manufactured Western style. *Shi* is simply a word for paper. Japanese papers with the words *gampi*, *kozo* or *mitsumata* in their names denote that they are made with these plant fibres. It is, however, worth checking with your paper supplier the percentage of the relevant plant fibre used in a paper's production, because many Japanese papers intended for export have wood pulp added to keep the price down.

For printing wood engravings, select papers with the smoothest surface and always print on the smoother of the sheet's two sides, as their fabrication process results in one side being smoother than the other. Avoid 'laid' papers because the visible lines of the paper-making mesh show up in engravings as pale stripes. Among the many smooth 'wove' papers, gampi papers print wood engravings particularly well, as they pick up their details while holding a good dense black from uncut areas. When trialling different papers, you will find that some print fine details but not a good dense black, while others print a good black but details may fill in. Gampi papers are, however, generally more expensive than kozo or mitsumata and are often only tissue-thin (albeit very strong). That thinness may not suit all your printing needs.

Production of these specialist papers is in gradual decline and various types, which I've used for years, are no longer made. My favourite, but for which fabrication was discontinued years ago, is the ivory-white Gampi Vellum. It comprises a gampi tissue laminated onto a more robust paper of different plant fibres. It combines the excellent printing qualities of gampi on a heavier-weight sheet. The lamination process produced a paper with a surface like washed silk – a characterful appearance which I love, though many other engravers prefer a pure white European paper without any distinctive surface other than the ability to take a good clear impression from the block.

Paper choices are very personal. They vary from artist to artist, depending on what seems to suit the nature and cutting of their blocks. To try out Japanese papers, buy sample packs from a printmaking supplier or directly from a manufacturer such as Awagami. You often get ten or more small sheets in a pack at anything from A4 to A6 size and they come with labels identifying each paper's name and weight. Use them until you find one or more that suits your work. Don't buy full-size sheets until you've found one that works for you. You can get many small prints from a large single sheet, but individual sheet prices can be high.

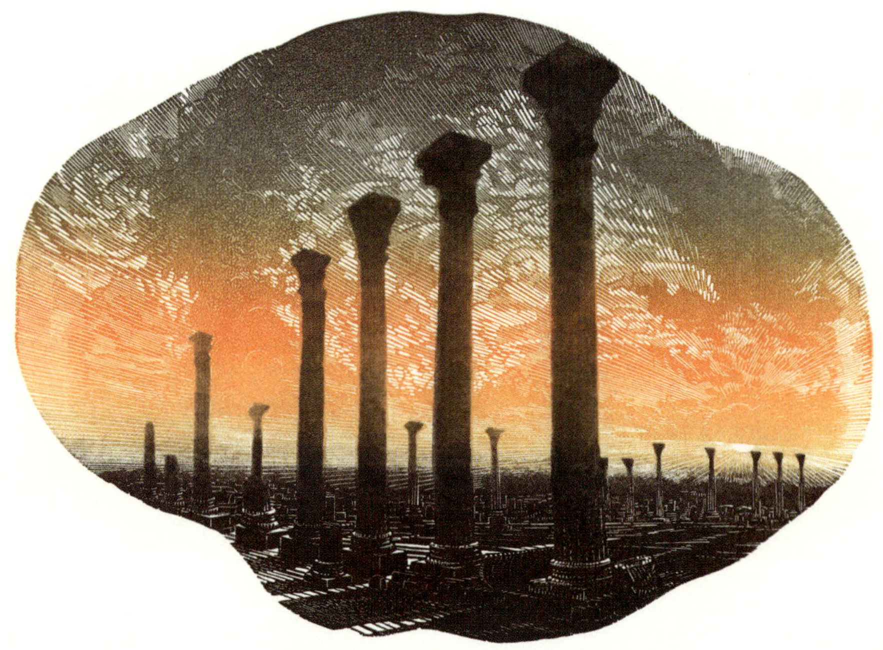

End of Empire (2018), engraving on boxwood, 13 × 17.4cm (5 × 6¾in), with stencil and pochoir, on Gampi Vellum paper. The woodblock (printed with a black/orange/grey colour blend) was press-printed. The stencil and pochoir areas were hand-printed.

In Japan, an old print in which the paper has darkened is valued more than a new print. The paper's ageing is associated with a sense of increasing beauty and history and is a greatly admired quality. It is therefore the case that, in making contemporary papers for printmakers, while not usually made with wood pulp (acids of which cause papers to brown), Japanese manufacturers don't add anything to their papers to inhibit a tendency to darken so, if you use them, be aware that white papers may turn pale pinkish-grey and ivory-toned ones will likely develop a darker, cream tone. These changes happen if works are exposed to strong sunlight, even for a short time, but not if prints are stored in the dark – in a plan chest for instance, or an archival solander box such as those which museums use. Before printing an edition, stick a paper sample in a sunny window while putting the other sheets in a drawer. After a week or two, compare the two. The window sample is now likely to be a different tone from the rest but, assuming you don't dislike it, don't be deterred from printing on it. Like the Japanese, if you like the way the paper ages, it needn't be a barrier to using these beautiful papers.

Have fun with papers: try printing, for instance, on map-pages, marbled papers, patterned origami sheets or giftwrap. They may not be either light-fast or acid-free but can yield surprising, often beautiful results.

When I first started printing, the first paper I used was a smooth, ivory-toned, opaque, lightweight, European wove paper called Basingwerk Parchment, used by many engravers until the 1990s when stocks ran out, it having been discontinued. In the 1980s, the accomplished wood engraver Edwina Ellis (b.1946) worked with London's John Purcell Papers to develop an excellent new paper for wood engravers, using a German paper mill. This was Zerkall: an extra-hot-pressed, beautifully smooth paper that printed wood engravings exceptionally well. Like Basingwerk, Zerkall was particularly suitable for press printing though both papers, with care, could be hand-printed. Tragically, however, the centuries-old Zerkall Papermill, in hilly countryside between Cologne and Aachen, was devastated by flash-floods in July 2021. Since then, research is ongoing to develop a new paper for wood engravers, perhaps to the Zerkall recipe. Among the best so far are Liber Charta

Proofs of my *Mersey Light* engraving on assorted Japanese paper samples. Some printed better than others and some of the paper tones suited the image better than others. Making test prints on paper samples will help you decide what works best for your blocks.

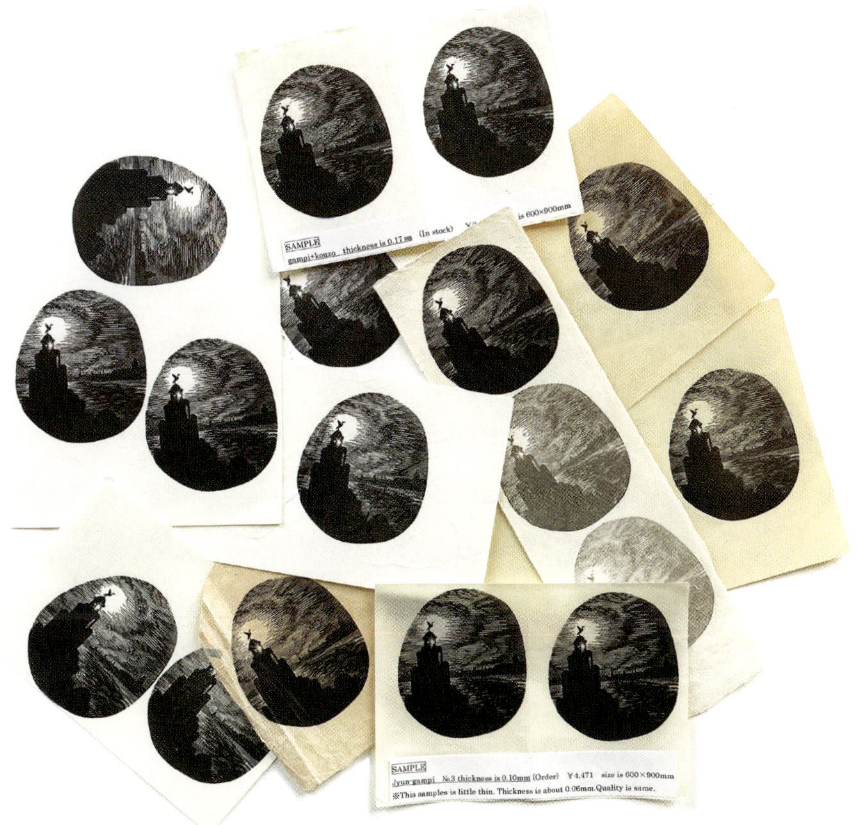

Home (1991), wood engraving on boxwood, 3.5 × 3cm (1½ × 1¼in), on China White paper.

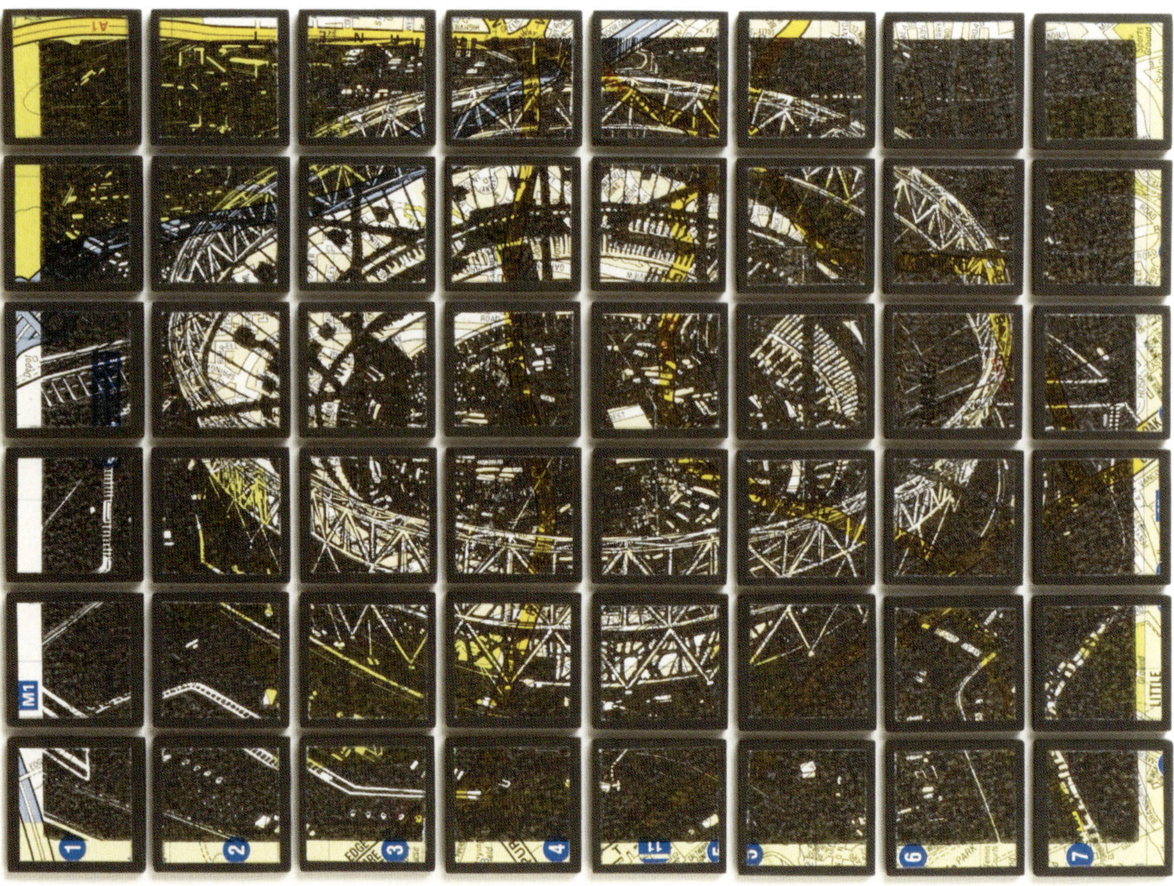

Olympic Site Map (2010), wood engraving printed on London-map page collaged on 48 ceramic mosaic tiles, 15 × 20.4 × 0.3cm (6 × 8 × 1/8in). The coloured map paper shows through in the pale parts of the image giving it a more layered appearance and adding a relevant location marker.

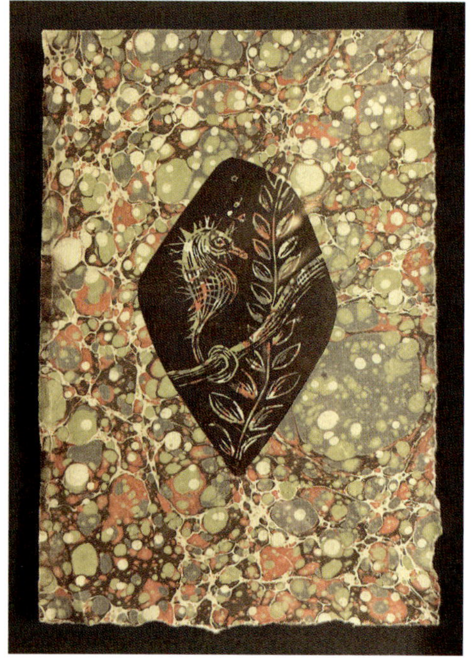

Nikki Tait engraved this tiny seahorse, c.6 × 5cm (2¼ × 2in), on a practice block, as a student on a course I ran at Gainsborough's House Print Workshop in Suffolk (2011). Printing it on marbled paper seemed to complement the image, suggesting a watery habitat.

and Hereford: inexpensive, smooth, white papers of 145gsm. Similar to Zerkall, they can be printed by hand but are especially well suited to press printing. Smooth, heavier papers, such as Somerset Satin 200gsm can be press-printed successfully, but are too thick for effective hand-printing of engraved blocks. European printmaking papers tend to be less varied in visual character than their Japanese counterparts, but they print very well, offer whiter whites, are acid-free and reasonably resistant to age- or light-related tonal changes.

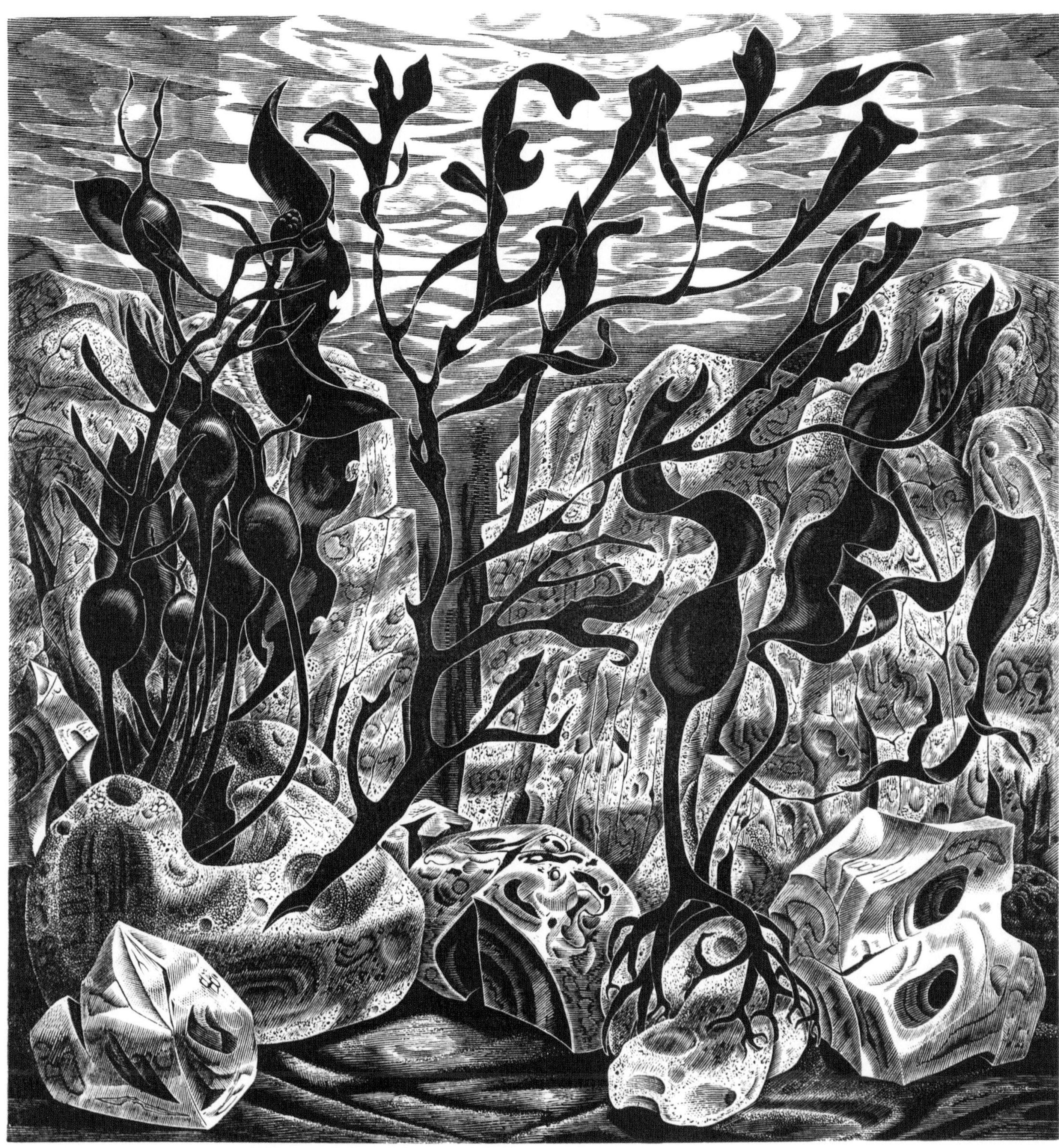

Under Water (1986), wood engraving, 22.5 × 20.7cm (8¾ × 8¼in), on Zerkall paper by Monica Poole. © Estate of Monica Poole. This extraordinarily fine engraving was printed using complex paper overlays to enhance dark tones and enable the lightest possible printing of paler areas. In my print collection I have equally fine examples by her on Basingwerk Parchment paper.

PRINTING BY HAND

This is a quick and easy process, but you need to prepare your work space properly for best results.

A clean space

Clear your desk (or use your kitchen table) to create a clean, uncluttered, printing space. You need good light to print by so, ideally, your desk should be near a window. If working without daylight, ensure there is strong artificial top- or side-light and that you don't set up your printing station such that you cast shadows on ink and block while working. Cover the desk or table in newspapers or plastic sheeting to protect it from printing ink. Wear an apron or old shirt to protect your clothing.

Preparing paper

When you buy it, apart from Japanese samples, individual sheets are generally large and you can get at least four prints per sheet (allowing for generous paper margins all around the image) or six, eight, or many more per sheet if the block is small and you give it narrower margins.

If printing a single block, it can be attractive to tear (rather than cut) sheets to whatever size is required as this gives a pleasing, slightly wavy edge to each one – though if you prefer the look of precision-cut, straight edges (or if you're printing a multiple-block print that needs perfect registration) you should cut the sheets instead. To tear (or cut) paper efficiently: put the sheets flat, in a neat stack, printing side downwards, onto a large self-healing cutting mat on a clean, smooth worktop. Having calculated the optimum number of pieces per sheet (avoiding wastage), use an extra-long steel ruler to place a line of four or five carefully measured pencil dots on the paper to guide your first tear (or cut). Using the ruler aligned along those dots, press down on it firmly with one hand while tearing the paper with the other, very carefully, one sheet at a time along the ruler's edge (or cut along the ruler's edge using a sharp cutting knife or scalpel). Having removed the first torn sheet, leave the ruler in place and tear or cut the next three or four sheets in the stack, one at a time, without re-measuring. As you tear or cut the paper to size, you can use the increasingly smaller sheets as templates to guide tearing or cutting the rest to the size you want. It's better to work from the back rather than the printing side because the steel ruler leaves a strong impression on the paper edge.

Assembling equipment

You will need: engraved block; square-ended chisel tool; stiff brush (cheap shaving brush, old toothbrush, or artist's bristle brush); small inking slab (toughened glass is ideal); barrier cream or disposable latex/plastic gloves if you want to protect your hands; palette knife or old store-card for spreading ink; small Durathene roller for a small block – or equivalent rubber roller; tube of oil-based relief printing ink; clean rags and paper towels; printing paper torn or cut to your preferred size; some small sheets of tissue or tracing paper (optional); metal teaspoon (for hand-printing); small bottle of cooking oil and your preferred liquid cleaner.

Taping

It's really helpful to place the inking slab on a sheet of clean white paper. This enables you to see what you're doing very clearly and especially aids colour mixing on the slab. Tape around the inking slab's edges with sticky tape to fix it to the worktop and prevent it from sliding about while you're working.

Drying

You'll need somewhere to put your prints, for a day or two, to dry after printing. Either lay them out on a clean worktop as you print each one. Otherwise, improvise an indoor washing line with clothes pegs or, for larger spaces, there are more elegant print hanging systems or drying racks that you can buy.

Block checking

Run your fingers over your block's engraved surface. It should feel smooth, despite being engraved. Sometimes, especially if you've engraved stippled dots and haven't flipped out each tiny speck of wood effectively, or if the block was a bit too spongey in the cutting, you may find that patches of it feel rough. If you print without remedying this, the roller won't make full contact with the block in those areas, but will simply leave tiny amounts of ink on top of every lump, each one of which will print as a little black dot surrounded by a white halo, rather than providing a clear impression of the engraved marks.

These tiny raised lumps can easily tear the paper while you're hand-printing. To get rid of them, take a flat chisel tool (which should have a blade width of at least 0.6cm/¼in). Holding its blade completely flat on the wood's surface, use it like a wood plane, moving it back and forth extremely gently (no gouging!) to level off those tiny, raised lumps until the block's surface feels uniformly smooth. Don't use the chisel at even a very shallow angle, as this will cause scratches and dents in the wood. You must keep it completely flat so it can only skim the surface and not dig into it. Don't plane the entire block, but only any localised rough areas. Don't use a square scorper as a chisel substitute as its narrower blade makes it almost impossible to use like a plane and it will scratch the block.

If you don't have a chisel, re-engrave each problematic dot with whatever tool you used to create it – taking care, this time, to ensure all the engraved wood is cleared away to leave the surface completely smooth.

Block brushing

Whether or not you've needed to apply chisel to wood, use a stiff brush (a small, flat-tipped, bristle brush from an art materials' supplier is ideal, but a clean, dry, shaving brush or even an old toothbrush will do the job) to clear out specks of sawdust from the block's surface (and/or talc/white chalk if you had rubbed any into the cuts). Any specks, if not removed, will inevitably find their way onto the ink slab or inked roller and spoil your print.

Protecting your hands

Rub barrier cream on your hands or wear disposable gloves if desired. Printing can, in fact, be done tidily without getting inky fingers, but soap and water and a good nailbrush will clean ink off your hands. (At art school, decades ago, I was taught to wash my hands with white spirit after printing. This is now known to break down the skin's natural protective layers, so it's absolutely not recommended and isn't something I do any more.)

Inking

For a very small block, squeeze a pea-sized ink blob from tube onto ink slab and roll it out into a neat rectangle. Keep the inked area contained in the middle of the slab. The more ink you spread about, the more likely you are to get it on your hands and on the printing paper. Also, the wider you spread it, the faster it will dry up and the more ink you'll need. Obviously, the bigger the block, the larger the length and diameter of roller required plus larger amounts of ink and a bigger slab. For blocks small enough to be held comfortably in one hand, you rarely need more ink than you would put toothpaste on a brush, and, for a really tiny block, a pea-sized blob is ample.

Rolling ink

1. When you start to roll it, the ink will make a noticeable slurping sound and may initially look a bit thick, with an orange peel-like texture. Very quickly, that sound should change to a gentle hiss and, when sufficiently rolled, should be a really thin ink layer that looks like fine, smooth, black silk with no ripples, lines, lumps or other glitches.

2. If you put more ink on the slab than intended, don't roll it out further across the slab to achieve the desired consistency. Scrape some off with the palette knife (or old store card). You can use it later to top up the slab.

3. Lift the roller right up, at the end of each roll. If you simply roll back and forth while leaving roller in constant contact with slab, you may only be inking the same part of the roller each time and not its entirety. By lifting it up at the end of each pass through the ink and placing it back down again for every new roll, you ensure the roller gets fully charged, ready to ink the block.

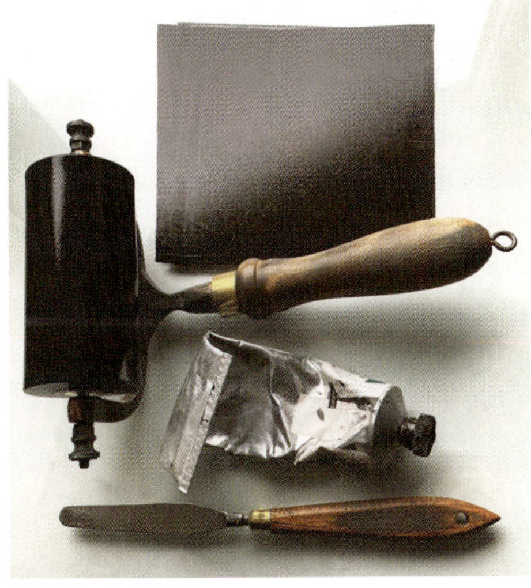

Stiff black letterpress ink rolled out in a thin shiny layer on the inking slab, ready for inking a block.

4. With the tip of a palette knife, pick out any flecks of dust, sawdust or hairs in ink or on roller and continue to remove any such debris as you go along.

5. When the slab is rolled and the roller fully charged with a thin, even, layer of the stiff ink (the work of barely a minute), hold your small block, engraved surface up, in your free hand (keeping your fingers well down its sides so as not to impede the roller's path) and, with the other hand, pass the roller across the block's surface. If the block is larger than would comfortably fit in your hand, it's better to place it on a clean flat surface for rolling but, personally, I find it easier to ink small blocks in my hand.

6. Unless it's a very lightweight roller, don't press down as you roll as that can squeeze ink into the engraved marks. You usually just need the roller's own weight to ink the block.

7. Without recharging the roller with fresh ink, roll the block about half a dozen times, ideally from at least two different directions, to ensure ink gets spread evenly and consistently across the surface, taking special care that all corners and edges are inked.

8. If the block is irregular in shape, it's easier to roll from a straight edge (if it has any) rather than from curved sides. Also, if you have cut away a noticeable amount from one or more edges, avoid rolling from any of those sides as the roller may dump more ink there than you want. Where possible, roll from edges that have the least cutting and therefore need the most ink to print to best effect.

9. Make sure, when rolling ink on block, that you lift the roller right off the block with each pass – exactly as earlier described for rolling ink on slab. Otherwise, you won't be using the roller's full inking surface and you may also not be inking the block's edges adequately.

Ready to print?

When inked, hold the block up to the light (daylight, ideally) and tilt it slightly back and forth. The thin surface layer of ink should glisten evenly all over as it catches the light. If it does, it's ready to print. But if it has dull patches, you probably missed a bit, so give it another couple of rolls (without re-charging the roller) before you print. Alternatively, if you see any raised ink lines on the block, you have probably caught a roller edge on it so, again, give the block another few rolls (without re-charging the roller) until the ink looks even and consistent over the block's entire face.

Spoon-printing

1. Put the inked block on a clean surface and place a piece of printing paper on top. You must be decisive: once you've placed the paper, don't adjust its position as that will cause a misprint. Pat the paper down gently. The ink will act like mild glue to keep the paper in place.

2 Take a metal teaspoon. Hold it with the handle in the palm of your hand and the spoon's bowl beneath the pad of your index finger. Press down so that the spoon's convex surface makes firm contact with the paper and the block beneath. Move the spoon in small circular motions, pressing down firmly all the time, while also holding the paper in place with a finger of the other hand. You may need slightly firmer pressure to spoon-print uncut areas and less for extensively engraved parts.

3. If printing on semi-transparent paper, you will see a back-to-front version of the image appearing through the back, as you burnish, much as if you were making a brass-rubbing. You will see clearly where your spoon-printing has succeeded and areas you've missed. Continue rubbing until the entire image shows through clearly.

4. Again, with semi-transparent paper, you can significantly affect the look of images by the pressure with which you burnish. If you want a part to print paler but your cutting hasn't created adequate tonal differentiation – do this simply by lightly rubbing (rather than spoon-burnishing) with your finger, so that much less ink transfers from block to paper in that part, and spoon-burnish firmly the rest of the block. This is only feasible if the paper is semi-transparent because you can see the image coming

through the back of the paper as you burnish, so you can see where to stop burnishing and where, simply, to finger-rub. If you can find a burnishing spoon with slightly rounded rather than sharp edges, you can also burnish with those edges to print very specific parts of the block that you want strongly printed, while leaving other parts lightly finger-rubbed.

5. Be extra careful burnishing the block's edges and corners as the spoon may slip off, creasing the paper.

6. With opaque paper, you won't be able to see the image coming through the back, but this is no barrier to a successful print. Start by carefully burnishing all around all the block's edges which, even with relatively thick paper, will show up sufficiently, once burnished, for you to be able to see the position of the entire block. Then print the rest using small circular motions with the spoon as already described.

7. If you're unsure whether you're pressing hard enough, peel up a corner to check your progress but be careful to hold the paper in place on the block with your other hand as, if the paper comes right off, it will be impossible to put it back in precisely the right position for more burnishing.

8. When hand-burnishing, I like to feel the spoon in direct contact with the paper and, through it, to the wood. However, if you press too hard, this risks ripping the paper. Also, if you have any ink smuts on spoon or fingers, it will transfer to the back of paper. So, consider inserting a small sheet of tissue or tracing paper between burnishing spoon and printing paper to minimise those risks.

9. When you've burnished the entire block, lift off the paper. Hopefully, you will have a perfect small print. A teaspoon is a surprisingly effective printing tool for small blocks, though you can buy special burnishing tools (of polished wood or bone) if you prefer. The smooth, rounded, wood handle of an engraving tool can also be an effective hand-printing implement but, if you use it, be careful not to cut yourself on the blade. As friction causes metal to heat up, a smooth wooden spoon is better for burnishing larger blocks.

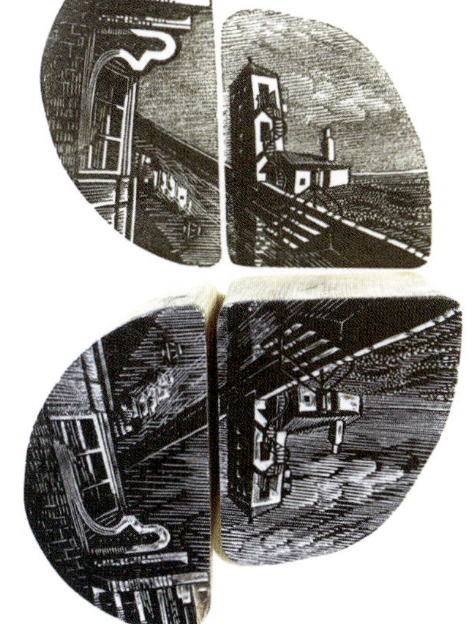

Tower after Rain (2013), engraving (inspired by Aldeburgh Beach Lookout, Suffolk, where I was artist in residence) on boxwood blocks printed by hand-burnishing on Kozu-shi, total printed area: 6.5 × 8cm (2½ × 3¼in). The buildings and beach were spoon-burnished while the sky was lightly finger-rubbed to create a paler grey.

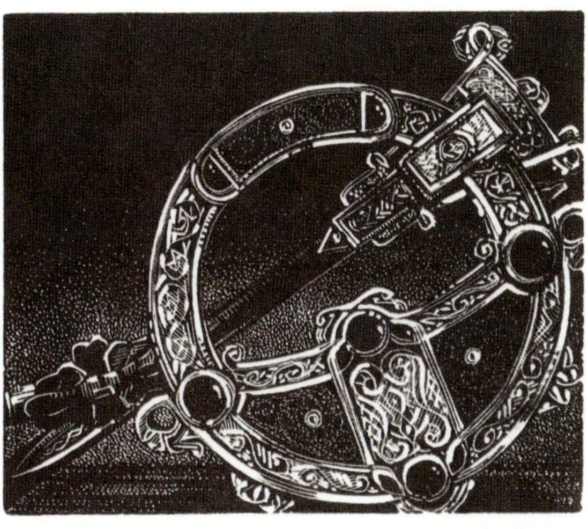

Tara (2012), engraving on boxwood, 6.1 × 7.1cm (2½ × 2¾in), on Gampi Vellum paper. A small block like this can be printed equally easily and successfully either by hand or by press.

Reprinting

The first print is usually paler than subsequent ones because a tiny amount of ink may sink into the end grain, so the first printing effectively also seals the block. To print further impressions, don't clean the block first. Just re-charge the roller from the ink slab and repeat all inking and printing steps already described for each new printing. Place each print face up, side by side, on a clean worktop or hang them up for a day or two to dry. When you've finished printing, clean inking slab and roller as described earlier.

Cleaning inked blocks

To clean the block, rub its inked surface with old newspaper or paper towel followed by a clean rag until it feels clean with no ink deposits coming off on your fingers or the rag. Take special care to wipe excess ink off its edges. The block will probably be clean now but, if you can see any ink in its engraved indentations, take a blob of Blu-Tack, roll it into a small ball and press it firmly all over the block's engraved parts. Any residual ink will lift out onto the putty leaving the block perfectly clean. (Don't use White-Tack. It's softer and stickier and may get stuck in the engraved indentations.)

Alternatively, if you don't mind solvents, a small amount of white spirit or lighter fuel on a clean rag, rubbed all over the block's surface, will clean it well but it won't be printable for a few days afterwards as the residual spirit will repel ink. Also, liquid solvents can soften a block's surface, making it harder to re-engrave. If you've used solvents, put the block aside for a day or two to dry thoroughly before undertaking further engraving on it.

PRINTING PRESSES

Various presses are suitable for printing wood engravings. Platen presses, perhaps the ones most frequently used, involve pulling a lever to cause a cast-iron flat plate (the platen) to exert downward pressure on block and paper to transfer inked image to paper. I print on an Albion: a particularly well-designed variety of platen press used for all forms of relief printing. It's made of cast-iron (with wooden and brass accessories) and weighs about half a ton. Mine was fabricated in London in 1859 yet is in perfect working order in my home studio. It isn't especially large – its press bed is only 50 × 36cm (19¾ × 14¼in) and its platen size is 40.5 × 28cm (16 × 11in) so the largest block it can print, without too much effort, is only about 29 × 19cm (11½ × 7½in). Although larger blocks fit on its bed, the pressure required to print them is more than I have strength to achieve. Generally speaking, the bigger the block, the larger the press you need to print it. While you can successfully print tiny blocks on very large presses, it's much harder to print a large block on a relatively small press.

My printing studio floor is reinforced to take the weight of the Albion press (and the copy press between its feet). The cloth-covered frame visible on the press is a tympan. To its right, a toughened glass inking slab sits on top of a small filing cabinet.

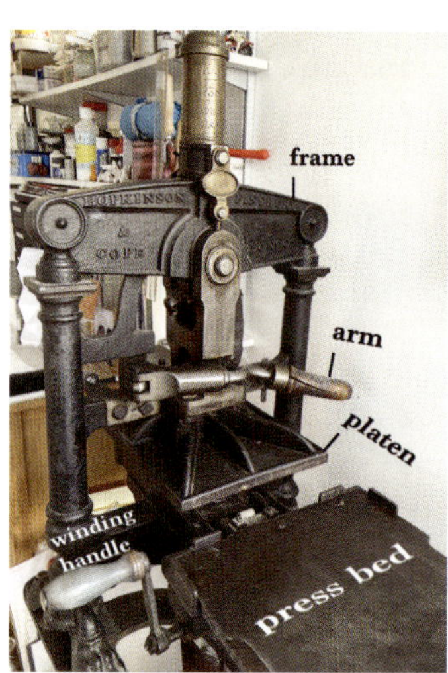

Albion press: close-up of parts revealing the press bed.

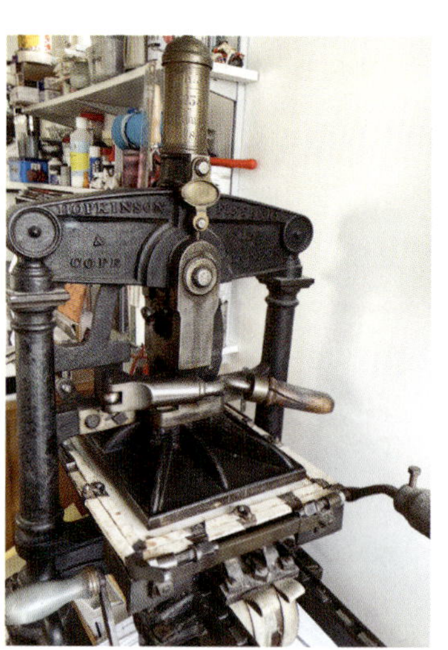

Albion press: with press bed and tympans rolled underneath the platen. You can see the bed rails (metal tracks) along which the press bed rolls.

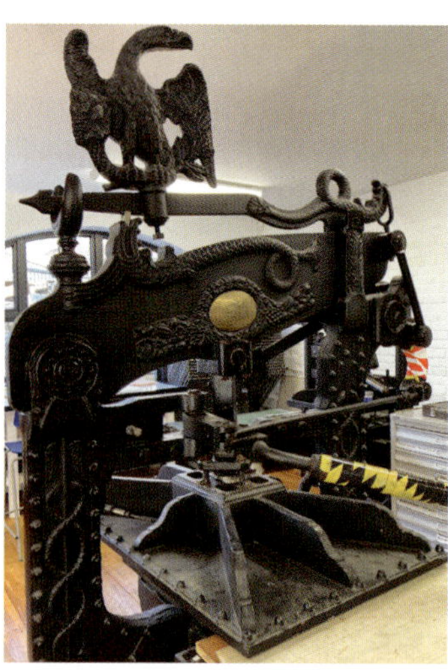

This Columbian press belonging to the Curwen Print Study Centre in Suffolk was made in 1837 and is still in good working order.

Other cast-iron platen-printing presses – all dating back to the 1800s and early 1900s – include the Columbian (with a distinctive counter-weight in the form of an eagle), Britannia, Alexandra, Stanhope and Reliance.

Many such presses are still in use in print workshops, schools and colleges, and in private homes and studios in Britain and overseas. They occasionally come up for sale, advertised in printmaking publications and online. Some years ago, UK press engineers Harry Rochat Ltd started remaking the Albion based on historic templates but with improved engineering. These can be ordered, bespoke, but at a significant price. They are wonderful machines, well worth having if you have the inclination, the budget and the (reinforced) floor space.

Cast iron screw presses, also known as book- or nipping-presses (wooden prototypes of which were developed by the Romans in the first century CE to press grapes and olives) and smaller copying presses can all be used effectively for printing wood engravings, as can certain types of cylinder press in which a heavy roller, wound across the top of the block, applies, as it rolls, pressure along the block's length. Book presses and copying presses can often be found via eBay, antique shops and specialist printmaking and paper suppliers and are quite affordable. There are also various small, portable and inexpensive wooden printing presses on the market (such as the Pooki and Woodzilla relief printing presses), which can print very small blocks effectively.

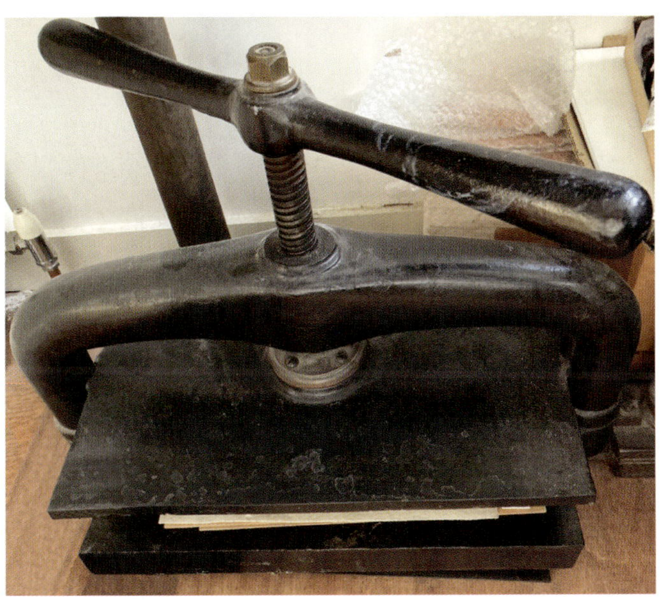

Small nipping (copy) press which sits underneath my Albion. I printed quite a few engravings on this in the early 1990s. These days I don't use it for printing but it's handy for book-binding.

PRESS PRINTING

If printing with a platen press, I'm assuming you have your own studio or access to a print workshop, which will have an inking station for your use. If you're not familiar with presses, you should always go to a print workshop and get some training in using a press safely before you ever use one unsupervised.

If you have your own press, keep its moving parts well-oiled and have it serviced by a press engineer from time to time to keep it in perfect working order.

Prepare block, paper and printing equipment exactly as described for hand-printing but, if the image is to involve multiple layers of printing on each sheet of paper, you may need to cut, rather than tear, your paper sheets in order to be able to use a registration system effectively for paper to contact block in exactly the same place with every printing.

Make sure you have a hanging system, clean worktop, or drying rack available for your prints to dry.

Registration system

Create a registration system to enable you to place paper on block in the desired position for each print. If the image will only involve a single printing from one block, registration can be very simple: place a piece of paper identical in size to your printing paper on the press bed as a template. Place the block printing face up on that paper in exactly the position where you'd like it to be in each print. Draw around the block's edges onto the paper beneath, then use this template as your guide to positioning block on press each time you print it, and use the template's edges as a guide to positioning the printing paper in the right place on the inked block. Tape template to press bed, with sticky tape along at least one edge, so it can't slide around, positioning it so that the block sits exactly in the middle of the press bed for each printing.

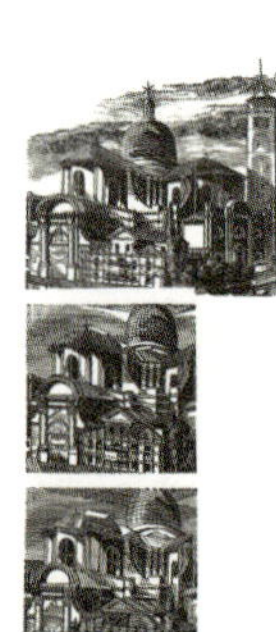
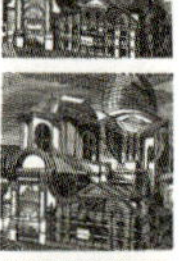
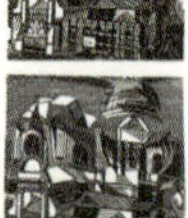
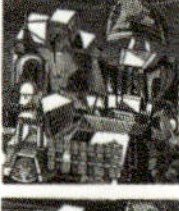
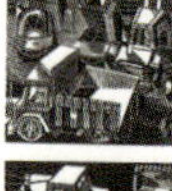
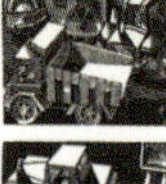
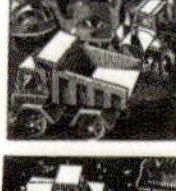
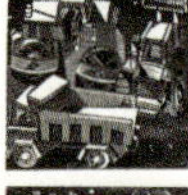
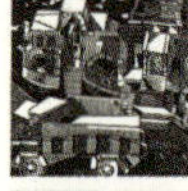
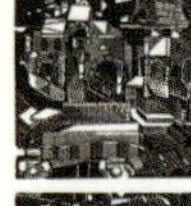
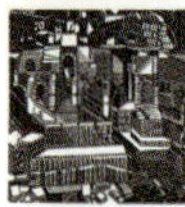
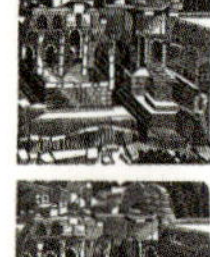
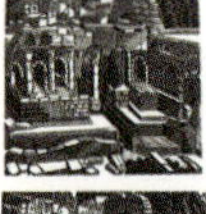
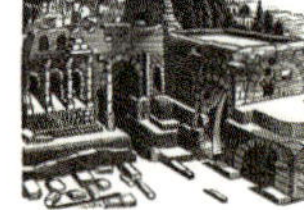

◀ *Building Blocks* (1994), 16 engravings on boxwood, on China White paper, total printed area: 78.7 × 6.5cm (31 × 2½in). Each part of this architectural/industrial metamorphosis was engraved on a separate block and press-printed.

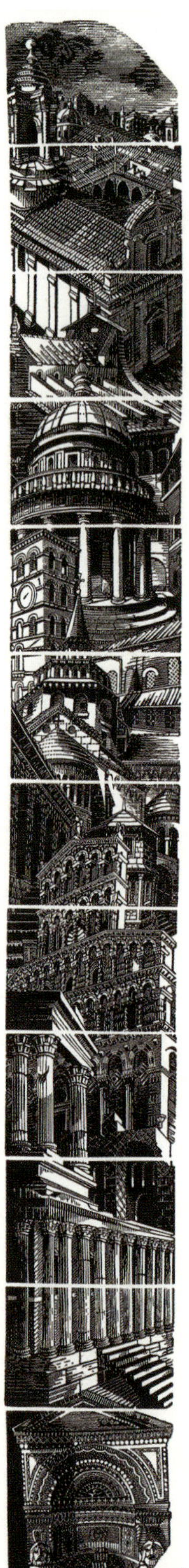

▶ *Reconstructing the Ruins* (1992), engraving on 13 boxwood blocks, total printed area: 43.2 × 4.5cm (17 × 1¾in), on China White paper. I press-printed this on a large Albion press in south London in the studio of painter-etcher Richard Fozard (1925–2000) whose work, like mine, was much influenced by a Rome Scholarship in Printmaking.

Pressure testing

1. Before you roll ink, it can be useful to test the pressure needed for the block before inking it. Although platen presses are designed for type-high blocks, the block's overall surface area and whether it's a square or rectangle or a more irregular shape will all affect the pressure needed to print it. Additionally, although blocks are, in theory, type-high, in practice their height often varies by several millimetres, and they may not be perfectly level.

2. Place the un-inked block in the centre of the press within the template you've created. Place a small piece of your chosen printing paper on top – this should entirely cover the block but you don't need to use a piece with extravagant paper margins.

3. If your press doesn't have tympans, place some packing (half a dozen pieces of newspaper will suffice) directly on top of the printing paper to soften the immediate impact of cast iron on wood.

4. Gently lower the tympans to cover block and paper. Slowly wind the press's handle so that the press bed rolls along its rails. Stop winding when the bed is directly beneath the platen. Always turn the handle slowly and stop turning before the bed reaches the ends of the rails at either end. Most presses have an inbuilt 'stop' to prevent the bed from jumping its rails if you wind too far, but many such stops are quite shallow so that, if you wind the handle too fast in either direction, the bed could still tip off at either end. Even if it only tips fractionally, it's extremely heavy and may take several people to lift it back onto its tracks. I've never seen a press bed tip right off and onto the floor but, if that happened, its weight could crush your feet so extreme caution is needed.

5. Now pull the press arm towards you – either as far as it will go or, if you feel resistance before it's pulled to its full extent, stop pulling as you may already have sufficient pressure – but keep in mind how far you had pulled the arm, if not to its maximum extent, as you may need to remember this for subsequent printings. Move the arm back to its resting position. (NB Never let the arm out of your grip until it's back in its resting position

as, uncontrolled, it will slam, with force, back into its original position and this may well damage the press.)

6. Slowly wind the bed out from under the platen, raise the tympans and lift printing paper off block. If you had sufficient pressure, you should see an extremely faint hint of the block's outlines on the paper.

7. If too much pressure, the paper will be embossed which means, when you ink and print the block, you shouldn't pull the arm quite so far across so as not to print it too heavily. (Doing this pressure test with the block already inked risks forcing ink into the engraved marks, if the pressure is too great, which could spoil subsequent prints.)

8. If too little pressure so you can't see even the faintest impression of block on paper, repeat the test (still without inking) but, this time, before rolling press bed under platen, add some old newspaper or magazine pages either on top of the printing paper or under the block (or some on top and some below) to increase the pressure when you pull the arm. Don't adjust the press's bolts. This won't affect the pressure and may simply loosen the platen, making the press dangerous to use. You should, instead, add sheets of paper to increase the pressure or, if the block is significantly lower than type-high, add one or more pieces of mount card to build up its height on the bed. (If doing this, I slide the card underneath my registration template, under the block. I also usually have some paper packing on top of the printing paper, above the block.)

Fish 4 engraving, 4 × 4cm (1½ × 1½in), in black ink (press-printed) on Somerset Satin paper with the boxwood block and *Fish 5* (a blind-embossed print from the same block) on Somerset Satin paper (all 2009).

9. Repeat this experiment using different quantities of packing above and/or below the block until you achieve an extremely light impression as previously described. (When you ink and print the block, any noticeable paper embossing is likely to result in a print with filled-in details.)

10. If your engraving is quite emphatic both with pronounced uncut and completely cleared out areas, you can get an interesting blind-embossed result by printing it with no ink but with far more pressure than you'd ordinarily use for printing. This might be a worthwhile result in its own right, but should never be done with an inked block as it will force ink into the engraved indentations.

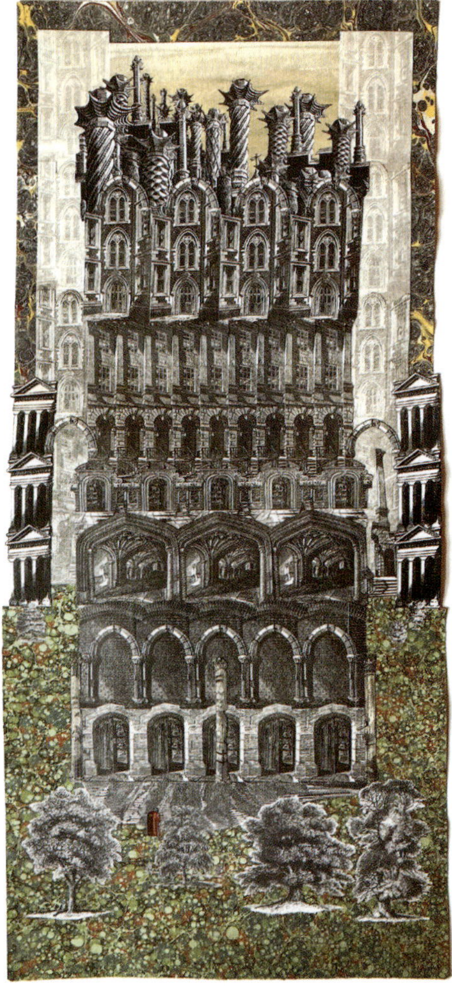

Lincoln's Inn – Past, Present, Future (2023), commissioned collage of press printed wood engravings, lithographs, linocut and found papers on marbled papers, 69 × 31.3cm (27 × 12in). The extremely pale printed sections at left and right were created by repeatedly press printing a particular block without re-inking between printings.

Platen printing

1. The press's tympan is a metal frame usually covered with stretched sailcloth (or other smooth fabric, or sometimes strong packing paper). If fully intact, it has a removable inner frame (also called a tympan), also covered with cloth. You can put all your packing materials between these two parts though, if you do that, you should ensure that each piece of packing is large enough not to slide about as you raise and lower the tympans for each print. Personally, I don't use the tympans in this way as the first presses I ever used at art school no longer had the second (inner) tympan still intact, which meant you couldn't use them in the way originally intended, so I got used to a system of adding packing, as necessary, directly on the press bed, either above or below the block. Many an old press, still in use today, has no tympans at all as they will have been broken or removed at some point in the press's long history.

2. Roll the ink out on the slab and ink the block exactly as already described for hand-printing (except that, if it's a larger block, you may need a slightly larger blob of ink and to re-charge the roller once or twice, while inking, as larger blocks usually require more ink).

3. Place the block on your template on the press bed. If necessary, add any packing materials that your pressure tests indicated. If your press doesn't have tympans, use about half a dozen packing sheets anyway to protect the block but, otherwise, use only if necessary.

4. If you don't need any packing, that's fine unless you're printing with very thin paper with which there's a danger that, when printed, the ink may squeeze through and offset onto a tympan. To avoid that risk, lay a thin sheet of packing paper on top of the printing paper. (Conversely, sometimes tympans in print workshops and art schools are dirty from years of use and might offset smuts onto the back of your printing paper unless you protect it in the same way.)

5. Close the tympans. Wind the bed under the platen. Pull the arm to the optimum position (as indicated by your pressure tests) to print the block. Hold for a second, then gently move the arm back to its rest position. Turn the handle to wind the bed out from beneath the platen. Lift the tympans. Remove your packing papers and gently peel off the printing paper to reveal the print.

6. If it's too pale, re-ink the block and print on a fresh sheet of paper. The second print is often darker than the first but, if it still prints pale, add some more packing paper before you pull the next one. If the print is too heavily printed, remove some packing paper before you pull another.

7. Lay out or hang up your print to dry.

8. Print as many impressions as you want, taking care to check each one carefully for printing problems as you go and take appropriate actions (described below) if problems arise.

9. You will need to refresh the ink with a pea-sized blob on the slab after every two or three prints, but it's impossible to say exactly how frequently because printing is affected by factors beyond your control, such as the weather.

10. When you've finished, clean roller, inking slab and block as described earlier. An alternative way of cleaning the block is to print half a dozen impressions on clean paper, without re-inking. Each impression will be successively paler. When there is virtually no imprint at all, the block is sufficiently clean. These pale impressions can be useful for collage-making, so don't throw them away.

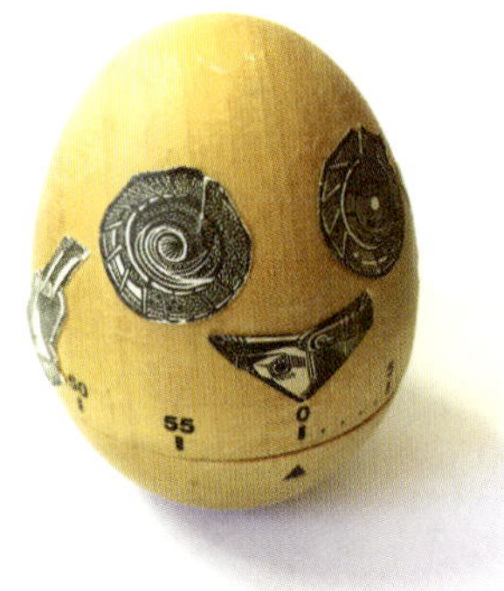

Wooden egg timer collaged with wood engraved prints (press-printed) on paper, 7.7 × 6.5 × 6.5 cm (3 × 2½ × 2½in).

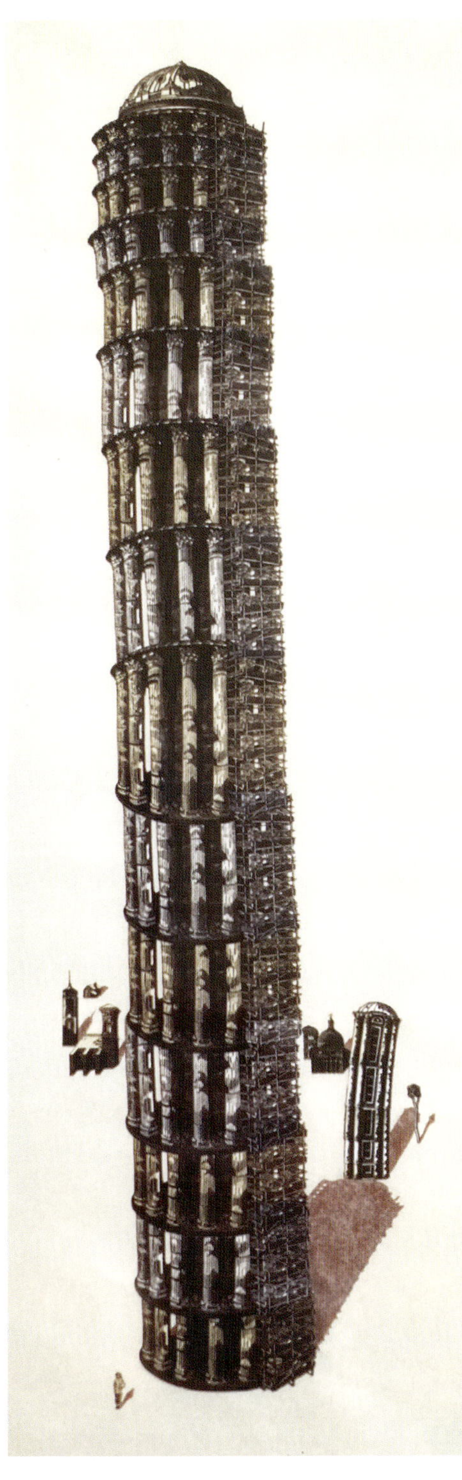

■ *Self Portrait with Towers* (1994), collage of wood engravings (with added pencil drawing) comprising, primarily, multiple press printings, on white and cream papers of one engraving block (of Rome's Temple of Hercules Victor), which were then cut out and reassembled to create this stretched tower form.

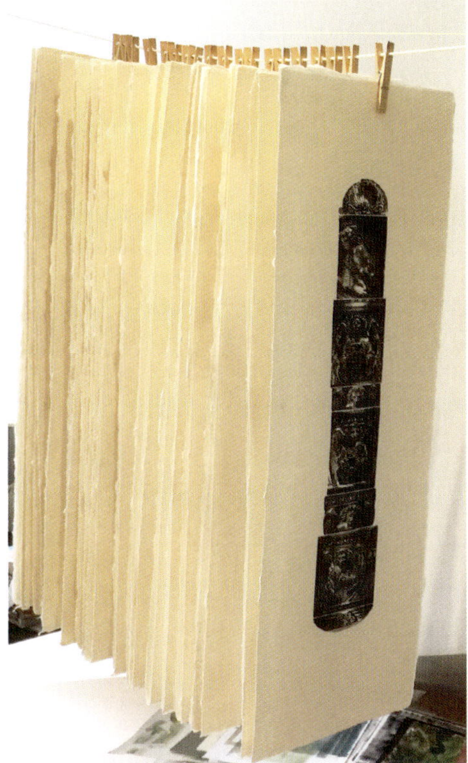

■ On this indoor 'washing' line, wooden pegs are drilled with holes and threaded along it so that freshly printed engravings can hang at right angles to the taut line with a small space between each one. I hang two prints, back to back, per peg. This section alone holds over 50 prints.

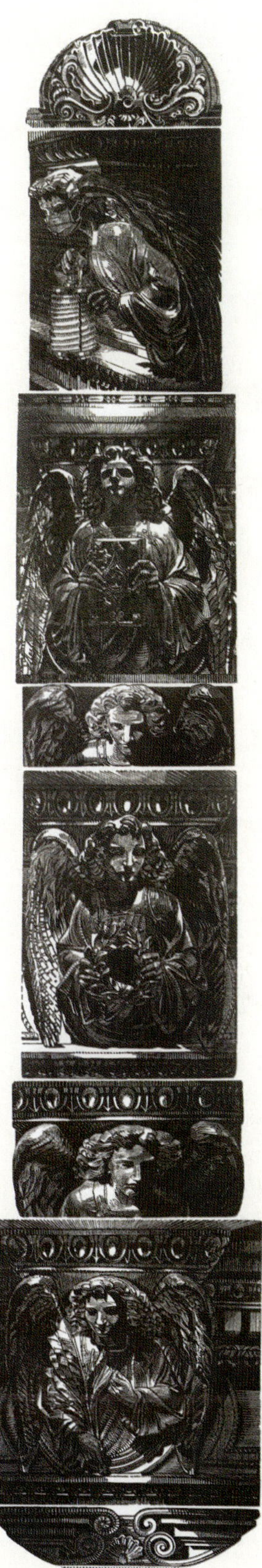

■ *Tower of Angels* (2020), eight engravings on boxwood, press-printed on Gampi Vellum paper, 52.3 × 9cm (20½ × 3½in). I printed the first block in the middle using a registration template. The rest were printed one at a time, placed by eye, above or below each adjacent component, and working outwards towards the top and bottom of the paper.

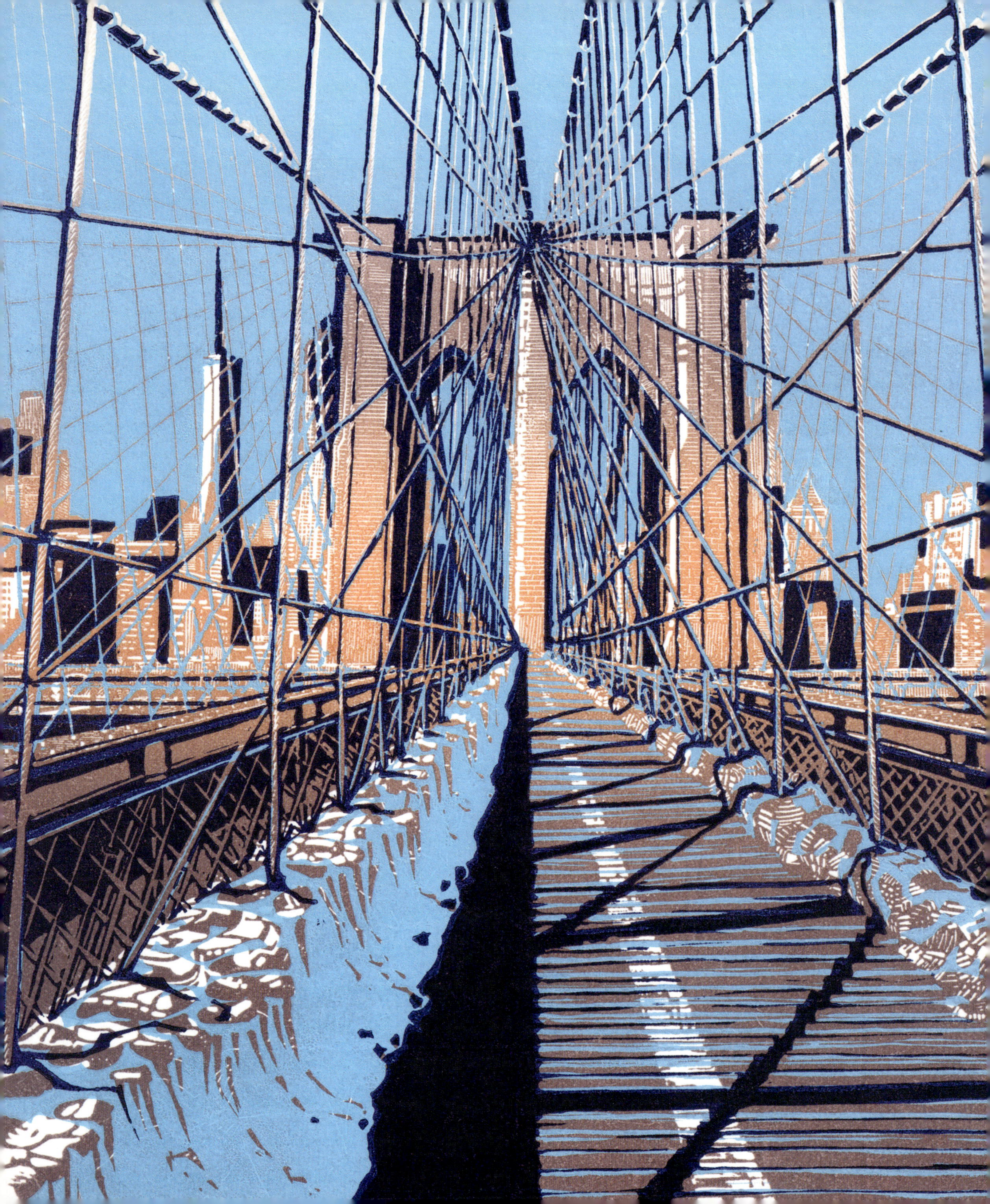

CHAPTER 7

COLOUR PRINTING AND MAKE-READY

Although, traditionally, wood engravings (especially in commercial usage as book or newspaper illustrations) have tended to be printed in black ink on white papers, and although they are exceptionally well-suited for printing in black because of the incredible tonal range possible in the engraving, there is no reason not to use colour, which can work wonderfully well in wood engravings.

COLOUR BLENDS

For a blend to run from left to right in your print, choose a roller a bit wider than the width of your block. For a top to bottom blend, the roller must be a bit wider than your block's full length.

1. On the ink slab, place a small blob of one colour. Then, at about the roller's width away, place a blob of another colour. (Use colours directly from the tubes or create your own by mixing different hues together.)
2. With a clean palette knife for each colour, drag each ink blob in a smear towards the other until they meet in the middle.
3. Roll the ink to the same stiff yet thin consistency described earlier, but be careful only to roll from one direction. (If you turn the roller and roll from a different direction, the blend will instantly disappear.)
4. When fully rolled, you will have a two-colour blend on slab and roller.
5. Roll this onto the block, again rolling only in one direction so as to maintain the blend across the block.
6. Print by press or by hand by the methods already described.
7. For a multicoloured or rainbow blend on one image, place as many small blobs of different hues as you want, on the slab, and roll them as already described. You can include extender with the ink blobs if you want highly translucent or transparent colours.

Brooklyn Bridge: Afternoon (2015), detail of an engraving on lemonwood printed in a brown colour blend, with two linocut blocks printed in opaque blue and purple, press-printed on Gampi Vellum paper.

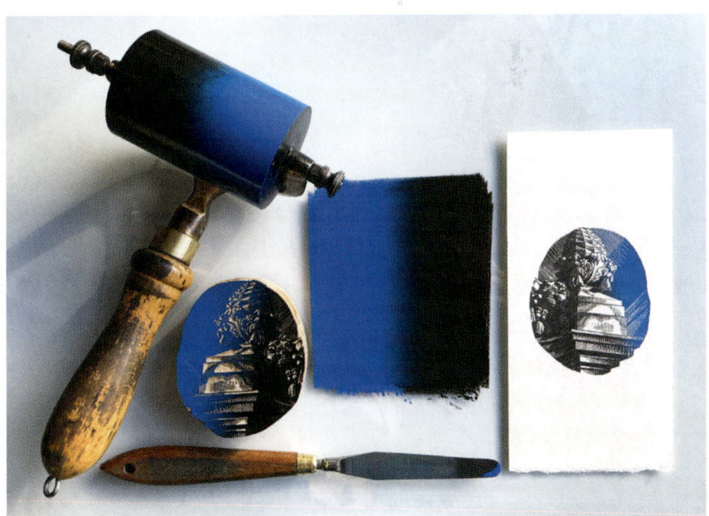

Pineapple (2016), engraving on boxwood, 8 × 6.4cm (3¼ × 2½in), on Gampi Vellum paper. For this image, I wanted the two-colour blend to run left to right (so my roller needed to be wider than the block's width). I rolled in only one direction (from bottom to top of this block) for each print.

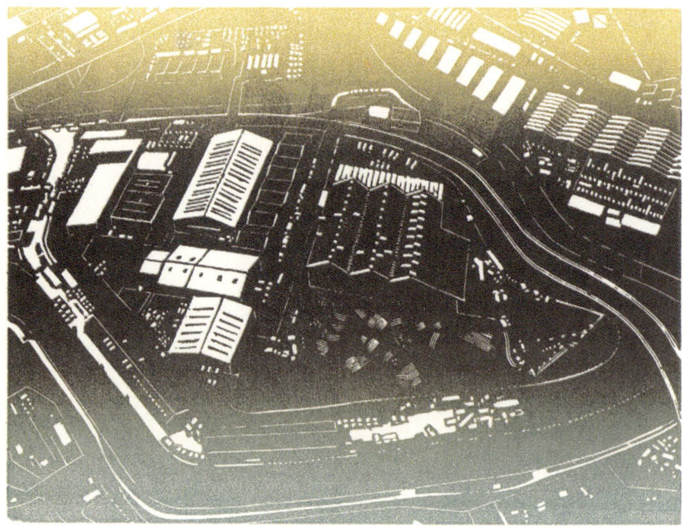

Hackney Olympic Site I (2009), engraving on boxwood, 10 × 13cm (4 × 5in), on Gampi Vellum paper. This has a three-colour blend running top to bottom. It involved rolling out small blobs of mustard-yellow (with extender), black and extended grey-blue inks to create a blend, and inking the block left to right.

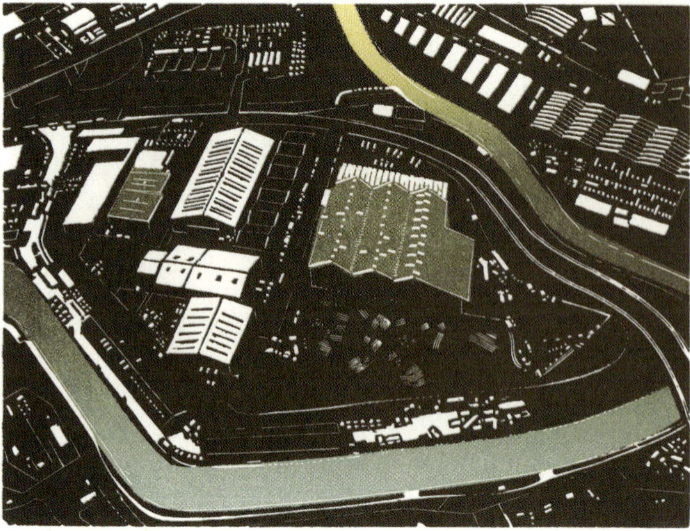

Hackney Olympic Site II (2009). First printed with a colour blend, I then masked out rivers and rooftops with paper stencils. I inked the block in black, laid stencils in place and press-printed it in precise alignment over the previous printing. The stencil-masked parts are the only areas where the underlying colour blend shows through.

COLOUR LAYERS

There are many other ways of using colour in an engraving. One is reduction cutting on a single block (described in the next chapter). Another is cutting multiple blocks, each of which is printed, one after another, in perfect registration on the same sheet to build up a single multicoloured image.

Different registration systems suit different artists, but you will need one if printing multi-layered prints. My own method is very basic and, even for images in multiple layers, usually involves a paper template for positioning the first block, then placing each successive block, very carefully by eye, face down onto the earlier printing(s) and press-printing them this way around. It's simple and effective, but needs a high degree of accuracy and steadiness of hand to place the block perfectly each time. For effective colour-layer printing:

1. Some papers take a single colour print beautifully, but are less good for multiple layers so test out layered printings on sample papers to see which best suits your needs.
2. If printing wood engravings in multiple layers, print on dry rather than dampened paper as damp paper drying between printings will adversely affect registration of each layer because paper can expand or contract as it dries.
3. Print tests to ensure you're happy with your chosen colours and their opacity or transparency before printing an edition.
4. Keep each layer's inking as thin as possible, as thicker ink layers will interfere with the paper's capacity to receive subsequent ink layers effectively.
5. After printing each layer, offset it onto blotting paper (either by spoon- or baren-burnishing or press-printing) to remove excess ink. This will keep the paper as receptive as possible to subsequent ink layers.
6. Leave at least a day between printing each layer to allow it to dry thoroughly. If you print directly onto a still-wet layer, you may get muddy-looking results.

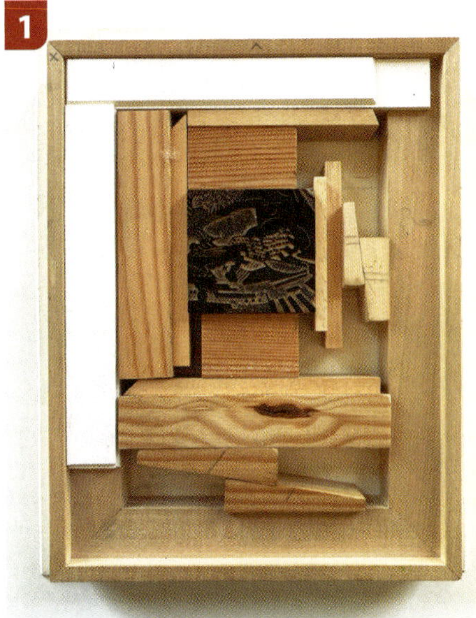

One of Roy Willingham's registration systems involving pieces of wood collated within an outer frame. The four roughly triangular-shaped wooden pegs can easily be moved to release the block for inking. They slot in place to lock the block in exactly the same position for each press-printing.

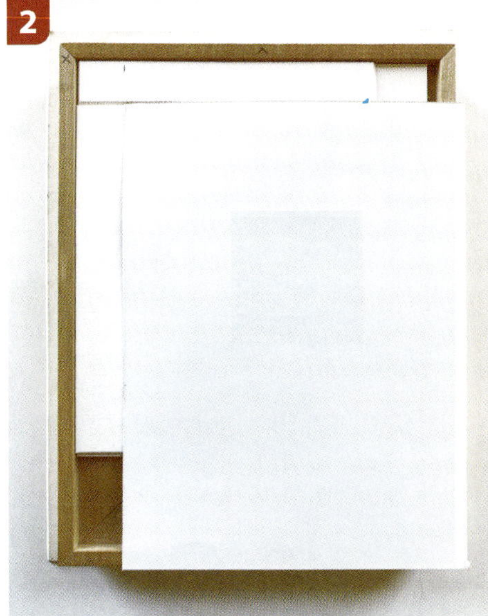

Two strips of mount-card provide a rigid L-shaped corner in which to slot the printing paper for perfect registration each time.

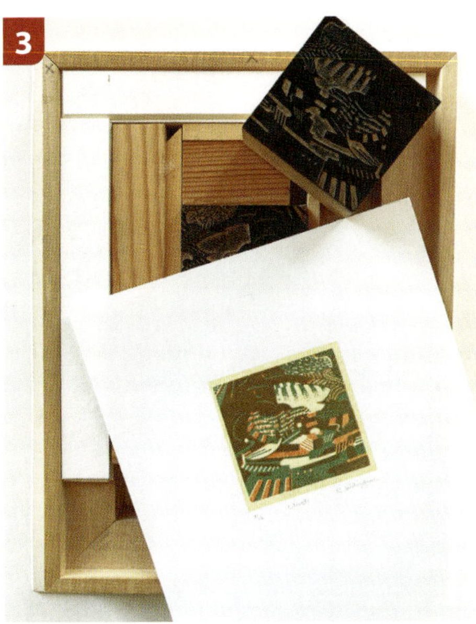

Multi-colour prints by Roy Willingham often involve multiple linocut layers. This one: *Uliveti* (1990–2018), 5.1 × 5.1cm (2 × 2in), on Zerkall paper, involved just three boxwood blocks: one uncut to print the cream tone, the other two engraved and printed in extended colours.

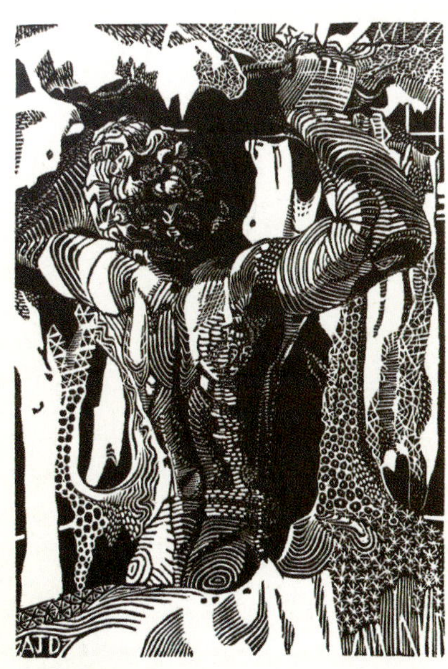

Icy Triton (1986), engraving on maple, 15 × 10cm (6 × 4in), on Basingwerk Parchment paper. This is one of my earliest engravings press-printed in a single colour.

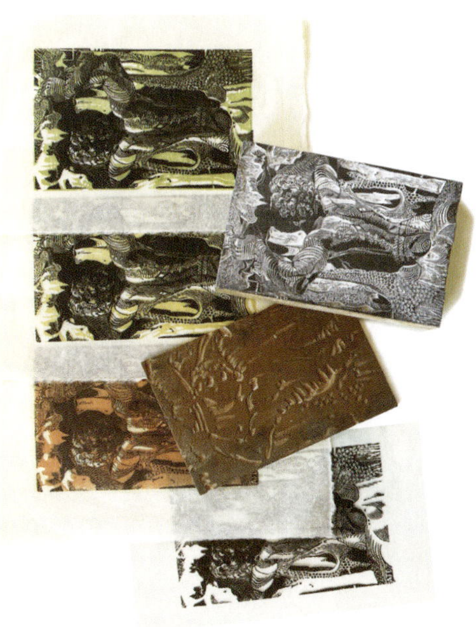

In 2015 I printed the woodblock on acetate and, while the ink was wet, offset-printed it onto a lino block of exactly the same size. This print served as a guide for cutting the lino to make a two-colour version of *Icy Triton*. Shown here are colour proofs on Kozu-shi, which takes colour layers beautifully.

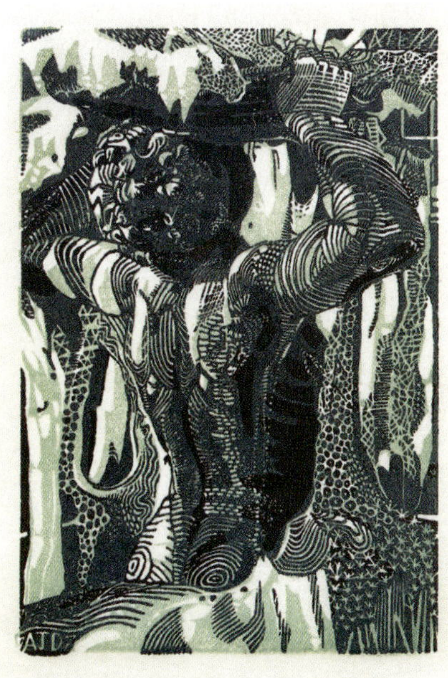

Frozen Fountain (2015), engraving on maple, 15 × 10cm (6 × 4in), printed with lino block on Kozu-shi. This involved press-printing the woodblock in black and the lino block on top in pale green with some opaque white in the mix, to create a blue-grey tone where it overprints the black.

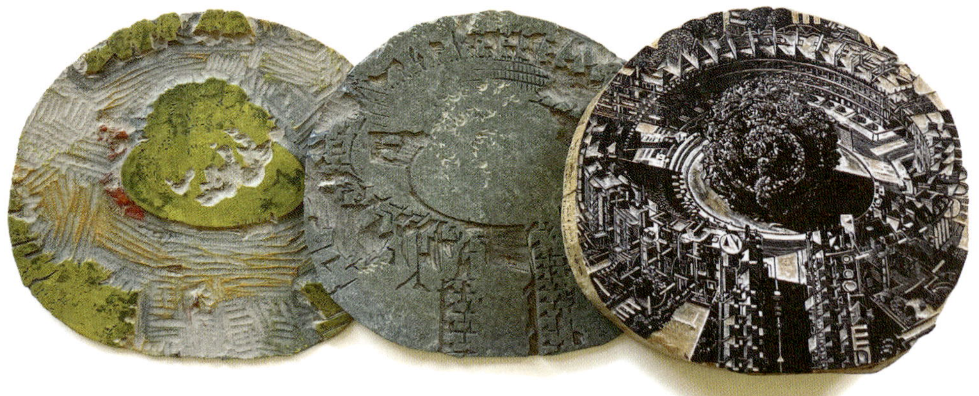

Having printed several monochrome editions from this boxwood roundel, 12 × 13cm (4¾ × 5in), I cut two lino blocks of exactly the same size to create a version in full colour.

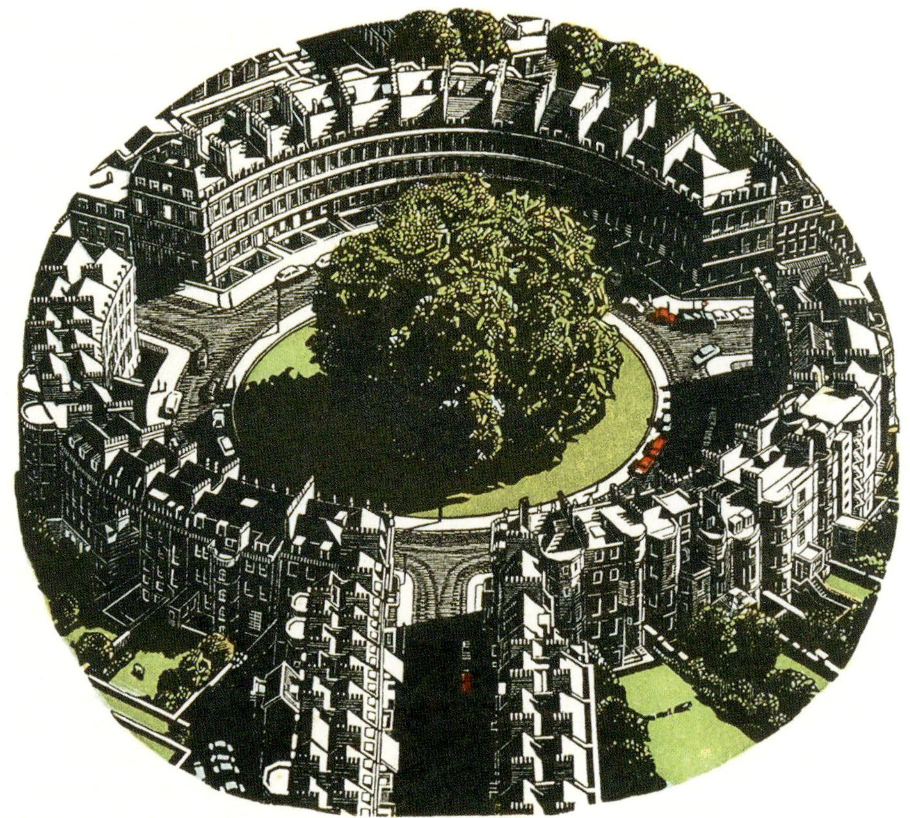

Bath Circus III (1998), wood engraving with two lino blocks, on Gampi Vellum paper. This involved first press-printing the woodblock for the black parts, then the lino blocks inked with extremely extended ink were printed, one after the other, in pale blue and yellow/green, with localised red dots applied to one of them with a cotton bud.

7. When printing colour layers, I like a lot of translucency to make them look like delicate watercolour washes. I like the fact that, with semi-transparent colours, tertiary hues appear where two colours collide. The inks, straight from the tubes, are very intense, opaque hues so, to make them more transparent, as well as mixing different colours of my choice, I mix them with oil-based extender (aka reducing medium). I often use only a tiny dot of colour to a bean-sized blob of extender but, if you prefer more intense, opaque colours, you will need a different ratio of ink to extender or you may not need extender at all. It's best to use the same brand of extender as the ink you're using. Sometimes, different brands don't mix well together.

8. It's often easiest to start printing in a pale tone before adding subsequent layers in increasingly darker tones or colours, though you can achieve equally great results working dark to light.

9. If working dark to light and you want paler colours to show up on top of darker ones, use little or no extender for the paler layers to retain the ink's opacity.

10. If working dark to light and you want paler colours to read like watercolour washes on top of a darker image, use plenty of extender in each colour layer to render them more transparent and thus virtually invisible printed directly over black or other dark tones.

MAKE-READY

Make-ready is a term for thin sheets of paper torn or cut and applied either to the back of the block or to a template on a tympan of the press in order to get the best possible impressions from the block. This can be really useful if particular parts of the block are printing less satisfactorily than others or if you want to exaggerate different tones in localised areas of the print. If printing a reduction-cut block, be aware that, if make-ready is needed at any stage of cutting, you may need to change it after each subsequent cutting and printing, because the block's printing needs at each stage will certainly vary.

Underlay

1. If one side of the block prints noticeably lighter than the other, the block may not be level and you may need to build up the back of it, corresponding to its paler-printing edge, with three or four torn sheets of paper attached with the tiniest smear of glue-stick or taped around the block's edges.

2. Arrange the torn sheets in stepped tiers.

3. Use torn, not cut, sheets because impressions of cut paper edges, even when applied to the back of the block, can show through as faint lines in a print.

4. You may need to adjust these layers – adding more torn paper or taking some away – when you've taken another print and can assess how well or otherwise this paper layering, known as 'underlay', is working.

5. Unless the press has been maintained impeccably over generations of users, it may print a block's edges more heavily than the centre. Alternatively, a block that prints paler in the middle than at the sides may be due to the block itself dishing fractionally in the middle. (This problem tends only to affect larger blocks.) In either case, it can help to make half a dozen roughly torn thin paper circles, each slightly smaller than the last and the largest fitting within the block's outer margins, leaving a clearance between it and the block's edges of at least 3–4cm (1¼–1½in) all round. Stick these (using tiny smears of glue stick) one on top of the other, going from largest to smallest. Then, when you take each print, place that composite of concentric paper circles either directly underneath the block as underlay or use as overlay on top of the printing paper but below any packing papers. This is unsophisticated but can be highly effective. If using these circles as underlay, avoid using more than about four of them for fear of creating too much variation in pressure and cracking the block. If used as overlay, you can safely add a few more and their impact on the print may be more marked.

■ Torn pieces of thin paper attached in layers to the underside of a block. This block wasn't level so, without the underlay, the printing from the image side was consistently too pale along that top edge.

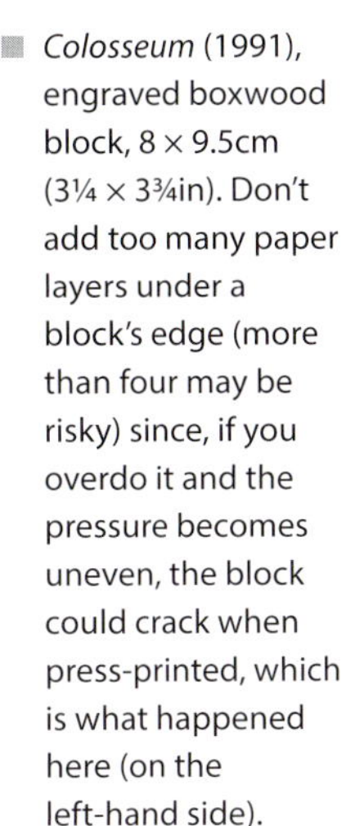

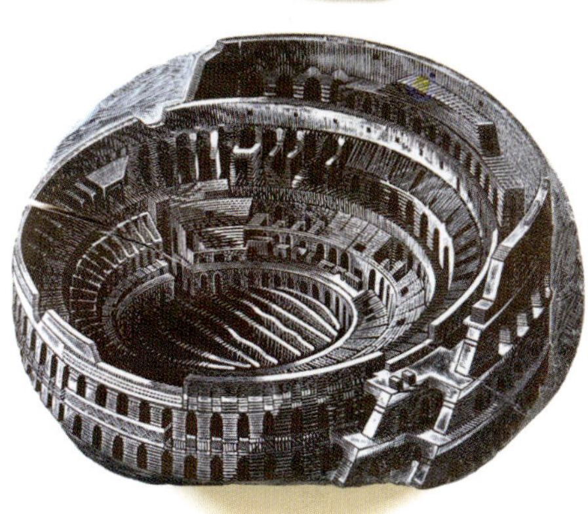

■ *Colosseum* (1991), engraved boxwood block, 8 × 9.5cm (3¼ × 3¾in). Don't add too many paper layers under a block's edge (more than four may be risky) since, if you overdo it and the pressure becomes uneven, the block could crack when press-printed, which is what happened here (on the left-hand side).

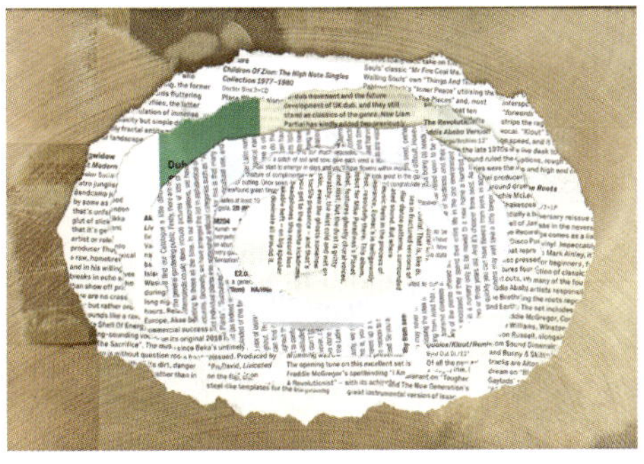

■ Make-ready torn paper composite (used as overlay or underlay) to correct a block that's printing too pale in the middle.

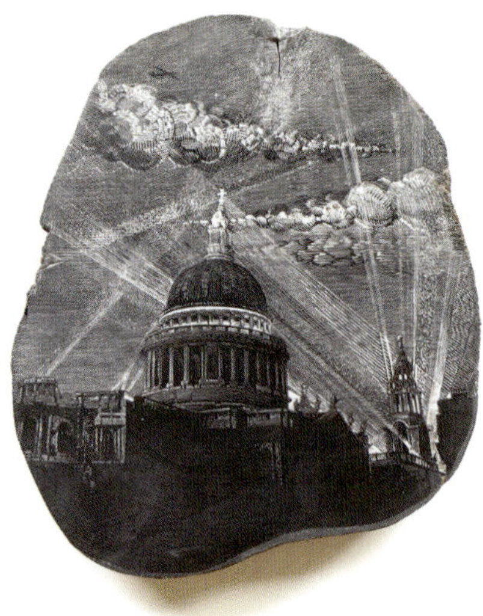

The engraved holly block, 22.5 × 17.3cm (8¾ × 6¾in), after press-printing the final image in a sequence of five reduction prints of St Paul's cathedral. The vertical crack near the top of the block occurred during its seasoning. I touched up all the prints in pen by hand to disguise it.

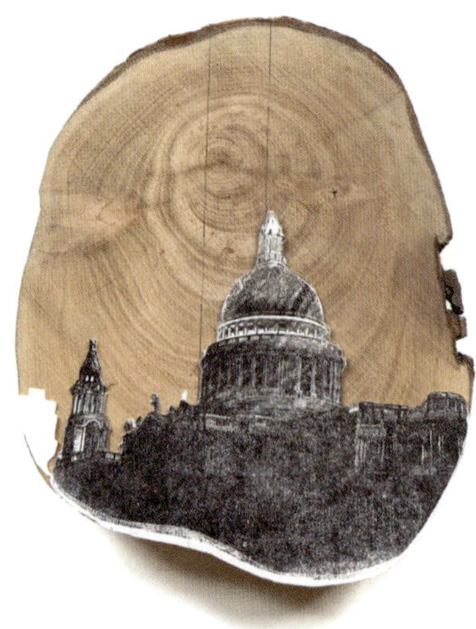

The reverse of the block with a detail from a proof attached as underlay to strengthen the intensity of printing of cathedral relative to sky.

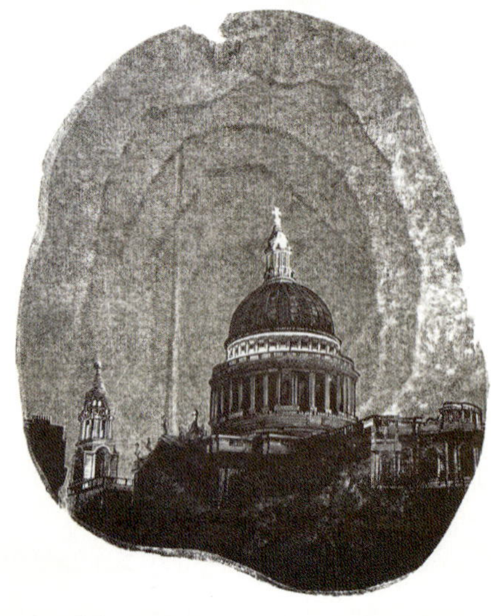

Initially, the block printed too pale in the middle. Torn paper circles, each smaller than the last, applied as an overlay, produced this result: the edges of each make-ready layer are visible in the print. After some adjustments and further proofs, these rings stopped printing and the block printed evenly.

Overlay

Overlay can have more precise effects on the tones in a block's printing and may replace some of the packing.

1. Print five good test prints (proofs) from the block on your preferred printing paper (if not too thick) or on newsprint and analyse them carefully to determine whether you're getting optimal results. Consider which areas of the image could be improved by being paler and which darker.
2. Create a rigid registration system – with an L-shape of thick card taped securely to the press bed (using double-sided sticky tape) – into which you slot the same corner of the block for each printing. Attach a sheet of clear acetate or tracing paper to the front tympan (the one which will lower directly onto the block and printing paper on the press bed), sticking the acetate to it along its bottom edge and both sides with masking tape.
3. Insert any packing papers behind the acetate using its one untaped top edge as a pouch.
4. Ink the block, lay it in position on the press bed, close the tympans (which will cause the block to make direct contact with the acetate) and print the block. After printing, slowly lift the tympans to separate the printed acetate from the block, taking care not to let acetate become detached from tympan in the process.
5. Using the first of the five earlier paper proofs as a base layer, cut up (or tear) specific pieces of the second proof that equate to the parts of the print that you would like to print darker. Attach those with tiny smears of glue stick to the base layer in precisely the right positions using the base-layer-print itself as a guide.
6. Cut all unprinted paper margins off the template to leave a precisely block-sized piece of make-ready and stick it, with glue stick, in perfect alignment, on top of the acetate printing already attached to the tympan, or leave a small paper margin on the template and stick it, with masking tape along its edges, behind the acetate but in perfect alignment with the acetate print.

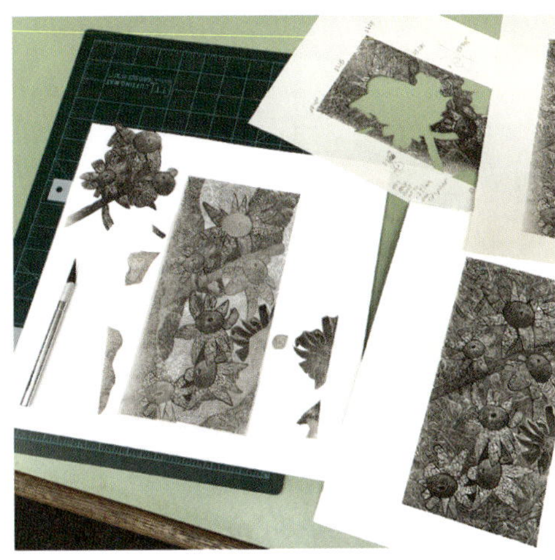

Wisconsin-based wood engraver Tony Drehfal scalpel cuts selected areas of his proofs to create often complex make-ready overlays to allow more printing pressure to be exerted on the few black areas of his intricately engraved maple blocks and less pressure in paler, more delicately cut parts.

7. Re-ink the block and place it exactly in its registration slot on the press bed as before. Print it on a fresh sheet of paper, using the make-ready now in place on the tympan. If the template is in front of the acetate, insert a sheet of thin paper or acetate between printing paper and make-ready to reduce the likelihood of edges of make-ready printing visible lines on your print.

8. Examine the new print. Tear or cut up parts of the third proof you printed earlier and add them to the template in specific areas that may still need to print darker.

9. Torn paper edges will give a softer printed effect. Cut ones will create sharper tonal distinctions.

10. Print the block again using the revised template and examine the results.

11. Keep adding to the template pieces from the fourth and fifth proofs as necessary to improve tonal variations, but probably using no more than four layers of overlay make-ready anywhere on the template, as more than this would risk creating excessively unequal pressure on the block and might cause it to crack.

12. This whole process might take half an hour or a day to get right and may involve additions or subtractions to the template along the way, but the results can make the effort well worthwhile. In my work, I tend to rely heavily on the marks I engrave to provide all the tonal range I want, or I use paper stencils (described later) to achieve stronger variations, but make-ready overlays, especially for getting best results from larger blocks, are definitely worth investigating and can make a vast difference to how a print looks.

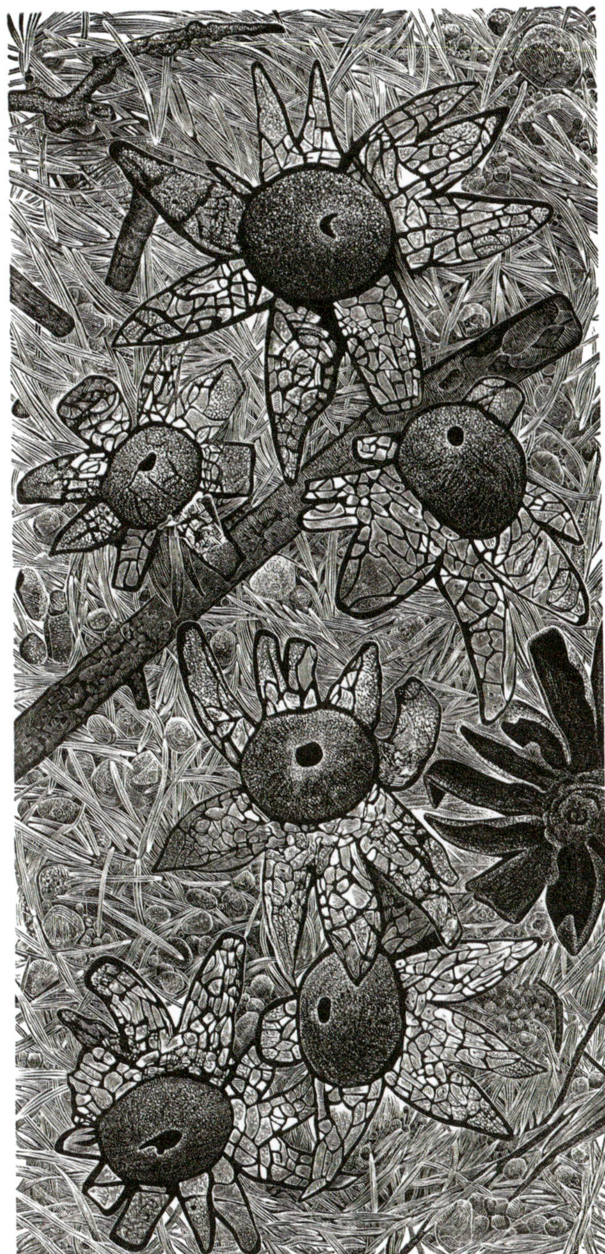

Barometer Earthstar Mushrooms (2023), engraving on maple, 24.4 × 11.4cm (9½ × 4½in), on Mohawk Superfine Smooth White paper by Tony Drehfal (b.1956). Printing with a complex make-ready overlay plus layers of underlay yields the optimal result from this block.

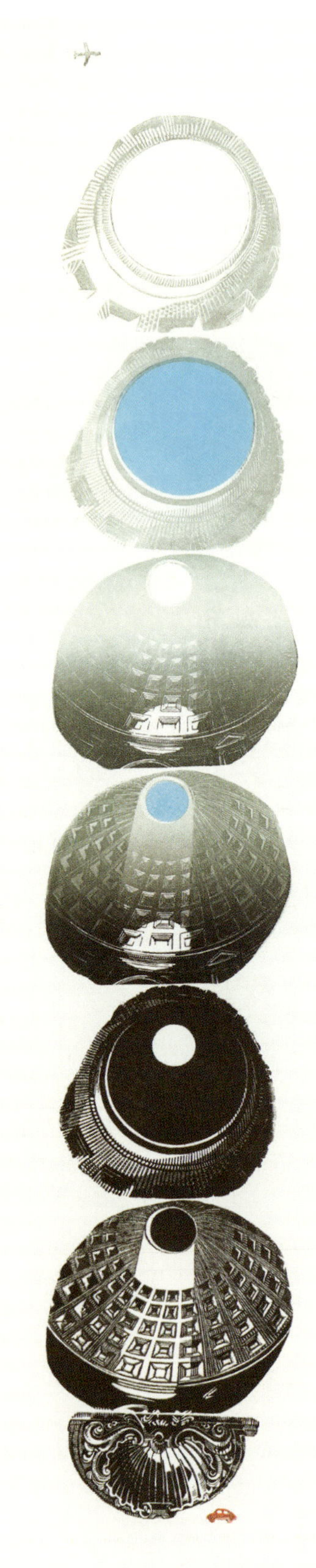

Lightwell (2021), total printed area: 54 × 8.5cm (21¼ × 3¼in), on Gampi Vellum paper. Inspired by the oculus of Rome's Pantheon, this was created from three boxwood blocks (two of which were printed using colour blends and stencils), and also a linocut block and two rubber eraser prints (car and aeroplane).

PRINTING PROBLEMS AND HOW TO FIX THEM

Pale patches

For under-printed, pale areas, check if those parts correspond with patches on the block where the ink still looks shiny. If so, then you missed those bits when hand-burnishing and should spend longer burnishing the next print more thoroughly. If the problem occurred when the block was press-printed, you may need to apply make-ready overlays or underlays to the block to persuade it to print more effectively.

Dust

If there are any tiny dots of ink surrounded by little white halos on the print, or other tiny dots or dashes that don't correspond to your engraved marks, you have probably got a speck or two of dust on the block. Carefully lift those off the block with your fingernail (or edge of a palette knife), re-ink and reprint it. Alternatively, many tiny white dots on a print can simply be an indication that the block was under-inked.

Correcting faults

If it's a good impression except for the odd glitch: a small white spot from a bit of grit on the block or roller perhaps, you can correct this straight after printing. Take a dressmaker's steel pin – and, using its rounded end, gently push a little of the print's wet ink from an area right next to the white spot to fill it in. If there isn't enough wet ink to completely fill the spot, use the pin to lift some more from the slab and smear on the tiniest amount to complete the repair.

Disguising errors

Alternatively, you can disguise any small white spots, lines or scratches directly on the print, without difficulty, if it has been printed in black. When it is dry (after about two days), take a good-quality, fine-line, drawing pen (one with water- and fade-proof ink). With great care, make tiny black dots in the problem areas. Avoid 'colouring in' more emphatically because this can damage and roughen the paper's surface and sometimes causes pen marks to end up looking darker than the printing ink, making your repair too visible. Keep an eye on the rest of the print while you're applying the dots and stop when the tone of the corrected part matches that of surrounding areas. Sometimes the pen mark looks a slightly different shade of black – more brownish perhaps, or it looks matt whereas printing ink may have a slight sheen. If either of these new problems occurs, take a not-quite sharp HB or B pencil and lightly stroke its tip over the corrected area. The pencil leaves a faint shiny mark simulating the printing ink's sheen and counteracts any tonal differences so your eye reads only one, consistent, shade of black.

Blurring

If the print shows a double image or blurriness in a single-layer print, either the paper slipped while you were hand printing or, if press printing, you laid paper on block but then it shifted slightly before printing. If hand printing, you may have burnished too vigorously, thus shifting the paper, or the ink may be too dry or too thinly rolled and is not gluing paper to block adequately during printing. The solution is to add a bit more ink to the slab, re-roll it and reprint on a fresh piece of paper.

If you get blurriness in a multi-layer print, your registration system may not be accurate enough or you may need to lay paper on block more carefully next time.

Over-inking

Often the first print from an end grain block prints paler than subsequent impressions. The second and subsequent prints will often look darker. Don't add more ink to the slab to roll for the second print as this risks over-inking the block. Just re-charge the roller and block from the ink already rolled.

Under-inking

If the printed impression looks pale but there isn't visible ink residue left on the block and it wasn't the first print pulled, the ink may be rolled too thinly and thus you don't have enough on the block or, if several prints have already been taken, there may not have been enough ink left on the slab or it may be drying out, so the block was under-inked. In either case, top up ink on slab with a small squeeze from the tube, roll it to the appropriate consistency, re-ink the block and reprint.

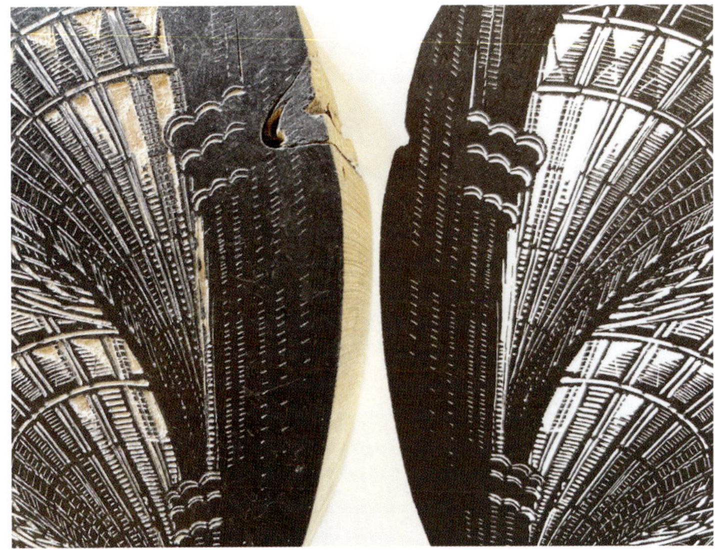

Detail of an engraving and its block in which a notable flaw is evident which prints as a white patch. On the print, I used a black fine-line drawing pen to fill in the problem area.

Adjusting pressure

Alternatively, a pale print that was press-printed may indicate that the block needs more pressure to print effectively. If so, add more packing paper as necessary, re-ink the block and reprint. Remember, too, that mount card and packing papers will get indented with each printing and, over the course of an edition, this can affect the pressure, so you may need to substitute fresh packing card or add an extra sheet of packing paper from time to time if necessary.

Uneven printing

If one side of the block prints noticeably paler than the other, before adding any underlay, try reprinting it, still in the middle of the press bed, but turned around so that the top edge of its image area is in line with a different side of the press bed. One alignment may print better than others. However, if the same area still prints pale, you will know the problem lies with the block and can proceed to build up the shallower edge with underlay. If, having changed the block's orientation on the press bed, a different part prints paler, then the problem may be with press rather than block. In that case, check and replace any packing materials that may have become indented from previous printings and may be adversely affecting the printing.

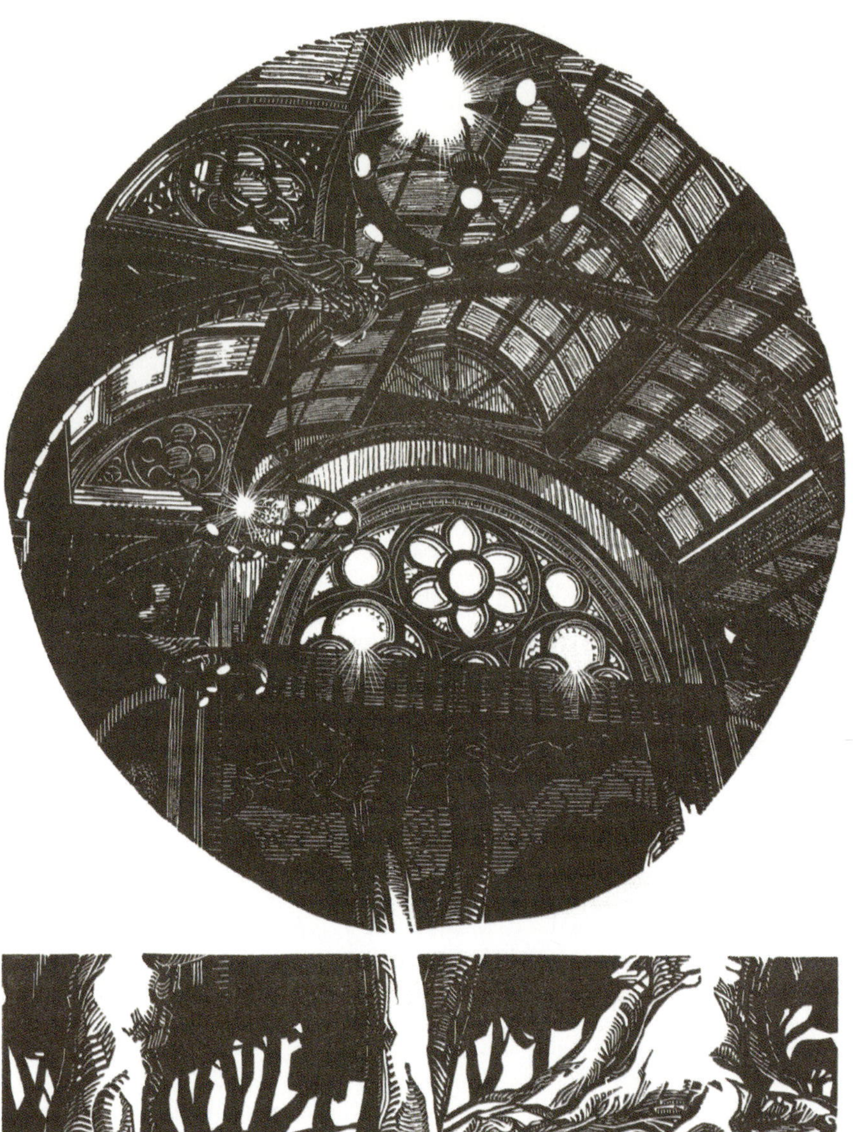

■ *Living History* (2019), engraving on two boxwood blocks, total printed area: 16.5 × 13cm (6½ × 5in), press-printed on Zerkall paper. Commissioned by Dulwich College, London, to mark its 400th anniversary.

Ink build-up

Sometimes a build-up of ink along a block's edges impairs the print. To avoid this, try not to let the roller slip off the block's edges while you're inking it, but lift it off at the end of each pass. If the build-up still occurs, take a clean rag and gently wipe along each inked edge from time to time to remove that residue. If you're not holding the block in your hand but have it on a clean flat surface for inking, try putting two woodblocks (each a bit longer than, and the same height as, your block), one on either side of it, as you roll it with ink. Assuming the roller's length is wider than the block's shortest edge, these two blocks will act as roller bearers, making it less likely to dump excess ink along the edges.

Uneven inking

If you get patchily printed areas or dark lines, you probably didn't ink the block consistently or you caught the roller's edges on the block, dumping more ink in those areas than intended. To solve both problems, re-ink it, taking care that the block looks evenly rolled before you print it.

Muddy details

If the engraving's fine details look muddy or have filled in, you may have over-inked the block or printed with too much pressure, forcing ink into the engraved marks. If press-printing, try printing a few impressions onto newspaper, without re-inking between printings. This will lift off all or most of the excess ink. If hand-printing (or if the press-printing hasn't totally cleaned the block), wipe the block's surface clean with dry newspaper, cotton rag or paper roll. Then take a small blob of Blu-tack and press it all over the block's surface, right into the engraved marks. When you lift it up, any excess ink will have attached itself to the putty, the block will be clean and you can then re-ink it and carry on printing, adjusting the amount of ink or the pressure, if necessary.

Heat and humidity

The day's temperature and humidity or your home/studio's central heating will affect the ink, which will dry up faster on some days than others. In hot weather, ink can be runnier and prone to filling in engraved details. Some papers take better or worse prints depending on the day's temperature and humidity. I always print on dry paper and choose papers that print good dense blacks (or other colours), while also printing every finely engraved detail. Some papers print particular images better than others depending on the size, nature and complexity of the engraving and the ratio of uncut to cut parts, so try out different papers if you aren't getting good results from the one you've selected, or else halt printing and try again on another day in different weather conditions.

Damp paper

Many engravers prefer printing on damp paper. I don't, because damp paper may dry with cockling and then needs pressing flat – an extra step I find annoying! But those who print damp invariably assert it can give a richer denser tone in uncut parts of the block – especially for larger blocks – while printing fine cutting very well too. But the paper's degree of dampness is significant and should be restrained: a fine mist of water sprayed in the air above one sheet at a time should be ample – or use steam from a hot kettle. Then pack up all the dampened sheets straight away in polythene/plastic wrapping, weigh the package down to avoid cockling, and print the paper within a day or so of misting.

Re-engraving

If fine marks still won't print cleanly, your cutting may not be quite deep enough. If you suspect this, clean the block and, with the greatest care, re-engrave the problem lines and dots, cutting slightly more emphatically to deepen their marks. Rub a little talcum powder into the cuts as you go to help you to see the engraving more clearly since, however carefully you clean the block, there will be some ink staining after printing so newly engraved marks may look too bright relative to older ones. Remember to brush the talc off before you reprint.

Nipping press

If using a nipping press, get a metal plate cut to the size of the press bed (an etching plate is ideal), which you can slide in and out of it. You can position block and printing paper (and packing papers) on this plate before sliding all of it into the press for printing. This is much easier than trying to position block and paper on the press's fixed and somewhat inaccessible bed.

Safety first

With a nipping press, though it may be quite small, it's probably made of cast iron and immensely heavy. Turning its screw handle for full pressure can cause the entire press to rotate, which could be extremely hazardous as it could fall off a table. To avoid that, before using it, buy some sturdy G-clamps to attach to the front edge of the table to hold the press firmly in place.

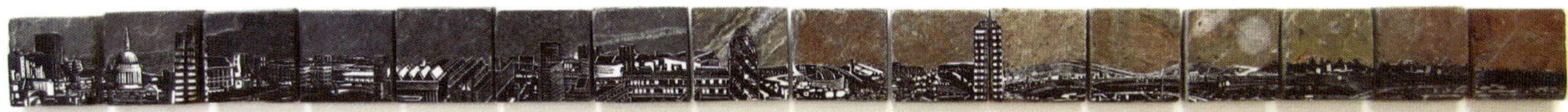

■ *Sense of London* (2012), wood engraved prints on paper collaged on 16 ceramic mosaic tiles, 2.5 × 42 × 0.5cm (1 × 16½ × ¼in).

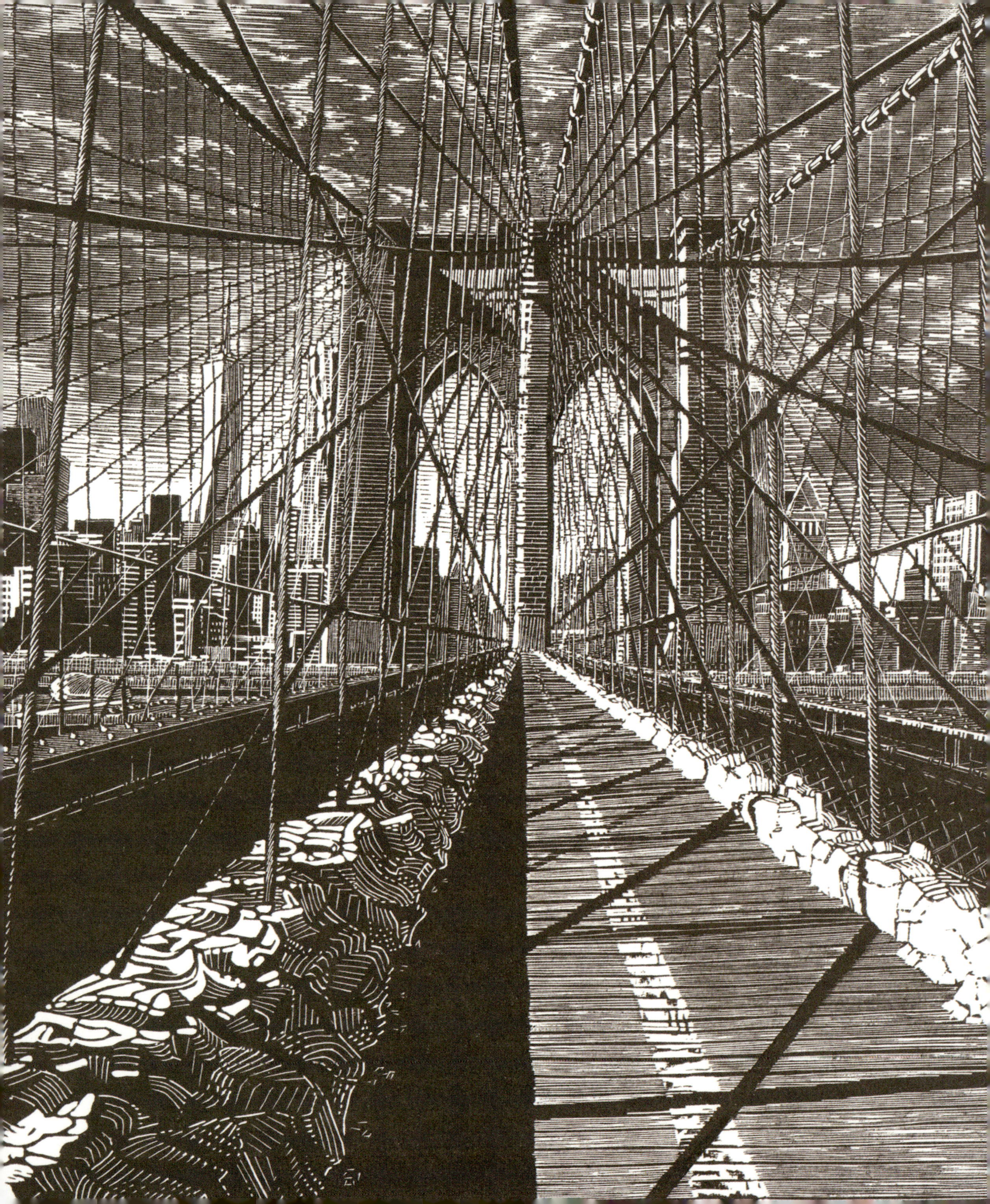

CHAPTER 8

ONE BLOCK, MULTIPLE POSSIBILITIES

An unusually shaped block may inspire an image more readily than a standard rectangle. For me, the question *why* I am making an engraving is just as important as *how* I am making it. I have long been interested in ideas of gradual change, transformation and metamorphosis: images which suggest time passing and hint at humankind's successes, failures, triumphs and tragedies along the way. I'm not a speedy engraver, so the weeks and sometimes months that a complex engraving might take seem to make it a very suitable medium for contemplating the slow passage of time. But there are, of course, many and varied reasons why anyone might be drawn to this glorious medium.

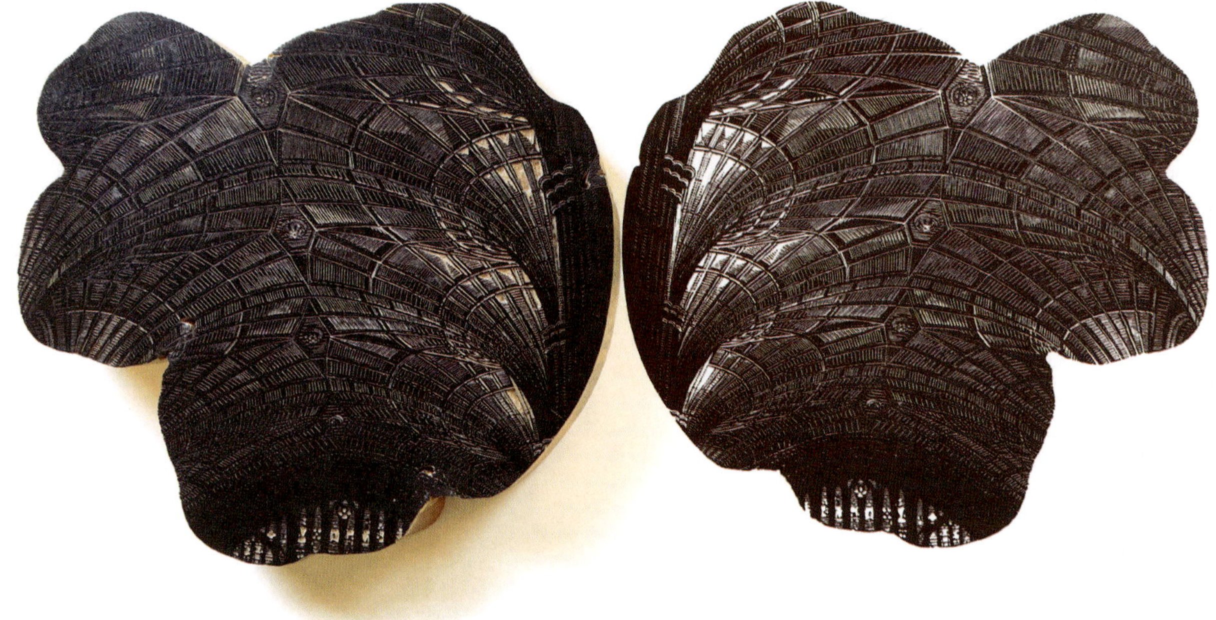

Fan Vault (2016), engraving on boxwood, 16 × 16.7cm (6¼ × 6½in), on Japanese paper. As artist-in-residence at Eton College (2016), I worked on several odd-shaped blocks including this one, which I used to depict the school's chapel. Using such unusual roundels facilitated, for me, a heightened focus on how the compositions might meld to best effect within each odd shape.

Brooklyn Bridge: New Day (2015), detail of an engraving on lemonwood on Zerkall paper. This is one of a series of seven different editions all produced from the same block at different stages of its engraving and, in some cases, with the addition of various linocut blocks and stencils.

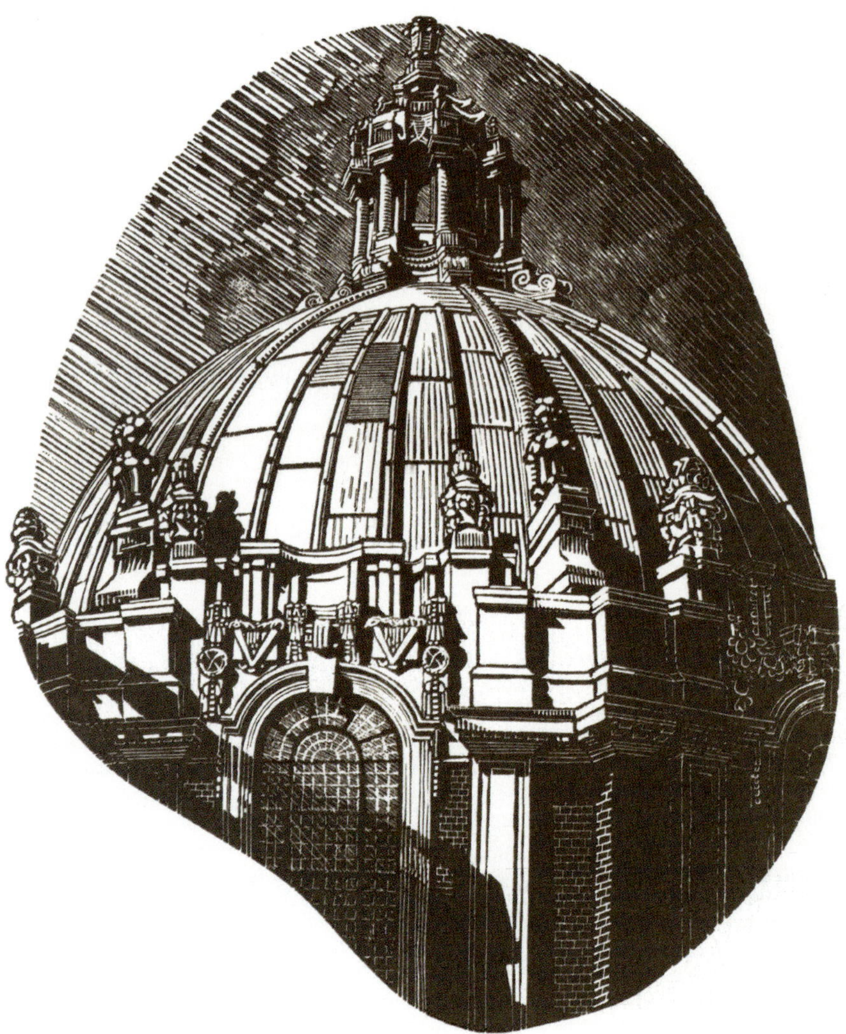

Library Dome (2016), engraving on boxwood, 14 × 11.5cm (5½ × 4½in), on Japanese paper. Another Eton view, its appearance on an odd-shaped roundel suggests a fragment of something larger and, like salvaged fresco fragments, might hint at a literal or metaphorical 'bigger picture'.

STENCIL EFFECTS

Paper stencils can radically change how a wood engraving looks. They can be made easily on tracing paper (or glassine, which is slightly thinner), tracing the desired outlines directly from print or block. They can be used to mask out parts of the image by placing them directly on the inked block prior to printing. They can also be used to lift off a layer of wet ink in selected parts of an inked block, enabling more dramatic tonal shifts than would be possible without them – though, for this purpose, you need a fresh stencil for each printing because it quickly becomes too clogged with ink to be reuseable.

When used directly on an inked block and where a stencil meets any of the block's edges, leave a little extra stencil extending beyond the block's margins to enable you easily to peel it off the block after printing. Stencils can also be used to great effect to mask out and frame areas on the print itself, rather than on the block, enabling you to apply localised colour to selected parts of the print, by finger-printing or with a brush or small dabber in a technique known as *pochoir*. For this usage, one stencil can be used to print an entire edition.

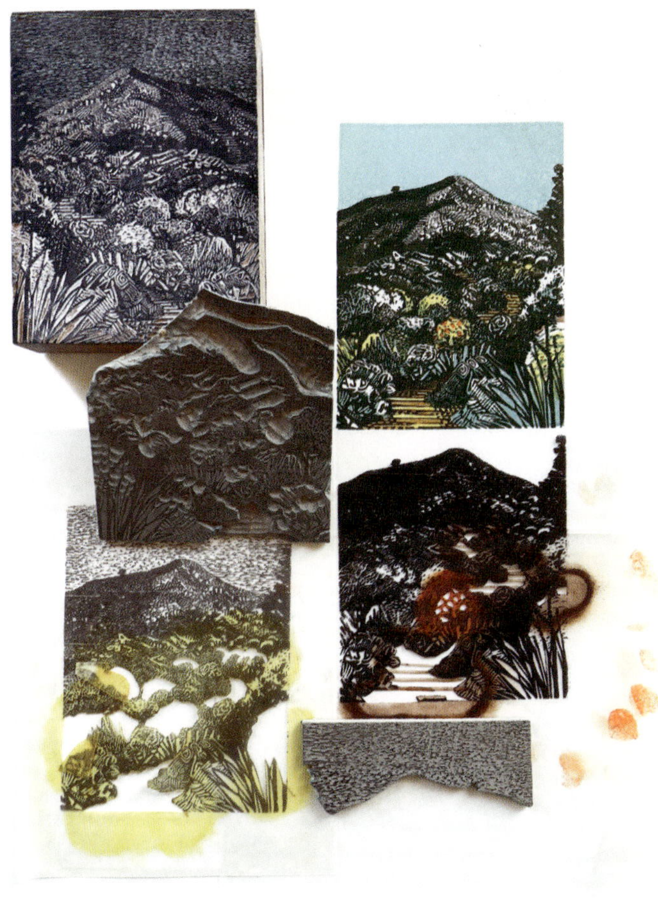

Pelagos Revisited (2019), engraving on maple, 10.1 × 7.5cm (4 × 3in), with linocut and stencils, on Zerkall paper. I press-printed the woodblock in green (with sky area masked out with a stencil), then press-printed both lino blocks to print the blue sky and darker green landscape. To finish, I finger-printed orange and yellow highlights through paper stencils.

A tracing paper stencil masks out three sides of this boxwood block. I hinged stencil to block along one edge, lifting it aside for inking and easing it back (where it stuck to the wet ink) for each press-printing. This saved time I would otherwise have had to spend cutting away substantial amounts of wood in these areas.

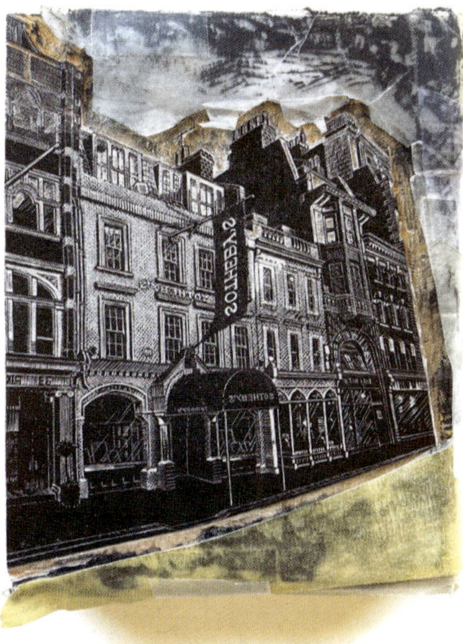

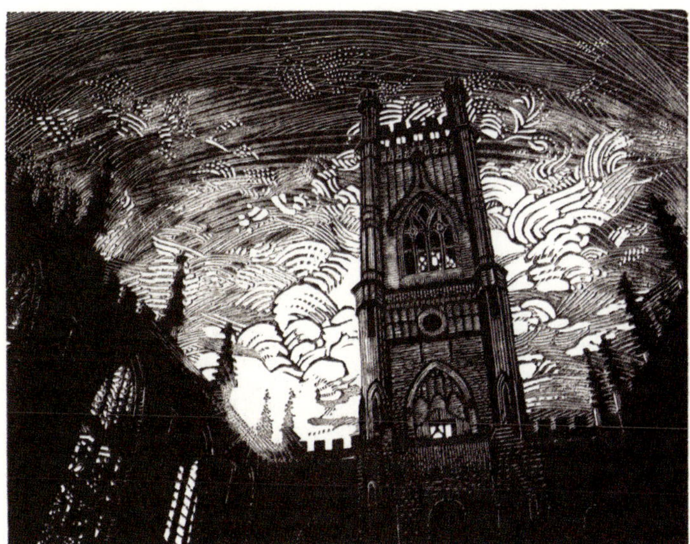

Bold Street – Black Sky (2014), engraving on pearwood, 10 × 12.3cm (4 × 4¾in), on Gampi Vellum paper, of St Luke's: Liverpool's 'bombed-out church'. Printed in black, it demonstrates a wide range of tool marks and some printing problems caused by the unusually soft block, which generated burrs during its engraving.

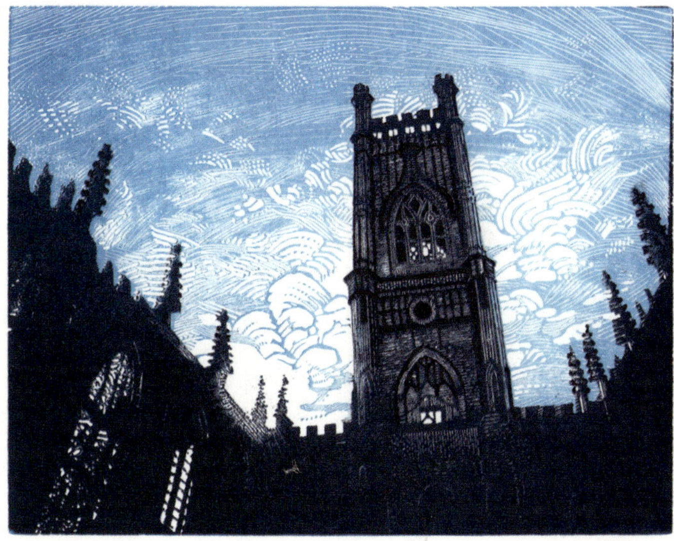

Bold Street – Blue Sky (2014). Here, I printed the block in blue. Then I re-inked the block in black, stuck a paper stencil on it to mask out the sky area (the ink acting like glue), placed the block face down onto the blue printing and press-printed it again, in perfect registration with the first printing to create a two-colour result.

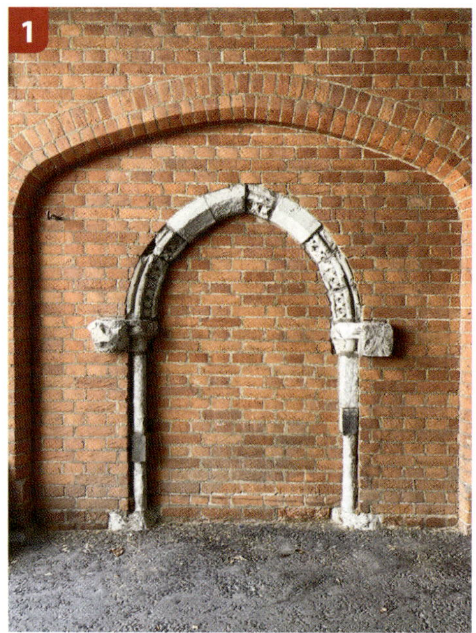

The oldest extant arch in London's Lincoln's Inn, this photo was the source material for two commissioned wood engravings.

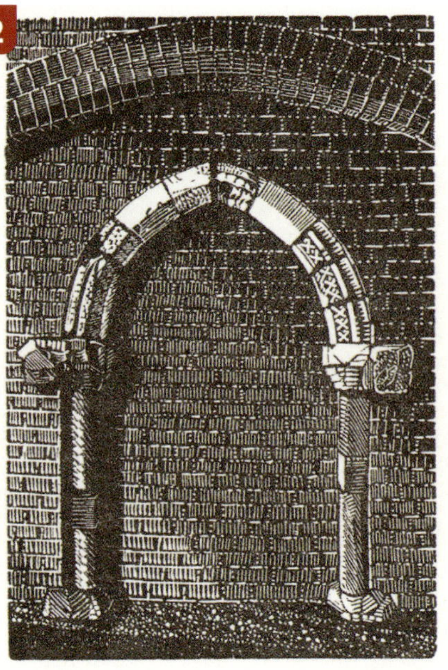

Old Hall (2022), engraving on boxwood, 7.7 × 5.1cm (3 × 2in), in black ink on Gampi Vellum paper. This was commissioned for London's Lincoln's Inn Law Chambers' 600th anniversary.

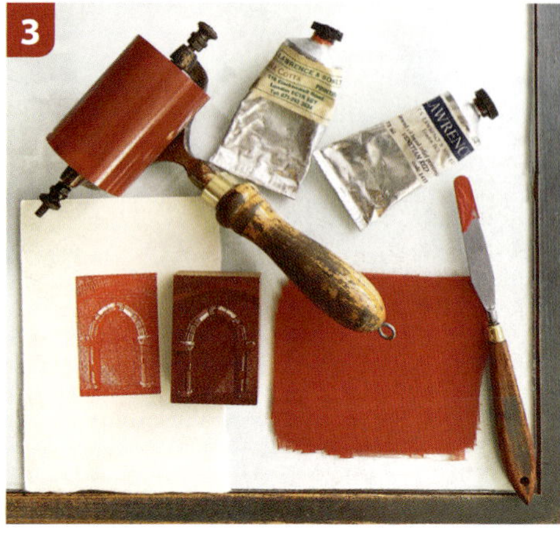

I inked and printed the same block in a red-brown mix of terra cotta and Venetian red inks.

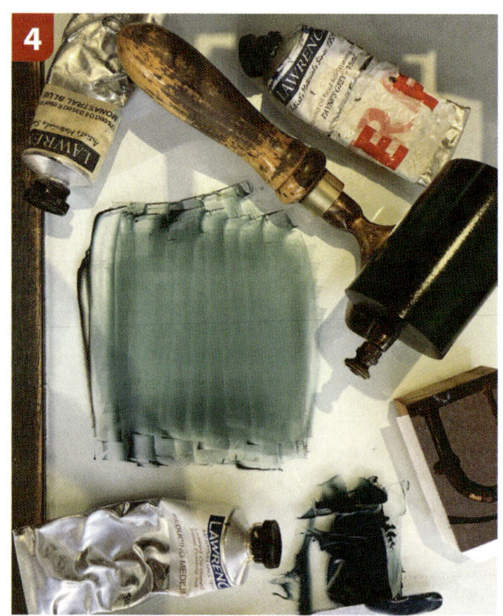

Then I re-inked the block in semi-transparent blue/grey ink involving a mix mostly of reducing medium (extender) and tiny amounts of Payne's grey and Monastral blue.

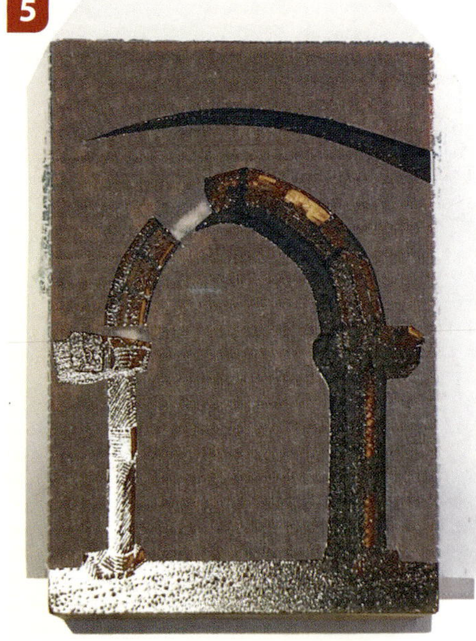

I applied a tracing paper stencil to the wet ink and press-printed it on top of the previous red-brown printing.

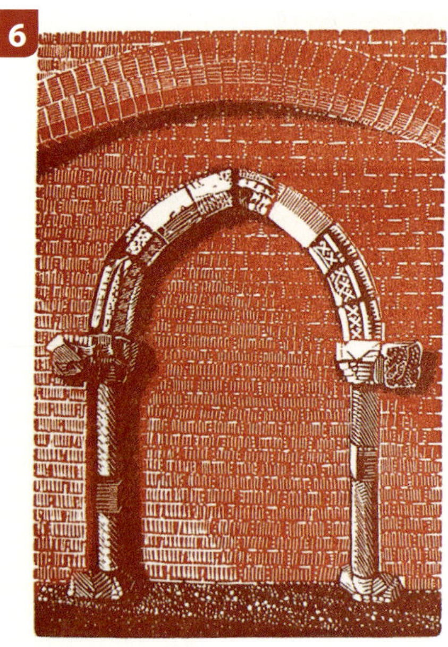

Medieval Arch, Lincoln's Inn (2022). The darker printed areas in the finished print represent the only parts of the block that weren't masked by the stencil.

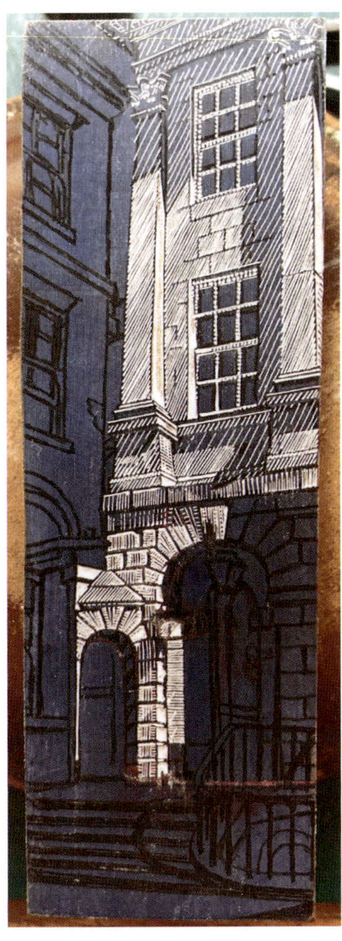

Boxwood block for *Stone Buildings* at an early stage of cutting.

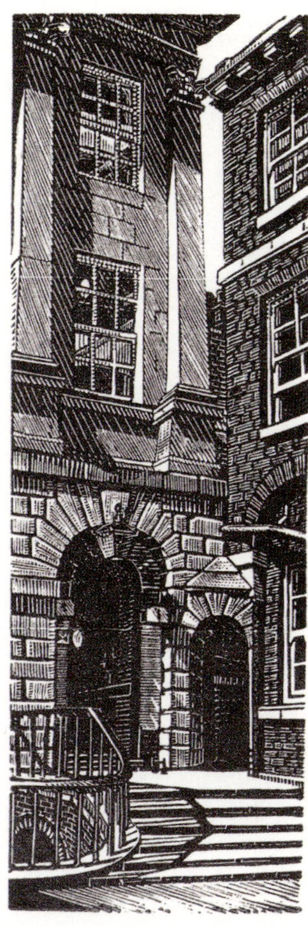

Stone Buildings (2022), engraving on boxwood, 11.5 × 3.8cm (4½ × 1½in), on Gampi Vellum paper. This small, commissioned monochrome engraving shows another detail of Lincoln's Inn.

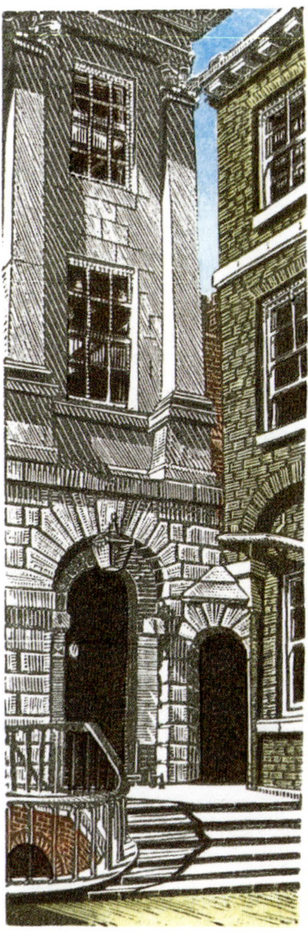

Legal London, Lincoln's Inn (2023). I printed the same block in grey, cut a stencil to frame the sky (on print, not block) which I finger-printed in blue. Through various other stencils I press- or finger-printed yellow and red-brown parts plus darker windows and doorways.

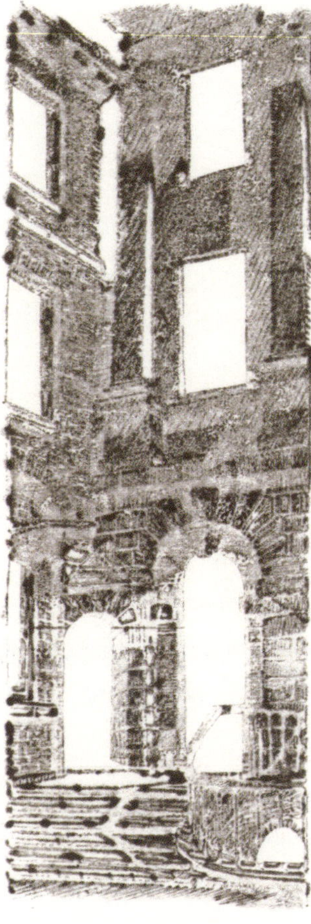

In Living Memory (2022), stencil print, 11.5 × 4cm (4½ × 1½in). To evoke a bombed-out ruin, I printed the stencil I had just used to mask out black parts of the *Legal London* print, spoon-printing it, still wet with ink, onto Gampi Vellum paper.

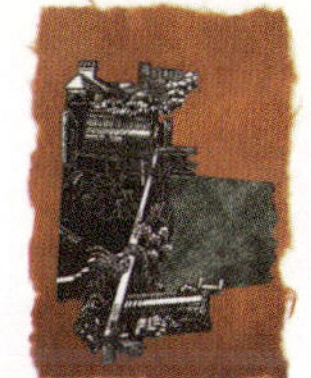
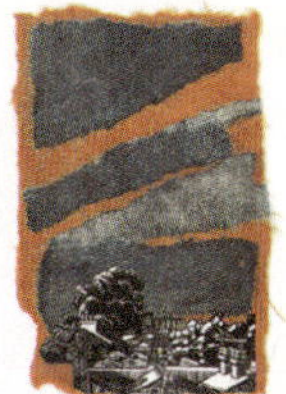
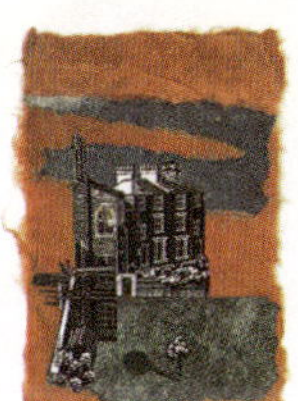
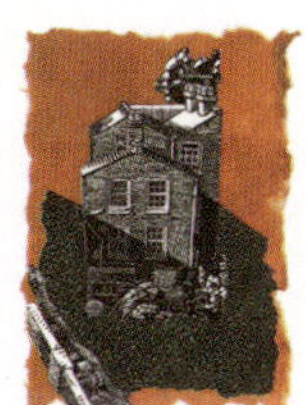
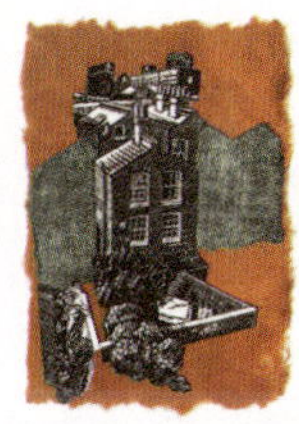
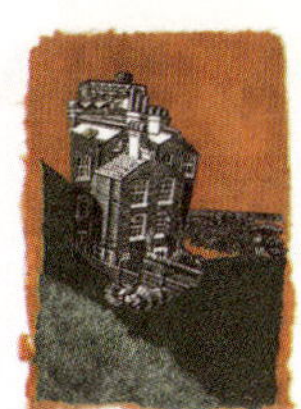
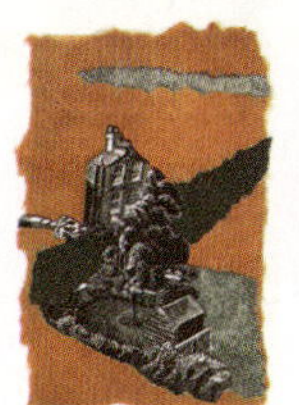
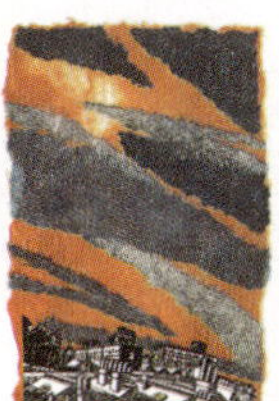
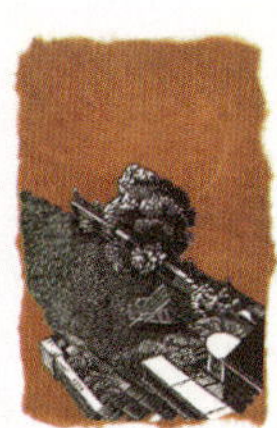

Hackney Vignettes (2003), pieces of one particular wood engraving (of a view across my London back garden to the houses beyond) collaged with colour-lino-printed paper and gold leaf on Nepalese paper, 7.6 × 73.7cm (3 × 29in).

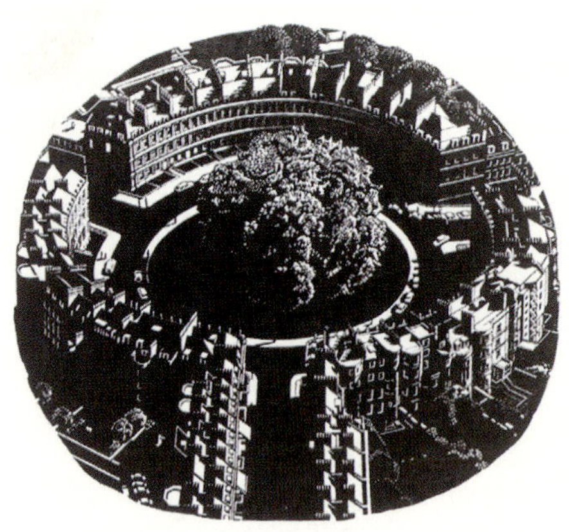

Bath Circus I (1997), engraving on boxwood, 12 × 13cm (4¾ × 5in), on Gampi Vellum paper. Here I had engraved only the brightest whites of the image.

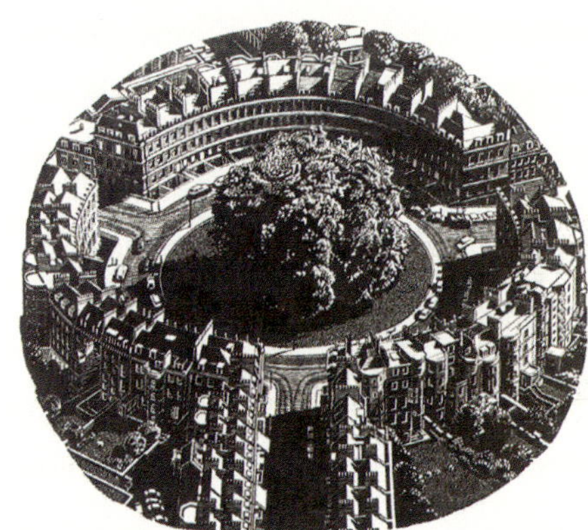

Bath Circus II (1997). In this next version, reduction-cut from the same block, I added a range of mid-tones to introduce extra light and more detail.

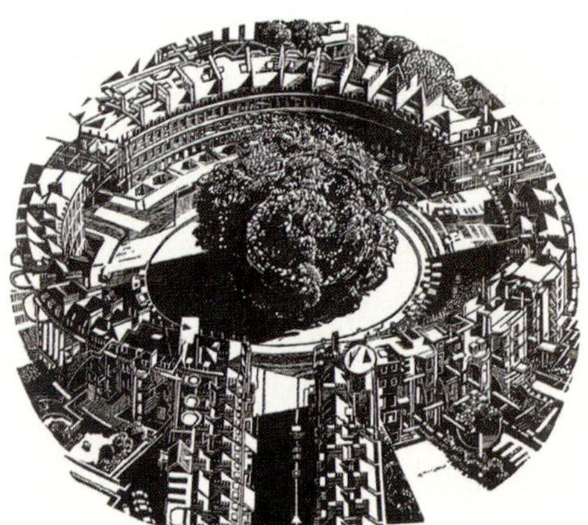

Bath Circus IV (2000). In this version, Roy Willingham engraved the same block further, taking my composition in a more abstract direction.

REDUCTION CUTTING

It's possible to generate different variant prints from one block at different stages of its engraving by a method known as reduction cutting: the process gradually reduces the uncut surface of the block as the image develops. Having cut away anything from the block's surface, you can't readily put it back, so ensure you print enough impressions at each stage to ensure that, should you cut away more than intended, you have good prints from earlier stages. Reduction cutting can be used to create sequences of gradually transforming images from one block, each stage of recutting and reprinting introducing more light and more detail into the image. The contrast between the first and final prints from a reduction block can be dramatic. If you were to continue the process to its ultimate conclusion over many cuttings and printings, there would be no uncut surface left on the block.

Reduction cut layers

Reduction cutting can also be used to make multiple layers on a single image. I use extender in my colours to make them print in semi-transparent layers. If printing layered reduction prints, be sure to print a reasonable number and perhaps in various tones and colours at each stage of the block's cutting because, once you've cut the block and overprinted with each subsequent colour, you can't return to reprint any earlier stages so, if you don't like the colours you chose, or if the colour or opacity of any layer doesn't gel harmoniously with the rest, or if you misprint a layer, there's no possibility of reprinting and your potential edition will dwindle. Also print a range of colour-variant options unless you're absolutely sure which colours and tones will best suit the image.

Reduction engravings with other interventions

While reduction cutting alone presents many possibilities for an image's development, it can also create logistical problems which may need inventive solutions. The aim behind a series of five reduction-cut engravings of mine was to present an idea of twelve hours in London during the World War Two blitz, starting at dusk one evening until dawn the next day. I decided I needed to cut the block for each printing in the same order as the intended image sequence, which solved some potential problems while

Towards the Light (2018), reduction engraving on pearwood, on Gampi Vellum paper, total image area: 58.4 × 12.6cm (23 × 5in). This sequence began with the darkest part in which only a few highlights were cut. Over three successively engraved stages, further light and detail were added.

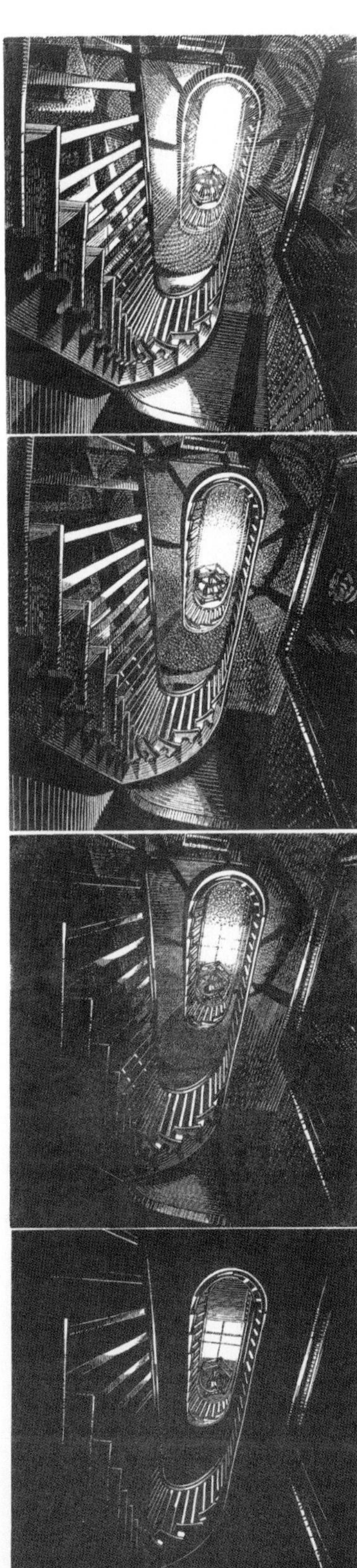

Further Towards the Light (2019) continued the cutting on the same block until, by the final print, there was little of the surface left uncut, and the image is flooded with light. The soft pearwood was helpful here, making cutting away large areas of wood relatively easy.

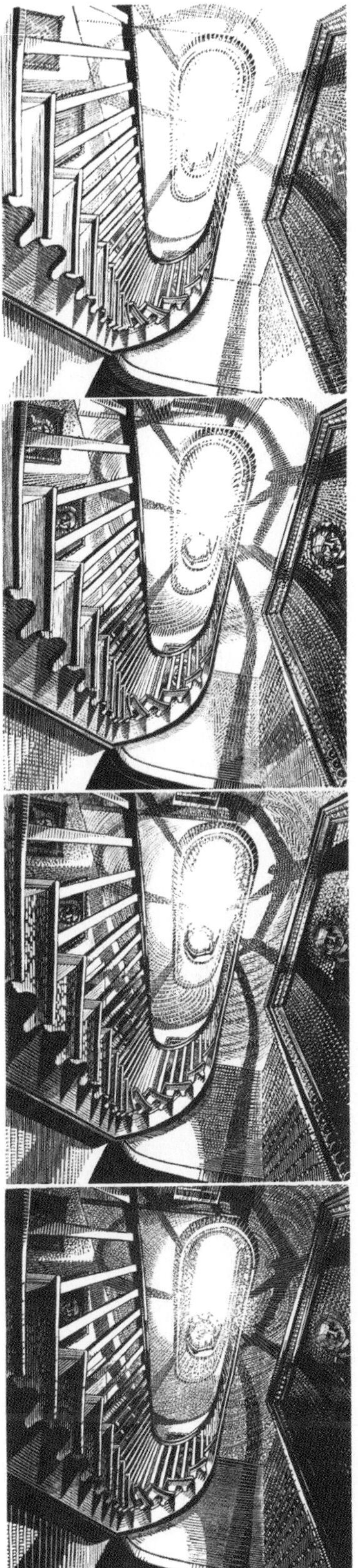

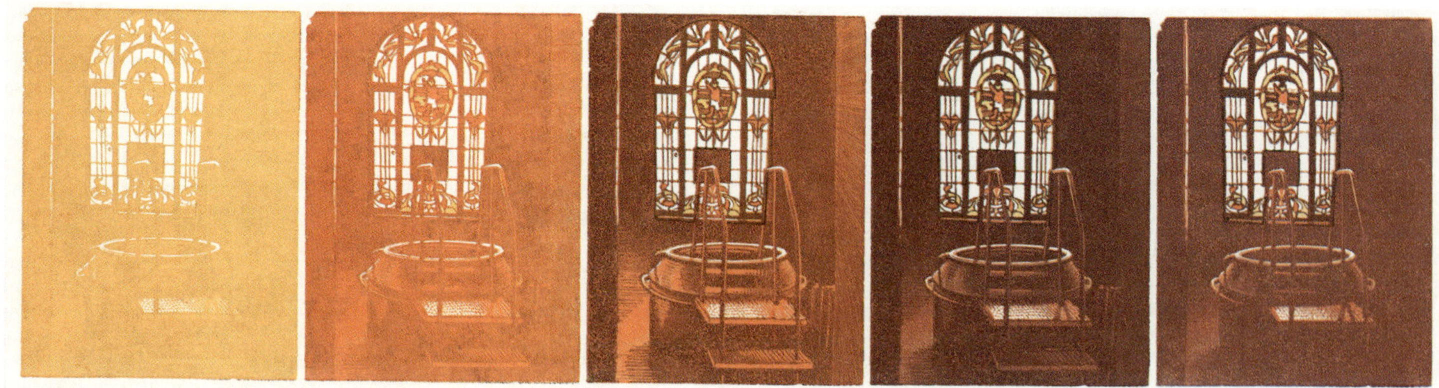

Shades of Memory (2007), reduction wood engraving from one lemonwood block, 10 × 7.5cm (4 × 3in), total printed area: 10.1 × 38.2cm (4 × 15in), on Gampi Vellum paper. In successive cuttings and printings, in which the yellow printing underlies the rest, I engraved the block before overprinting parts in orange, then cutting and overprinting successively in three shades of brown.

creating others. Had I, for instance, engraved tones to produce the grey sky of the first image, I couldn't have printed a black sky from the same block for later variants but, likewise, had I engraved stars or searchlights for a night sky straight away, I couldn't have removed them to print a calm, featureless, paler evening sky. Reduction cutting combined with stencils and some monotype drawing directly into the wet ink on the inked block provided creative solutions. Because, in this case, each stencil was designed to lift off some printing ink, causing the sky areas to print grey rather than black, I had to make a new, identical, stencil for each printing because wet ink on a stencil prevents it from effectively lifting ink off the freshly inked block in subsequent printings.

The marks you make on any block can be many and varied and can create highly varied tonal illusions, as well as indulging a pure love of pattern. When you've been engraving for years, it's easy to start repeating marks – be it a particular way of arranging stippled dots or closely spaced lines – rather automatically, on each block, once you've found a particular set of marks that works for you. This isn't necessarily a fault and is what some engravers prize as their signature 'style'. However, it can make the prints look rather repetitive, even if they are varied in subject matter. There is no right or wrong approach but it is certainly vital to keep yourself interested in the cutting during the time each block takes to engrave or the results may start looking a bit mechanical, a bit dull. I had felt this danger in my own work so, in the print in my *St Paul's* sequence featuring searchlights in a night sky, I set myself the challenge of engraving those lights without resorting to fine parallel lines. I didn't entirely succeed, but I did introduce more patterns than had I not set myself the challenge. The print is livelier and visually stronger because of it!

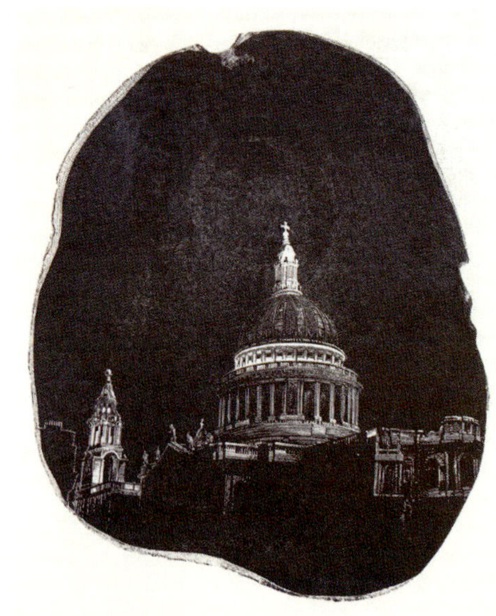

Proof of *St Paul's Dusk* (2014), engraving on holly roundel, on Gampi Vellum paper. This was the block's first printing. The uncut sky printed black, but I wanted it paler, without engraving it.

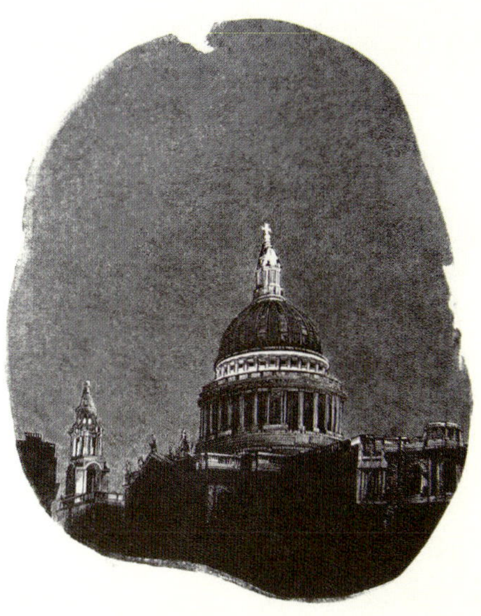

St Paul's Dusk (2014), engraving on holly, 22.5 × 17.3cm (8¾ × 6¾in), on Gampi Vellum paper. I masked out the block's totally uncut sky area with a stencil and press-printed it. Then I peeled up the printing paper just enough to remove the stencil, smoothed the paper down and press-printed again.

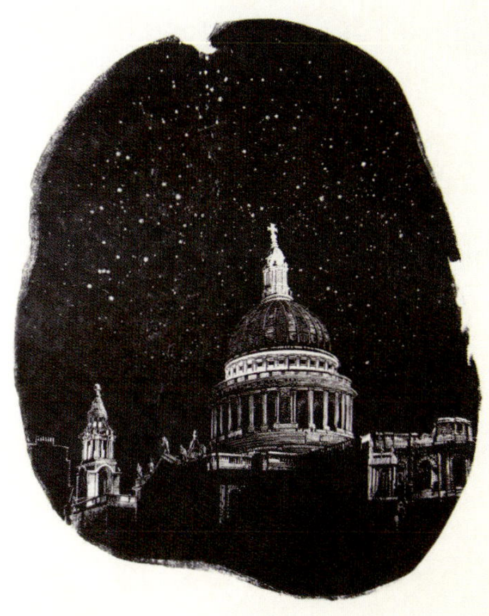

St Paul's Stars (2014). For this version I cut stars into the sky on the same block (another roundel that originated from a tree from the garden of my family home in Liverpool) and press-printed it without stencils.

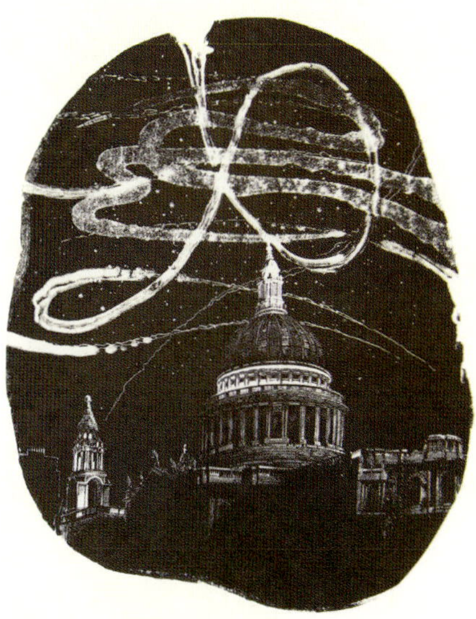

St Paul's Night Flight (2014). I re-inked the block, drew vapour trails in its wet ink (with biro nib and cotton bud), laid a vapour trail-shaped stencil on top, press-printed it, removed the stencil keeping printing paper in place, then finger-rubbed the sky part. The ink residue on the block (where the stencil had been) printed as grey vapour trails.

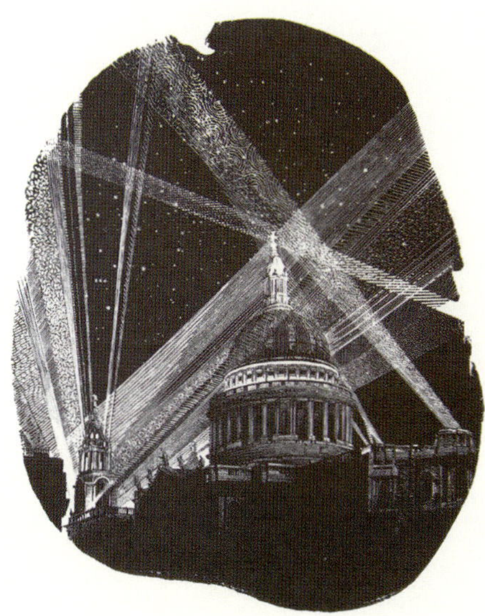

St Paul's Lights (2014). I engraved different patterns into the sky area to suggest wartime anti-aircraft searchlights in the night sky, then inked and printed the block again.

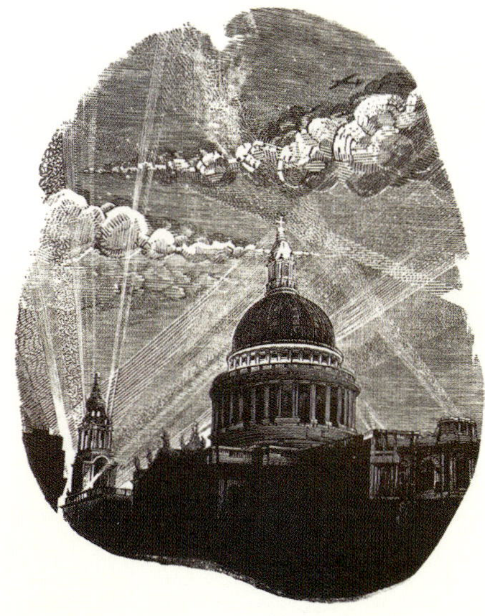

St Paul's Dawn (2014): trial proof. I re-engraved the block extensively to lighten the sky. I left a small uncut area as the silhouette of a tiny aeroplane. When printed, this version was still darker than I wanted.

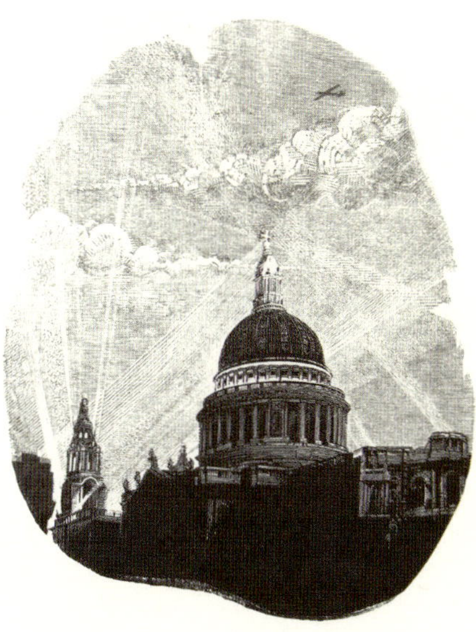

St Paul's Dawn (2014). I masked the sky part with a stencil, printing exactly as for the *Dusk* variant except that, to keep it very pale, rather than press-printing again after removing the stencil, I finger-rubbed the back of the printing paper. The tiny aeroplane now printed too pale so, once dry, I strengthened it with black pen dots.

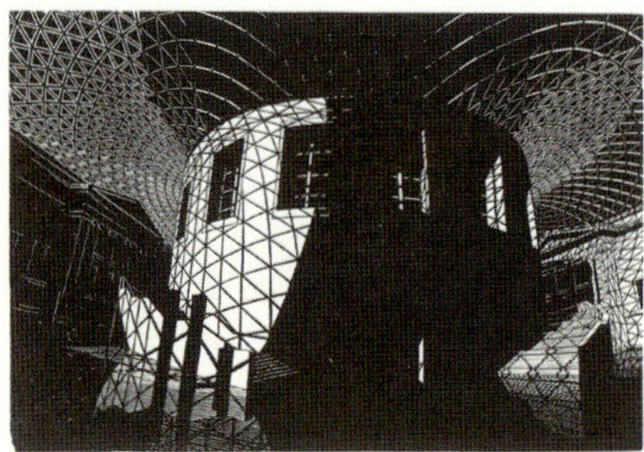

British Museum Series No. 1 (2004), engraving on lemonwood, 17.4 × 24.8cm (6¾ × 9¾in), on Gampi Vellum paper. This is press-printed in black directly from the minimally engraved block.

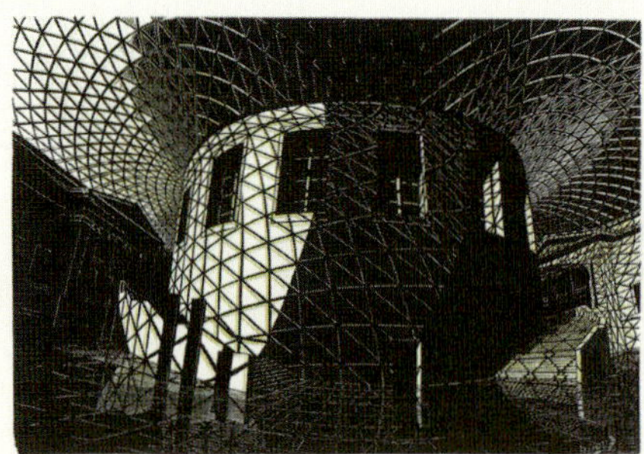

British Museum Series No. 2 (2005). I re-engraved and reprinted the block. Then I re-inked it in extended green and, with a stencil masking out selected parts, placed block face-down on print (for press-printing) but intentionally out of register so the green would print next to the black to suggest shadows fragmenting into colours.

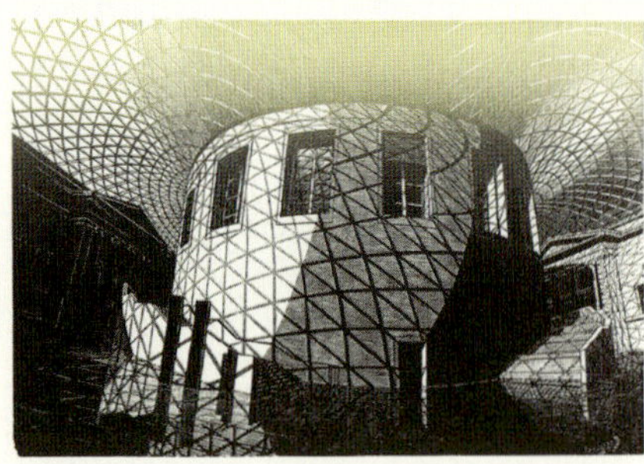

British Museum Series No. 3 (2005). I engraved more light and more detail on the block then inked and printed it with a yellow/black blend to suggest sunlight coming through the glass roof.

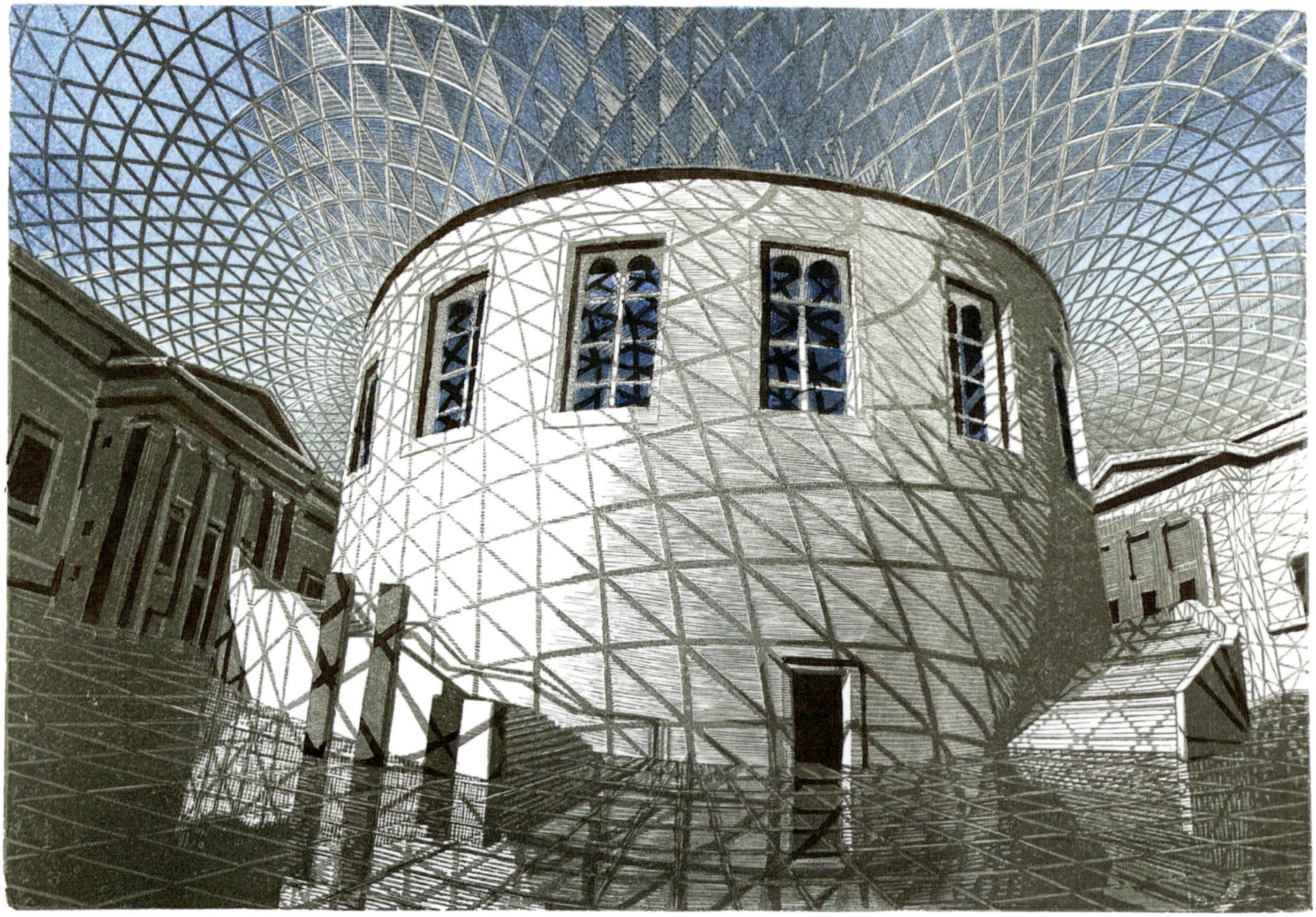

British Museum – Blue Sky (2023) on Zerkall paper. After further engraving, I printed the block in mid-grey. I printed a lino block with foreground details in darker grey, and another with the string-vest roof in a blue tonal blend. The blue and black window details were finger-printed through paper stencils.

USING MORE THAN ONE BLOCK FOR A SINGLE IMAGE

To transfer (or offset) the image from the 'key block' (usually the block that prints the 'black' of the image and all its most important features) to other blocks, as a guide to cutting additional blocks intended for the same image:

1. Ink the key block in an opaque, dark colour (black is ideal) and print it onto clear acetate.

2. While still wet, put the acetate print side down on your next block (which, if a woodblock, you'll have stained in advance to darken its surface) and either press-print it onto the block or spoon-burnish it.

3. The second block must be exactly the same size as the key block and you must position the wet print in perfect alignment for it to make an accurate guide to cutting the next part of the image.

4. You can offset freshly printed acetate impressions on to as many blocks as you require and then work on each of them to create a multicoloured, multi-layered single image.

5. Because of the expense of end grain wood, and because secondary blocks often need much less complex cutting than the key block, it is often cheaper (and speedier in cutting) to use, for example, a woodblock as key block but use lino blocks or stencils for extra colour layers, or to alter the appearance of the image in other ways.

My *Manhattan series* (all press-printed) was created in a similar way to the *Brooklyn Bridge* sequence, except that I printed various initial stages of several images before recutting the engraved block to complete any of them. So, I had several different prints all underway simultaneously.

Ultimately, this series yielded ten different images from, essentially, one woodblock supplemented with lino blocks and stencils. Although different prints from the same block run the risk of being rather dull if all one does is change the colour, with a bit of planning and using, perhaps, colour blends, different ink translucencies, plus stencils or additional blocks, it's possible to generate extensive, highly varied series with just one engraving as the starting point. I find this way of working inspiring, as it facilitates different ways of depicting various times of day and different light and weather conditions, but it's worth trying out simply to gain surprising new results from any of your engravings.

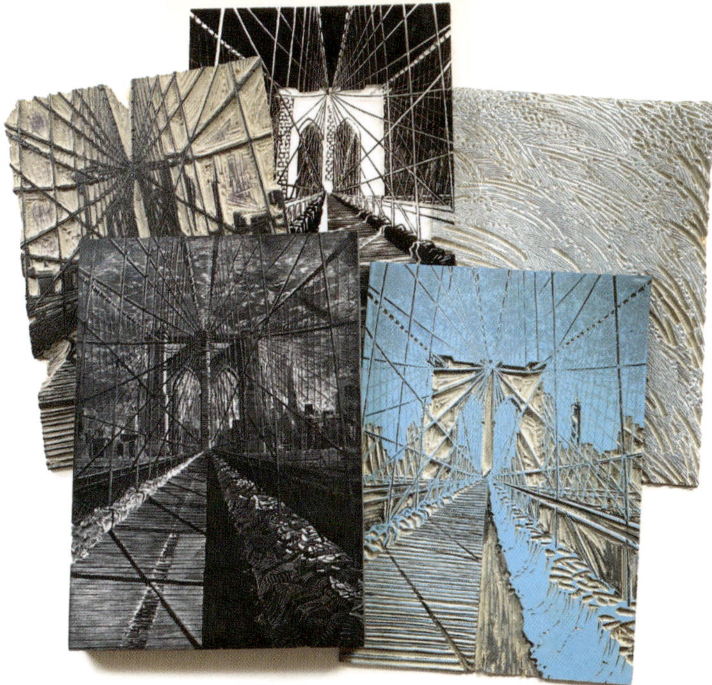

The engraved block for my *Brooklyn Bridge* series with three lino blocks made to create variant prints from it, plus an acetate print from the lino block (here showing residual blue ink), used to offset that image to another lino block for subsequent cutting.

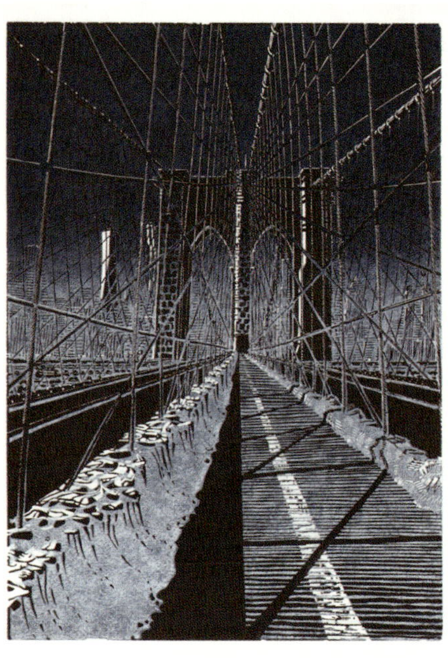

Brooklyn Bridge: Night Ice (2015), 24.6 × 17.3cm (9¾ × 6¾in), on Gampi Vellum paper. I engraved a lemonwood block and printed in black. I then cut a lino block, using it to overprint the black with opaque white in a colour blend using extender to make the ink increasingly transparent towards the image's top edge.

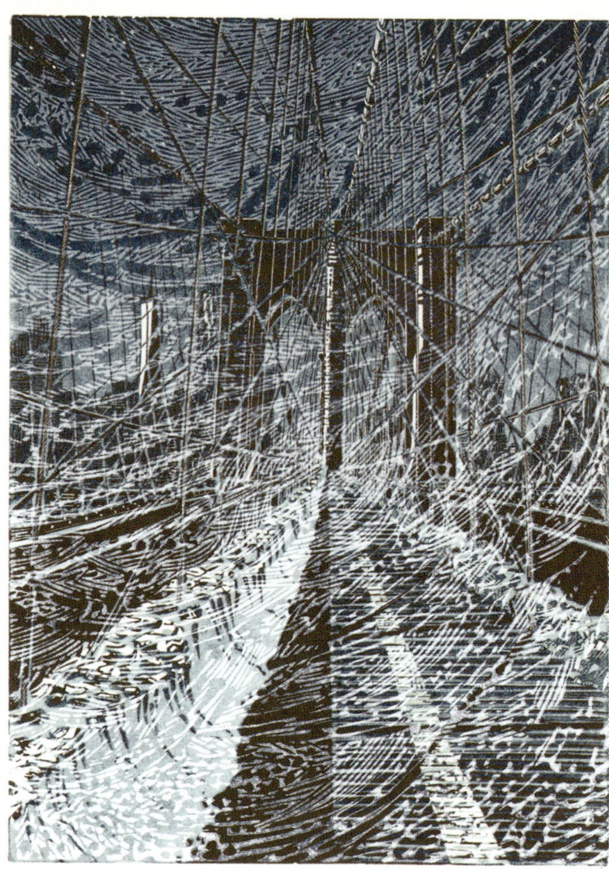

Brooklyn Bridge: Blizzard (2015). I repeated both stages of the *Night Ice* version but added another lino block, cut with marks to suggest a snowstorm, inked and printed, again, in a colour blend of opaque white graduating to pure transparent extender.

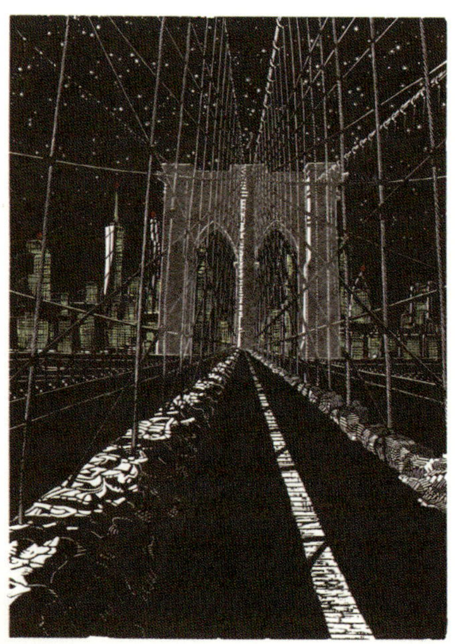

Brooklyn Bridge: Stars (2015). I engraved stars on the block and printed it black, masking the bridge with a stencil. Extracting the stencil without shifting the paper, I reprinted the block to print the bridge grey. Using a rubber eraser cut with crosshatching, I printed opaque yellow through another stencil onto the skyscrapers, and red highlights using a cotton bud.

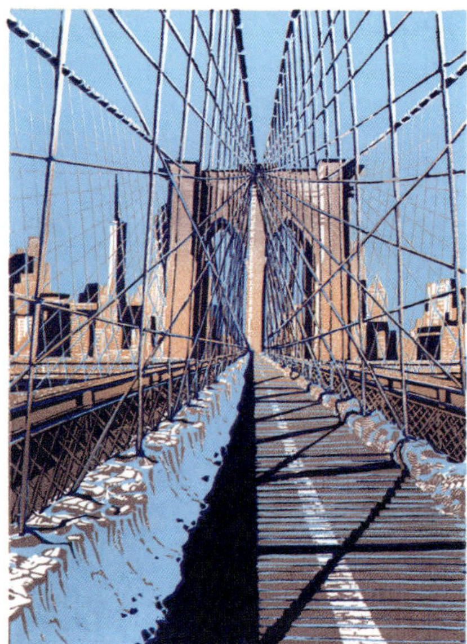

Brooklyn Bridge: Afternoon (2015). I engraved more detail on the woodblock, reprinting in a colour blend of orange-brown before overprinting it with the lino block made for the *Night Ice* variant, but this time inked in opaque sky blue. An additional lino block printed in purple completed the image.

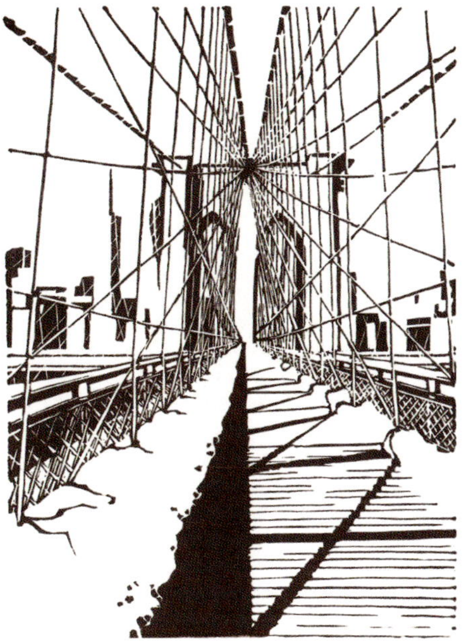

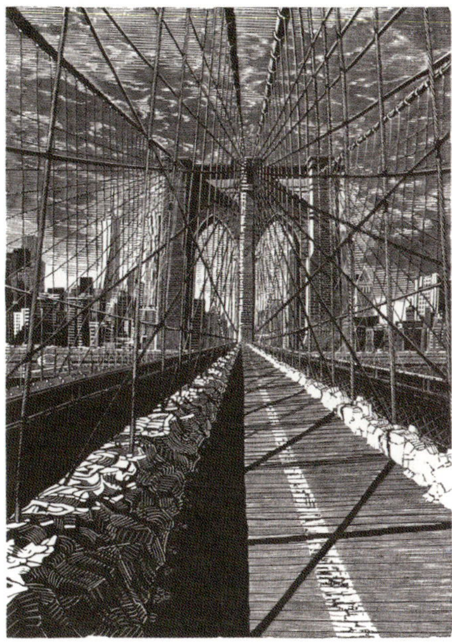

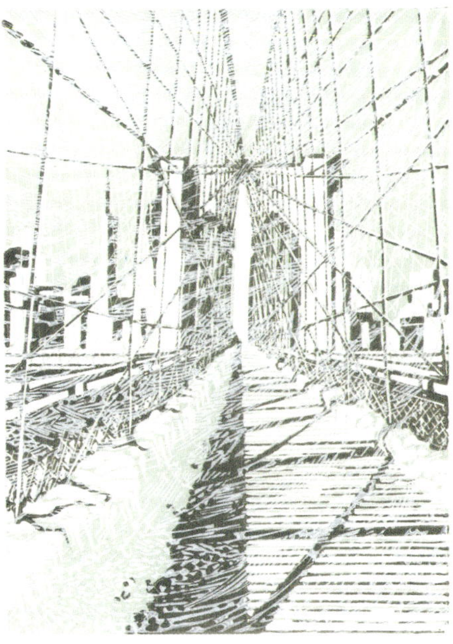

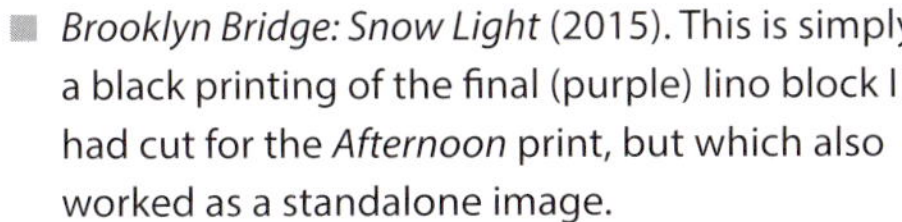

Brooklyn Bridge: Snow Light (2015). This is simply a black printing of the final (purple) lino block I had cut for the *Afternoon* print, but which also worked as a standalone image.

Brooklyn Bridge: New Day (2015). I cut away much more of the woodblock to introduce more detail and more tones. I printed it in black, with no additional blocks or stencils.

Brooklyn Bridge: Snow on Snow (2015), printed in grey, green and white on Zerkall paper. This brings together all three lino blocks cut for earlier variants in my *Brooklyn Bridge* series into a new image without printing the woodblock here at all.

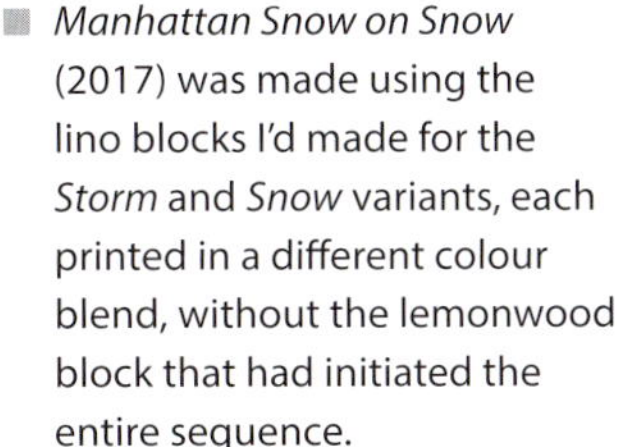

Manhattan Snow on Snow (2017) was made using the lino blocks I'd made for the *Storm* and *Snow* variants, each printed in a different colour blend, without the lemonwood block that had initiated the entire sequence.

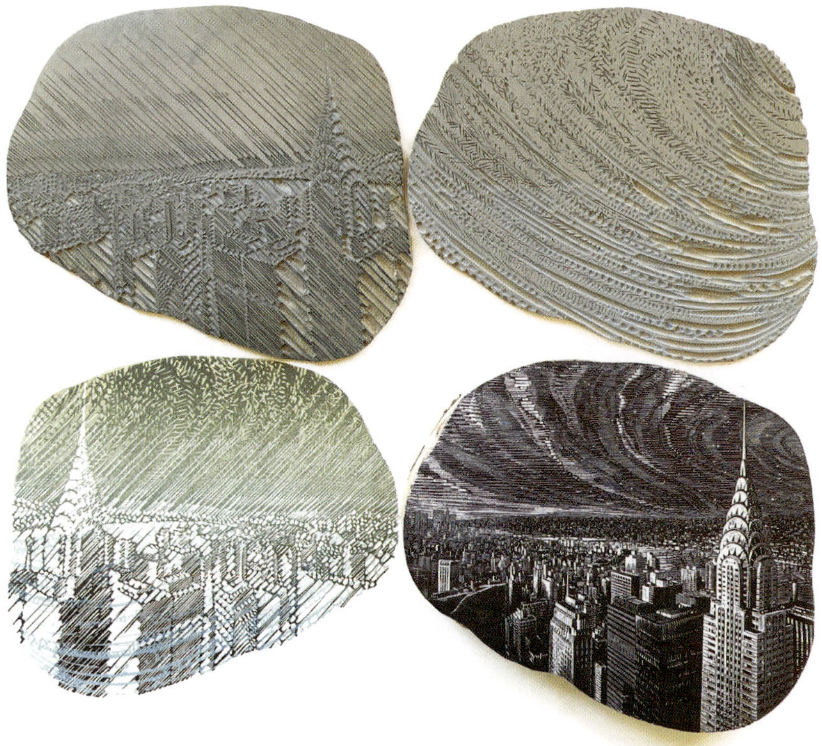

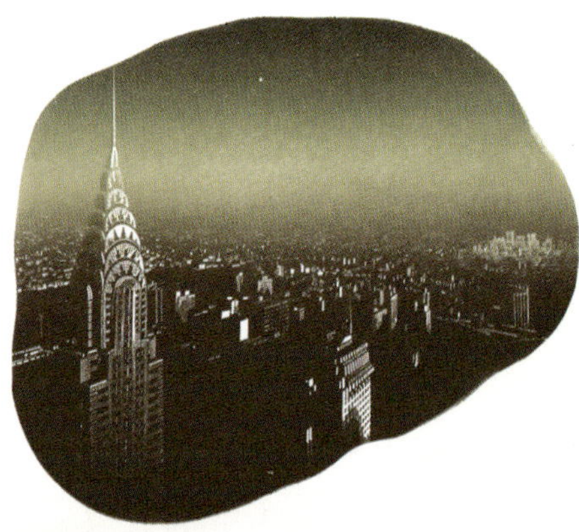

Manhattan Twilight (2017), engraving on holly roundel, 19 × 20.3cm (7½ × 8in), on Zerkall paper. I engraved the block so that skyscrapers, Hudson River and background were defined but not detailed. I printed it in a grey/cream/black horizontal blend with stencil-work on the Chrysler Building's spire to darken one side.

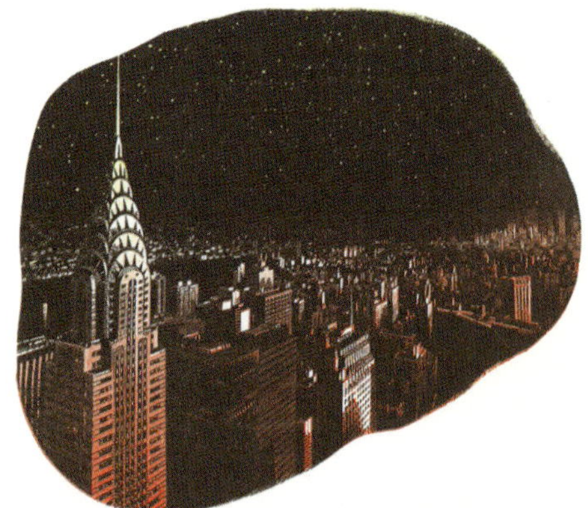

Manhattan Stars (2017). Here I reprinted the woodblock in a yellow/red blend. I then engraved it further, cutting a starry sky and more details in the skyscrapers. I inked it in black, overprinting the yellow/red layer.

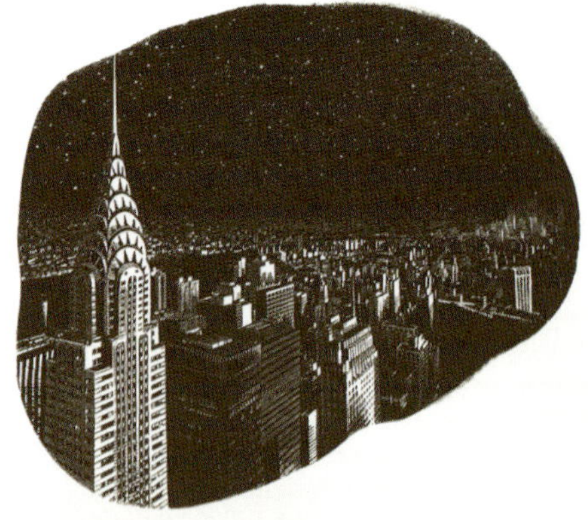

Manhattan Night (2017). This variant is a simple black printing of the block at this particular stage of cutting.

Manhattan Sun (2017). Before recutting the woodblock with a starry sky and more detail in the buildings, I inked it with a blue/amber blend diagonally across the block. Then I re-inked it (now at the next cutting stage) in a mid-brown blend, masking out the print's sky so the new inking would only overprint the cityscape.

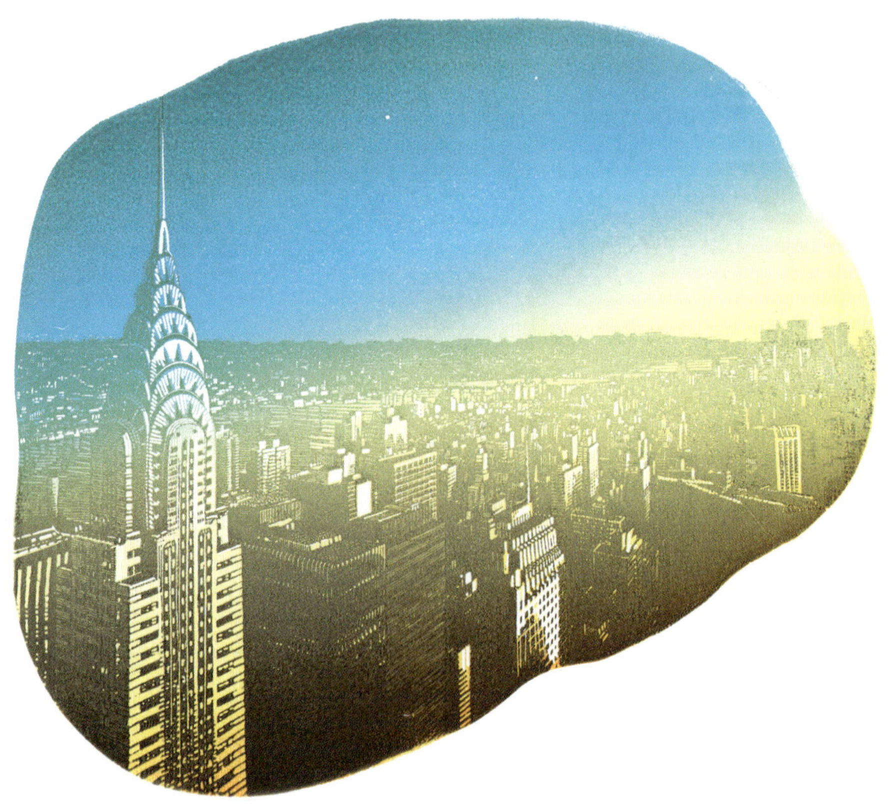

Manhattan Storm (2017). Before recutting the woodblock with stars or detailed skyscrapers, I printed it in black for the first stage of this print. I cut a lino block with mostly diagonal lines (recalling Japanese prints of rain) and overprinted the black using a blend of increasingly transparent grey/white.

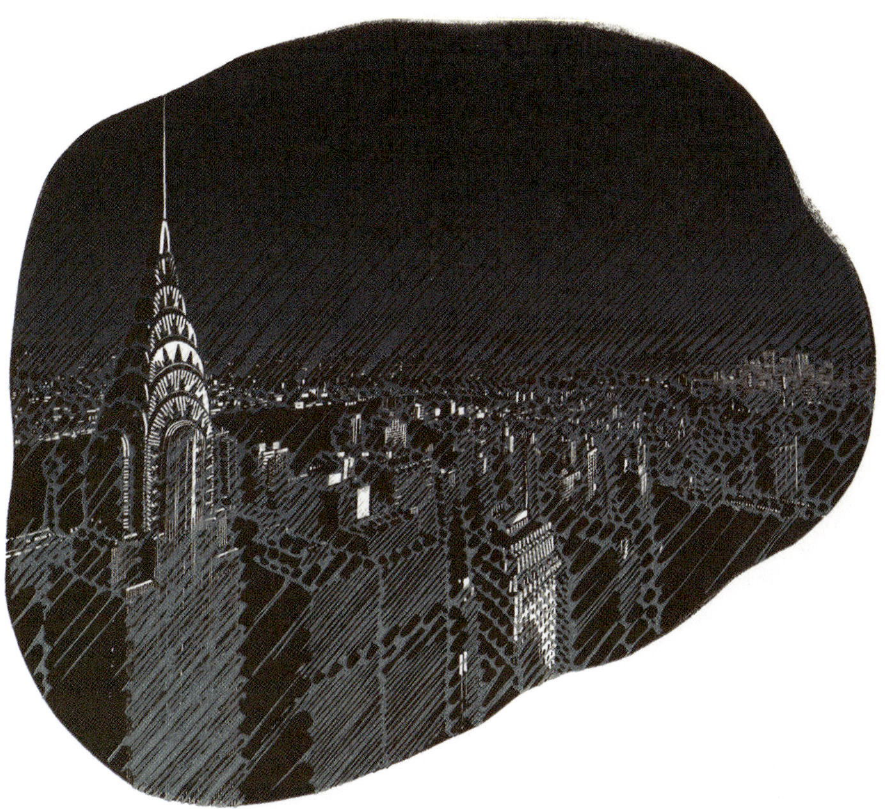

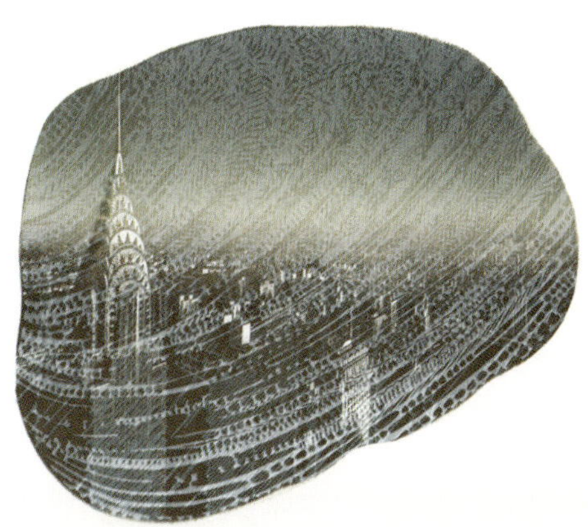

Manhattan Snow (2017). Before re-engraving with stars, I reprinted the woodblock in a grey/beige/black blend and printed the lino block from the *Storm* print in a grey/white semi-transparent blend on top before adding a new lino block cut with swirls and dots to suggest a blizzard, printed in a grey/white blend.

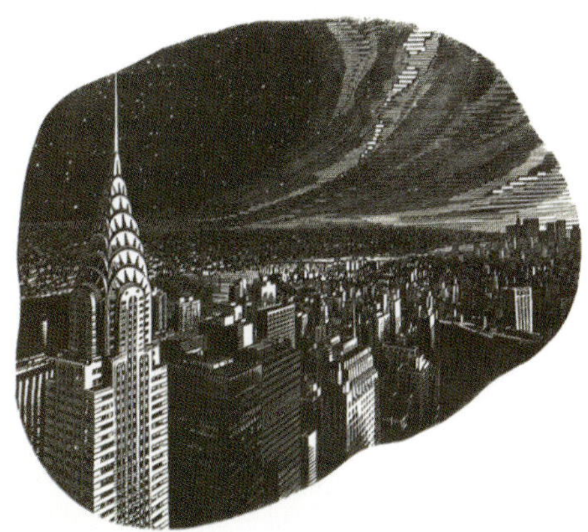

Manhattan Night Becomes Day (2017). Having completed the variants already described, I started engraving the woodblock with horizontal lines to suggest daylight. I hadn't initially planned to print at this stage of cutting, but I liked the way the cutting grew like a veil drawing over the night. (The version with a fully daylit sky is shown in Chapter 2.)

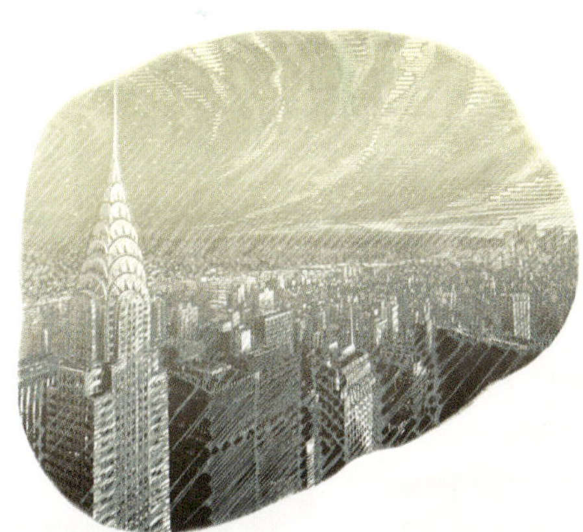

Manhattan Rain (2017). I printed the woodblock, now extensively engraved, in a yellow/grey blend, overprinting with the diagonally cut lino block I'd used in the *Storm* variant, printed in a grey/blue extended blend to suggest daytime rain in a sulphurous sky.

ARTISTS' BOOKS

Even tiny blocks can be put to complex use either as standalone miniatures or as parts of a larger multiple-block complete image (assembled like a jigsaw for printing) or maybe as *ex libris* designs or as the components for handmade books. I have printed various small books on concertina-folded pages using a nipping press, which I also used to press the book covers flat, once I had pasted on their cloth bindings. To date, I have only ever made four artists' books, so I'm not an expert in this area which deserves – and has – extensive tomes of its own! These examples are the tiniest taste of an enormous creative field in which wood engraving has a long history. Books without words such as the graphic novels of Belgian engraver Frans Masereel (1889–1972) or American Lynd Ward (1905–85) have long demonstrated impactful presentations of wood engraving, as have fine illustrated books (with text) by Robert Gibbings (1889–1958), Clare Leighton (1898–1989), John Farleigh (1900–65), Blair Hughes-Stanton (1902–81), Joan Hassall (1906–88) and many others.

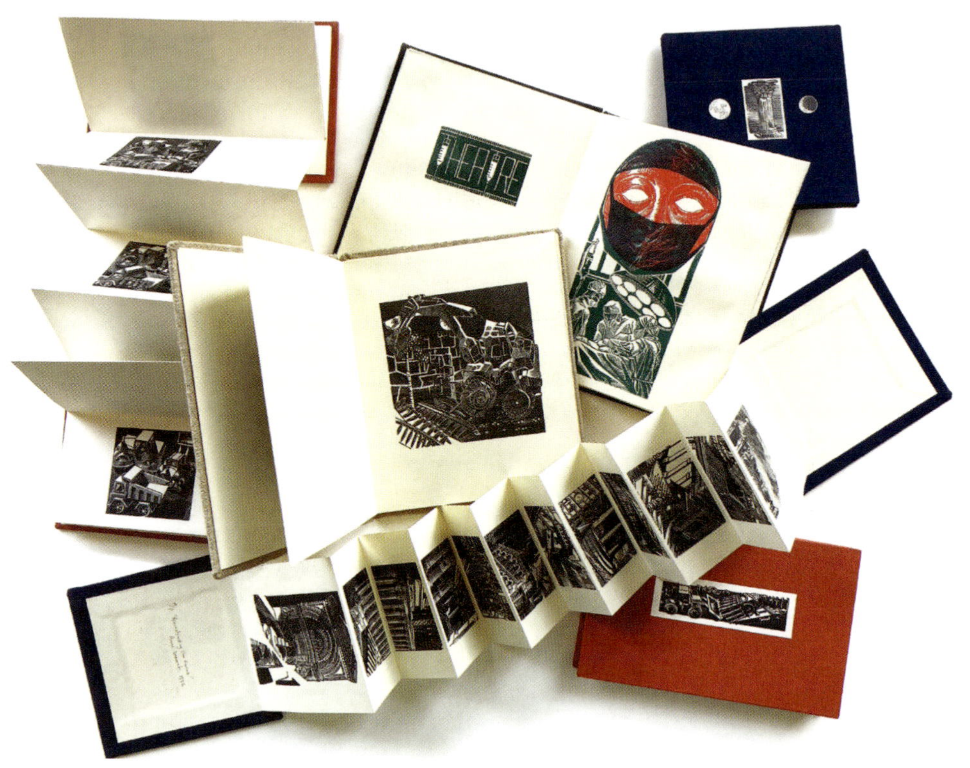

My concertina-folded artist's books (1988–94) printed with my wood engravings and bound with cloth-covered archival card (using my nipping press). Each book provided a way of showing metamorphosing sequences of diverse small images. None of these books (closed) is larger than 14 × 11cm (5½ × 4¼in).

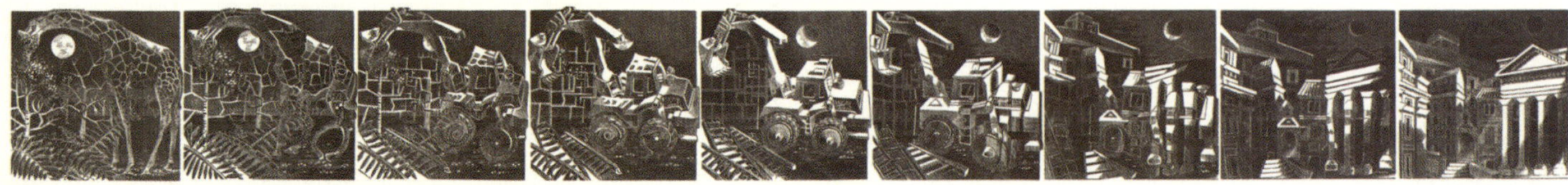

Progress/Progression? (1988–90), engravings on nine separate lemonwood blocks, each 7.5 × 7.5cm (3 × 3in), on Basingwerk parchment paper. I printed this both as a single-sheet print (as shown here) and in book form on concertina-folded pages.

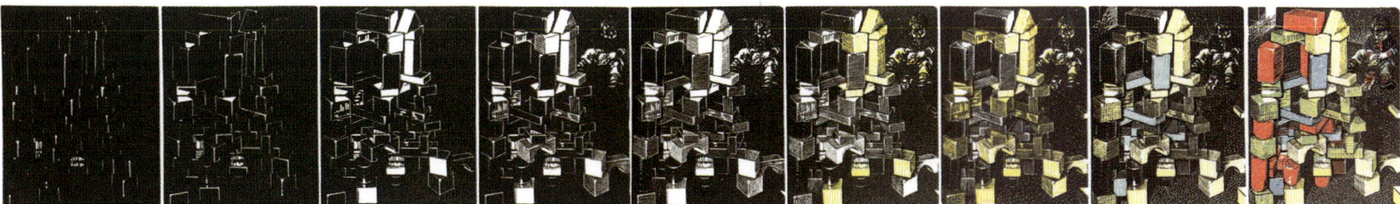

Building Development (2002), reduction engraving from one pearwood block, printed nine times on Zerkall paper, with three lino blocks. Total printed area: 6.6 × 46cm (2½ × 18in). Suggesting skyscrapers evolving into my toddler-son with his building-block tower, this sequence might have made a good book but that didn't occur to me in time. As it was a reduction print, I couldn't reprint it.

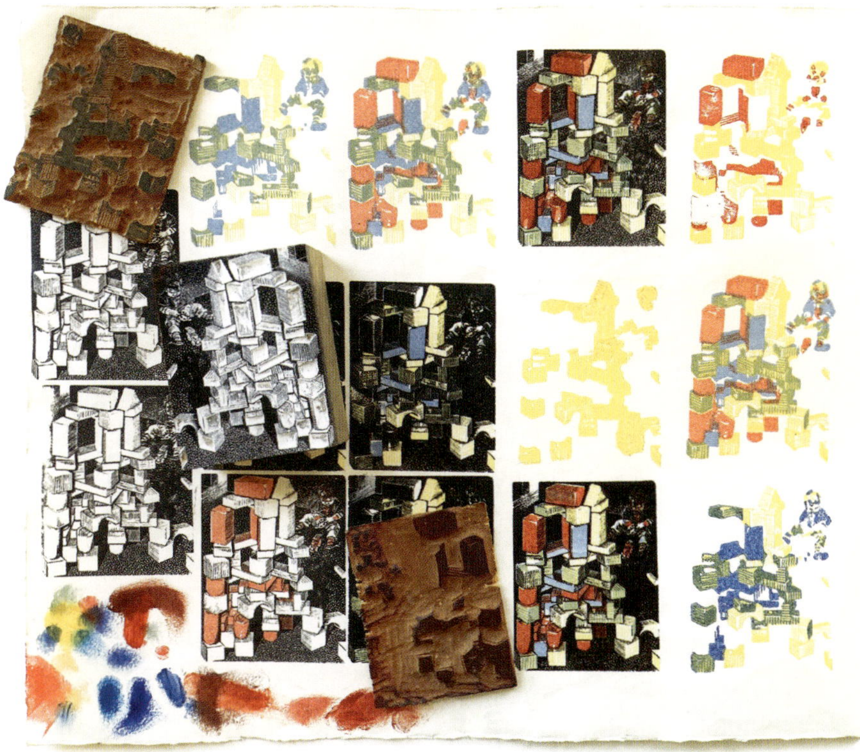

Because *Building Development* was a reduction cut, I couldn't print more if anything went wrong, so I made sample prints on a worksheet to test the colours of three additional lino blocks (two shown here) before printing them on the final image.

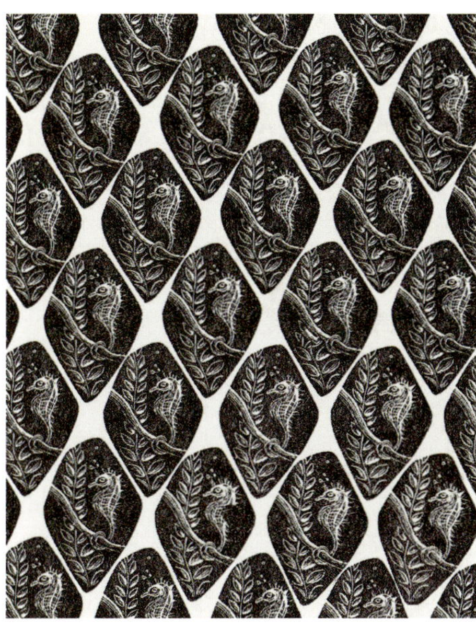

This striking potential endpaper for a fine book was spoon-printed by me (in 2011), using a tiny block engraved by one of my students, Nikki Tait, on a course I was teaching. It demonstrates the huge potential applications even of the tiniest practice blocks.

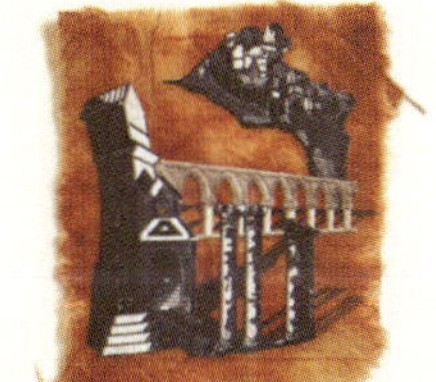
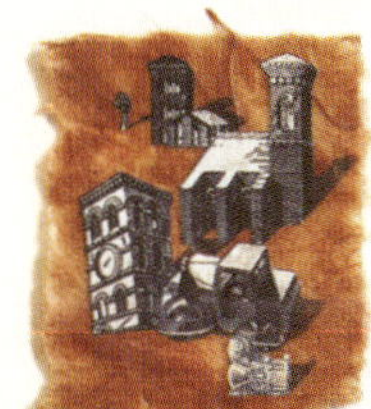
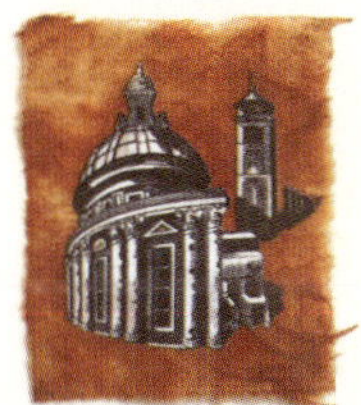
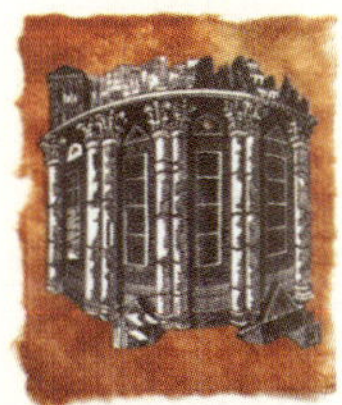

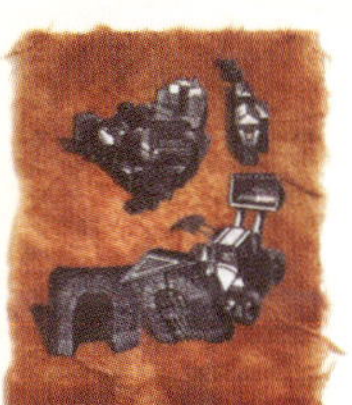
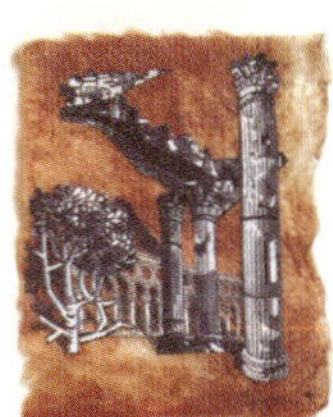

Illuminations (1994), wood engravings, pencil drawing, Italian lire banknote fragments, and gold leaf collaged on Nepalese Lhokta paper, 9.3 × 70.5cm (3¾ × 27¾in). I created this as a long narrow sequential image but each of its parts could have worked equally well as pages in an artist's book, perhaps concertina-folded.

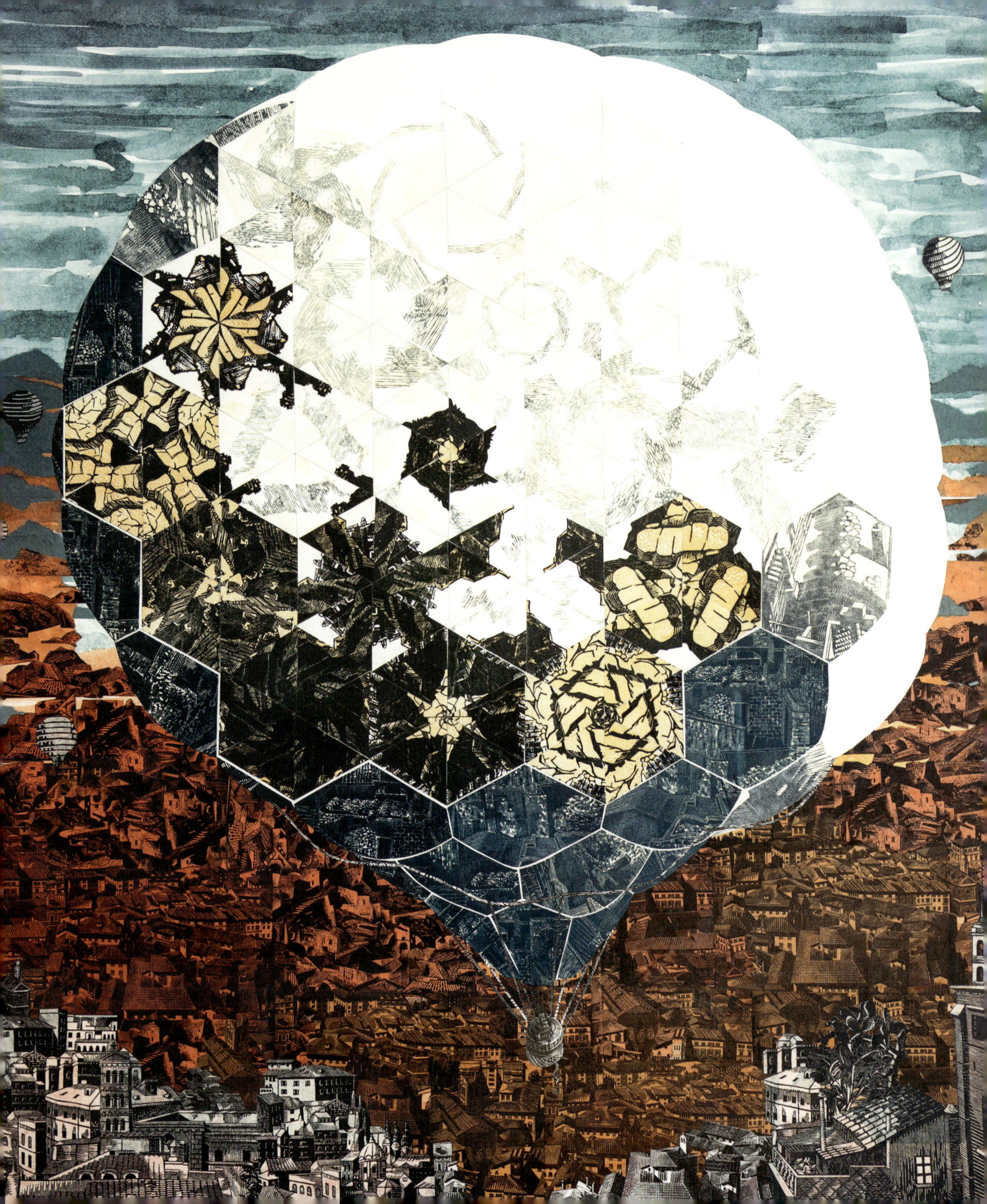

CHAPTER 9

WOOD ENGRAVING AND COLLAGE

When I finished at art school and started trying to make a living as an artist, I was, at that point, working almost exclusively as a wood engraving and linocut printmaker, printing just a single image in a limited edition from each block (as is the traditional practice). Being quite a slow worker, with some of my complex prints taking months to complete, I started to feel frustrated that I had so many ideas in my head, yet I'd need many lifetimes to engrave them all. Also, when working on one image at a time, as I tended to do, if I got stuck – unsure of what marks to make next – my work rate would get slower and slower and I found myself breaking off for too many tea breaks and other distractions!

I have subsequently discovered that it's best to have several works on the go at the same time, especially if one allows for more spontaneity and is less labour-intensive than the other. Instead of ploughing on with one that's reached a difficult patch, stop and swap to another (which for me is usually a collage). When you resume engraving, having focused on a totally different image and different ways of working for a while, invariably a solution to the earlier problem seems to present itself.

When I was living and working in Rome in 1989, I had engraved a small self-portrait on boxwood and printed some impressions in orange-brown ink. I wasn't happy with it and tried reprinting in black, but I liked that version less and tore up both printings into shreds and went into the city to spend the rest of the day sketching. On returning to my study bedroom, the first thing that caught my eye was the way the torn paper strips had landed on the floor, creating intriguing orange/black stripes with hints of imagery. This accident directly inspired my first collage.

Early Flight (2022), detail of a mixed-media work comprising wood engraving and linocut prints on paper collaged on museum board, with pencil drawing and watercolour, 81 × 71cm (32 × 28in).

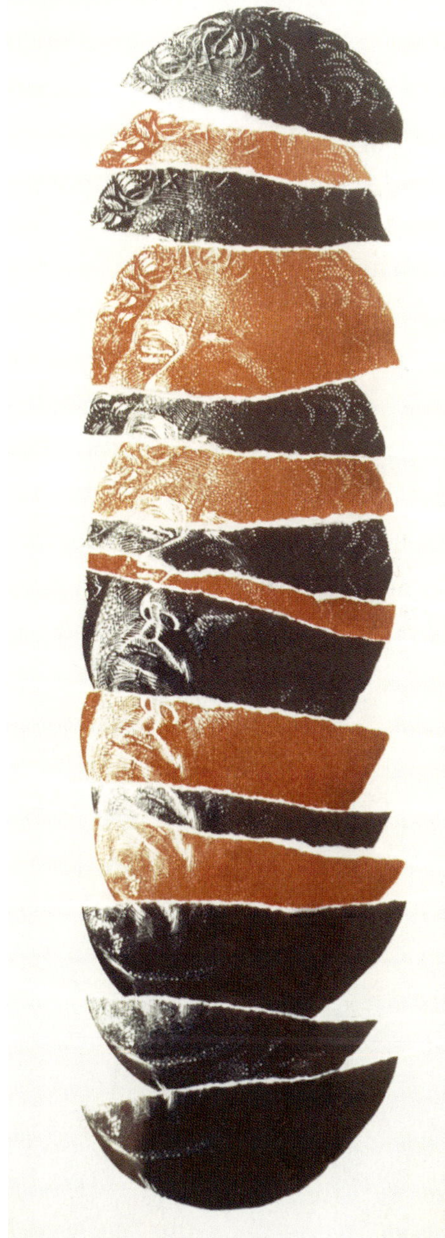

Self-Portrait (Tower) (1990), wood engraved collage on Basingwerk Parchment paper, 20.5 × 5.5cm (8 × 2¼in). This was my first collage made as a unique piece. I was later commissioned to make a small edition of four more of the same image, two of which are now in the Ashmolean and Whitworth collections.

WHY COLLAGE?

Wood engraved prints on paper are fantastic source material for entirely new and convincing collaged compositions. The nature of printmaking too means that you are never short of prints to cut up and play with! When printing your woodblocks, if you want to try collage, don't throw away impressions that were perhaps too pale or not the colour you'd intended – but were otherwise well printed. A drawer full of such 'mistakes' can be a perfect starting point for collage.

In the thirty-five years I have been making collages alongside wood engravings, I have found, often, that some element of an engraving might spark its own idea for a collage, which I can make by printing plenty of spare prints from that finished block, cutting out the same detail from those identical prints (part of a colonnade perhaps, or other architectural details), reassembling them and collaging them together to create new, invented structures.

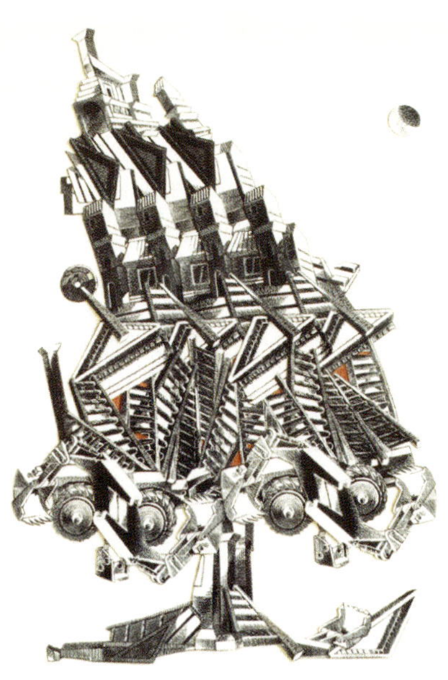
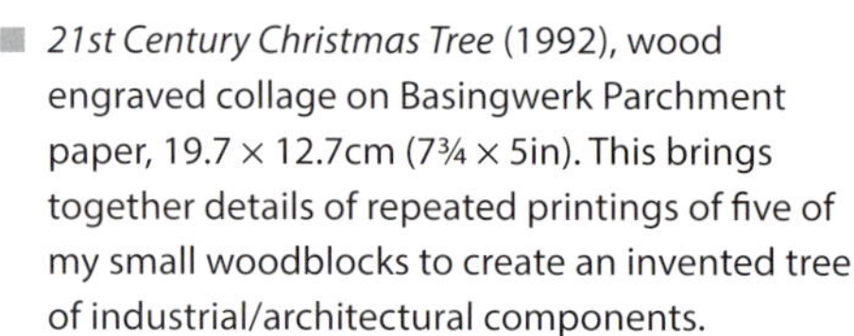

21st Century Christmas Tree (1992), wood engraved collage on Basingwerk Parchment paper, 19.7 × 12.7cm (7¾ × 5in). This brings together details of repeated printings of five of my small woodblocks to create an invented tree of industrial/architectural components.

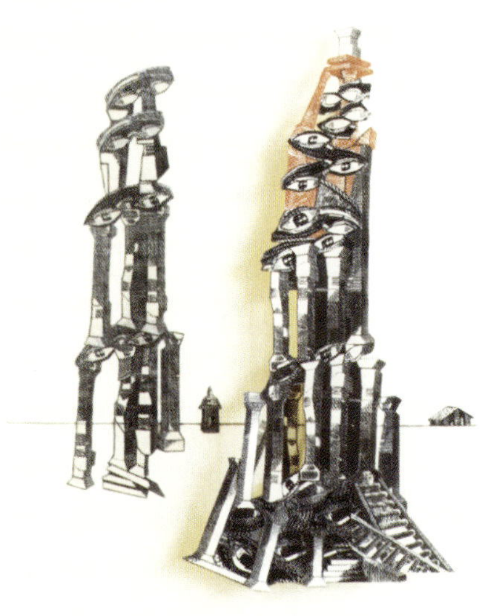

Watchtowers (1992), wood engraved collage and cotton thread (horizon line) on Basingwerk Parchment and Kozu-shi papers, 16.5 × 14 × 0.7cm (6½ × 5½ × ¼in). The larger tower sits on a small block of mount card so it sits in front of the base layer and casts a shadow.

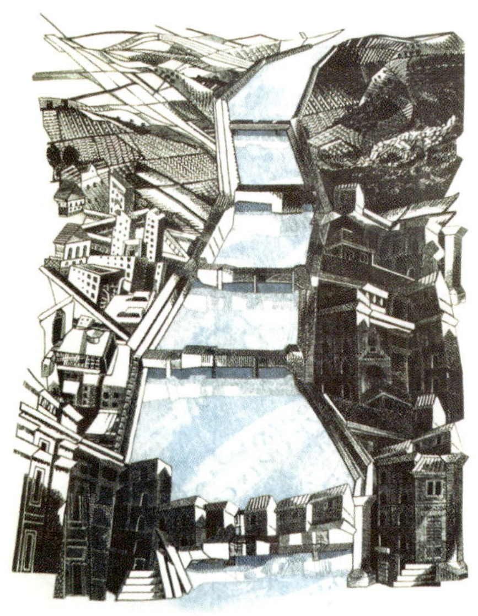

Il Fiume e I Ponti (1992), wood engraving on Basingwerk Parchment paper collaged on Japanese paper with Italian paper sweet wrappers and wood engraving details collaged on the back of the semi-transparent Japanese paper to suggest reflections in water. 22 × 17cm (8¾ × 6¾in).

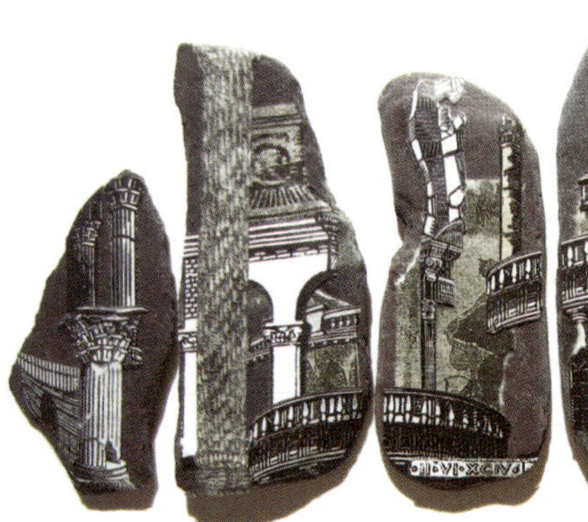
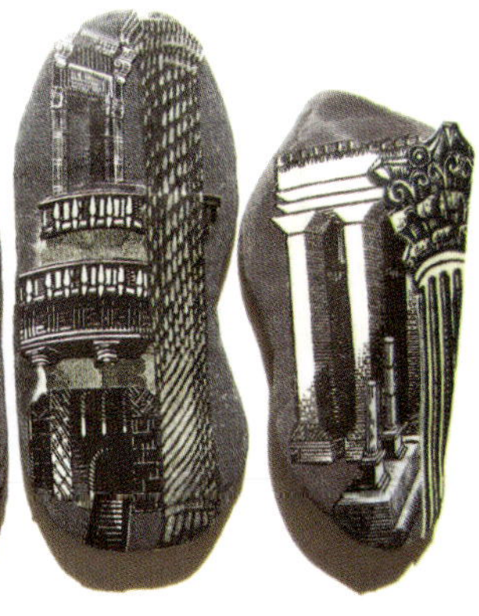

Traces of Rome (2012), wood engraving, linocut and solarplate prints on paper collaged on five slate shards, 15.8 × 7.7 × 0.5cm (6¼ × 3 × ¼in).

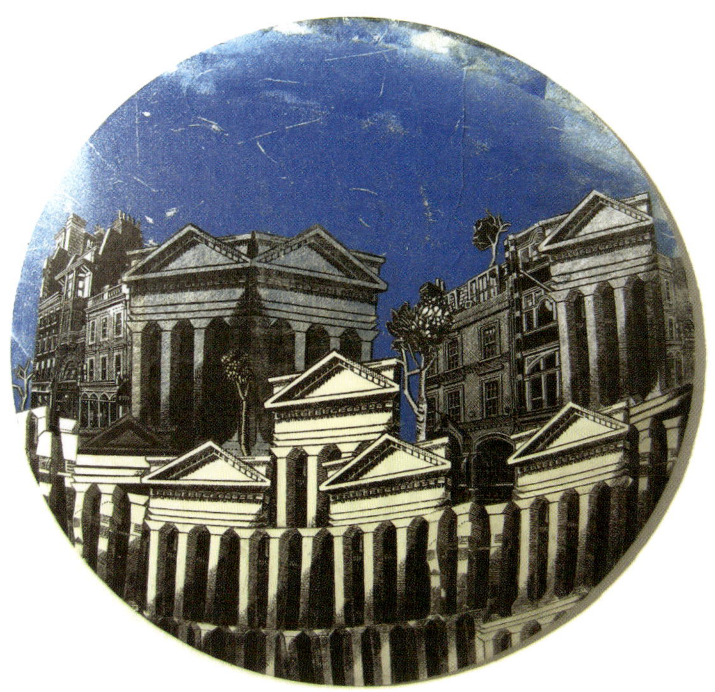

Temple Steppes (2012), wood engraving (on opaque Basingwerk parchment paper and semi-transparent Japanese tissue) collaged on a print (in blue ink on Kozu-shi) taken from a piece of salvaged floor lino, all collaged on convex glass, diameter: 18cm (7in).

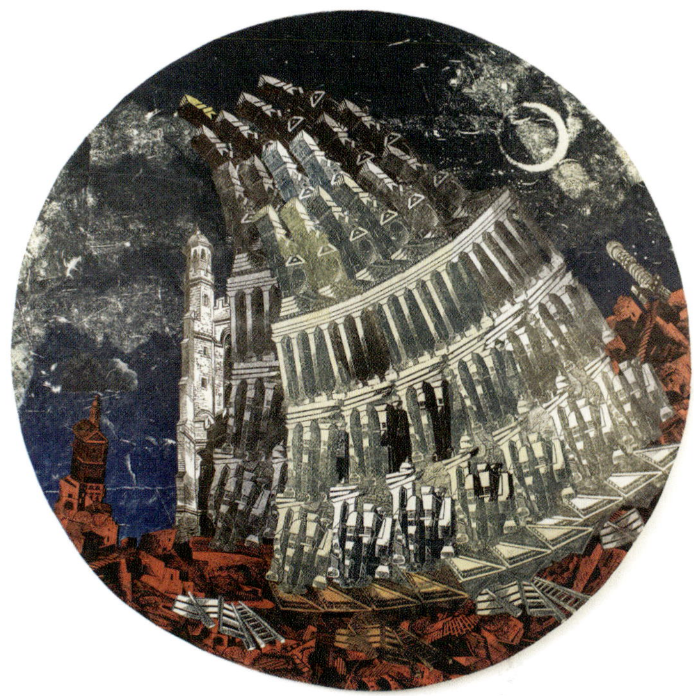

Babel Moon (2018), wood engraving, solarplate and monotype prints collaged on paper under convex glass, diameter: 33cm (13in). This uses repeated details from earlier engravings printed on white and rust-red papers assembled to create a new tower form.

THEMES AND VARIATIONS

The Tower of Babel and other comparable architectural reimaginings and inventions are enduring themes and have inspired many of my collages. Many feature reused pieces from a tiny engraving, *Babel Tower in pieces* (illustrated in Chapter 5) but each one, in collaged form, looks very different from its counterparts. Again, it's the use of repeated architectural elements from multiple printings of just a few blocks that, for me, inspires the creation of whole new invented architectural forms.

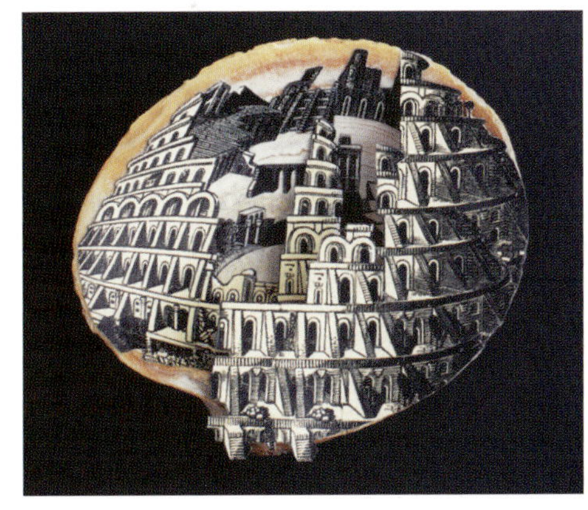

Babel Shell (2005), wood engraving on Zerkall paper collaged on seashell, 7.5 × 8 × 1cm (3 × 3¼ × ½in). Parts of this tiny collage are glued in layers so that the front parts cast shadows on parts further back, enhancing its three-dimensional illusion.

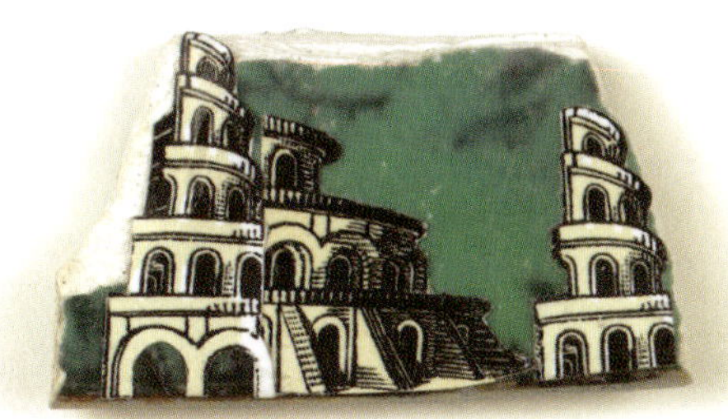

Tiny Babel (2018), wood engraving prints on Zerkall paper collaged on tiny green-glazed pottery fragment, 2.5 × 4.3 × 0.5cm (1 × 1¾ × ¼in).

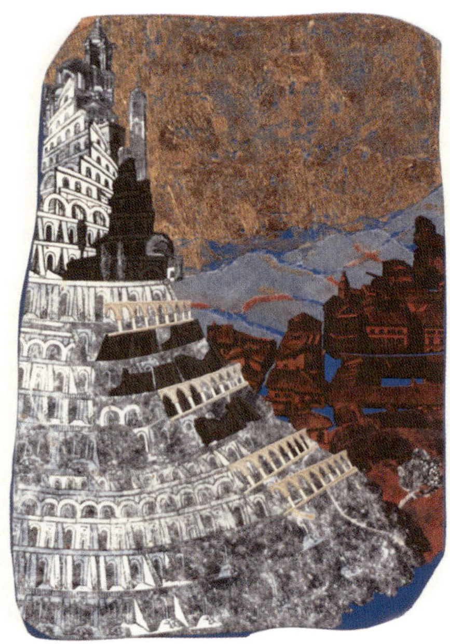

Babel Fragment (2005), wood engravings and solarplate prints on Japanese paper with Italian banknotes and gold leaf collaged on painted wood panel, 31 × 21cm (12¼ × 8¼in). This is one of my collages intended to suggest ancient fresco fragments.

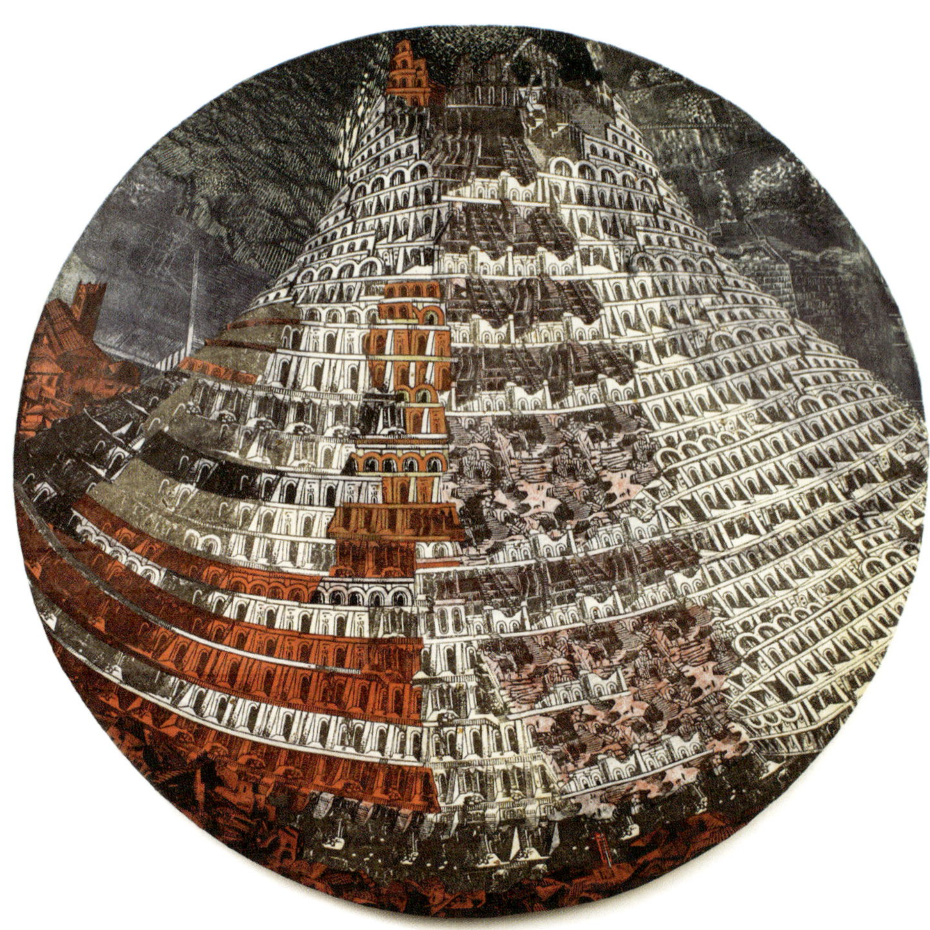

Babel Tower Revisited (2018), solarplate, linocut and wood engraving prints collaged on paper under convex glass, diameter: 46cm (18in). A complex work involving layered prints on papers of different transparencies and colours, all used to create various tonal effects.

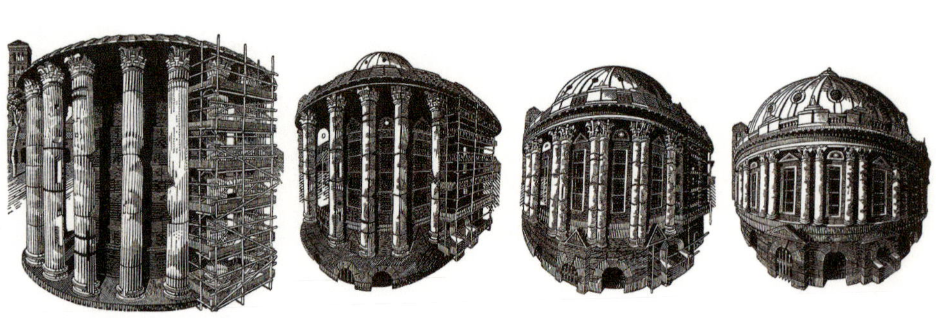

Rotunda × 4 (1993), engravings on four boxwood blocks, total printed area: 10.2 × 33.2cm (4 × 13in), on China White paper. This shows the Ancient Roman temple of Hercules Victor morphing into Oxford's neo-classical Radcliffe Camera. Its various columns feature in many of my collages.

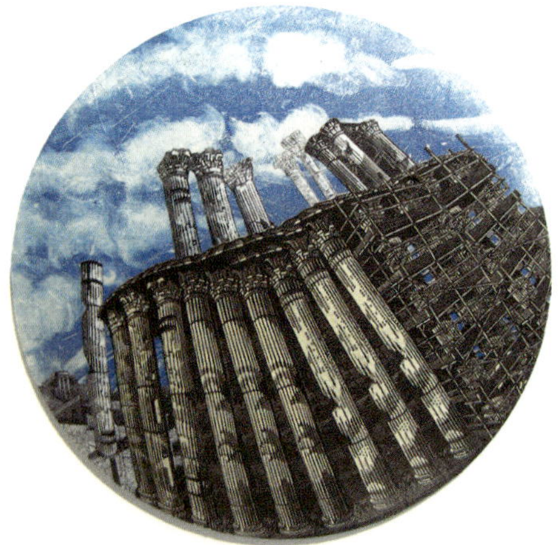

Roman Order (2012), wood engraving and monotype prints on white, cream and semi-transparent Japanese papers collaged on convex glass, diameter: 18cm (7in). This collage re-works and expands the temple in my *Rotunda × 4* engraving.

CHINE COLLÉ EFFECTS

In intaglio prints such as etchings, artists can create subtle tonal effects in a technique called *chine collé*. This involves laying down pieces of differently toned or coloured, dampened, printing papers, with a thin layer of glue on the back of each one, onto an inked metal plate, laying the white printing paper on top and then printing this metal and paper sandwich on an etching press, the intense pressure of which fuses the papers together, while printing the etching. In the final result, the different fused papers can look like subtle watercolour washes or sometimes stronger colour areas across the image. Wood engravings can't be printed using this same chine collé method, because even the subtlest variation in thickness between different papers applied across one inked block would cause the image to print too heavily in some areas and too lightly in others. However, with collage, you can certainly simulate chine collé effects.

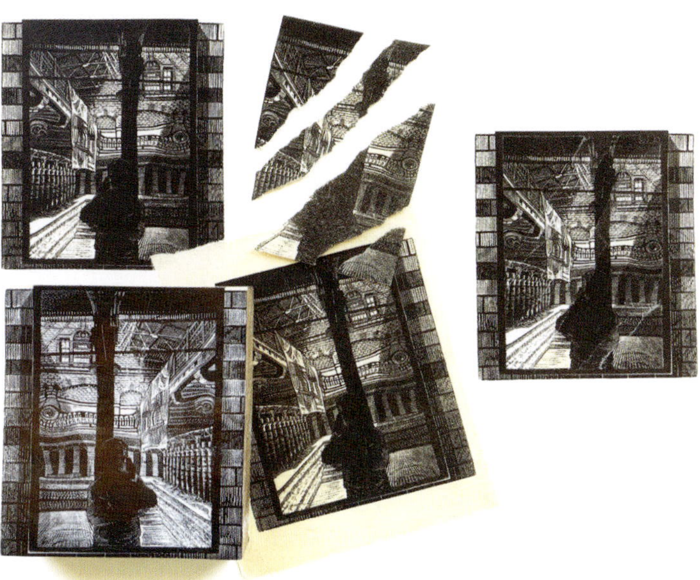

Poolside Reflection (2006), boxwood engraving, 10 × 9cm (4 × 3½in). To evoke a rusting, distorting mirror in an abandoned swimming pool, I printed the block on white Zerkall paper, then reprinted it on off-white, Kozu-shi before collaging strips of the off-white onto the white print to create a two-tone effect like chine collé.

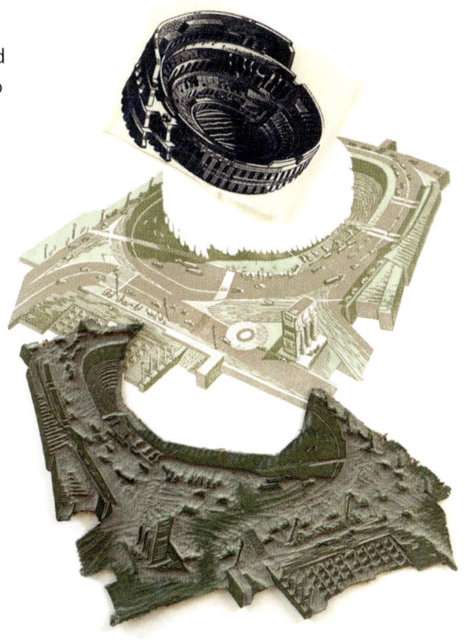

I made a three-colour reduction linocut to add geographical context to a boxwood engraving of Rome's colosseum I had made earlier. I printed the woodblock (in deep blue) on semi-transparent Japanese paper (Kozu-shi) before cutting it out and collaging it on the linocut.

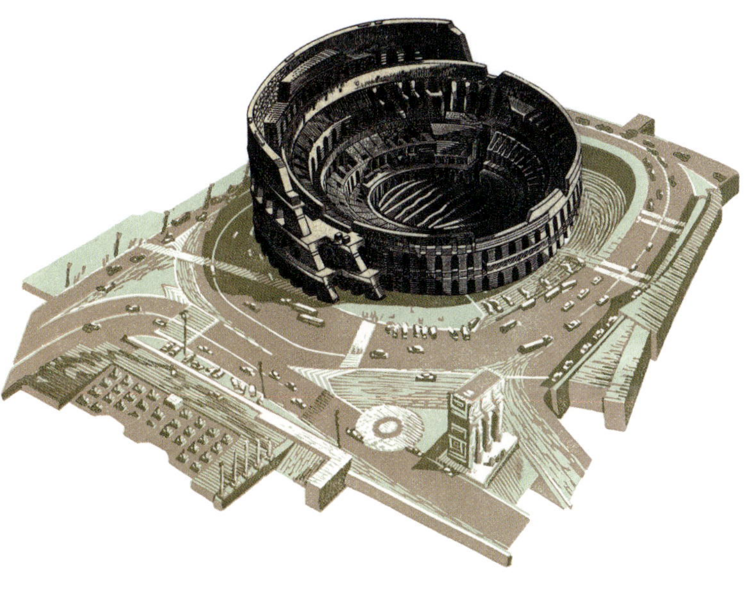

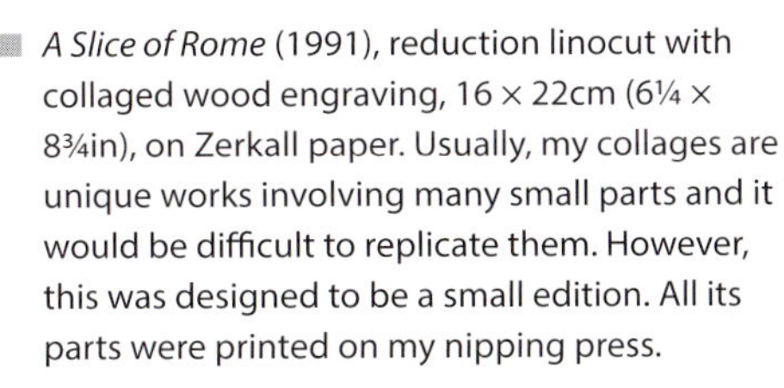

A Slice of Rome (1991), reduction linocut with collaged wood engraving, 16 × 22cm (6¼ × 8¾in), on Zerkall paper. Usually, my collages are unique works involving many small parts and it would be difficult to replicate them. However, this was designed to be a small edition. All its parts were printed on my nipping press.

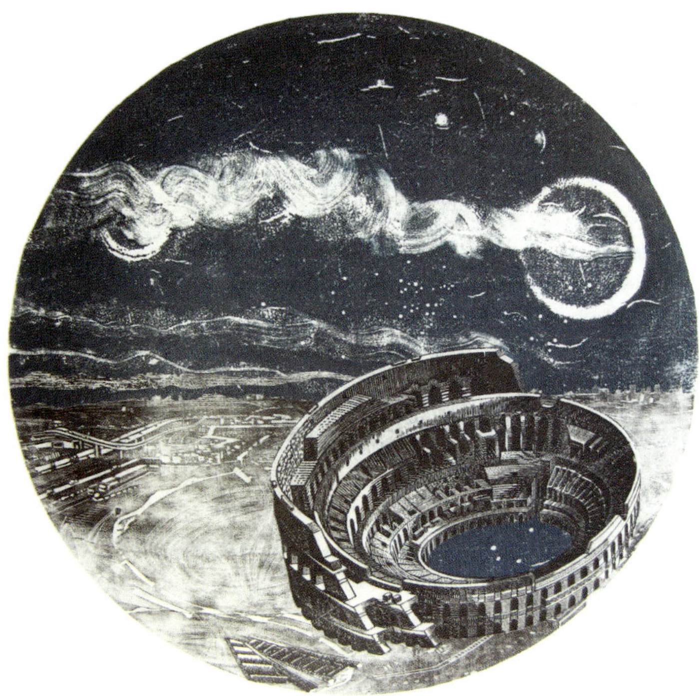

Moonlit Colosseum (2013), wood engravings and monotype print from salvaged floor lino, on Kozu-shi collaged on convex glass, diameter: 18cm (7in). This same colosseum image has provided the basis for various of my collages.

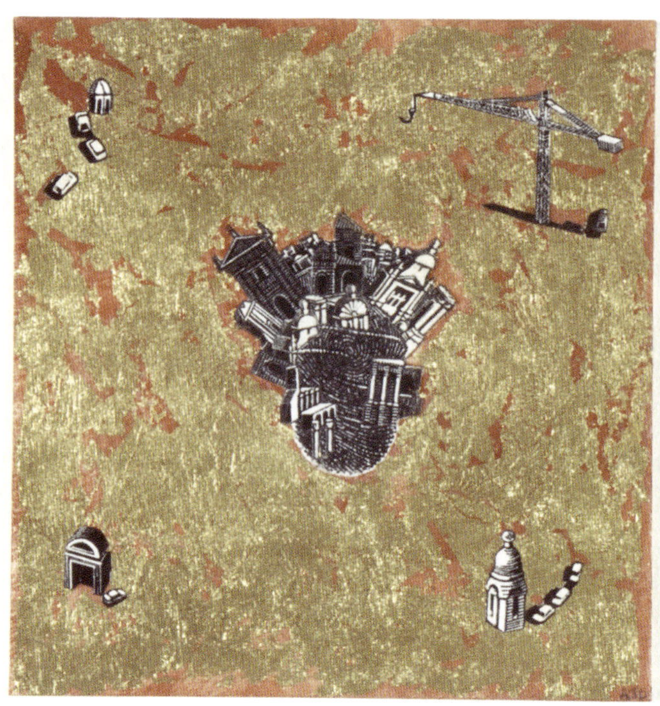

Fingerprint City (2000), my fingerprint (in black ink) with collage, 9.5 × 8.9cm (3¾ × 3½). I painted the white base paper in rust-red watercolour, then collaged wood engraving details onto it, as if the fingerprint was spontaneously sprouting tiny buildings. The gold leaf was intended to suggest a medieval altarpiece.

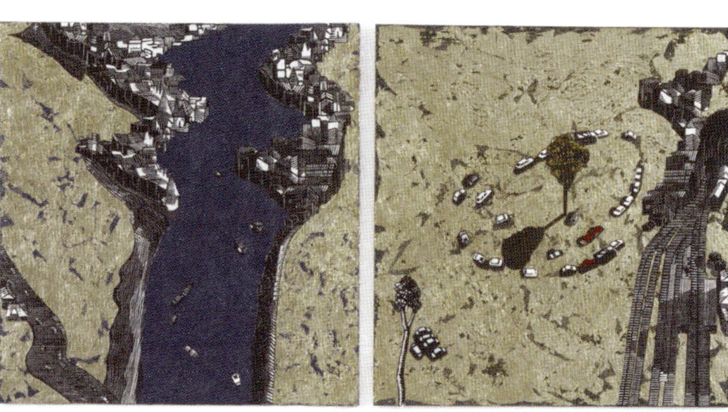

Rivers Roads Railways (2000), wood engravings on paper and gold leaf collaged on two pieces of paper, 9.4 × 18.1cm (3¾ × 7in). This was made in a similar way and is a similar scale to *Fingerprint City*.

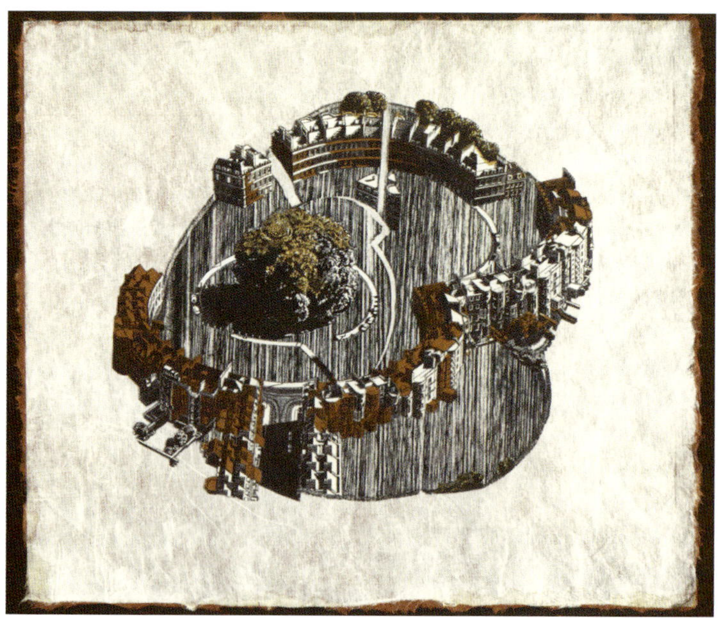

Trunk Roads (2002), on Japanese paper, 15.5 × 17.8cm (6 × 7in). This uses details from my engravings of Bath Circus (on cream and rust-brown papers) collaged on a print of a roughly sawn holly roundel. Its pattern of vertical black lines was generated by the saw. The cracks in the block, printing as white lines, inspired this composition.

MIXED MEDIA AND ABSTRACTION

Collage is a great way to combine elements of images made by diverse processes and thus displaying different qualities of mark-making and various nuances of light and dark tonality. Collage lets me play with the scale of compositional elements, as well as the varied visual effects of mixing together different types of prints. It can also facilitate playing with visual forms to create more abstract results.

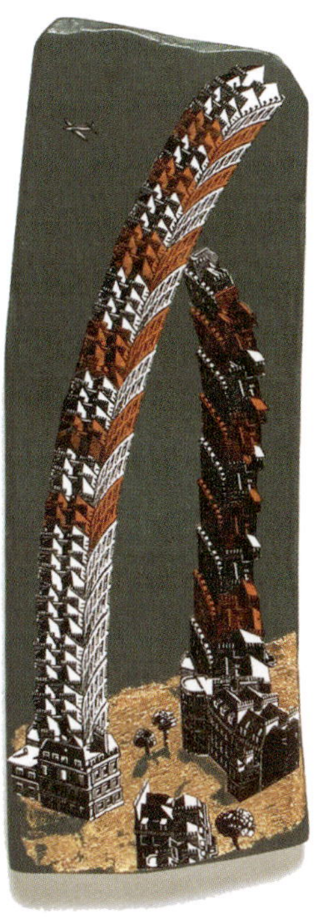

A Delicate Balance (2002), wood engraving on white and coloured papers, gold leaf and pen drawing on paper collaged on deep-green painted wood panel, 19.7 × 6.7 × 0.6cm (7¾ × 2¾ × ¼in).

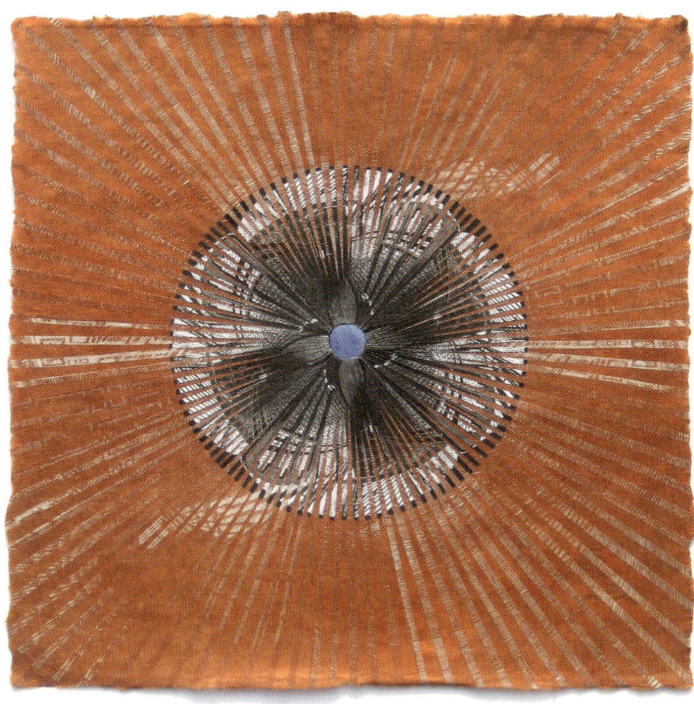

Wall Flower (2008), collage on Nepalese Lhokta paper, 43.2 × 43.2cm (17 × 17in), involved printing several impressions of a small engraving: *Passage of Light*, cutting the prints into strips and reassembling them on strips of an architectural linocut in orange-red hues. In the middle is what looks like a blue paper circle but is actually a tiny mirror (photographed outdoors).

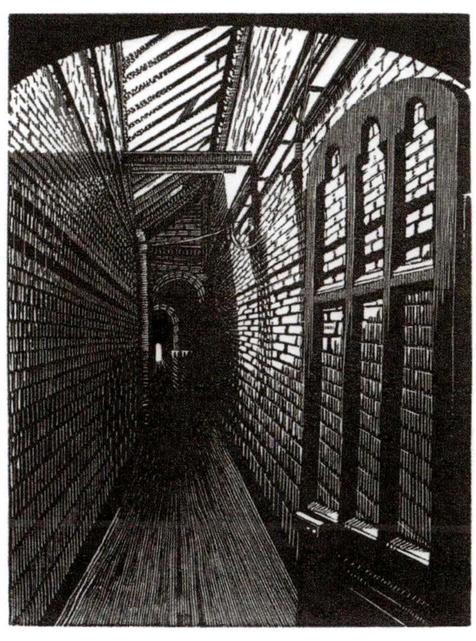

Passage of Light (2007), engraving on boxwood block, 10 × 7.5cm (4 × 3in), on Zerkall paper. Elements of this small engraving have provided the basis for several of my larger collages.

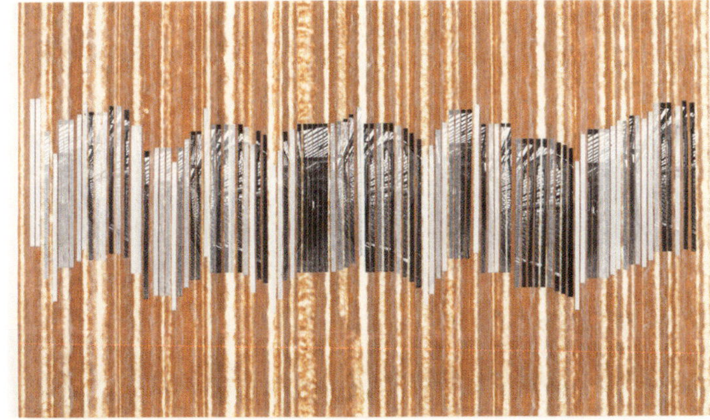

Repeat till Fade (2008), wood engraving collage, 28.8 × 47.5cm (11¼ × 18¾in). This comprises strips of black and grey printings of *Passage of Light* collaged on striped, rust-red paper.

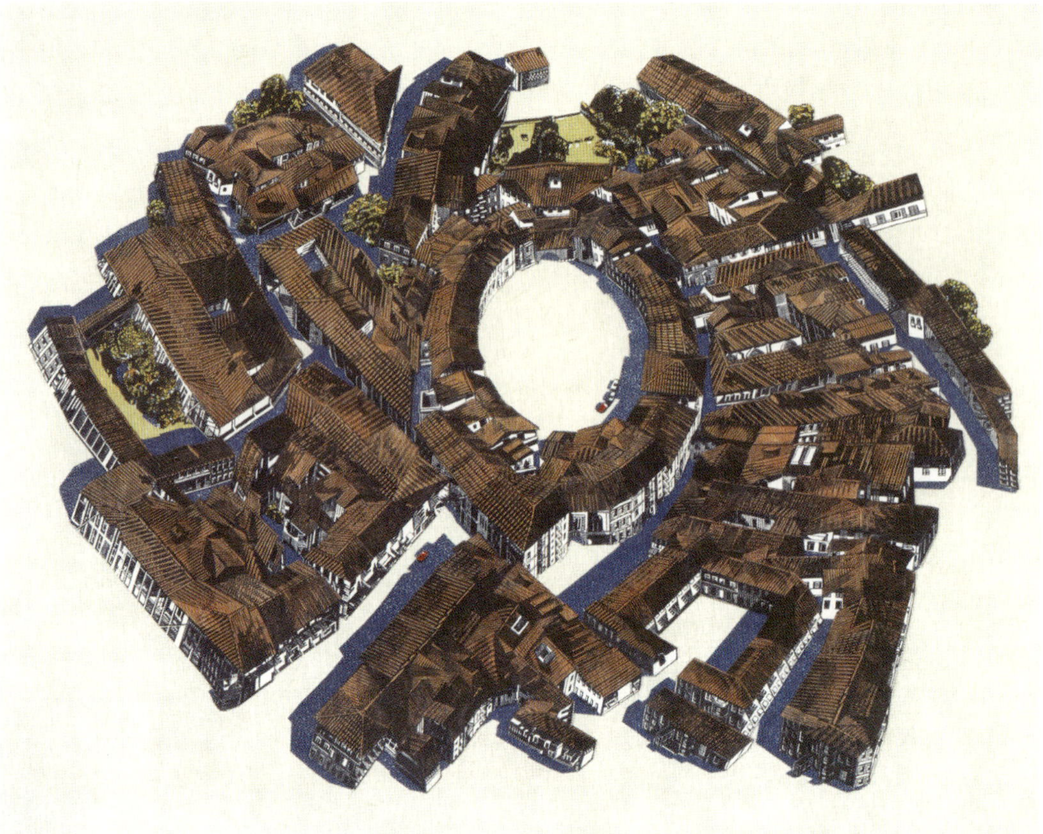

Lucca (2000), 30.5 × 35.2cm (12 × 13¾in), uses buildings and rooftops from my engraving *Panorama* (illustrated in Chapter 4) to create an aerial impression (inspired by a postcard) of Lucca in Tuscany. I first printed some of the woodblocks on rust-red Nepalese Lhokta paper and used details from those and other engravings and linocuts to create this collaged composition.

Collage equipment

What you need for making collages is:

A large clean **work surface**.

Old newspapers or magazines for gluing on.

A supply of **spare prints** in black and white and/or colour as preferred and a box or large drawer to store them in.

Other **interesting materials** including, perhaps, papers painted with watercolour or else manufactured map pages, marbled papers, redundant bank notes and patterned paper packaging of various sorts (though some are not acid-free so may discolour over time.)

Scissors or **sharp scalpel** and **self-healing cutting mat**. (I almost always use sharp scissors rather than a scalpel; my favourite are Fiskars embroidery scissors, which cut paper crisply.)

Sharp pencil (useful to outline areas of print for cutting or to map out guides for sticking down pieces of collage on more complex compositions).

Glue: I use the readily available glue stick, Pritt, for almost all my collages. Archival pastes available from specialist paper and printmaking suppliers are fine too, except that, after pasting maybe half a dozen collage pieces in place, you need to press the work under heavy books or in a nipping press overnight (between blotters) to prevent paper cockling. As some of my collages involve hundreds of pieces of paper glued in place, the necessity to keep pressing them flat at frequent intervals would make it impossible for me to finish them because the creative momentum would be lost in those forced breaks. Pritt, by contrast, dries flat, so you can carry on working until the collage is finished. Although it may seem surprising that such a non-specialist glue could be suitable for artists' collage-making, it's actually non-toxic, solvent-free and acid-free (actually very slightly alkaline), and is apparently made from over 90 per cent natural ingredients such as water and potato starch.

Filmoplast P90: this is an archival, self-adhesive, paper tape I often use when making larger collages. If gluing many small components together for a large collage, which may or may not later be glued to a more rigid surface, the weight of adding successive small pieces of paper and the composition's expanding size may cause the structure to start pulling apart. Before that happens, it's useful to turn the glued composition onto its face from time to time, and strengthen the back of it by sticking strips of this tape along all its paper edges, at the back, to ensure that all the glued parts are reinforced and firmly held together. (I often end up with quite a dense, overlapping mat of tape strips across the back of my collages.)

Substrates on which to glue your compositions. Often, collages are on paper or card (preferably archival/acid free if you don't want them to discolour). But I also enjoy collaging on unexpected surfaces including razor- and oyster-shells; flat stones, pebbles and fragments of roofing slate; ceramic and mosaic tiles, ceramic bowls and pottery shards; broken mirror fragments and convex clock glass of different dimensions. Paper can be collaged onto all sorts of unusual and surprising surfaces such as these. So long as the substrates are clean, dry, hard, reasonably smooth, non-acidic and resistant to mould, discolouration or general decay, they should be fine for collage.

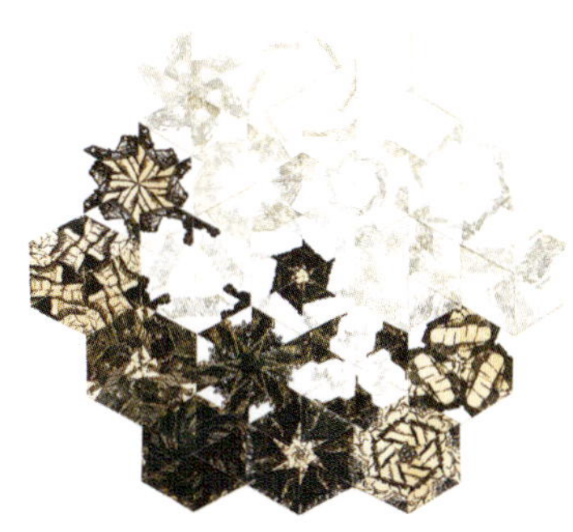

The balloon canopy for *Early Flight* comprised linocuts cut into equilateral triangles and reassembled in kaleidoscopic patterns.

The triangles were attached to one another at the back using Filmoplast P90 – a self-adhesive archival paper tape.

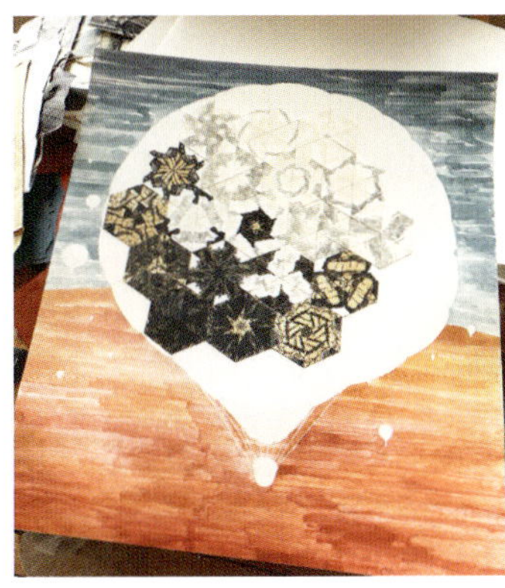

Here the hexagons comprising the balloon canopy have been glued to a base of museum board painted with watercolour.

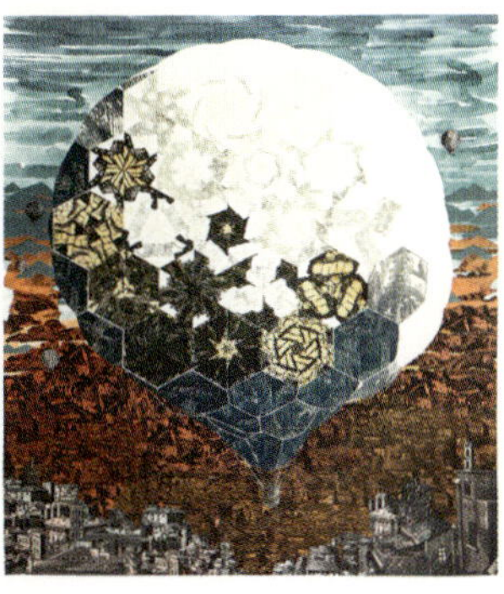

Early Flight (2022), collage on museum board, 81 × 71cm (32 × 28in), incorporates the same rooftops used in the *Lucca* collage, adds a foreground of linocut-printed buildings and a balloon canopy of linocut fragments on a watercolour background.

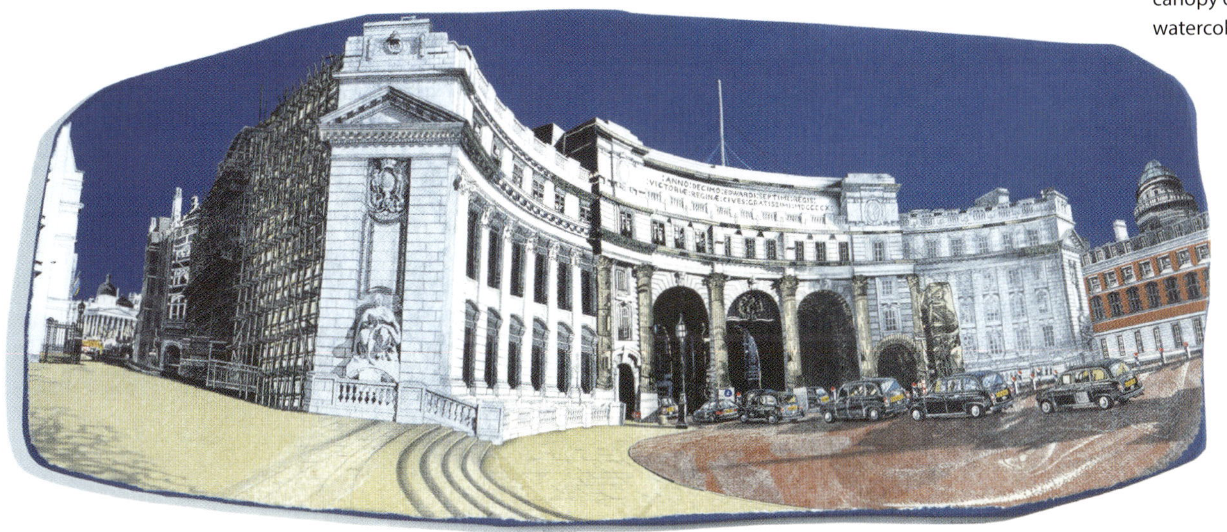

London, February Sun (1997). Pencil, pen and coloured pencil drawing with linocut, wood engraving, gold leaf and found papers collaged on painted wood panel, 31.1 × 69.8 × 0.6cm (12¼ × 27½ × ¼in).

Collage dos and don'ts

While I don't want to deter any creative experimentation, for best results, bear these factors in mind:

1. Don't glue heavier weight papers onto lighter ones. While Pritt dries flat without cockling, paper naturally expands and contracts depending on the temperature and humidity of its environment. So, if you glue heavier weight papers to a substrate of lighter weight paper, while the whole artwork may be flat in the short term, you may later find that, while its collaged parts have remained flat, there is cockling in the lighter weight substrate surrounding those collaged areas. This is because heavier and lighter papers expand and contract at different rates. If you collage lighter papers to a heavier paper substrate, this problem doesn't cause visible cockling though the paper support may become slightly wavy over time. To collage on, for instance, a light Japanese paper, for optimal results you should first laminate it to thin archival card to create a base layer of greater rigidity for the collage.

Greek Fragment (2018), parts of a 1000-drachma Greek banknote and wood engraving prints on Japanese paper collaged on oyster shell, 7.5 × 7.9 × 2.2cm (3 × 3¼ × ¾in).

2. Make sure the ink on your engravings has had time to dry thoroughly before you start cutting and collaging them, to avoid accidentally smudging printed components or of getting inky fingers, which will inevitably mar the image.

3. Japanese papers are exceptionally good for collaging because their long fibres bond very securely when you glue them down, but all printing papers, Eastern and Western, that print wood engravings well, will also perform well for collage.

4. Avoid ultra-smooth or shiny papers such as heavily coated photographic ones. They may not adhere well.

5. Pritt glue works particularly well for collages on entirely rigid substrates, which will ultimately be framed and glazed and thus are not vulnerable to being flexed in any way. If you've ever tried using it to stick paper ephemera in scrapbooks, you may have noticed that they can come unstuck. This is because the flexing of pages as you turn them breaks the glue's bond. For this reason, depending on the papers used, it may not always be ideal to use Pritt to collage images into books.

6. Don't use other household glues or glue sticks without checking their ingredients and pH value. Although some may adhere very well, they may change colour over time and discolour the paper.

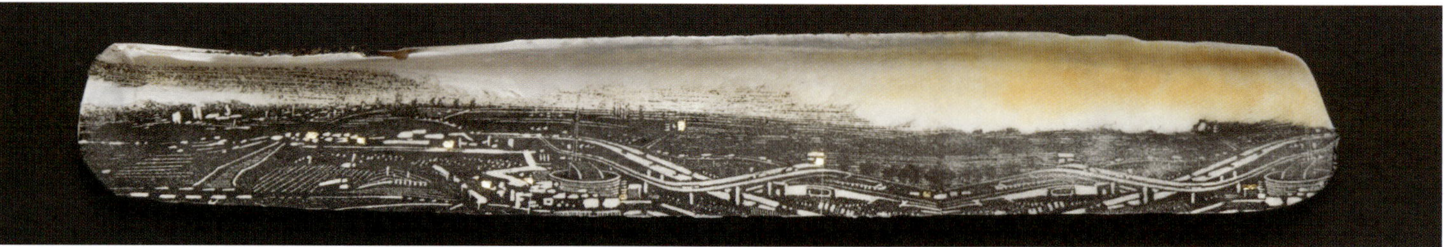

Hackney Marshes Dawn (2010), wood engraving on Kozu-shi and gold leaf collaged on razor shell, 2.5 × 18 × 0.6cm (1 × 7 × ¼in). The shell's orange streak suggested a dawn sky. The thin paper collage blends in as if the imagery was directly printed on the shell. With thicker paper, edges would be visible and the illusion less convincing.

7. If using collage to decorate an object (*découpage*), and if it's made of an acidic substance such as wood or household cardboard, paint its surface with a few layers of acrylic primer (as if you were preparing a canvas for oil painting) to seal its surface, thus creating a buffer between the acidic surface and the paper collage. If directly in contact with one another, the acids in the wood or card would quickly discolour the paper collage.

8. After the découpage is complete, paint at least six layers of a good-quality artists' clear varnish (either matt, satin or gloss as you prefer) all over the image area to seal and protect it from dirt or abrasions. Once dry, the surface can be wiped, if necessary, with a damp cloth to keep it clean. (Be aware that some varnishes may yellow with age.)

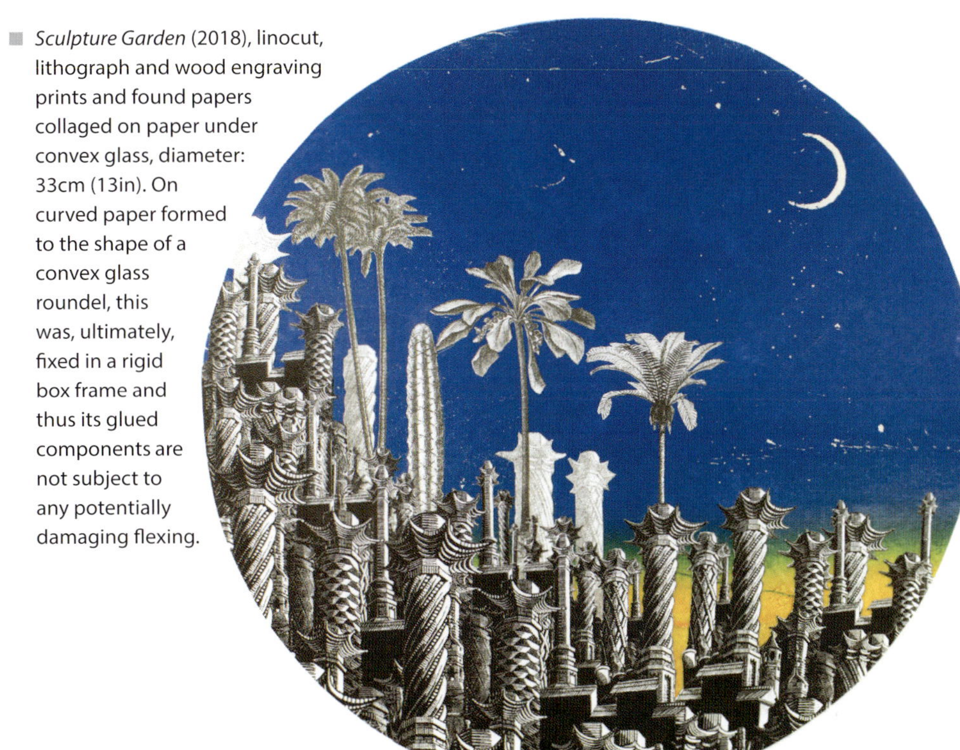

Sculpture Garden (2018), linocut, lithograph and wood engraving prints and found papers collaged on paper under convex glass, diameter: 33cm (13in). On curved paper formed to the shape of a convex glass roundel, this was, ultimately, fixed in a rigid box frame and thus its glued components are not subject to any potentially damaging flexing.

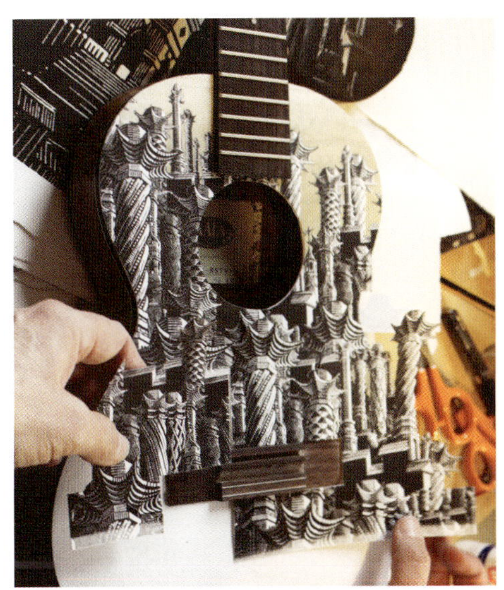

This wooden ukulele was collaged for a charity fundraiser. Before applying collage, the wooden surface was primed with acrylic primer.

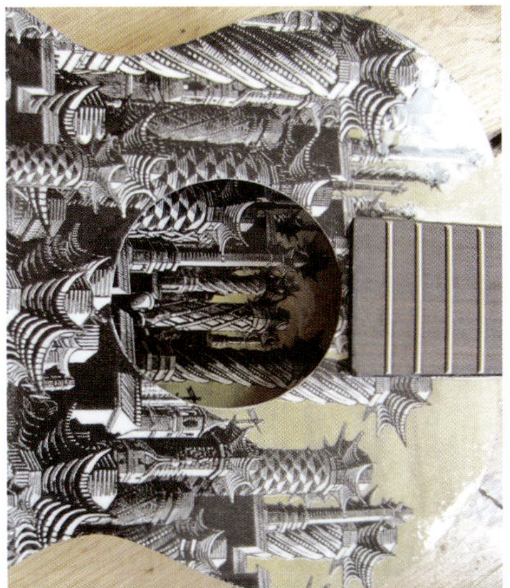

Notice the shiny surface of the layers of clear varnish used to seal the collaged surface.

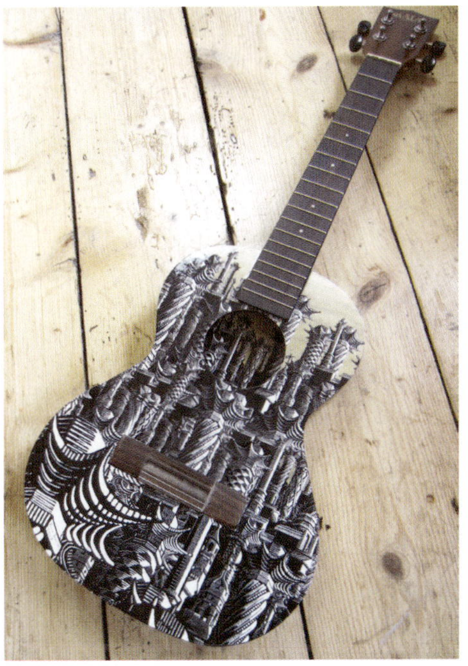

Tudor Rhythms (2017), commissioned by the Hepatitis C Trust. Lithographic prints (developed from wood engravings) on Somerset Satin paper collaged on wooden ukulele and varnished, 61 × 22.5 × 7cm (24 × 8¾ × 2¾in).

9. If collaging with heavier papers, you may notice distracting, visible, white lines of the paper edges at the edge of each glued piece. If the collage is essentially black and white, you can disguise visible edges by colouring them in with a water- and fade-proof black pen to create a seamless look to your work with invisible or barely visible joins.

10. If the collage will be framed and glazed or otherwise maintained in a dust-free environment like your prints (such as in a storage box or plan-chest drawer), there's no need to varnish it.

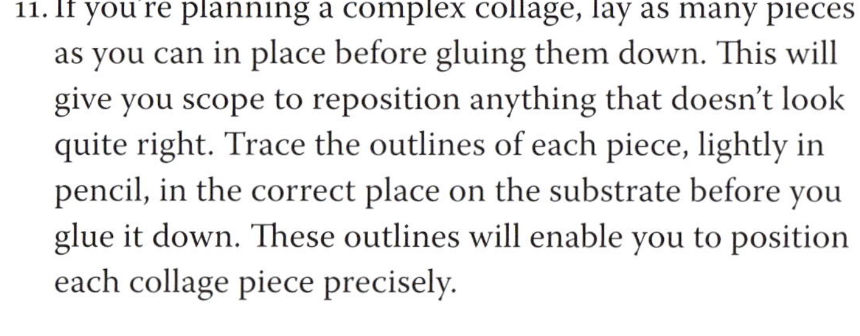

11. If you're planning a complex collage, lay as many pieces as you can in place before gluing them down. This will give you scope to reposition anything that doesn't look quite right. Trace the outlines of each piece, lightly in pencil, in the correct place on the substrate before you glue it down. These outlines will enable you to position each collage piece precisely.

12. Take a photo of the laid-out pieces, for constant reference while you're working, before you move them out of position to apply glue to each one.

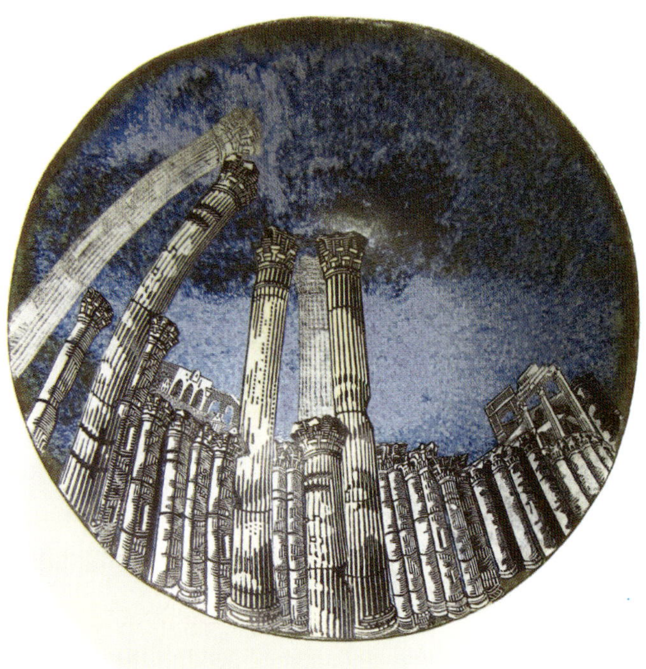

Palmyra Approaching Storm (2015), wood engraving prints on Japanese cream, white and semi-transparent China White and Kozu papers collaged on the concave surface of a fired, glazed, ceramic bowl, diameter: 12cm (4¾in). The collage was not varnished because the bowl was framed and glazed for display.

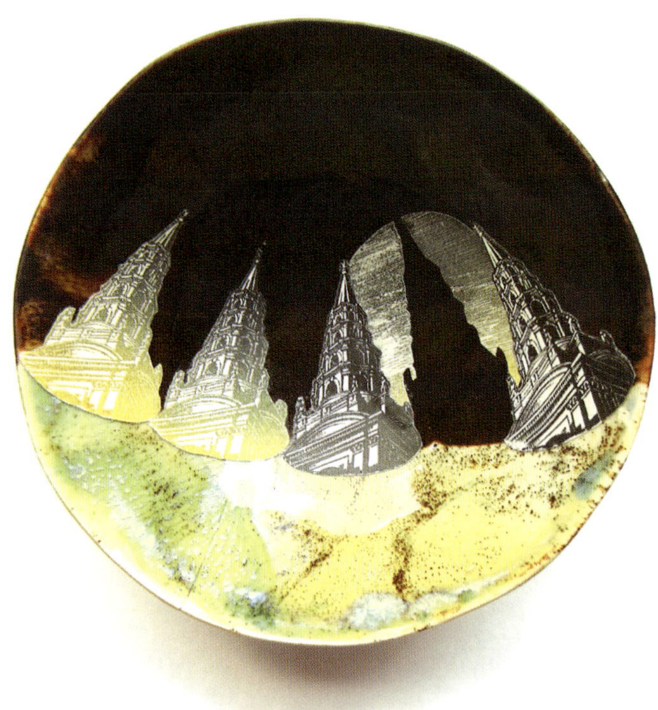

Four Weddings and a Funeral (2014), wood engravings on Gampi Vellum paper collaged on the concave surface of a fired, glazed, ceramic bowl, diameter and depth: 10.5 × 3.5cm (4 × 1½in).

Greek Idyll (2019), wood engraving on Gampi vellum paper and fragment of Greek (pre Euro) banknote collaged on glazed ceramic disc, diameter and depth: 4 × 0.3cm (1½ × 1/8in).

Using glue-stick effectively

Gather some old newspapers or magazines (ones without staple-binding, ideally). Open one out to its centre pages and lay it out, flat, on the worktop.

Don't hold paper to be glued in one hand while you glue it, in mid-air, with the other – that is messy and inefficient! Place the paper to be glued face-down in the middle of the opened newspaper. Press the glue stick firmly down into its mid-point and push it in a straight line heading towards an edge, and continuing right off onto the newspaper. Repeat this action many times, starting always in the middle, to create a series of radiating, overlapping, glue lines out from the middle of the collage paper and making, in effect, a star shape in glue on its back. Work quickly as Pritt dries fast.

As you work, tiny paper fibres (more visible on Japanese papers) will be pulled by the glue to fan out slightly at the paper's edges, which will help hold the paper in place on the newspaper.

If by any chance the collage paper shifts while you're gluing it, which might cause glue residue on the newspaper to transfer to the front of the collage, lift up the affected piece, move it to a clean area of newspaper and continue pasting these radiating star lines until the back of the paper is completely coated.

Check that the paper is well and truly coated because, if you miss gluing any parts of it, they may form air blisters in the collage later. While pasting, check for lumps of glue on the back of the paper. (These may create unwanted bumps on the front of the collage.) If there are any, work from the middle outwards with the glue stick to push them all off onto the newspaper.

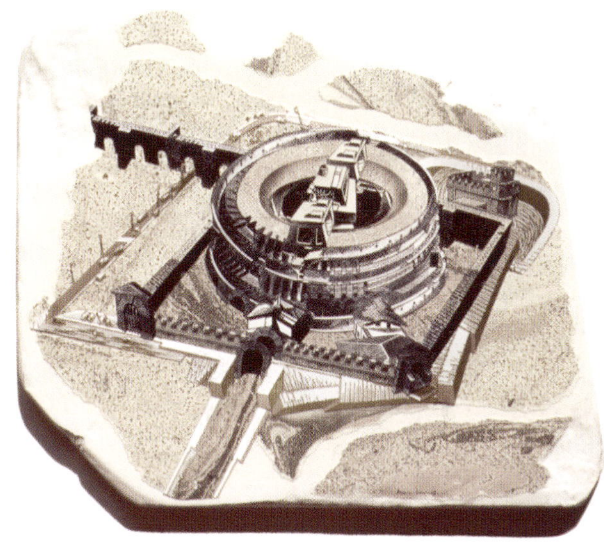

Castel S Angelo (1996), wood engraving, linocut, pencil and marbling on paper on painted wood panel, 19.7 × 22.2cm (7¾ × 8¾in).

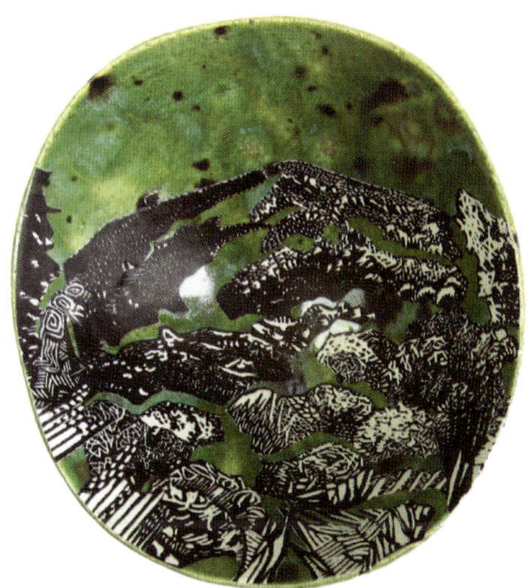

Greek Island I (2015), wood engraving prints on Basingwerk Parchment paper collaged on the concave surface of a fired, glazed, ceramic bowl, diameter: 9.8cm (3¾in).

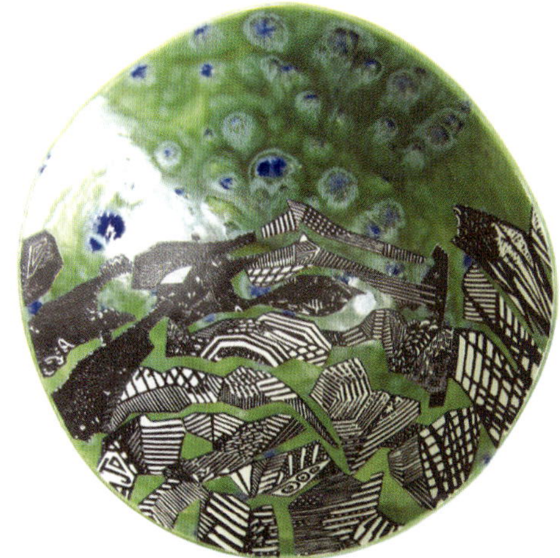

Greek Island II (2015), wood engraving prints on Basingwerk Parchment paper collaged on the concave surface of a fired, glazed, ceramic bowl, diameter: 12cm (4¾in).

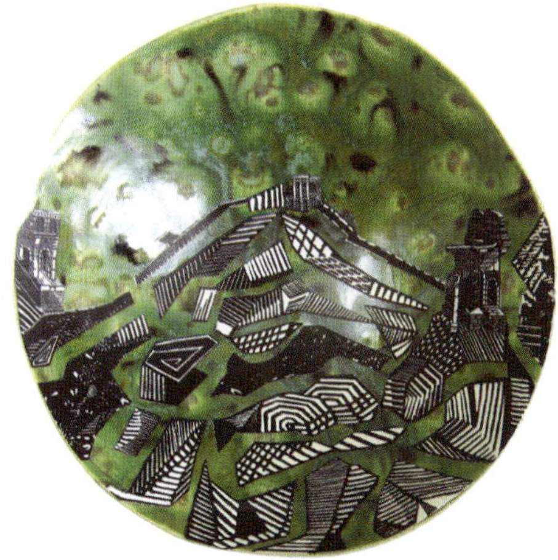

Greek Island III (2015), wood engraving prints on Basingwerk Parchment paper collaged on the concave surface of a fired, glazed, ceramic bowl, diameter: 12cm (4¾in)

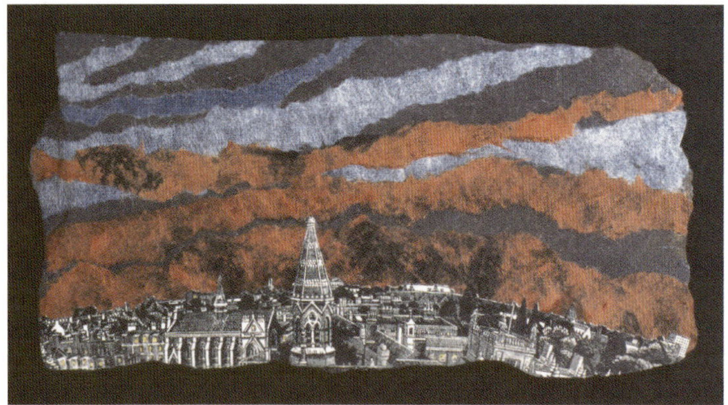

Oxford Storm (2005), wood engraving on paper with gold leaf and coloured Nepalese and Japanese papers collaged on slate, 8.3 × 16.3 × 0.6cm (3¼ × 6½ × ¼in). The long fibres on layered Japanese papers make an extremely secure bond when glued. This collage is in the V&A collection.

Try to avoid a build-up of glue at the edges of the paper because, when you press the glued piece into position, any excess glue may squeeze out around the edges, and this can spoil the image. If this happens, carefully lift off the excess with a scalpel blade straight away, being careful to avoid smearing it, which will stain. Otherwise, leave it to dry completely and then carefully cut away the dry glue lump with a scalpel.

Avoid gluing very large pieces of paper all in one go. It is usually easier to cut or tear them into smaller, more manageable, pieces. As Pritt dries fast, gluing a piece of paper much larger than, say, the full span of your hand, can be problematic. It's also easier to smooth smaller glued pieces into position within a collage than large ones where the paper (especially if it's thin) may crease or wrinkle as you're working on it.

When you've applied an even layer of glue all over the back of the paper and removed any glue lumps, stick the glue stick back down on it (either in the middle or towards an edge – wherever you prefer), press it down gently and lift it up. The paper, if it's not too heavy, will stick to the glue stick and lift up easily off the newspaper. You can move it, still attached to the stick, to place it on the developing collage, thereby keeping fingers reasonably glue free.

Check that the piece you've just glued is in exactly the desired position before pressing it down firmly. If it isn't, peel it up gently (either with fingers or a pair of tweezers) and adjust accordingly. You can usually do this successfully only once, before the glue dries, but ideally try to get it right first time.

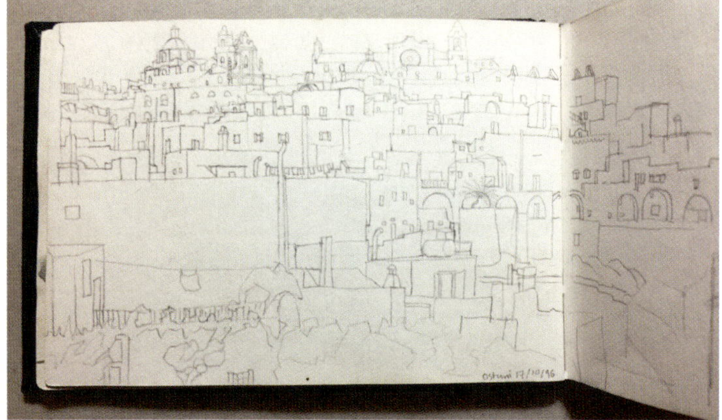

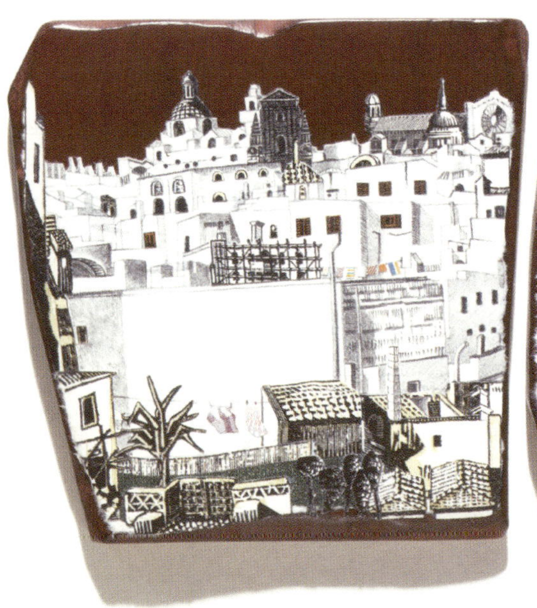

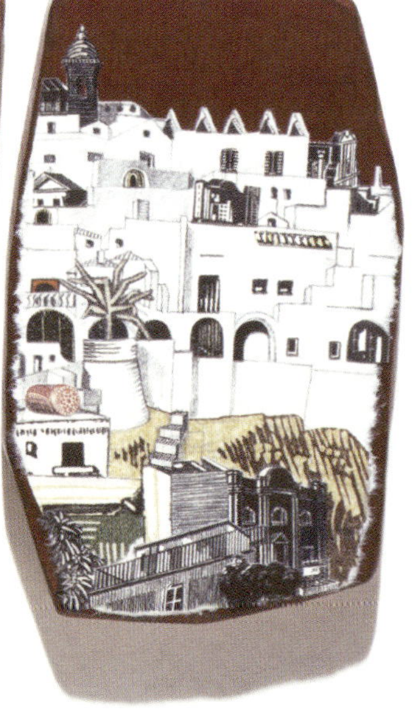

The pencil sketch above, 10 × 14cm (4 × 5½in) of the Italian hilltown of Ostuni inspired this collage, *Ostuni* (2000), pencil, pen and coloured pencil drawing on paper with collaged wood engraving and linocut, all collaged on painted wood panels, total area: 14.3 × 19 × 0.9cm (5½ × 7½ × ½in).

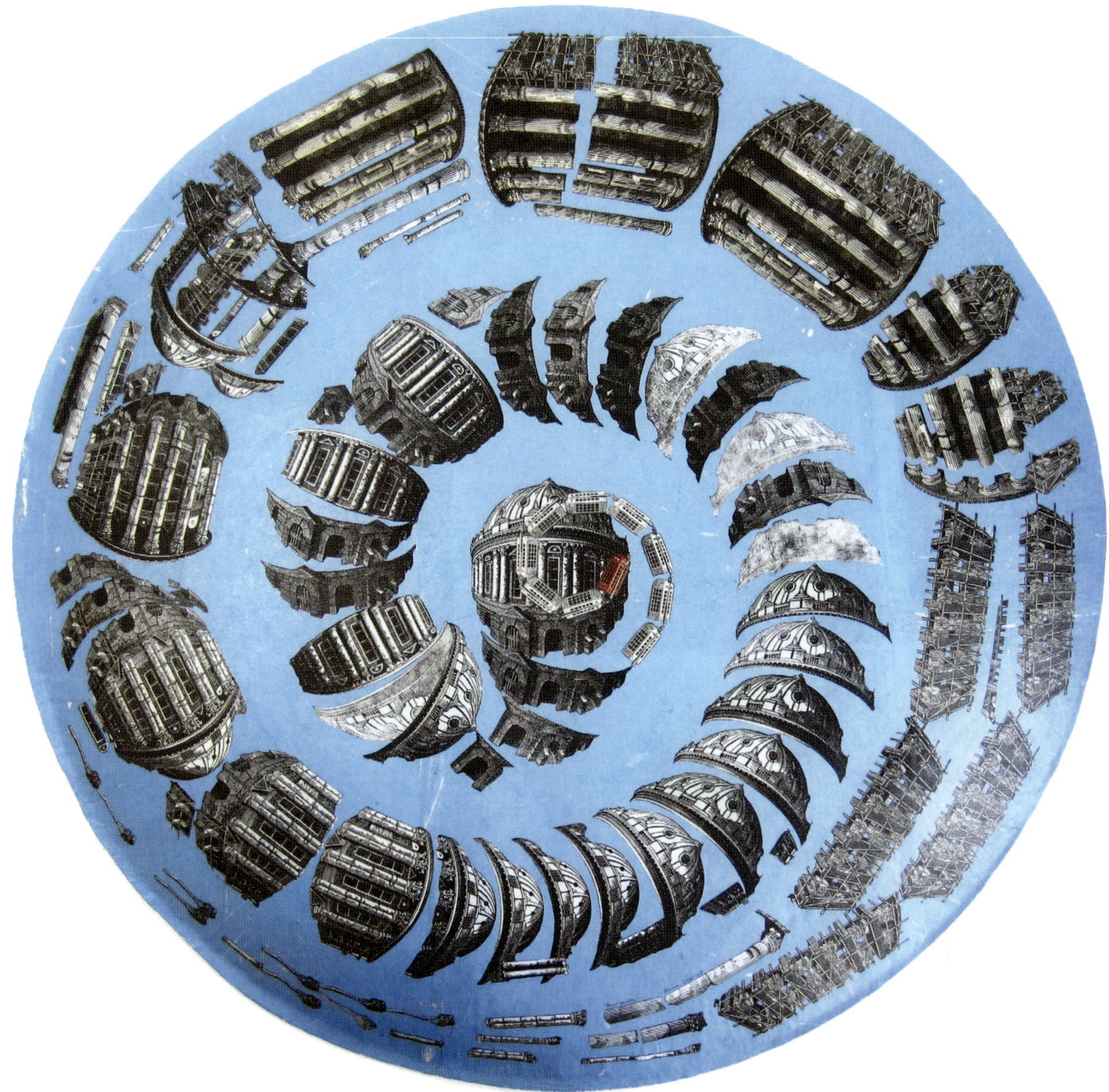

Ammonite (2015), wood engravings on China White and off-white Kozu papers and linocut prints on paper collaged under convex glass, diameter: 51cm (20in). To maintain a perfect ammonite-like whorl, I drew a faint outline around each component so that I would be able to reposition it in exactly the right place once I'd applied glue to it.

Smooth the freshly glued piece down with your finger (make sure your hands are clean). To avoid getting unwanted wrinkles in the paper, work from the middle of the glued piece outwards (roughly replicating with your finger the star shape you made in glue on the back) and ensure that you press down every part firmly so that its entire surface is fully bonded.

Repeat this procedure for every piece of collage, throwing away the newspaper sheets as they become contaminated with glue and working on the clean sheets immediately underneath in your stack.

If the glue stick is drying out and getting hard to use, discard it and get a new one. Old, dry glue sticks never perform well and may tear your papers while you're trying to glue them.

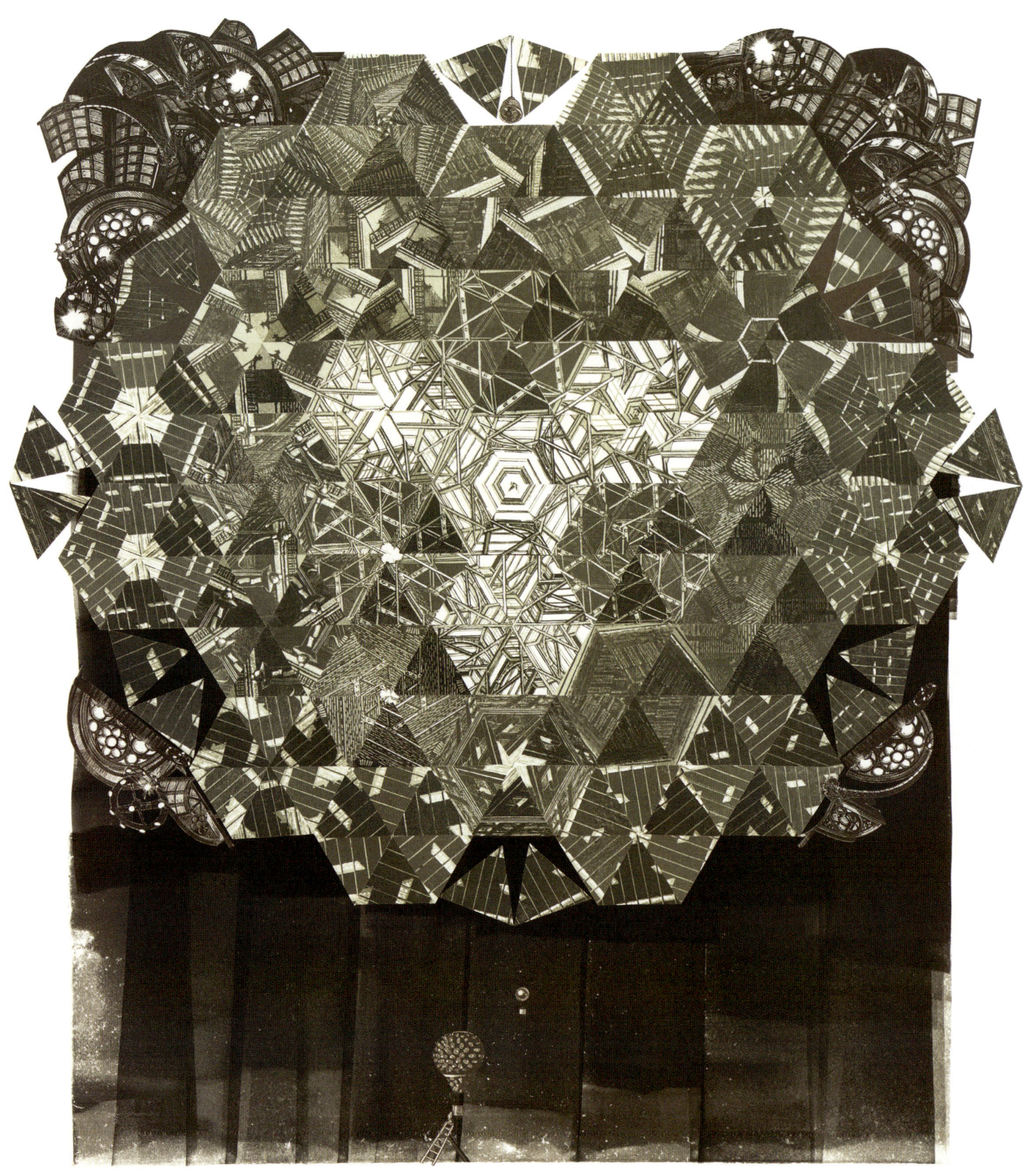

CHAPTER 10

COLLAGE ON UNUSUAL SURFACES

The collage base – be it seashell, mirror shard or pottery fragment – is not a random choice. Sometimes it may suggest its own image. At other times its choice may relate visually and conceptually to a theme I'm working on. The possibilities of collage are as endless and various as the possibilities of wood engraving. Substrates I've used thus far have been fairly wide-ranging but haven't yet extended to metals, plastics or textiles – all of which could have properties worth exploring.

RAZOR SHELLS

If using any found object for collage (especially if found outdoors), wash it thoroughly before use. Even if it appears clean, it may have salts or other invisible chemicals on the surface that might affect the paper at some point in the collage's future. Don't use soaps or detergents. These may deposit chemical residues of their own, which may later affect the collage adversely. If any shells have, for instance, extensive oil or tar deposits on them that wouldn't be cleanable without detergent, then discard them.

I wash found objects in my home sink. I leave them to soak in warm water for a few minutes and then scrub them thoroughly but carefully with a stiff nailbrush. If a razor shell breaks at this stage, as sometimes happens, it demonstrates that it wouldn't have been strong enough as a collage

Fragile Earth (2022), wood engravings, linocuts and lithographs on various papers collaged on 40 razor shells collaged on archival board, 14 × 85 × 1.5cm (5½ × 33½ × ½in). The natural mauve colouration of the delicate shells seemed to suggest a bruised sky and, by extension, our Earth's fragility and thus the idea for the collage.

Flight Of Fancy (2021), collage on museum board, 69 × 60.5cm (27¼ × 23¾in), involved linocut and wood engraving printed on relatively lightweight (Japanese) Gampi Vellum and (German) Zerkall papers collaged on heavier (British) Somerset Satin paper rolled with black ink, all collaged on archival, acid-free, mount board.

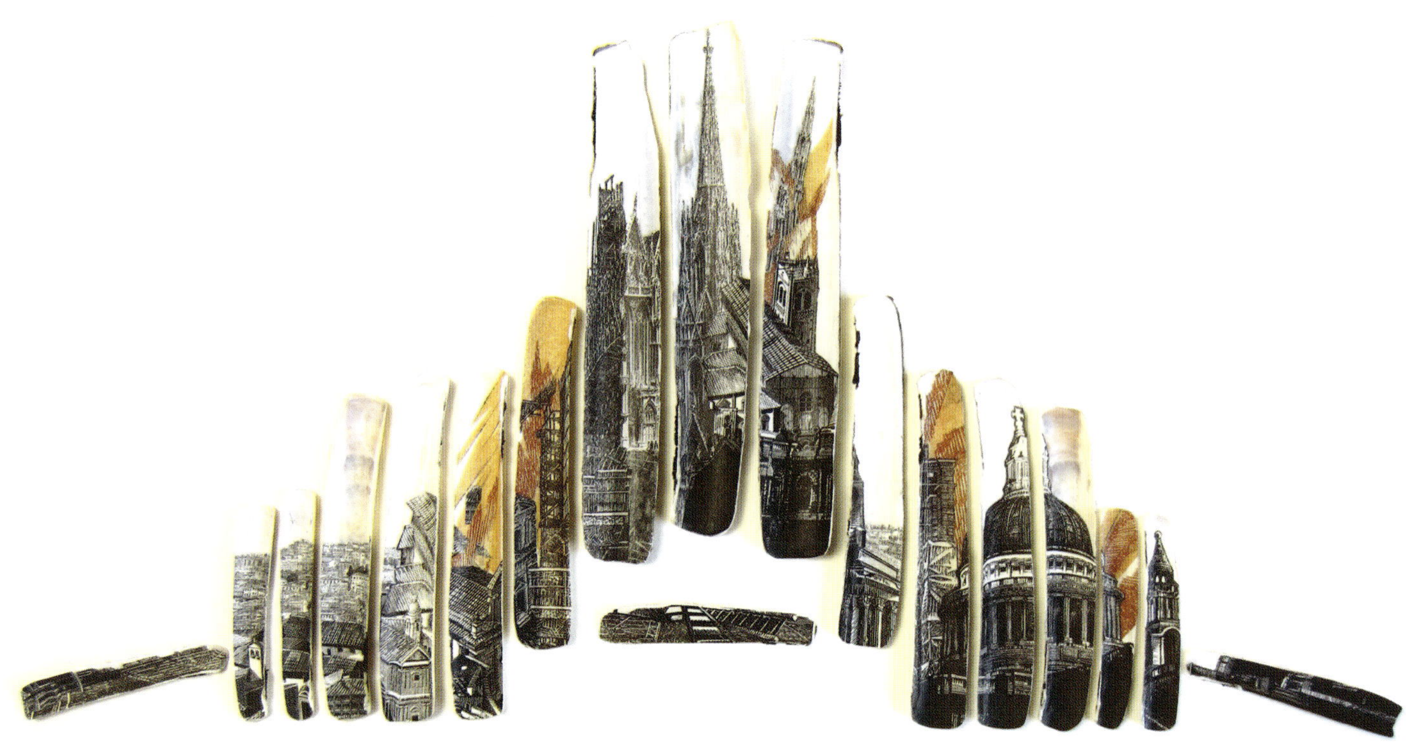

Fires of London (2015), wood engravings on Gampi Vellum, linocuts on Kozu-shi and found papers collaged on 18 razor shells, 23 × 45.5 × 1.5cm (9 × 18 × ½in). This collage, on shells arranged in a church-like shape, presents aspects of London history through a focus on St Paul's cathedral. This work is in London's Guildhall Art Gallery Collection.

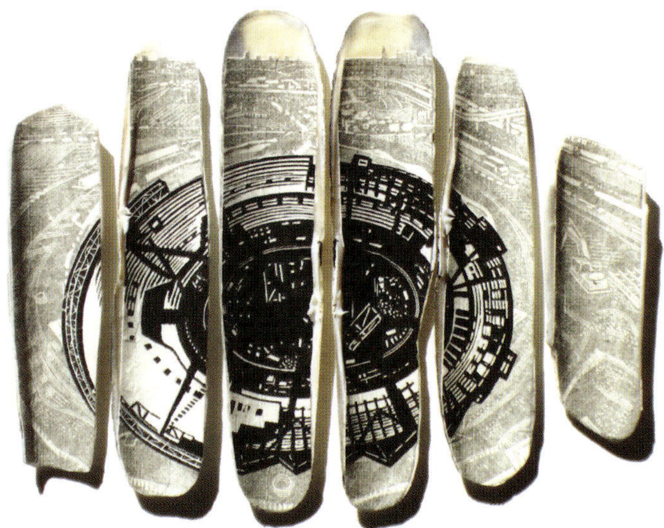

Fragile Hope (2012), wood engravings on Gampi Vellum paper collaged on six razor shells, 11 × 13.5 × 1.5cm (4¼ × 5¼ × ½in). It's easier to use very lightweight papers for collage on such delicate curved surfaces as these. Japanese papers are ideal. This collage and the adjacent example were both responses to London's developing Olympic site on former marshland.

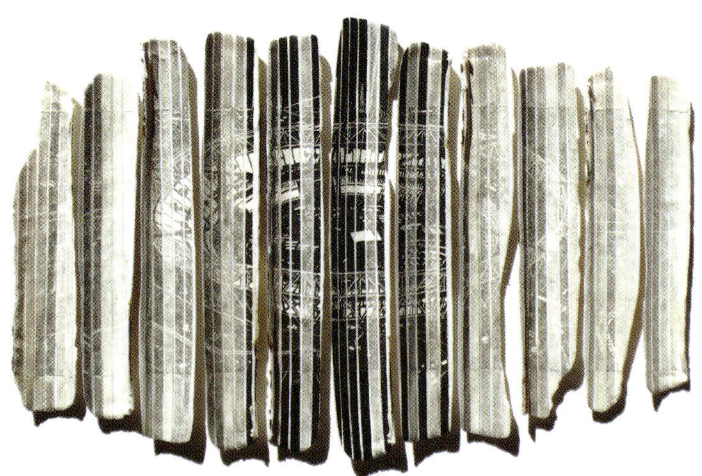

At the End of the Day (2012), wood engraving on Gampi Vellum paper collaged on eleven razor shells, 19 × 29.3 × 1.5cm (7½ × 11½ × ½in). For subtly graduated greys, use prints easily produced as part of the block-cleaning process after editioning: press-printed impressions on paper made without re-inking between printings.

base, so the cleaning becomes a useful self-selecting process for eliminating unsuitable materials. After washing, I leave the intact shells either to air dry naturally or I dry them with clean cotton rag or paper roll.

Before I start a razor-shell collage, I strengthen these fragile shells by sticking strips of self-adhesive, archival, paper tape (Filmoplast P90) to the back of each one, pressing it firmly in place with my fingers and moulding it exactly to the contours of the convex outer surface. I trim excess tape away with sharp scissors. Once the collage is finished, I attach the shells to a firm base of archival board using long hinges of the same self-adhesive tape applied along the length of each shell, at the back, and pressed into place on the base-board with my finger.

Before gluing each piece of paper to the shell's concave surface, it can help to roll it, image side inwards, around a tubular marker pen. Although you then apply the glue to each piece on a flat surface, once you press the glued paper to the shell's concave curve, the paper fibres will remember the equivalent curve you'd created around the pen and will adapt readily to the shell without creasing. (If you collage on the outer, convex, surface of such a shell, the paper is less likely to crease, so it won't need pre-rolling).

OYSTER SHELLS

Collage on non-smooth surfaces, such as, especially, the outer (though sometimes also the inner) surface of an oyster shell, is also best carried out with thin Japanese papers which, when glued, can be moulded with your fingertips into the ridges of the shell. However, bear in mind that the thinner and more transparent the paper, the more the substrate's underlying colour will show through it when glued in place. So, for a more highly contrasted effect of white paper on a darker surface, you will need a heavier paper. Much as an irregular-shaped wood engraving block can suggest a composition and the appropriate scale of the elements within it, so too can the shape or colouring of a naturally formed structure such as an oyster shell.

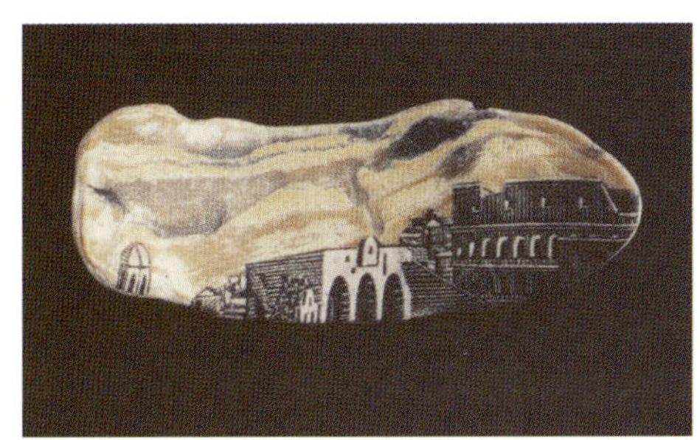

Roman Sky (2005), wood engraving on paper collaged on seashell fragment, 2.1 × 5.2 × 1cm (¾ × 2 × ½in).

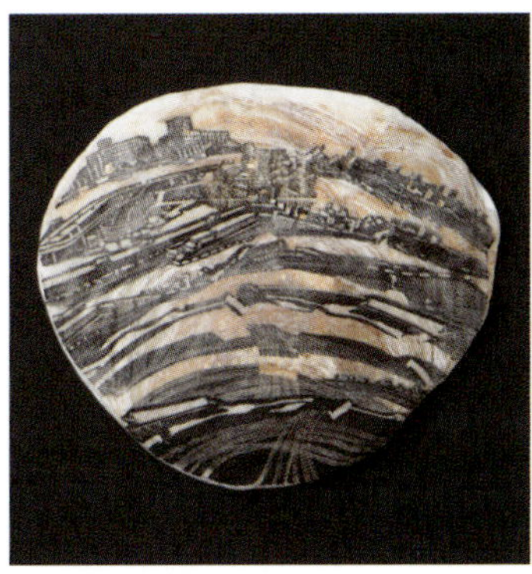

Hackney Marshes Dusk (2010), wood engraving on semi-transparent Kozu-shi with gold leaf collaged on the convex surface of a seashell, 8.3 × 9.5 × 0.6cm (3¼ × 3¾ × ¼in).

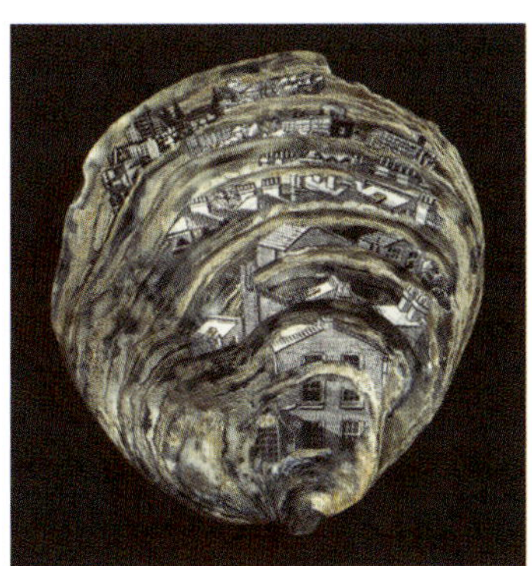

Skylines (2003), wood engraving on opaque off-white paper with pen drawing and gold leaf collaged on the uneven convex surface of an oyster shell, 9.3 × 8.3 × 0.6cm (3¾ × 3¼ × ¼in). Each paper piece was cut or torn to follow the shell's ridged edges.

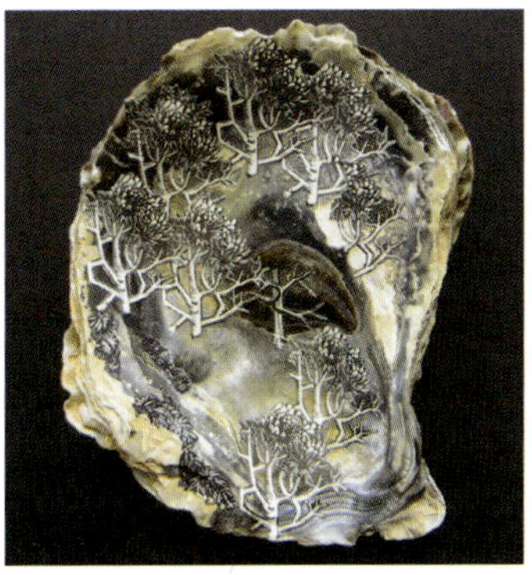

Drowned Forest (2005), wood engraving on paper collaged on the smooth (concave) surface of an oyster shell, 12.8 × 10.5 × 2.8cm (5 × 4 × 1in).

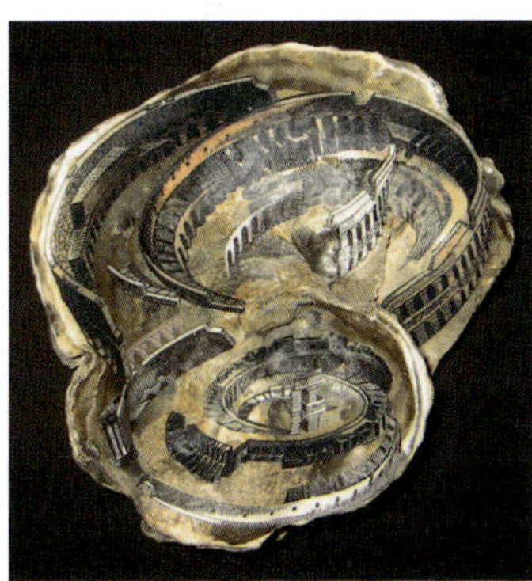

Whirlpool (2005), wood engraving on paper with coloured pencil drawing and fragment of Italian 1,000-lire-banknote collaged on oyster shell, 12 × 11 × 3cm (4¾ × 4¼ × 1¼in). Developed using my *Colosseum* engraving, this collage is in the V&A collection.

Glimpse of Pompeii (2012), wood engraved prints on paper collaged on stone, 4.3 × 2.8 × 1.5cm (1¾ × 1 × ½in). The less flat the pebble, the harder it is to attach to a backing board should you wish to present such a work framed. This one proved quite a framing challenge!

PEBBLES AND SLATE

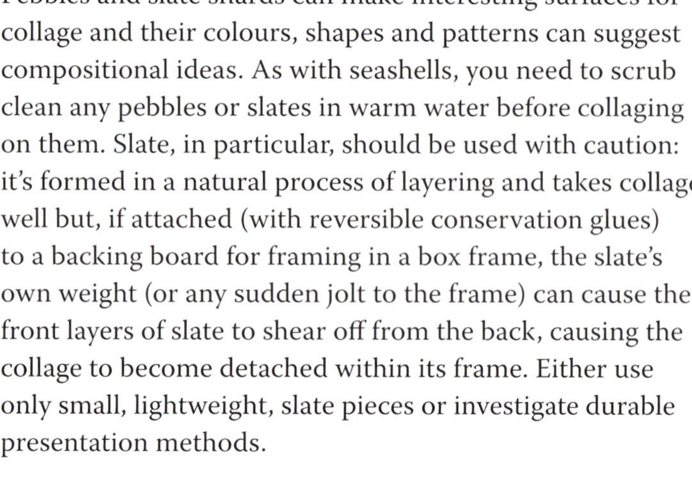

Pebbles and slate shards can make interesting surfaces for collage and their colours, shapes and patterns can suggest compositional ideas. As with seashells, you need to scrub clean any pebbles or slates in warm water before collaging on them. Slate, in particular, should be used with caution: it's formed in a natural process of layering and takes collage well but, if attached (with reversible conservation glues) to a backing board for framing in a box frame, the slate's own weight (or any sudden jolt to the frame) can cause the front layers of slate to shear off from the back, causing the collage to become detached within its frame. Either use only small, lightweight, slate pieces or investigate durable presentation methods.

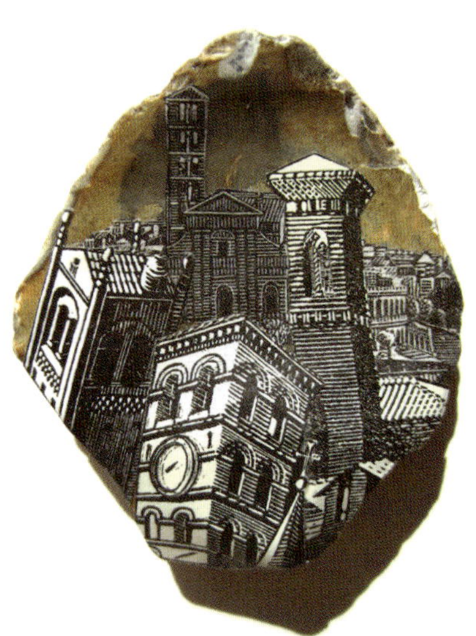

Various Towers (2012), wood engraved prints on paper collaged on stone, 6 × 5 × 1.8cm (2¼ × 2 × ¾in). A pebble of subtle colouring such as this can make a warm, atmospheric background for a collage.

MDF PANELS

I have often used painted panels of medium-density fibreboard as collage substrates. I like to use them to create collages that suggest an aged fragment of a larger whole – an ancient fresco fragment perhaps. To create this effect, I start by sawing the panels to the desired sizes and shapes. I then sand the edges to smooth them off. Then I paint each panel's intended front and edges with at least four layers of casein-based paint, which provides a tough, resilient, opaque, plaster-like layer. This also provides a necessary buffer between the MDF and the intended paper collage, which would otherwise be susceptible to damage from the wood's acids.

After each paint layer is dry, I sand down the surface (and edges) to a smooth finish (using the same sharpening and polishing papers I use for sharpening wood engraving tools) before applying the next layer. Sometimes I polish the final layer to an eggshell-like smoothness. Sometimes I leave it unpolished to give an effect of matt plaster. Both are very receptive surfaces for paper collage. The colour (or colours) chosen for the base layer significantly affect the look of the finished works.

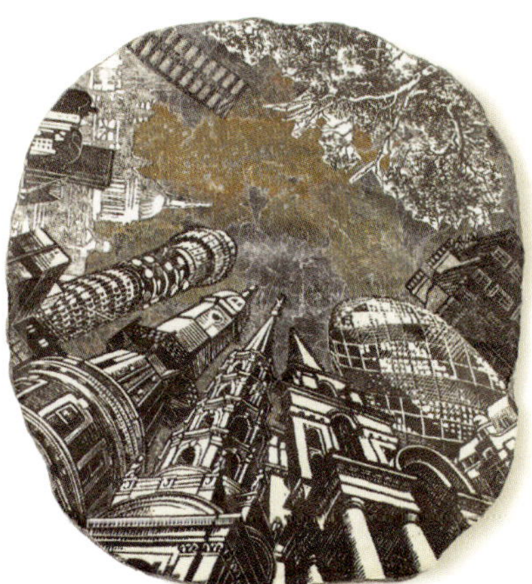

London Landmarks (2018), wood engraved prints on Gampi Vellum, Zerkall and Kozu-shi papers and found paper collaged on slate, 8.2 × 7.5 × 0.4cm (3¼ × 3 × 1/8in). The slate's colouration seemed to suggest a thundery sky which inspired the collage.

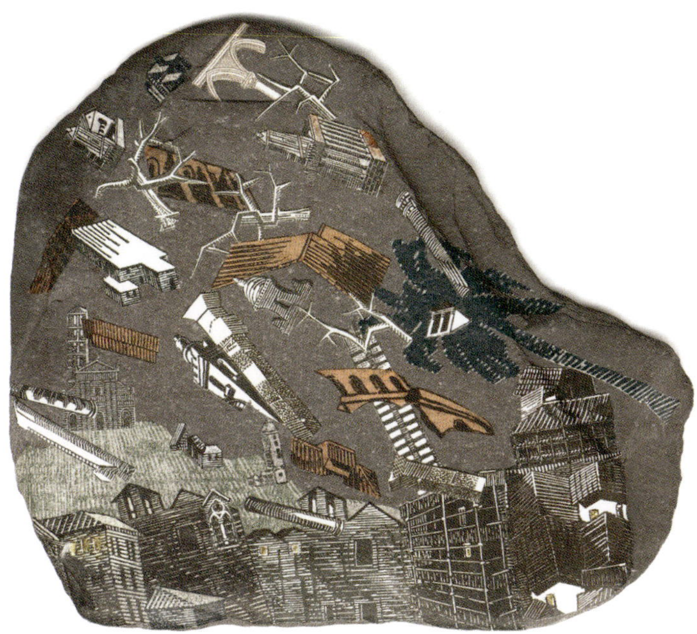

Hurricane with Flying Roofs (2005), wood engraving and linocut prints on paper with fragments of Italian 1,000-lire note and gold leaf collaged on slate, 12 × 13 × 0.8cm (4¾ × 5 × ¼in).

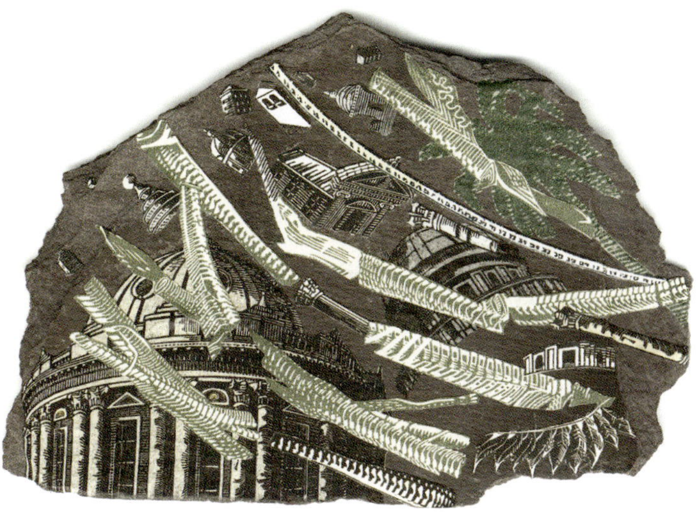

Hurricane with Palm Trees (2005), wood engraving and linocut prints on opaque and semi-transparent Japanese papers with gold leaf collaged on slate, 9.5 × 13.2 × 0.5cm (3¾ × 5¼ × ¼in).

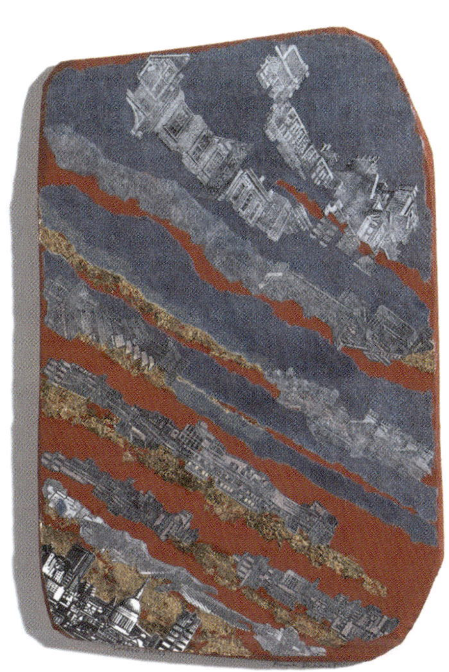

London Skies (2003), wood engravings on opaque and semi-transparent papers with gold leaf and colour-lino-printed paper collaged on deep-red painted wood panel, 17.8 × 11.4 × 0.6cm (7 × 4½ × ¼in).

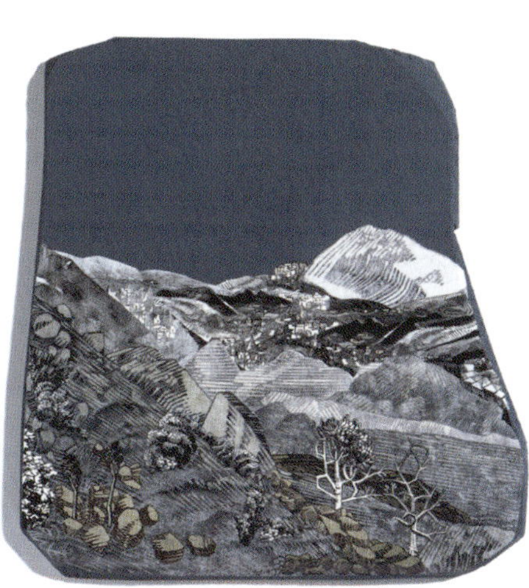

Approaching Storm (2003), wood engraving and linocut prints on white and cream toned Japanese papers, with gold leaf, collaged on blue/grey-painted wood panel, 20.3 × 19 × 0.6cm (8 × 7½ × ¼in).

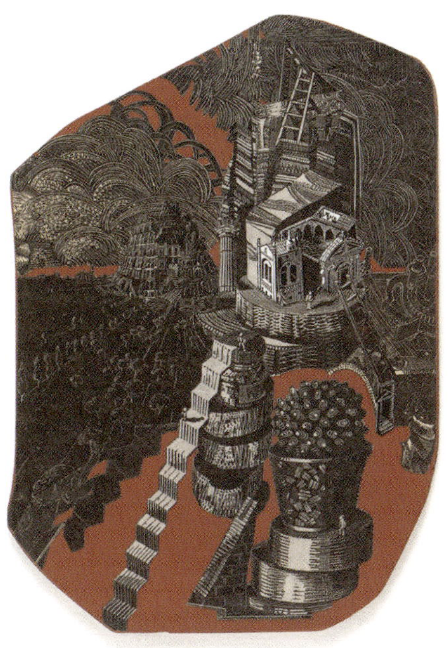

Ambitions and Blind Alleys (2022), wood engravings on Gampi Vellum paper collaged on deep red-painted wood panel, 20.5 × 14.3 × 0.6cm (8 × 5½ × ¼in).

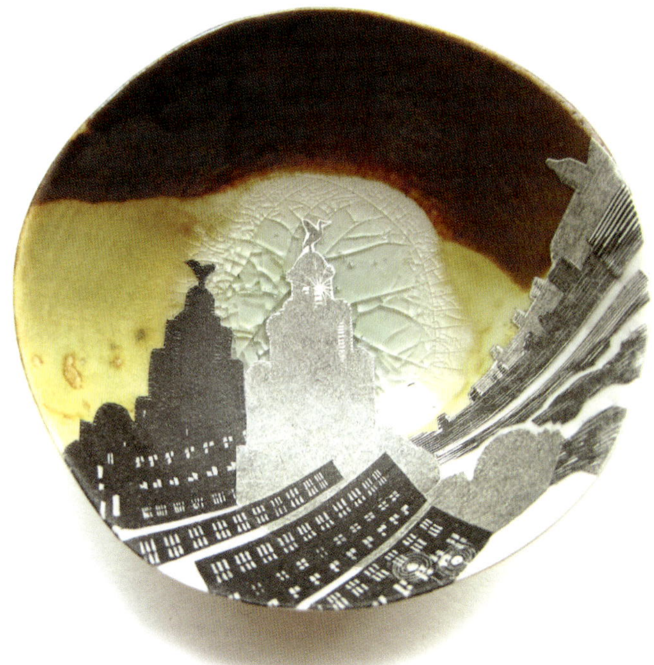

Mersey Morning (2014), wood engravings on Gampi Vellum paper collaged on glazed ceramic bowl (with irregular brown, yellow and opalescent green glaze), diameter: 7.5cm, depth: 3cm (3 × 1¼in).

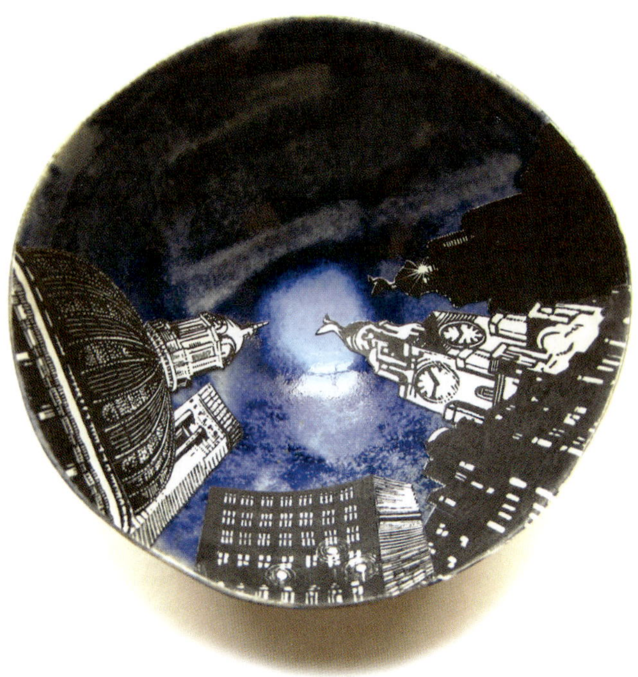

Three Graces (2016), wood engravings on Gampi Vellum paper collaged on glazed, ceramic bowl, diameter: 8.4cm, depth: 4.5cm (3¼ × 1¾in). The bowl's deep blue glaze with pale centre suggested a blue moon in a night sky, inspiring this composition.

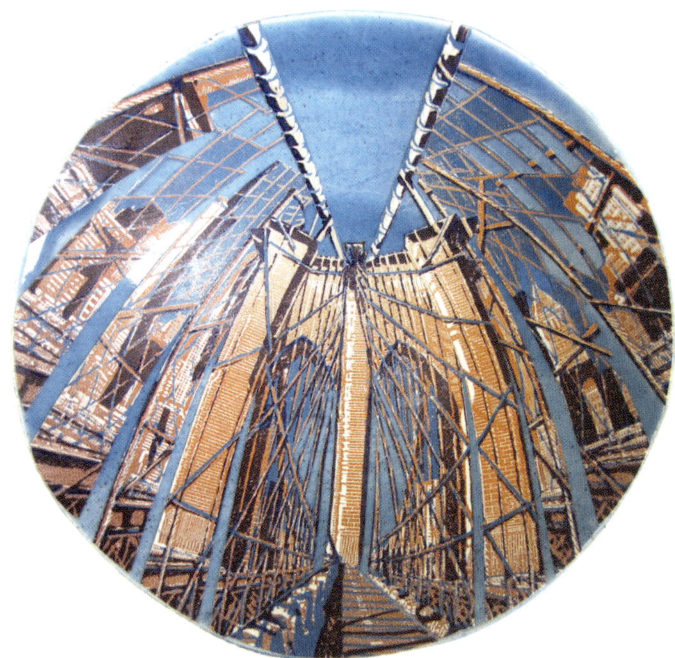

Entering Manhattan (2015), wood engraving and linocut on paper collaged on glazed, ceramic bowl, diameter: 12cm, depth: 4.5cm (4¾ × 1¾in). The glaze suggested a bright blue sky and inspired this composition which uses parts of one of my prints with a similar blue-sky tone.

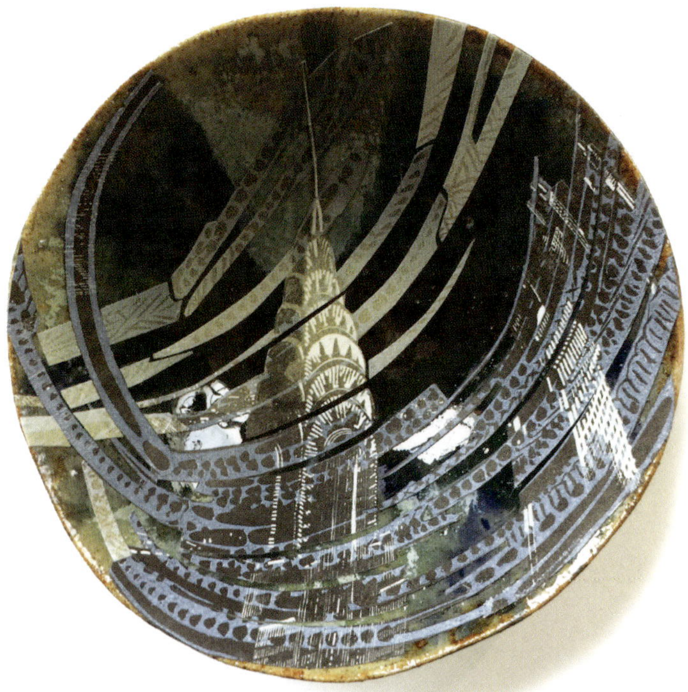

Manhattan Hurricane (2018), wood engraving and linocut prints on Japanese papers collaged on glazed ceramic bowl, diameter: 11.7cm, depth: 4.5cm (4½ × 1¾in). Paper can be distorted by pronounced curves like this bowl's, so it's easier to work with smaller paper pieces to avoid them creasing or not aligning exactly where you had intended.

CERAMIC BOWLS AND POTTERY SHARDS

Fired, glazed ceramics can provide inspiring substrates for collage. If well varnished after the collage's application, such collages could be displayed without framing and cleaned by wiping with a slightly damp cloth, but I have always presented them unvarnished, as wall-mounted pieces in deep box frames. Many of the substrates I use are found materials, as I like recycling and reusing natural and manmade objects where possible. Many of the bowls I've used were purchased at a school fête years ago. Made by an East London ceramist, they were her seconds, with patterns and irregular shapes she didn't much care for, while for me those features were exactly what I found inspiring.

Like pebbles and seashells, found pottery shards, after careful cleaning, can provide worthwhile substrates for collages of different shapes, sizes, formats and compositions. Others can be made from any accidentally smashed crockery. In all cases, the shards' shapes or patterns seem to suggest the subject and nature of each collage.

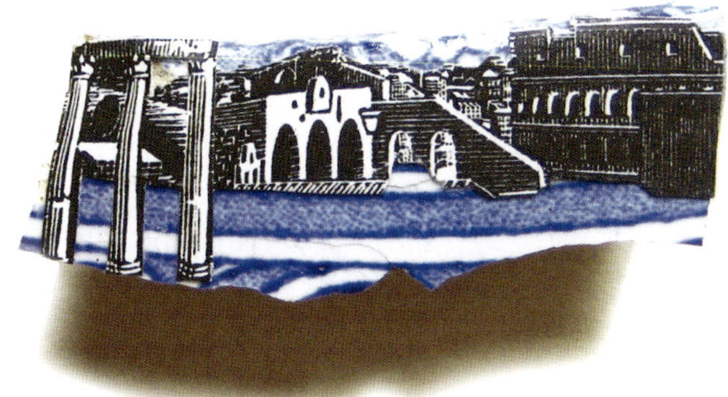

Forum Fragment (2012), wood engraved prints on Zerkall paper collaged on blue tile fragment, 2.5 × 5.4 × 1.3cm (1 × 2 × ½in). The pottery shard base was found in my London garden.

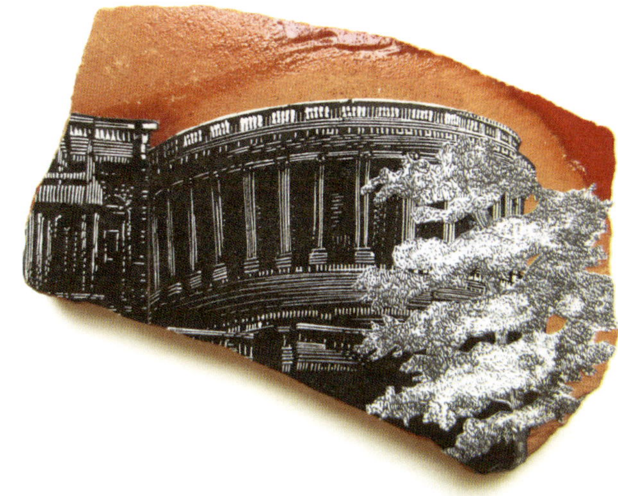

Library with Red Sky (2016), wood engravings on paper collaged on pottery shard, 6 × 8.5 × 1.5cm (2¼ × 3¼ × ½in).

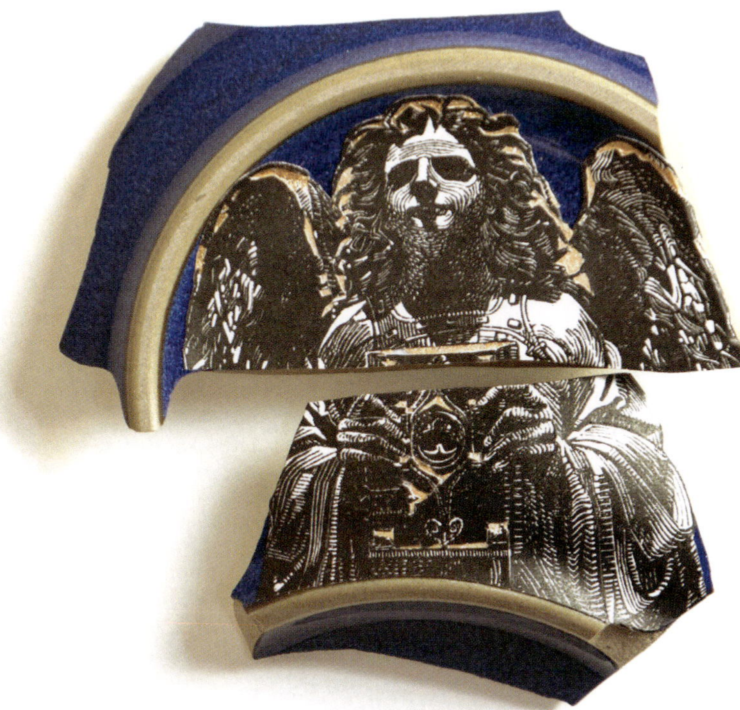

Angel Fragment II (2021), wood engraving on paper and gold leaf collaged on two glazed pottery shards, 9 × 8.5 × 1.5cm (3½ × 3¼ × ½in). This was made from an accidentally smashed bowl from my kitchen cupboard.

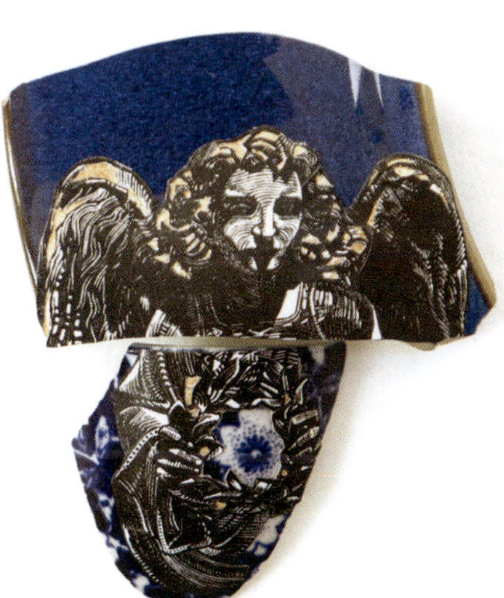

Angel Fragment I (2021), wood engraving on paper and gold leaf collaged on two glazed pottery shards, 8.5 × 7.5 × 1.5cm (3¼in × 3 × ½in).

WALL TILES AND MOSAICS

When collaging cut or torn prints on paper on glazed ceramic wall tiles, the colour and texture of the tiles become an integral part of the design. If intended for display unframed, they would require varnishing to protect the paper collage, but mine have always been framed and so I have never varnished them.

Ceramic and also glass mosaic tiles can be satisfying surfaces for collage. Having created and printed wood engraving blocks or prints in other techniques, it may be that, while the end results are what you had intended, it is also often the case that there are small details in each print that are interesting in their own right. Collaging those details on mosaic tiles is a way of homing in on them, but presenting them as semi-abstract compositions. Just as one engraving may inspire another, one collage too may directly inspire another.

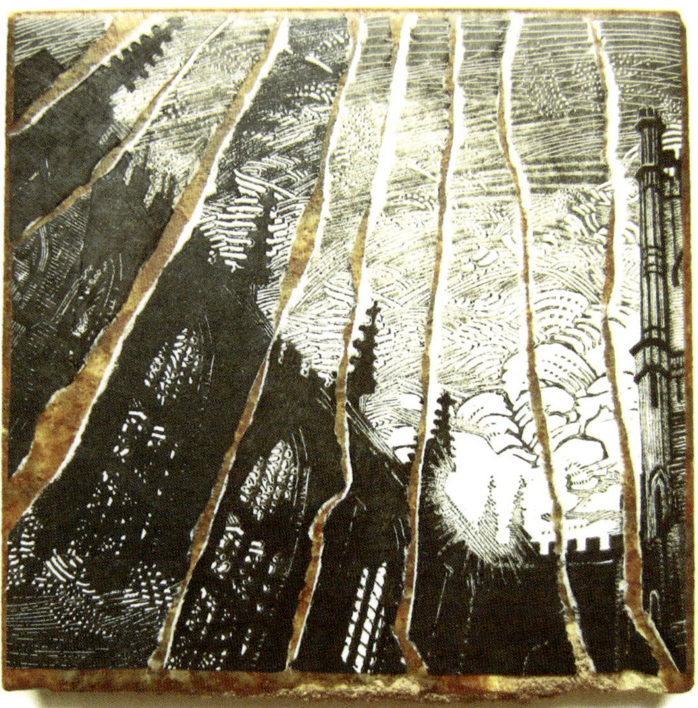

St Luke's Splintered Light (2016), torn strips of wood engraving on Gampi Vellum paper collaged on ceramic tile, 10.3 × 10.3 × 0.8cm (4 × 4 × ¼in). The torn white paper edges of prints can be used to good effect in a collage.

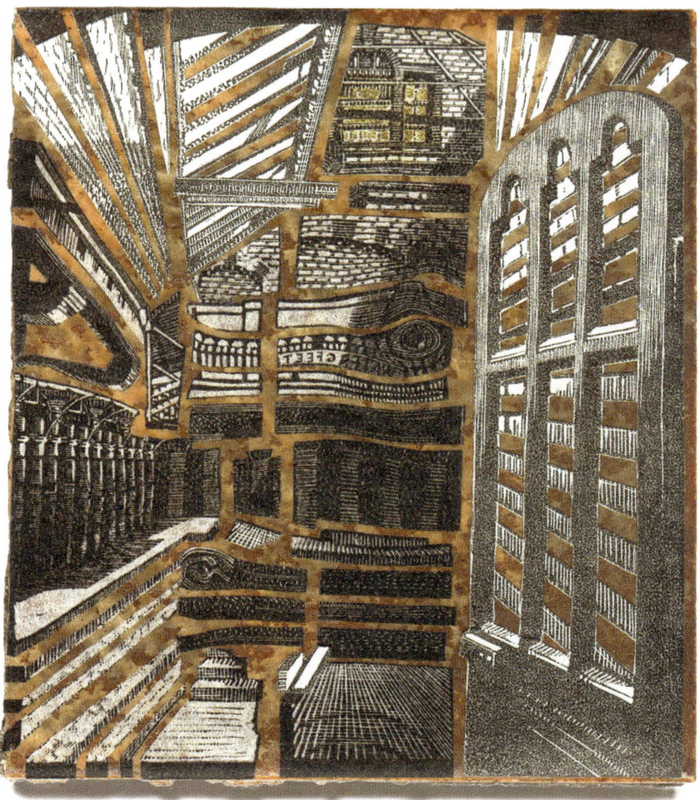

Interior Shards (2007), wood engraving on paper and gold leaf collaged on ceramic tile, 10.3 × 9 × 0.8cm (4 × 3½ × ¼in). This collage's pieces were all cut rather than torn.

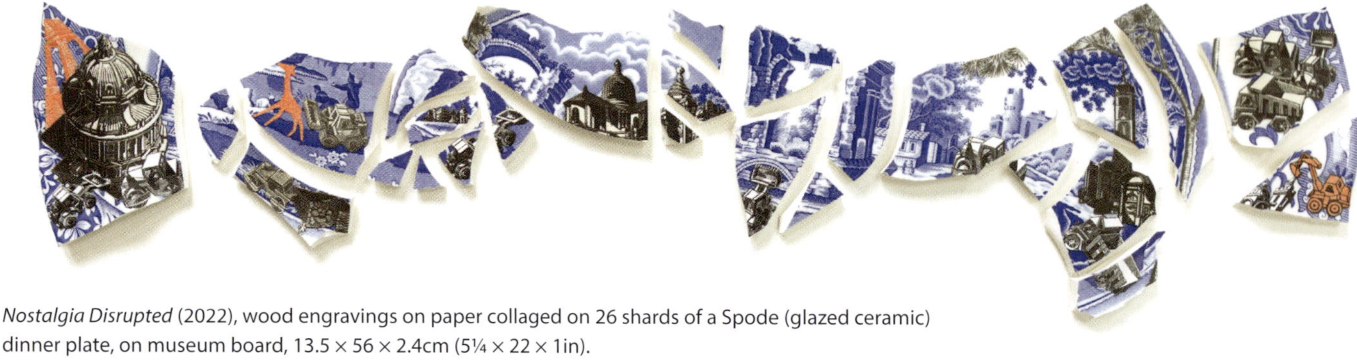

Nostalgia Disrupted (2022), wood engravings on paper collaged on 26 shards of a Spode (glazed ceramic) dinner plate, on museum board, 13.5 × 56 × 2.4cm (5¼ × 22 × 1in).

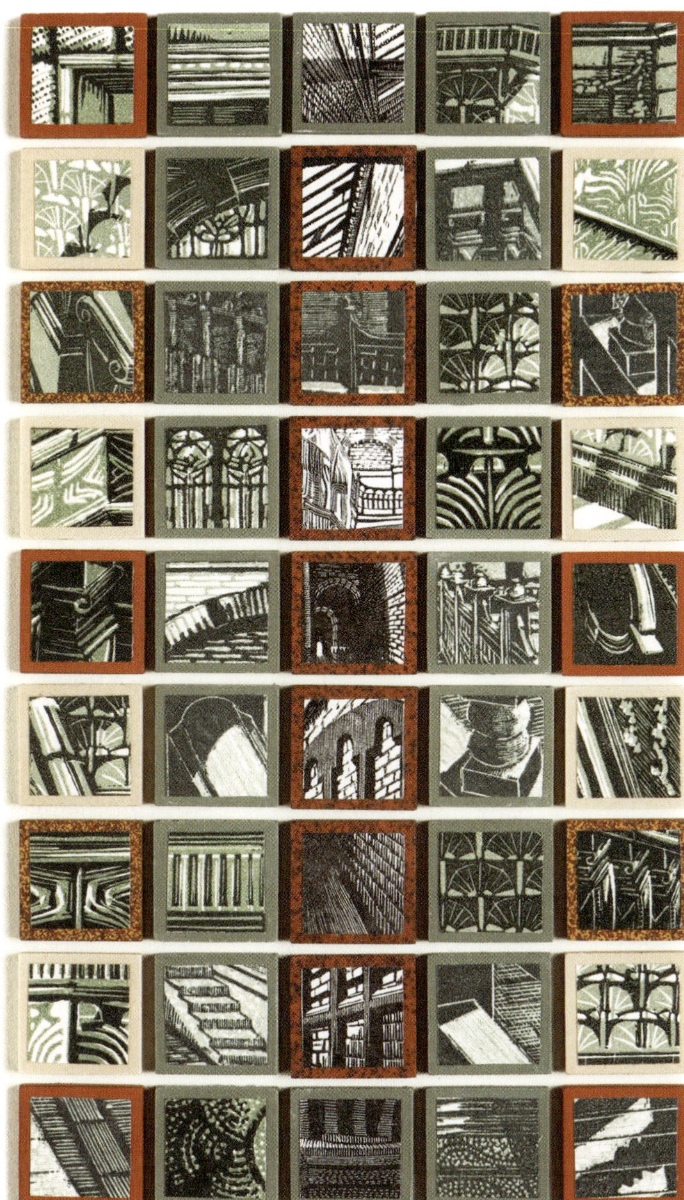

Tiles and Tesselations I (2007), wood engravings and linocuts on paper collaged on 45 ceramic mosaic tiles, 22.5 × 12.5 × 0.4cm (8¾ × 5 × 1/8in), attached to museum board.

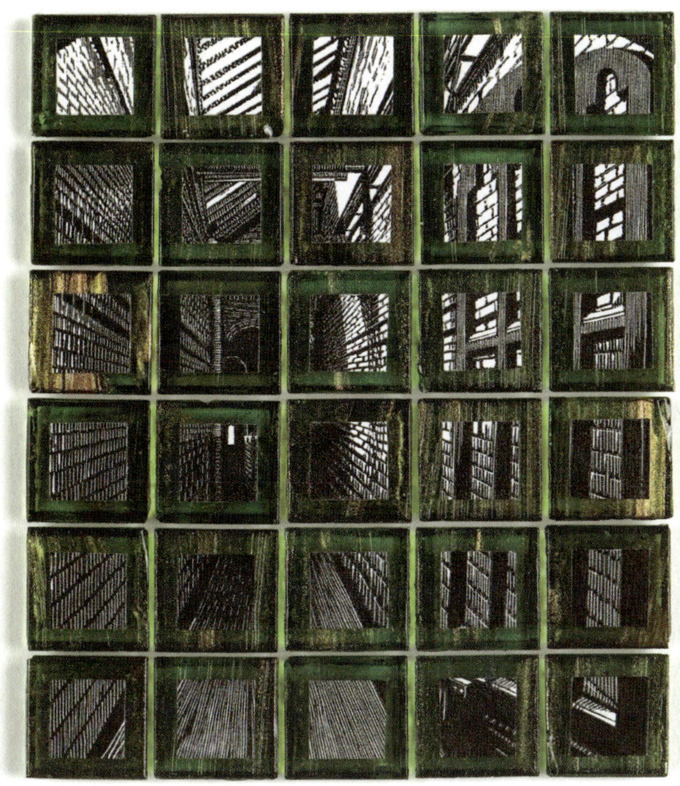

Green Glass Light (2007), wood engraving on paper collaged on 30 green glass tesserae, 12.2 × 10.3 × 0.4cm (4¾ × 4 × 1/8in), attached to museum board. Based on my wood engraving *Passage of Light* (illustrated in Chapter 9), this work is in the Whitworth collection.

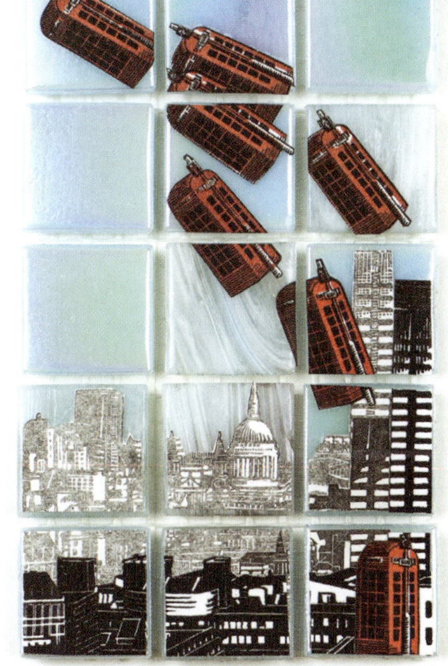

Nearly Gone (2018), wood engraving and linocut prints on paper collaged onto fifteen glass mosaic tiles, 10.8 × 6.5 × 0.4cm (4¼ × 2½ × 1/8in), on museum board. A grid of mosaic tiles may be a useful way of presenting a figurative image broken down into tiny, related components.

GLASS AND MIRRORS

Glass and mirror shards can also be used for collage. Some of mine, on broken glass, like some of those on pottery shards, were accidental discoveries dug up in my garden. You can collage on the front or back of a piece of glass and use its transparency to good effect.

Inspired by the many convex glass mirrors built into the fabric of London's Georgian Sir John Soane's Museum, I have explored ways of creating collage using a base of convex clock glass (which can be purchased online in many sizes) and then placing identical glass roundels over the collage's surface to create an effect reminiscent of those mirrors. The effect was what I wanted but there is a danger with this kind of glass 'sandwich' (with the paper collage as filling) that the paper may be unduly susceptible to temperature changes and, if even the minutest drop of condensation formed between the two layers, this could cause mould to develop on the paper, ruining the artwork.

A safer method is to collage on a base of *papier mâché*, moulded, in advance, to the form of the convex glass which, when the collage is finished, provides its lid. As with collaging on concave surfaces, such as ceramic bowls, it is best to build such collages up using many small paper pieces rather than trying to stick larger pieces in place, which may wrinkle or distort over the curved surface. I have also made entire clocks into collaged works.

Wood engraved imagery seems to be especially effective in collage, creating a means of presenting seemingly infinitely expansive miniature worlds.

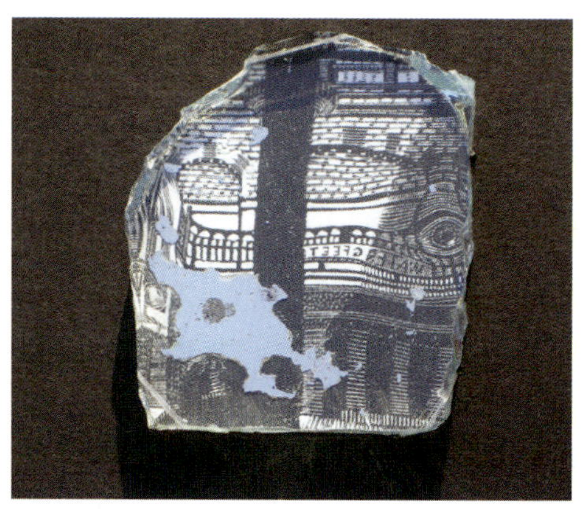

Reflected Fragment (2007), wood engraving on paper collaged behind glass with a trace of silvering (showing blue as it was photographed outdoors), 5 × 4.3 × 0.7cm (2 × 1¾ × ¼in). A thin layer of Pritt glue attaching paper to glass isn't visible through the front of the finished collage as Pritt dries to a colourless film.

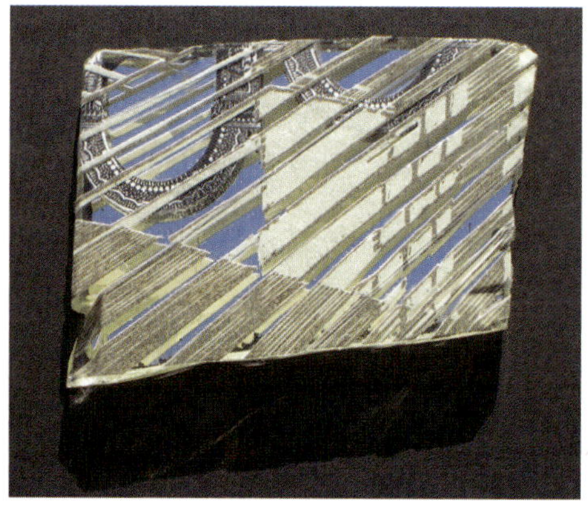

Floor Reflection (2007), wood engraving and linocut on paper collaged on the front of a mirror shard, 6.4 × 9 × 0.6cm (2½ × 3½ × ¼in). Again, the mirror looks blue as it was photographed outdoors under a blue sky.

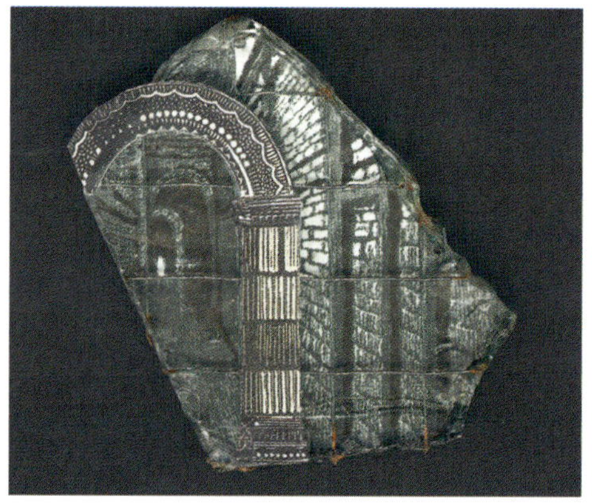

Through a Glass Darkly (2007), wood engraving on paper collaged on the front and back of reinforced glass (a fragment originally found in my garden), 6.2 × 6.2 × 0.7cm (2½ × 2½ × ¼in). This is in the Whitworth collection.

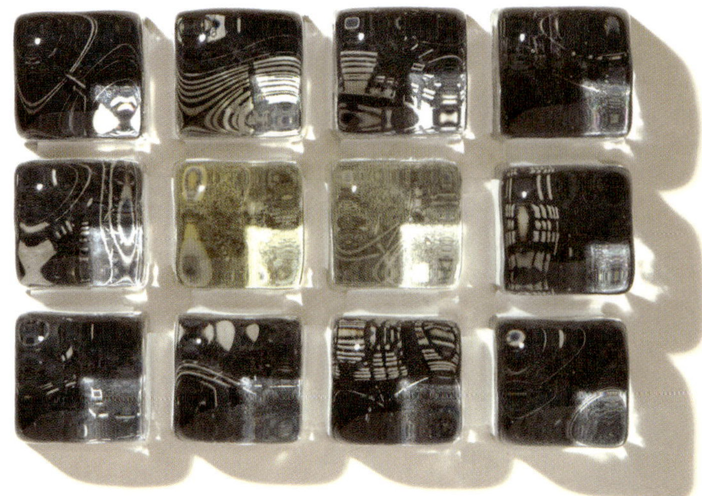

Olympic Memory (2010), wood engraving on paper collaged behind 12 glass cubes, total collage area: 8.1 × 12 × 2.8cm (3¼ × 4¾ × 1in). The glass cubes create an interesting distortion of the image behind them.

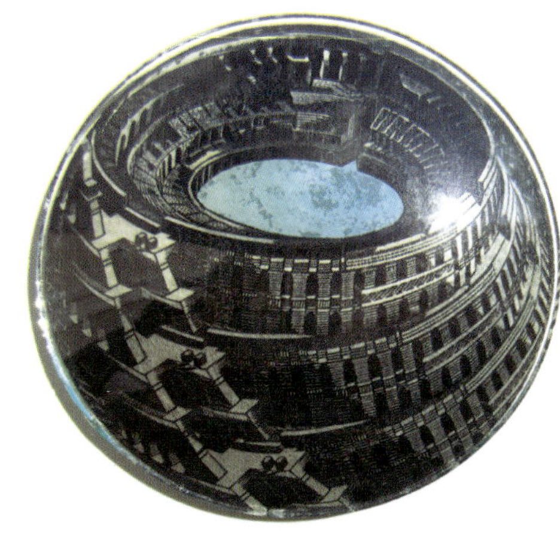

Lake Colosseum (2012), wood engravings and screenprint on paper collaged on convex glass, diameter: 10cm (4in). To avoid reflections, most of my collages under convex glass are photographed without their glass lids but this one shows its lid in place.

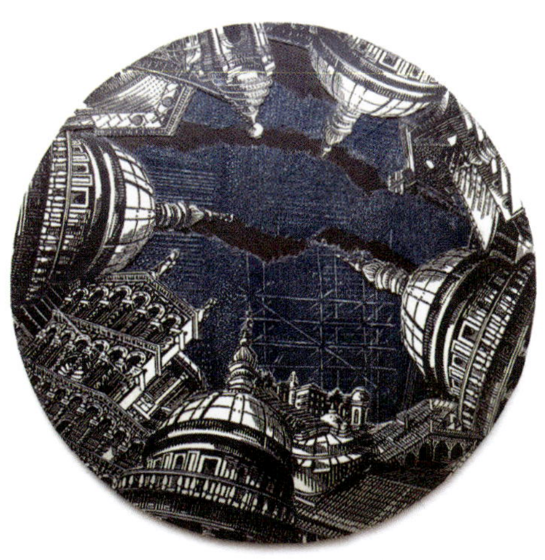

Domes Duomi (2012), wood engraving and linocut prints on paper collaged on convex glass, diameter: 10cm (4in). This collage doesn't have a glass lid but, instead, the surface is varnished to provide a sheen.

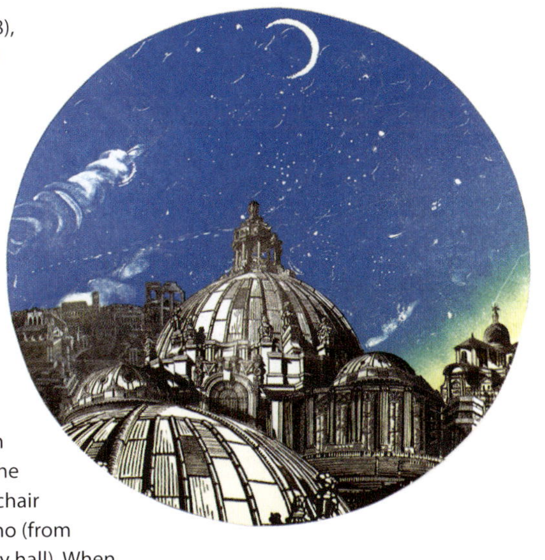

Italian Light (2018), lithograph, wood engraving and print (in sky-blue ink, from salvaged lino block) on paper collaged under convex glass, diameter: 28cm (11in). The crescent moon impression was created via the indentation of a chair leg in the floor lino (from a school assembly hall). When printed, it created this moon-like image.

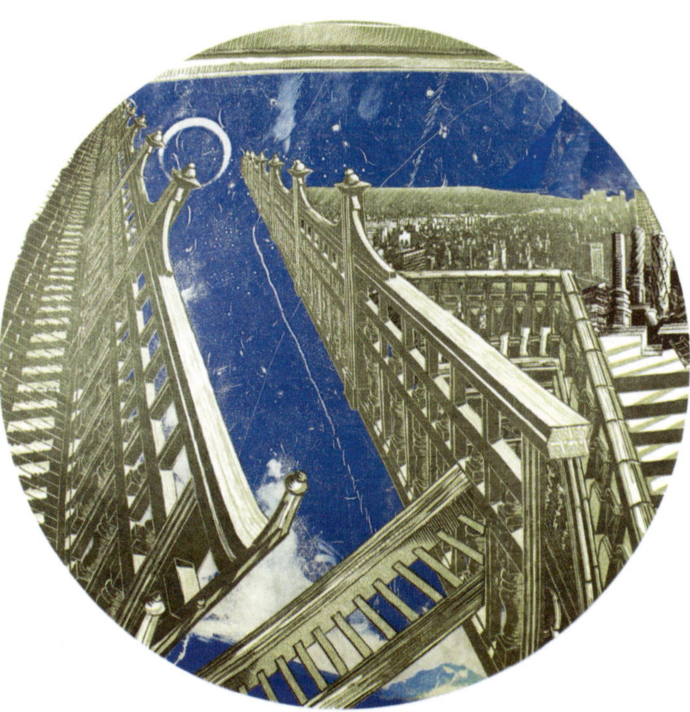

Seems Like Heaven (2018), linocut, wood engraving, lithograph and monotype print (using salvaged floor lino block) on paper collaged under convex glass, diameter: 33cm (13in).

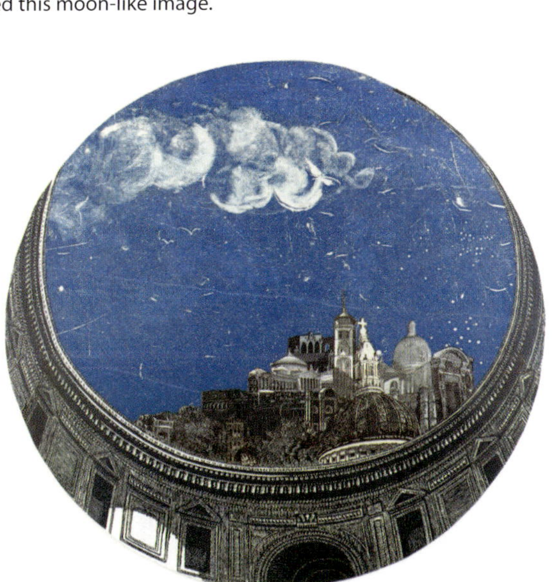

Into the Blue (2018), linocut, wood engraving and monotype prints with Italian postage stamp fragment collaged on paper under convex glass, diameter 20.3cm (8in).

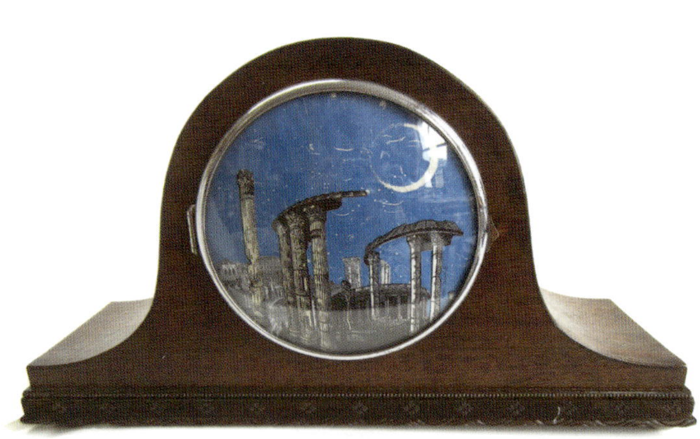

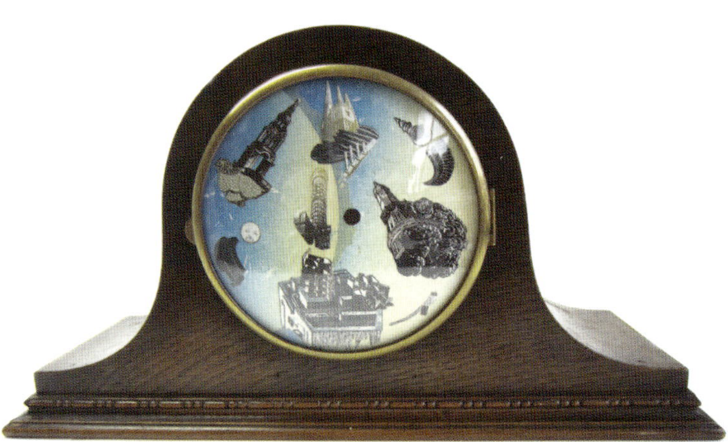

Moonlit Afternoon above, and *Worlds Within Worlds (Homage to Cornell)* below (both 2015), wood engravings, solarplate prints, linocuts and monotypes (printed from salvaged floor lino) on paper collaged under the convex glass clock faces of two wooden Napoleon Hat clocks (dating from c.1920s), each 23 × 42 × 13.5cm (9 × 16½ × 5¼in).

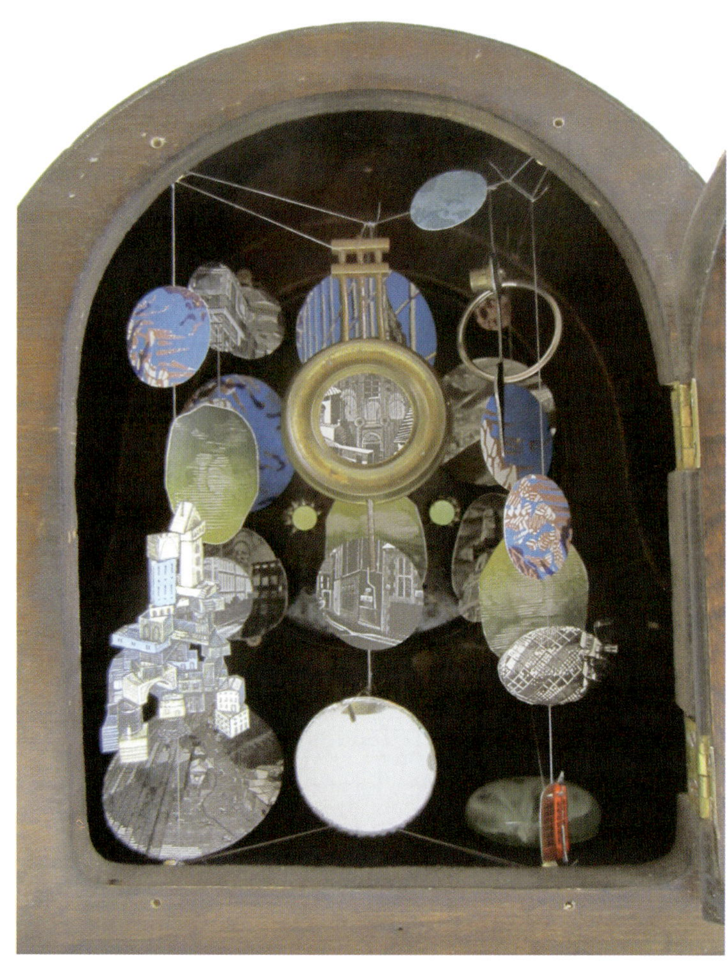

Worlds Within Worlds (verso, detail) (2015), collage of linocut and wood engraving prints on paper plus small mirror and other found objects hung on nylon thread inside the back of the adjacent clock, behind the hinged wooden door where the clock's mechanism was formerly housed.

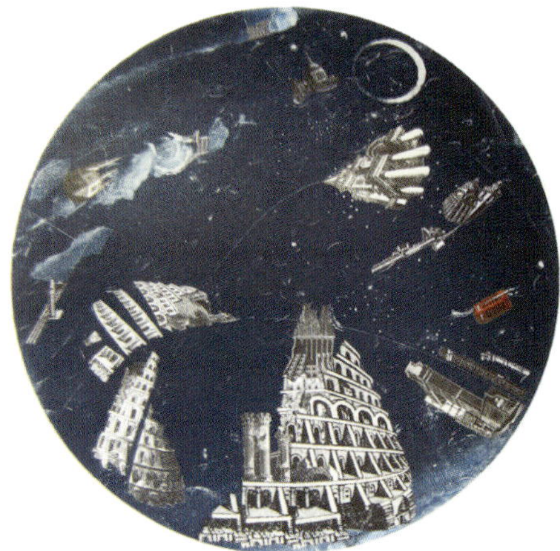

Moonlit Fantasy (2013), wood engraving, solarplate, linocut and monotype prints on paper collaged on convex glass, diameter: 26cm (10in). Wood engraved buildings, liberated from their original compositions, are freed here to fly about like spaceships in a night sky.

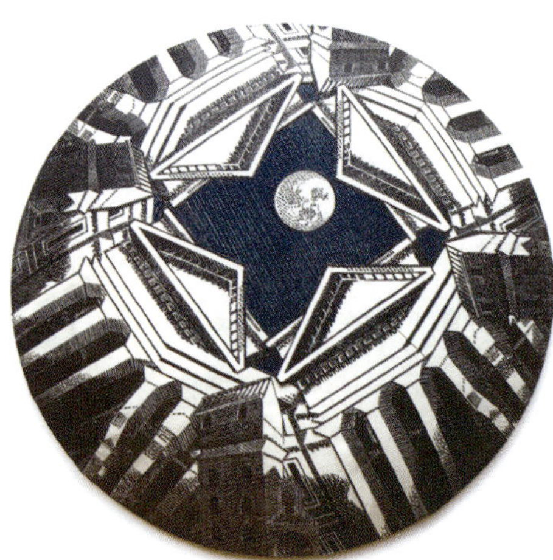

Moonlit Temples (2012), wood engraving and linocut prints on paper collaged on convex glass, diameter: 10cm (4in).

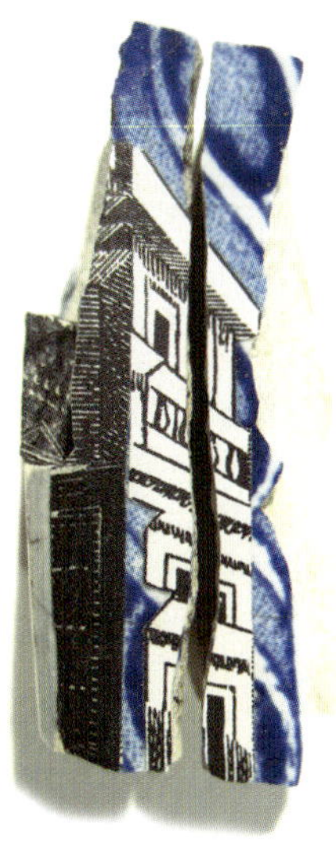

Roman Remains (2012), wood engraved prints on Basingwerk Parchment paper collaged on two blue tile fragments, 6 × 3 × 3 cm (2¼ × 1¼ × 1¼in).

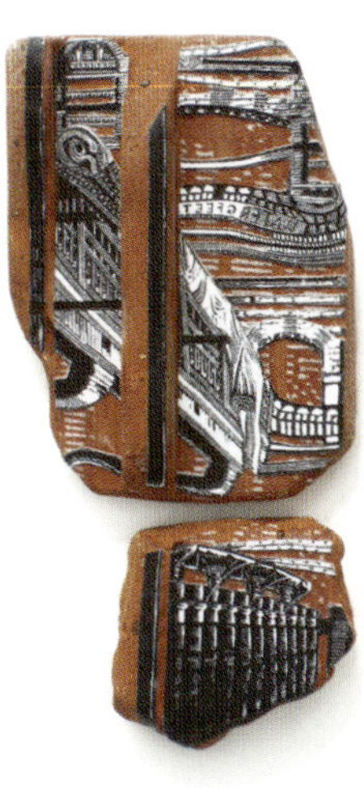

Small Ripples (2008), wood engraving and linocut on paper collaged on red roof-tile fragments, 9.5 × 5 × 1.3cm (3¾ × 2 × ½in).

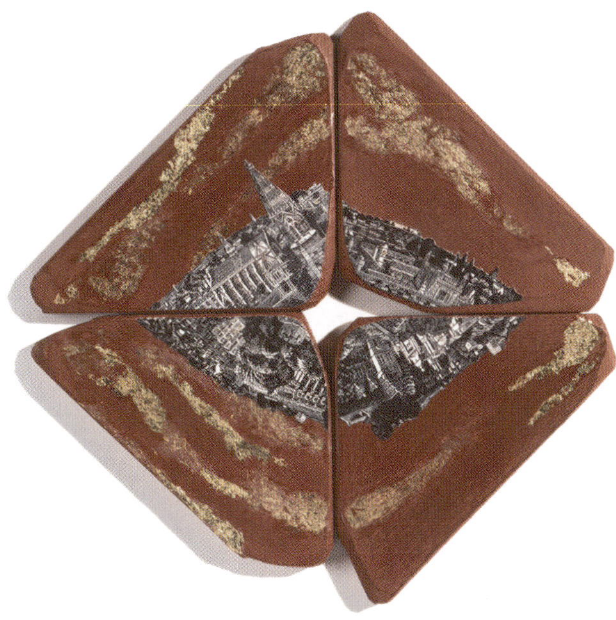

Oxford Skies (2003), wood engraving on Gampi Vellum paper and gold leaf collaged on four red-painted wood panels, 20.3 × 20.3 × 0.9cm (8 × 8 × ½in).

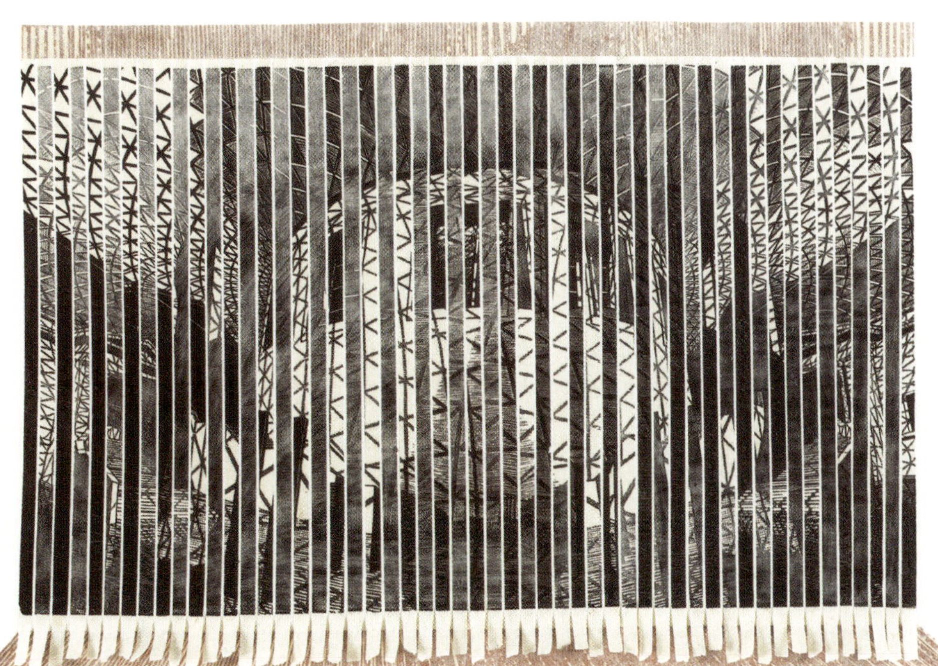

British Museum Verticals (2005), wood engraving and linocut prints collaged on archival card, 21 × 31.5cm (8¼ × 12½in). This involved printing my British Museum woodblock on Kozu-shi, then cutting the prints into vertical strips. I turned over every other strip for the image to read through alternate sides of the semi-transparent paper as black and grey stripes.

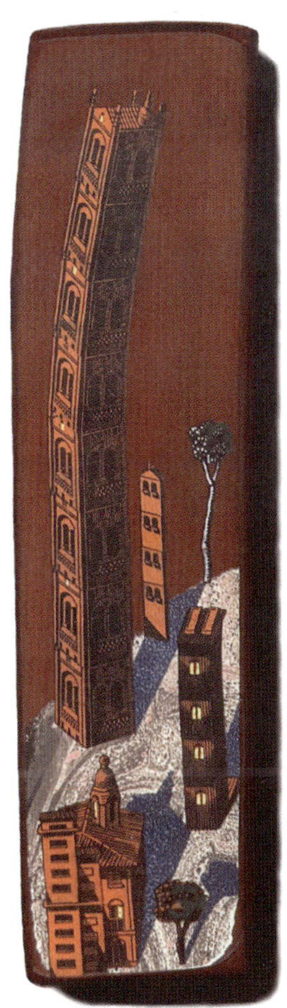

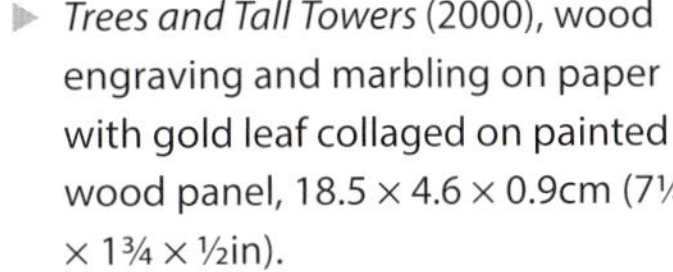

Trees and Tall Towers (2000), wood engraving and marbling on paper with gold leaf collaged on painted wood panel, 18.5 × 4.6 × 0.9cm (7¼ × 1¾ × ½in).

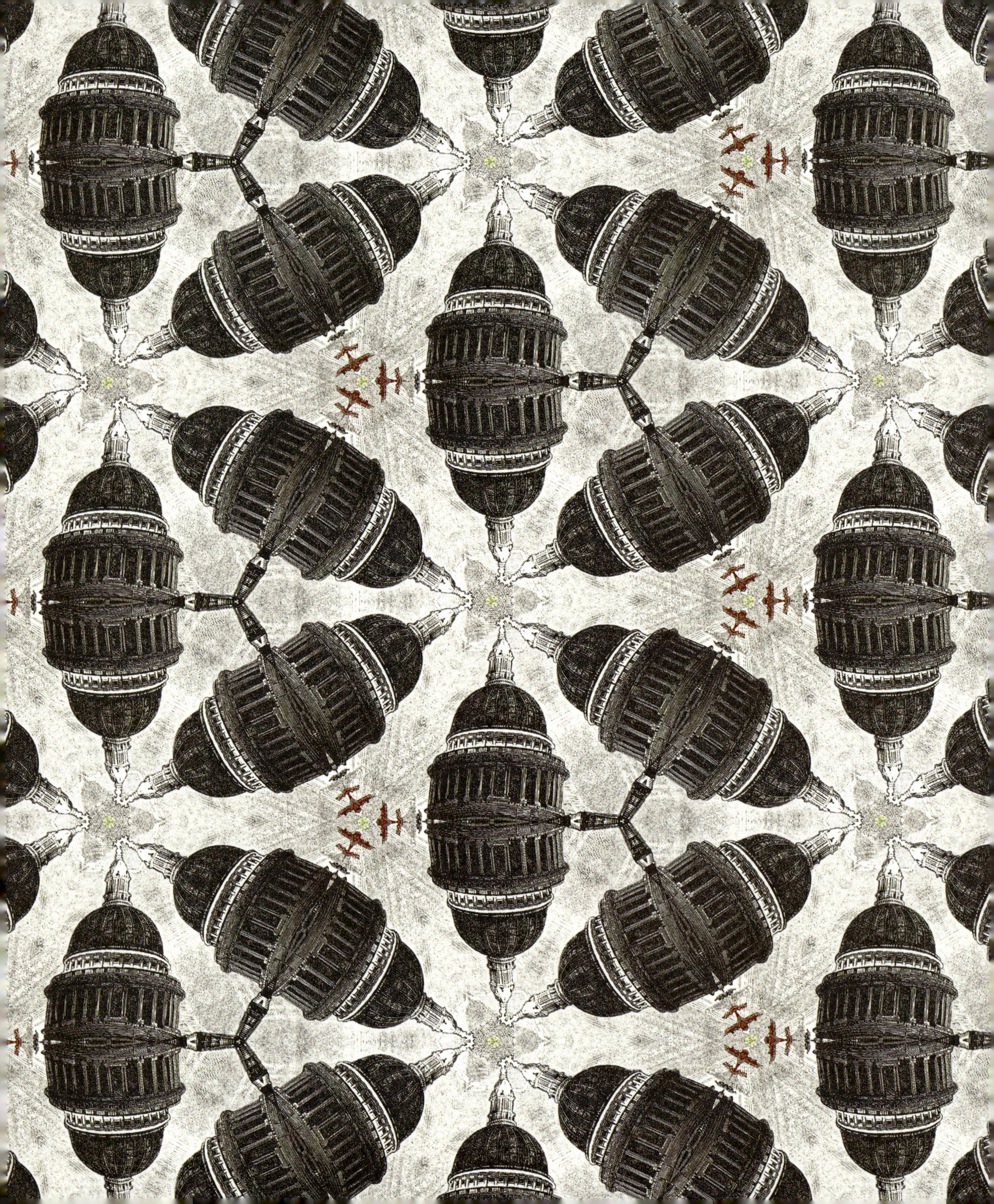

CHAPTER 11

ENGRAVING INTO DIGITAL

Just as wood engravings can inspire unique collages created with scissors and glue, engravings can also be source material for original, digital collages made by copying, cutting and pasting them in image creation software.

DIGITAL ADVANTAGES

As well as facilitating the reassembling or repetition of compositional elements to make entirely new compositions, working digitally lets you change the scale of a composition or of selected elements within it. It also gives you options of stretching or otherwise distorting elements and of using mirror image versions of engravings rather than their original-way-round viewings. You can add or subtract colours and tones as desired, with either opaque or transparent effects. Much as I love making collages in the traditional way, the potential of digital collage can definitely expand the engraving medium in fruitful and hitherto unseen directions.

I'm no digital expert, having worked in this field only intermittently and for barely a decade. I still use relatively few of the available software tools and my version of Photoshop is old, yet it does what I need. The point of mentioning my own limitations is to say that, if I can master enough skills to create effective digital images, you definitely can!

■ *St Paul's Dance* (2023), digital print developed from a wood engraving using a kaleidoscope app, 52.6 × 37.8cm (20¾ × 15in), on Somerset Satin paper (printed at Jealous Print Studio, London).

I can't describe the process for each digital print in specific detail as that would fill a whole other book and the frequency of software updates would speedily date it. Online step-by-step videos on using image creation software are useful guides that are regularly updated. Although I have only used Photoshop, other photo-editing and image manipulation software is available. There are some points worth mentioning, however, which I find helpful in my own digital printmaking. But you should take the advice below as tips rather than a complete instruction kit.

Settings

1. For printing digital collages to optimum effect, the images should be high-resolution files of at least 300 dots per inch.

2. For printing rather than purely viewing digitally, set the image mode to CMYK rather than RGB colour.

3. Although you can successfully print an image at smaller scale than its digital file size, if you print it larger, it will lose some definition.

4. For digital collage, I usually start with a blank background layer set to the maximum size I might want the collage to be and definitely larger than the largest image file I plan to import into it. I then import successive layers of imagery on to that background, much like working with physical paper and scissors. If the background layer later turns out to be too large, it can easily be trimmed down digitally later.

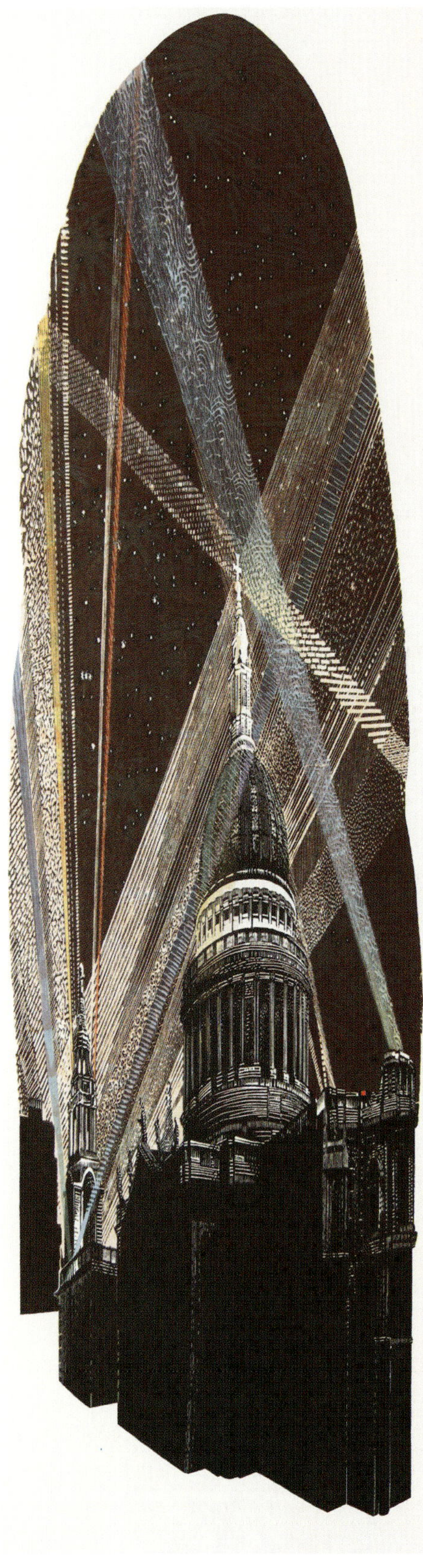

St Paul's Summer Night (2022), digital print (developed from wood engraving) on Somerset Satin paper, 73.6 × 23cm (29 × 9in), printed at Jealous Print Studio. I enlarged and stretched a scan of an earlier wood engraving to exaggerate the tool cuts in its sky area. I added colour and overlaid a semi-transparent scan of an etching to create texture in the sky.

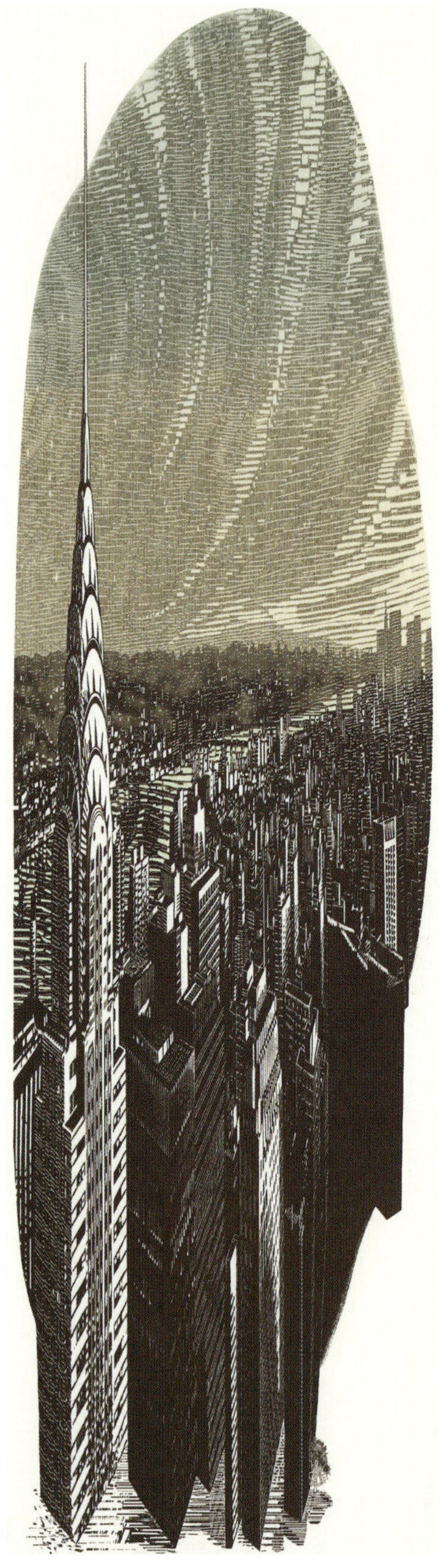

Manhattan Microclimate (2022), digital print (developed from wood engraving) on Somerset Satin paper, 73.6 × 23cm (29 × 9in), printed at Jealous Print Studio. I stretched a scan of a wood engraving to distort and lengthen the Chrysler building and emphasise the tool cuts in the sky to which I added subtle colours and drawing (in Photoshop) at the bottom edge.

5. Set the resolution size of the background layer to a minimum of 300 dpi.

6. Save it as a tiff file – .tif – or, if using Photoshop, it can be saved as .psd. Either file type allows you to save an image with multiple layers.

7. Before importing any scans of engravings or any other material you might want to use, check, for each one, that it is in excellent focus, at high resolution, and set to the same dpi as the background layer.

8. Make sure the lighting across any scans or photographs you plan to use is balanced across the whole image. Avoid working from digital files that are visibly paler along one side than the other. This can cause difficulties later in achieving the optimal tonal balance for your collage.

9. When copying and pasting multiple new layers into a composition, each will appear at a relatively different scale depending on the size of the original engraving you scanned or the resolution of the photograph you made of it. You can easily reduce the size of anything in each layer but, be careful, if enlarging anything, that you don't lose the necessary high resolution of any layer by enlarging its contents beyond its original file size. This can cause blurred, pixilated areas.

Useful tools

1. Move the contents of each different image layer to its desired compositional position using the Move tool. While doing this, it's helpful to reduce the opacity of the relevant layer, perhaps by over 50 per cent, rendering it partially transparent, so you can see precisely what is on the layer(s) underneath and thus position the element you're moving with total accuracy. You can then readjust the opacity of that layer back to 100 per cent if desired.

2. There are various tools that enable you to cut and paste irregularly shaped details of an engraving into your collage. I've not yet mastered any of them! Instead, I open the file for each engraving I want to use and cut the image down, digitally, using the Crop tool, so that I end up with a series of new high resolution jpegs of small details: a Corinthian column from one image, a doorframe from another, a tree from another, for instance, with which I can create layers in my collages, much as if I had cut and pasted them with actual scissors. When cropping, it's important to save each cropped version with a new filename so as not to overwrite the original images. A benefit of this method is that, having saved these details as separately named image files, I can reuse them, if desired, for other digital collages whereas, for traditional collage, I'd need to cut out those separate details anew, from paper prints, each time.

3. Each of these rectangular components may contain bits of the original source material that perhaps aren't needed. Once imported into the new composition, I use the Eraser tool to rub out any surplus bits on the relevant layer, leaving me with only the part I wanted (exactly as if I had cut around it first as a rectangle on the paper and then, accurately, as a more irregular shape, with scissors).

4. Save your digital collage frequently while making it and also save it, from time to time, with a new filename so that, if you do anything you don't like and can't work out how to correct your mistake, you can revert to working on an earlier version before the error occurred.

5. I sometimes use the Sharpen Unsharp Mask tool to make the overall focus look slightly sharper if necessary. This can be useful to help digital images print with the same crispness you'd expect from an actual woodblock print, but use this tool with caution. Set at too high a percentage, it can exaggerate a composition's most emphatic marks while damaging its subtleties.

6. In CMYK mode, you can adjust the colour balance in highly nuanced ways using the Curves tool in the Image menu. This enables you to alter the relative balance of the cyan, magenta, yellow and black hues, which comprise the entire image, and to make separate adjustments for each colour, adjusting the intensity in different parts of the image as required. You can make sophisticated adjustments which might, for instance, maintain the intensity of a particular colour or tone in one part of an image while fractionally or more radically modifying it in other parts.

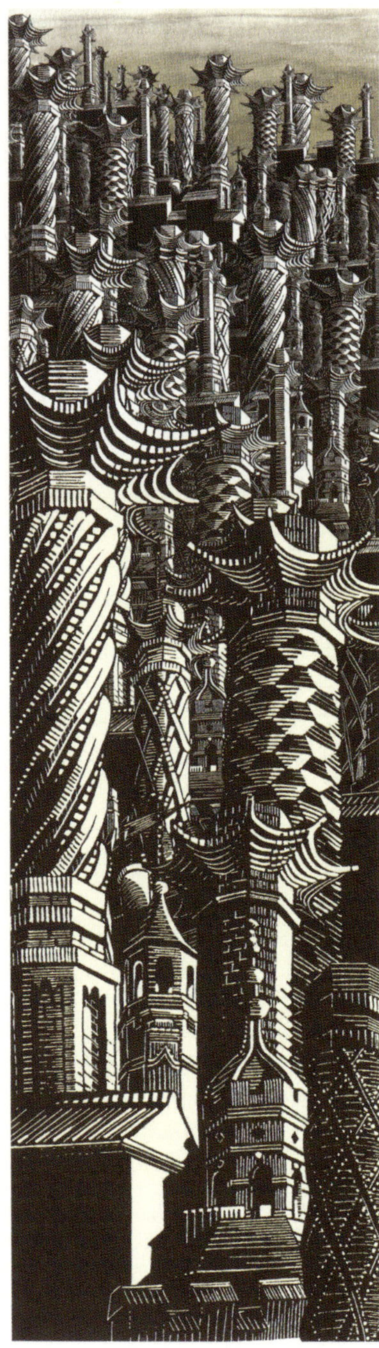

Urban Jungle (2016), four-plate lithograph, 73.6 × 20.3cm (29 × 8in), on Somerset Satin paper (printed at Hole Editions, Newcastle), was developed as a collage in Photoshop from repeated and radically rescaled chimneys (both reduced and enlarged) from a smaller engraving: *Towers and Tudor Chimneys* (illustrated in Chapter 4).

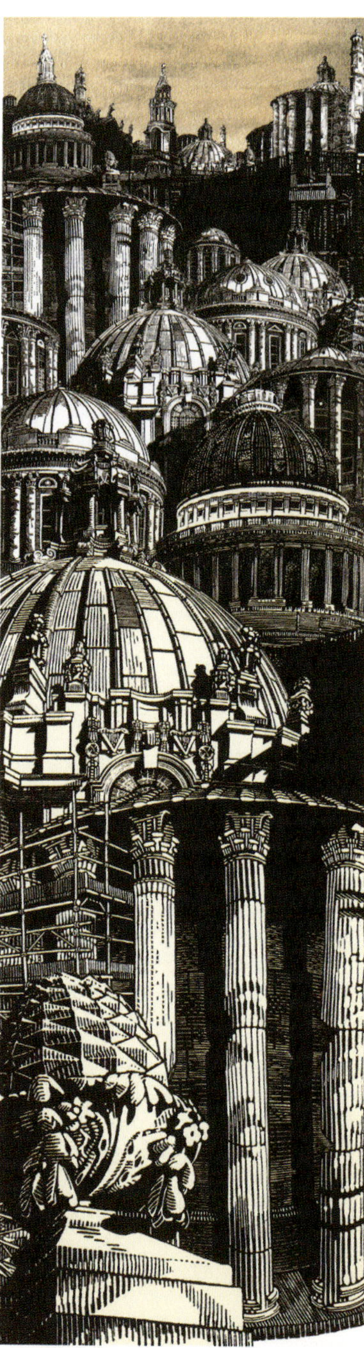

Rotunda × 20 (2016), four-plate lithograph, 73.6 × 20.3cm (29 × 8in), on Somerset Satin paper (printed at Hole Editions, Newcastle), was developed as a collage in Photoshop from parts of about six of my engravings. The sky tones were scanned from one of my sketchbook studies.

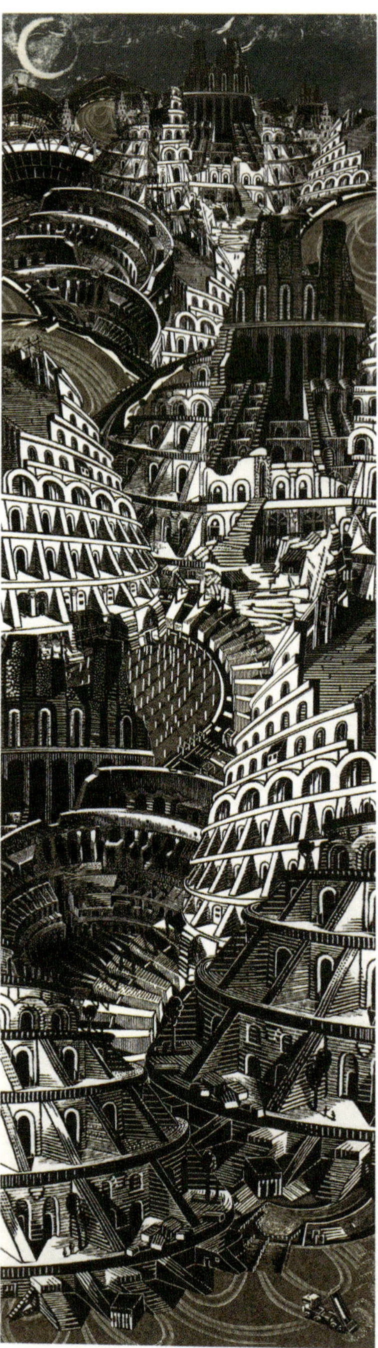

Uncharted Terrain (2021), digital print 73.6 × 20.3cm (29 × 8in), was developed as a collage in Photoshop from elements of about six of my engravings and a scan of a print from a piece of salvaged floor lino (for the sky), printed on Somerset Satin paper by Jealous Print Studio.

Colour balance

1. Curves offers much more specific control over individual parts of the tonal/colour balance than the Brightness/Contrast tool which, while sometimes useful, affects all parts of an image at once.

2. Even very low levels of colour – as little as 5 or 6 per cent – can print darker than they appear on screen. If you want any of your final image to print at virtually page-white, adjust the cyan, magenta and yellow in those areas to no more than 2 per cent.

3. Consider reducing, slightly, the intensity of black and cyan (and sometimes magenta) in the darkest, most high-contrast, areas. While unadjusted levels look great on screen, they sometimes cause fine details to fill in when printed – especially if using engravings in digital collage since very strong dark tones in a digital image tend to fill in any fine details when printed (exactly as in an over-inked engraving).

4. For colour washes, I usually scan one of my watercolours or colour prints. These (or details) can be imported as layers in the digital collage. Adjusting the opacity for the relevant layer(s) can considerably affect the transparency or luminosity of the colour(s) exactly as if you had painted a watercolour or printed a colour woodblock.

5. Even if all the source material, as wood engraving prints, was originally printed in the same black (or other colour) on identical paper, because you may have scanned or photographed each engraving in varying light conditions, the tonal balance across the digital image may be uneven. In combination as digital layers in the composition, some of those blacks may appear dark blue or brown, or their background tones may look yellow, pink or blue. For a composition of homogeneous, seamless parts, adjust the tonal balance of each layer individually before you merge the layers down.

Proofing and printing

1. When satisfied that all compositional components are in the right positions and relative scale and that the tonal and colour balance of each layer and of the whole composition looks right, save the file again, still with its individual layers intact. Then flatten the image (in other words: merge its layers to make a single-layered image) and save it again as a tiff file (or high-resolution jpeg) for printing.

2. My home printer doesn't print to a high enough resolution, nor can it print artists' quality papers, so I always send my image files to a specialist digital printer. It's sensible to make a trial proof (exactly as if you were printing from an engraving block) and then inspect it, checking for problem areas that might need adjusting. Digital images, backlit on screen, always look more luminous – stained-glass-like – than the final printing in which colours don't always look as vivid, so proofs are necessary, enabling you to modify the digital file as necessary before printing an edition.

3. Having proofed it and if it needs altering, depending on what needs doing, you may need to revert to the previous image file, before you merged its layers, as this version will allow you to make minor changes to individual layers, rather than adjustments affecting the entire composition.

4. Always print proofs on the same printer as the intended edition. Digital prints from the same image file but printed on different printers can yield startlingly dissimilar results.

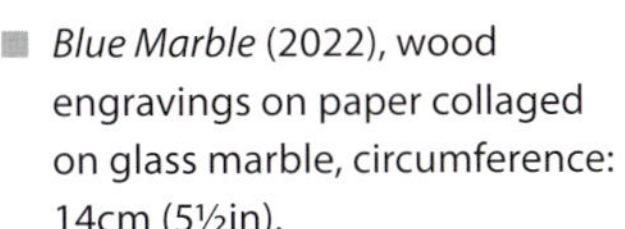

Blue Marble (2022), wood engravings on paper collaged on glass marble, circumference: 14cm (5½in).

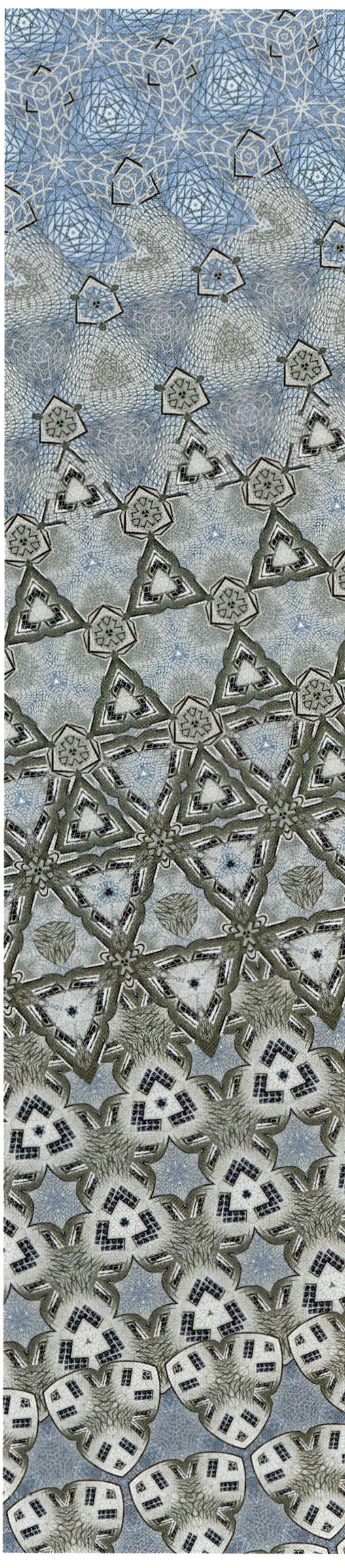

British Museum Kaleidoscope 3 (2023), digital print, 74 × 16.5cm (29¼ × 6½in) on Somerset Satin paper printed by Jealous Print Studio. I developed it, via a kaleidoscope app, from my *British Museum – Blue Sky* engraving (illustrated in Chapter 8).

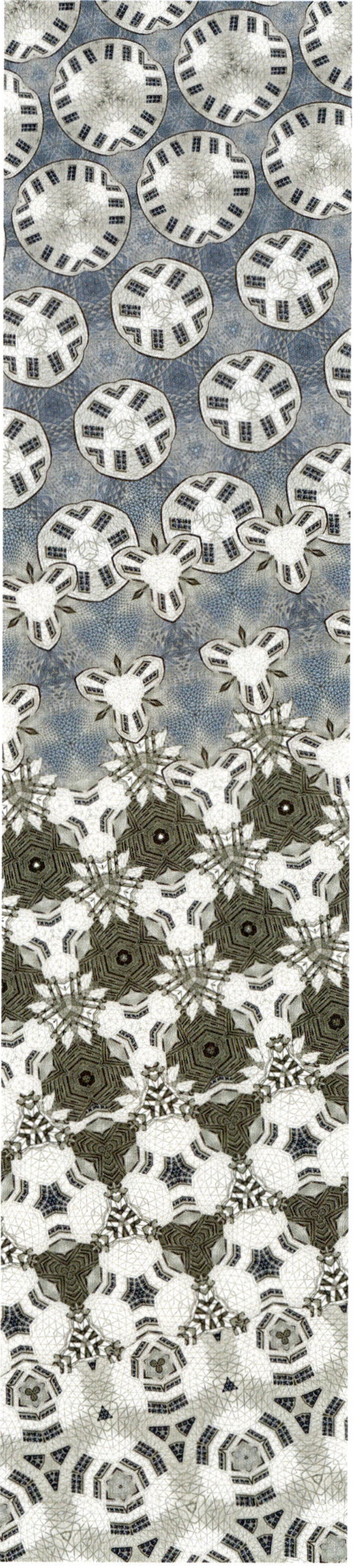

British Museum Kaleidoscope 4 (2023), digital print, 74 × 16.5cm (29¼ × 6½in), on Somerset Satin paper printed by Jealous Print Studio. For each of these related images, I joined five photos made via the kaleidoscope app then used the clone tool in Photoshop to link the components together to create a seamless Escher-like metamorphosis.

CLONE TOOL

I use the Clone tool extensively – probably more than any other Photoshop tool. Perhaps I'm drawn to it because its image icon is a miniature printing stamp! It's incredibly useful and versatile and can be set to many and various brush diameters from very large to extremely tiny.

You can adjust its settings from a completely solid intensity to an effect of slight blurring around the edges. It works by cloning a small (or larger) circle of an image, which you can then move to a different place. It works a bit like a rubber stamp, letting you 'pick up' part of your image (as if plunging a rubber stamp into an ink pad) and then press it down somewhere else to leave a duplicate mark. I use it for many purposes, including these:

- If there are imperfections in my digital file of an engraving, such as specks of dust in the image area or its paper surround, I select and clone a clean area immediately adjacent to the problem, using one of the tool's smallest brush sizes (sometimes using a less-than-full intensity level). I then position the tool over the speck and place the cloned detail on top, thus obliterating the imperfection.
- I use it to copy and replicate large areas of a design or very small marks to affect the composition either quite radically or very subtly.
- The component parts of a digital collage, just like cut-and-glued paper pieces, can sometimes show white edges. If that happens, I use the clone tool to pick up a relevant line of colour from a nearby part of the image to fill in those unwanted white edges – just like using a pen on paper.
- I use the same method for making other modifications to the collage, exactly like adding pen drawing to a paper collage.

KALEIDOSCOPE APP

In an ongoing series of digital prints, I have tried to emulate some effects of non-digital collages that I had earlier created by cutting up and reassembling some of my representational images into carefully calculated equilateral triangles and hexagons, to create abstract compositions inspired by kaleidoscopes.

Using a simple children's kaleidoscope – of a variety (technically called a teleidoscope) with a faceted lens that breaks up any view you are looking at into light-filled, geometric reconfigurations (as opposed to the more familiar kaleidoscope with a sparkly internal bead box that generates its own patterns), I created a digital collage (commissioned by the gallery to celebrate its fortieth anniversary) which combined a photographic view of a handsome stairwell at Chichester's Pallant House Gallery with a wood engraving.

To do this, I took photographs on my iPhone, but placed the kaleidoscope over its lens to break up each view into a kaleidoscopic rearrangement. In Photoshop, I made an image file from one of these images, then added an extra layer: a scan of a wood engraving I had made of a chandelier (from the same stairwell). Then I removed the white paper background colour of the chandelier layer so that the colours of the photographic layer underneath showed through it exactly as if I had inked the woodblock and printed it directly on the digital photograph rather than on a separate piece of paper.

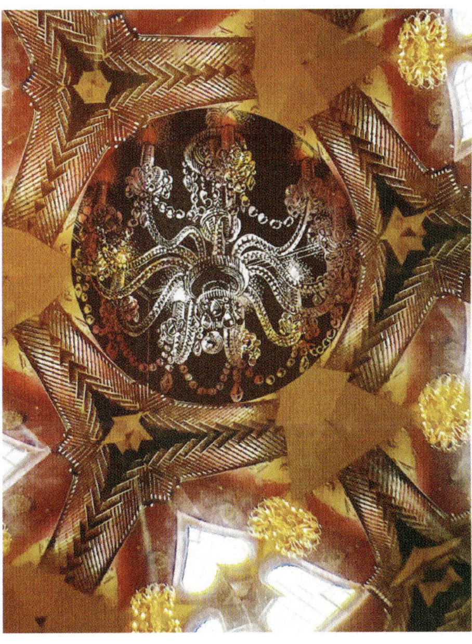

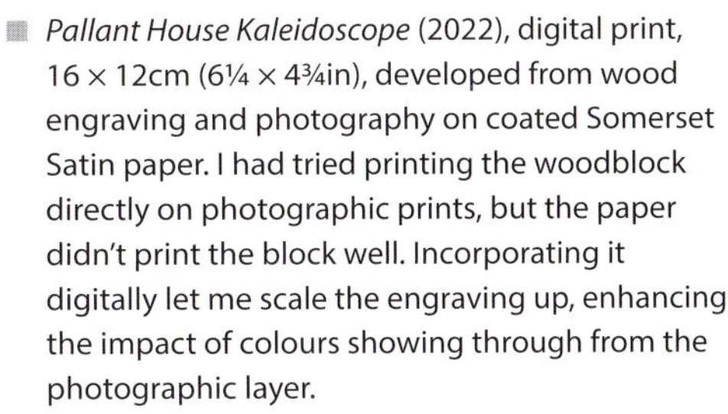

Pallant House Kaleidoscope (2022), digital print, 16 × 12cm (6¼ × 4¾in), developed from wood engraving and photography on coated Somerset Satin paper. I had tried printing the woodblock directly on photographic prints, but the paper didn't print the block well. Incorporating it digitally let me scale the engraving up, enhancing the impact of colours showing through from the photographic layer.

In subsequent digital images expanding the kaleidoscope theme, I have been using a kaleidoscope app to photograph some of my pre-existing wood engravings. Some of the resulting high-resolution images have become bases for new digital prints. In some, I have stitched together different images, digitally, to create new compositions with an intentionally metamorphosing, sequential character. In others, I have added colour layers that weren't in the original engravings. Apart from involving the app, however, all other aspects of these digital prints were made using techniques already described.

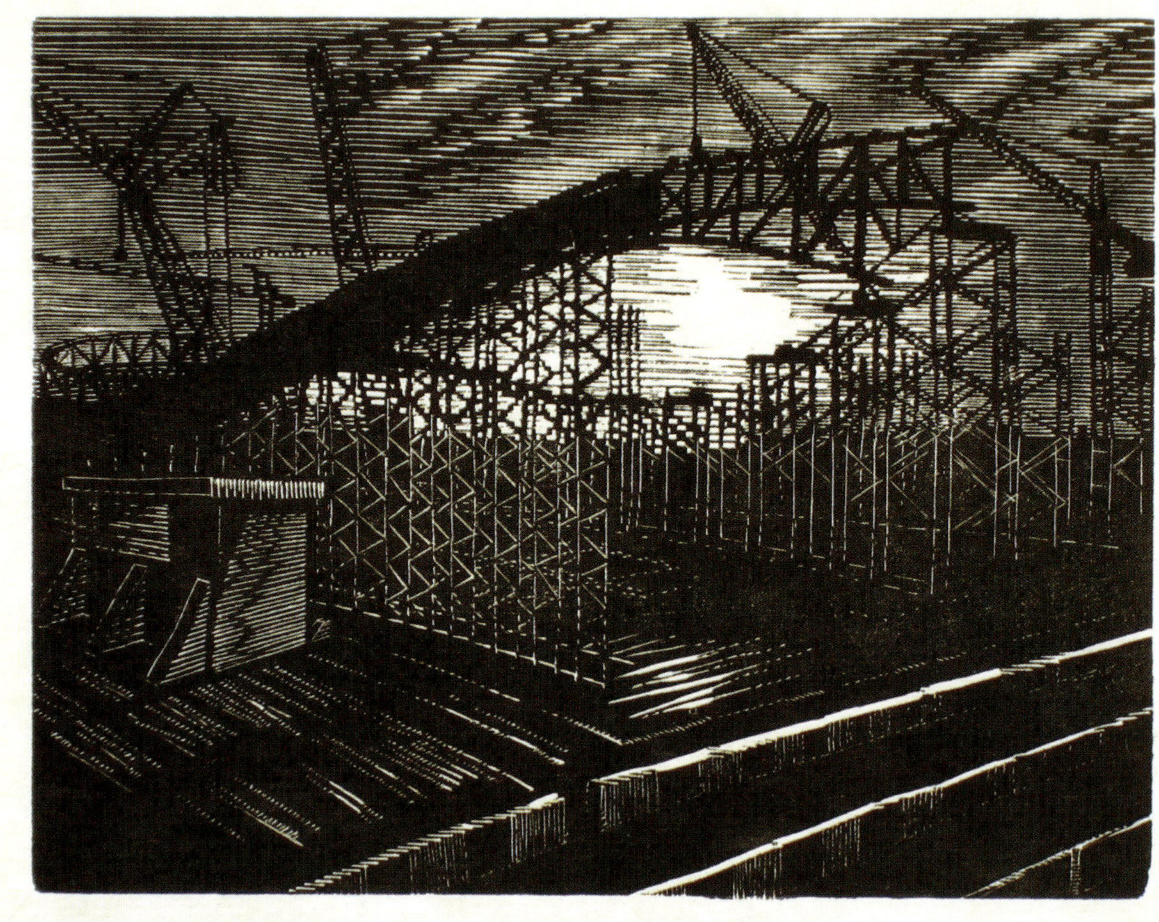

Olympic Aquatic Centre in Construction (2012), engraving on boxwood, 9.7 × 12.4cm (3¾ × 5in), on Gampi Vellum paper, based on one of my sketchbook drawings, was later the basis for *Olympic Legacy*: a kaleidoscope-inspired digital print.

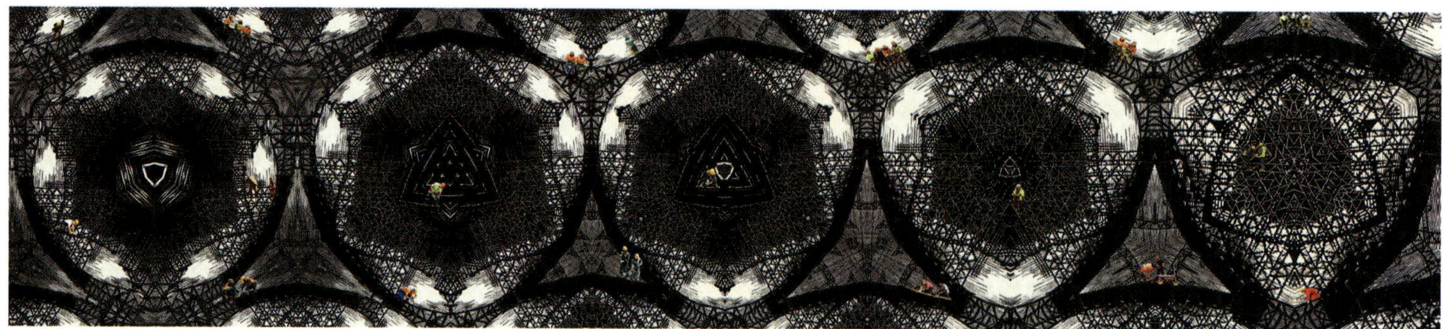

Olympic Legacy (2023), digital print, 17 × 74cm (6¾ × 29¼in), on Somerset Satin paper, united in Photoshop photos of the engraving, made using the kaleidoscope app, into one composition with lace-like traceries. I added tiny brightly-coloured construction workers to suggest that the structure represents a building. The final work was printed by Jealous Print Studio.

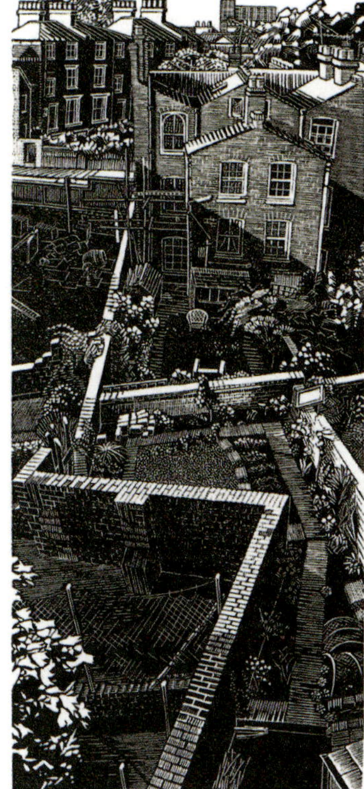

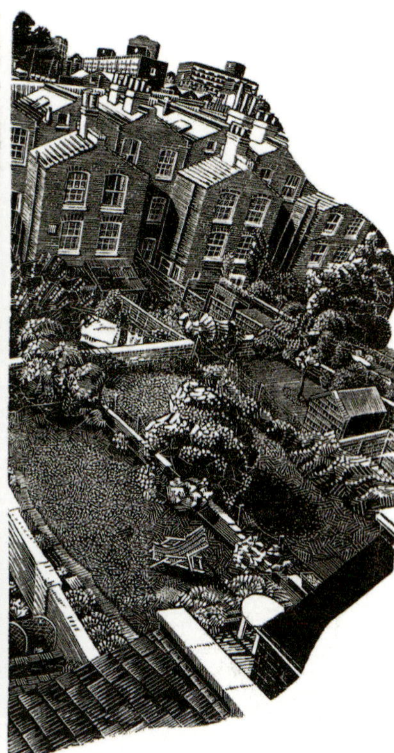

London Gardens (Diptych) (1997), engraving on two boxwood blocks, 12.5 × 12cm (5 × 4¾in), on Gampi Vellum paper. This view from the top floor of my home has more recently formed the basis of two new digital collages.

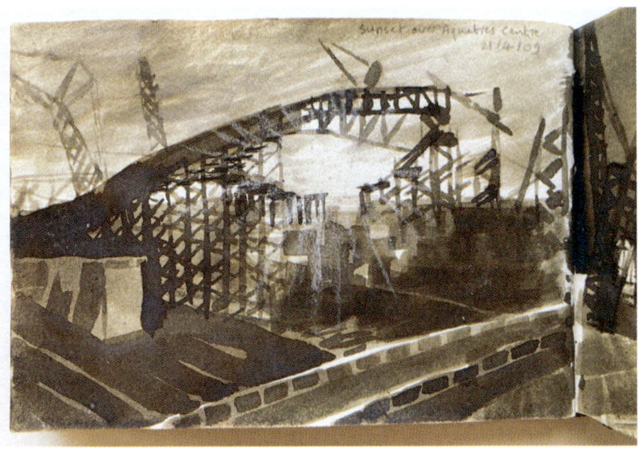

Small sketchbook drawing (2009), 10 × 14 cm (4 × 5½in), made in grey ink wash and white crayon, showing Zaha Hadid's London Olympic Aquatic Centre in construction.

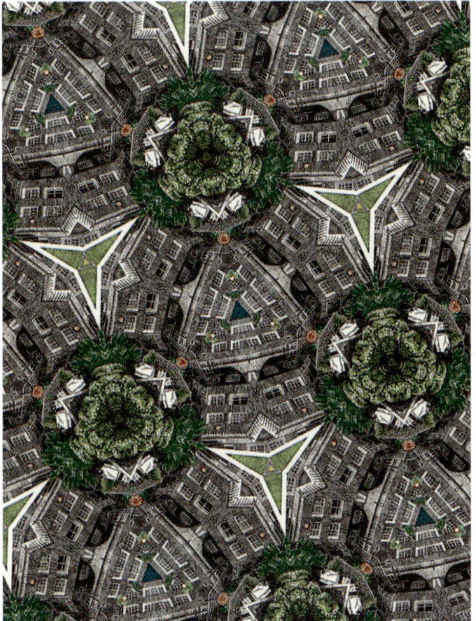

London Gardens Kaleidoscope I (2023), digital print, 27.6 × 20.7cm (10¾ × 8¼in), was developed from my engraving, using a kaleidoscope app with colours added in Photoshop, on Somerset Satin paper, printed by Jealous Print Studio.

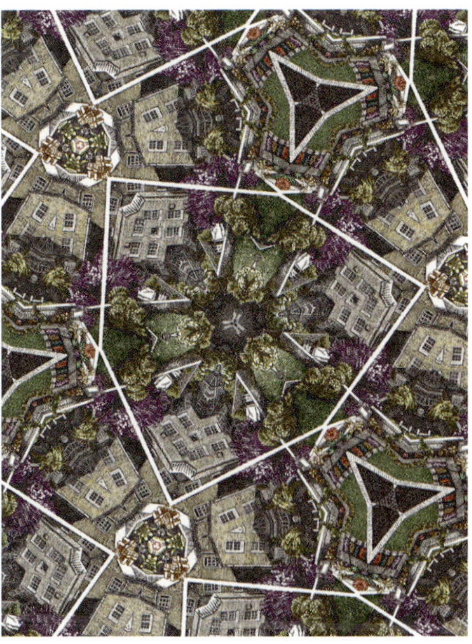

London Gardens Kaleidoscope II (2023), digital print, 27.6 × 20.7cm (10¾ × 8¼in), was developed from the same engraving using the same methods as for its companion print.

LASER CUT PRINTS FROM WOOD ENGRAVINGS

Although you can certainly cut woodblocks using laser cutters rather than hand-tools, I don't think a laser cutter can yet simulate the finesse or the appearance of tool marks hand-engraved in boxwood, nor the very individual shapes of each tool cut. In fact, to replicate them, you would first need to simulate them somehow in the source imagery with which you program the laser. In the time it would take to create such a highly finished image to include every semblance of hand-engraving that you might like – your time might be better spent engraving a woodblock!

I have, however, found laser cutting useful for generating cut paper images developed from my engravings. For each one, I scanned an engraving, then worked on the scan in Photoshop to simplify and enlarge its palest areas. Because my intention was to laser cut the final result on black paper, the laser-cut holes equating to white areas in the original engravings, it was necessary, in Photoshop, to simplify each image and make sure none of its white marks joined up to make an unbroken shape. After working on each image to ensure that no white marks linked up in this way, the Photoshop file was translated into a vector programme from which the laser cutter could be programmed. The final

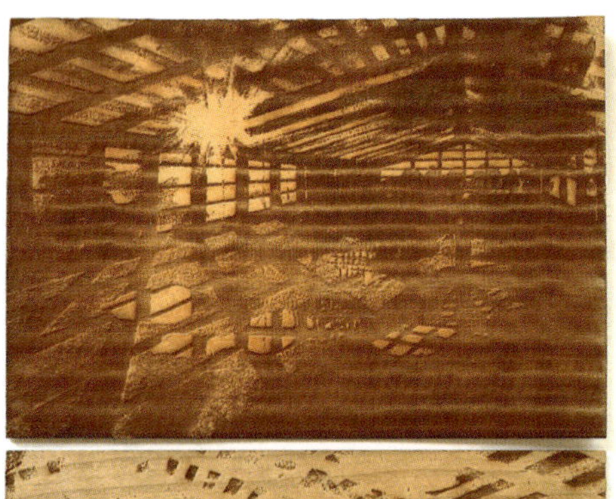

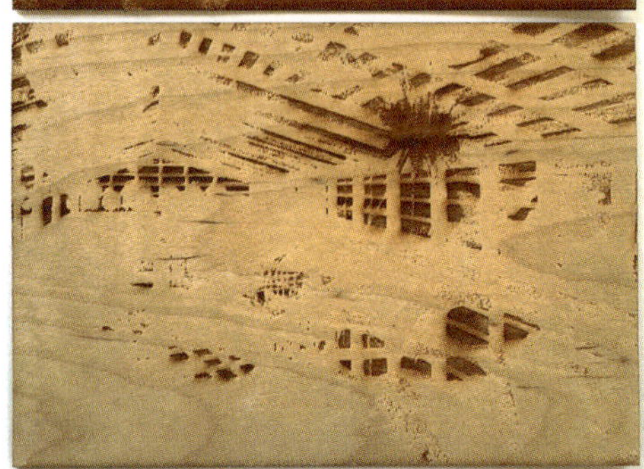

These laser-cut plywood test blocks were made using a sketchbook drawing, much modified in Photoshop, as source material. At the time (2010), the laser cutter couldn't cut wood – either long grain or end grain – to remotely the finesse of a hand-engraved block, but technology has no doubt improved vastly since these unsuccessful tests were made.

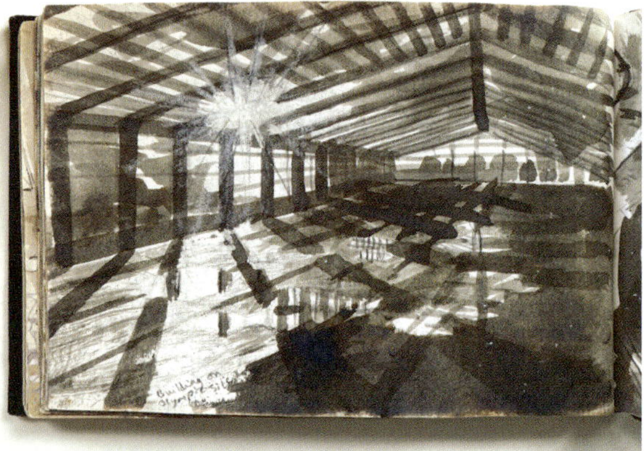

This grey wash, pencil and Chinagraph pencil sketch, 10 × 14.5cm (4 × 5¾in), of a derelict warehouse on what was to become London's Olympic site, was the basis for my initial unsuccessful experiments to laser-cut an end grain block with an image as fine as a hand-engraved block.

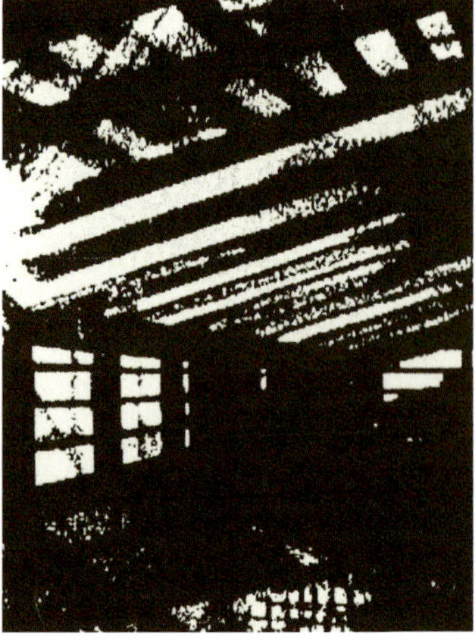

Prints from my laser-cut lemonwood block looked fuzzy and unresolved. In this detail, you can see that the laser coped poorly with cutting clean diagonals on the dense block. All its diagonal lines appear jagged.

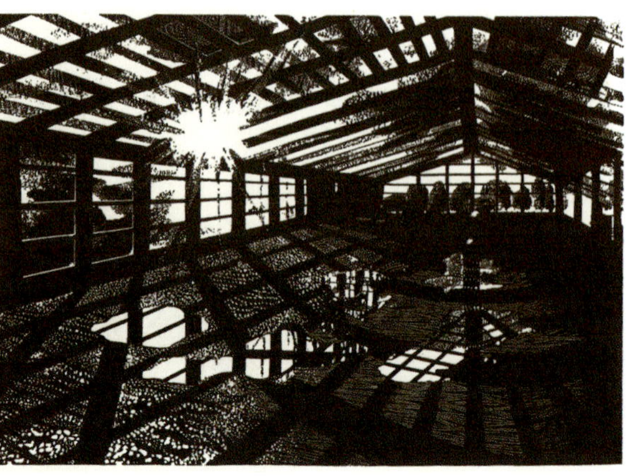

Derelict Warehouse, Olympic Site (2010), engraving on lemonwood, 12 × 16.6cm (4¾ × 6½in), on Gampi Vellum paper. The larger white parts were laser-cut on the block but to a shallow depth, so they picked up ink, and every diagonal line looked jagged. I had to recut and refine the engraving by hand and add tonal cuts to get this acceptable result.

prints were presented in deep box frames with an LED light panel in the inside back of each frame, arranged to shine through the laser-cut holes in the black printing paper to create effects of illuminated buildings in a night sky.

I haven't yet explored the possibilities of AI in any of my image-making as I would far rather work from visual sources that I created myself. However, a student on one of my most recent engraving classes used ChatGPT to translate his cityscape photos and a fellow-student's watercolour sketch into variants simulating black and white relief prints. While, initially, this seemed helpful to gain a sense of how one might interpret colour imagery in order to create monochrome prints, both students then proceeded to copy, rather too assiduously, the AI versions of their source material to make their own engravings rather than interpreting their own much livelier and subtler original imagery for themselves. While, at the time of writing, I have reservations about AI because of its potential to subvert one's own autonomous creativity, the technology is moving so fast that it is certainly worth watching and may become a useful tool.

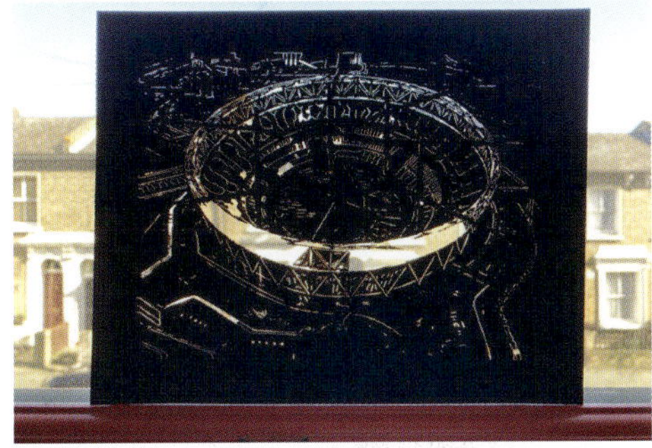

If my image file had rendered the circumference of this stadium out of interlinked white lines, when the laser cut the image, its entire oval shape would have become detached from the rest of the paper. In this test proof (shown in my studio window) two large sections have fallen away where too many white lines linked up.

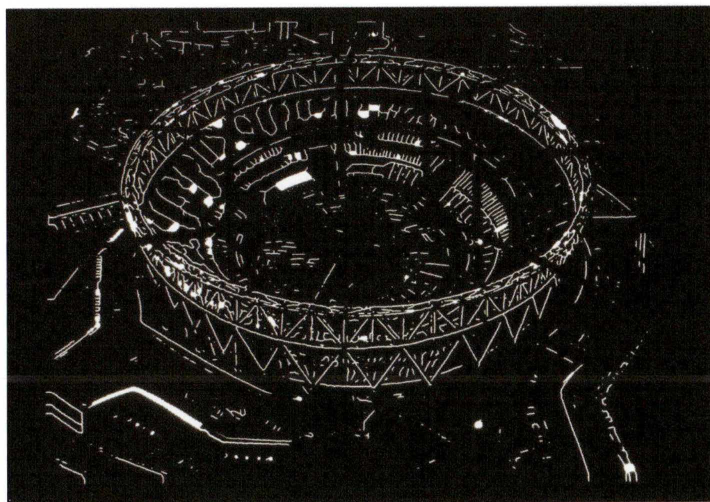

Olympic Light (2010), laser cut print on black Somerset paper, developed directly from wood engraving, and presented as an LED light box, 20.3 × 24cm (8 × 9½in).

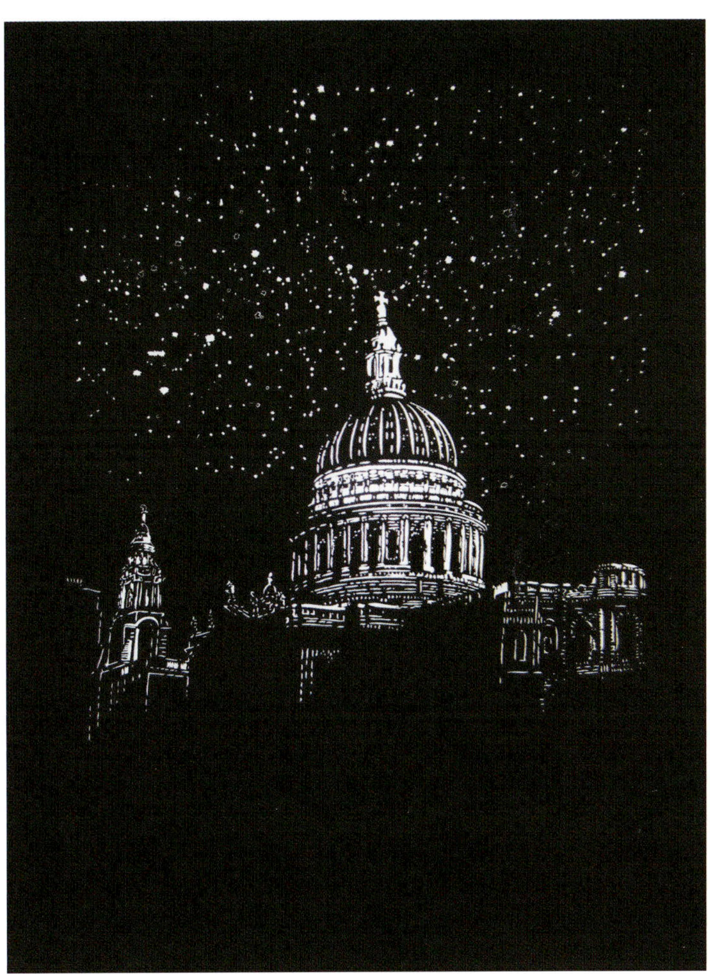

London's Secret Stars (2015), laser cut print on black Somerset paper, developed directly from wood engraving, and presented as an LED light box, 22 × 17cm (8¾ × 6¾in).

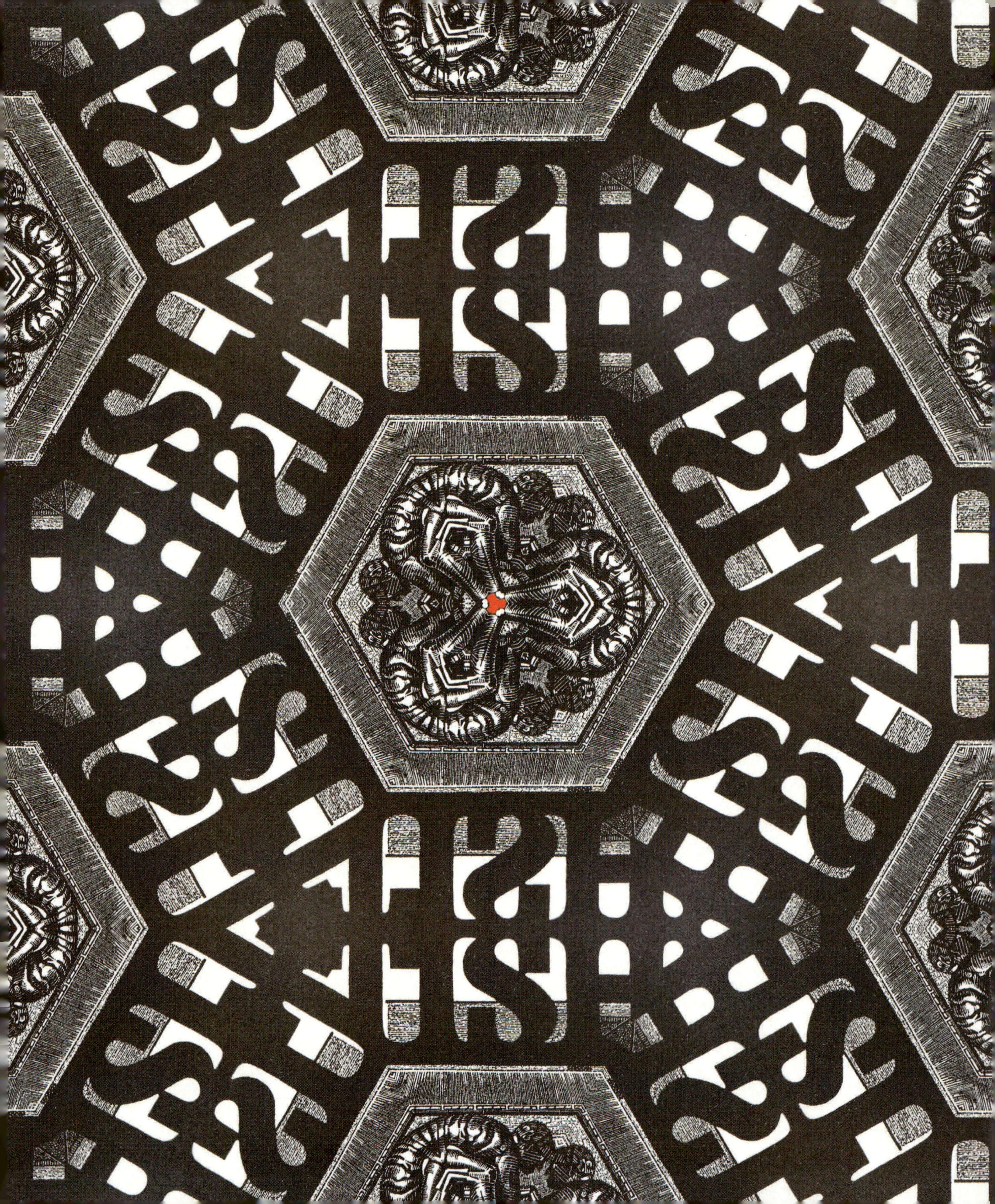

CHAPTER 12

EDITIONING, PRINT CARE AND DISPLAY

Boxwood blocks can be inked and printed thousands of times before the block might show wear – which is why wood engraving was so successful in commercial applications. The limited edition is a relatively recent Western invention by printer-publishers/gallerists keen to establish a specific market value for their wares, which was harder to do if images could be printed in almost infinite numbers.

Reconstructing the Ruins Revisited (2021), wood engravings on Gampi Vellum paper collaged on painted wood panel, 54.5 × 16 × 0.6cm (21½ × 6¼ × ¼in).

EDITIONING ETIQUETTE

The practice arose, during the late nineteenth and early twentieth century etching boom, of generating each new print in a limited edition of however many the publisher anticipated selling. Numbers written like this on a print – 8/100, for instance – denote that the print is the eighth impression in an edition of a hundred.

Because, historically, Western print publishing was controlled by printer-publishers rather than by artists, the artist would be paid a fee for the edition, which the publisher would then own and sell. Simultaneously, therefore, the convention arose of printing proofs for the artist's own use. These didn't usually exceed 10 per cent of the edition so, in an edition of 100 there would also be ten artist's proofs indicated as AP (or A/P). (In France, A/P becomes E/A for *épreuve d'artiste*.) In addition, there may be assorted trial or state proofs indicated as TP (T/P) or SP (S/P): either

British Library – Kaleidoscope (2023), digital print, 32 × 24cm (12½ × 9½in), on Somerset Satin paper, developed via a kaleidoscope app and Photoshop from a 1997 (commissioned) wood engraving I had made of the front gate of the British Library with the statue of Sir Isaac Newton by Eduardo Paolozzi (1924–2005) visible in the forecourt.

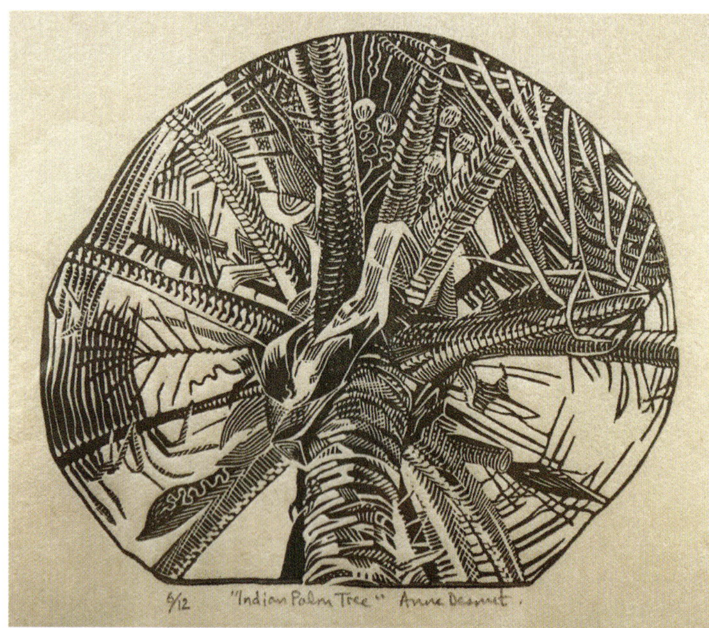

Small engraving showing edition number, title and signature. *Indian Palm Tree* (1986), boxwood engraving, 9 × 10cm (3½ × 4in), on buff Japanese paper.

subtly or sometimes radically different from the final edition, being experiments to determine how a block should best be printed. A print labelled BAT means *bon à tirer* or 'good to pull'. The printer uses this as the perfectly printed measure the edition needs to match. PP (P/P) is the printer's proof, which they keep, though artists who do their own printing sometimes make their own PP. Rarely seen now but common in the last century is HC (H/C) or *hors de commerce*. This denotes a sample print, not for sale and often carried about in a portfolio to show clients an artist's work without endangering any of the actual edition.

Having printed a first edition, if you print a second from the same block, you should write either (2nd ed.) after each new edition number, or else number each print entirely in Roman numerals, for instance iv/xx denotes print 4/20 from a second edition. Some artists print the entire edition in one go and others print as sales arise. Usually, but not necessarily, all prints in an edition are printed on the same type of paper.

When an edition is complete, by convention you should engrave a line across the block to 'cancel' it. I have never done this – partly because the blocks are lovely objects that I wouldn't want to deface, but also because I sometimes reprint them, long after editioning, to use for collage.

Keeping the block intact after editioning can be a form of insurance: if a print was irreparably damaged and had to be thrown away, you could print a replacement for the edition.

If an edition sells out and the block is intact, you have the option to print a second edition. There is no rule against this, though not everyone considers it good practice. But it's difficult to second-guess what might sell and what your future circumstances might be. An alternative approach, which many artists use, is to write a large edition total for the first edition, not printing them all but retaining the option to do so as and when, so never needing a second edition.

CARE OF PRINTS

When dry, prints should be signed, titled (if desired), numbered, then the edition wrapped in acid-free tissue until you need it. (Write the print title in pencil on the outside so you can easily identify the package's contents.) Prints are best stored horizontally in a drawer or archival box. If the drawer is wooden, line it with acid-free paper or card as a buffer between wood and prints.

Small prints can be packed in sturdy flat packages for posting and larger ones rolled into mailing tubes. Either way, wrap them first in acid-free tissue. I only buy mailing tubes with a minimum diameter of 8cm (3¼in) so as not to roll the print too tightly, thus avoiding paper creases. Most papers have an optimal rolling direction: one side may feel stiffer and more resistant to rolling than the other, so let the paper guide you. If unrolling a print, never roll it back on itself to flatten it, as this will disrupt the paper fibres and crease the paper. Instead, gently unroll it and lay it under weights (a stack of books or paper will work fine) for a few weeks.

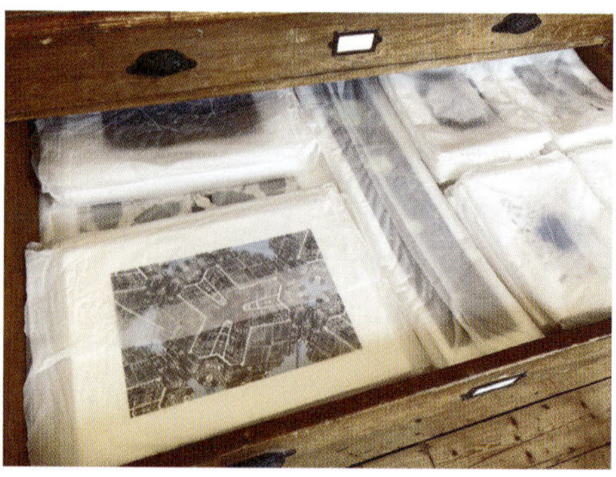

A plan chest drawer containing tissue-wrapped editions.

PRESENTATION

Wood engravings can be displayed framed and glazed or in other display arrangements. Framing protects them but is expensive and bulky to store. A plain wood moulding or one painted or stained a neutral colour (plus or minus a white or off-white acid-free window mount) is a conventional, elegant solution. Always use acid-free paper or fabric tabs to hinge prints (at their top corners) either into an acid-free window mount or on an acid-free backing board. Never tape the printing paper down along any edges: this will cause cockling.

Prints can also look great floated in shallow box frames, which are also excellent for three-dimensional collages (such as those on razor shells). Keep prints away from direct sunlight, which may cause papers to darken and colours to fade. Framing using glass with strong UV protection is worthwhile.

Some galleries use magnetic wall paint, enabling unframed prints to be displayed using small magnets at each corner. Others present them sandwiched between sheets of lightweight Perspex. A tall narrow work might be presented with minimal hanging fixtures at top and bottom edges, like a Chinese scroll. Display methods for all kinds of work – especially works on paper – are becoming increasingly various and imaginative.

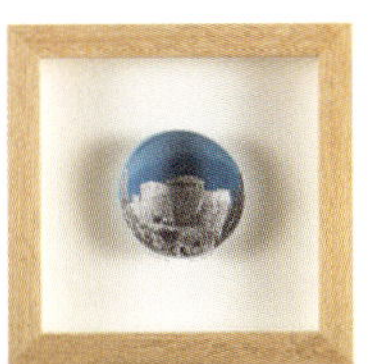

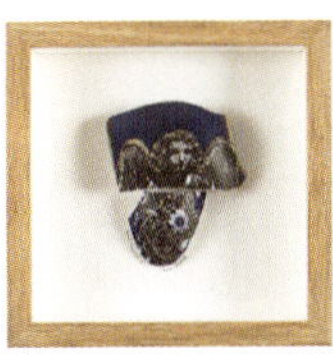

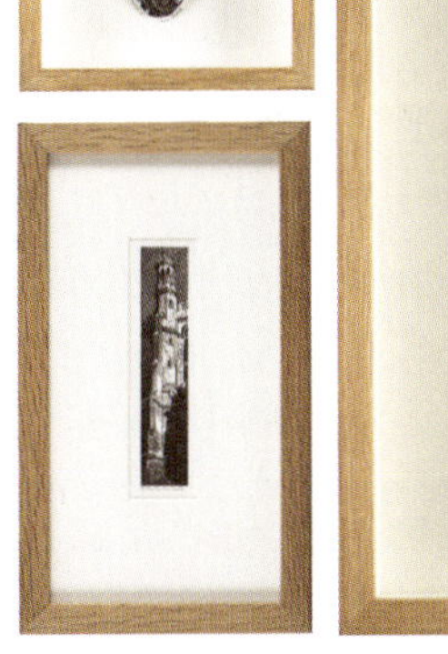

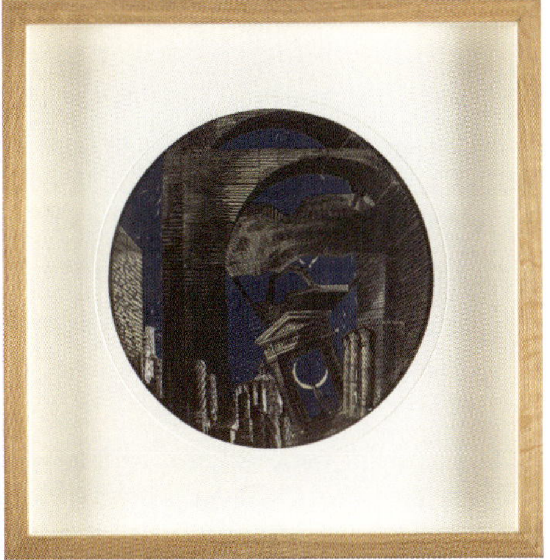

Some of my framed prints and collages. The engraving *Chapel Tower* (bottom left) has an archival window mount, as does the convex glass collaged roundel next to it. The roundel and the other collages on paper, ceramic bowl and pottery shards respectively, are presented in deep box frames.

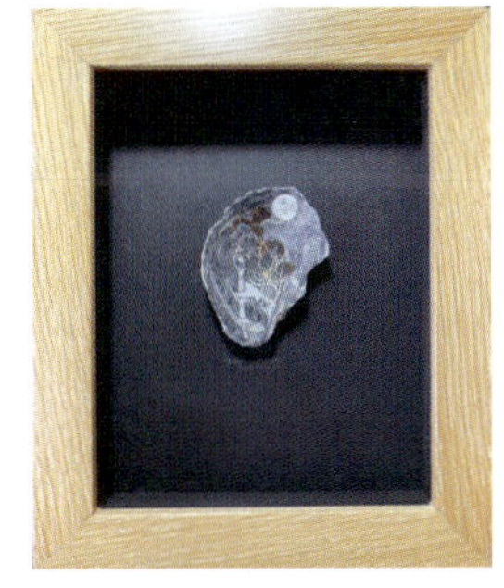

This collage of wood engravings on seashell, *Underwater World* (2005), 6.3 × 4.7 × 1cm (2½ × 2 × ½in) was floated on black card to accentuate the impact of its bright full moon. Non-reflective glass was therefore used to present it to best effect.

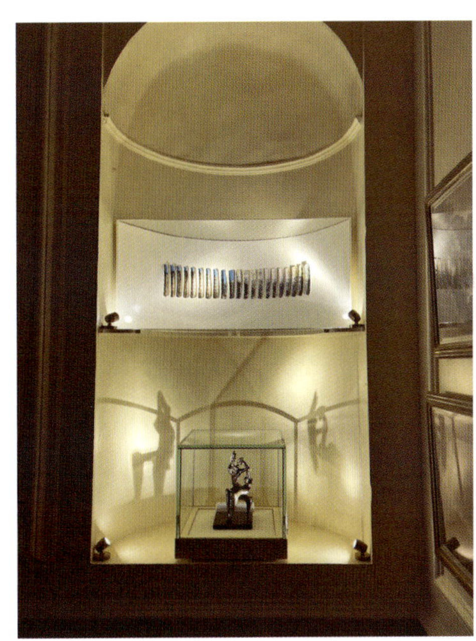

Echoes of Empires (2016), commissioned by Worcester College Oxford, comprises wood engravings and linocuts on paper collaged on 21 razor shells collaged on archival board, all framed in a bespoke Perspex box built to fit a semicircular curved shelf. Collage dimensions, 13 × 45 × 1.5cm (5 × 17¾ × ½in).

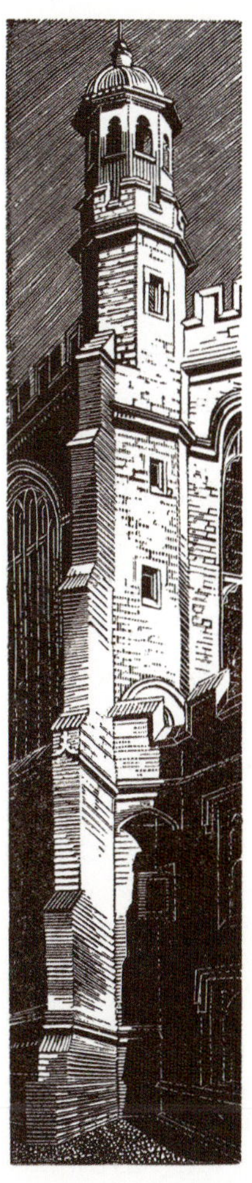

Chapel Tower (2016), engraving on boxwood, 15.7 × 3.1cm (6¼ × 1¼in), on Gampi Vellum paper.

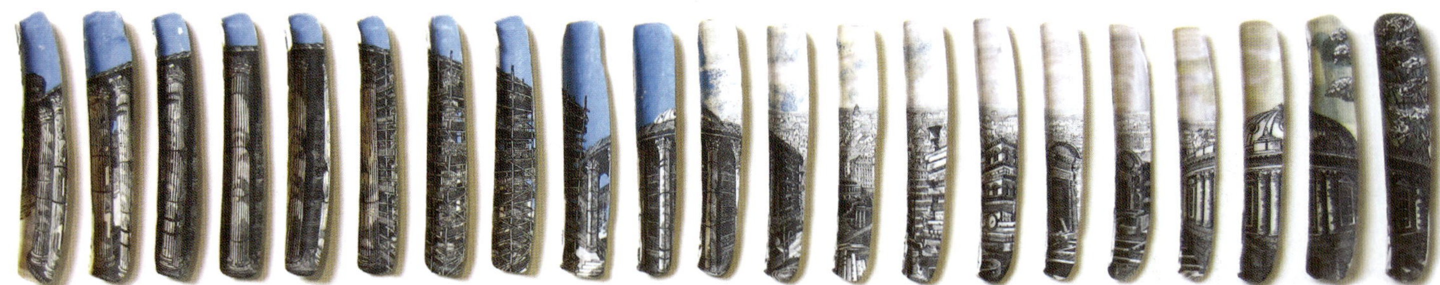

Echoes of Empires is shown here photographed flat before the archival board to which the razor shells are attached was fitted into the gentle curve of its Perspex frame.

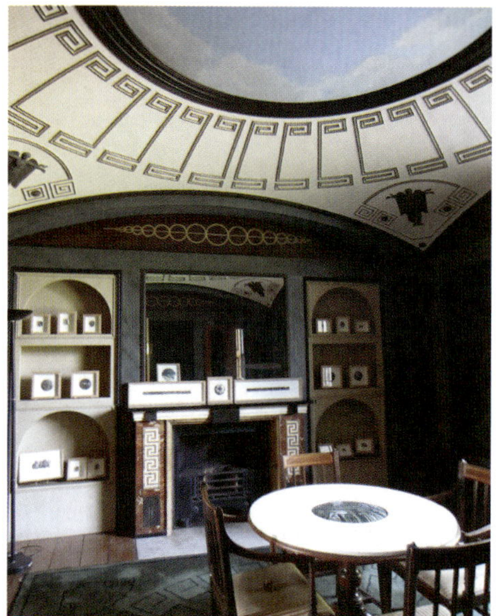

In 2012 I had an exhibition at Pitzhanger Manor, London. Designed to fill empty niches and a mantelpiece with an installation of framed collages suggestive of the Sir John Soane Museum and a historic Grand Tour, a collage behind convex glass on a round table was displayed simply behind a window mount.

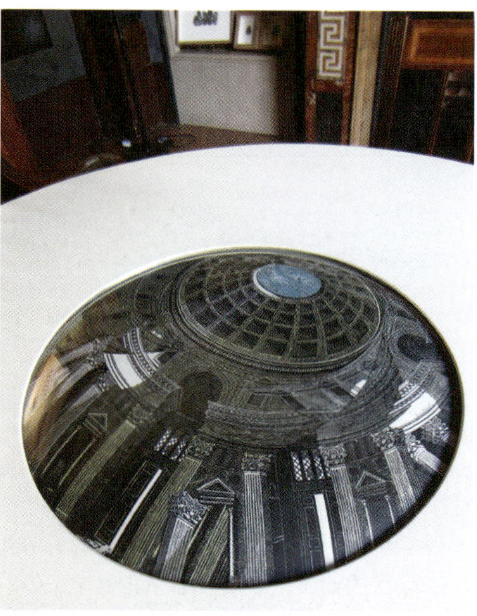

Pantheon (Oculus) (2012), linocut and screenprint on paper collaged behind convex glass, diameter: 36cm (14¼in), shown behind an archival window mount cut to the diameter of the table on which it was placed. It was framed in an oak box frame after the exhibition.

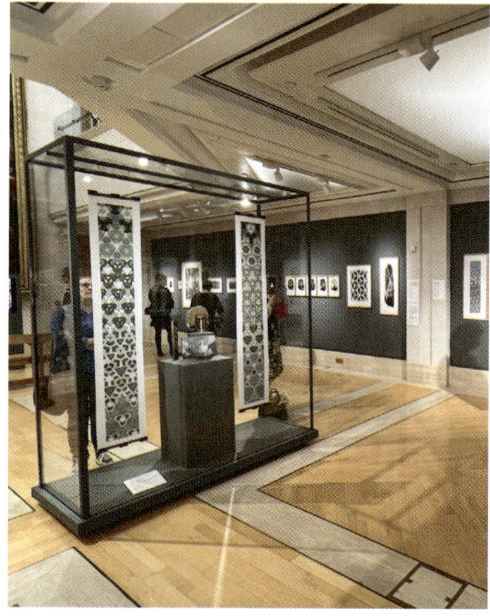

British Museum Kaleidoscope 1 and 2 (both 2023), digital prints (developed from wood engravings) on Somerset Satin paper, each 168 × 20.7cm (66 × 8¼in), printed by Jealous Print Studio. These tall narrow prints were shown displayed as hanging scrolls in my museum exhibition at Guildhall Art Gallery, London, in 2024–25.

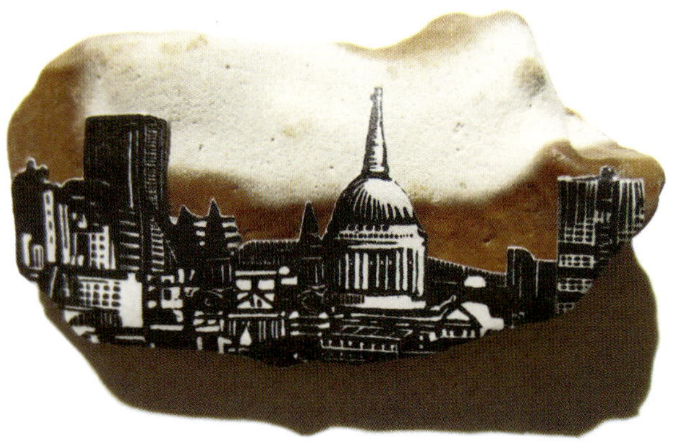

St Paul's Stone (2012), wood engraved print on paper collaged on pebble, 2.8 × 5.1 × 1.1cm (1¼ × 2 × ½in). This collage, framed in a tiny box frame, is one of the works I exhibited in the Pitzhanger Manor's breakfast room in 2012.

Build Your Own Babel Tower (2022), linocuts and wood engravings on paper collaged on museum board with pencil drawing and watercolour, 81 × 71cm (32 × 28in).

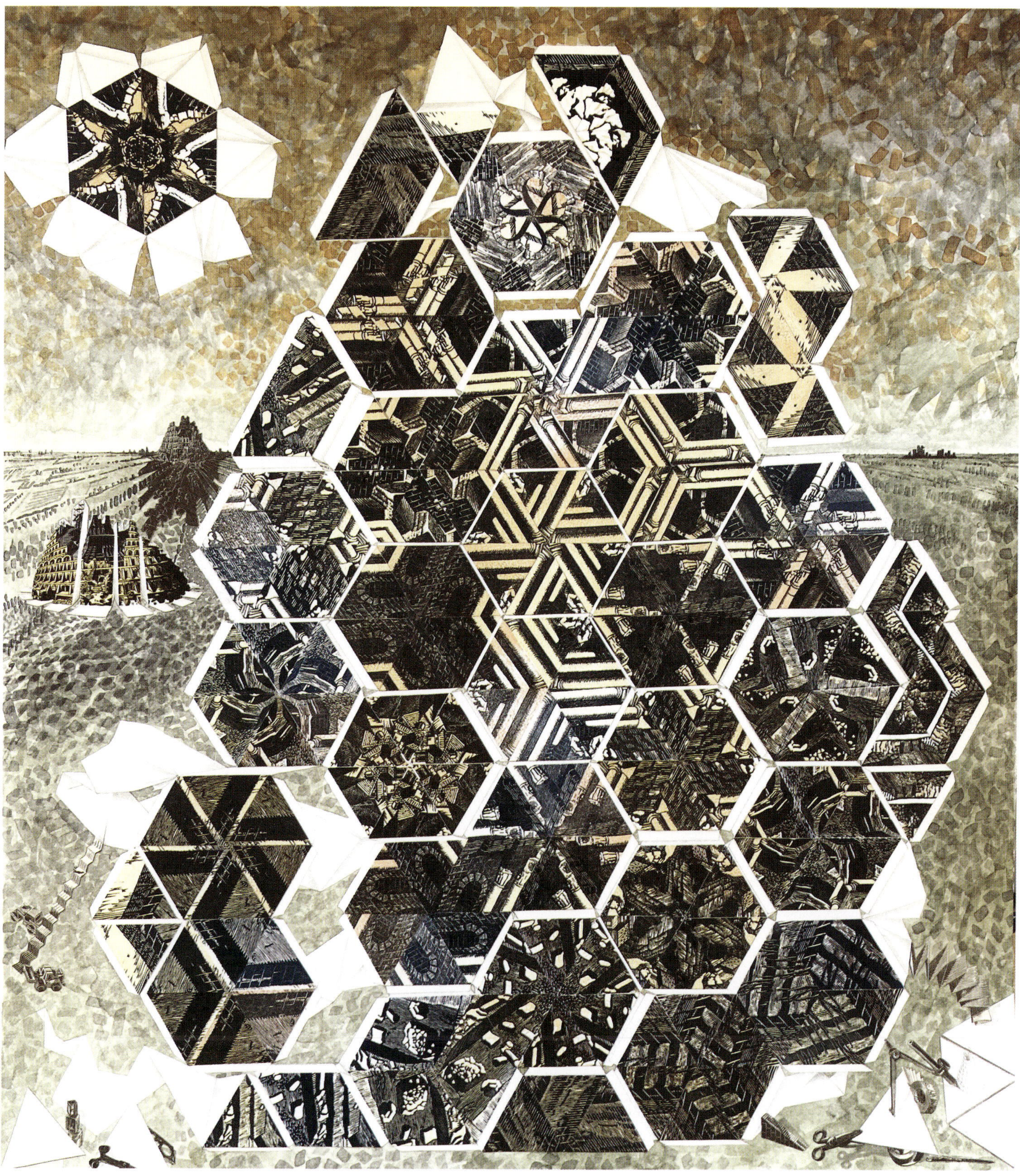

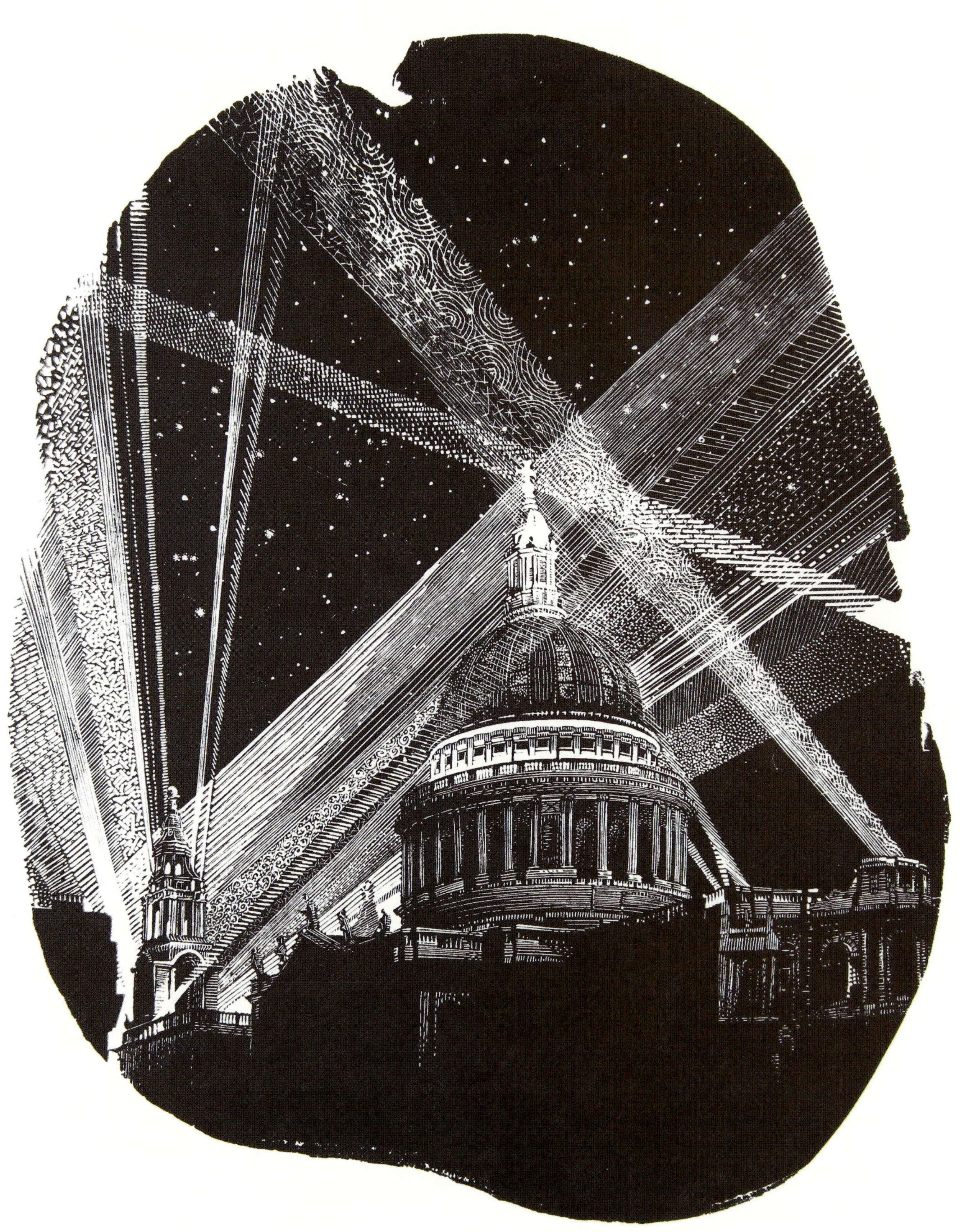

RELEVANT ORGANISATIONS AND PUBLICATIONS

Illustration
cellopress.co.uk
(magazine inc. historic and contemporary wood engraving)

International Fine Print Dealers Association (IFPDA)
ifpda.org
(the world's leading organisation of premier print dealers and galleries, established in 1987)

Journal of The Print World
journaloftheprintworld.com
(journal on antique and contemporary prints)

Letterpress Today
letterpress.today
(information source for letterpress and printmaking inc. presses for sale)

London Original Print Fair (UK)
Londonoriginalprintfair.com
(major annual event featuring British and International print galleries and dealers working with historic and contemporary prints and including wood engravings)

Pressing Matters
pressingmattersmag.com
(magazine on contemporary printmaking)

Printmaking Today
cellopress.co.uk
(journal on contemporary printmaking)

Print Quarterly
printquarterly.co.uk
(academic journal on historic and modern printmaking)

The Art Workers' Guild (UK)
artworkersguild.org
(body of c.400 artists and craftspeople inc. wood engravers working at the highest levels of excellence)

The Printmakers Council (UK)
printmakerscouncil.com
(non-profit artist-run group promoting use of both traditional and contemporary print processes)

The Royal Society of Painter-Printmakers (UK)
reprintmakers.com
(one of the world's leading printmaking organisations established in 1880)

The Society of Wood Engravers (SWE) (UK)
societyofwoodengravers.co.uk
(UK-based society founded in 1920 to promote wood engraving; it publishes a regular online newsletter, printed journal and runs an annual open submission wood engraving exhibition that tours the UK)

The Wood Engravers Network (WEN) (USA)
woodengravers.org
(non-profit arts organisation committed to furthering public recognition and appreciation of wood engraving and providing educational and exhibition opportunities in the medium)

Woolwich Contemporary Print Fair (UK)
woolwichprintfair.com
(annual London-based contemporary print fair, including wood engravings)

St Paul's: Lights (2014), fourth in a series of five reduction engravings on holly, on Gampi Vellum paper, 22.5 × 17.3cm (9 × 6¾in).

MATERIALS' SUPPLIERS

UK

AMR Logan Press
amrloganpress.co.uk
(press engineering, removals, servicing, supplies of presses and printing equipment)

Art Equipment Ltd
art-equipment.co.uk
(Albion press removals, refurbishments, servicing; nipping press sales)

Chris Daunt
chrisdaunt.com
(wood engraving block-maker and wood engraving equipment; endorsed by The Society of Wood Engravers)

Cranfield Colours Ltd
cranfield-colours.co.uk
(manufacturer of inks and transparent extender for wood engravers and other printmakers)

Deerness Tools
Ian Corrigan
e: deerness55@gmail.com
(bespoke wood engraving tools with hand-turned hardwood handles; tool shortening and sharpening services)

G Ryder & Co. Ltd
ryderbox.co.uk
(bespoke archival boxes for print storage and presentation purposes)

Harry F Rochat Ltd
harryrochat.com
(presses inc. bespoke Albions, press engineering, servicing, removals)

Hawthorn Printmaker Supplies
hawthornprintmaker.com
(printmakers' supplies inc. presses, rollers, inks)

H S Walsh & Sons Ltd
hswalsh.com
(jewellers' tool suppliers inc. emery polishing papers, magnifying lenses)

Intaglio Printmaker
intaglioprintmaker.com
(printmaking supplies inc. Lyons and bespoke wood engraving tools, Japanese woodcutting tools and papers)

John Purcell Papers
johnpurcell.net
(fine art and printmaking papers)

L Cornelissen & Son
cornelissen.com
(fine art and printmaking supplies)

LION Picture Framing Supplies Ltd
lionpic.co.uk
(picture framing mouldings, mountboards etc)

Pooki Presses
Pookipresses.co.uk
(small portable wooden printing presses)

R K Burt & Company Ltd
rkburt.com
(fine art and printmaking papers)

Shepherds London
store.bookbinding.co.uk
(bookbinding, specialist papers and paper conservation products)

Stuart R Stevenson
shop.stuartstevenson.co.uk
(gilding materials, archival boxes, print racks)

T N Lawrence & Son Ltd
tnlawrence.com
(specialist printmaking supplies inc. wood engraving tools, blocks, inks, papers)

Trotec Laser
troteclaser.com
(specialist plastic for engraving and laser cutting)

USA

Apex Printers Rollers Co.
apexrollers.com
(printing rollers)

Atlantic Papers
atlanticpapers.com
(printmaking papers)

Edward C Lyons Company
eclyons.com
(makers of wood engraving tools)

Jim Reynolds
e: jmreynolds@wi.rr.com
(block-maker of maple blocks and block resurfacing)

Laird Plastics
Lairdplastics.com
(Styrene plastics for engraving)

Legion Paper Corp.
legionpaper.com
(printmaking papers)

Light Impressions Corp.
lightimpressionsdirect.com
(archival storage materials, framing)

McClain's Printmaking Supplies
imcclains.com
(printmaking supplies inc. wood engraving tools, sandbags)

Moore Wood Type
moorewoodtype.com
(maple, holly, pear woodblocks)

NA Graphics
nagraph.com
(letterpress supplies)

Tom Veling
e: awr@nu3c.com
(engraving block-maker and resurfacing)

East Asia

Awagami Factory
Awagami.com
(Japanese printmaking papers inc. sample packs)

Kaiming Li Wood Engraving Supplies
Instagram.com/kaimingli99
e: kaimingli1999@gmail.com
(block-maker and wood engraving tool supplier)

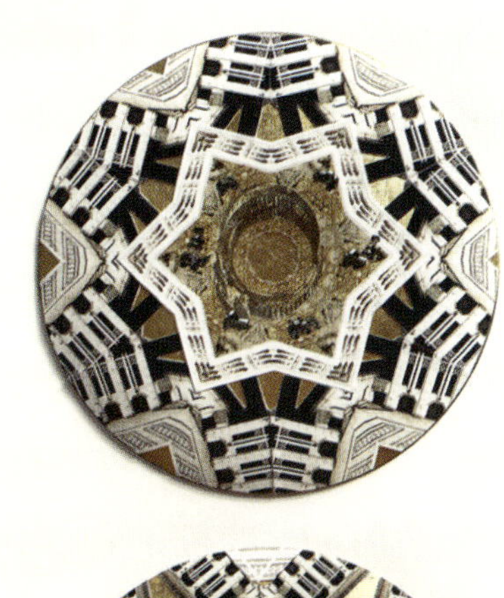

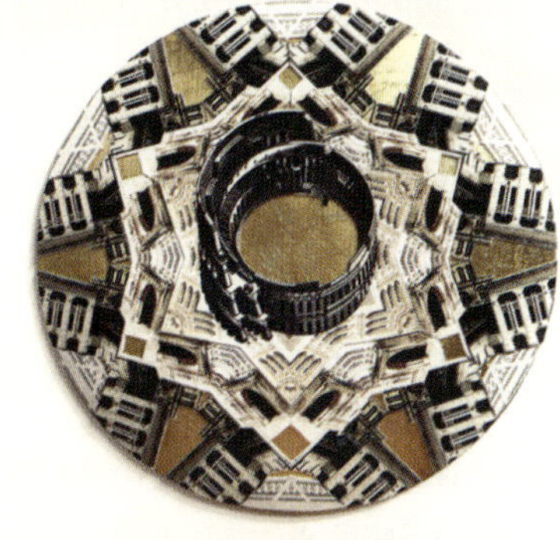

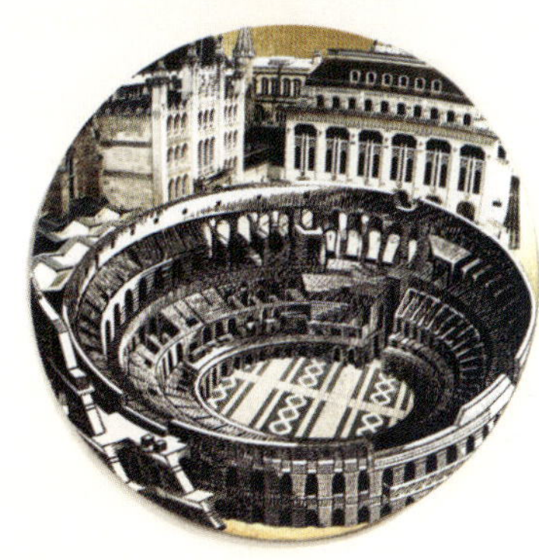

Colosseum Kaleidoscope (2024), digital prints (developed from my photos and wood engravings) on Somerset Satin paper collaged on three roundels of convex glass (diameter of each one: 21.7cm/8½in) with gold-coloured metal foil. Commissioned by London's Guildhall Art Gallery.

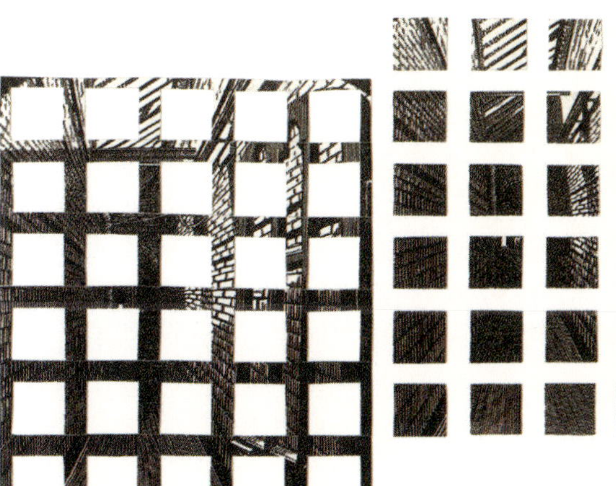

Light Grid Displaced (2008), wood engraving on paper collaged on museum board, 10.2 × 15.1cm (4 × 6in).

FURTHER READING

This list makes no attempt at completeness but includes relevant books I have found useful or inspiring.

BARTRUM, Giulia, *Albrecht Dürer and His Legacy*. British Museum Press, London, 2002.

BIGGS, John R, *Classic Woodcut Art and Engraving*. Blandford Press, London, 1988.

BLISS, Douglas Percy, *A History of Wood Engraving*, J M Dent & Sons, London, 1928.

BRABY, Dorothea, *The Way of Wood Engraving*, The Studio Publications, London and New York, 1953.

BRETT, Simon, *An Engraver's Globe – Wood Engraving World-Wide in the 21st Century*. Primrose Hill Press, London, 2002.

BRETT, Simon, *An Engraver's Progress – Simon Brett: Fifty Years of Wood Engraving*. Oblong Creative, Yorkshire, 2013.

BRETT, Simon, *Engravers – A Handbook for the Nineties. Compiled for the Society of Wood Engravers*. Silent Books, Cambridge, 1987.

BRETT, Simon, *Engravers Two – A Handbook Compiled for the Society of Wood Engravers*. Silent Books, Cambridge, 1992.

BRETT, Simon, *The Life and Art of Clifford Webb*. Little Toller Books, West Dorset, 2019.

BRETT, Simon, *Wood Engraving – How to Do It. Silent Books*, Cambridge, 1994; revised ed. A&C Black, London, 2010.

CHAMBERLAIN, Walter, *The Thames and Hudson Manual of Wood Engraving*. Thames & Hudson, London, 1978.

DAUNT, Chris, *The Art and Craft of Wood Engraving*. The Crowood Press, Wiltshire, 2023.

DESMET, Anne, *Box of Delights – Wood Engravings from the Ashmolean Collection*. Ashmolean Publications, Oxford, 2020.

DESMET, Anne, *Scene through Wood – A Century of Modern Wood Engraving*, Ashmolean Publications, Oxford, 2020.

DESMET, Anne and ANDERSON, Jim, *Handmade Prints – An Introduction to Creative Printmaking without a Press*. A&C Black, London; Davis, USA; & Haupt, Germany, 2000.

DESMET, Anne and DYSON, Anthony, *Printmakers – The Directory*. A&C Black, London, 2006.

DIGBY, John and DIGBY, Joan, *The Collage Handbook*. Thames & Hudson, London, 1987.

ESCHER, Maurits Cornelis, *M C Escher – The Graphic Work*, Benedikt Taschen, Berlin, 1990 (English translation of the Dutch version published in 1959).

FORTY, Sandra, *M C Escher*. Taj Books International, Surrey, 2006.

FRANCIS, Julian, *Tom Chadwick and The Grosvenor School of Modern Art*, Fleece Press, Yorkshire, 2012.

GARRETT, Albert, *A History of Wood Engraving*. Bloomsbury, London, 1986 (1st published by Midas Books, 1978).

GARRETT, Albert, *British Wood Engraving of the 20th Century – A Personal View*. Scolar Press, London, 1980.

GARRETT, Albert, *Wood Engravings and Drawings of Iain Macnab of Barachastlain*. Midas Books, Kent, 1973.

GENTLEMAN, David, *Wood Engravings of David Gentleman*. David Esslemont, Montgomery, Wales, 2000.

GOLDMAN, Paul, *Victorian Illustrated Books 1850–1870. The Heyday of Wood-Engraving*. British Museum Press, London, 1994.

GREENWOOD, Jeremy, *The Graphic Work of Edward Wadsworth.* Wood Lea Press, Suffolk, 2002.

GREENWOOD, Jeremy, *The Wood Engravings of John Nash.* Wood Lea Press, Liverpool, 1987.

GREENWOOD, Jeremy, *The Wood Engravings of Paul Nash.* Wood Lea Press, Woodbridge, 1997.

HAMILTON, James, *Wood Engraving and The Woodcut in Britain c.1890–1990.* Barrie & Jenkins, London, 1994.

HARLING, Robert, *The Engravings of Eric Ravilious.* Faber & Faber, London, 1946.

HOSKINS, Stephen and CRAINE, Michael, *Ink for Printmaking – The Art, Craft and Chemistry of Ink. Bloomsbury*, 2025.

HOSKINS, Stephen, *Inks (Printmaking Handbooks).* A&C Black, London, 2004.

HUGHES-STANTON, Penelope, *The Wood Engravings of Blair Hughes-Stanton.* Private Libraries Assoc., Pinner, 1991.

JAFFE, PATRICIA, *Women Engravers.* Virago, London, 1990.

JONKER, Pieter, *Het labyrinth in zwart en wit Houtgravures van Peter Lazarov.* Krips Repro Meppel, The Netherlands, 1991.

KALASHNIKOV, Anatoly, *500 Ex Libris.* Evrika, Moscow, 1993.

LEEPER, Janet, *Edward Gordon Craig: Designs for the Theatre.* Penguin Books, Middlesex, 1948.

LEIGHTON, Clare, *Four Hedges – A Gardener's Chronicle.* Sumach Press, St Albans, 1991 (1st published by Victor Gollancz Ltd, 1935).

LEIGHTON, Clare, *The Farmer's Year – A Calendar of English Husbandry.* Little Toller Books, Dorset, 2018 (1st published by Collins, 1933).

LEIGHTON, Clare, *Wood-Engraving and Woodcuts, How to do it series, No. 2.* The Studio Publications, London and New York, 1932.

LOCHER, J L (editor), *Leven en werk van M C Escher.* Meulenhoff, Amsterdam, 1981.

MACKLEY, George E, *Monica Poole: Wood Engraver.* Florin Press, Biddenden, 1984.

MASEREEL, Frans, *Passionate Journey, a novel told in 165 woodcuts.* Redstone Press, London, 1987.

MASEREEL, Frans, *Story Without Words and The Idea, two novels told in woodcuts.* Redstone Press, London, 1986.

MASEREEL, Frans, *The City: A Vision in Woodcuts.* Dover Publications, New York, USA, 2006.

MEYRICK, Robert and HEUSER, Harry, *C F Tunnicliffe Prints: A Catalogue Raisonné.* Royal Academy of Arts, London, 2017.

MEYRICK, Robert, *Sydney Lee Prints: A Catalogue Raisonné.* Royal Academy of Arts, London, 2013.

NASH, John, *Poisonous Plants: Deadly, Dangerous and Suspect*, edited by Dr A W Hill, FRS. Frederick Etchells and Hugh Macdonald, Hazelwood Books, London, 1927.

PAYNTER, Hilary, *Full Circle – Hilary Paynter Wood Engravings.* Woodend Publishing, Somerset, 2010.

POOLE, Monica, *The Wood Engravings of John Farleigh*, Gresham Books, Oxfordshire, 1985.

RAYNER, John, *Wood Engravings by Thomas Bewick.* Penguin, London, 1947.

RUSSELL, James, *In Relation: Nine Couples who Transformed Modern British Art.* Sansom & Co., Bristol, 2018.

RUSSELL, James, *Ravilious.* Philip Wilson Publishers, London, 2015.

RUSSELL, James, *Tirzah Garwood: Beyond Ravilious.* Bloomsbury, 2024.

RUSSELL, Judith, *The Wood Engravings of Gertrude Hermes.* Scolar Press, Hampshire, and Ashgate Publishing, Vermont, USA, 1993.

SALTER, Rebecca, *Japanese Woodblock Printing.* A&C Black, London, 2001.

SEE-PAYNTON, Colin, *The Incisive Eye: Colin See-Paynton, Wood Engravings 1980–1996.* Scolar Press, Hants/Glynn Vivian Art Gallery, Swansea, 1996.

SELBORNE, Joanna, *British Wood-Engraved Book Illustration 1904–1940. A Break with Tradition.* The British Library, London/Oak Knoll Press, New Castle, Delaware, USA, 1998.

SELBORNE, Joanna and NEWMAN, Lindsay, *Gwen Raverat: Wood Engraver*, British Library, London/Oak Knoll Press, New Castle, Delaware, USA, 2003.

SIMMONS, Rosemary, *Collecting Original Prints – A Complete Guide.* A&C Black, London, 2005.

SIMMONS, Rosemary and CLEMSON, Katie, *The Complete Manual of Relief Printmaking.* Dorling Kindersley, London, 1988.

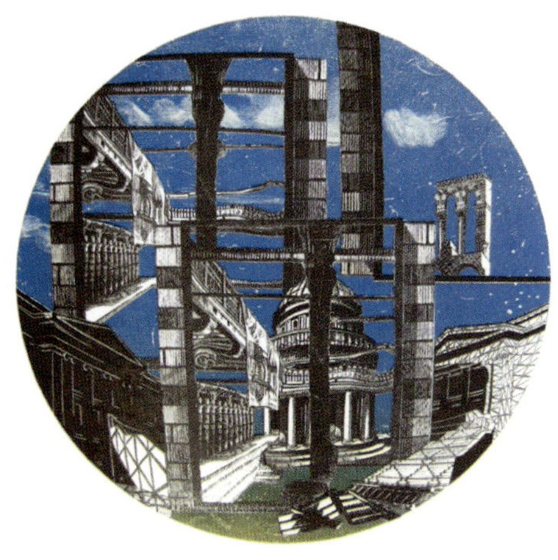

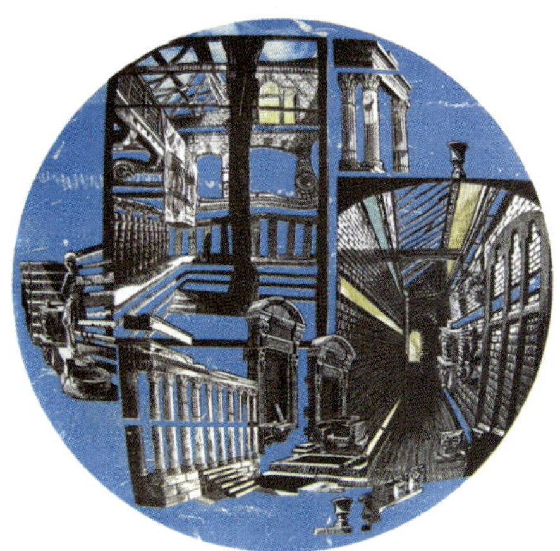

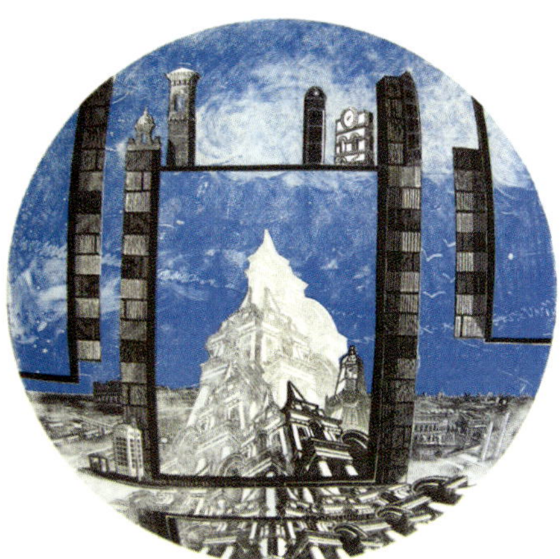

■ *Constructed Space I*, *Constructed Space II* and *Constructed Space III* (all 2013), wood engraving, linocut and monotype prints (using salvaged floor lino block) on paper collaged on convex glass, diameter of each one: 18cm (7in).

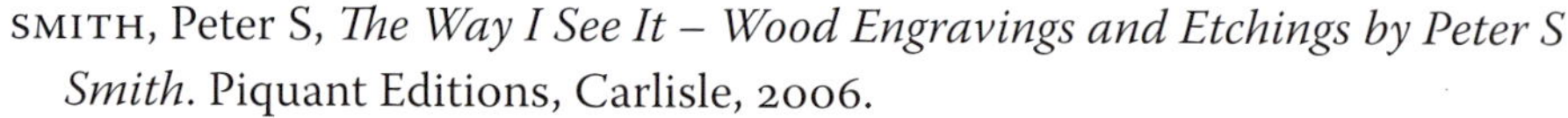

SMITH, Peter S, *The Way I See It – Wood Engravings and Etchings by Peter S Smith*. Piquant Editions, Carlisle, 2006.

SPIEGELMAN, Art (editor), *Lynd Ward: Six Novels in Woodcuts*. The Library of America, New York, 2010.

STEVENS, Anne, *Monica Poole*. Ashmolean Museum, Oxford, 1993.

TWOHIG, Edward, *Print REbels. Haden, Palmer, Whistler and the origins of the RE (Royal Society of Painter-Printmakers)*. RE, Bankside Gallery London, 2018.

WADSWORTH, Barbara, *Edward Wadsworth, a Painter's Life*, Michael Russell, Wiltshire, 1989.

WEBB, Brian and SKIPWITH, Peyton, *David Gentleman – Design*. Antique Collectors' Club, Suffolk, 2009.

WEBB, Brian and SKIPWITH, Peyton, *Edward Bawden and Eric Ravilious*. Antique Collectors' Club, Suffolk, 2005.

WEBB, Brian and SKIPWITH, Peyton, *Paul Nash – Design – John Nash*. Antique Collectors' Club, Suffolk, 2006.

WILLIAMS, Graham, *Make-Ready – An Essential Skill for Wood Engravers and Letterpress Printers*. The Florin Press, Kent, 2024.

WILLIAMS, Graham, *Understanding Paper. Assessment and Permanence for Artists and Fine Printers*. The Florin Press, Kent, 2021.

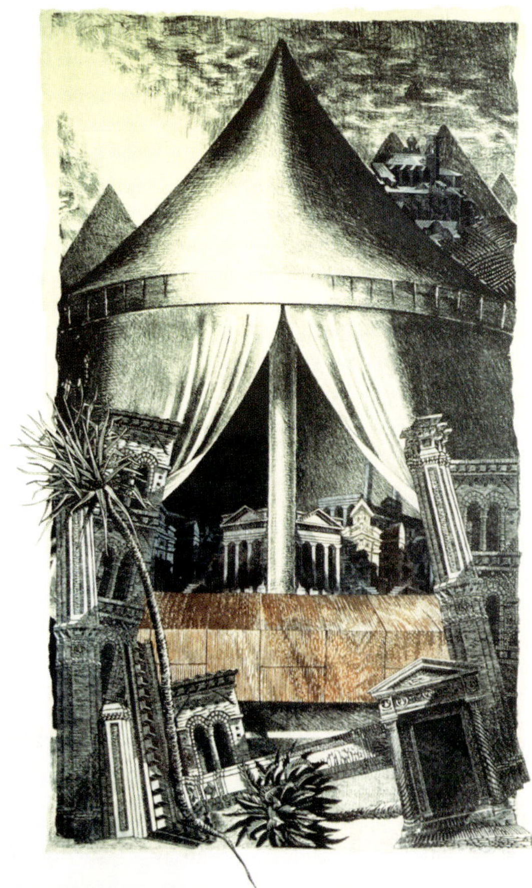

■ *City Within Tent* (1992), stone lithograph, linocut and wood engraving prints collaged on paper, with black pen drawing, 58.5 × 34.3cm (23 × 13½in). This combines elements of at least six prints. The tent is a stone lithograph; the foreground architecture is linocut; the smaller architectural parts are wood engravings.

GLOSSARY OF TERMS

Artist's book: book (or artwork with book traits), usually self-published by an artist or specialist press, usually involving original artwork.

Artist's proof: finished print identical to those in the edition, usually retained by the artist, and identified on the print as AP or A/P.

Black-line engraving: a characteristic of the wood engraving technique wherein the design appears, when printed, as black lines on a paper-white background, closely resembling a pen and ink drawing.

Bon à tirer: print that sets the standard for producing the rest of an edition, meaning 'good to print' and marked as BAT on the print.

Boxwood: traditional wood used for wood engraving from the common box tree (*Buxus sempervirens*). Lemonwood (not the fruiting lemon tree, but a close-grained tree with leaves that give a citrus scent when rubbed), holly, pear, cherry, American maple and other alternatives are also used.

Bruising: dents or other non-engraved indentations in a woodblock, sometimes caused accidentally by the sharp belly of a tool.

Bullsticker: engraving tool with a leaf-shaped cutting face, a variation on a spitsticker.

Burin/Graver: generic term for engraving tools.

Chine collé: a printmaking technique in which a thin piece of paper is glued to a heavier backing paper as part of the process of printing (usually) an etching plate in order to introduce new colours or textures to localised parts of the image.

Chisel: tool for wood engraving, woodcutting or linocutting; generally used for clearing/smoothing areas of a block's surface.

Copper engraving: intaglio print produced from a smooth copper plate, into the surface of which the artist engraves a design, using steel burins.

End grain: block of hardwood sawn across the trunk and used for the technique of wood engraving in which cuts made run at right angles to the wood grain.

Engraving: the act of incising marks, the incised block itself and any prints taken from it. It describes a print produced by cutting into a metal or end grain woodblock with sharp tools. Metal engravings are usually printed intaglio whereas wood engravings are printed in relief.

Etching: general term for using a mordant to bite the surface of a printing plate (usually metal or lino), the etched plate itself and any prints taken from it. The process was developed in medieval Europe where it was first used to decorate metal armour.

Ex Libris: (Latin: 'from the books of') is a bookplate usually comprising a small printed, decorative paper label pasted into a book, often onto the inside front page, to indicate ownership. The designs are often created as wood engravings.

Frisket: part of a platen press comprising a metal frame (hinged to the tympans) to which is attached a stretched sheet of strong paper with a woodblock-sized hole cut in the middle and the printing paper is placed behind that hole for each printing. The stretched paper of the frisket protects the area of the printing paper that is not desired to print.

Grain: directional pattern of fibres in wood and paper.

Hand-burnishing: printing with a hard, smooth, hand-held implement, such as a wooden or metal spoon, or Japanese baren.

Hors de commerce: 'not for commerce/not for sale' prints used as display samples by artists and publishers.

HP (hot pressed), Not or **CP (cold pressed)** and **Rough**: different surfaces of paper produced by different manufacturing processes. Extra hot-pressed papers tend to have very smooth surfaces suitable for wood engraving.

Imprint/impression: a print.

Ink (printing): pigment suspended in semi-liquid oil-based or water-based medium, prepared to a particular consistency suitable for printing.

Inking slab: smooth hard surface (such as toughened glass) for mixing, spreading and rolling out printing ink.

Intaglio: from the Italian *intagliare*, meaning to engrave or incise a design into a surface.

Intaglio print: imprint produced by a method in which ink is rubbed into the grooves of a design made in a (usually metal) printing plate. Printing is on an etching press used to force damp paper into the plate's inked grooves to pick up the impression. Developed since the sixteenth century, intaglio processes have been used by artists such as Dürer, Rembrandt and Goya.

Japanese paper: strong paper (sometimes handmade) made from long fibres of mulberry and other indigenous Japanese plants; Japanese printmaking papers offer particularly receptive surfaces for printing wood engravings and woodcut prints.

Jigsaw block: printing block cut into entirely separate pieces which are inked (sometimes in different colours) and reassembled, like a jigsaw, for printing.

Key block: printing block carrying the primary features of a design involving several separate blocks.

Laid paper: the imprint of light lines produced by wires comprising the mesh base of a mould for handmade paper and imitated in machine-made papers.

Limited edition: finite number of identical prints, each numbered as part of the total.

Linocut: print produced from a linoleum block, onto the surface of which the artist cuts an image using steel gouges. The areas of the block to be printed are left uncut (in relief) while areas not intended to take printing ink are cut away. Although linoleum is a floor covering dating to the 1860s, linocut printing was used first by artists of Die Brücke in Germany between 1905 and 1913.

Lithography: printing process, developed in Bavaria in c.1796 by Alois Senefelder, which relies on the antipathy of grease and water. The image is drawn onto a limestone block or special metal plate, using greasy crayon or ink (tusche). The greasy image is chemically fixed to the stone/plate which is dampened with water and rolled with oil-based ink. The oily ink adheres to the grease of the image and is repelled by the water in surrounding areas. Lithographs are press-printed, each colour requiring a separate stone/plate. It was popular with French artists including Toulouse-Lautrec in the 1890s and widely used by twentieth century artists.

Lozenge graver/square graver: engraving tool made from a square- or lozenge-shaped steel rod, used both for copper-plate intaglio and end grain relief engraving, it is usually used for engraving straight lines of varying thicknesses.

Make-ready: thin (often tissue) paper overlays or underlays used to increase pressure on specific areas of an engraved block when printing.

Matrix: general term for a printing block or plate.

Mixed media: any artwork created by several diverse methods; artists' prints combining more than one basic method, for example, woodcut and screenprint.

Monoprint: impression printed from a reprintable block, such as a linoblock or woodblock, but printed in such a way that only one of its kind exists, for example, a printed image incorporating unique hand-colouring or collage.

Monotype: one-off print in which there is no re-usable printing matrix so the work is unique and cannot be replicated exactly.

Multiple-block printing: method using more than one block to produce an image – usually in overlapping colours.

Multiple tool: tool for wood engraving. Its cutting edge comprises a row of tiny steel teeth; it is used for cutting several short parallel lines simultaneously.

Offset printing: method of transferring a still-wet impression from one surface to another and often used to transfer a key-image to subsequent blocks to guide the cutting of multiple-block prints.

Plate (printing): general term for a sheet of plastic, metal etc. from which a print is taken. It is largely interchangeable with **Block** or **Printer** but usually used to describe thinner printers than blocks, which often refer to wood.

Platen: cast-iron plate of a relief printing press which supplies the pressure and weight to print a wood engraved block.

Pochoir: subtle stencil-based printing technique popular from the late nineteenth century through the 1930s, with its centre of activity in Paris. It is still used by artists and illustrators today.

Press bed: The (usually) movable cast-iron base plate of a printing press, which supports the block when printing.

Printing press: machine (hand operated or mechanized) designed to print repeatable impressions. Different types are required to print images created via the various different printing processes, for example, platen (or relief) presses are used to print woodcuts and other relief prints, while etching (or intaglio) presses print etchings, copper engravings etc. Lithography requires another type of press and there are many different types, sizes and designs of press for each print process.

Printing/printmaking: process of transferring an impression from one object onto another – rather than directly painting or drawing.

Proofs: trial impressions taken prior to editioning a final version of an image – often called **State Proofs** or **Trial Proofs**.

Reduction method: process of making a multi-colour (or tonally graded) print from one block. The block is cut and printed in stages. Between each printing, further cutting is carried out – thereby gradually reducing the block's uncut surface.

Registration: alignment of multiple printings onto the same surface to ensure that each printing falls in precisely the correct position relative to the first one.

Relief print/surface print: impression produced by applying ink to the surface of a printing plate. The block's uncut surface is the area which is inked and printed; cut (or indented) areas show as the paper colour.

Resin blocks: acetal resin polymer products simulating many qualities of end grain boxwood. These are used by some artists as alternatives to engraving wood.

Roller/brayer: tool for rolling ink out evenly onto inking slab and printing block (especially for relief prints).

Sandbag: cushion made of two circular pieces of leather sewn together and packed tight with sand. It is used as a surface on which to rest the end grain woodblock and to facilitate rotating the block beneath the tool.

Scorper: tool for wood engraving. Its cutting tip is either rounded or squared off (for round or square scorpers accordingly). It is used to engrave round- or square-shaped stippled dots, relatively broad lines, and to clear away areas of a block's surface.

Screenprinting/serigraphy/silkscreen: printing using a frame covered in a fine taut mesh through which ink is forced onto paper (or other material) beneath. Areas of the screen are masked off using hand-drawn or photographic stencils to define an image. It was popularised as an artists' medium by American Pop Artists Andy Warhol and Roy Lichtenstein in the 1960s, though the basic technique seems to date back to c.500 BCE in Japan.

Side-grain/long-grain: wood sawn in planks, along the grain. It is used for woodcut prints in which the cuts the artist makes run parallel to the block's grain and the pattern of the grain is often (but not necessarily) a feature of the print.

Solarplate aka **Flexograph**: printing plate comprising a light-sensitive, polymer layer on a thin metal backing sheet which is 'etched' using a light-box or sunlight to remove or create texture in polymer areas not masked by stencils. Such plates can be printed either in intaglio or in relief.

Spitsticker: wood engraving tool with a fine, sharp, cutting edge and slightly rounded underbelly designed to facilitate engraving curving lines of varying thickness.

Stencil: template for a design, sometimes involving cut-out shapes from stiff paper, card or acetate.

Tint tool: wood engraving tool with an extremely fine cutting edge used to make delicate lines of uniform width.

Tympans: a pair of interconnected metal frames, each of which is covered with taut paper or fabric. The tympans are parts of a platen printing press and are used to hold packing materials to adjust the pressure on the block being printed. They attach with hinges to the press bed.

Type high: the height of metal (or, formerly, wood) type in letterpress printing. It is usually 2.33cm (approximately 1in) but varies slightly in Europe and elsewhere. Because wood engraving blocks (especially in early commercial applications in the 1800s) were often printed with set type, engraving blocks were all made 'type high', a convention which continues today.

U-gouge: tool for creating woodcut or linocut prints but not suitable for wood engraving. U-shaped in section, it is used for broad marks and lines and to clear away large areas of the block's surface.

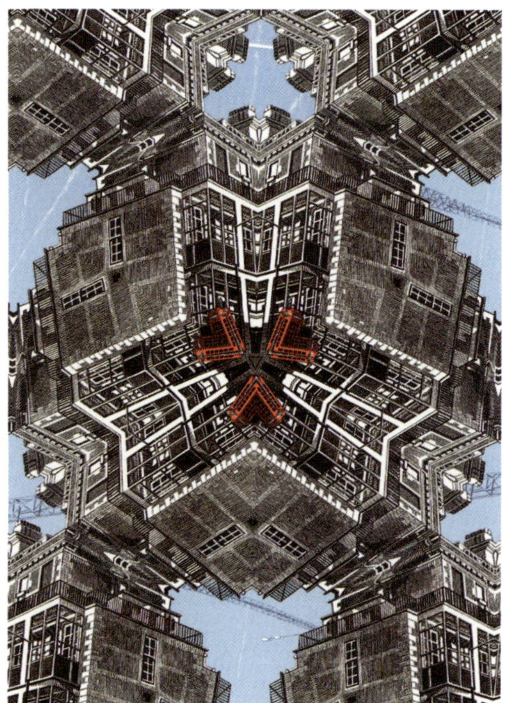

Changing London (2023), digital print (developed from wood engraving and stone lithograph) on Somerset Satin paper, 30 × 21.2cm (11¾ × 8¼in).

V-gouge: tool for creating woodcut or linocut prints but not suitable for wood engraving. V-shaped in section, it is used to make fine lines.

White-line engraving: characteristic of the wood engraving technique wherein the design appears, when printed, as white lines on a dark background.

Woodblock print: Western term for traditional Chinese or Japanese woodcut printed using water-based colours.

Woodcut: perhaps the oldest printing process, first appearing in China (c.800 CE). An image is drawn onto a block of side-grain wood (plank). The artist then cuts away areas of the block leaving, in relief, the intended image. Ink is dabbed or rolled onto the block's cut surface and the inked block is pressed onto paper. Tools used are usually steel gouges or specialist cutting knives. The term 'woodcut' is often used indiscriminately to describe all prints produced from a wooden block, but a more specific use of the term describes prints from side-grain blocks whereas wood engraving describes, specifically, prints produced from end grain blocks. These differentiations are helpful because different tools are required for each process and the prints made by each method are notably different in character.

Wood engraving: a relief print produced from a block of end grain wood into the surface of which the artist engraves a design using fine, steel, cutting tools and prints it either by hand or by press. This technique is widely credited to Thomas Bewick in Newcastle, England, in 1768 though there are earlier examples. The term describes the process and the printed result.

Wove paper: paper produced using a mould containing a finely woven metal mesh upon which paper pulp is applied and dried, creating a smooth, uniform surface. Most papers suitable for printing wood engravings are wove.

Xylography: derived from the Greek for 'wood', this is a word used to describe woodcutting and wood engraving.

INDEX

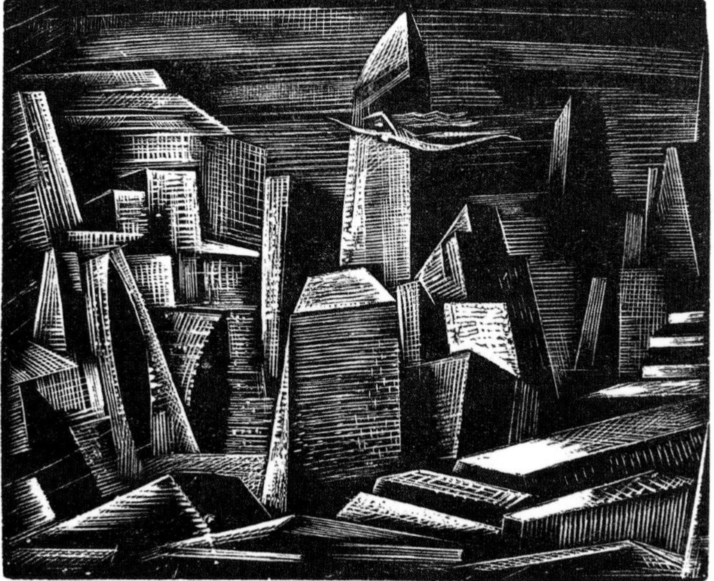

Das Rheingold, Scene 1 (1925) by Paul Nash, wood engraving, 7.7 × 9.2cm (3 × 3½in), on Japanese paper (this impression printed from the block in c.2004). This engraving shows the influence of the previous century's trade engravings yet with modern vigour in its cutting style and dramatic chiaroscuro effects.

The British Library (1998), engraving on lemonwood, 14.4 × 12.7cm (5½ × 5in), printed on Somerset Satin paper. This was commissioned by the British Library and I later used it as the basis for a kaleidoscope-inspired digital print.

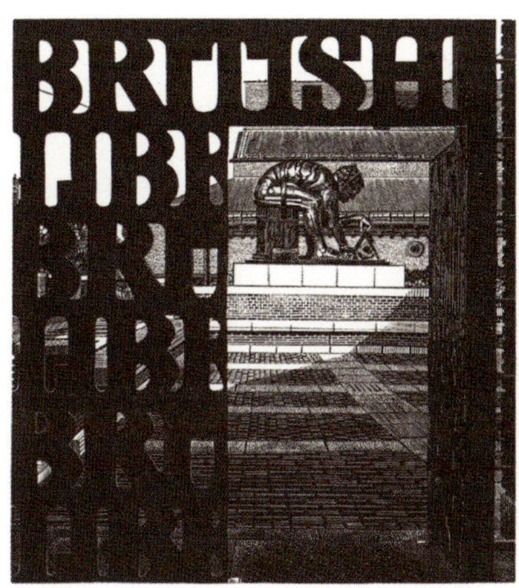

Babel Vesuvius (2002), linocuts, wood engravings and solarplate prints collaged on paper, 86.3 × 78.7cm (34 × 31in).

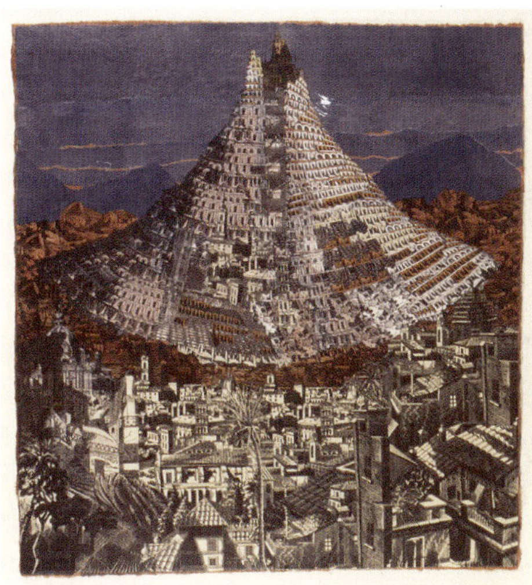

September (2025), digital print (developed from several of my wood engravings collaged and entirely reconfigured in Photoshop) on Somerset Satin paper, 17.7 × 19.5cm (7 × 7¾in).

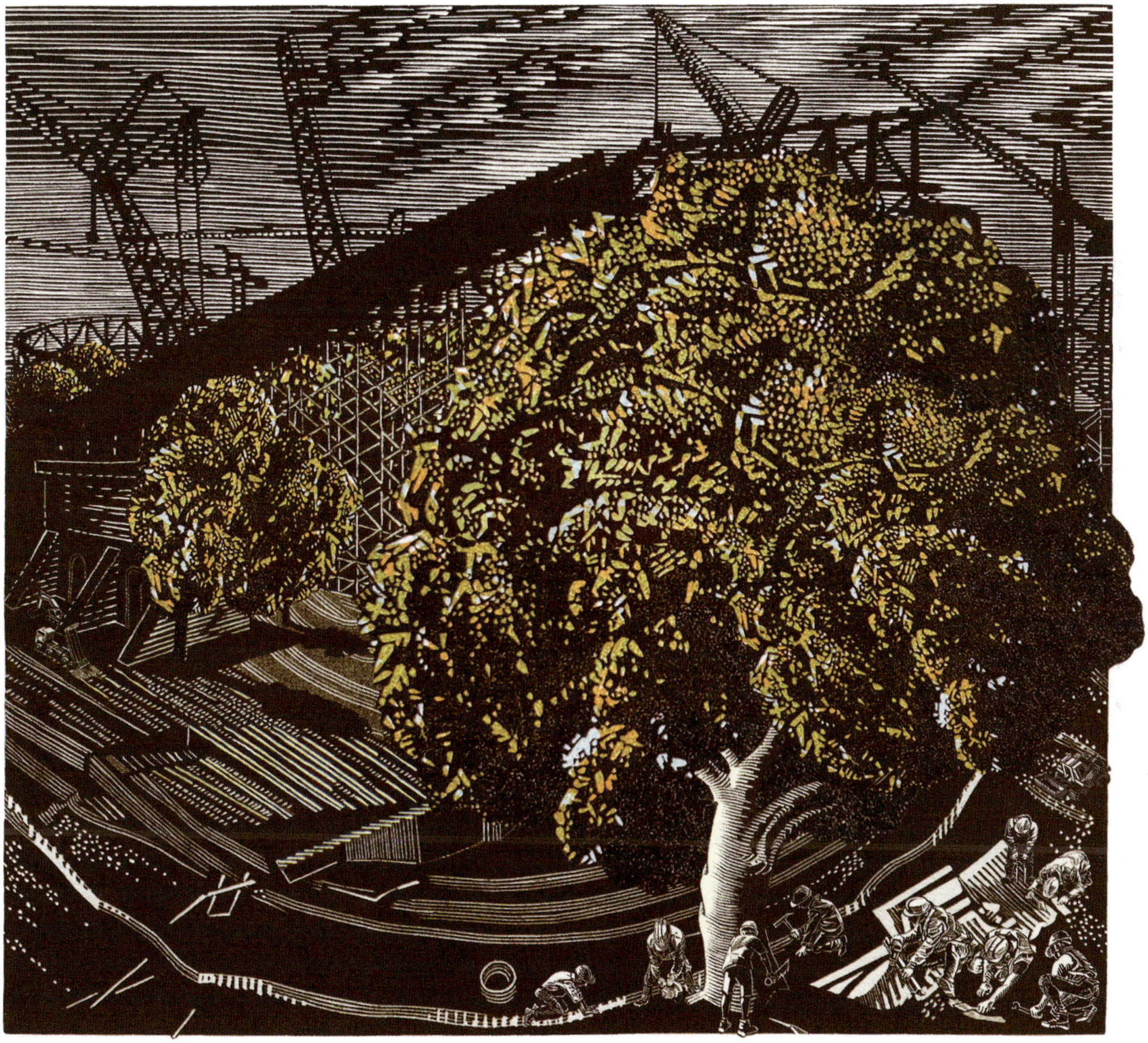

First published in 2025 by
The Crowood Press Ltd
Ramsbury, Marlborough
Wiltshire SN8 2HR

enquiries@crowood.com
www.crowood.com

British Library Cataloguing-in-Publication Data
A catalogue record for this book is available from the British Library.
For product safety-related questions, contact:
productsafety@crowood.com

ISBN 978 0 7198 4587 1

Graphic design and typesetting by Peggy & Co. Design
Cover design by Sergey Tsvetkov
Printed and bound in India by Parksons Graphics

Dedication

To my wonderful Roy for just being your unique self. Never a dull moment!

Acknowledgements

Many thanks to The Crowood Press for inviting me to write this book and for their hugely helpful suggestions and edits. Thanks too to those amazing wood engravers, past and present, whose work never fails to inspire me. Special thanks to all the artists (and their families) who have kindly allowed me to illustrate their works here, but especially to Jean Lodge, without whom I might never have been introduced to wood engraving 40 years ago. Many thanks also to my son, Tom Willingham, for taking most of the photographs of my work included here. Finally, thanks to the peerless wood engraver Simon Brett (1943–2024) whose encouragement over many decades meant a lot to me, and whose own excellent books on wood engraving set the benchmark impressively high.

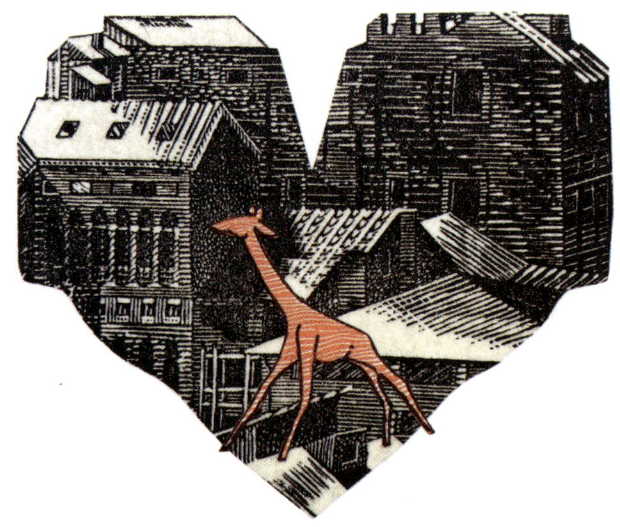

■ *Surreal Valentine* (2023), wood engraved collage with pen drawing on paper, 5.6 x 6.5cm (2¼ x 2½in).

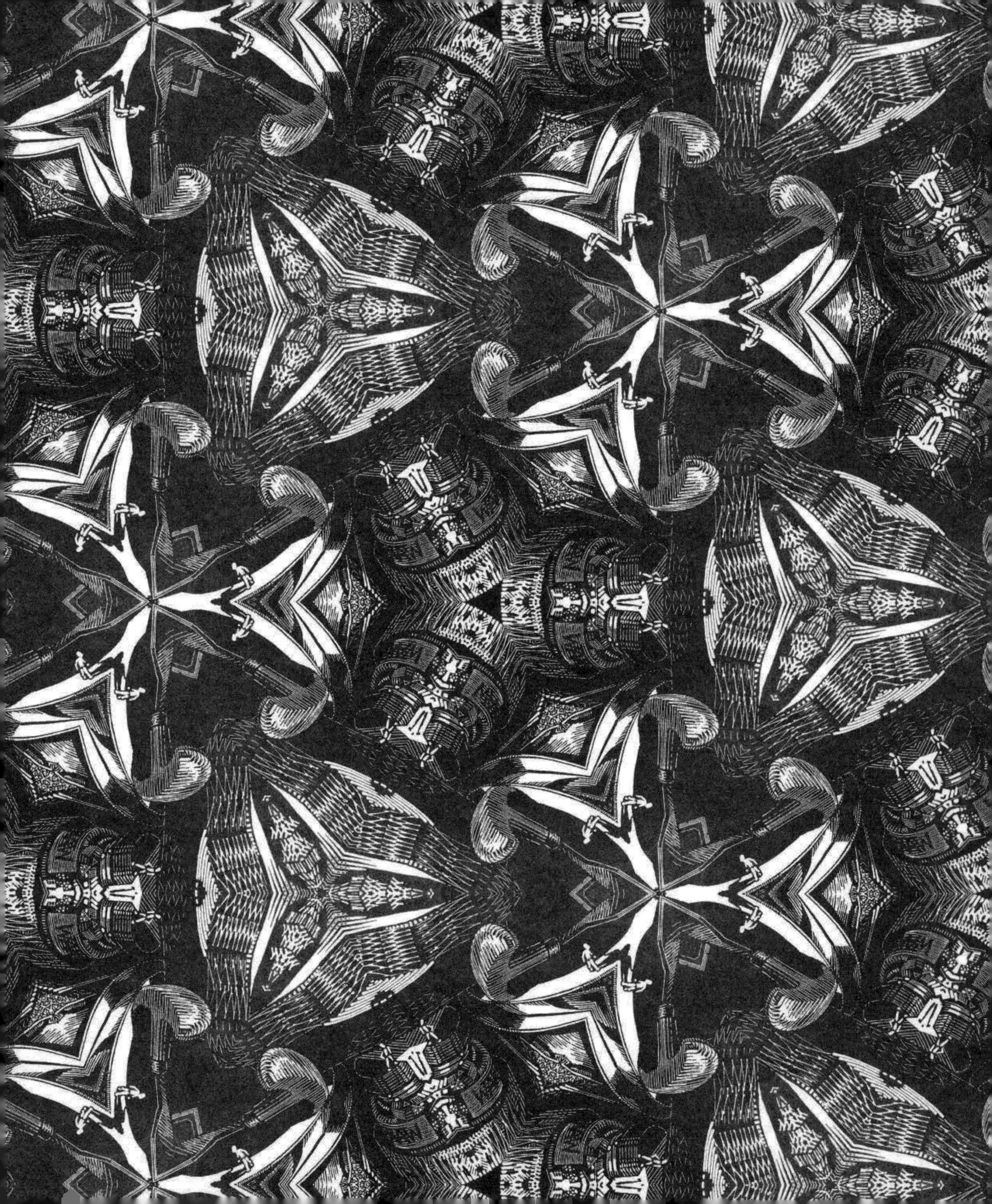